MW01074609

The GOSPEL *of* JOHN

A Theological Commentary

DAVID F. FORD

BakerAcademic
a division of Baker Publishing Group
Grand Rapids, Michigan

Published by Baker Academic
a division of Baker Publishing Group
PO Box 6287, Grand Rapids, MI 49516-6287
www.bakeracademic.com

Printed in the United States of America

Library of Congress Cataloging-in-Publication Data
Names: Ford, David F., 1948– author.
Title: The Gospel of John : a theological commentary / David F. Ford.
Description: Grand Rapids, Michigan : Baker Academic, a division of Baker Publishing Group, [2021] | Includes bibliographical references and index.
Identifiers: LCCN 2021009305 | ISBN 9781540964083 (cloth) | ISBN 9781493432271 (ebook)
Subjects: LCSH: Bible. John—Commentaries.
Classification: LCC BS2615.53 .F67 2021 | DDC 226.5/077—dc23
LC record available at https://lccn.loc.gov/2021009305

Baker Publishing Group publications use paper produced from sustainable forestry practices and post-consumer waste whenever possible.

22 23 24 25 26 27 28 8 7 6 5 4 3

For Deborah

Contents

Acknowledgments

The account given in the epilogue of the writing of this commentary over a twenty-year period includes many of those to whom I am most indebted: my wife, Deborah Ford; her father, Daniel Hardy; Micheal O'Siadhail; Peter Ochs; Frances Young; Hans Frei; Sarah Snyder; Giles Waller; Simeon Zahl; Frances Clemson; Paul Nimmo; Rachel Muers; Michael Volland; Jean Vanier;[1] Justin Welby; Peter McDonald; Jonathan Aitken; Maria Dakake; Richard Hays; Richard Bauckham; Margaret Daly-Denton; Susan Hylen; Dorothy Lee; Vittorio Montemaggi; Loraine Gelsthorpe; and Ian Randall.

The epilogue also names some of the groups and institutional settings that have been important, and to which I am very grateful: the Faculty of Divinity at the University of Cambridge, where I was teaching during fifteen of the twenty years, and where the final year undergraduate course on the Gospel of John and a masters course in theology that included study of John were especially helpful; the Lyn's House community in Cambridge; those who responded to eight Bampton Lectures on John at the University of Oxford; the symposium on John sponsored by the McDonald Agape Foundation; the students who took a course on John in Candler School of Divinity, Emory University; the Community of St. Anselm at Lambeth Palace; a great many diocesan, clergy, and lay conferences of the Church of England and other churches; the Rose Castle Foundation; and the multifaith Scriptural Reasoning community.

Elsewhere in the commentary other significant companions on the journey are noted: Tom Greggs, Jeremy Begbie, Richard Chartres, Amy Plantinga Pauw, Ashley Cocksworth, Paul Murray, Lesslie Newbigin, Andrew Lincoln, Trond

1. For more on Jean Vanier see the section "Ongoing Drama" in the epilogue.

Dokka, Kate Sonderegger, Susannah Ticciati, Judith Lieu, Donald MacKinnon, Peter Carnley, and Mike Higton.

But these are not all! There are other communities and groups significantly related to my thinking about John: three church congregations in Cambridge in which my wife, Deborah, has successively served as a priest—St. Bene't's, St. James' Wulfstan Way, and now St. Andrew's Cherry Hinton—and in which I have preached and taught on John; the chaplaincy team at Addenbrooke's Hospital in Cambridge, in which Deborah also serves, and the wider network of healthcare chaplains in the United Kingdom; the Theological Retreat Group hosted by Justin Welby in Canterbury; the Cambridge Muslim College; Minzu University in Beijing; Dev Sanskriti Vishwavidyalaya in Haridwar; the Society of St. Francis; the Monastery of St. Barnabas the Encourager in Wales; St. Mary's Abbey West Malling; two weeklong gatherings with prisoners in Louisiana State Penitentiary (known as "Angola") initiated by Peter Kang; four gatherings of the primates of the Anglican Communion, 2000–2003; the Council of Christians and Jews theology project led by Tony Bayfield; L'Arche UK and the L'Arche International Federation; the Ministry of Religious Affairs in Muscat, Oman; Kalam Research and Media; Faith in Leadership; and the Elijah Interfaith Institute in Jerusalem.

Then there are the many others with whom I have had encounters and relationships that have helped in diverse ways to shape this commentary. Even the long list to come is just a representative sample, and it covers only the two decades of the writing. It was tempting to try to shorten it or to limit it to those still living, but at every name gratitude took over. So my thanks to each of you: Anna Abram; Nick Adams; Donald Allchin; Abdullah Al-Salmi; Mother Anne; Brother Anselm, SSF; Fergus and Frank Armstrong; Michael Barnes, SJ; Tony Bayfield; Barbara Bennett; Georgette Bennett; Hanoch Ben-Pazi; You Bin; Dave Bookless; James Broad; Rob and Joanna Brown; John Casson; Frank Clooney, SJ; David Clough; Chris Cocksworth; Drew Collins; Ken Costa; Dick and Lena Curtis; Tim Dakin; Ellen Davis; Lejla Demiri; Beth Dodd; Ben Evans; Miriam Feldmann-Kaye; Jennifer and Sean Fields; Jim Fodor; Alan Ford; Annie Ford; Phyllis Ford; Nicolas and Virginie Fournier; Jason Fout; Ben Fulford; Joseph Galgalo; James and Judith Gardom; Sister Gemma, CJ; Nigel Genders; Julie Gittoes; Rachael Gledhill; Paula Gooder; Alon and Thérèse Goshen-Gottstein; Thomas Graff; Matthias Grebe; Heather Greggs; Robin Griffith-Jones; Isabelle Hamley; Perrin Hardy; Annie and Alan Hargrave; Richard Harman; Sarah Hills; Cameron Howes; Yang Huilin; Peter and Catherine Ievins; Denise Inge; Carole Irwin; Tim Jenkins; Anderson Jeremiah; Greg Jones; Emily Kempson; Steve Kepnes; Karen Kilby; Daniel King; Graham Kings; Basit Koshul; Dominic Krautter; Catriona Laing; Patrick Leckie; Robbie Leigh; Doug Leonard; Natan Levy; Miriam

Lorie; John and Wenna Marks; Ed Marques; Victoria Mason; Georgia and Owen May; Edward McCabe; Ian McFarland; Christine McGrievy; Patrick McKearney; Dominic McMullen; William McVey; Suzie Millar; Walter Moberly; Aref Nayed; Rachel Noel; Madeleine O'Callaghan; Amiel Osmaston; Chinmay Pandiya; Theresia Paquet; Jean-Christophe Pascal; Janette Pearson; Antti Pentekainen; Chase Pepper; Stephen Plant; Leonard Polonsky; Philip Powell; Ben Quash; Alex Radford; Krish Raval; Chloë Reddaway; Kavin Rowe; Miikka Ruokanen; William Salomon; Brother Sam, SSF; Christoph Schwöbel; Bryan and Dorothy Scrivener; Greg Seach; Jutta and Martin Seeley; Hugh Shilson Thomas; Sarah Simpson; Nicola Slee; Daniel Smith; John Snyder; Janet Soskice; Gillian Spence; John Swinton; Nadiya Takolia; Lindsey Taylor-Gutharz; Jonathan Teubner; Gabby Thomas; Angela Tilby; Margie Tolstoy; Graham Tomlin; Iain Torrance; Miroslav Volf; Karin Voth-Harman; Jim Walters; Daniel Weiss; Caroline Welby; Jo and Sam Wells; Christina Weltz; Jerry White; Andy Wolfe; Alison Wood; John Wood; Alexandra Wright; Tom Wright; Jon and Sophie Young; Peter Young; Bonnie Zahl; and Laurie Zoloth.

Finally, there are our children and their partners, Rebecca and Joe, Rachel and John, Daniel and Alex; and our grandchildren, Solomon and Azalea. They have been vivid signs of the abundant life, light, and love that John speaks of, and have influenced what has been written here in so many more ways than they can imagine. My thanks to them, and above all to the one to whom this book is dedicated, Deborah.

Preface

Earlier in its life, this book was signed up as a contribution to the Westminster John Knox Belief series of commentaries on the Bible by theologians. As will be clear to those who know any of the volumes in that excellent series, it is aimed at a broad readership, especially those within churches of many traditions and in many regions, but also anyone in our varied cultures who is open to an intelligent faith that engages as deeply as possible both with the Bible and with the contemporary world. As the original editors, William Placher and Amy Plantinga Pauw, wrote, "These commentaries have learned from tradition, but they are most importantly commentaries for today. The authors share the conviction that their work will be more contemporary, more faithful, and more radical, to the extent that it is more biblical, honestly wrestling with the texts of the Scriptures."[1]

That manifesto excited me, and I have tried to fulfill its many demands. My aim has been to seek Christian wisdom for today through the Gospel of John. The Belief series sets the two core questions around which my introduction and epilogue are shaped: "Why John?" and "Why Now?"[2] Guided by them, I have experienced both a responsibility and a liberation.

The responsibility has been to be as well grounded as possible in the areas of scholarship and theology that are most relevant to interpreting the Gospel of John today. The two main ones are biblical studies and the field that is variously called doctrinal, systematic, dogmatic, or constructive theology. There are (rightly) very specialist, technical aspects of each of those areas—one thinks,

1. See the "Series Introduction" in each volume of the series, beginning with William Placher's posthumously published *Mark*.

2. The Belief series also encourages authors to reflect in the epilogue on the process of writing the commentary, and that, too, is part of this one.

for example, of the vast scholarly literature on the dating, authorship, original audience, historical reliability, language, literary craft, intertextuality, and similar issues relating to the Gospel of John, and also of the theological and philosophical concepts and debates surrounding the doctrines of the Trinity and Christology in which this Gospel has played a central role. I have written on some of these topics elsewhere (as the epilogue describes), but in this commentary the aim is to be sure-footed in relation to the specialist literature and discussions, without entering into them at any length.

The liberation has been to be able to pursue the deep, life-shaping questions raised by the Gospel of John, not only with reference to biblical studies and a range of theologies, but also through poetry, history, Christian living, interfaith engagement, involvements in largely secular settings and thought-worlds, and more. The first words of Jesus in John's Gospel are "What are you looking for?" (1:38), and I have found that repeated rereadings of this Gospel have inspired passionate searching, and in the process have offered an education of desire. So the result is as much a spirituality as a theology, both of them centered on the first question of the Gospel, "Who are you?" (1:19). Even further, there has been a glimpse of how promising, and how relevant to our time, is the prospect of a Johannine renaissance.

When this commentary grew to a size that was around double the norm for the Belief series, there was a friendly agreement that it did not (literally) fit there, being far longer than any of the others. I remain very grateful to Westminster John Knox Press, and especially to Amy Plantinga Pauw, for many years of encouragement, patience, and support.

Baker Academic's welcome of the commentary has been warm and generous. Not only has their first-class team gone to work on the many tasks involved in publication, offering valuable advice, and then making sure that all necessary support is in place. There has also been the experience that every author longs for: an editor, Dave Nelson, who has read the book closely, appreciated it, commented perceptively, and given clear guidance for what more needs to be done. It has been a delight to work with someone who has such broad and rich experience of the field, and such reliable judgment. In addition, James Korsmo has been an extraordinarily helpful project editor, whose alertness and expertise have proved most valuable.

A final word is about a striking feature of the Gospel of John: it combines being accessible to those who are new to it with the capacity to go on challenging and feeding those who have reread it many times. This commentary is written in the hope that both groups will find in it something of worth, and that those in the first group will, over time, migrate into the second.

Introduction

Why John? Why Now?

Gospel of Abundance

"From his fullness we have all received, grace upon grace" (John 1:16). John is a Gospel of abundance. The prologue first sounds this note; the first sign that Jesus does turns a huge amount of water into good wine; the Spirit is a wind that blows where it will and is given "without measure" (3:34); the "living water" that Jesus gives is "a spring of water gushing up to eternal life" (4:14); when Jesus feeds five thousand with five loaves, there are twelve baskets of fragments left over; through Jesus there is abundance of glory, healing, light, life, truth, fruitfulness, joy, and love; the last sign that Jesus does brings about a large catch of big fish; and John's closing sentence responds to the impossible task of writing all that could be said about what Jesus did: "If every one of them were written down, I suppose that the world itself could not contain the books that would be written" (21:25).

This abundance stretches the thought and imagination of readers, and it is intensified by John's[1] way of writing. Common words are used both in their everyday, ordinary sense and also with deeper meanings—try following through this Gospel terms such as *word, in, all, life, light, darkness, come, world, receive, believe, as, father, son, see* (that is just a selection of some from the prologue), and you will find yourself led into the depths of John's meaning. This is what I call the "deep plain sense," which invites the reader to search for deeper meaning in plain words. It is enriched by John's use of ambiguity and double meanings, as in the conversation between Jesus and Nicodemus in John 3 (where one

1. On the authorship of this Gospel, see comments on 21:24–25, which is where the authorship is raised by the Gospel itself. I refer to the author simply as John.

Greek word can mean both "from above" and "again," another can mean both "wind" and "spirit"), by his use of repetition with variation, by inexhaustibly rich imagery, by complex portrayal of characters, and in other ways.

But by far the most important way is through relating to other texts, above all that of his own Bible. John may well have known Hebrew, but the main text that he uses is the Septuagint (LXX), the translation of the Hebrew Bible into Greek done by Jews in Alexandria a couple of centuries before he wrote his Gospel. This is the great connecting text between the Jewish and the Christian Scriptures, and John was steeped in it. His opening words are its opening words: "In the beginning . . ." (Gen. 1:1; John 1:1). He often quotes it and, even more frequently, echoes[2] it. Every chapter is, as it were, marinated in it. Without it, his meaning is shallowly understood, or misunderstood, or key points missed. With it, the reader is drawn into a constant to and fro, reading and rereading both John and the Septuagint, and finding that one text usually leads into a network of texts. This is what I call John's use of "intertexts," which invite the reader to interrelate what John writes with another text. I will frequently draw attention to John's intertexts, and sometimes quote them, but only occasionally will I have the space to explore their interaction at length—the reader is encouraged to take time to do so.

While the Septuagint is plainly an intertext, John also had some relationship with the Synoptic Gospels—Matthew, Mark, and Luke—or with the sources that fed into them. Many scholars now are of the opinion that John knew the actual Synoptic Gospels, or at least Mark and Luke, and I think that he knew all three (see comments on John 6). It can be very illuminating to ask why or how John includes, interprets, alters, or omits a particular Synoptic passage, and I will do so frequently.

One fascinating fruit of following how John reads his own Bible (and the Synoptics) is that *we learn how he wants us to read his own text.* Many scholars agree that John understood himself to be writing Scripture. If that is so, then in interpreting his Bible he is modeling how we are to read what he himself writes. In this commentary I try to learn from John how to read John and to share that with readers.

The commentator on John is faced not only with the superabundance of meaning generated by his rich text and its intertexts but also with nearly two thousand years of other people responding to this Gospel and to one another's readings. The responses are by no means only in the form of commentary,

2. A superb study of this aspect of all four Gospels is Hays, *Echoes of Scripture,* whose sections on John are the best condensed study of his ways of relating to his Bible. For a response to Hays, which also gives a fuller account of the approach to John taken in this commentary, see Ford, "Reading Backwards, Reading Forwards."

but also include hymns, songs, music, and poetry; prayer and spirituality; liturgy and ritual; art and architecture; drama and film; theology and philosophy; accounts of reception history; ethics and politics; and (perhaps most fitting of all) the lives of people and their communities. The present work (which has the form of a commentary in that it moves through the text chapter by chapter, but also tries to do justice to other genres—the index is intended to be a help in making connections between leading themes) has been profoundly shaped by many elements of that history of reception, but they can only rarely be explicitly pursued. There has been a repeated and often painful process of selection and rejection, but I hope that the result is helpful to the reader by offering one way through an immense mass of material. A similar challenge was faced by the author of John's Gospel, as he says at the end of both John 20 and 21: there were "many other signs" (20:30) and "many other things" (21:25) that Jesus did. Just as John's selection is immensely significant (see comments on 20:31 and below in the "Why John Now?" sections), so, in lesser ways, are each respondent's decisions about where to focus.

Yet on John there is one text that might be considered the response that deserves pride of place. The First Letter of John may have been written by the author of the Gospel of John, or else by someone in the same tradition and steeped in the Gospel—the language is Johannine. It is written to a Christian community with problems, and it calls them back to the essentials of the Gospel. And it is clear that the essentials all have love at their heart, reaching a crescendo in the repeated statement "God is love" (1 John 4:8, 16). Jesus is the embodiment of this love and is the Savior of the world, and the most important thing for those who believe in him is to receive his Spirit and to love one another (1 John 4:7–21).

This work tries to do justice to those as the essentials of John's Gospel, where they are most fully expressed in the Farewell Discourses (John 13–17). The resulting three main emphases are given under three headings below; but before coming to them, we must note a further striking feature of John's Gospel. This Gospel is a text that has proved to be both accessible to those meeting it for the first time and increasingly challenging the more it is reread. Its Greek is fairly straightforward, and it was my first text when I began to learn New Testament Greek, at the age of twelve. Yet now, over half a century later, as I look back at the twenty years during which I have been working on John, it stands out as the most challenging project I have ever undertaken.

More will be said about this in the epilogue, which tells something of the personal story behind this commentary, but I am by no means alone in this experience with John. Beginners can find something comprehensible and attractive, but the more they take this to heart—and, in particular, the more they take Jesus to heart—the more dimensions of the abundance of this Gospel open up. Places in the text where before they could paddle now stretch their swimming ability, like the water flowing from the temple and becoming deeper and deeper in Ezekiel's vision (Ezek. 47:1–12), which is one of John's intertexts.

The three interrelated answers to the question Why John? that follow are given as three "waves" of meaning, a form of presentation common in John—his very first sentence (1:1) is a concise example.

Why John? (1): Who Jesus Is

The abundance of John's Gospel is given above all through Jesus. Who is Jesus? is the leading question running through the whole Gospel. This is, of course, a core concern of the other Gospels and of the rest of the New Testament, but John concentrates on it in a distinctive way and develops it further. John's is an understanding of Jesus that has had the benefit of long reflection on eyewitness testimony, on the Synoptic Gospels, and probably also on the teaching of Paul,[3] and also of many years living and teaching in a Christian community.[4] *It is the culmination of New Testament testimony to Jesus.* The commentary will trace in detail how this is done, but it is worth summarizing now how this is the primary concern in each section of the Gospel.[5]

The Prologue's Horizon and Focus on Jesus

The prologue (1:1–18) gives John's "manifesto," setting the Word (*logos*), later identified with Jesus, within the ultimate horizon of God and all reality. The headline description of Jesus as the Word of God, who became flesh, and through whom "all things came into being" (v. 3), not only identifies Jesus simultaneously as one with both God and humanity but also relates him to the whole of the Jewish Scriptures, to the Hellenistic civilization of the Roman Empire, and to all creation.

3. On the relationship between John and Paul scholars differ, as on so much else about John. I am persuaded by those who think that John knew teachings of Paul and his "school," and in particular see John combining the Synoptic narrative approach with some of the main pillars of Pauline theology, such as the glory of God, love, faith, "in Christ," the Holy Spirit, and abundance.

4. Where? I am persuaded by those scholars who argue, on a variety of grounds, for Ephesus, in Asia Minor (on the Aegean coast of modern Turkey). This would give a connection with Paul's churches, and especially with the Letter to the Ephesians, which is one of the most fruitful intertexts to read with John.

5. I assume that the way many readers engage with a commentary such as this is not to read it through from first page to last but to consult it on particular passages or topics. It can therefore be helpful to get some sense of the whole from an introduction. Besides attempting to do that here, in the commentary itself I take into account its piecemeal use by employing some "repetition with variation" of key points. John too, as will become clear, frequently uses repetition with variation.

As the prologue continues, the reader is invited to begin to think about Jesus imaginatively in relation to light and darkness; to attend to testimony (beginning with John the Baptist); to be open to the possibility of being part of a family, the children of God, who believe and trust in his name (who he is); and to recognize that an event has happened, a human person has come, in whom there is the full meaning and reality of God in relation to us—God's abundance incarnate, "the glory as of a father's only son, full of grace and truth" (v. 14). This "fullness" has been shared; it is the "grace and truth" of the "law . . . given through Moses," now come in person through Jesus Christ (vv. 16–17).

Then comes the climax (v. 18). It combines the mystery of the invisible God, the relationship of love at the heart of God and all reality—"God the only Son, who is close to the Father's heart"—and the mission of Jesus, to make God "known."

The "Who" Question Headlined (1:19–51)

The first and leading question of the Gospel is then posed: "Who are you?" (v. 19). It comes as the brief prologue leads into the primary form in which the message of this Gospel is given: dramatic narrative in which Jesus is central. The question is addressed to John the Baptist, but he makes clear that it should be asked not about himself but about the one whose way he is preparing. He then gives a series of pointers to who this is, the first being the most daring of all: "the Lord" (v. 23). Almost as surprising is the next: "Here is the Lamb of God who takes away the sin of the world!" (v. 29). More answers to the "who" question follow: the one on whom the "Spirit" descends and remains; "the one who baptizes with the Holy Spirit"; and "the Son of God" (vv. 33–34).

The rest of John 1 has an avalanche of identifications of Jesus, with one title after another, each resonating through the rest of the Gospel, to be filled with further meaning through the events, teachings, and controversies: "Rabbi" or "Teacher" (v. 38); "Messiah" or "Christ" (v. 41); "him about whom Moses in the law and also the prophets wrote, Jesus son of Joseph from Nazareth" (v. 45); "Son of God" (v. 49); "King of Israel" (v. 49); and the only one from the lips of Jesus, "Son of Man" (v. 51).

So, overall, the first chapter could hardly make it clearer where the primary focus of this Gospel is concentrated: who Jesus is.

Jesus Doing Signs, Having Encounters, Giving Teaching (Chaps. 2–17)

This concentration continues during the following sixteen chapters.

John's favorite term for key actions of Jesus is "signs," emphasizing their wider meaning. As this meaning unfolds, in conversations around the signs, in discourses before or after them, and in authorial comments, the key issue again and again is who Jesus is. The headline statement by the author, after telling of the initial sign, is focused on the revelation of who he is and the primary response to that—believing in, having faith in, trusting him: "Jesus did this, the first of his signs, in Cana of Galilee, and revealed his glory; and his disciples believed in him" (2:11). The man healed at the Beth-zatha pool is asked, "Who is the man who . . . ?" (5:12), and this leads into a long discourse (vv. 19–47) by Jesus about himself in relation to his Father. The longest discourse of all follows the feeding of the five thousand, and it spirals around John's most distinctive characterization of who Jesus is, the "I am" statements—here, "I am the bread of life. . . . I am the bread that came down from heaven. . . . I am the bread of life" (6:35, 41, 48). The controversy in John 9 around the man born blind likewise turns on who Jesus is, as does the raising of Lazarus in John 11.

The encounters and conversations of Jesus, both friendly and hostile, also have who he is as their leading theme. The headline for these is the clearing of the temple in John 2, during which he identifies his body with the temple. This also makes explicit a key factor in John's characterization of Jesus: his combination of preresurrection and postresurrection standpoints (see more below). Then, the conversation with Nicodemus merges into a discourse on believing "in the name of the only Son of God" (3:18). Next, the conversation with the Samaritan woman at the well leads into identifying Jesus as "prophet," "Messiah," "I am," "Rabbi," and "Savior of the world" (3:19, 25, 26, 29, 31, 42). The controversies in John 7–10 likewise return again and again to who Jesus is. By the time the public ministry of Jesus ends in John 12, the question of who he is has become utterly central.

The Farewell Discourses (chaps. 13–17) then go deeper into who he is. This theme is opened up through the footwashing, fundamental statements such as "I am the way, and the truth, and the life" (14:6), Jesus as the friend who lays down his life, Jesus as the vine (or vineyard), the inseparability of love in action from prayer in the name of Jesus, and, deepest of all, the revelation of who Jesus is in his definitive relationship to his Father in his prayer in John 17.

Arrest, Trial, Crucifixion, and Resurrection (Chaps. 18–21)

There could hardly be a more graphic indication of the importance to John of who Jesus is than his distinctive way of telling of the arrest of Jesus. This has two "who" questions and three "I am" statements (18:4–8). Later, the trial before Pilate pivots around the identity of Jesus, summed up in Pilate's question, "Are you the King of the Jews?" (18:33). The commentary will bring out the subtle ways in which John's narrative of the trial and crucifixion handles this identity issue.

Then, in his first resurrection appearance Jesus asks the weeping Mary Magdalene, "Whom are you looking for?" and he addresses her by name, "Mary!" "Rabbouni!" she replies (20:15–16). This dramatic "who to who" meeting is then complemented by the climactic and unsurpassed affirmation of who Jesus is by Thomas: "My Lord and my God!" (20:28). Finally, the epilogue suggests the ongoing, permanent presence of Jesus by a threefold repetition that usually is lost in translation: "It is the Lord!"—literally, "The Lord is!" (*ho kyrios estin* occurs twice in 21:7 and once in 21:12). The third repetition of this third-person variation on the "I am" of Jesus is fittingly paired with a final repetition of the "who" question that first appeared in 1:19: "Now none of the disciples dared to ask him, 'Who are you?' because they knew it was the Lord" (21:12).

All those points will be expanded upon in the course of this book, and the overall conclusion is very clear. The first answer to the question Why John? is because this is the culminating New Testament testimony, abundantly rich and profound, to who Jesus is.

Why John? (2): The Spirit Given without Measure for the Ongoing Drama of Loving

The second answer is dependent on and inseparable from the first, and brings together further distinctive elements in John's Gospel.

The Holy Spirit

First, John says far more about the Holy Spirit than do the other Gospels. Readers are reminded of the Spirit right through John's Gospel.

This begins in the opening chapter when John the Baptist testifies to the Holy Spirit remaining/abiding on Jesus (1:32–33). This means that every word and action of Jesus, and his whole person, are to be understood as at one with the Spirit, inspired through the Spirit, and indicators of the character of the Spirit. So the Spirit is always to be understood as involved even when not mentioned (as, e.g., in the prayer of Jesus in John 17). In Jesus's conversation with Nicodemus, the Spirit is seen as generative for life in the kingdom of God (for which John's preferred term is "eternal life," or "life in all its abundance," on both sides of death), and as pervasive and surprising as the wind (3:1–16). Jesus is sent to baptize with the Holy Spirit (1:33), and "he whom God has sent speaks the words of God, for he gives the Spirit without measure" (3:34). The Samaritan woman is told that "true worshipers will worship the Father in spirit and truth" (4:23). The longest of Jesus's discourses comes to a dramatic climax when he says, "It is the spirit that gives life; the flesh is useless. The words that I have spoken to you are spirit and life" (6:63). And at the climax of the Festival of Booths Jesus cries out, "Let anyone who is thirsty come to me, and let the one who believes in me drink. As the scripture has said, 'Out of the believer's heart shall flow rivers of living water.'" And John adds, "Now he said this about the Spirit, which believers in him were to receive; for as yet there was no Spirit, because Jesus was not yet glorified" (7:37–39).

The most intensive focus on the Spirit comes in the Farewell Discourses as Jesus prepares his disciples for his death and for their part in the ongoing drama afterward. Just as the Spirit was seen by John the Baptist to abide on Jesus, so the Spirit is promised to the disciples, "to be with you forever. . . . You know him, because he abides with you, and he will be in you" (14:16–17). The Spirit is the *paraklētos*, the Encourager, Helper, Comforter, Advocate, the one who "cries out alongside" us. Given "without measure" (3:34), distributing the abundance of Jesus, the Spirit "will teach you everything, and remind you of all I have said to you" (14:26). Jesus is even able to say, "I tell you the truth: it is to your advantage that I go away, for if I do not go away, the Advocate will not come to you" (16:7). This is "the Spirit of truth" who "will guide you into all the truth" (16:13), a further astonishing promise (especially given the horizon of God and all reality opened up in the prologue). The fascinating, mysterious interrelation of Jesus, the Spirit, and the Father in the Farewell Discourses was later to be at the heart of the development of Christian thought in its early centuries, as it slowly arrived at the momentous affirmation of God as Trinity.

This commentary agrees with those interpreters who find the first giving of the Spirit by Jesus in his final act of dying: "Then he bowed his head and gave up [literally, "handed over" or "passed on"] his [literally, "the"] spirit [or "Spirit"]" (19:30). The Greek can simply mean that he stopped breathing and died; but its deep plain sense can be that this is simultaneously the moment of his death and the beginning of new life given through his death—also symbolized by the blood and water that flow from the side of the dead Jesus when a soldier pierces him to ascertain that he really is dead (19:31–37).

The final mention of the Spirit is when the crucified and resurrected Jesus breathes on his disciples and says, "Receive the Holy Spirit" (20:22). This connects the giving of the Spirit as closely and intimately as possible with Jesus himself. But what Jesus has just said also connects this gift as closely as possible with the ongoing drama.

The Ongoing Drama

Just before the breathing of the Spirit, Jesus has commissioned his disciples: "As the Father has sent me, so I send you" (20:21). John is far more explicitly concerned than other Gospels with what I call the ongoing drama of following Jesus after his crucifixion and resurrection—much of the Farewell Discourses is about this, and so is much of his last two chapters. What are the implications of Jesus sending his disciples as he himself was sent?

First, it requires *continual learning from how Jesus was sent,* as seen in the drama of his ministry (especially gathering a new family of disciples/learners, doing life-giving signs, entering into deep and challenging conversations, and setting an example of witnessing to the truth, loving service, friendship, and intimate prayer) and in his passion, crucifixion, resurrection, ascension, and giving of the Holy Spirit.

It also encourages *continual improvisation in the Spirit of Jesus,* in line with what I call the capacious "as . . . so . . ." of that commissioning, of his footwashing command (13:12–20), and of his love commandments (13:34; 15:12–17). As Jesus loved, so disciples are to love. Followers are to be inspired to act daringly in love and service, to spring surprises as Jesus did, even to do "greater works" than Jesus did (14:12). *This is to be an ongoing drama of inspired loving.*

Inseparably, there is to be *continual prayer in the name of Jesus* (14:13; 15:16; 16:23–24), above all inspired by his own prayer in John 17, which is where this Gospel sounds its greatest depths, reaches its greatest heights, opens up its innermost secret of intimate mutual indwelling, and orients the desires of readers toward union with the ultimate desire of Jesus.

And *all this is aimed above all at you,* the readers of his text, as directly addressed: "But these are written so that you [plural] may come to believe [or "may continue to believe"] that Jesus is the Messiah [or "the Christ"], the Son of God, and that through believing you may have life in his name" (20:31). That is John's core motive in writing his Gospel, and it is wise to keep it in mind when reading each chapter. His passionate desire is for us, his readers, to encounter the living Jesus to whom he is testifying. This is the main reason he combines preresurrection and postresurrection perspectives: he wants us to understand who Jesus is, and that even as we read about what he did and said, we are in the presence of this crucified and risen one who says "I am," who loves us incomparably, and who longs above all for us to trust, love, and follow him now. This good shepherd calls each reader by name into the ongoing drama. But, strikingly, the model disciple, "the disciple whom Jesus loved" (21:20), to whom the writing of this Gospel is attributed, is not named—perhaps to allow every follower to self-identify as loved by Jesus.

So the second answer to the question Why John? is because it gives profound and practical inspiration and guidance to disciples committed to the ongoing drama of living in the Spirit of the crucified and risen Jesus.

Why John? (3): God and All People, All Creation

The third answer reaches far beyond the circle of the committed followers of Jesus in order to take seriously the vision of the God of love, light, and all reality that this Gospel opens up.

The prologue, as already noted, first opens up this horizon that embraces all things, all life, and all people. Intertexts here include Genesis on creation, and Wisdom of Solomon, which brought Jewish Scriptures into rich engagement with the culture, learning, and wisdom of Greek-speaking Hellenistic civilization. This openness across the boundaries of any single community, type of person, or other distinction continues through the rest of the Gospel.

The first question that Jesus asks his first disciples is, "What are you looking for?" (1:38), probing their core desire. The whole Gospel is an examination and education of human desire, as later chapters will show. The desire of Jesus is expressed most fully in his prayer in John 17, but, before that, through the signs that he does, he shows his desire that people (whether they are following him or not) may "have life, and have it abundantly" (10:10). He begins by providing a huge quantity of wine for a wedding, an archetypal celebration of life, love, and commitment. His feeding and healings are about sustaining, restoring, and enhancing life for anyone in need, without regard for their religion, race, gender, power, wealth, or status. His conversation with the Samaritan woman at the well engages across divisions of religion, ethnicity, and gender. "I am the light of the world" (8:12) sees no limit to his relevance.

Yet there is no triumphalist "global solution"; rather, the deepest secret of Jesus's relationship to all people and things lies in his death. In John 12, in response to an approach to him by some foreigners, Greeks, Jesus begins to speak of his death, its fruitfulness, and its capacity to draw people of all sorts together: "And I, when I am lifted up from the earth, will draw all people [or "all things"] to myself" (12:32). The Farewell Discourses prepare his disciples for this event, and for receiving the Holy Spirit flowing from it, culminating in the final prayer of Jesus in John 17. That gives the vision of what he is laying down his life for, his ultimate desire: the fullest conceivable unity in love and peace.

The process of actually giving his life is one in which betrayal by one of his closest followers and the combination of religious, political, economic, and military power represented by the Roman Empire and the temple hierarchy work together against him. The ongoing drama likewise will involve his followers in such things, as warned in the Farewell Discourses and predicted in the martyrdom of Peter (21:18–19). Some interpreters see John's own Christian community as "sectarian," turned inward by such pressures, concerned with love for one another rather than love of enemies, and with hard boundaries over against "the world." This commentary sides with those who see the thrust of this Gospel (however it was actually lived by John's community, about which there are contradictory speculations but little evidence) being toward doing life-giving signs for all who are in need, daringly crossing deep divisions, seeking more and more truth, engaging critically and constructively with the civilization of which it is a part, prophetically challenging the pathologies of power, modeling servant leadership, and building communities of prayer, love, and friendship that serve God's love for all people and all creation, seeking to be part of the fulfillment of the desire of Jesus in his final prayer.

So the third answer to the question Why John? is because it nurtures in readers a global horizon that can unite them with the desire of Jesus for an ultimate unity of all people and all creation in love and peace.

Why John Now? (1): Jesus Now

Each of those three dimensions of John proves to be deeply and practically relevant today.

The "I am" of Jesus is the most direct and profound pointer to his ongoing relevance. John relates Jesus to all time. As regards the past, in the prologue John the Baptist says, "He who comes after me ranks ahead of me because he was before me" (1:15, repeated in 1:30); Jesus says, "Very truly, I tell you, before Abraham was, I am" (8:58); and he prays, "So now, Father, glorify me in your own presence with the glory that I had in your presence before the world existed" (17:5; cf. 17:24). As regards the future, he looks beyond his death to preparing "a place" for his disciples (14:1–7); and his last words assume a future to which his desire and his coming are central: "If it is my will [*thelō*, "I desire"] that he remain until I come, what is that to you?" (21:23). *Yet the primary concentration is on the present—any and every present time. But this is not a momentary or fleeting present; it is defined by the presence of Jesus, who is present as God is present.* A key word for this ongoing presence is "abide/remain/dwell," which is used of Jesus, his Father, the Holy Spirit, and those who trust and love them. Their mutual indwelling culminates in the prayer of Jesus in 17:20–26, expressed through the rich use of "in," and explicitly embracing those who come after the first disciples. No Gospel insists more strongly on the relevance of Jesus to every "now."

The ways in which this ongoing presence of Jesus is brought home to readers are multiple. Among the most important are the following three, all thoroughly interrelated.

Most obvious and emphasized is the gift of the Holy Spirit. The Spirit by no means replaces the presence of Jesus or the presence of his Father—all three are always together, while also differentiated and interrelated. They signify the rich presence of the God of love, as later understood and expressed in trinitarian thinking, prayer, and worship down through the centuries. The promise for every "now" is that the Spirit "abides with you, and he will be in you" (14:17). The interrelationship with Jesus and the Father is clear: "The Advocate, the Holy Spirit, whom the Father will send in my name, will teach you everything, and remind you of all that I have said to you. . . . He will glorify me, because he will take from what is mine and declare it to you. All that the Father has is mine. For this reason I said that he will take from what is mine and declare it to you" (14:26; 16:14–15).

Second, note the repeated mention of what Jesus has said or declared. Elsewhere, too, this is emphasized alongside the Spirit: "He whom God has sent speaks the words of God, for he gives the Spirit without measure" (3:34); "The words that I have spoken to you are spirit [or "Spirit"] and life" (6:63). Essential to the life of abiding in Jesus is that "my words abide in you" (15:7), and part of his summary, in prayer to his Father, of what he has been able to do is, "The words that you gave to me I have given to them, and they have received them and know in truth that I came from you" (17:8). When Jesus finally breathes the Spirit into his disciples, the breath carries his words (20:22). It is hard to overstress how important for the Gospel of John is this interrelationship of the words of Jesus with his Father, the giving of the Spirit, abiding, abundant life, and faith. The Gospel is written to invite readers into this dynamic set of relationships (cf. 20:31). *Reading and hearing this text, and letting its words abide in us, is how to experience the presence of Jesus and his Spirit now.* The words breathe his Spirit as his breath carries the words. It is hard to imagine a more vivid picture of minute-by-minute living presence than that of breathing. The mutual indwelling of Jesus and those who trust and love him means that that first breathing continues now through engagement with his words and the testimony to him.

Yet, third, the text itself points beyond the text. Partly, it does this through intertexts, through connecting Jesus with the creation of all things, life, and people, and through the promise that the Spirit will lead into more and more truth. But central to all that is who Jesus is, present, active, and alive with the life of God. *Jesus is free to be present and to communicate in many ways, and to spring surprises*—as he did during his ministry, especially after his resurrection. Knowing the text (but who ever knows this text well enough?) does not give an overview of Jesus and his activity. His core commands to wash feet and to love, and his final commissioning that sends his disciples into the ongoing drama, have an open, capacious "as . . . so . . ." that invites into improvisation and innovation, open to risk-taking and surprises. If Jesus now is present as God is present—in all situations, to all people, and to all families, cultures, businesses, religions, nations, and environments—then finding him and meeting him calls for continual openness to new encounters. All the postresurrection encounters were surprises, and they were not obvious or straightforward. There is no reason to think that recognizing the free self-revelations of Jesus now will be any less challenging and surprising, or that either the current followers of Jesus, or anyone else, will be able to anticipate to whom or how they will be granted.

Jesus Then: The Historical Jesus and John

Jesus now assumes Jesus then, the historical Jesus. This has been a matter of special interest in recent centuries, with the rise of historical-critical methods of studying the past. There has been a great variety of approaches and results, too large to survey here.[6] For my approach, the following three points (which can be pursued further through the literature referred to) are particularly important.

First, testimony is essential to John, and it is appropriate to cross-examine this testimony, as scholars and others do.[7] As in a court of law, after such cross-examination there is a judgment to be made about whether the testimony is basically trustworthy, by which I mean whether it is a reliable testimony to who the crucified and risen Jesus is. I, along with many others, am convinced that it is.[8] There are many differences among the Gospel accounts of Jesus,

6. In this commentary I try to be sure-footed in relation to historical criticism. That is, I would be prepared to defend my judgments, both explicit and implicit, but do not go into the detailed discussion of various positions that would be required if this were a work of technical historical scholarship. Plenty of commentaries and other works do this, but my attempt to not take many detours is in the interests of my main goal, which is to relate the Gospel to life now—thinking, imagining, praying, living in community, and loving—which is rightly not the leading concern of historical scholarship. I also try to be sure-footed in relation to historical, doctrinal, and systematic theology (again, I would be prepared to defend my judgments, but do not develop full positions on, for instance, Christology—though here other works mentioned in the epilogue are relevant); and the same applies to literary criticism, hermeneutics, spirituality, ethics, philosophy, and other discourses.

7. One standard account of the scholarly historical examination of the New Testament testimony to Jesus that coheres with the approach of this commentary is Young, "Prelude: Jesus Christ."

8. For an overall account of my approach, see Ford, "Who Is Jesus Now?"; for more detailed discussion of a theological understanding of Jesus that takes historical and biblical scholarship

but all four testify to who he is by telling about what he said and did, his encounters and conflicts, his passion, crucifixion, and resurrection. There is plenty of convergence on key elements, and the divergences (which are greatest between the Synoptics and John) often offer fruitful ways of reflecting further on him.

Second, the pivotal event for relating Jesus then to Jesus now is his resurrection. All the Gospels, and the other New Testament books, are written in the light of the resurrection, but John is more explicitly concerned to give both pre-resurrection and postresurrection perspectives on him, as will be clear through this commentary. This goes with his greater emphasis on the Spirit and on the ongoing drama of postresurrection discipleship, and also with his horizon of God, all people, and all creation. Doing justice to this combination of perspectives involves taking into account and making judgments about the relevance of a range of matters to a theological interpretation such as this, including how history, biography, and theology could be combined in the literature of the time; how rewriting sacred and other texts was a way of receiving and interpreting them in new situations;[9] and the importance to John of being continually led into further truth through the Spirit.

Third, the resurrection of Jesus cannot be understood simply as a historical event alongside others, such as his crucifixion. As the interpretation of John 20 below will discuss, in John it is a "God-sized" event in which God acts, Jesus appears, and the disciples are transformed through the Spirit. Testimony that can be cross-examined is important to it, but so is faith that recognizes who God is, who Jesus is, and responds with personal trust and love—the double "my" in "My Lord and my God!" (20:28).[10]

Jesus between Then and Now: The History of the Reception of John's Jesus

John's Gospel has perhaps been the most influential single text on Christian thought during the past two millennia. Its effects have been so pervasive that a history of its reception would be a history of a huge amount of Christian

---

and interpretation into account, see Ford, *Self and Salvation*, chaps. 7, 8; Ford, *Christian Wisdom*, chaps. 2, 5.

9. It is worth remembering that authors who wished to convey fresh insight or emphasis in telling a story would feel free to tell the story differently, while keeping what they considered essentials. This is seen in the Bible not only in the four Gospels but also in the divergences between Exodus and Deuteronomy, or between 1–2 Chronicles and the earlier books 1–2 Samuel and 1–2 Kings. On Jewish and Hellenistic rewriting, see Brodie, *The Quest for the Origin of John's Gospel*.

10. Perhaps the most important single book on Jesus and his resurrection has for me been *The Identity of Jesus Christ* by Hans Frei, who is especially illuminating on the interrelationship of realistic narrative, historical testimony, and resurrection. This is backed up by Frei's other works, such as *The Eclipse of Biblical Narrative* and *Types of Christian Theology*.

thought, liturgy, music, art, and so on. Out of all that, I focus now on just four representative elements that are relevant to my interpretation.

One is the formative effect of this Gospel on the development of the mainstream doctrines of Jesus Christ and the Trinity. It was considered the fullest revelation of Jesus, and in the Greek tradition its author was simply known as "The Theologian." Perhaps the most divisive doctrinal issue in the early centuries of the church was teaching about the person of Christ, Christology, which is also central to the Gospel of John. This convergence on who Jesus is as the key question not only points to what was considered to lie at the heart of Christian faith, but also suggests that Christians need to be very wary of dividing the church over any issue not directly related to that. More will be said about Christology, Trinity, and unity at various points in the coming chapters.[11]

The second is the fruitfulness of intensive attention to the reception of John in particular periods and authors. To take just one of many in this genre, Paul Cefalu's work on John in early modern English literature and theology has repeatedly given stimulation and illumination.[12] I am especially attracted by his concept of a "Johannine Renaissance,"[13] since I think that would be something of great benefit to the twenty-first-century church and world.

The third is the impact of John on Christian thought in the past century. It is striking how leading thinkers and movements have found this Gospel extraordinarily fruitful. Even some of those with deep differences from one another, such as Karl Barth, Rudolf Bultmann, and Hans Urs von Balthasar, have taken John as their leading theological guide among the Gospels. The same has been true of diverse Christian traditions around the world—Catholic, Orthodox, Anglican, Lutheran (John was Luther's favorite Gospel), Reformed, Methodist, and Quaker (John was George Fox's favorite Gospel)—and in the ecumenical movement there has been no more influential single text than John 17:20–26.[14] In the years to come it will be of particular interest to see how Pentecostal and Charismatic theologies integrate John on the Holy Spirit with

11. The most influential scholar on my own understanding of Jesus and the Gospel of John in the context of the relation of doctrine and Scripture in the early centuries of Christianity has been Frances M. Young, especially in *Ways of Reading Scripture*; *Exegesis and Theology in Early Christianity*; *Biblical Exegesis and the Formation of Christian Culture*; *From Nicaea to Chalcedon*; and her forthcoming magnum opus, which she has shared as it is being written, "Doctrine as Making Sense of Scripture."

12. Cefalu, *The Johannine Renaissance*.

13. "Renaissance" means "rebirth" and is one of John's generative images for seeing and entering the kingdom of God, receiving the Spirit, believing and trusting in Jesus, having eternal life, and living and acting "in God" (3:1–21). Furthering a Johannine renaissance is a theme in my own continuing work, such as Ford, *Meeting God in John*; Ford and Cocksworth, *Glorification*.

14. See Ford, "Mature Ecumenism's Daring Future."

their understandings of Luke-Acts and Paul, which so far have usually been dominant.[15]

Finally, standing for the many artistic responses to John, is Johann Sebastian Bach's *St. John Passion*.[16] Bach integrates in it the three leading themes that I have identified in this introduction. Right from the start in the opening chorus, and then immediately in the arrest scene, there is the primacy given to who Jesus is, intensified by passionate personal address to him in the first chorale: "O great love, O love beyond measure, that brought You to this path of martyrdom!"[17] There is a parallel concern with the ongoing drama of following Jesus, as in the early aria: "I follow You likewise with happy steps, and do not leave You, my Life, my Light. Pursue your journey, and don't stop, continue to draw me on, to push me, to urge me." This is expressed both in individual solos and corporate chorales. Bach's music and words communicate the stretching of mind, heart, and action in discipleship: "I cannot grasp with my mind, how to imitate Your mercy. How can I then repay Your deeds of love with my actions?" Throughout, there is a shaping of desire and longing: "O beloved Lord! Only give me what You earned, more I do not desire!" And the third theme of God, all people, and all creation is expressed in words, but above all in the integration of the words with the music, as the verbal meaning combines with the physicality of sounds, instruments, and voices, and the abundance of melodies, rhythms, harmonies, tonal and theological symmetries,[18] repetitions with variations, and cadences.[19] This *St. John Passion* has proved through three centuries to be attractive and accessible far beyond the company of the followers of Jesus.[20] It

15. For an account of the range of Christian theologies of the past century, see Ford and Muers, *The Modern Theologians*.

16. A major work on this is Chafe, *J. S. Bach's Johannine Theology*. He shows the connections of Bach's scriptural understanding with classic patristic and medieval "senses of Scripture," with intertextuality (especially with the Synoptic Gospels and Psalms), and with the liturgical year, as well as the specific influence of Bach's own Lutheran tradition.

17. Chafe is clear about the centrality of the name of Jesus, and other indicators of his identity, such as "I am," to the *St. John Passion*, and he sees Bach's musical expression of who Jesus is as "perhaps the strongest evidence for the fact that Bach should be ranked with other artistic interpreters of the Gospel," such as Leonardo da Vinci in his painting *The Last Supper* (*J. S. Bach's Johannine Theology*, 30).

18. A favorite theme throughout Chafe, *J. S. Bach's Johannine Theology*.

19. On the interplay of theology and music, see the perceptive writings of Jeremy S. Begbie, including *Resounding Truth* and *Theology, Music and Time*. I am grateful to Jeremy for the time spent listening together to the *St. John Passion* with its score in front of us and Jeremy suggesting connections between the music and theology. Specifically on the cosmic dimension of Bach's *St. John Passion*, see Plantinga, "The Integration of Music and Theology in the Vocal Compositions of J. S. Bach."

20. Michael Marissen, in his original musical and conceptual study *Lutheranism, Anti-Judaism, and Bach's St. John Passion*, also shows how Bach resists Luther's anti-Semitism—e.g., by assigning responsibility for the death of Jesus to all of sinful humanity, not just the Jews.

continues to communicate, across many boundaries and differences, a sense of abundant life that is not overcome by evil, sin, suffering, or death.

Why John Now? (2): The Church Now

Each of the three leading themes seems to me to be of vital importance to the twenty-first-century church and therefore to encourage a Johannine renaissance in the church now.

Who Jesus is, now and always, alive and present as God is present, longing to share this life of love with others in the Spirit, is the reality at the heart of the church. The primary response to recognizing this is amazed acknowledgment that leads into commitment and worship: "My Lord and my God!" (20:28). John wants both to enable an initial encounter with Jesus, one by one and one to one, sensitive to each person, each called by name, and to embrace each in a family community of love. It is a community of learners, whose main question is, Who are you, Jesus? The learning is endless, and it involves learning to read John in constant intertextual relationship with other texts, learning to think within the horizon of the prologue and the rest of the Gospel, learning to pray within the horizon of John 17, and above all learning to love and serve as Jesus loved and served.

Such a learning community, besides its positive focus on reading, thinking, praying, and loving in ways that center on who Jesus is, needs to be alert to whatever distracts people from this concentration. John selects from a mass of material (20:30; 21:25) what he considers essential for readers, "that through believing you may have life in his name" (20:31). Any Christian or church therefore needs to be extremely wary of considering as essential things that John does not emphasize, and to be constantly aware of the many desires, concerns, issues, plans, and conflicts that might distract from attending primarily to who Jesus is.

The Holy Spirit is inseparable from who Jesus is and who his followers are. At the heart of the ongoing drama of following Jesus together is the intimate relationship of Jesus with those into whom he breathes his Spirit bearing his words. In this relationship his followers can constantly learn more and more of what is involved in being loved by Jesus and loving him. One striking feature of the ongoing drama as taught by John is its daring openness to more truth and to innovative loving and serving—all on condition of ringing true with who Jesus is.

And the horizon for this is nothing less than God and all reality. That constantly challenges individuals and whole communities to stretch their thinking, imagining, and praying to do justice to the Word of God, through whom all things were created, and who continues to relate to them all. The desire of Jesus for the coming together of all people and all creation is the inspiration for a church that is here for the sake of the whole world, as Jesus is. One implication of this is a prophetic questioning of boundaries, dividing walls, and the often opposed, conflictual identities that the walls surround. Jesus is constantly moving, speaking, and acting across boundaries, and the risen Jesus is, whether acknowledged or not, present to those on both sides of all divisions. What that might mean for his followers, both locally and globally, is one of their most profound challenges. Jesus in John's Gospel makes sure that this is first of all faced at home, in one's own face-to-face community. The challenge is in the "if" of his love command, "By this everyone will know that you are my disciples, if you have love for one another" (13:35), and even more radically in the "completely" of his prayer, "that they may become completely one, so that the world may know that you have sent me and have loved them even as you have loved me" (17:23).

Yet there are two very serious qualifications, one negative, the other positive, regarding this picture of the followers of Jesus today and their community, the church now.

The negative reality is that, to use a favorite image of John, the darkness continues—not least in the church. There is, as this commentary seeks to show, a tragic dimension to this Gospel. It is not only starkly realistic about the ways the world goes tragically wrong; it shows the same grim realism about the community of those who follow Jesus. Disciples are shown to be mistaken, misled, inadequate, wrongly confident, lacking in faith and love, fearful, disloyal, thieving, and traitorous. These are the ones Jesus has chosen and taught in person! The Gospel picture of the fallible followers of Jesus is not just preresurrection: the final incident in the Gospel is provoked by false rumors in the church, and the First Letter of John reinforces the picture of a church of sinners, divided in doctrine and urgently needing encouragement to love.

This fallible community has continued through history in its tragic vulnerability to all sorts of sin, including those most emphasized by John: lack of trust in and commitment to Jesus, blindness and deafness to the truth, and lack of love. Perhaps most disgraceful of all has been a lack of unity in love, trust, peace, and joy, contrary to the desire of Jesus in his final prayer. The reception history of the Gospel of John has been problematic in many ways. One that has deservedly received much recent attention has been its polemical use against Jews and Judaism, and its share in the appalling history of anti-Semitism and anti-Judaism, both of which still continue. Interpretations of John down through the centuries, including those by leading figures such as Augustine and Martin Luther, have repeatedly fed the teaching of contempt for Jews, and of supersessionism in relation to Judaism.

This commentary faces these and other painful issues at several points.[21] The overall approach is to try to identify how John has been drawn on in problematic ways, and yet to seek how John, his intertexts, and other strands in the tradition can be drawn on now to help in repairing damage, healing wounds, and generating a better reception history for the future. Any Johannine renaissance in the church that fails to follow such an approach is in danger of reenacting some of the worst in Christian history.

The positive qualification to the positive vision of the church is that there is no suggestion in John that the presence and activity of Jesus are restricted to the community of his followers. We who follow Jesus are loved, illuminated, sent as he was sent, given the Spirit without measure, and invited to trust, serve, pray, and love in response. But, however we respond, the ongoing drama is far greater than that of the church. The world is also loved, and Jesus freely relates to it. That is the further dimension of the question, Why John Now?

Why John Now? (3): The World Now

The prologue's horizon of God and all reality opens up an abundance of meaning, of life, and of love, none of which can be imagined as confined to those who follow Jesus.

Meaning

Meaning is signaled in the prologue by the lead concept of "the Word," *logos*, identified with God, connected with the creation of all things and with light, the source of fullness, and also identified with Jesus Christ. The present work tries to think through the unlimited significance of Jesus, but in ways that do not imply that I have an overview of it. Only the Word, one with God, has that. The rest of us see glimpses. The desire for meaning, understanding, knowledge, and truth is unlimited, and leads now along paths similar to those followed by John: reading Scriptures and other texts; attending to testimony and personal experience; engaging with the surrounding culture and civilization; thinking and praying in community with others; trying to distinguish truth from falsehood; experimenting with forms of communication; and stretching minds, hearts, and imaginations to do justice to questions, doubts, and discoveries. In all this the Spirit of truth blows freely across the boundaries of historical

21. Issues include predestination; power and authority; gender; Eucharist; ethical and political implications and orientations; relations between faiths; evil, sin, and death; and personal and social identity.

periods, genders, cultures, arts, media, religions, disciplines, political allegiances, classes, abilities, and other sources of meaning and identity. *Openness to Jesus and the Spirit he breathes involves openness to meaning and truth wherever they are found, and therefore values sustained openness to fresh understanding, to new ways of seeing things, to changing our minds, and to rethinking and reimagining both ourselves and reality.*

Yet falsehood, fake news, misunderstanding, lies and deception, unreliable testimony, ignorance, distortions and manipulations of knowledge and desire, energetic promotion of shallow or prejudiced or hate-filled opinions, character assassination, incitements to violence, ideologies in the service of money or racism or gender inequality or dominating power, and worldviews with habits of thought and imagination that find no life-giving meaning and lead to despair—these, and more such things, also are real. The prologue says, "The light shines in the darkness, and the darkness did not overcome it" (1:5). That both recognizes the continuation of darkness and gives confidence in the ongoing drama of seeking and witnessing to the truth. "For this I was born, and for this I came into the world, to testify to the truth. Everyone who belongs to the truth listens to my voice" (18:37). Jesus said this at his trial, leading to his death, and witnesses to the truth are now, daily, being humiliated, tortured, and killed. One of the greatest challenges for followers of Jesus, who are sent as he was sent, is to learn the truth, belong to it, witness to it, and be in solidarity with others (often surprising others) who also witness to the truth.

Life

Life is one of John's core categories, essential to the presentation of who Jesus is and to following him, and also to reaching out to embrace all humanity and all living creatures. The prologue headlines it: "What has come into being in him was life, and the life was the light of all people" (1:3–4). *As with truth, the vocation and mission of Jesus are explicitly connected with life, and so commitment to full, multifaceted life is vital for those who are sent as he was sent*: "I came that they may have life, and have it abundantly" (10:10).

Yet disease, mental illness, disability, hunger and thirst, poverty, bitter division, violent conflict, forced migration, pollution of water and air and land, extinction of species, injustice, cruelty and torture, exploitation and slavery, humiliation and misery of many sorts, mistrust and despair, and death—these, and much else like them, are also the reality of our world now. To follow Jesus is to be part of a drama in which we trust, for ourselves and others, that none of those have the last word, and that Jesus, crucified and risen, is the first, present, and last word. This commits us to enduring our own share in such evils, and, when possible, doing life-giving signs, sometimes in collaboration with unlikely people and organizations, and often in long-term, costly, and largely hidden service.

Love

Love is subtly headlined in the prologue's culminating picture of the Son being "close to the Father's heart" (1:18). Then it is first mentioned in the programmatic statement, "For God so loved the world that he gave his only Son, so that everyone who believes in him may not perish but may have eternal life" (3:16). *This love for the world, springing from the heart of God and embodied in Jesus, is the single most important reality to which John testifies, inseparable from Jesus, his Father, and the continuing, Spirit-inspired drama into which all are invited.* The Farewell Discourses open up its mutuality and its breadth, length, depth, and height; the crucifixion of Jesus enacts it, and initiates a new family, with the disciple Jesus loved and the mother of Jesus at its heart; and, after the resurrection, Jesus breathes his own Spirit of love into his followers, sending them as he was sent—in love for the world.

Yet lack of love, distorted love, wounded love, disappointed love, tragic love, failure in love, exploited or exploiting love, deceitful love, betrayal of love, one-sided and rejected love, illusions of love, misunderstood love, inability to love, hardheartedness and refusal to love, and humiliated love—these, and other pathologies of love, are the experience of multitudes of people right now. *The greatest challenge of the Gospel of John is to trust the love of Jesus and to respond in love.* Time and again the reader is invited (sometimes in ways that seem more like shock therapy) to face the decision to trust or not to trust, and to love or not to love. Both the enemies of Jesus and those closest to him demonstrate the pathologies of love. The way of love's abundance is through the crucifixion, and being willing to put one's life on the line, or even to give one's life for love of others: if the "single grain . . . dies, it bears much fruit" (12:24).

Here in love the three leading elements in this Gospel come together: who Jesus is, and the abundance of meaning, life, and love in him; the Spirit given without measure for the ongoing drama of loving, centered in the intimate mutuality of being loved by Jesus and abiding in him; and the world that is loved by God and is the subject of the astonishing promise, "And I, when I am lifted up from the earth, will draw all people [or "all things"] to myself" (12:32). We can have no overview of the mysteries of this love, or of the forms it can take, both among and beyond the followers of Jesus. But this Gospel (together with its intertexts) encourages desiring it, receiving it, trusting it, inhabiting it, being radically open to its surprises, and responding to it imaginatively and with daring.

Now

The world now, as I write, is coping with an unprecedented surprise: the global COVID-19 pandemic. Inseparable from that are other unprecedented global developments, especially two: the intensifying ecological crisis and the impact of electronic communication in shaping an "information civilization" with computers, smartphones, internet, virtual interactions and communities, remote working and education, online business and gambling and worship, social media, new addictions, expanding surveillance, electronic warfare and crime, and accompanying massive inequalities of wealth, power, and knowledge.

What happens when such surprises are met by the surprises and the abundance that come through reading and rereading John? There is, of course, no answer in advance of it happening. And it happens differently for different people, groups, nations, regions, and religions. The Spirit is given to draw us readers of John closer to Jesus and his Father in ever-deepening understanding and love, at the same time as drawing us deeper into community with one another, and drawing us deeper and further into the world in love. Global challenges, such as the pandemic, the ecological crisis, and a pervasive information culture, are joined with very particular, personal, and local challenges each person faces in the areas of meaning, life, and love. There is no overview of all this, even within our own group or family—"If it is my will that he remain until I come, what is that to you? Follow me!" (21:22). A Johannine renaissance, like the European Renaissance so perceptively described by Stephen Toulmin,[22] is about an abundance of signs of creativity and life, thousands of flowers blossoming, each with a name, yet many hidden.

For me, in my small sphere of living and loving, as I continue to reread John by myself and with others during this time,[23] amidst the continuing abundance

22. Toulmin, *Cosmopolis*.

23. During the pandemic, beside conversation with my wife, Deborah, and with the staff team at St. Andrew's Cherry Hinton, Zoom meetings with Ashley Cocksworth and Robbie Leigh, Zoom Scriptural Reasoning sessions, and Zoom discussion on John's Gospel with members of the research community of the Queen's Ecumenical Theological Foundation in Birmingham, there have been two especially fruitful engagements in connecting John with the three global developments mentioned. Margaret Daly-Denton, whose Earth Bible commentary on John will figure later in this commentary, has shared the initial results of rereading John in relation to the pandemic. And Micheal O'Siadhail and I together have been both rereading John and reading alongside it a number of works relating to our information civilization and the ecological crisis, while also reflecting on the pandemic. Of these contemporary intertexts with John, three of the most fruitful (all recommended by my children) have been Zuboff, *The Age of Surveillance Capitalism*; Krznaric, *The Good Ancestor*; Tsing, *The Mushroom at the End of the World*. Tsing's book is a social-anthropological study of the culture, economics, and multispecies ecology related to "the most valuable mushroom in the world," the matsutake mushroom (see the quotation from Tsing in the sidebar). It is premature

Searching has a rhythm, both impassioned and still. Pickers describe their eagerness to get into the forest as a "fever." Sometimes, they say, they didn't plan to go, but the fever catches you. In the heat of the fever, one picks in the rain or snow, even at night with lights. One gets up before dawn to be there first, lest others find the mushrooms. Yet no one can find a mushroom by hurrying through the forest: "slow down," I was constantly advised. Inexperienced pickers miss most of the mushrooms by moving too fast, for only careful observation reveals those gentle heaves. Calm but fevered, impassioned but still: the picker's rhythm condenses this tension in a poised alertness.

Pickers also study the forest. . . . Some pickers mention that they pay attention to the dirt. . . . But when I press for specifications, they always demur. One picker was probably tired of my asking, and so he explained: the right kind of soil is the soil where matsutake grows. So much for classification. Discourse has its limits here.

Rather than a class of soils, the picker scans for lines of life. . . . Life lines are entangled: candy cane and matsutake; matsutake and its host trees; host trees and herbs, mosses, insects, soil bacteria, and forest animals; heaving bumps and mushroom pickers. Matsutake pickers are alert to life lines in the forest; searching with all the senses creates this alertness. It is a form of forest knowledge and appreciation without the completeness of classification. Instead, searching brings us to the liveliness of beings experienced as subjects rather than objects.

—Anna Lowenhaupt Tsing, *The Mushroom at the End of the World*, 242–43

one thing has become very clear: *now John is as relevant as ever, and in fresh, generative ways.* The main way to discover this is simply to read and reread this text, with appropriate intertexts, by oneself and with others. Discovery happens as the reading, thinking, and conversations are motivated by a passionate desire for meaning, life, and love. The aim is the sort of searching Anna Lowenhaupt Tsing describes among the pickers of matsutake mushrooms (see the quotation from Tsing in the sidebar).

I hope that you readers of this commentary, as you try to discern how to read, think, and live in the world now, will find yourselves drawn into such searching—impassioned, slow, alert to entangled lines of life, and above all alert to the Subject who is to be encountered through reading and trusting what is written in this Gospel.

---

to come to conclusions now, but we hope that these engagements will in time result in published poetry and theology.

Conclusion: To the Single, Beloved Reader

This introduction ends where it began, with reading John. Up to now, the readers have been plural; here I concentrate on the single reader of John and of this commentary's reading of John. The first words of Jesus in this Gospel are "What are you [plural] looking for?" (1:38). Near the end, the crucified and risen Jesus says to Mary Magdalene, "Whom are you [singular] looking for?" (20:15). My own individual account of reading John over many years is given in the epilogue. Here I address you singular, whoever you are.

Of all the Gospels, John is most concerned with the individual, both in encounters with Jesus and in his teaching. The good shepherd calls each by name. *Because Jesus is risen and present as God is present, the event of reading about Jesus can also be the event of meeting him, one to one.* What this means is that you yourself are in his presence, loved by him as was the author of the Gospel, and invited deeper, broader, higher, and forever into an abundance of meaning, life, and love. My chief desire is to help you accept that invitation. By far the best way for that to happen is by reading, thinking, trusting, praying, and living John; and you are promised the Spirit "without measure" (3:34) as you seek to do so. This book is just one intertext that may be helpful. John's text is given in bold print. Please concentrate mainly on that. And be open to surprises.

John 1:1–18

The Unsurpassable Horizon

God and All Reality, Jesus and Us, Ultimate Mystery and Intimacy

John's prologue, the first eighteen verses of the Gospel, is perhaps the single most influential short passage in the history of Christian theology. It is a daring, innovative account of God and all reality, and this is the context for making sense of the ongoing drama of Jesus Christ and his followers. The prologue is not ascribed to Jesus; it is a mature theology springing from long and hard thinking about Jesus. The author[1] explores the depth and breadth of the significance of Jesus, while being in intimate relationship with him and taking part in the Christian community of the friends of Jesus.

> 1 In the beginning was the Word, and the Word was with God, and the Word
> was God. 2 He was in the beginning with God. 3 All things came into being
> through him, and without him not one thing came into being. What has come
> into being 4 in him was life, and the life was the light of all people. 5 The light
> shines in the darkness, and the darkness did not overcome it.
> 6 There was a man sent from God, whose name was John. 7 He came as
> a witness to testify to the light, so that all might believe through him. 8 He

1. On the authorship of John, see comments on 21:24–25. I refer to the author simply as John, while recognizing that whoever wrote the Gospel we have now was also part of a community of recollection and interpretation.

> himself was not the light, but he came to testify to the light. [9] The true light,
> which enlightens everyone, was coming into the world.
>
> [10] He was in the world, and the world came into being through him; yet
> the world did not know him. [11] He came to what was his own, and his own
> people did not accept him. [12] But to all who received him, who believed in
> his name, he gave power to become children of God, [13] who were born, not
> of blood or of the will of the flesh or of the will of man, but of God.
>
> [14] And the Word became flesh and lived among us, and we have seen
> his glory, the glory as of a father's only son, full of grace and truth. [15] (John
> testified to him and cried out, "This was he of whom I said, 'He who comes
> after me ranks ahead of me because he was before me.'") [16] From his full-
> ness we have all received, grace upon grace. [17] The law indeed was given
> through Moses; grace and truth came through Jesus Christ. [18] No one has
> ever seen God. It is God the only Son, who is close to the Father's heart,
> who has made him known.

This introduces key themes, images, and essential categories of the Gospel: God, Word, creation, all things, all people, life, light, darkness, John (the Baptist, the forerunner of Jesus), witnessing and testimony, believing, the world, knowing, Jesus's own people, the name of Jesus, power, children of God, birth from God, flesh, glory, father, only son, grace, truth, fullness, law, Moses, Jesus Christ, seeing, and the intimacy between Jesus and his Father. These might be seen as large containers into which more and more is poured as the Gospel progresses, deepening and expanding the meaning.

The prologue can be read as a poetic hymn and as a fresh interpretation of Scripture in the light of Jesus Christ; it is also crafted as an introduction to the entire Gospel, and it suggests that it is to be considered as itself Scripture. It opens (1:1–5) with the Word related to God and all things, affirming a God-centered, meaningful universe. It then (1:6–17) plunges into the complexity and messiness of history and ordinary life, as the Word becomes a human being. Its culmination (1:18) is about the intimacy between Jesus and his Father into which the Gospel invites all its readers.

Those ("we" [1:14]; "we . . . all" [1:16]) who accept this invitation are "children of God" (1:12), who, as the rest of the Gospel shows, receive the Spirit that is breathed by Jesus into his disciples (literally, "learners"), leading them "into all the truth" (16:13) and inspiring them to do even "greater things" than Jesus did (14:12). *So the unsurpassable extensity of the prologue's horizon, embracing God and all reality, combines with the ultimate intensity of intimacy between Jesus and his Father, and this frames and introduces not only the drama of Jesus's life, death, resurrection, and giving of his Spirit, but also the ongoing drama of following Jesus in the company of his friends (21:19, 22).*

Beginning with Scripture: Learning to Read with John (1:1)

"In the beginning" (*en archē*) is the opening of the Septuagint, John's Greek translation of the Hebrew Bible.[2] They are the first words of the first verse of the book of Genesis. John begins with Scripture, and this whole Gospel is steeped in allusions to it, so that in order to understand it we have to read it alongside other texts. One of its main ways of inviting us deeper into its meaning is to lead us to reread both what is written and the Scriptures to which it refers. So throughout this commentary there will be suggestions for such fruitful "intertexts."

This way of opening the Gospel is just one of many indications that it has been written as Scripture. That is especially important for how we are being invited to read it: as a text that is to be reread repeatedly, savored and meditated upon, inhabited through prayer and practice, connected to other scriptural texts, and continually shared with other readers.

But even more than that, if John is writing Scripture, then his own way of interpreting Scripture can be a guide to his readers in interpreting what he himself writes—*John's way of reading can be a model for ours.* How does John read Genesis 1:1 in this prologue? Thoughtfully, daringly, surprisingly, as no one, so far as we know, had ever read it before. Instead of continuing the quotation from Genesis to say "In the beginning God created" (*en archē epoiēsen ho theos*), he takes from Genesis that God created through speaking ("Then God said, 'Let there be light'" [Gen. 1:3]) and says "In the beginning was the Word." Then in the rest of the prologue he takes this further and identifies the Word with God and also with Jesus Christ as God's full self-expression. What might this mean for our reading John? There are at least three guidelines that can be drawn initially from the prologue and confirmed in the rest of this Gospel.

- The text is to be taken very seriously in its plain sense, but this is a "deep sense," with abundant meaning. Rereading need not simply lead to repeating Genesis or John, or previous interpretations of them, but needs to be open to further meaning. If the Holy Spirit has led John into more truth (16:13), then likewise, since the Spirit is shared with others too (20:22) and is given "without measure" (3:34), his readers are to be open to further

2. The translation was by Jews in Alexandria, Egypt, over two centuries before Christ, and it was the Bible used by most of the New Testament authors.

truth. Just as John improvises afresh in his reading of Genesis, so his readers might improvise on what he writes.

- This improvisation is not arbitrary, or a matter of "anything goes." Not only is the text taken seriously in its plain sense, but also there is a basic discipline and criterion: Jesus Christ.[3] He is the inspiration for John's rereading of Genesis. But the understanding of Jesus also is not just a matter of repeating what previous texts or testimonies have said. John himself improvises on the Synoptic Gospels. One of the most important things to do while reading any passage in John is to ask how it connects with passages in the other Gospels (e.g., reflecting on John 1:1 alongside Mark 1:1, "The beginning of the good news of Jesus Christ, the Son of God"—that looks like the theme on which John's prologue improvises, embracing "beginning," testimony, and the relation of Father and Son, with John affirming and deepening each). There are other affirmations, omissions, additions, and transformations, and by thinking through them we can be led deeper into understanding who Jesus is and appreciating better both the Synoptics and John.
- The double improvisation on the Scriptures of the Septuagint and the Synoptic Gospels is not just about reading texts but is also a model for practical living and is meant to shape it. New "light" and new "life" go inseparably together in the prologue and the rest of the Gospel. John above all is concerned with the ongoing drama of a community (the prologue's "we") being led by the Spirit of Jesus, following Jesus into new situations where there is no choice but to improvise and into new engagements with realities and people within the prologue's horizon of "all things" and "all people."

3. John's subtle, profound reading and writing of Scripture is beautifully illustrated by the way he both affirms and transforms the opening words of Gen. 1:1. The plain sense of Genesis, affirming creation by God, is clearly intended. But where the direct quotation from the Septuagint breaks off is before the words *epoiēsen ho theos*, meaning "God created." The Greek for "created," *epoiēsen*, can also mean "did" or "made," and it is a favorite verb in John's Gospel, often associated with Jesus. And what do we find at the end of the Gospel? In both "endings," 20:30–31 and 21:25, John says "Jesus did," *epoiēsen ho Iēsous*. This is Gen. 1:1 with "Jesus" as "God." It is as if John completes the quotation but transforms it by this substitution. In John 1:1 he breaks it off before "God created" and suspends it all through the Gospel. Then in chapter 20 he takes it up again: just after Thomas has addressed Jesus directly as "My Lord and my God!" he says "Jesus did/made/created" (20:30), improvising a new continuation. And finally, in a conclusion that refers to "the world" (*ho kosmos*), he repeats it: "There are also many other things that Jesus did/made/created" (21:25). The further meaning does not compete with or contradict Gen. 1:1; indeed, the whole Gospel might be seen as his account of why this is deeply true to Genesis. This is just one example of John's understated literary craftsmanship leading readers into deep theology; others will emerge through the Gospel, and it is likely that many are yet to be discovered. The "deep plain sense" of the Septuagint, the Synoptic Gospels, and John's own Gospel is inexhaustibly rich, and John writes so as to open attentive readers up to their multiple depths.

The Sense of the Word: Self-Expression, Scripture, and Civilization (1:1, 14)

In the beginning was the Word, and the Word was with God, and the Word was God. . . . And the Word became flesh and lived among us, and we have seen his glory (1:1, 14). Why does John use **the Word** (*ho logos*) as his key opening term? Of the many suggestions made over the centuries about this, there are three that together seem to me to be least inadequate.

First, and most obvious, John is beginning a writing that is made up of words and is trying to communicate the most important meaning and truth he knows, which he traces to God. At the heart of his conception of God is the relationship of Jesus to his Father (see 1:14, 18), which is one of mutual indwelling. They are utterly, inseparably involved with each other, yet can also be distinguished from each other. "Word" captures this combination of communication, identification, intimacy, and differentiation.

As so often, John is not only taking up a meaning but is also transforming it. The rest of his Gospel fills out what he means by "Word." Most speech only expresses something of the person speaking; it is a partial self-expression. This is full self-expression. *God is free to express completely in Jesus who God is.* Such a unique act of self-revelation in history has to be told mainly through the medium best suited to unique events involving people: testimony in story form. So most of the Gospel is in the form of a dramatic narrative. But, if one wants a key summary term for an initiative in which the truth of God's own reality is shared with human beings, then "Word" makes good sense. This has been confirmed by the fruitfulness of "Word" in Christian theology century after century and across cultures, worldviews, and civilizations. The two remaining points give some of the main reasons for that.

Second, "Word" leads into an engagement with the whole of Scripture. The obvious plain sense of the term *logos* is rooted in the Septuagint. There *logos* and related words for "saying" are used for ordinary human speech and also for God speaking, as in the creation narrative of Genesis 1. Besides creation by God's word, *logos* can also be used in relation to each of the three parts of the Septuagint: Torah (Law), Prophets, and Writings. It can refer to Torah—the Ten Commandments, for example, can be called the "ten words" (Decalogue, *deka logoi*); it is used for "the word of the Lord" that is spoken by the Prophets; and among the Writings it can refer to wisdom, and frequently occurs in Psalms. So John's key opening term resonates with the whole of his Bible: it recalls creation, law, prophecy, and wisdom, and the response to God in worship.

In addition, there is the use of *logos* in the rest of the New Testament. It often means the Christian good news (Luke 8:11; 2 Tim. 2:9; 1 John 1:1; Rev. 1:9), the

Gospel message as given by apostles (Acts 6:2), Paul (Acts 13:5; 1 Thess. 2:13), or Jesus (Luke 5:1). The main, and very important, theological point is that the Synoptics show through their narratives the inseparability of the message, or *logos*, of Jesus from his person—the emphasis on his teaching and actions during his ministry moves into a climax centered on what happens to him in person, his death and resurrection; and John's prologue, combined with his "I am" sayings and the narrative of Jesus's teaching, signs, death, and resurrection, is the most explicit and direct of all in its insistence on the identification of his person with his message and work. *For John the question Who is Jesus? is utterly central, his opening way of answering it is "the Word," and the meaning of this resonates with all Scripture. As Martin Hengel says, "The Prologue is a witness to a theology of the whole Bible"*[4] (see the further quotation from Hengel in the sidebar).

Third, there is another plain sense that is rooted in the Greek-speaking world of John's time. There, *logos* not only has a range of ordinary meanings, including verbal expression and the human reasoning faculty, but it also appears in many types of philosophical discourse, with meanings as various as the Platonic form or idea, the Stoic rational principle of all reality and its verbal expression, and the Neoplatonist divine emanation or mind. Greek-speaking Jews, notably Philo, could relate philosophy to Jewish biblical thought with the help of this term. This Hellenistic background to John is a matter of continual debate, but it is clear that in the Septuagint and its interpretation John inherited centuries of Jewish use of words such as *logos* that were also common currency in the wider culture. *His Scripture and his civilization come together in this term.*

The theological potential of the choice of this fundamental term is therefore immense. The way John uses it encourages intercultural theology, since one can be confident that Jesus Christ is already involved with all peoples and cultures, so that "seeds of the word" can be sought in them, found, and cultivated. In the strongly rhetorical culture of the Hellenistic world, a word-led theology was

> How simple and how extraordinary a symbol, yet how complex and how inclusive! As a stimulus to the imagination, it was able to fuse together aspects of human experience that normally tend to fly apart: hearing and doing, thinking and feeling, remembering and hoping, the liturgical and the ethical, the doctrinal and the mystical, the inaudible and the audible, the eternal and the historical.
>
> —Martin Hengel, "The Prologue of John," 289

4. Hengel, "The Prologue of John," 289.

especially attractive. In a more intellectual mode, *logos* was closely associated with thought and rationality, so Christian thinkers have been encouraged by the prologue to engage with the best in their civilization's thinking in philosophy and all other branches of understanding and knowledge.

The horizon of God and the whole of reality means that no limit can be set on what is relevant to Christian thought and imagination, and all forms of discourse are potentially fruitful. The twentieth and twenty-first centuries have perhaps been the most theologically fruitful in the history of Christianity. There have been many new voices, those of women above all, together with others from many continents, cultures, identities, backgrounds, and academic disciplines. The result has been a blossoming of Christian thought and imagination, and lively engagements not only with the classic topics of theology (such as God, creation, sin and evil, providence, Jesus Christ, the Holy Spirit, salvation, the church, ethics and politics, and the future) but also with art, poetry, drama, dance, film, the natural and human sciences, other religions, and much else. John's embracing horizon of "all things" and "all people" has continually inspired Christians and others to stretch their minds and imaginations in these ways.

Rethinking God in Relation to Jesus: Intimacy, Incarnation, and Invisibility (1:1–9, 14–15, 18)

> [1] . . . and the Word was with God, and the Word was God. [2] He was in the
> beginning with God. [3] . . . What has come into being [4] in him was life, and
> the life was the light of all people. [5] The light shines in the darkness, and the
> darkness did not overcome it. . . .
>
> [14] And the Word became flesh and lived among us, and we have seen his
> glory, the glory as of a father's only son. . . . [18] No one has ever seen God. It
> is God the only Son, who is close to the Father's heart, who has made him
> known.

All the New Testament authors write in the presence of God known through Jesus Christ, and they reach for language that might do justice to an amazing, unprecedented reality. John's prologue faces head-on the most profound double question: Who is God? Who is Jesus?

Intimacy at the Heart of Reality

John answers not only with the concept of **the Word**, which allows him to speak of Jesus as the full self-expression and self-revelation of who God is (resonating, as we have seen, with the whole of the Bible and of his civilization and enacted dramatically in the way he tells the Gospel story), but also with the concept of relationship in God, **God the only Son, who is close to the Father's heart.**

This is the climactic insight of the prologue. *Here John is pointing to the deepest secret of reality: the relationship between the Father and the Son.* Love is not mentioned at this point, but the rest of the Gospel makes it clear that this is above all a relationship of love. This love is at the heart of the unsurpassable horizon of God and "all things," "all people" (1:3, 5). The prologue moves from that breadth to this depth and intimacy. One of the most distinctive features of John's Gospel is its fascination with the relationship of Father and Son. It is a repeated theme, as in no other New Testament writing. The culminating insight into it is given in John 17 in the long prayer of Jesus on the eve of his death. That is also the most vivid affirmation of this relationship being open to all who enter it in trust and love.

Indeed, the whole Gospel can be read as an invitation to take part fully in the love between the Father and the Son. The imagery in 1:18 is significant: the Greek literally speaks of the Son being "into the bosom [*kolpon*] of the Father" (John McHugh translates, "who is now returned into the bosom of the Father").[5] This imagery is later used at the Last Supper of the disciple "whom Jesus loved" on his first explicit appearance: he reclined "on the bosom of Jesus" (the NRSV's "next to Jesus" fails to mention the Greek *kolpos*, "bosom") (13:23). This "Beloved Disciple" is never named, but he appears at key points (Last Supper, crucifixion, empty tomb, final meeting with the resurrected Jesus), and the whole Gospel is ascribed to him (21:24). One persuasive explanation of his anonymity is that he not only is a particular person but also stands for all followers of Jesus. He is the model of discipleship, defined by being loved by Jesus, resting on the breast of Jesus as Jesus does on his Father's, and testifying to Jesus. He has accepted the invitation into this love. Readers are reminded at the very end of the Gospel of him resting on the breast of Jesus at the Last Supper (21:20). Jesus's final words are about him: "If it is my will that he remain [*menein*] until I come, what is that to you?" (21:22, repeated in 21:23). As we will see,[6] that word *menein*, meaning "remain, abide, rest, dwell, live, stay, last, endure, await," is one of the most important in the Gospel. By the end of the Gospel, the Beloved Disciple has taken the mother of Jesus into his home, so that is where he is literally dwelling, in a family-transcending community formed by Jesus on the cross (19:26–27).

5. McHugh, *John 1–4*, 49.

6. See especially the section "Ongoing Life: Where Are You Staying/Abiding/Dwelling?" in the comments on 1:35–42 and the comments on 14:1 and 15:1–17.

The imagery of Jesus "now returned into the bosom of the Father" and of the disciple he loved being on his breast and sharing a home with his mother connects the beginning, the climax, and the ending of the Gospel, and the connectivity is above all that of love.

Darkness and the Drama of Incarnation

But there is no leap from the broad horizon of the opening of the prologue to the intimacy between Father and Son in its final verse, nor is there any disconnection between them. Some thinkers have mainly emphasized the broad horizon, and the need for a philosophy and theology that makes sense of the whole of reality, offering a worldview suited to intelligent faith. Others have emphasized the intimacy of relationship with Jesus and his Father, and John's Gospel has been a favorite in spirituality, mysticism, and other practices of prayerful communion. Both are genuinely inspired by John, but John's test of their faithfulness to Jesus is given in the central part of the prologue, which also points to what the rest of his Gospel is mainly focused on: the drama of God's involvement in history with all its darkness, messiness, sin, evil, and death. Both the big picture and the spirituality are decisively shaped by who Jesus is, as described in the story of his words, actions, relationships, suffering, death, and resurrection.

Darkness is introduced early, in 1:5, and recurs through the Gospel. What is darkness? There are two classic mysteries in Christian theology—the dark mystery of evil, sin, suffering, and death, and the bright mystery of God—and both are present in the prologue. They are not mysteries in the sense of realities that are to be simply regarded as insoluble problems, accepted as brute facts, and not thought about further. On the contrary, they are so central and pervasive that we need to think about them again and again; and if we are open to reality in all its puzzling complexity, they will challenge us again and again. Neither has a neat, packaged "solution," and one of the great dangers is to claim to have one—this is a special temptation for theologians and all sorts of ideologists seeking cut-and-dried certainty. They are mysteries in the sense of needing to be wrestled with continually, and it is always possible to develop our understanding of them, which often in practice means being open to fresh insights and surprises that lead us to rethink what we thought we knew.

Perhaps the most profound biblical lesson about this is in the book of Job. Job's friends offer him confident, packaged answers to his terrible suffering, but Job rejects these and wrestles on, stretching his mind and imagination to rethink the mystery of God, creation, and what goes wrong with creation. At the end of the book, his questioning and anguished immersion in mystery is decisively affirmed.[7]

In the culture of Western civilization, a profound lesson in sustained engagement with the mystery of evil, sin, suffering, and death can be learned through tragic drama, especially the Greek tragedians (Aeschylus, Sophocles, and Euripides) and Shakespeare. Like John, their response to the mystery is not primarily through concepts or arguments or explanations (though these are not excluded) but through dramatic narrative, characters, and events in interaction, and multiple perspectives that resist any simple overview or solution. Most cultures have in fact recognized the priority of this sort of story-shaped reality in coming to terms with life, as in our own popular culture of films, "soaps," fiction, and news stories.

After engaging with Job, Shakespeare, or John, we are left still in the midst of the drama of living, but with our understanding of it somehow changed. Above all, we enter the future of our own little drama informed by their dramas. Perhaps the single most important thing to be said about meeting the challenge of darkness in its many forms is that it is a practical problem. How do we actually carry on living in the face of it? John's Gospel is above all practical in this sense. It gives not a theoretical solution but a practical way forward. It says: go forward in intimate relationship with Jesus, learning who he is through his story, and then living in his Spirit. John 1:5 gives the basic encouragement that the darkness does not **overcome** (or "comprehend," or "master") the light and life that are in the Word, but there is no suggestion that the darkness has already disappeared or is harmless. The darkness continues. Just as Jesus was sent into a world where there was deep darkness, so his followers are sent into darkness at other times and places. In the final scene of the Gospel, Peter, after affirming the love between himself and Jesus, is told that he will suffer and die (21:15–23). *The Gospel is written to draw people into this ongoing drama of love that follows Jesus into darkness, in the confidence that love, not darkness, has the last word.*

After recognizing the character of human life in its interplay of light and darkness, we come to the central statement of the prologue: **And the Word became flesh and lived among us** (1:14). This affirms the incarnation (meaning literally, "in or into flesh"), God becoming a particular human being. It is an astonishing, daring conception: the Word, who has already been identified with the God who created all things, became flesh.

What is flesh? Here it stands for the full humanity, the human selfhood, of Jesus. It is important that John does not imply a dualism in which flesh is an

7. Some of my own wrestling with Job is described in Ford, *Christian Wisdom*, chap. 3, "Job!," and chap. 4, "Job and Post-Holocaust Wisdom."

inferior—or, even more negatively, a dangerously sinful—partner to the human soul or spirit. In Christian history "fleshly" or "carnal" has often carried very negative content, frequently sexually loaded. What flesh does imply in John is, as Dorothy Lee says, "fragility and finitude, limitation, and susceptibility to pain, sorrow, grief, rejection, oppression, and death."[8] But, as Lee shows, "flesh" in John means much more than this. Because the one who became flesh is also the one through whom "all things came into being" (1:3), any glory seen in his flesh extends to the whole of creation, whose fragility and vulnerability have become especially clear in our time. The rest of the Gospel shows John expanding the significance of the flesh of Jesus through signs, sayings, and events.[9] By the end of the Gospel the difference between God and flesh remains, but astonished acknowledgment of the union of the two in Jesus has culminated in Thomas's "My Lord and my God!" (20:28). What began with a "cool," sober statement in the prologue has been given its fullest content through the drama leading up to that intense, "hot" cry.

This has, century after century, evoked amazement and even offense. It is sometimes called "the scandal of particularity"—the universal God of all things embodied in one particular person. The hymns, poetry, and theology of incarnation are full of ways of expressing it that bring out how surprising, counterintuitive, and apparently paradoxical it is (see the quotation from Gregory Nazianzus in the sidebar).

> Oh the new mingling! Oh the blend contrary to all expectation! The one who is, becomes. The uncreated is created. The uncontainable is contained through a thinking soul, mediating between godhead and the thickness of flesh. The one who enriches becomes a beggar; for he begs for my own flesh, so that I might become rich in his divinity. The one who is full becomes empty; for he empties himself of his glory for a little time so that I might share in his fullness. . . . I received the image and I did not protect it; he received a share in my flesh so that he might even save the image and make deathless the flesh.
>
> —Gregory Nazianzus, *On the Holy Passover* 45.633–36

8. Lee, *Flesh and Glory*, 50.

9. Jesus's body is identified with the temple, the central place of God's glory (2:18–22); to eat his flesh and drink his blood is to have eternal life (6:54); the blood and water that flow from his side, when his dead body is pierced by a soldier's spear (19:33–37), have deep symbolic resonance (see commentary on 19:31–37); and the resurrected body of Jesus that has come through death still has the marks of that spear and of the crucifixion nails (20:26–29). Through his account of Jesus and of the Holy Spirit, John redefines the meaning of "flesh" just as he redefines the meaning of "God."

Those who question or reject the possibility of incarnation draw a more commonsense conclusion from its surprising character: it is therefore unlikely to be true. But the prologue, together with other parts of the Gospel of John and of the New Testament, points to the form of truth that is best suited to a surprising event and person: testimony. If something happens that is genuinely new (and what could be more genuinely new than a free initiative of the God who creates everything out of nothing?), then it is likely to require fresh categories and concepts, bursting the bounds of the old ones. So the old ones are unlikely to be the best guide to doing justice to the new event or person, and if we take them as conclusive we will not be open to the new. In this situation the possibility of the new cannot be conceived in advance: its possibility is shown only by it actually happening. It is news and must be witnessed to be known. There is no way for others who have not witnessed it to know it other than by trusting testimony. *History cannot be rerun, it is one-off, and so its primary form of truth is testimony.* As in a courtroom, testimony can be endlessly cross-examined (and there is a whole scholarly industry engaged in cross-examining the Gospel of John), but in the end the question is, Do the judge and jury believe the witnesses? **John . . . came as a witness to testify to the light, so that all might believe through him. He himself was not the light, but he came to testify to the light. . . . (John testified to him and cried out, "This was he of whom I said, 'He who comes after me ranks ahead of me because he was before me.'")** (1:6–8, 15).

Even if this surprising testimony is trusted, there is the further challenge to make sense of it. John faces this squarely and thinks it through in a way that had not been done before. The result is his idea of the Word incarnate as the full self-expression and self-giving of God in love, actualized in signs, teaching, crucifixion, resurrection, and the sharing of his Spirit. This generated hundreds of years of further thinking and discussion that, under the pressure of the New Testament testimony, led to classic teachings: the person of Jesus Christ is "of one being" (*homoousios*) with God; and this one God of love is intrinsically relational, a Trinity of Father, Son, and Holy Spirit. So the testimony to Jesus led to a rethinking of the second classic mystery, that of God. *In John the term that brings together both mysteries, dark and bright, is "glory."*

The Glory and Invisibility of God

John says of the Word incarnate, **We have seen his glory** (1:14). In the Bible glory is strongly associated with God, evoking the divine presence, holiness, radiance, self-communication, and transcendence that yet can come near and overwhelm people. The Word has already been identified with God. But then in 1:18 John says: **No one has ever seen God**. These apparently paradoxical or contradictory statements invite us deeper into John's theology. At the heart of John's rethinking of God in the light of Jesus is his reconception of glory.

This begins here in the prologue when John connects the glory of God with the Word made flesh. The glory is described in an analogy: **glory as of a father's only son**. As will emerge later, one of the most important theological terms in John is that little word "as."[10] Here the suggestion that the language of father and son, which is so important in John, is an analogy, and not a simplistic identification of God as masculine, can act as a check on taking the male imagery of God literally. Other checks include such elements as John's language for the humanity of Jesus (e.g., "flesh," "body," and "human being" [*anthrōpos*] are not gender-specific), the prominence of women in this Gospel, the use of wisdom language, and the abundance of other imagery (e.g., light, bread, water, birth, wind). Part of the particularity of Jesus is his maleness, but is his maleness more "scandalous" than being Jewish, speaking one language rather than another, being poor, or living in first-century Palestine? Some say it is, and there is ongoing debate.[11]

But what does **glory as of a father's only son** mean? As discussed above, it is illuminated by 1:18, the **only Son, who is close to the Father's heart**: this is the glory of deep, intimate love. Further content is given to both glory and love as the Gospel unfolds, notably in the prayer of Jesus in John 17.[12] Then the pivotal moment, in which glory and love are realized and revealed most fully, comes in the crucifixion of Jesus. Jesus laying down his life is both an act of supreme love (15:13) and the hour of his glorification (e.g., 7:39; 12:16, 23; 13:31). *There the mystery of darkness and the mystery of God come together in the person on the cross.* Glory and love are there revealed in flesh. C. K. Barrett calls this "the paradox which runs through the whole gospel: the δόξα [*doxa*, "glory"] is not to be seen *alongside* the σάρξ [*sarx*, "flesh"], nor *through* the σάρξ as through a window; it

10. See the section "'As . . . So . . .': A Daring Theological Imagination" in the comments on 3:11–21, and the comments on 10:11–21; 13:15, 31–35; 15:12; 17:18; 20:21.

11. Lee, *Flesh and Glory*, gives an account of it as it stood at the beginning of this century (see introduction, chaps. 2, 4, 5, 6, and 8, and conclusion), and I agree with her conclusions. See also Soskice, *The Kindness of God*, chap. 4, "Calling God 'Father,'" and chap. 6, "Trinity and the 'Feminine Other.'"

12. Each of these, glory and love, is a lens through which the whole Gospel can be viewed. On love, see comments on 3:16; 13:1–38; 15:12–17; 17:20–26; 21:15–23. On glory, see Ford, "'To See My Glory'"; Ford, "Ultimate Desire"; see also comments on 2:11; 11:4, 40; 12:28; 13:31–32; 17:1–5, 20–26; 21:19. Whereas in the Synoptics the glory of Jesus is glimpsed in episodes, above all in the transfiguration of Jesus, John headlines glory from the first—transfiguration pervades his Gospel. It is not only here in the prologue; glory is emphasized in the first of Jesus's signs (2:11) and the conclusion of the so-called book of signs (12:23, 28; cf. 12:43); it also appears early in the Farewell Discourses (13:31–32) and in Jesus's concluding prayer (17:1–5, 10, 22, 24). So glory frames the first two parts of the Gospel, and in the process it is redefined, above all by seeing Jesus's death as his glorification.

is to be seen *in* the σάρξ and nowhere else."[13] The central, burning question of the Gospel is therefore, *Who is this person, utterly flesh and utterly divine?*

Yet what about **No one has ever seen God** (1:18)? This radically rejects any idolatry of the humanity of Jesus and, by extension, resists making absolute or definitive any representation of God, whether in language or in another form. It is only through some medium that there is knowledge of God, and here that mediation is in Jesus, **who has made him known** (1:18). It is the "glory" of God that has been seen, not God. And there is only one God, the God of creation (1:1–2) and of Moses (1:17), who sent John the Baptist (1:6) and sent Jesus. Just after glory is evoked most intensely and comprehensively by Jesus in his final prayer (17:1), he says, "And this is eternal life, that they may know you, the only [*monos*] true God, and Jesus Christ whom you have sent" (17:3). The utter unicity and uniqueness of the one God has been profoundly reaffirmed and explored in recent theology by Katherine Sonderegger.[14]

The invisibility of the one God is underlined the second time glory is mentioned in the Gospel. This is when Jesus turns water into wine at a wedding, and the story concludes: "Jesus did [*epoiēsen*, "did/created"] this, the first [*archē*, "beginning"] of his signs, in Cana of Galilee, and revealed his glory; and his disciples believed in him" (2:11). It is described in terms as close as possible to a divine act of creation, but God is not seen. Jesus creates a sign, something that can be seen and, in this case, tasted. But it also has a meaning that draws some to acknowledge who he is: "his glory" is revealed, and "his disciples believed in him."

This is the pattern in the rest of the Gospel: signs, symbols, conversations, and events of rich, abundant meaning that all relate to who Jesus is, giving testimony that may or may not be believed but that always affirms the uniquely one God. The prologue introduces the question of believing or not believing—**His own people did not accept him. But to all who received him, who believed in his name, he gave power to become children of God** (1:11–12)—and it also strikes the note of abundance: **From his fullness we have all received, grace upon grace** (1:16). Both of these statements, together with the core testimony, **We have seen his glory**, raise a further question vital to the meaning of the prologue and the whole Gospel: Who are "we"?

We, the Children of God: Abundant Life, Believing, and Conflict (1:10–13, 16–18)

Alongside the three main themes of the prologue already explored—the framework of God and all things, the drama of the incarnation, and the intimate love

13. Barrett, *The Gospel according to St. John*, 165.
14. See Sonderegger, *The Doctrine of God* and *The Doctrine of the Holy Trinity*.

of the Father and the Son—is a fourth: the community to which John belongs, his "we." This mainly figures as part of the drama of history, but it is also deeply involved with the other two.

The opening of the prologue, **In him was life, and the life was the light of all people** (1:4), embraces these people too. Jesus came to bring abundant life (10:10). John continually emphasizes this abundance, imaginatively pointing to it in many ways: large quantities of wine, the wind of the Spirit blowing freely, water welling up to eternal life, surplus baskets of bread, perfume filling a house, a huge catch of fish, and more. "Eternal life" is his most common phrase for it, and this is a life of love, beginning now, to which community is intrinsic: it is life together with others. The end of the prologue indicates the fullest expression of this life: the love between the Father and the Son, into which all are invited. Coping with an abundance of love might be seen as the central challenge of John's Gospel.

In between the all-embracing extensity of the opening and the intimate intensity of the conclusion comes the complexity of historical life. **He was in the world, and the world came into being through him; yet the world did not know him. He came to what was his own, and his own people did not accept him. But to all who received him, who believed in his name, he gave power to become children of God, who were born, not of blood or of the will of the flesh or of the will of man, but of God** (1:10–13). This might refer directly to Jesus coming, being rejected, and gathering a community; or it might be about the Word in Israel's history before the incarnation is introduced in 1:14. I think, with B. F. Westcott,[15] that it is about both—John often writes so as to allow for more than one meaning. This passage raises at least three major issues that are important for the whole Gospel.

First, what about Israel and Judaism, "his own people"? Some of the sharpest disputes surrounding the Gospel of John concern its alleged anti-Judaism or anti-Semitism because of what it says about "the Jews." This will be discussed in commenting on John 2, and especially when we come to chapter 8, in which the conflict between Jesus and the Jews reaches its bitterest intensity. In the prologue the question also arises later in 1:17: "The law indeed was given through Moses; grace and truth came through Jesus Christ." The more general question of John's relation to Israel's history and Scriptures has already been discussed and recurs throughout this commentary.

15. "It is impossible to refer these words simply to the historical Presence of the Word in Jesus as witnessed to by John the Baptist. The whole scope and connexion of the passage requires a wider sense. The Word acts by His Presence as well as by His special Advent. The continuance and progress of things, no less than their original constitution, are fitted to make Him known." Westcott, *The Gospel according to St. John*, 8.

Second, what does it mean to "believe in his name"? The Greek verb *pisteuein*, meaning "believe, trust, have faith in," is a favorite of John. In 20:31 he sums up the whole purpose of his Gospel as being written so that "you may come to believe that Jesus is the Messiah, the Son of God, and that through believing you may have life in his name." There is a textual variation in some manuscripts, so that instead of "come to believe" the meaning could be "continue to believe." That happily illustrates a surprising feature of the Gospel of John that has often puzzled commentators.

On the one hand, John's Gospel is *very accessible to beginners* and is often given to inquirers or new Christians. Its language is straightforward, its stories well crafted, its imagery (especially from nature—water, wind, light and dark) is easily understandable, and its ethical teaching is simplified into a few core commands centered on love and service.

On the other hand, for experienced Christians, who "continue to believe," John can be *the most challenging text in the Bible*, with every rereading opening further depths, inviting us to stretch our minds and imaginations further and further. At the heart of it all there is continual engagement with the crucified and risen Jesus, whose radical summons is to love as he loves, to receive his Spirit and be sent as he was sent, and even to do greater things than he did.

In John's Gospel believing has sometimes been seen as an either/or decision, to believe or not believe, to live in the light or in the dark. But I am convinced by those who have a more nuanced view.[16] The Gospel describes many ways and stages of believing, and its approach to believing and trusting makes room for questioning, doubting, ambiguity, testing, gradual as well as sudden realization, growing, and maturing. It is a teaching Gospel for disciples (*mathētai*, "learners"). Its pedagogical methods are those of a skilled and experienced teacher and will be explored through this commentary. The main method is that of telling a good story with a variety of characters and viewpoints, drawing readers into a drama through which they are invited to trust, love, and follow the main character, Jesus, now. Who he is, what "his name" means, is given above all through his story, so relating to him in trust and faith involves following the story and entering more and more deeply into what it means.

So believing has many facets and forms, but in its full sense it embraces the whole of a person's life with God and other people: entering into that love, trust, and mutual glorification between Father and Son, and living from there, with all aspects of life affected—praying and worshiping, knowing and understanding, ethics and politics, suffering and dying.

16. See Hylen, *Imperfect Believers*; Dokka, "Irony and Sectarianism in the Gospel of John."

Third, what about John's own community, the immediate "we" that he refers to? An immense amount has been written about "the Johannine community." There is almost no historical evidence about it apart from the Gospel and the three Letters of John in the New Testament. So there is much speculation, and very little agreement, based on interpretations of those texts. Some scholars find in the Gospel a number of stages of composition, each reflecting a different period in the history of the Johannine community, and especially in its relations with its parent Jewish community.[17] These readings are often suggestive or provocative and can be theologically fruitful (somewhat like allegorical readings, which similarly see another meaning behind a text's plain sense), but on the whole I am content to remain agnostic about their historical reconstructions, which differ greatly among themselves.

Rather than speculating about the Johannine community, the approach in this commentary is to focus mainly on two other communities about which the Gospel has a good deal to say explicitly. The first is the community that figures in the story, those learners gathered around Jesus. The second, in continuity with that one, is the ongoing community of believers, down to today and beyond. John has more to say of relevance to this ongoing community than any of the other Gospels. Indeed, the "you" in the stated purpose of the Gospel, that "you may have life in his name" (20:31), is, in the light of the prologue and other passages, to be seen as potentially embracing all humanity, and the life is eternal life with no temporal limit. The drama of Jesus and his followers continues today, and this Gospel is a rich source of guidance and inspiration for today's followers as they seek to follow Jesus into new situations, improvising faithfully and daringly "in his name."

There is one final key question about the Johannine community that must be faced: Was it "sectarian," in the sense of an exclusive, closed community, the insiders sharply differentiated from outsiders? The case for this includes John's dualistic language (light/dark, truth/falsehood, life/death), the acute conflict with "the Jews," expectation of the world's hatred (e.g., 15:18–20), and the command to love one another (not neighbors or enemies). It does seem to have been a community under outside pressure, subject to hatred and enmity.

But, whatever the community's response to such pressures, the evidence of what John says about the two other communities, the one around Jesus in

17. See Martyn, *History and Theology in the Fourth Gospel*; R. Brown, *The Community of the Beloved Disciple*. The more recent account that I find most stimulating is Ashton, *The Gospel of John and Christian Origins* (see note 3 in the comments on 17:1–26). I am attracted by the "plea for caution" with which David Lamb ends his study, *Text, Context and the Johannine Community*, and by his modest description of it as "an embryonic *textual community*" (p. 209) in which reading and interpretation were vital and formative.

the story of his life, death, and resurrection and the ongoing one envisaged especially in the Farewell Discourses and the resurrection stories, points to something very different from sectarianism. The horizon is universal: Jesus is sent out of his Father's love for the world; he relates to diverse people from many communities; he washes the feet of Judas; and his death is to draw all people to himself.[18] And the ongoing community envisaged in the Farewell Discourses is centered on the nonsectarian Jesus, with open boundaries, a community of love that draws in many others. The God-centered intensity of the community's life is an attractor: "As you, Father, are in me and I am in you, may they also be in us, so that the world may believe that you have sent me" (17:21). If this believing is in line with what has been said above, then the community envisaged here is no more sectarian than is Jesus.

The Prologue as a Companion through the Gospel

There is so much more to be drawn from the prologue than has been done here: whole libraries of writing on it still do not exhaust it, not to mention conversations, sermons, prayer, liturgies, hymns, music, and all the other arts. How can readers cope with the prologue's extensity, depth, and density? I have explored it from a number of angles, especially its relation to the rest of the Bible; its comprehensive horizon; the concepts of incarnation, glory, and belief; its rethinking of God; and the community behind it, within it, and generated through it. *The picture that has begun to emerge is of a Gospel that is both disciplined and daring in its theology and encourages readers to be disciplined (by the Scriptures, and above all by attention to Jesus Christ) and daring (in thoughtful and imaginative interpretation, and above all in action) in theirs.*

As we move into the rest of the Gospel, it is worth making one further point: the prologue can act as a companion through the Gospel. It is fruitful to reread the prologue alongside every chapter, going back and forth between them. This both allows the prologue to be understood more fully, as further meaning is poured into its imagery and concepts, and also sets each new chapter in the primary context that the author wants it to have. This commentary will do that explicitly on only some chapters, but readers are recommended to do it for themselves with all.

18. "In the death of his Son the Father offers life *to his enemies*. This is the 'ultimate insanity' of the revelation that this narrator is trying to convey to his readers. To believe in that insanity is what requires a rebirth through the Spirit. The hostile world *is* the beloved world; the beloved world *is* the hostile world." Minear, *John: The Martyr's Gospel*, 41.

John 1:19–51

The Formation of a Learning Community

Now the drama begins. John the Baptist has already been mentioned twice in the prologue.[1] Now he appears in person, as does the other figure named in the prologue, Jesus. Jesus then starts to gather a community of disciples (literally, "learners"). This is the prologue dramatized, and the final fascinating and mysterious vision of intercourse between earth and heaven (1:51) can be seen as an image of Jesus, "close to the Father's heart," making God known (1:18).

John is confronted by the authorities from Jerusalem asking, "Who are you?" The "who" question proves to be central to the whole Gospel. Later John sees Jesus, identifies him as "the Lamb of God who takes away the sin of the world" and as "the Son of God," and testifies to the Holy Spirit coming and remaining/abiding on him. John then witnesses to two of his own disciples, and when they meet Jesus there is an exchange of fundamental questions: "What are you looking for?" asks Jesus; "Where are you staying/dwelling/abiding?" ask the disciples. This new community begins with two-way questioning.

One of these disciples, Andrew, extends the chain of testimony by finding and witnessing to his brother Simon Peter. The circle of learners then grows as Jesus finds and calls Philip, and Philip finds and witnesses to Nathanael. In the course of these conversations there is a flood of further identifications of who Jesus is, culminating with the only one on the lips of Jesus: "the Son of Man."

1. For a fuller discussion of John the Baptist, see the section "Love and Joy" in the comments on 3:22–36.

The passage is full of important theological content, multifaceted images and titles, and words and phrases whose meaning will extend and deepen as the Gospel proceeds. These are embedded in an open-textured story, pivoting around those three many-leveled, fundamental questions: "Who are you?" "What are you looking for?" and "Where are you staying/dwelling/abiding?" The rest of the Gospel might be seen as a response to these.

"Who Are You?" and the First Wave (1:19–28)

> 19 This is the testimony given by John when the Jews sent priests and Le-
> vites from Jerusalem to ask him, "Who are you?" 20 He confessed and did
> not deny it, but confessed, "I am not the Messiah." 21 And they asked him,
> "What then? Are you Elijah?" He said, "I am not." "Are you the prophet?"
> He answered, "No." 22 Then they said to him, "Who are you? Let us have an
> answer for those who sent us. What do you say about yourself?" 23 He said,
>
> "I am the voice of one crying out in the wilderness,
> 'Make straight the way of the Lord,'"
>
> as the prophet Isaiah said.
>
> 24 Now they had been sent from the Pharisees. 25 They asked him, "Why
> then are you baptizing if you are neither the Messiah, nor Elijah, nor the
> prophet?" 26 John answered them, "I baptize with water. Among you stands
> one whom you do not know, 27 the one who is coming after me; I am not
> worthy to untie the thong of his sandal." 28 This took place in Bethany across
> the Jordan where John was baptizing.

When John the Baptist is asked, **"Who are you?"** his first answer is, **"I am not the Messiah"** (*Christos*, "Christ," "anointed one"). Since, soon afterwards, Jesus is called the Messiah, this answer, and John's other two negatives, clear the space for the question that dominates this Gospel: *Who is Jesus?* John's "I am not . . ." prepares for the many later statements of Jesus beginning with "I am . . ."

John's string of negatives leads into the rest of the chapter's positive identification of Jesus in four waves of meaning.[2] The first wave centers on a quotation from the prophet Isaiah, and it suggests both a humble role for John as a **voice**, a witness, and also a daring answer, in line with the prologue, to the question

2. For this Gospel's way of giving its most important teaching in successive waves of meaning, see discussion of Nicodemus in the comments on 3:1–36. The archetype of this in its most condensed form is the first verse: "In the beginning was the Word, and the Word was with God, and the Word was God" (1:1).

of who Jesus is. If John the Baptist has come to **make straight the way of the Lord**, and if this is about testifying to Jesus, then Jesus is being identified with the Lord—that is, with God.

This first wave ends with John identifying Jesus as **among you** but unknown, **the one who is coming after me**. From now on, this "who" is central to the drama, just as he has been central in the prologue.

The Second Wave, the Next Day (1:29–34)

> 29 The next day he saw Jesus coming toward him and declared, "Here is the
> Lamb of God who takes away the sin of the world! 30 This is he of whom I
> said, 'After me comes a man who ranks ahead of me because he was before
> me.' 31 I myself did not know him; but I came baptizing with water for this
> reason, that he might be revealed to Israel." 32 And John testified, "I saw
> the Spirit descending from heaven like a dove, and it remained on him. 33 I
> myself did not know him, but the one who sent me to baptize with water
> said to me, 'He on whom you see the Spirit descend and remain is the one
> who baptizes with the Holy Spirit.' 34 And I myself have seen and have testi-
> fied that this is the Son of God."

The Lamb of God Who Takes Away the Sin of the World

The second wave of meaning is centered on the surprising cry, **"Here is the Lamb of God who takes away the sin of the world!"** This has become an iconic statement resonating down through the centuries in Christian liturgies, symbolism, art, hymns, and poetry. Yet here it is startling, very different from the titles that John the Baptist has just rejected. Can its freshness and challenge to the imagination be renewed today?

Denise Levertov, in "Agnus Dei" (Lamb of God),[3] offers a probing meditation on it (see Levertov's poem in the sidebar). The poet herself said later that in the course of writing this "the unknown began to be revealed to me as God, and further, God revealed in the Incarnation."[4] Thomas Gardner sees through her poem "the terrible and utterly unexpected vision of vulnerability captured in the Baptist's words." He asks how God could "turn to the broken world *in* brokenness" so that the "icy heart" could be "stirred and warmed

3. The last poem in a six-part "agnostic Mass" entitled "Mass for the Day of St. Thomas Didymus" by Denise Levertov, in *Candles in Babylon*, 113–15; also in Levertov, *The Collected Poems*, 677–78.

4. Levertov, "A Poet's View," 241.

by the vulnerability of God expressed in Jesus," grasped through "the lamb's pungent fragility."[5]

The image of the lamb also has many biblical resonances. Above all there is the Passover lamb in the foundational story of Israel's liberation from Egypt led by Moses (Exod. 12). In the Gospel of John's account of the crucifixion Jesus dies at the time the Passover lambs are being killed. Exodus imagery and references to Moses begin in the prologue and continue through the Gospel, and they invite repeated rereading in conversation with the texts to which they allude. The same is true of many other relevant lamb references, perhaps the most significant of which are the "sacrifice" of Isaac in Genesis and the songs of the Suffering Servant in Isaiah.

When God tests Abraham by telling him to sacrifice Isaac, his only, beloved son, as they are on their way to the place of sacrifice, Isaac asks where the lamb for the sacrifice is. Abraham answers, "God himself will provide the lamb for a burnt offering, my son" (Gen. 22:8). This is a lamb of God; and the other title John the Baptist uses for Jesus in this passage is "the Son of God" (1:34).

In Isaiah's Servant Songs,[6] which were extraordinarily important in the New Testament and later church traditions as ways of understanding who Jesus is, the servant is described in ways that could be seen as an expansion of **the lamb of God who takes away the sin of the world**: "But he was wounded for our transgressions, crushed for our iniquities. . . . He was oppressed, and he was afflicted, yet he did not open his mouth; like a lamb that is led to the slaughter, . . . he did not open his mouth. . . . The righteous one, my servant, shall make many righteous, and he shall bear their iniquities. Therefore I will allot him a portion with the great, . . . because he poured out himself to death, and was numbered with the transgressors; yet he bore the sin of many, and made intercession for the transgressors" (Isa. 53:5, 7, 11, 12). Strikingly, too, that song opens with the servant being "lifted up" (Isa. 52:13), which is one of the Gospel of John's most distinctive images for the crucifixion.[7]

In Christian theology one recurrent theme is that of the person of Jesus (who he is) in relation to the work of Jesus (what he has done).[8] "The Lamb of God who takes away the sin of the world" combines the two inseparably, as does the rest of John's Gospel. There is no doubt that the leading and most distinctive emphasis is on the "who." The good news of the Gospel is primarily

5. Gardner, *John in the Company of the Poets*, 27, 29.

6. Isa. 40–55, especially 42:1–7 and 52:13–53:12.

7. John 3:14; 12:32–33.

8. In theological terminology this is the relationship of Christology (doctrine of Jesus Christ) to soteriology (doctrine of salvation, reconciliation, or atonement).

"Agnus Dei"

Given that lambs
are infant sheep, that sheep
are afraid and foolish, and lack
the means of self-protection, having
neither rage nor claws,
venom nor cunning,
what then
is this "Lamb of God"?

This pretty creature, vigorous
to nuzzle at milky dugs,
woolbearer, bleater,
leaper in air for delight of being, who finds in astonishment
four legs to land on, the grass
all it knows of the world?
With whom we would like to play,
whom we'd lead with ribbons, but may not bring
into our houses because
it would soil the floor with its droppings?

What terror lies concealed
in strangest words, *O lamb*
of God that taketh away
the Sins of the World: an innocence
smelling of ignorance,
born in bloody snowdrifts,
licked by forbearing
dogs more intelligent than its entire flock put together?

God then,
encompassing all things, is
defenseless? Omnipotence
has been tossed away, reduced
to a wisp of damp wool?

And we
frightened, bored, wanting
only to sleep till catastrophe

has raged, clashed, seethed and gone by without us,
wanting then
to awaken in quietude without remembrance of agony,

we who in shamefaced private hope
had looked to be plucked from fire and given
a bliss we deserved for having imagined it,

is it implied that *we*
must protect this perversely weak
animal, whose muzzle's nudgings
suppose there is milk to be found in us?
Must hold to our icy hearts
a shivering God?

•

So be it.
Come, rag of pungent
quiverings,
dim star.
Let's try
if something human still
can shield you,
spark
of remote light.

—Denise Levertov, *Candles in Babylon*, 113–15

of "life in his name" (20:31), relating to him in person, being loved by him, trusting him, being friends of his, being animated by his Spirit. Yet that life is one of action, above all of love, and is continually inspired by what Jesus has done. Jesus later says, "Just as I have loved you, you also should love one another" (13:34). This can even extend to laying down their lives, as he has done.

This also is a pointer to the meaning of **the sin of the world**. The basic sin indicated in the Gospel of John is lack of faith/trust/belief, inevitably involving lack of love. The desire/will of God is for a love inseparable from trust. The ultimate desire of Jesus, expressed above all in his climactic prayer in John 17, is for people to be united in trust and love with God and one another through him, a unity in which the whole of creation is embraced. This is the "summit of love," the joy, the "eternal life," the peace, for which people are created and into which they are invited, and whatever prevents or distorts or falsifies or opposes this is sin.

Yet for all the participation in him, extending to mutual indwelling ("Abide in me as I abide in you" [15:4]), and for all the doing as he does, extending even to doing "greater works" than Jesus has done (14:12), there is never any doubt about who is greater, who is Lord, who alone can say "Before Abraham was, I am" (8:58). This decisive distinction is first made insistently by John the Baptist: "He who comes after me ranks ahead of me because he was before me" (1:15, repeated in 1:30), and "I am not worthy to untie the thong of his sandal" (1:27). This uniqueness of the person of Jesus is especially important for understanding his death and what it might mean that he **takes away the sin of the world.**[9] Just as the Gospel points to his death here, but draws readers only gradually into its meaning, so we will return to this central matter at several points later, especially in John 12 and the Farewell Discourses.

The Holy Spirit Abiding on Jesus

This second wave of meaning goes even further. John the Baptist gives testimony to the Holy Spirit coming down and "remaining/abiding" (the Greek verb is *menein* [see further below]) on Jesus, which directly leads to John testifying that **this is the Son of God**.

The Gospel of John has far more to say about the Holy Spirit than do the Synoptic Gospels, just as it is more explicitly and repeatedly concerned with the question of who Jesus is. *Those two strikingly distinctive things about each of the four Gospels—on the one hand, the person of Jesus, and, on the other hand, the giving of the Holy Spirit—are intensified and deepened by John.* He omits many of the details of Synoptic accounts and many important Synoptic events (birth stories, temptations, transfiguration, institution of the Eucharist, ascension)[10] in order to combine simplicity with concentration, above all on who Jesus is. The effect is often an account that has a "deep plain sense."[11] This invites further exploration through rereading and reflection; through relating to other parts of John; through rereading the Synoptic Gospels, Paul's Letters, and the Septuagint; and through openness to fresh meaning from ongoing life. Other Scriptures and writings, of course, also have such deep plain sense, but John is unusual in the degree and thoroughness with which he integrates literary craft, theology, improvisation on his sources, and confidence that the Spirit will

9. Another poem by Denise Levertov, "On a Theme from Julian's Chapter XX," powerfully makes this point. See comments on 19:28–29.

10. Though it is possible to find references to each of these implied by John.

11. On this term, see the introduction and the comments on 1:1–18.

"guide you into all the truth" (16:13)—that "you" including both himself and those who come after him.

Here, a comparison with the Synoptic accounts of the baptism of Jesus shows what John wants us to concentrate on: the Holy Spirit remaining on Jesus as **the one who baptizes with the Holy Spirit**, and on Jesus identified as **the Son of God**. John does not mention that John the Baptist baptized Jesus, though probably that is assumed. Nor is there mention, as in the Synoptics, of the voice from heaven saying, "You are my Son, the Beloved; with you I am well pleased" (Mark 1:11; cf. Matt. 3:17; Luke 3:22)—that has already been implied in the Son being "close to the Father's heart" (1:18). *Instead, the focus is on the Spirit being permanently intrinsic to who Jesus is (remaining on him) and to what he does (baptizing with the Holy Spirit).* This is reinforced later, since the climactic events of the giving of the Spirit in the Gospel of John are when the dying Jesus "gave up [or "handed over"] his spirit [or "the Spirit"]" (19:30), and when the resurrected Jesus "breathed on them and said to them, 'Receive the Holy Spirit'" (20:22). So the Spirit is connected as closely as possible with Jesus himself and the culminating events of his crucifixion and resurrection.

How does this relate to the prologue? It might seem as though the Spirit does not figure there, but if one rereads the prologue after having read the whole Gospel in the context of the Septuagint and the Synoptic Gospels, the Spirit is implied at every turn. The opening words from Genesis recall the *pneuma theou* (spirit or wind of God) over the water (Gen. 1:2). The Word and the life of Jesus the Word are closely related to the Spirit: "It is the spirit that gives life; the flesh is useless. The words that I have spoken are spirit and life" (6:63). Witnessing to Jesus is one of the main things that the Spirit does and inspires (1:7–8, 15; cf. 15:26–27; 16:12–15). "Power to become children of God" and being "born of God" (1:12, 13) are also related to the Spirit (e.g., 3:1–10). So are light, truth, and fullness; and in John as in the rest of the New Testament (and through the history of Christian theology), grace (1:14, 16, 17) is one of the main ways of talking about the Holy Spirit. *So the whole prologue breathes the Spirit,* and this is important for the influence it had on the development of the understanding of God as Trinity.

The Third Wave, the Next Day: The Teacher Forms a Community of Learners (1:35–42)

> 35 The next day John again was standing with two of his disciples, 36 and as
> he watched Jesus walk by, he exclaimed, "Look, here is the Lamb of God!"
> 37 The two disciples heard him say this, and they followed Jesus. 38 When

Jesus turned and saw them following, he said to them, "What are you looking for?" They said to him, "Rabbi" (which translated means Teacher), "where are you staying?" [39] He said to them, "Come and see." They came and saw where he was staying, and they remained with him that day. It was about four o'clock in the afternoon. [40] One of the two who heard John speak and followed him was Andrew, Simon Peter's brother. [41] He first found his brother Simon and said to him, "We have found the Messiah" (which is translated Anointed). [42] He brought Simon to Jesus, who looked at him and said, "You are Simon son of John. You are to be called Cephas" (which is translated Peter).

The third wave of meaning covers some of the same ground as the earlier waves, with John the Baptist pointing two of his disciples to Jesus as **the Lamb of God**. Then follows, in this and the fourth wave and on into the final verse, a veritable avalanche of titles: **Rabbi/Teacher**; **the Christ/Messiah/Anointed**; **him about whom Moses in the law and also the prophets wrote**, **Jesus son of Joseph from Nazareth**; **the King of Israel**; **the Son of Man**. The rest of the Gospel, as will emerge, pours more meaning into each of these titles.

So, if anything is clear, it is that we are to focus on who Jesus is. John's first chapter is dominated by this, and it is hard to overemphasize its importance. In a classic statement on its priority, Dietrich Bonhoeffer argues that the question "Who are you, Jesus Christ, Word of God, Logos of God?"[12]—the question of encounter with Jesus—is at the heart of Christian theology. It is certainly at the heart of the Gospel of John. Most of the Gospel is devoted to Jesus in encounter with other people, and the key question in most of those meetings is who Jesus is. The theological implications of this are immense. Not only should questions about Jesus begin with the "who" question, first of all addressed to the living Jesus in prayer (Bonhoeffer gives one of the clearest discussions of what this means as regards other questions); every other theological question is also affected by the answer to this one. The way to the doctrine of the Trinity is opened up. Who Jesus is also changes what it means to be human. The understanding of salvation is transformed if each aspect (suffering, sin, death, faith, discipleship, community, ethics, politics, hope for the future) is thought through with reference first to who this person is. What John's Gospel gives is not answers to all the questions (on many it gives far less explicit guidance than do other parts of the Bible) but a clear pointer to how to seek answers: be part of a community within which you can think through the issues with others by rereading Scripture

12. Bonhoeffer, *Christ the Center*, 32.

and engaging afresh with the drama of Jesus, living, thinking, and praying in the spirit of that drama; and abiding in him, open to being led further into the truth.

DNA of the Learning Community around Jesus

The character of that community is the other leading theme of John 1. It is inseparably interwoven with the question of who Jesus is. We have already explored the community element in the prologue; now in the rest of the chapter the drama of the community's formation begins. It is first of all about gathering disciples, or learners. This passage gives something like the DNA, the basic "code," of the church as a learning community.

Everything anyone understands of Jesus—or of Christian faith, hope, and love, together with practices of speaking, reading, thinking, questioning, praying, following, relating to others, belonging, and so on—has been learned. One of the most important questions in anybody's life is, Who teaches me? One of the most important questions for any community is, What sorts of learning form us? *And within any learning community the dynamism and depth of learning begins with the dynamism and depth of the questions that grip and animate it.*

We have already explored how for this Gospel the central question that grips the community around Jesus is, Who are you? What types of teaching and learning are in line with that question?

Testimony and Total Teaching

John the Baptist embodies the first answer: testimony. This Gospel strips away most of the details about John the Baptist that are given in the Synoptics—his parents, his birth and naming, his mother's relationship with the mother of Jesus, what he wore and ate, his call to repentance, even his actual baptizing of Jesus, and more—in order to concentrate mainly on his utter dedication to the task of testifying to Jesus.[13] In this Gospel it would be more fitting to call him John the Witness.

If we have not met someone in the flesh (and, often, even if we have met them), the main way we know who they are is through testimony. In order to know anyone who lived before us, we are completely dependent on testimony. It can be tested and cross-examined, but in the end we are always faced with the question, Do we trust it? There is an inescapable correlation between testifying and believing (or not). The whole of John's Gospel is testimony inviting readers to believe it in order to trust who Jesus is, so that "through believing you may

13. Yet this Gospel also adds elements to the Synoptic picture; see the comments on 3:22–36.

have life in his name" (20:31). Who bears that name, and what it means, are known only through the testimony of witnesses.

Further, if the one to whom testimony is given calls us to follow him and to entrust our whole lives to him, then that affects the sort of teaching and learning involved in knowing and believing in him. Noting that the cry "Here is the Lamb of God who takes away the sin of the world!" (1:29), with its sacrificial associations, is closely followed by the gathering of a learning community, Thomas Brodie makes a profound comment: the passage, he says, "transforms the self-giving of sacrifice into the self-giving of total teaching."[14]

The teaching is "total" because it is by no means only about information, or "head knowledge." It is about that, but also about a rich, close, face-to-face interpersonal relationship of wholehearted trust. In that context of meeting in depth it involves looking, seeing and being seen (1:36, 38, 39, 42, 46, 47, 48, 50, 51), hearing (1:37, 40, and throughout), following (1:37, 38, 40, 43), being turned to and faced by Jesus (1:38, 42), seeking, searching, questioning, and doubting (1:38, 46, 48, 50), translating between languages (1:38, 41, 42), coming (1:39, 46), staying/remaining/abiding/living with (1:38, 39), finding (1:41, 43, 45), witnessing/testifying (1:36, 41, 45, 46, 49), naming and recognizing (1:36, 42, 45, 47, 49), reading Scripture (1:45), knowing and being known (1:48), believing/trusting (1:50), and being part of a new relationship between earth and heaven centered on Jesus (1:50–51). Almost every element in that list is a basic activity whose content is enriched and deepened in the course of the rest of the Gospel, culminating in chapters 20–21, where most of them recur. It is, as Raymond Brown says, "a conspectus of Christian vocation."[15]

Growth in Learning and the Education of Desire: "What Are You Looking For?"

This learning and understanding are not something that happens all at once. They involve progress and growth, and what is told of the last two days recounted in chapter 1 (1:35–42, 43–51) exemplifies this. *There is a deepening and broadening during this time, and the rest of the Gospel continues this pedagogy.*

This is partly indicated by the titles of Jesus. In the third wave he is called **Lamb of God** and **Rabbi/Teacher**, followed by **Messiah/Christ/Anointed**; in the fourth he is still, significantly, **Rabbi/Teacher**, but is also **Son of God**, **King of Israel**, and, in the final mysterious verse, **Son of Man**. These titles of the final day are the most important for the rest of the Gospel, and their developing content will be noted in later chapters. Their connection with "Rabbi/Teacher"

14. Brodie, *The Gospel according to John*, 159.
15. R. Brown, *The Gospel according to John*, 1:77.

underlines Brodie's insight into "the self-giving of total teaching": this is a teacher in utter solidarity with God and human beings, for whom he will die as Lamb of God. The final occurrence of "lamb" in the Gospel (though a different Greek word is used than in 1:29, 36) is when the resurrected Jesus says to Peter, "Feed my lambs" (21:15), and then predicts Peter's death as a martyr: the leading witness, pastor, and teacher is to be ready to give his life. The final occurrence of the title "Rabbi" occurs in what is perhaps the most moving person-to-person encounter in the Gospel, after the resurrected Jesus has asked Mary Magdalene, "Whom are you looking for?" (20:15–16).

The verb used there by Jesus, translated as "look for" (*zētein*), is one of the key terms in the Gospel of John. Its range of meaning includes "seek, search, try, attempt, strive for, want, desire, ask, ask for, demand, require, expect, deliberate, examine, investigate." It is an activity that is at the heart of progress in learning, and in this Gospel it is used first in the first words Jesus says: **"What are you looking for?"** (1:38).

That the first words of Jesus are a question underlines the learning that is essential to discipleship. This is a community of inquiry, searching, and reflection. That the question is about what the disciples are "looking for" points to the concern of Jesus both to educate and to fulfill the desires of those he encounters. This is an attractive community, one of abundant life and love. At its heart is the attraction of the love of Jesus: "And I, when I am lifted up from the earth, will draw all people to myself" (12:32); and the love within the community is meant to attract others: "By this everyone will know that you are my disciples, if you have love for one another" (13:35).

The whole Gospel can be read as an education of desire. The disciples have much to learn and frequently get things wrong; their faith—their understanding of and trust in Jesus—needs to grow and mature; and their imagination and horizon need to be enriched and expanded by the signs Jesus does, the encounters he has, the teaching he gives, and above all by his crucifixion and resurrection. The deepest secret of what is to be desired is revealed in the prayer of Jesus: "Father, I desire that those also, whom you have given me, may be with me where I am, to see my glory, which you have given me because you loved me before the foundation of the world" (17:24). The first sign of that glory which Jesus gives is at the wedding at Cana (2:1–11), an occasion celebrating fulfilled desire, joy together, and the promise of new life. And at the heart of the secret in 17:24 is the "I am" (*egō eimi*) of Jesus, who Jesus is. So by the time the resurrected Jesus meets Mary Magdalene, his opening question, "What are you looking for?" (1:38), has become "Whom are you looking for?" (20:15). He has triggered the recognition of who he is by naming who she is: "Mary!" (20:16).

Ongoing Life: "Where Are You Staying/Abiding/Dwelling?"

That questioning is fundamental to this community is further emphasized when the disciples reply to the question of Jesus with their own question: **"Where are you staying?"** The verb used, *menein,* has a range of meaning that includes "remaining, abiding, resting, dwelling, living, staying, lasting, continuing, enduring, awaiting." It is one of the most fascinating words in the Gospel.

It has already appeared twice in the first chapter, describing the Holy Spirit remaining on Jesus, and now is used three times more as the new disciples ask Jesus where he is staying. Its immediate plain sense is, of course, where he is being accommodated, what his physical lodging is. But readers of the prologue will have read that Jesus is "close to the Father's heart" (1:18), in the bosom of the Father. *So we are invited by that, and by the use of the verb in relation to the Holy Spirit and Jesus, to be alert to a deeper plain sense.*

Anyone who has read the Septuagint will already be alert to this. Two of this Gospel's favorite intertexts are Psalms and Isaiah. In both, *menein* is used of God or God's wisdom, righteousness, or word, enduring forever (our English translations from the Hebrew often do not reflect the terms used in the Septuagint's translation into Greek, but John's primary text was the Septuagint): "You, O Lord, are enthroned forever [*eis ton aiōna meneis*]" (LXX Ps. 101:13 [ET 102:12]; cf. LXX Pss. 9:8; 32:11; 110:3; 116:2 [ET 9:7; 33:11; 111:3; 117:2]); "The word of our God will stand forever [*menei eis ton aiōna*]" (LXX Isa. 40:8; cf. LXX Isa. 14:24; 30:18; 66:22). In this way *menein* is also closely linked with the Greek phrase *eis ton aiōna* ("forever") and the adjective *aiōnios* ("eternal, everlasting"). These are very common in the Septuagint, and John especially uses the adjective in his key term "eternal life."

As the Gospel proceeds, the meaning of *menein* and its derivatives broadens and deepens. The link with eternal life is made explicitly: the food that the Son of Man gives "endures for eternal life" (6:27). A little further on, the key idea of mutual indwelling is introduced: "Those who eat my flesh and drink my blood abide in me and I in them" (6:56). Later, *menein* is connected with true, long-term discipleship: "Then Jesus said to the Jews who had believed in him, 'If you continue [*meinēte*] in my word, you are truly my disciples'" (8:31). In the Farewell Discourses the noun *monē,* derived from the verb, is used in an intriguing way to suggest what seems like an ultimate diversity: "In my Father's house are many dwelling places [*monai*]" (14:2). Later, *menein* also describes the relationship of Jesus to his Father: "the Father who dwells in me" (14:10); and of the Holy Spirit to the disciples: "He abides with you, and he will be in you" (14:17). But the most intensive use of the verb, twelve times in twelve verses, is in the parable of the vine (or vineyard) in chapter 15, where the embracing organic imagery is used to gather up many of the earlier uses and take them further. So mutual indwelling has practical consequences: "Those who abide in me and I in them bear much fruit" (15:5). And it is about love: "As the Father has loved me, so I have loved you; abide in my love" (15:9). This dynamic of mutual indwelling in love is taken even further in the prayer of Jesus in chapter 17, though there *menein* is no longer used because its essence is distilled and expressed repeatedly in the simple, yet unfathomably deep, preposition "in" (17:10, 11, 12, 13, 17, 19, 21, 23, 26).

Yet, while this word can lead us into the depths of the Gospel, other uses of it are ordinary references to place and time, as in this initial question of the new disciples. It is characteristic of John to use language like this—for example, with the verb *poiein*, meaning "do, make, create"—and it can be seen as a linguistic expression of incarnation: abiding as simultaneously an ordinary human activity and a divine activity, allowing for both an obvious surface sense and also level beneath level of deeper sense.

What Sort of Community?

So this first questioning of the disciples opens onto some of the most important themes of the Gospel. Within the context of a chapter whose main task is beginning to answer the central question, Who is Jesus? these two further questions go to the heart of relating to Jesus by being part of the community around him. What sort of community is portrayed here?

The fundamental features are that, within a horizon of God and all reality, it is about recognizing and testifying to who Jesus is, following him with others, and learning from him with others. It is a community whose desires are stimulated, educated, and fulfilled in relationship with Jesus, and whose minds and imaginations are stretched through being questioned, called, and taught by him. The long-term question for all in the community is about whether they share in the life of Jesus, in the Holy Spirit who rests on him, and in his relationship with his Father and the world—whether they abide in him and he in them. The disciples took the first steps into this life when **they came and saw where he was staying** [*menei*], **and they remained** [*emeinan*] **with him that day**. *The rest of the Gospel can be seen as a journey into learning what that remaining/abiding/dwelling/enduring means.*

The Fourth Wave, the Next Day: Life with Jesus—Scriptural, Surprising, Intercultural, Experiential, and Interpersonal (1:43–50)

> 43 The next day Jesus decided to go to Galilee. He found Philip and said to
> him, "Follow me." 44 Now Philip was from Bethsaida, the city of Andrew and
> Peter. 45 Philip found Nathanael and said to him, "We have found him about

> whom Moses in the law and also the prophets wrote, Jesus son of Joseph from Nazareth." [46] Nathanael said to him, "Can anything good come out of Nazareth?" Philip said to him, "Come and see." [47] When Jesus saw Nathanael coming toward him, he said of him, "Here is truly an Israelite in whom there is no deceit!" [48] Nathanael asked him, "Where did you get to know me?" Jesus answered, "I saw you under the fig tree before Philip called you." [49] Nathanael replied, "Rabbi, you are the Son of God! You are the King of Israel!" [50] Jesus answered, "Do you believe because I told you that I saw you under the fig tree? You will see greater things than these."

Several elements in this wave have already been discussed. The questions continue, and there are also other instructive pointers to aspects of this community.

- It is scriptural, seen not so much in direct quotations as in multiple allusions that take for granted a scriptural world of meaning. Yet Scripture is not simply repeated: John is writing fresh Scripture because something new and unprecedented has happened.
- This means being open to surprises, the great one of the coming of Jesus and the Holy Spirit generating many more: **"Can anything good come out of Nazareth?" . . . "Where did you get to know me?" . . . "You will see greater things than these."**
- It is multilingual and intercultural. Three times we are given translations (1:38, 41, 42), and the names are both Jewish and Greek.
- It is strongly experiential, about meeting, hearing, coming and seeing, finding, sharing life together, and being amazed.
- It spreads through individual initiatives, face-to-face networking (not least within kinship groups), and seizing opportunities as they arise amid the contingencies of life.

The Mysterious Final Verse (1:51)

> [51] And he said to him, "Very truly, I tell you, you will see heaven opened and the angels of God ascending and descending upon the Son of Man."

What of the final verse, which Raymond Brown says "has caused as much trouble for commentators as any other single verse in the Fourth Gospel"?[16]

16. R. Brown, *The Gospel according to John*, 1:88.

Nathanael has been presented as one who could be expected to know what **Moses in the law and also the prophets wrote**; Jesus has called him **truly an Israelite in whom there is no deceit**, which suggests a contrast with Jacob's use of deceit in Genesis; and Nathanael has called Jesus not only **Son of God** but also **King of Israel**. So here we are in the world of Israel and its Scriptures, and the final verse is a mysterious "tiny midrash"[17] on Jacob's dream in Genesis 28:10–22. It is an invitation to the imagination, using the poetic or mythological imagery of a dream; and, as so often, the evangelist is offering a theologically daring reading of it. John Ashton identifies the challenge to many (see the quotation from Ashton in the sidebar).

When Jacob in Genesis wakes up, he says, "Surely the Lord is in this place—and I did not know it!" and calls the place Bethel, meaning "house of God" (Gen. 28:16, 19). Here at the end of this encounter with Nathanael, Jesus, by fusing Jacob's dream ladder with himself as Son of Man, is doing several things.

- *First and foremost, in a climactic*[18] *statement, he focuses on who he is: he himself is the place of God's presence, of communication between earth and heaven.* This is an imaginative, midrashic parallel to the culmination of the prologue, with Jesus "close to the Father's heart" and making him known (1:18). The God of Jacob is also the God of Jesus—and now present in this person.
- The title "Son of Man" is given pride of place by being last, prefaced by the authoritative "very truly" (*amēn amēn*), and it is the only title put on the lips

> This is a common experience of twentieth-century Westerners: as they look at myth, they feel compelled, somehow, to demythologize. But why should a demythologized myth be any more use than dehydrated water? The medium is the message—it does not contain it or hold it imprisoned like a genie in a bottle, waiting to be released. Somehow, then, we have to allow the picture of the ladder, base on earth and top in the clouds, to fuse with that of the Son of Man, and at the same time to allow the busily climbing angels, some going up and others going down, to convey the message with which the evangelist has charged them. But what is this message? It lies in *the picture*: it is simply that there is no other *route* between heaven and earth than the Son of Man.
>
> —John Ashton, *Understanding the Fourth Gospel*, 249–50 (italics original)

17. Ashton, *Understanding the Fourth Gospel*, 250.
18. Literally—*klimax* is the Greek word for "ladder."

of Jesus in this chapter. It is a title around which there are long-running scholarly battles. It is hard to deny the commonsense implication that Jesus is identifying with other human beings. But the background to the term includes a heavenly, kingly, glorious, apocalyptic figure in the book of Daniel (7:13–14).[19] In the Synoptics (where, as in John, "Son of Man" is only used by Jesus), alongside this triumphal, future aspect are sayings about the Son of Man as one who suffers. John combines the humanity, the kingship, the glory, and the suffering in Jesus, and downplays the future aspect in favor of his personal presence. In theological terms, John places Christology at the heart of eschatology: the most important thing about the ultimate future is not when or how it happens but trusting the one who is central to it, Jesus; and the focus as regards time is not on the epic end of the world but on the ongoing drama of loving now (see comments on 21:20–23).

- The image of ascending and descending is important in the rest of the Gospel and has already been partly introduced in John the Baptist's vision of "the Spirit descending from heaven" (1:32). Ashton sees one function of the little dream-based midrash in 1:51 being to "discourage the reader from an overliteral interpretation."[20] It can be seen as paralleling the prologue by offering a framework of God and the whole of reality[21] within which to place the drama to come.
- There is a striking change of person in the later part of what Jesus says to Nathanael. Up to verse 51 Jesus addresses him in the second-person singular. Then in verse 51 he changes to the plural: **"I tell you** [plural], **you** [plural] **will see . . ."** The effect is to open out the conclusion beyond Nathanael and embrace every reader—a "making known" in line with the last words of the prologue.
- The implied identification of the person of Jesus with Bethel, the House of God, points forward to the next chapter's cleansing of the temple in Jerusalem, when Jesus speaks of his body as the temple.

That is just a little of the meaning that has been discovered in this verse. An original further suggestion is made by John McHugh that there is a reference to Isaiah 64:1: "O that you would tear open the heavens and come down." It

19. It is noteworthy that this passage in Daniel is part of a "night vision" and that the Septuagint translation contains several Johannine terms relating to Jesus: heaven, authority, all, glory, eternal, kingship/kingdom.

20. Ashton, *Understanding the Fourth Gospel*, 276.

21. The encompassing character is reinforced by the content of Jacob's dream, which includes a promise that "all the families of the earth shall be blessed in you and your offspring" (Gen. 28:14).

expresses a passionate longing for return from exile, and McHugh draws on rabbinical exegesis of this passage after the destruction of the temple in 70 CE in which the Messiah, repentance, and the return of the Shekinah (the presence of God) to the temple sanctuary are "all urgently desired."[22] In an exercise of reading for what I have called the deep plain sense, he goes on to connect the opening of heaven with the Holy Spirit and baptism (as in 1:32), and with the Eucharist (as in the bread from heaven in chap. 6).

Conclusion

This second, narrative beginning of the Gospel has been paid far less attention than the prologue, but it is comparable in theological richness and in opening up key themes to come in later chapters. Like the prologue, it is worth rereading and rethinking alongside every other chapter of John's Gospel and in dialogue with other scriptural texts,[23] as its leading questions (Who is Jesus? What are you looking for? Where are you abiding/dwelling?) are responded to, and its encounters, characters, titles, words, images, and concepts are filled with further meaning.

22. McHugh, *John 1–4*, 167.

23. The following biblical texts are especially fruitful if read alongside John 1:19–51: Deut. 18; Ps. 2; Isa. 7; 9; 40; 53; Ezek. 34; Zeph. 3.

John 2:1–25

Signs of Glory and New Life

Two vivid scenes continue the beginning of the Gospel. The first is unique to John.

In Cana, at a wedding, Jesus does the first, or beginning (*archē*), of his signs (2:11). Chapters 2–12 are sometimes called the Book of Signs. These are, above all, signs of who Jesus is and of the life Jesus gives. Their meaning is enriched by conversations Jesus has with a range of people and by resonances with the Synoptic Gospels, the Septuagint, and the surrounding culture. Their imaginative power is produced by combining dramatic narrative craft with symbols of abundant life (10:10): marriage, wine, birth, wind, water, bread, health after severe illness or disability, and even life restored after death. All of these are focused on who Jesus is and what he does, especially through "I am" statements, which are both absolute (4:26; 6:20; 8:24, 28, 58) and descriptive: "I am the bread of life" (6:35, 41, 48), "I am the light of the world" (8:12), "I am the good shepherd" (10:11, 14), "I am the resurrection and the life" (11:25). Where the Synoptic Gospels use "miracle" (*dynamis*), John prefers to use "sign" (*sēmeion*). This emphasizes the meaning dimension, but the miraculous is by no means downplayed; on the contrary, John has far fewer signs/miracles than the Synoptics, but those he chooses to include are often especially striking.

The second scene in this chapter is set in the holy city of Jerusalem. The time is Passover, the annual reenactment of the exodus, the liberation of the people of Israel from slavery in Egypt. The stage is the temple, the building centered on God's presence in the holy of holies. Here Jesus forcefully interrupts the trading and money-changing in order to affirm the temple's dedication to his

Father. When confronted with a request for a sign, he responds by speaking of the destruction and raising up of the temple, interpreted as referring to his own body, which will die and be resurrected. So the foundational drama of Israel, the exodus, is connected with the drama of Jesus, and the place of God's presence in Israel is identified with the person of Jesus as God's Son. In the process, John gives a lesson in levels of meaning, a further stage in teaching how to read Scripture and his own text.

The wedding at Cana is a headline for the signs that Jesus does, signifying abundant life. The clearance of the temple is a headline for the drama of the central conflict of his life, centered in Jerusalem, leading to his death and resurrection there, and above all focused on who Jesus is. The two are interconnected by Jesus referring to "my hour" (2:4) at Cana, by the demand for a sign in the temple, by the explicit mention of glory revealed at Cana and glory's strong association with the temple in Scripture, and by the emphasis in both stories on believing in Jesus.

There is also a further element in common: just as Jesus at the wedding not only meets the problem posed by his mother but also does something more than necessary (Richard Wilbur's "sweet excess" [see "A Wedding Toast" in the sidebar later in this chapter]), so here the demand for a sign to justify the action of Jesus is met by a response pointing to the heart of John's message, the "sign" of Jesus, his death and resurrection, that goes far beyond anything imagined by the questioners.

The First Sign: Dramatic, Biblical, and Universal (2:1–12)

> 1 On the third day there was a wedding in Cana of Galilee, and the mother of Jesus was there. 2 Jesus and his disciples had also been invited to the wedding. 3 When the wine gave out, the mother of Jesus said to him, "They have no wine." 4 And Jesus said to her, "Woman, what concern is that to you and to me? My hour has not yet come." 5 His mother said to the servants, "Do whatever he tells you." 6 Now standing there were six stone water jars for the Jewish rites of purification, each holding twenty or thirty gallons. 7 Jesus said to them, "Fill the jars with water." And they filled them up to the brim. 8 He said to them, "Now draw some out, and take it to the chief steward." So they took it. 9 When the steward tasted the water that had become wine, and did not know where it came from (though the servants who had drawn the water knew), the steward called the bridegroom 10 and said to him, "Everyone serves the good wine first, and then the inferior wine after the guests have become drunk. But you have kept the good wine until

now." [11] Jesus did this, the first of his signs, in Cana of Galilee, and revealed his glory; and his disciples believed in him.

[12] After this he went down to Capernaum with his mother, his brothers, and his disciples; and they remained there a few days.

This first sign, paradigmatic for the rest, is a well-crafted dramatic scene telling a surprising story with brevity and precision. At the same time, without taking away from the drama, it is a classic example of deep plain sense. Read with the rest of John's Gospel, the significance of characters in this story—Jesus, the mother of Jesus, and his disciples—is developed further, the meanings of key terms, such as "my hour," "did/made/created," "sign," "glory," and "believed in," are enriched and expanded, and the connections of this wine with later statements such as "my blood is true drink" (6:55) and "I am the true vine" (15:1) deserve much meditation. Read in conversation with the Old Testament, the Synoptic Gospels, surrounding Hellenistic civilization, and any culture that celebrates weddings, the meaning deepens and broadens further.

The Drama: The Puzzle, the Sign/Miracle, and Two Lessons

The scene is at Cana in Galilee partway through a wedding feast (Jewish weddings at the time often lasted seven days) at which the wine has run out. This is the home village of Nathanael, so what happens is probably meant to be a sign of the fulfillment of what Jesus promised Nathanael in 1:51: "You will see greater things than these." **The mother of Jesus**, who is unnamed and appears in John only here and at the crucifixion of Jesus (19:26–27), is present, and she tells Jesus about the lack of wine.

Then comes the puzzling response of Jesus: **"Woman, what concern is that to you and to me? My hour has not yet come."** It seems rude, or at least brusque and distancing, to address his mother as "woman," which he does again in 19:26. Coupled with the reference to "my hour," which in John refers to the death of Jesus, it connects with the dedication of Jesus to his mission that relativizes his family relationships. The puzzlement increases when his mother tells the servants, **"Do whatever he tells you,"**[1] and Jesus tells them to fill large purification jars with water that then turns into wine. So, after initial reluctance, he does something completely surprising. Reluctance followed by appropriate action happens elsewhere in John, especially in the raising of Lazarus. *Both signs emphasize Jesus's freedom to do things his way, as well as the good surprises that come from trusting him despite appearances.*

1. Typical of John's deep plain sense, her instruction is also a basic maxim of discipleship.

This surprise is a quiet one; it seems that only the servants and the mother of Jesus know what has happened (though clearly the disciples come to know). The central focus is on what Jesus says and what happens as a result of that. Jesus is completely part of the event as a wedding guest with his mother and disciples, yet also he is differentiated from others: he is the only named person in the story, he is looked to for help, his mother directs the servants to do what he says, he takes charge by issuing instructions to the servants, and the result is superabundant wine. What he does is inseparable from what others do—his mother's initiative, the servants' hard work in filling the jars—but also somehow is primary, the crucial factor without which the problem would not be solved.

It is striking how hidden the actual transformation of the water into wine is. In the text it is a subordinate clause, **that had become wine**. The "become" translates the same Greek verb (*ginomai*) used repeatedly in the prologue: "All things *came into being* through him, and without him not one thing *came into being*. What *has come into being*" (1:3); "*There was* a man sent from God" (1:6); "The world *came into being* through him" (1:10); ". . . power *to become* children of God" (1:12); "And the Word *became* flesh" (1:14); "He who comes after me *ranks* ahead of me" (1:15); "Grace and truth *came* through Jesus Christ" (1:17). It is a broad word signifying "happening" (as straightforwardly in 1:28) without specifying an agent, but often implying divine agency. There is no overt action by Jesus at all, apart from him speaking. The testimony to it is given, with dramatic irony, by the steward, who does not know how it came about.

What has happened? Jesus has brought about something completely unexpected yet, in retrospect, both completely appropriate to the situation and more than a response to it—there is an abundance that goes beyond all needs. This, in the terms John has given us already, is creative speech by "the Word," through whom "all things came into being" (1:3), a manifestation of his "glory" (1:14; 2:11), an overflow of "his fullness . . . , grace upon grace" (1:16), an action in the Spirit by the one on whom the Spirit "descended and remained" (1:32, 33), and an example of the "greater things" that are to be expected through him (1:51). The main concern of the narrator is clearly the glory of Jesus, but this is not first of all a concept or image or doctrine. It cannot be abstracted from the drama of incarnation and its embodiment in life, relationships, contingencies, people in interaction, initiatives, and responses. It can be manifested again and again and is inexhaustibly rich, generative, surprising—and even intoxicating. And when it happens, often in quiet ways, some perceive it and some do not, then as now.

What does this say about the miraculous? Perhaps the most striking thing is the way the ordinary and the extraordinary come together without any sense of tension or contradiction. *It is as if our usual concept of the ordinary simply needs to be enlarged to take account of the reality of God and God's creativity, freedom, and generosity.* When that is taken seriously, then there will of course be surprises, and we need to be open to unprecedented things happening. It is a God-centered understanding of reality in which the regularities of the world (what today we might call "laws of nature") are due to the constancy and faithfulness of God, who wants us to be able to live in a reliable, mostly predictable order; but God is, of course, also free to do new things, to relate to people in new ways, and to answer prayer—though, as in the response here by Jesus to the appeal by his mother, answers are not necessarily in line with what we might expect. Perhaps the core meaning of this as the first sign is that it acts out the prologue: *the creative Word utterly involved in material reality, living among us, and showing the glory of a God of love, abundance, and grace by both being in solidarity with and transforming what he is part of—in this case, a wedding in crisis.*

This drama gives two overt lessons. The first is in the steward's statement: **"But you have kept the good wine until now."** That is underlined by being the final words of the story. It is a typical multilayered statement. Within the story its meaning is obvious. But, for the readers, the steward's surprise suggests the greater, God-centered, surprise of which this is a sign. And it is notable that the phrase is "until now," not "until the end." This "now" is important for John, and to follow the idea through the rest of the Gospel (Greek *arti*, and also *nyn*, whose meaning is mostly the same) is to see how the presence of Jesus in person is utterly central. Time itself is relative to him, as in the absolute "I am" sayings. The instantaneous transformation of water into wine might be seen as a symbol of the acceleration or concentration of time, or of the freedom of God with time, or, in Johannine terms, of "eternal life." The coming of Jesus is the arrival of eternal life "now," good wine that does not run out; and "now" is also this point in the Gospel drama, the first of Jesus's signs.

The second lesson is given in a comment by the narrator: **Jesus did this, the first of his signs, in Cana of Galilee, and revealed his glory; and his disciples believed in him.** This offers four basic theological categories in which to think about the story. These not only encourage rereading this story but also provide terms for interpreting the rest of the Gospel.

- The first is **Jesus did**, which can also be translated as "Jesus created." This phrase has been commented on already in the discussion of the prologue and above on the miraculous. The action of Jesus, at one with the agency of the God who creates (here emphasized by the use of "first," *archē*, "beginning," as in 1:1), is a fundamental category in the Gospel, perhaps most strikingly expressed in raising the dead: "Indeed, just as the Father raises the dead and gives them life [*zōopoiei*; literally, "life-makes/life-creates"], so also the Son gives life [*zōopoiei*] to whomever he wishes" (5:21). It is this that makes the dramatic content of people and events in interaction so important, so that the theology of the Gospel is primarily communicated through its narrative, with Jesus as the main character. It also makes human action crucially significant and is a measure of the astonishing promise that the one who believes/trusts in Jesus "will do [*poiēsei*] the works that I do and, in fact, will do [*poiēsei*] greater works than these" (14:12).

- The second is **signs**, as already discussed above, which by stressing the meaning dimension of Jesus's symbolic actions and miracles encourages extensive and repeated reflection on them.
- The third is **glory**. The revelation of glory has a major role in John's theology, the most distinctive feature of it being the centrality of the crucifixion to Jesus's glorification. This first sign suggests the cross through the reference by Jesus to "my hour" (2:4), but it mainly points to what is especially associated with his glory in the prologue: living among us, abundance, and a new community of family and more than family, as his mother and his disciples feast together at a wedding.
- The fourth is **his disciples believed in him**. The learning of faith in Jesus is the purpose of the Gospel (20:31), and the signs are part of this. This thoroughly pedagogical Gospel draws readers into one meeting with Jesus after another and constantly invites them to understand more and trust more. This world of meaning has horizons that are open toward God and all created reality, while having at its heart the loving intimacy of believing "in him." Uniting the infinite horizon with the depth of love, the dramatic narratives are also dense with further meaning, some of which the next section will try to open up.

Weddings and Wine: Wider Resonances

John's decision to set Jesus's first major act at a wedding is striking. Contrast Matthew, who, after Jesus calls his disciples, describes him teaching, healing, and exorcising, and then, in a first "set piece," Jesus gives the Sermon on the Mount (Matt. 4:23–7:29); or Mark, who tells of teaching, an exorcism, and a healing (Mark 1:21–31); or Luke, who, even before Jesus calls his disciples, has him give a controversial programmatic proclamation based on Isaiah in the synagogue in Nazareth, followed by an exorcism and a healing (Luke 4:14–39). Unlike each of the next six "signs" in John, there is no direct Synoptic parallel for the Cana wedding.

What might John mean by this? Eventually, in 2:11, he gives us his own categories for understanding it, but even before we reach there we can gather something of his thrust. A wedding is a burst of joy, a celebration of the beginning of a new family, with new naming and the anticipation of new life. It resonates across cultures and generations. At the same time, it runs through the Scripture, with marriage as a leading image for the core relationship of the whole Scripture: the covenant between God and Israel. For example, to read Isaiah 62 is to realize some of the scriptural connotations of John 2:1–12 and its wedding: there is mention of glory, light, salvation, a new name, beauty, delight, wine, praise, and a sign for the peoples—all around the central metaphor of the people of Israel being married to God:

> 2 The nations shall see your vindication,
> and all the kings your glory;
> and you shall be called by a new name
> that the mouth of the LORD will give.
> 3 You shall be a crown of beauty in the hand of the LORD,
> and a royal diadem in the hand of your God.
> 4 You shall no more be termed Forsaken,
> and your land shall no more be termed Desolate;
> but you shall be called My Delight Is in Her,
> and your land Married;
> for the LORD delights in you,
> and your land shall be married.
> 5 For as a young man marries a young woman,
> so shall your builder [*or* your sons] marry you,
> and as the bridegroom rejoices over the bride,
> so shall your God rejoice over you. (Isa. 62:2–5)[2]

If to the wedding resonances are added those of abundant wine, we are drawn further into celebration, feasting, joy, and the expectation of future blessing in the presence of God, as earlier in Isaiah:

> 6 On this mountain the LORD of hosts will make for all peoples
> a feast of rich food, a feast of well-aged wines,
> of rich food filled with marrow, of well-aged wines strained clear.
> 7 And he will destroy on this mountain
> the shroud that is cast over all peoples,
> the sheet that is spread over all nations;
> he will swallow up death forever.

2. The particular focus of Isa. 62 on Jerusalem also links into the next scene, the cleansing of the temple.

8 Then the Lord God will wipe away the tears from all faces,
and the disgrace of his people he will take away from all the earth,
for the Lord has spoken.
9 It will be said on that day,
Lo, this is our God; we have waited for him, so that he might save us.
This is the Lord for whom we have waited;
let us be glad and rejoice in his salvation.
10 For the hand of the Lord will rest on this mountain. (Isa. 25:6–10)[3]

In the Synoptic Gospels the wedding feast features in parables of the kingdom of God (e.g., Matt. 22:1–14); Jesus himself is represented by all four Gospels as a bridegroom (Matt. 9:15; Mark 2:19; Luke 5:34; John 3:29), and in the Synoptics this is linked to a saying about new wine; and Jesus is portrayed by his opponents as a wine drinker (Matt. 11:19; Luke 7:34). There are also the Synoptic accounts of the Last Supper, with Jesus sharing the cup of wine representing his blood (Matt. 26:27–28; Mark 14:23–24; Luke 22:20), and John 6:54–56; 15:1.

So the wedding and the wine have rich associations for those who know the texts, traditions, and rituals of John's Christian community, but they can also resonate across cultures and religions. In the Hellenistic world there is an especially strong association of abundant wine with myths of the god Dionysus (also known as Bacchus) and with his festivals. Scholars differ about whether this might have been intended by John; but, whether he intended it or not, many Hellenistic readers would have made the connection. And beyond that civilization, in one culture after another, weddings have been and are celebrated and are generally among the most wholeheartedly joyful events we experience.

Then there is Song of Songs: "For your love is better than wine. . . . We will exult and rejoice in you; we will extol your love more than wine" (1:2, 4). The whole of Song of Songs can be fruitfully read in conversation with the Gospel of John, with intensity of mutual love and abundance of life through natural imagery, helping each to enrich the other. The horizon and tone are set for such reading by the first sign taking place at a wedding.

One of the most perceptive contemporary interpretations of the wedding at Cana is by the great American poet Richard Wilbur, who wrote "A Wedding Toast" for his son's wedding (see Wilbur's poem in the sidebar). It simultaneously celebrates a family occasion and suggests the heart of John's Gospel: the "sweet excess" and overflowing reality of love; the ordinary water of life becoming extraordinarily good wine. Thomas Gardner comments, "So, I would argue,

3. Cf. Isa. 55:1 and Joel 3:18, both of which combine abundance of water and wine; Hosea 2:22; Amos 9:14.

"A Wedding Toast"

St. John tells how, at Cana's wedding-feast,
The water-pots poured wine in such amount
That by his sober count
There were a hundred gallons at the least.

It made no earthly sense, unless to show
How whatsoever love elects to bless
Brims to a sweet excess
That can without depletion overflow.

Which is to say that what love sees is true;
That the world's fullness is not made but found.
Life hungers to abound
And pour its plenty out for such as you.

Now, if your loves will lend an ear to mine,
I toast you both, good son and dear new daughter.
May you not lack for water,
And may that water smack of Cana's wine.

—Richard Wilbur, *The Mind-Reader*, 12

with all of John's signs—the more we allow them to unfold within us, the more they 'smack of Cana's wine.'"[4]

Drama in the Temple: God, Money, and Deeper Meaning (2:13–25)

13 The Passover of the Jews was near, and Jesus went up to Jerusalem. 14 In
the temple he found people selling cattle, sheep, and doves, and the money
changers seated at their tables. 15 Making a whip of cords, he drove all of
them out of the temple, both the sheep and the cattle. He also poured out
the coins of the money changers and overturned their tables. 16 He told those
who were selling the doves, "Take these things out of here! Stop making
my Father's house a marketplace!" 17 His disciples remembered that it was
written, "Zeal for your house will consume me." 18 The Jews then said to
him, "What sign can you show us for doing this?" 19 Jesus answered them,

4. Gardner, *John in the Company of the Poets*, 39.

"Destroy this temple, and in three days I will raise it up." [20] The Jews then
said, "This temple has been under construction for forty-six years, and will
you raise it up in three days?" [21] But he was speaking of the temple of his
body. [22] After he was raised from the dead, his disciples remembered that
he had said this; and they believed the scripture and the word that Jesus
had spoken.

[23] When he was in Jerusalem during the Passover festival, many believed
in his name because they saw the signs that he was doing. [24] But Jesus on
his part would not entrust himself to them, because he knew all people
[25] and needed no one to testify about anyone; for he himself knew what
was in everyone.

Theological History-Writing

The theological significance of Jerusalem and its temple is immense, as indicated by the huge number of references to them in the Scriptures of Israel. Likewise, the exodus from slavery, celebrated annually in early spring at Passover, is fundamental to Israel's relationship to God. The psalms and the prophets also frequently speak of the exodus, Jerusalem, and the temple. So the scriptural resonances in this story of Jesus clearing animals and traders out of the temple at the time of Passover are dense and pervasive, made explicit in a quotation from Psalm 69. The passage is a condensed evocation of Jewish identity in relation to God, as described in Scripture.

There are also strong resonances with the Synoptic Gospels. One question is historical: Is this John's version of the "cleansing" of the temple that occurs in each of the Synoptics (Matt. 21:12–13; Mark 11:15–17; Luke 19:45–46)? But that comes in those Gospels at a different point in the story, the week before Jesus's death. Some say that there were two similar events; others that there was one event and that John's dating at the opening of Jesus's ministry is right; others (the majority of academic biblical commentators today) that there was one event and the Synoptics date it correctly. Rudolf Schnackenburg sums up John's approach as "theological history-writing," which rings true. John is concerned with testimony to who Jesus is, as illuminated by reflection on Scripture and other testimony to him, drawing more and more meaning from events and texts and encouraging readers to continue this process.

How does John interpret the Synoptics? C. K. Barrett is impressed by what John does here: "This Johannine narrative, at first sight artless and simple, is in fact a very striking example of the way in which John collects scattered synoptic material and synoptic themes, welds them into a whole, and uses them to bring out unmistakably the true meaning of the synoptic presentation of

Jesus, who acts with an authority he will not, and cannot, explain, and focuses this paradoxical authority upon his death and resurrection."[5] So John integrates the cleansing of the temple, Passover, Jesus speaking of God as his Father, the destruction of the temple, questions about signs and authority, conflict with Jerusalem Jews, quotation from Scripture, the body of Jesus, and his death and resurrection—all of which occur in the Synoptics—and makes this a headline event for the public ministry of Jesus. It is typical of John's distinctive way of distilling meaning from his sources in order to make deeper theological sense.

What is that deeper sense here? It is seen especially in elements that are fundamental to the whole of John's Gospel: the relationship of Jesus to his Father; incarnation, death, and resurrection; the theme of dwelling or abiding; and retrospective understanding.

My Father's House; the Temple of His Body; God and Money

"Stop making my Father's house a marketplace!" Unlike the Synoptics, here the temple is called "my Father's house," emphasizing Jesus as the Son of God. Also unlike the Synoptics, the traders and money changers are not called robbers. Rather, the objection is to the temple being a marketplace. The prophetic act of Jesus is a judgment on those in the temple, but not for dishonesty so much as for failing to acknowledge adequately its primary purpose: the worship of God. This point is made in the Synoptics too, most comprehensively by Mark with his quotation from Isaiah 56:7: "My house shall be called a house of prayer for all nations" (Mark 11:17). Jesus's point in John about the marketplace resonates with his Synoptic teaching: "You cannot serve God and wealth [mammon]" (Matt. 6:24; Luke 16:13). John characteristically takes this God-centeredness further by making the connection with Jesus. He not only adds the identification of God as the Father of Jesus—as Dorothy Lee writes, "The Johannine Jesus declares, right from the beginning, a unique relationship with God that entitles him to call God not 'our Father' (Matt. 6:9 par.) but 'my Father' (cf. Luke 2:49; also Matt. 26:39). . . . Jesus' possessive mode of address for God is decisive for his identity and ministry, and the basis and justification for his 'works.'"[6] In addition, John goes on to identify the temple with the body of Jesus.

This is a momentous move, echoing his key statement in the prologue: "And the Word became flesh and lived among us, and we have seen his glory, the glory as of a father's only son, full of grace and truth" (1:14). John's temple drama again affirms the sonship of Jesus and the importance of his physical life, this time going beyond the prologue by emphasizing his death and resurrection.

5. Barrett, *The Gospel according to St. John*, 196.
6. Lee, *Flesh and Glory*, 115.

The temple was also supremely associated with the glory and presence of God, especially in the holy of holies, the sanctuary at its heart. In 1:14 the Greek word for "lived" could be translated as "tented," and the cognate noun *skēnē* is used in the Septuagint for the "tent of meeting" or tabernacle, which was the locus of God's presence and glory and the predecessor of the holy of holies in the temple. Here in chapter 2 John underlines the connection of Jesus with the sanctuary by using different Greek words for "temple" when talking about the traders in verses 14–15 (*hieron*) and about the destruction and raising of the temple and the body of Jesus in verses 19–21 (*naos*). The former refers to the whole temple site; the latter can refer specifically to the sanctuary, the holy of holies.

So there is a concentration on the presence and glory of God inseparable from the body and person of Jesus as Son of God, and this is intensified by the quotation from Psalm 69: **Zeal for your house will consume me** (see next section below). John's Gospel has far more than the Synoptics about Jesus in the temple and at festivals in Jerusalem. *This headline scene tells us: read all those scenes in the light of this one; they can lead us deeper into who God is and who Jesus is, by thinking of the temple and the festivals in terms of Jesus and Jesus in terms of the temple and the festivals.*

Here the distinctive phrase **my Father's house**, together with seeing the body of Jesus in terms of this house, opens up an even more comprehensive dimension of John's Gospel than the temple and festivals: the theme of dwelling, abiding. We have already noted it as a key theme in chapter 1: the Word made flesh, who "lived among us," the Son in the bosom of the Father, the Holy Spirit abiding on Jesus, the first question of the disciples to Jesus about where he was staying, and the culminating reference to Jacob's dream at the place called Bethel, "the house of God." It also connects with the wedding theme: in this culture the bride was taken to the house of the father of the bridegroom.[7]

Further, in the light of the rest of the Gospel (especially chaps. 15, 17), where there is mutual indwelling of Jesus, his Father, and his disciples, this identification of the body of Jesus with the temple also points to a new community life of learning, love, and prayer, participating in the intimacy of Jesus, who is "close to the Father's heart" (1:18). This was a transformation in the meaning of temple and sacred space. In the ancient world temples were primarily homes for the gods, usually served by priestly servants, but not places where the people as a whole gathered. This is also seen in the holy of holies of the Jerusalem temple being a place of the presence of God, entered only by the high priest

7. Rereading the opening chapters of John from the standpoint of 3:29–30, where Jesus is seen as the bridegroom and John the Baptist the friend of the bridegroom, one might see various aspects of this theme: the role of the friend in matching Jesus with his disciples, the wedding at Cana, the bridegroom's father's house, and, in the Nicodemus story, new birth.

once a year. Now that sanctuary is being identified with the body of Jesus as a dwelling place, a home, and the rest of the Gospel is an invitation to all who follow him to enter it and base their lives there. Mary Coloe has suggested a rich Johannine understanding of community and spirituality centered on the themes of dwelling and the household of God (see the quotation from Coloe in the sidebar). This transformation is discussed further by Jesus in his meeting with the Samaritan woman at Jacob's well in 4:20–26, where worship "in spirit and truth" is linked to the "I am" of Jesus.

Yet the transformation comes with a sharp challenge. This account of the cleansing of the temple asks a radical question, perhaps even more relevant to our world of global capitalism than it was to first-century Jerusalem. As Jean Vanier puts it, "Is the world only a marketplace?"[8] The twentieth century saw defeats (though who can tell for how long?) for race-centered fascism and class-centered communism, opening the way for the global dominance of money-centered capitalism. How can God be worshiped and loved with all our heart, mind, soul, and strength in the face of the attraction and power of money? How can imaginations and desires shaped by advertising, economic incentives and imperatives, and fear of need be freed to delight in and serve God and other people? Can zeal for God and the worship of God compete for attention and time with the attractions of earning money and consuming?

John takes this fundamental issue about human desires, commitments, and practices in relation to God and money, places it prominently at the opening of the public ministry of Jesus, then leaves his readers to be led further on the matter. We can reflect further on the large number of relevant texts in the Old

> This book began by proposing that "household" provides the best living metaphor of the Johannine community. In their lived experience of Jesus' presence still with them, mediated through the Spirit, community members perceived themselves as the locus for God's dwelling. Where the physical body of Jesus could be called the Temple or House of God because of Jesus' unique relationship with his Father (1:1, 18; 2:16, 19, 21), in the post-Easter period they too experienced the indwelling presence of Father, Spirit, and Jesus (14:10, 27, 23, 25). . . . A community of believers becomes the dwelling place of God in becoming part of Jesus' "family" at the cross and so being drawn into his Father's household (19:25–30).
>
> —Mary Coloe, *Dwelling in the Household of God*, 102

8. Vanier, *Drawn into the Mystery of Jesus*, the title of chap. 5.

Testament and in the Synoptics, especially in the Gospel of Luke, about economic justice, forgiveness of debts, generosity to the poor and marginal, and being "rich toward God" (Luke 12:21).

Above all, we can reread this story in the light of the rest of John's Gospel. By the end of it, the theme of mutual indwelling has been developed in depth (especially in chaps. 15, 17), the zeal shown here by Jesus *has* consumed him, and this Passover has led to a later one in which Jesus, the Lamb of God, has been killed at the time the Passover lambs are killed. But after his resurrection he has sent his disciples as he was sent and has breathed his Spirit into them to enable them to follow him (20:21–22). We who receive that commission are sent into one situation after another where the attractions of God and of money are at least in tension and at worst in opposition. As we pray and live in the reality of mutual indwelling—"Abide in me as I abide in you" (15:4)—John gives this headline story of the prophetic action of Jesus in his Father's house and poses the question that is perhaps the most important of all for his disciples: *If we are sent as Jesus was sent, how do we act now in the same Spirit?*

John also here gives guidance about how to go about discerning answers to that question, as he describes a journey of ever-deepening understanding.

"His Disciples Remembered": Retrospective Understanding and Believing

We have already reflected on John's way of teaching us to read his text through the way he reads his Scriptures.[9] So far, that teaching has been implicit; but now, as Jesus makes his first public appearance, John underlines its importance by beginning to make it explicit.

As often in John, what is repeated—here, **his disciples remembered**—points to what is significant. The first time, it is the immediate response to the prophetic action and words of Jesus by disciples who know their Scriptures.[10] This is relevant but limited. The lesson seems to be that it is right to be steeped in Scripture and connect it with current events like this.

What follows shows that they needed to be open to further understanding. The second time, their remembering is after the death and resurrection of Jesus, and in the light of that they grasp and believe what Jesus meant by speaking of the destruction and raising up of the temple.

9. See the sections "Gospel of Abundance," "The Ongoing Drama," "Why John Now? (1): Jesus Now," and "Conclusion: To the Single, Beloved Reader" in the introduction, and comments on 1:1–18.

10. Luther emphasizes how ordinary people like the disciples knew their Scriptures by heart, while Calvin sees this as a much later remembering by the disciples (Farmer, *John 1–12*, 81, 82).

This passage gives at least three key lessons that are enriched and expanded in the rest of the Gospel. First, fuller believing and trusting in Jesus happens only after his resurrection. John is clear about his own standpoint being postresurrection (leading to the insight in this passage: **But he was speaking of the temple of his body**), and this pervades this Gospel more obviously than it does the Synoptics. It matches his insistence that the Holy Spirit is given only after the resurrection (e.g., 7:39). He crafts his Gospel as a pedagogy of understanding, desiring, and believing, giving diverse examples of how people and groups come, or fail to come, into various types of understanding, desiring, and believing, with full believing in Jesus happening for the first time after his resurrection. In 20:8 the disciple Jesus loved is the first to come to this sort of believing in Jesus, without seeing him, and this is the model for readers—"Blessed are those who have not seen and yet have come to believe" (20:29).

The conclusion of this temple drama underlines the different types of believing in 2:23–25: **many believed in his name because they saw the signs that he was doing**, but Jesus was clear that this was not sufficient for full trust on his part—it is not fully mutual, not yet the believing of mutual indwelling.

Second, retrospective understanding involves figural interpretation. In his major work on retrospective reading of Israel's Scriptures in all four Gospels, Richard Hays defines "figural interpretation" as "the discernment of unexpected patterns of correspondence between earlier and later events or persons within a continuous temporal stream."[11] The identification of the body of Jesus with the temple and the accompanying comments about remembering and resurrection are seen by Hays as a paradigm for John's whole approach to Scripture, teaching us to read figurally and symbolically in the light of Jesus. In this passage, "*Jesus now takes over the temple's function as a place of mediation between God and human beings.*"[12]

Elsewhere, John suggests figural interpretations of Abraham, Jacob, Moses and the exodus, Elijah, Isaiah, David in many psalms, Israel's festivals, many titles of Jesus, several symbols for Israel, and more. The verdict is that "even more comprehensively than the other Gospels, John understands the Old Testament as a vast matrix of symbols prefiguring Jesus."[13] Readers are encouraged to have their imaginations continually shaped by this matrix through reading and rereading John in interplay with a host of other texts. It is about the formation and exercise of what the theologian David Tracy calls "the analogical imagination"—constant alertness to the resonances of symbols and metaphors,

11. Hays, *Echoes of Scripture*, 347.
12. Hays, *Echoes of Scripture*, 312 (italics original).
13. Hays, *Echoes of Scripture*, 343.

to the similarities and differences of patterns, characters, and stories, and to the ways in which they can inspire fresh improvisation today.

Third, fuller faith, further following, and richer worship are fed by deeper understanding of Scripture and Jesus together. The result of the disciples remembering after the resurrection of Jesus was that **they believed the scripture and the word that Jesus had spoken**. This full postresurrection believing embraces the whole of life, following Jesus, and abiding in him and he in believers. For this community, Scripture and Jesus together are the main inspiration, guidance, and nourishment. It is significant how John brings together Scripture and the word of Jesus. That is a pointer to how he sees his own text: since he testifies here to "the word that Jesus had spoken" and in the prologue to Jesus as "the Word," he is regarding what he writes as on the same level as Scripture and to be believed, reread, learned, and "indwelt" as Scripture is.

Read in the light of the rest of John's Gospel, the plain sense of verse 22 deepens. Any chapter could be an example of this; for now, I will connect it only with three passages.

First, the prologue is recalled by the use here of "word" (*logos*) with Jesus. That sets the horizon for breadth of understanding after the resurrection: God, Jesus, all creation, all people, and the whole of Scripture.

Second, in John 6, Scripture, in the form of Moses, the exodus, and the feeding of the people of Israel in the wilderness, comes together with the word and action of Jesus as he feeds five thousand people and then, unlike in the Synoptics, gives a lengthy teaching about its meaning. This rich discourse will be explored in due course, but for now two points are important. First, as in this temple drama, there is a strong concentration on the body of Jesus, this time not in the imagery of dwelling but as food: "The bread that I will give for the life of the world is my flesh" (6:51). Second, Jesus responds to disciples, who say, "This teaching [*logos*] is difficult" (6:60), by bringing together a postresurrection perspective, the Spirit, his own words, and believing: "Does this offend you? Then what if you were to see the Son of Man ascending to where he was before? It is the Spirit that gives life; the flesh is useless. The words that I have spoken to you are Spirit and life. But among you there are some who do not believe" (6:61–64). That identification of the words of Jesus with Spirit and life again suggests how John sees his own text, as a bearer of the Spirit and abundant life.

Third, in the Farewell Discourses (chaps. 13–17) that reference to the Spirit is intensified, and the postresurrection life of the disciples is above all shaped by the Holy Spirit, named the Paraclete, the Encourager/Advocate/Comforter/Helper. The Paraclete is associated with truth (14:17; 15:26), with abiding/indwelling (14:17), and with judgment (16:8–11)—all relevant to the cleansing of the temple. But especially to be noted is the Spirit's role in teaching, both reaching back to what Jesus said, prompting the disciples to remember, and reaching forward into more and more truth. The Holy Spirit "will teach you everything, and remind you of all that I have said to you" (14:26) and "will guide you into all the truth" (16:13). *The double dynamic of, on the one hand, remembering more fully and deeply and, on the other hand, entering into more and more truth is essential to John's own theology and writing and to his conception of life following Jesus.*

The plain sense of verse 22 can go on deepening and broadening indefinitely as more and more Scriptures are related to Jesus. And, since there are many other writings testifying to Jesus, they too can be brought into consideration—above all, the rest of the New Testament. I agree with those scholars who think that John knew the Synoptic Gospels and Paul's Letters; but even if he did not, his capacious theology of the Spirit guiding into all the truth allows for others, in and before his own time, down through the centuries, and around the world today, to be inspired by the Spirit in their remembering, analogical imagining, understanding, and openness to truth, within the horizon set by the prologue.

If we return from that vast scriptural horizon to the one specific text quoted in the story of this event, there we find "scripture" and "the word of Jesus" coming together as the disciples respond to his words and actions by quoting Psalm 69. But the quotation they use is in the first person, so here "scripture" and "the word of Jesus" are being identified: **Zeal for your house will consume me.** As Margaret Daly-Denton says about this, in her fine study of Psalms in the Gospel of John: "Just as Jesus' speech is, in some sense, Scripture, so Scripture is, in a very real sense, his speech."[14]

This verse looks back to the prologue's "He came to what was his own, and his own people did not accept him" (1:11) and foreshadows the conflict and death to come. In particular, given the Passover setting, it looks back to Jesus being called "the Lamb of God" (1:29, 36) and forward to Jesus being killed at Passover. The twist given to the Septuagint, by turning its "consumed" into "will consume," also directs attention to the future. The imagery of eating resonates with both the Passover and the discourse about the feeding of the five thousand in chapter 6. Within Psalm 69, too, the psalmist's life is at stake, and verse 9 of the psalm is in line with this.

Psalm 69 is a key text in the New Testament and early Christian literature for describing the passion and death of Jesus, and to read it alongside John and the other Gospel accounts generates further relevant analogies. John's innovation is in bringing this (and other psalms) into the earlier part of his Gospel, whereas the Synoptics confine Psalms quotations to their passion stories. It

14. Daly-Denton, *David in the Fourth Gospel*, 121.

is especially appropriate to draw on a psalm here in the context of the temple, where psalms were at the heart of the liturgy.

About 60 percent of John's scriptural quotations are from the psalms, and three-way conversation between them, John, and the ongoing drama of following Jesus in Christian community is one of the most fruitful ways to learn to read his Gospel as John is teaching us to read it. The psalms are the part of the Bible that probably is most fully part of Christian (and Jewish) personal and community prayer and worship, most committed to memory, most set to music, most important in shaping the imagination. They take up into poetry and worship leading themes of Israel's Scriptures and the main elements of its faith and practice—creation, patriarchs, the exodus, the law, prophecy, wisdom. Both Jesus and John were, clearly, steeped in the psalms, and continually reading the psalms in conversation with the Gospels deepens understanding and nourishes fuller faith, further following, and richer worship.

Further Reflections: Does Jesus Replace the Temple? Is John Supersessionist?—John and the Challenge of Jewish-Christian Relations

One of the most important questions for Christians is how they relate to Jews. In the history of this relationship the Gospel of John has often played a very problematic role. There has been intensive discussion about this aspect of John in recent decades, and the topic will recur in the course of this commentary, in particular on John 8, where the polemics between Jesus and "the Jews" are most intense and bitter. For now, these further reflections on the cleansing of the temple set out the broad lines of an approach that will be given more content later.

The particular focus on whether Jesus replaces the temple contributes to the more general question about what is called "supersessionism," or "replacement theology." According to this, Christianity supersedes or replaces Judaism, its "new covenant" abrogating the Jewish "old covenant." Jews are seen as outside the covenant and rejected by God unless they become Christians, and so have no theological rationale for their continuing existence as Jews. This theological delegitimation has fed into persecution and attempts to eliminate them physically. I am not here attempting to define just what degree of responsibility "fed into" implies, but Christian contempt for and persecution of Jews is one of the darkest themes in Christian history, and interpretations of the Gospel of John have played a part in it. The Holocaust or Shoah, in which six million Jews were murdered, brought about a thorough reassessment of Christian theology in relation to Jews. There have been decisive rejections of replacement theology by many Protestant churches and by the Roman Catholic Church, and also by many other Christian churches, groups, scholars, theologians, and individuals, though this is by no means unanimous.

What about John's account of the cleansing of the temple?

It has often been interpreted as the body of Jesus replacing the temple. The truth in this is that when John was writing, the temple had been destroyed, and there was competition with the synagogue-centered Judaism of his day over a shared heritage. What emerged were a Christianity and a rabbinic Judaism that both claimed continuity with the temple, the festivals, and the Scriptures of Israel, but in very different ways.

The recognition of Jesus as Messiah, and more than Messiah, deeply divided Jews then and has continued to divide most Jews from Christians. But this does not mean that Christians have to be supersessionist, and it is a tempting misreading of John, both here and elsewhere, to see him as offering a replacement theology. Ruth Edwards summarizes a great deal of scholarship in showing (I think convincingly) that on one topic after another, not only on the temple but also on other Jewish elements (Scripture, Torah, circumcision, covenant, Sabbath, dietary laws, purity laws, festivals, worship, ethnicity, and monotheism), John is not offering a replacement theology.[15] His concept of "fulfillment" could be, and often has been, distorted to imply replacement, just as his daring use of divine language for Jesus could be seen as an abandonment of monotheism; but neither perception is correct. John does not see Jesus superseding the covenant of God with Israel but rather as opening it to all. "And just as Moses lifted up the serpent in the wilderness, so must the Son of Man be lifted up, that whoever believes in him may have eternal life" (3:14–15). John never mentions the word "covenant," but his Gospel is pervaded by covenantal language and testifies to a dramatic opening of the covenant, not to its supersession or abrogation.[16]

In John's cleansing of the temple, there is a clear affirmation and honoring of it as **my Father's house** (and therefore also no rejection of "institutional religion," which is one of the interpretations sometimes given). The quotation from Psalm 69 is an affirmation and honoring of Scripture that refers to the temple and so carries over its meaning into the time beyond the temple's destruction. Rabbinic Judaism, too, took Scripture as a bearer of meaning through the destruction of the temple. The Christian rereading in relation to Jesus in the New Testament was very different from the rabbinic rereading eventually embodied in the Talmud, but neither has a theology of replacement. Something

15. R. Edwards, *Discovering John*, chaps. 11–12.

16. One might say that, without ever using the word "covenant," John's account of Jesus as the Word enacts what Jeremiah speaks of: a "new covenant" that is the old covenant written on the heart, indwelling people in an abiding way (Jer. 31:31–34).

new certainly is happening in both, but B. F. Westcott's verdict on John could be applied to the self-understanding of both emergent traditions: "The old Church is transfigured and not destroyed. The continuity of revelation is never broken."[17]

Yet the differences between the two have been deep and often bitter. In John's time, the power to persecute was with the synagogue; later, it lay with the church, and the result was an often tragic history of alienation, misunderstanding, and violence.

That history poses a major challenge to Christians today. The Gospel of John, one of our authoritative texts, has been interpreted repeatedly in supersessionist and anti-Jewish ways. Can it be reread authentically so as to contribute to the healing of that history and the shaping of a better future? One of the purposes of this commentary is to give substance to the answer: Yes! This is based partly on continually reading the Gospel of John and other Scriptures with Jews during more than two decades in the practice called Scriptural Reasoning (on this see the epilogue to this commentary). This has by no means led to theological agreement but rather to what might be called an improved quality of disagreement and a commitment to ever-deepening mutual engagement. This commentary gives a reading of the Gospel of John that encourages Christians not only to reject the supersessionism that has been so prominent in their history but also to enter into a new phase of Jewish-Christian relations that includes learning from rabbinic Judaism.[18]

John's headline text for this is in the prologue: "The law indeed was given through Moses; grace and truth came through Jesus Christ" (1:17). There are conflicting interpretations of that verse, some supersessionist. I agree with Ruth Edwards, who sees it explicating the previous verse's "one grace after another." She comments, "John acknowledges Torah as God's gracious gift; but he sees the revelation provided by Jesus as even greater."[19] Yet I would qualify her use of "greater." It is not about size—both Torah and Jesus reveal the same God of superabundant grace, so there can be no quantitative comparison;[20] rather, the difference is between being *given* as Word or instruction (*logos*) through Moses and *coming* in person as *logos* made flesh, Jesus. John 1:17 contains the first mention of Jesus Christ by name in the Gospel. The prologue has already connected the *logos* with God, creation, and the history of Israel, and it is a term that gathers

17. Westcott, *The Gospel according to St. John*, 43.

18. For an example of Jewish-Christian engagement that, during its five years of dialogue and writing (in which I was privileged to take part), was accompanied by the practice of Scriptural Reasoning, see Bayfield, *Deep Calls to Deep*.

19. R. Edwards, *Discovering John*, 144.

20. I find a thorough and profound nonsupersessionist Christian doctrine of God in Sonderegger, *The Doctrine of God* and *The Doctrine of the Holy Trinity*.

under its umbrella all parts of the Septuagint—Torah, Prophets, and Writings. The distinctive novelty is the later identification of all this with the particular person, Jesus as the Christ or Messiah, and the dramatic narrative of his life, death, and resurrection that John is about to tell. There can be no avoiding the Christian distinctiveness of this grace, but neither should there be any denial by Christians of the other grace, "given through Moses," which is a gift of God, cosmic in scope, and of continuing importance to both Jews and Christians.

The engagement between Christians and rabbinic Jews is at best "deep to deep." In this there can be multiple deepenings and broadenings, going together further into one's own texts and traditions, into the other's, into understanding the world created and sustained by God, into collaboration for the common good, into agreements and disagreements, into understanding, obeying, and praising God, and into the new sort of community made up of those who are involved in such engagement. It is desirable for the Gospel of John to be one resource for that engagement as part of the ongoing drama of Jewish-Christian relations in the twenty-first century.

Conclusion

This chapter has headlined two events with implications through the rest of the Gospel. The wedding at Cana has been a sign of the abundant life available through Jesus, a "sweet excess" that resonates with experiences of marriage, celebration, wine drinking, and good surprises. It opens up rich levels of meaning, the relationship of Jesus with his mother and his disciples, and above all his relationship with creation and with God.

The dramatic Jerusalem confrontation likewise has multiple dimensions. In the setting of two fundamental bearers of meaning in his Jewish experience and practice—the temple and the Passover celebration of the exodus—Jesus has claimed the temple as his Father's house, challenged its relationship to money and markets, and pointed to "the temple of his body."

For the reader, these two events dramatically perform key elements of the prologue, are an imaginative preparation for further signs and confrontations, and, above all, reveal further who Jesus is, enriched by many intertexts. The rereader is invited by the author to join in retrospective interpretation, from a position after the resurrection, in a community that experiences the presence of the risen Jesus understood through testimony and Scripture, as combined in this text of John.

John 3:1–36

Astonishing Teaching

This is a chapter with two sets of teachings on core themes of the Gospel. The first comes in a meeting with Nicodemus, the first of several significant encounters in which Jesus engages with individuals (more occur in chaps. 4, 5, 9, 11). The second comes through another appearance of John the Baptist. Both contain astonishing statements.

A Teacher Is Taught: New Birth; Spirit Birth; God's Love, God's Son, and Eternal Life (3:1–2)

Nicodemus, a Jewish leader and teacher, comes to Jesus by night and recognizes him as a teacher from God. In three waves of teaching, each introduced by **"Very truly, I tell you,"** Jesus opens up the surprise of the Gospel. Just as both the Cana wine sign and the response of Jesus to being challenged in the temple exceeded any expectations, so here Nicodemus is bewildered and amazed by responses that go far beyond anything he could have anticipated.

> [1] Now there was a Pharisee named Nicodemus, a leader of the Jews. [2] He came to Jesus by night and said to him, "Rabbi, we know that you are a teacher who has come from God; for no one can do these signs that you do apart from the presence of God."

Nicodemus is not mentioned in other Gospels, but he appears here and at two other points in the Gospel of John: at 7:50–52, where he challenges the Pharisees by standing up for due legal process in relation to Jesus and is met by mockery; and at 19:38–42, when he and Joseph of Arimathea lay the body of Jesus in a tomb, Nicodemus bringing a large amount of costly myrrh and aloes. Commentators down through the centuries and today have been divided about whether Nicodemus became a full believer, or represents failure to understand and believe in Jesus, or is an ambiguous, in-between figure.

I think that the third option fits him best.[1] Coming **by night** suggests that he was not wanting to be openly involved with Jesus but was fascinated by him, and his first words are (for someone in his position) daringly open to Jesus as a **teacher who has come from God**. Then he is challenged radically in his core identity by mind-blowing ideas, and his final statement is an open question: **"How can these things be?"** His later appearances in the drama show that he stayed concerned with Jesus and was willing to speak up for him and to go to great expense to honor him in death; but that does not amount to what the Gospel of John means by full faith in Jesus. So, in a story aimed at drawing readers into full believing (20:31), Nicodemus is a figure who raises profound questions for readers who are searchers, and he is in some ways a model; but others, above all "the disciple whom Jesus loved,"[2] are models of the goal of full discipleship.

The First Wave: Kingdom of God, New Birth from Above, and Jesus (3:3–4)

> [3] Jesus answered him, "Very truly, I tell you, no one can see the kingdom of God without being born from above." [4] Nicodemus said to him, "How can anyone be born after having grown old? Can one enter a second time into the mother's womb and be born?"

The first words of Jesus to Nicodemus raise some important questions, three in particular.

The Kingdom of God

First, what is **the kingdom of God**? Readers of the Synoptic Gospels of Matthew, Mark, and Luke (and I think that John not only knew them in some form but also expected his readers to know them) will know that in them the central message of Jesus is about the coming of the kingdom of God through him, his teaching (especially in vivid parables), his ministry, and his death and

1. For a fuller discussion of Nicodemus, see Ford, "Meeting Nicodemus."
2. See comments on John 13; 19; 20; 21.

resurrection. John's Gospel does not repeat literally that message of the kingdom of God (in Matthew often called the kingdom of heaven—note the mention of heaven by John, too, in 3:12–13) or those parables, but does something both different and parallel that at the same time both helps readers to understand the other Gospels better and also gives fresh insights. Where the Synoptics speak of the kingdom of God, John often speaks of life, the Spirit, love, trusting and believing, light, truth, and, above all, eternal life.

What seems to be happening here is that John is teaching Synoptic readers to use different parallel terms and in this way to expand our ways of understanding the message and mission of Jesus. *We are invited to think of the kingdom of God or kingdom of heaven in terms of life (seeing and entering the kingdom of God is seen as birth, our entry into life), the Spirit or breath/wind* (see the second wave below), *and believing in Jesus, eternal life, love, light, and truth* (see the third wave below). And essential to all of this is the central concern of John: who Jesus is.

Why might John be doing this? I can think of at least three probable reasons, besides the obvious, embracing concern (that is clear throughout his Gospel) to lead us deeper into who Jesus is and what following and trusting him means.

One is about accessibility. "Kingdom of God" language is rooted only in Judaism and the Jewish Scriptures, whereas the language of life, Spirit, love, light, and truth is found not only in Judaism and the Jewish Scriptures but also in the surrounding culture of Hellenistic civilization, so that John's writing is more widely accessible.[3]

A second reason has to do with John's understanding of rule and power. He is less attracted to the hierarchical language of power and authority implied by "kingdom of God." In telling the story of the night before Jesus's death, John omits the institution of the Eucharist or Lord's Supper, which in each of the Synoptics involves the kingdom of God, and instead has Jesus washing his disciples' feet, turning upside down the hierarchy of king and servant. And in his account of the confrontation of Jesus with Pontius Pilate, John makes the issue of kingship central only in order to define it in terms of testifying to the truth (18:33–38).

A third reason is how he imagines the future in relation to Jesus. John has none of the vivid apocalyptic imagery of the coming kingdom of God that is found in, for example, Mark 13:26: "'the Son of Man coming in clouds' with great power and glory." He is clear that the future is completely bound up with Jesus, but eternal life is available now as well as beyond death. Rather

3. A similar point was made in discussing why John chose to open his Gospel with a focus on *logos*, "word" (see comments on 1:1–4). See also, on the words for "love," comments on 15:12–14 and 21:15–19.

than encouraging speculation, prediction, or apocalyptic imagining, the last, twice-repeated, words of Jesus in John's Gospel are about the ongoing, faithful abiding of the disciple he loved and assume both his own authority and his return: "If it is my will that he remain [*menein*, "abide"] until I come, what is that to you?" (21:22, 23).

So overall there is a shift in the balance of imagery. "Kingdom of God," or "kingdom of heaven," is not displaced, but the balance is now tipped toward emphasizing other social language (that is also present in the Synoptics and Old Testament) about family life as children of God ("born of God" [cf. 1:12–13]), a community of followers and learners inspired by the Spirit, the love of friends, or (most distinctively Johannine) mutual indwelling or abiding. The political remains while the relational is deepened and expanded.

Perhaps deepest and most expansive of all is the dynamic integration of earth and heaven, above and below, which reaches its climax in the desire for mutual indwelling and unity in love expressed in the prayer of Jesus in John 17. There, as will be seen, is the ultimate "beloved community."[4]

One practical effect of John's switch away from "kingdom of God" language after the Nicodemus encounter is to invite readers to reread his Gospel in conversation with the Synoptics. For example, all those parables of the kingdom of God as a place of wedding feasts and other celebrations illuminate and are illuminated by John's imagery of abundant wine, water, food, fish, life, Spirit, light, truth, and love. Similarly, Paul rarely uses "kingdom of God" language, and his vision of the church (in terms of the body of Christ, mutual indwelling, family, people of God, covenant, love, the Spirit, abundance, eternal life, and more) invites three-way intertextual reading with the Synoptics and John.

New Birth from Above

Second, what does **being born from above** mean? The Greek *anōthen* has more than one possible meaning—the Amplified Bible translates, "born again (anew, from above)." For large numbers of Christians, being "born again" goes to the heart of their identity. *As we will see, if being a "born again Christian" is understood through Nicodemus and this whole passage (3:1–21), that identity is transformative, deep, and multifaceted.* It involves the whole Gospel as John presents it—encountering and trusting the incarnate, crucified, and risen Jesus, understanding who he is in relation to his Father, having a new beginning given by

4. The phrase is from Josiah Royce, the American philosopher whose culminating work near the end of his life, *The Problem of Christianity*, represents a remarkable development in his thinking. The biblical dimension of Royce's thinking is mainly inspired by Paul's Letters; this commentary gives a complementary biblical dimension through John and his intertexts.

God, living in the Spirit and being open to surprises, being loved by God, and, in the ongoing drama of life before God, being faced continually with the crucial decision of fully trusting and believing in Jesus or not. Nicodemus, as already suggested, is a character who could decide either way, and so models anyone who is facing up to the challenge of Jesus.

All of that emerges from the whole passage, more clearly when it is reread in the light of the rest of the Gospel, even more when read in interplay with the Synoptics, with Paul, and with the rest of the New and Old Testaments, and most fully when understood within both the prologue's horizon of God and all reality and the Farewell Discourses' concern with the ongoing drama of following Jesus now. An obvious danger with a "born again" identity is that of being reduced to a one-off decision or a neat package, ignoring some of those dimensions, and so missing out on much of the abundance of light and life that Jesus came to bring.

John's use of the ambiguous *anōthen* is deliberate, as Nicodemus's misunderstanding and the rest of the passage makes clear: Nicodemus takes it to mean that one is to **enter a second time into the mother's womb and be born**. Two other plays on words with more than one meaning are in verses 6–8, where *pneuma* can mean "wind" or "spirit/Spirit," and *phōnē* can mean "sound" or "voice." To recognize this is to realize that John intends us to check any habit of thinking that what he writes has only one meaning: we are to look for more and more. One way of doing this is to follow through each meaning in turn as far as we can, trying to learn what John, in this passage about two teachers, is teaching his readers.

Taking first the meaning that Nicodemus takes, "being born again/anew," one lesson seems to be that readers should be alert to meanings that are not literal, be open to thinking metaphorically, imaginatively, symbolically. The rest of John's Gospel supports this; he loves to open up immensely rich metaphors, images, and symbols, and leave readers to explore them further. Nicodemus may have taken Jesus too literally, but the meaning of *anōthen* that he takes up, about "being born again/anew," is worth pursuing further, this time as a vivid image of what is involved in the kingdom of God, living in the Spirit, eternal life, being loved by God, and following Jesus.

For careful readers of John up to this point, being "born again" resonates with the prologue. This is about a new beginning given by God. The prologue opens with "In the beginning was the Word" (1:1) and then goes on to say that "to all who received" the Word, "who believed in his name, he gave power to become children of God, who were born, not of blood or of the will of the flesh, or of the will of man, but of God" (1:12–13). The One who is the ultimate beginner shares the power to give new beginnings. Here "born again" and "born from above" come together, and in the light of this the best translation of the phrase in 3:3 and 3:7 is "born again from above."

By speaking of birth in his prologue John probably intends us to read it in conversation with the stories of the birth of Jesus that are at the beginning of the Gospels of Matthew and Luke. For all their differences, both of them agree that the birth of Jesus is both a physical birth and from God. The metaphor of height, "from above" or "of God," is signaled by Matthew through the Holy Spirit (Matt. 1:18, 20), dreams (1:20–24; 2:12–13), the fulfillment of Scripture (1:23; 2:6, 15), and Jesus being called "Emmanuel," which means "God is with us" (1:23). Luke indicates it through the Holy Spirit (Luke 1:15, 35, 41, 67; 2:25–26), angels (1:11–19, 26–38; 2:8–15), many scriptural echoes, and Jesus being called "Son of the Most High" (1:32), a Davidic king of whose "kingdom there will be no end" (1:32–33), "Son of God" (1:35), and "the dawn from on high" (1:78). The account of Nicodemus meeting Jesus, besides the themes of birth, divine origin (3:2, 16–17), sonship (3:13–17), Spirit, kingdom, heaven, and height, also has a striking echo of the amazed response of Mary to the angel Gabriel. Mary says, "How can this be?" (Luke 1:34). Jesus tells Nicodemus, **"Do not be astonished,"** but his last words to Jesus are: **"How can these things be?"**

So John, in line with the themes of union with Jesus, mutual indwelling of Jesus and believers, and their sharing in his life and Spirit (which are explored most fully in the Farewell Discourses, culminating in the prayer of Jesus in John 17), here opens up further what the prologue means by being "born of God" and the connection of that birth with Jesus. This leads into the third question about this first wave of teaching.

No One? Who?

"No one can see the kingdom of God without being born from above." So has anyone actually been "born from above"? *Once the question is raised, John's answer is obvious: Jesus!* The next wave makes this clearer before the third wave makes it explicit.

The Second Wave: Water and Flesh; Wind/Spirit and Sound/Voice (3:5–10)

> [5] Jesus answered, "Very truly, I tell you, no one can enter the kingdom of
> God without being born of water and Spirit. [6] What is born of the flesh is
> flesh, and what is born of the Spirit is spirit. [7] Do not be astonished that I said
> to you, 'You must be born from above.' [8] The wind blows where it chooses,
> and you hear the sound of it, but you do not know where it comes from or

> where it goes. So it is with everyone who is born of the Spirit." 9 Nicodemus said to him, "How can these things be?" 10 Jesus answered him, "Are you a teacher of Israel, and yet you do not understand these things?"

Introduced by a second **"Very truly, I tell you,"** the next wave covers the same ground as the first but goes further up the beach. It is still about being "born from above" (3:3), but this is now explained as being **born of water and Spirit** (3:5). The following verse parallels Spirit with flesh: **"What is born of the flesh is flesh, and what is born of the Spirit is spirit"** (3:6). Here water (which is also associated with physical birth, and water in this Gospel so far has been the material for the first sign of Jesus, resonating with creation)[5] and flesh (whose main association in this Gospel so far has been with Jesus, the Word made flesh) seem to be used together to indicate both the material creation and its close association with Jesus, as in the prologue. So there is nothing negative about flesh here, but it is not all there is to someone.

The other dimension is called "spirit/Spirit" (*pneuma*). There are no capitals in the original manuscripts, and how John uses *pneuma* makes no simple distinction between the human spirit or breath of life, especially that of Jesus, and the Holy Spirit. For example, when he died, Jesus "gave up *to pneuma*," meaning "the breath/spirit/Spirit" (19:30); and when, after his resurrection, he shares the Holy Spirit with his disciples, the verb for "breathed" in 20:22 is the one used in the Septuagint in Genesis 2:7 for God breathing the breath of life into Adam. Spirit, too, has already in John 1 been connected as closely as possible with Jesus and also with what comes from above: "I saw the Spirit descending from heaven like a dove, and it remained on him" (1:32). Further, Jesus is called "the one who baptizes with the Holy Spirit" (1:33), and immediately after the meeting with Nicodemus, he and his disciples are described as baptizing with water, as John the Baptist did (3:22–23).[6] Water, like flesh and wind/breath, is a good creation, but there is a transformation brought by Jesus, symbolized by turning water into wine, just as the breath carrying the words of Jesus transforms the lives of the disciples.

There will be much more about the Spirit later in this Gospel, which has far more on this subject than the other Gospels, but here the key statement

5. See comments on 2:1–12.

6. There is considerable controversy about the extent to which John's Gospel is concerned with the sacraments of baptism and Eucharist (Mass, Holy Communion, Lord's Supper). I am persuaded that reference to them is part of the "deep plain sense" of this Gospel and that readers are right to explore their meaning with the help of such Johannine themes as birth, death, water, wine, blood, drinking, bread, body, eating, word, Spirit, light, darkness, sight, footwashing, and more. See especially comments on 6:25–65 and chap. 13.

that evokes astonishment in Nicodemus is 3:8. The reader already knows Jesus as the Word made flesh and the one on whom the Spirit remains. Within the drama of this scene, Nicodemus does not know this, but yet he does think, "We know that you are a teacher who has come from God" (3:2). Verse 8 explodes that confident knowledge. He may think he has a known role for Jesus as "a teacher" and a known origin for Jesus "from God," but while that is not wrong, it is an utterly inadequate understanding when compared to what the first two chapters have already said about who Jesus is. Verse 8 opens up a mystery that, like the wind, has no defining edge. *It evokes imaginatively a God who is free (the wind/Spirit* ***blows where it chooses****), who overflows our categories, who challenges our knowledge of origins and purposes (****where it comes from or where it goes****), who has an energy we cannot harness, who can spring endless surprises, who is unseen yet effective, and who can blow us in new directions.* In line with this, Tom Greggs offers an inspiring theology of the church, the love of God for the whole of creation, and the Spirit moving across boundaries and springing surprises (see the quotation from Greggs in the sidebar).

The image of wind/spirit, especially when understood in relation to other references to spirit in the rest of John and the Bible, can lead into surprising insights. Indeed, the reader is encouraged to explore the rest of Scripture like this by Jesus's question to Nicodemus, **"Are you a teacher of Israel, and yet you**

> There is no sense that the Spirit's particular act in the life of the church comes at the cost of activity in creation. The Spirit, of course, is boundless and free. . . . The Spirit is the one who in the Spirit's extensity is multiply intensely present within the creation. In freeing the human to love and to live the humanity for which she was eternally destined in loving those around her, the Spirit's work in *all* those who love unites the Christian and the non-Christian and demonstrates that the division between the church and the world is not absolute or ultimate, however significant and important it might be: the Spirit is Lord and the Spirit blows wherever the Spirit wills (cf. John 3:8), and the church is dependent on the Spirit—not the Spirit on the church. But the Spirit is also *intensely and particularly* present in the event of the Spirit's act that is the church as a body of those who participate actively by the Spirit in the body of Christ and in its form, and *knowingly* and *actively* desire to be conformed to the likeness of Christ and His love in its cruciform reality.
>
> —Tom Greggs, *Dogmatic Ecclesiology*, 1:413–14 (italics original)

do not understand these things?"[7] Jesus is a guide to what Nicodemus does not know, but it is not knowledge that is fixed, clear, and containable: as Jesus says in 16:13, it is guidance by the Spirit "into all the truth." Here the abundance of that truth and its uncontainability are symbolized by the wind.

Verse 8 has another significant wordplay. **You hear the sound** [*phōnē*] **of it** can also be translated as "you hear the voice of it." Both *phōnē* and *pneuma* are at the same time images from nature and connected with both believers and Jesus. John the Baptist has already been described as "the voice of one crying out in the wilderness" (1:23), pointing to Jesus. The voice of Jesus himself plays a role throughout the Gospel. This is emphasized most in his description of himself as the good shepherd, during which *phōnē* occurs five times (10:3, 4, 5, 16, 27), culminating in a statement that takes up the Nicodemus conversation's theme of eternal life: "My sheep hear my voice. I know them, and they follow me. I give them eternal life, and they will never perish" (10:27–28). Then in the next chapter the climax of the most dramatic of Jesus's signs, the raising of Lazarus from death, comes when Jesus at the opened tomb "cried with a loud voice, 'Lazarus, come out!'" (11:43).

The first step in understanding this surprising mystery is to recognize that **you do not know** (3:8) and **you do not understand** (3:10). The next step is amazed questioning, and that is what Nicodemus does: **"How can these things be?"** The response to that is the third, immense wave.

The Third Wave: Jesus, God's Love, Eternal Life, Darkness and Light (3:11–21)

> [11] "Very truly, I tell you, we speak of what we know and testify to what we have seen; yet you do not receive our testimony. [12] If I have told you about earthly things and you do not believe, how can you believe if I tell you about heavenly things? [13] No one has ascended into heaven except the one who descended from heaven, the Son of Man. [14] And just as Moses lifted up the serpent in the wilderness, so must the Son of Man be lifted up, [15] that whoever believes in him may have eternal life.

7. If Nicodemus had followed the word *anōthen* through the Septuagint, he would have found it meaning "from above" many times—e.g., "blessings of heaven above" (Gen. 49:25); "There I will meet with you, and from above the mercy seat, from between the two cherubim that are on the ark of the covenant, I will deliver to you all my commands for the Israelites" (Exod. 25:22; cf. 40:20); "When Moses went into the tent of meeting to speak with the Lord, he would hear the voice [*phōnē*] speaking to him from above the mercy seat" (Num. 7:89); "What would be my portion from God above [*apanōthen*]?" (Job 31:2); "Shower, O heavens, from above, and let the skies rain down righteousness" (Isa. 45:8). Likewise, the outpouring of the Spirit comes "from on high" (Isa. 32:15: *pneuma aph' hypsēlou*).

[16] "For God so loved the world that he gave his only Son, so that everyone who believes in him may not perish but may have eternal life.

[17] "Indeed, God did not send the Son into the world to condemn the world, but in order that the world might be saved through him. [18] Those who believe in him are not condemned; but those who do not believe are condemned already, because they have not believed in the name of the only Son of God. [19] And this is the judgment, that the light has come into the world, and people loved darkness rather than light because their deeds were evil. [20] For all who do evil hate the light and do not come to the light, so that their deeds may not be exposed. [21] But those who do what is true come to the light, so that it may be clearly seen that their deeds have been done in God."

Introduced by another **"Very truly, I tell you,"** the third wave has rightly been seen as a summary of the Gospel. It takes up again many of the themes already headlined in chapter 1, such as interplays with the Synoptics and Old Testament, knowing, testifying, seeing, receiving, believing and trusting, ascending and descending, Son of Man, the death of Jesus, Moses, God as Father, Son of God, the world, light and darkness, seeing, and truth—each of which gathers more meaning as the Gospel proceeds. But it also goes further. Like a further wave of introduction to the Gospel, it headlines new key themes: the **as . . . so . . .** pattern, **eternal life**, **love**, **judgment**, **evil**, and **in God**.

Just as John only headlines these new themes here, so that their further meaning can be unfolded later, so I will make some basic points now and indicate where they will be opened up more fully. But first there is the question of who is speaking and being spoken to here.

Who is speaking? The "I" of Jesus still continues for at least a while—some translations close the quotation from him at the end of verse 15 instead of verse 21 as in the NRSV. From verse 16 it could just as well be the voice of the Gospel's author. There are no quotation marks in the original Greek, so it is up to us readers to decide. Or do we need to decide? Like the wordplay with "from above/again," "wind/spirit," and "sound/voice," it can fruitfully be read both ways. But here there is an additional point. The fact that what Jesus says and what John writes can merge without clear distinction (not only here but also elsewhere in this Gospel) underlines the postresurrection standpoint of John, which has already been made clear in his account of the cleansing of the temple. If John understands himself to be guided by the Spirit, who can remind him of what Jesus has said and lead him into further truth in line with that (14:26; 16:13), then the distinction does blur, for it is the truth that matters.

To whom is the third wave addressed, Nicodemus or a wider audience? The whole passage of 3:1–21 switches between singular and plural.[8] Again, it appears that John wants us to think along both lines together, and this is confirmed by the number of times in 3:1–21 he uses a general singular, which can be individual or plural in sense: **no one . . . anyone**[9] **. . . no one . . . everyone . . . no one . . . whoever . . . everyone.**[10] So the third wave begins by addressing Nicodemus but by the end he has faded out of the picture and all the focus is on a general audience—indeed, on any reader. More sharply, readers are being radically challenged to believe and become committed to Jesus and to living in his light, with their actions done "in God" (v. 21).

The conclusion seems clear: John is teaching readers to understand his words in more than one way at the same time. This is part of what I have been calling his "deep plain sense." But it is by no means a matter of playing around with various meanings: *all of them converge on that summons to live and act "in God."*

The Way In: Trusting Testimony; Openness to Surprise; The One Who . . .

Already in chapter 1 testimony to who Jesus is has emerged as fundamental to the Gospel. Here in verses 11–13 the logic of that is followed through: the testimony of Jesus himself is the most important of all. It is a postresurrection perspective, and what has been implied in the first two waves is here explicit. Jesus is the exception to the "no one" in verses 3 and 5: **"No one has ascended into heaven except the one who descended from heaven, the Son of Man"** (v. 13). The whole of John's Gospel is an exercise in witnessing or testifying to Jesus (21:24–25). Testimony always raises the questions: Is it to be believed and trusted? Is the witness to be believed and trusted?

Those raise further questions: What is the framework within which we judge testimony? What if something or someone does not fit our current framework and expectations—are we open to changing our previous understanding? How confident are we that we have a comprehensive understanding of reality? *Are we open to a radical, divine surprise?* The whole New Testament is about someone

8. Nicodemus at the beginning of the conversation says "we know," and Jesus speaks in both the singular, "I tell you," "I said," and the plural, "we speak, "we know and testify," "we have seen." Jesus addresses Nicodemus in the singular "you" (vv. 3, 5, 7, 8, 10, 11) and the plural "you" (vv. 11, 12), with the switch happening in v. 11, which strikingly begins in the singular and ends in the plural: "Very truly, I tell you [singular] . . . ; yet you [plural] do not receive our testimony."

9. In v. 4 this is literally "a human being" (*anthrōpos*), which is what Nicodemus is called in v. 1, so here it is both very specific and very general. The plural *anthrōpoi* is used in v. 19, translated by NRSV as "people."

10. In vv. 18–21 the NRSV even has a string of plurals—"those who . . . those who . . . all who . . . those who"—all of which are singular in the Greek.

surprising, whose teaching, actions, death, and resurrection were astonishing news, accessible only through testimony to them. Nicodemus is being faced with a message and person not fitting within his previous understanding and is being challenged to change. The reader has already been given the framework of the prologue, but now in Nicodemus the reader is also given a vivid picture of someone who is not yet there, who is asking the question "How can these things be?" (v. 9).

In response, the first point (v. 11) has been about trusting testimony; the second (v. 12) about the need to be open to earthly and heavenly surprises; the third (v. 13) has pointed to the need to reframe the question from "how" to "who" in order to do justice to the surprise of the Gospel. Then (vv. 14–15) comes a veiled hint in fresh imagery at the shocking surprise central to who Jesus is.

The Son of Man Must Be Lifted Up: Preparing the Imagination (3:14)

From his opening chapter John prepares the reader's imagination for the eventual death of Jesus. He is first "the Lamb of God who takes away the sin of the world" (1:29; cf. 1:36); next, his "hour has not yet come" (2:4); then his crucified and resurrected body is identified with the Jerusalem temple: "Destroy this temple, and in three days I will raise it up" (2:19). On rereading, these and later images (such as in 10:11: "The good shepherd lays down his life for the sheep") enable us to go deeper in different ways and through relating to a variety of intertexts. Here in verse 14 two striking new elements appear.

One is the introduction of the image of Jesus being **lifted up**, which is later used again as a hint in 8:28 and then in 12:32–33 explicitly about the death of Jesus: "'And I, when I am lifted up from the earth, will draw all people to myself.' He said this to indicate the kind of death he was to die." This picture of his death as exaltation goes with John's distinctive presentation of the death of Jesus as his glorification. It also connects with the reimagining of the kingdom of God and the kingship of Jesus through washing his disciples' feet and his statements in his trial before Pilate. Here in 3:14 "lifted up" at once adds a twist to the previous language of height—"from above" and "ascended." Now the height is inseparable from a humiliating death.

All this is introduced gently, as it were an early wave of teaching to be followed by larger, later ones as the story moves to its climax. The shock of surprise is framed, its meaning is opened up, it is made less strange, by reference to other texts. There is a dense set of echoes here, both of the Synoptic Gospels and of the Jewish Scriptures.

One little word sums up the connection with the Synoptics: the **must** (*dei*) of 3:14. It is used by Matthew (16:21), Mark (8:31), and Luke (9:22) in predictions of the passion and death of Jesus as "Son of Man," suggesting that it is the will of God. The same suggestion is made by John, but with his own theology of the cross that intensifies the paradox of crucifixion as saving, attractive, uplifting. Whereas the Synoptics see the cross as humiliation and the resurrection/ascension as exaltation and glorification, John makes the cross intrinsic to the glory—what Rudolf Schnackenburg calls "a most important step in Christology"—because it shifts attention from a succession of events to the "who" question about Jesus, who is at the center of the events and is identified through them. His glory is simultaneously that of the crucified and risen one, the one who says "I am," redefining glory through who he is.

Moses lifting up the serpent in the wilderness (referring to Num. 21:8–9) to save the Israelites from poisonous serpents is a type of the salvific uplifting of Jesus. This is distinctively Johannine—there is no New Testament parallel to this interpretation of Numbers 21.

But the intertextuality is not just with Numbers. Above all, the verb "lift up" or "exalt" appears in a Septuagint text in the book of Isaiah crucial to early Christians: "My servant [*pais*, which also means "child"] will be exalted and greatly glorified" (Isa. 52:13). Here exaltation and glory are brought together in relation to a suffering servant of God.[11]

This densely intertextual verse not only begins to reimagine the death of Jesus but also is the first example of a characteristic and very important pattern of thought in John. This is the second new element in 3:14.

"As . . . So . . ." : A Daring Theological Imagination

Perhaps the richest theological words in John are "as . . . so . . ." and "in." Both occur in the Nicodemus story and recur throughout the Gospel.

The "as . . . so . . ." (sometimes only "as . . .") pattern often occurs at points that are vital to the thought and action of readers in their own roles in the ongoing drama of following Jesus, reaching a climax in the Farewell Discourses with the footwashing ("Do as I have done to you" [13:15]), the new love command ("Just as I have loved you, you also should love one another" [13:34]), and the

11. As often in John, the resonances of meaning go on and on. E.g., the Suffering Servant passage in Isa. 52:13–53:12 has many other Greek words used by John, besides "lifting up" and "glory," such as "astonish," "king," "hear," "understand," "Lord," "reveal," "thirst," "see," "know," "sin," "peace," "heal," "way," "sheep," "hand over," "judgment," "life," "transgression," "people," "death," "evil," "light," "serve." And the Num. 21:8–9 text itself is interpreted in Wisd. 16:5–7, which stresses that being healed or saved did not happen just because of looking at the serpent but through God "the Savior of all." This goes well with John's emphasis on the initiative of God and the response of faith in 3:16.

final prayer of Jesus ("As you have sent me into the world, so I have sent them into the world" [17:18; cf. 20:21]).

Each of those sayings gives the disciples a broad responsibility for thinking as fully as possible about both what the "as" means and how to act in line with that meaning in their own circumstances. What might the current analogies of footwashing be? Or, how has Jesus loved, and where might that lead in our situation? Or, how and for what was Jesus sent, and what might the current analogies of that be? Readers are encouraged to have an analogical imagination and to improvise further on what Jesus did and said. In the light of the teaching in the Farewell Discourses about the Holy Spirit, readers are being invited to be daring in their improvisations, even to the point of doing "greater works" than Jesus did (14:12). In the Spirit of Jesus, we are to stretch ourselves in imagination, understanding, and practice. This is a charter for doing theology analogous to that of John in the service of a life in the Spirit analogous to that of Jesus.

Here in 3:14 the thinking involves two complex events—Moses lifting up the serpent, and Jesus dying on the cross—each with a rich, expansive context of meaning. In Moses's case, the resonances ramify through the exodus story (with its naming of God as "I am"), the rest of the Pentateuch, later interpretations (as in Wisdom of Solomon), and the role of Moses and Torah in history. In the case of Jesus, the context is nothing less than God and all created reality, the full drama of his life, death, resurrection, and sharing his Spirit, and the other ways of understanding his death in John, the rest of the New Testament, and in Christian history. John brings the two together in this "as . . . so . . ." pattern and leaves his readers to explore further.

The "as . . . so . . ." pattern, especially in close connection with the "I am" sayings, is perhaps the most comprehensive way John has of inviting readers into doing for themselves the sort of meditatively daring theology that he himself models. He reads Numbers, Exodus, Isaiah, and other parts of the Septuagint together with the testimonies to Jesus in the Synoptics and other traditions and invites readers to read both them and his own writing, guided by the Spirit, in analogously deep, theological, and practical ways.

Eternal Life through Believing in Jesus: The Heart of the Gospel (3:15)

This verse is what John himself says his Gospel is all about for his readers: "that through believing you may have life in his name" (20:31). So this whole commentary is an interpretation of 3:15: **that whoever believes in him may have eternal life**.

The verb *pisteuein* has a rich range of meaning in John, including believing truths, trusting in a person, and committing one's life to someone. It has been discussed a little already,[12] and will be explored further at various points, especially on chapter 20, where John's drama of believing reaches its climax. A mistake that is often made is trying to understand what believing is only through John's explicit statements about it. Just as important is to see how it is understood through the characters and their interactions, such as Nicodemus in the present chapter. As has been noted, commentators have differed greatly about his faith or lack of it, and I think that part of John's intention is to provoke that sort of questioning and discussion so that his readers are challenged to have their faith stimulated, questioned, and deepened.[13]

"Life" has been a leading theme connected with Jesus from the opening of the Gospel: "In him was life, and the life was the light of all people" (1:4). It will also be explored later at various points. A new element in 3:15 is calling it **eternal life**. A common mistake about this has been to see it as life after death. It does include that—Jesus goes on to say in 11:25, "Those who believe in me, even though they die, will live." But it does not begin then; it has already begun, so that physical death is relativized and is not the most decisive event for a person. Eternal life is identified with Jesus, whose life is shared, before as well as after their death, with those who trust him. So the decisive events are the death and resurrection of Jesus, and eternal life means not just "life after death" but life after the death and resurrection of Jesus—which means life with Jesus now.

A second new element here is the connection of believing and eternal life with God's love in the next verse, where both are repeated.

God's Love for the World: The Deep, Dangerous Truth (3:16)

God so loved the world gives the deepest reason for the previous verse's basic affirmation. It is the first explicit mention by John of love, which he emphasizes more than do the other Gospels, the culmination coming in his final chapter. Like believing and life, love will be explored as it occurs through the story. For now, just two issues will be opened up: God giving his Son, and how God's love and the danger of perishing can go together.

The statement **He gave his only Son** is John's distinctive God-centered summary of what happens in the Gospel. We have already seen how he introduces it in the prologue: there the stress is on the Word of God, God's self-expression in Jesus, and the picture of "the only Son, who is close to the Father's heart" (1:18) connects it implicitly with love. Here the explicit emphasis is on the love of God, God's giving of Jesus, which in view of the rest of the Gospel (e.g., at

12. See the section "We, the Children of God: Abundant Life, Believing, and Conflict (1:10–13, 16–18)" in the comments on 1:1–18.

13. The commentary by Gail R. O'Day and Susan E. Hylen, *John*, is especially perceptive on this.

the conclusion of a later passage about the giving of the Father, Jesus says, "The Father and I are one" [10:30]) can be called God's self-giving in Jesus. God's free self-expression and self-giving have continued down through the centuries as primary Christian concepts for what God has said and done, as well as decisive pointers to who God is, and our reflections on God in John will culminate in chapter 20, in which Thomas cries out to Jesus, "My Lord and my God!" (20:28).

In the Synoptic Gospels the love of God for Jesus as his Son is articulated in events that John does not describe: the baptism of Jesus (John hints at it in 1:29–34) and his transfiguration. John not only distills the theology of those events into key statements, such as 3:16, but also distributes their significance across the whole of his Gospel by emphasizing more than do the Synoptics some key elements in those events, such as the Holy Spirit, glory, Moses, the exodus, and, above all, the Father-Son relationship of love. *John draws believers into the inner life of Jesus and his Father (especially through the prayer of Jesus in chap. 17), and God's love for the world is seen as an overflow of that divine life and love, just as the love among believers is intended to overflow and attract the world.*

What about the terrible possibility suggested by **may not perish**? God's love for the world is unqualified, the horizon of this Gospel from the beginning embraces all things, all life, and all people, and the promise is that the love of God embodied in Jesus on the cross "will draw all people to myself" (12:32). Yet at the same time this Gospel contemplates the appalling possibility of rejecting this love, cutting oneself off from it, and, as this passage goes on to say, being condemned for hating the light and doing evil. Whether God ultimately condemns anyone has been a deeply divisive issue down through the centuries, sharpened by teachings in some Catholic and Protestant traditions about God predestining some to salvation and some to damnation ("double predestination"). The question is discussed below at length in commenting on John 9. For now, here are three relevant points.

First, the emphasis on "all people" in John makes it appropriate to hope that the promise of 12:32 will be fulfilled. The position taken by Karl Barth, who radically challenged the theology of double predestination in his own Calvinist tradition, is that a Christian is one who, in the light of Jesus Christ, is permitted to hope for the best for all people, even Judas who betrayed Jesus.[14] This is not a claim to knowledge of the ultimate future or of the mind of God, but an act of trust and hope in the God who loves the world through giving his Son to be crucified. John's Gospel ends with an agnosticism about the fate of an individual that is at the same time an invitation to trust in Jesus and his love: "If it is my will

14. On Judas, see Barth, *Church Dogmatics* II/1.

that he [the disciple whom Jesus loved] remain [*menein*, "abide"] until I come, what is that to you?" (21:22, 23).

Second, Jesus ends that statement by saying to Peter, "Follow me!" (21:22). That shows the central orientation of this Gospel toward the ongoing drama of following Jesus. In that drama people can do horrendous things, and there is darkness, deceit, cruelty, evil, hatred, tragedy, denial, betrayal, violation, and murder. What does the right judgment of God on these involve? There is simply no human overview of this drama, and to assume that all will inevitably say yes to the love of God is to turn them into automatons, depriving them of freedom. One may rightly hope that all will say yes, but we have to take the ongoing drama and the decisions it demands with utmost seriousness. The world is not risk-free, and neither is relating to God.

Third, there is in the end only one person whose decision is in my hands: myself. That "Follow me!" is Jesus addressing Peter one to one. Jesus has just questioned him about his love, and he has told him to take care of the community for which he is responsible and to be willing to be taken "where you do not wish to go," to the point of a death by which he would glorify God (21:18–19). There is no inevitability that Peter will fulfill his responsibilities, and he had already denied Jesus just before the crucifixion. We all know that our relationships and lives can go wrong in serious ways and that marriages, friendships, and other commitments can end tragically. The drama, dangers, and meaning of real life would be ignored if we were to take an easy, risk-free, undramatic overview of how it is all bound to end. To try to step out of history like that would be to step away from Jesus and the meaning of his life, death, and resurrection. Above all, I know that in my own case there are crucial decisions to be made, paths to be followed, responsibilities to be fulfilled, calls to be answered, and people to be served and loved, and that it is all too possible for me to be blind, foolish, irresponsible, unloving, and worse. The "may not perish" of 3:16 is above all addressed to each person in relation to God in the midst of the ongoing drama, and it is a dangerous distraction from the path I am called to follow if I indulge in speculation or comparison with others: "If it is my will that he remain until I come, what is that to you? Follow me!" (21:22).

Judgment, and Believing or Not: The Personal Challenge (3:17–20)

In an era when many Christians and others are rightly concerned for religious freedom, respecting others in their beliefs and commitments, and engaging in dialogue with those of different traditions rather than in polemical confrontation and condemnation, how should 3:17–21 be understood? Many scholars see it reflecting the divisions and polemics between the community of Christians that John was part of and the Jewish synagogue community from which they are thought to have had a painful separation. If Nicodemus is a figure representing those Jews faced with a decision about which community to be part of, it would make sense to issue a sharp appeal for a decision. We look at John's account of "the Jews" in other chapters (especially above on chap. 2 and below on chap. 8). I will also discuss the implications of John's Gospel for Christian relations with other faiths when commenting on chapter 14.[15]

For now, the key point is that believing in, trusting in, and committing to (*pisteuein* means all three together) Jesus are essential if a relationship of love is to be mutual. There is an assurance from God's side that **God did not send the Son into the world to condemn the world, but in order that the world might be saved through him**. But the decision about whether there is to be mutual love and trust is in the balance, and the gift of love can be received only if its giver is trusted. Not to trust oneself to God's love is a self-judgment and of course means that there cannot be a life of love together. Gail O'Day and Susan Hylen state this well (see the quotation from O'Day and Hylen in the sidebar).

The essential thing to remember, as in the discussion of 3:16, is that this is above all a personal challenge, growing out of an encounter of Jesus with one particular person, and addressed to each reader. Opening ourselves to the

> Verses 17–18 reinforce that the incarnation, the Word-made-flesh, is about the possibility of new life, not judgment. The presence of Jesus as the incarnate Word confronts the world with the decision to believe or not, and making that decision is the moment of self-judgment. Belief is how people respond to God's gift of Jesus; the community can respond to the gift of God with the gift of faith. Because God's gift of Jesus is eternal life, to receive and welcome that gift is immediately to receive the life it offers. If one does not receive that gift, then one cannot receive the life it offers, and in John's vocabulary that means that one is condemned—not sharing in the gift of life that is offered. The language of condemnation needs to be read carefully. Eternal life and condemnation are the flip sides of the same experience. If one embraces the gift, one receives life; if not, one remains trapped in the realm of death and darkness.
>
> —Gail O'Day and Susan Hylen, *John*, 46

15. Especially 14:6: "Jesus said to him, 'I am the way, and the truth, and the life. No one comes to the Father except through me.'"

love and light of God is an ongoing daily challenge. It does not give access to anyone else's encounter, response, or future (and it is important that there is no timescale here—the timing is open), or to any overview about how others relate to God. About anyone else, we need to be confident in the love of God for the whole world and aware that the Spirit is free to move however God's love chooses, which is often in very surprising ways.

Deeds Done in God: The Ongoing Drama and Reading Now (3:21)

The inseparable connection between faith and action is clear throughout John's Gospel, with the action growing out of knowing and trusting that one is loved. "The disciple whom Jesus loved" is the model of this. The whole Gospel is oriented to guiding the ongoing drama of following the crucified and risen Jesus. That guidance comes through exposure to the light and truth of the Gospel, above all to who Jesus is and what he teaches. To act from within that relationship of faith, understanding, and love is to **do what is true**. And that relationship is rooted **in God**.

"In" is one of the richest theological words in John, its multiple dimensions culminating in the prayer of Jesus in John 17. Here, in the encounter of two teachers, there has been repeated emphasis on God. The movement of the story has been from Nicodemus speaking of Jesus being "from God" and doing signs that could not have been done "apart from the presence of God" (literally, "unless God were with him"), through Jesus speaking of "the kingdom of God" and "the Spirit," and then Jesus (or the author of the Gospel) saying that "God so loved the world that he gave his only Son." The culmination of this in 3:21 is the vital little phrase "in God." What does it mean? Later chapters will fill out the meaning, but at this point two comments are relevant.

First, one of the distinctive emphases of John is on participation in God, with John 17 the most concentrated expression of this. So if the mention of "in God" in 3:21 is reread in the light of the rest of the Gospel, the meaning of this verse is opened up further. But already in this passage the identity of God has been opened up further, in line with the prologue, through reference not only to the Father and the Son but also to the Spirit, love, and eternal life. God is one to whom eternal, dynamic relating in love is intrinsic.

Second, the most astonishing lesson for readers is the possibility of living their lives in this love of God, committing their lives to Jesus, and being energized by the Spirit. And this, of course, means that one of "their deeds" that "have been done in God" is reading and rereading the Gospel of John. This is how ongoing exposure to the light can happen now.

Voices of Love: Joy, the Measureless Spirit, and Trust (3:22–36)

The rest of chapter 3 marks the end of the beginning of the Gospel, and it both sums up and takes further the astonishing teaching of the first three chapters. John the Baptist, who was the first witness to Jesus in John 1, here makes his final personal appearance,[16] witnesses to Jesus as a friend, repeats his insistence on his own subordinate role, and bows out, leaving the spotlight on Jesus and his disciples. The stage is now set for the rest of the drama.

> 22 After this Jesus and his disciples went into the Judean countryside, and he spent some time there with them and baptized. 23 John also was baptizing at Aenon near Salim because water was abundant there; and people kept coming and were being baptized 24 —John, of course, had not yet been thrown into prison.
>
> 25 Now a discussion about purification arose between John's disciples and a Jew. 26 They came to John and said to him, "Rabbi, the one who was with you across the Jordan, to whom you testified, here he is baptizing, and all are going to him." 27 John answered, "No one can receive anything except what has been given from heaven. 28 You yourselves are my witnesses that I said, 'I am not the Messiah, but I have been sent ahead of him.' 29 He who has the bride is the bridegroom. The friend of the bridegroom, who stands and hears him, rejoices greatly at the bridegroom's voice. For this reason my joy has been fulfilled. 30 He must increase, but I must decrease."
>
> 31 The one who comes from above is above all; the one who is of the earth belongs to the earth and speaks about earthly things. The one who comes from heaven is above all. 32 He testifies to what he has seen and heard, yet no one accepts his testimony. 33 Whoever has accepted his testimony has certified this, that God is true. 34 He whom God has sent speaks the words of God, for he gives the Spirit without measure. 35 The Father loves the Son and has placed all things in his hands. 36 Whoever believes in the Son has eternal life; whoever disobeys the Son will not see life, but must endure God's wrath.

Scholars differ about the history and geography of this passage, including about how the followers of John the Baptist and of Jesus related to one another. Yet the thrust of this passage is clear: a joyful affirmation of Jesus as friend, bridegroom, Word of God, witness, giver of **the Spirit without measure**, beloved Son of the Father, who has **placed all things in his hands**; and a challenge to readers to trust, believe, and obey Jesus or not.

16. He is mentioned later in 5:33–36 and 10:40–41, both times with reference to his role as a witness.

The move now from Jerusalem **into the Judean countryside**, before Jesus goes into Samaria in chapter 4, means that here Jesus is still in Jewish territory. This is the last of a series of significant encounters with fellow Jews who respond very differently to him: the first disciples and others in chapter 1, his mother and those in the temple in chapter 2, and Nicodemus in chapter 3. The first encounter was with John the Baptist, and he now reappears to repeat and intensify his message. The account assumes that readers know the Synoptic Gospel accounts of John being **thrown into prison**, and this supports further the practice of reading them alongside John's Gospel.

Just as in the meeting with Nicodemus it is unclear whether the Gospel author's voice takes over from Jesus at 3:16, so here the author, rather than John the Baptist or Jesus, may be speaking from 3:31 (as the NRSV decides). In both cases the perspective is postresurrection, and the effect is to give an enriched theological framework in line with the prologue.

Love and Joy

Love, which becomes a major theme from chapter 11 onward, was not mentioned explicitly in the first two chapters; then God's love for the world was introduced in the fundamental statement of 3:16. Now love and the imagery of love are central to this culmination of the Gospel's beginning.

Key themes and imagery of the Gospel, that will continue to have their meaning filled out in later chapters, are reaffirmed: **God**, **Father**, **Son**, **Spirit**, **Messiah**, abundant **water**, **what has been given from heaven**, **witnesses**, **testimony** and its rejection, **sent**, **voice**, **speaks** and **words**, **fulfilled**, **what he has seen and heard**, **all things**, **believes**, **eternal life**, and **endures** (*menein*, "abide, remain").

But this is also a new wave, and it is above all about love. For the first time in this Gospel the relationship of God and Jesus is put in terms of love: **the Father loves** [*agapa*] **the Son**. The other key Johannine term for "love" (*philein*, "to love"), *philos* ("friend") (*philia* and *philein* are usually used interchangeably with *agapē* and *agapan*), is also used here for the first time: **the friend** [*philos*] **of the bridegroom**.

The imagery of the bridegroom and celebration not only resonates with love but also recalls the first sign of Jesus, at the wedding in Cana. Further, it invites a rereading of the earlier relationship of John the Baptist with Jesus. The bridegroom's friend in that culture was responsible for arranging the match with the bride, and John the Baptist introduces his disciples to Jesus, whom they then follow. In John's Scriptures Israel is spoken of as the bride of God,[17] and

17. E.g., Isa. 62:4–5; Jer. 2:2; Ezek. 16:8; 23:4; Hosea 2:19–20.

in the rest of the New Testament the church can be understood as the bride of Christ.[18] So the disciples can be seen as the bride whose coming together with Jesus is brokered by John the Baptist. Stretching the image still further, the wedding in Cana (complete with the disciples as new "bride," and the mother of the groom) is followed by the scene with the disciples in "my Father's house" (in this culture the bride went to live in the family home of the groom); there is the new family life through being "born anew from above" (3:3, 7); and, now that his role has been fulfilled, the bridegroom's friend can "decrease" and retire from the scene (3:30).

John the Baptist in this Gospel is often said to be purely a witness to Jesus, but this passage says more, mentioning him baptizing and keeping company with Jesus (**the one who was with you across the Jordan**), and it even adds to the Synoptic picture of John, which has no hint of joy, friendship, celebration, or love. The witness is also a friend. The Johannine note of abundant life and love sounds here, as the intensity of the relationship of John with Jesus in the joy of friendship is evoked. At the same time, John's complete trust and belief in Jesus are affirmed in his response to a dispute that seems to have involved competition between his followers and those of Jesus. In these early chapters of the Gospel the two people who utterly trust Jesus and what Jesus says are his mother ("Do whatever he tells you" [2:5]) and John the Baptist, who **rejoices greatly at the bridegroom's voice**.

The Bridegroom's Voice and the Superabundant Spirit

Perhaps the most fascinating new element in this passage is verse 34: **He whom God has sent speaks the words of God, for he gives the Spirit without measure**. Here Jesus, the Word of God "whom God has sent" and who speaks "the words of God," resonates with this passage's multifaceted theme of voice, speaking, and witnessing (by John, Jesus, and, of course, the author) and is connected with *the divine superabundance of the Spirit.*

This is one of the most important truths in John's Gospel. The inseparability of Word and Spirit is pictured from the beginning in the twice-repeated (1:32, 33) image of the Spirit remaining (abiding) like a dove on Jesus, who has just been identified with the Word of God. The identification of the words of Jesus with the gift of the Spirit is reaffirmed in the culminating part of the discourse on the bread of life: "The words that I have spoken to you are spirit [or "Spirit"] and life" (6:63). This message is also given in many other ways, above all in the Farewell Discourses, as will be seen. Finally, the resurrected Jesus shares the

18. E.g., 2 Cor. 11:2; Eph. 5:25–27; Rev. 21:2; 22:17.

Holy Spirit with his disciples by simultaneously breathing on them and speaking to them, sending them as he was sent by his Father (20:21–22). Overall, the Gospel of John is both intensively focused on Jesus and has far more to say than the other Gospels about the Spirit, and the two are inseparable.

This differentiated union of Word and Spirit has led Christian thinking deeper into the inexhaustible mystery of who God is, and it is also at the heart of the ongoing drama of following the risen Jesus together. Even the ambiguity of John's language serves to deepen the theology. Who is it that "gives the Spirit without measure"? The Greek text allows that it could be either Jesus or God. As with several terms in the Nicodemus story discussed above, this double meaning invites readers to explore both and then hold them together. If Jesus is the giver, we look first in the direction of the ongoing drama. If God is the giver, we look first to the relationship of Father and Son. Yet neither need exclude the other, and together they show why this verse is yet another pointer to why this Gospel was so crucial to the development of the doctrine of the Trinity, both "immanent" (God in God's own being, the "processions" of the eternal Son and the Spirit, and the interrelationship of Father, Son, and Spirit) and "economic" (God involved with creation and history, the "missions" of the Son and Spirit).

At this stage it is worth asking what it might mean for our reading of John's Gospel. If John writes down words of Jesus and believes these to be "Spirit and life" (6:63), then to read and believe his Gospel is nothing less than to receive the Holy Spirit and life. He is clear in addressing his readers that his intention in writing "this book" is "so that you may come to believe that Jesus is the Messiah, the Son of God, and that through believing you may have life in his name" (20:30–31). That name, those words, and that life bear the gift of "the Spirit without measure."

The rich, multileveled, "deep plain sense" writing of John, with its imagery of superabundant life—water, wine, wind, bread, light, fish, and more—can be seen as itself a performance of the Spirit that John has received to guide him "into all the truth" (16:13). To drink deeply, to savor, to be continually nourished by his writing, and to let Jesus's "words abide in you" (15:7) is to receive the Spirit that is intrinsic to the Word. "From his fullness we have all received, grace upon grace" (1:16). It is, as John the Baptist says, about being **the friend of the bridegroom, who stands and hears him**, and who **rejoices greatly at the bridegroom's voice**. It is **joy . . . fulfilled**. This is the desire of Jesus: "I have said these things to you so that my joy may be in you, and that your joy may be complete" (15:11).

God's Wrath

The drama, however, is not yet over. This Gospel itself is an appeal to readers in the midst of it—otherwise why write it? Just as the last section of the

Nicodemus story spoke of the possibility of condemnation, judgment, and the exposure of evil deeds, so here there is a radical, unflinching recognition of what Rudolf Bultmann calls a "dualism of decision."[19]

In the face of evil, sin, refusal of love and compassion, corruption, cruelty, denial or distortion of truth, destruction of life and goodness, betrayal of trust and friendship, and whatever else constitutes darkness and disobedience, God is not neutral: there is the reality of ***God's wrath****. God demands decision and commitment: there is no neutrality for us either.*

As was argued above in commenting on the Nicodemus story, in the light of Jesus Christ we are permitted to hope for the best for all people, we have no overview of how others will ultimately stand with God, and the only thing we can be sure of is that, given who God is, there will be great surprises. But for each reader there is a crucial decision to be made in response to the witness of the Gospel, one that is ultimately about deciding either for life, love, and joy or for whatever negates them.

19. Bultmann, *Theology of the New Testament*, 2:76.

John 4:1–54

Two Surprising, Life-Giving Encounters

The Gospel of John pays special attention to the one-to-one encounters of Jesus. After Nicodemus in chapter 3, now in chapter 4 there are two more, first with a woman at a well, then with a royal official. In each, Jesus is life giver: "The water that I will give will become in them a spring of water gushing up to eternal life" (4:14); "Your son will live" (4:50, 53).

Jesus has moved from Judea to the alien territory of Samaria, where he has a meeting that is doubly surprising and countercultural: not only with a Samaritan but with one who is a woman. Whereas Nicodemus was Jewish, male, a named high-status leader and orthodox teacher, she is a Samaritan, heterodox (to Jews), female, anonymous, and living with a man to whom she is not married. Yet whereas the encounter with Nicodemus (who comes to Jesus under cover of night) left him undecided, the Samaritan woman (who meets him at noon) is drawn into trusting and acknowledging Jesus and sharing her testimony to him with her city, as a result of which many others believe in him.

Then Jesus returns to Cana in Galilee, the scene of his first sign, and does a second sign, healing a dying child, through which a royal official and his household also come to faith.

A Story with Several Surprises, Many Gaps, and Far-Reaching Implications (4:1–42)

In the course of this story about a Samaritan woman and Jesus meeting at a deep well and crossing gender, ethnic, and religious differences, some important themes in John's Gospel are sounded: growing in faith and understanding; the symbolisms of water and thirst; marriage; food, hunger, and harvest; worship, truth, and the Spirit; work and witness. All through it runs the deepest theme of all: who Jesus is. The pointers to who Jesus is include him being called **a Jew**, **greater than . . . Jacob**, **a prophet**, **Messiah** (Christ), **a man** (*anthrōpos*, "person" [v. 29]), **Rabbi** (teacher), and **the Savior of the world**. And for the first time in this Gospel Jesus gives his most distinctive and daring self-description, the divine **"I am he"** (*egō eimi*—better translated simply as "I am" [v. 26]). Yet the story also has allusions, ambiguities, hints and gaps that raise many questions, and these, inseparable from the richness of the theological themes, invite continual rereading, exploring the far-reaching implications of the encounter.

A Permanent Thirst Quencher (4:1–15)

> 1 Now when Jesus learned that the Pharisees had heard, "Jesus is making and baptizing more disciples than John" 2 —although it was not Jesus himself but his disciples who baptized—3 he left Judea and started back to Galilee. 4 But he had to go through Samaria. 5 So he came to a Samaritan city called Sychar, near the plot of ground that Jacob had given to his son Joseph. 6 Jacob's well was there, and Jesus, tired out by his journey, was sitting by the well. It was about noon.
>
> 7 A Samaritan woman came to draw water, and Jesus said to her, "Give me a drink." 8 (His disciples had gone to the city to buy food.) 9 The Samaritan woman said to him, "How is it that you, a Jew, ask a drink of me, a woman of Samaria?" (Jews do not share things in common with Samaritans.) 10 Jesus answered her, "If you knew the gift of God, and who it is that is saying to you, 'Give me a drink,' you would have asked him, and he would have given you living water." 11 The woman said to him, "Sir, you have no bucket, and the well is deep. Where do you get that living water? 12 Are you greater than our ancestor Jacob, who gave us the well, and with his sons and his flocks drank from it?" 13 Jesus said to her, "Everyone who drinks of this water will be thirsty again, 14 but those who drink of the water that I will give them will never be thirsty. The water that I will give will become in them a spring of water gushing up to eternal life." 15 The woman said to him, "Sir, give me this water, so that I may never be thirsty or have to keep coming here to draw water."

The exchange between Jesus and the woman is complex. He asks for a drink; she challenges him, a Jew, asking her, a Samaritan, for water; he turns the tables by offering her **living water**; she challenges him again, apparently taking him to be speaking literally; he expands on what he means—anyone who drinks his water **will never be thirsty** again, and it **will become in them a spring of water gushing up to eternal life**; when she seems to take even that literally, there is an impasse. How will that be resolved?

The conversation opens up further one of the richest terms in John's Gospel, "water." Water has already been associated with baptism, the wedding at Cana, and being born anew from above; later in the Gospel it will have its meaning diversified in connection with healing, footwashing, a sword piercing of the side of the dead Jesus so that "at once blood and water came out" (19:34), and the final scene on and beside the Sea of Tiberias in chapter 21. And the cry of Jesus on the cross, "I am thirsty!" (19:28), is one of the most vivid demonstrations of the paradox at the heart of this Gospel: light shining in darkness, God become vulnerable flesh, the source of life-giving water who is thirsty, the life giver who dies.

The focus in chapter 4 is on water as thirst quenching and life giving. It is set against a scriptural background in which drinking water is frequently seen as a gift of God to meet physical need and also as representing how the deepest human desires are met through God's presence, wisdom, law, word, salvation, and Spirit.

Yet that scriptural background was not fully available to the Samaritan woman. The Samaritans recognized only the first five books of the Jewish Scriptures, in which references to water are many, but mostly literal. It is in the other two parts of Jesus's Scriptures, the Prophets and the Writings (the latter including Psalms, Song of Songs, and the Wisdom books) that the symbolic meanings of water are developed. It is worth savoring something of that development.

The Major Prophets, Isaiah, Jeremiah, and Ezekiel, are rich in water imagery in relation to God, salvation, and other themes in John 4, as headlined in Isaiah:

> With joy you will draw water from the wells of salvation. (Isa. 12:3)

Second Isaiah (chaps. 40–55), whose language especially pervades the Gospel of John, has an abundance of water. Particularly relevant to the present passage is the opening of Isaiah 44, where Jacob, water, God's Spirit, and the distinctive identity of Israel in relation to God all come together:

> [1] But now hear, O Jacob my servant,
> Israel whom I have chosen!
> [2] Thus says the Lord who made you,
> who formed you in the womb and will help you:

Do not fear, O Jacob my servant,
Jeshurun whom I have chosen.
3 For I will pour water on the thirsty land,
and streams on the dry ground;
I will pour my spirit upon your descendants,
and my blessing on your offspring.
4 They shall spring up like a green tamarisk,
like willows by flowing streams.
5 This one will say, "I am the LORD's,"
another will be called by the name of Jacob,
yet another will write on the hand, "The LORD's,"
and adopt the name of Israel. (Isa. 44:1–5 [cf. 41:17–20])

Perhaps even more strikingly relevant is the climax of Second Isaiah in chapter 55. This not only weaves together themes of abundant water, life, invitation, what is everlasting (or eternal—the Greek word is the same in Isa. 55:3, 13 and John 4:14), witness to those beyond Israel, and finding the God of Israel; it also embraces other key elements of John 4: food as well as drink, an abundant harvest, the Word of God as water sent by God, and God's surprising thoughts and ways:

1 Ho, everyone who thirsts,
come to the waters;
and you that have no money,
come, buy and eat!
Come, buy wine and milk
without money and without price.
2 Why do you spend your money for that which is not bread,
and your labor for that which does not satisfy?
Listen carefully to me, and eat what is good,
and delight yourselves in rich food.
3 Incline your ear, and come to me;
listen, so that you may live.
I will make with you an everlasting covenant,
my steadfast, sure love for David.
4 See, I made him a witness to the peoples,
a leader and commander for the peoples.
5 See, you shall call nations that you do not know,
and nations that do not know you shall run to you,
because of the LORD your God, the Holy One of Israel,
for he has glorified you.
6 Seek the LORD while he may be found,
call upon him while he is near;

7 let the wicked forsake their way,
and the unrighteous their thoughts;
let them return to the Lord, that he may have mercy on them,
and to our God, for he will abundantly pardon.
8 For my thoughts are not your thoughts,
nor are your ways my ways, says the Lord.
9 For as the heavens are higher than the earth,
so are my ways higher than your ways
and my thoughts than your thoughts.
10 For as the rain and the snow come down from heaven,
and do not return there until they have watered the earth,
making it bring forth and sprout,
giving seed to the sower and bread to the eater,
11 so shall my word be that goes out from my mouth;
it shall not return to me empty,
but it shall accomplish that which I purpose,
and succeed in the thing for which I sent it.
12 For you shall go out in joy,
and be led back in peace;
the mountains and the hills before you
shall burst into song,
and all the trees of the field shall clap their hands.
13 Instead of the thorn shall come up the cypress;
instead of the brier shall come up the myrtle;
and it shall be to the Lord for a memorial,
for an everlasting sign that shall not be cut off. (Isa. 55)[1]

The prophet Jeremiah has God twice self-identifying as "the fountain of living water" (Jer. 2:13; 17:13). Ezekiel 47 has a vision of a life-giving river flowing from the temple:

> On the banks, on both sides of the river, there will grow all kinds of trees for food. Their leaves will not wither nor their fruit fail, but they will bear fresh fruit every month, because the water for them flows from the sanctuary. Their fruit will be for food, and their leaves for healing. (Ezek. 47:12)[2]

If we remember that in John 2 the body of Jesus is identified with the temple and that in John 7 he cries out in the temple, "'Let anyone who is thirsty come to me, and let the one who believes in me drink.' . . . Now he said this about the

1. Third Isaiah (chaps. 56–66) adds more resonant imagery, as in the waters from God that "never fail" (58:11).

2. See comments on 7:25–52.

Spirit, which believers were to receive; for as yet there was no Spirit, because Jesus was not yet glorified" (7:37–39), then the water in chapter 4 can be seen as paralleling the wind in chapter 3 in offering dynamic images of the Spirit. A rich connection is also revealed between the two parts of Jesus's conversation with the Samaritan woman: first about water, then about worship "in Spirit and truth" (discussed below).[3]

Moving to the third part of Jesus's Scriptures, the Writings, there the Psalms are especially important for John; he quotes and alludes to them more than any other scriptural book. They "exerted a profound influence on his [John's] entire composition."[4] They speak passionately of the thirst for God, also connecting with the later exchange about worship between Jesus and the Samaritan woman:

> As a deer longs for flowing streams,
>   so my soul longs for you, O God.
> My soul thirsts for God,
>   for the living God. (Ps. 42:1–2 [cf. Pss. 63:1; 143:6])

The marriage theme later in the woman's conversation with Jesus also resonates with the imagery of water, both through the stories of marriages arranged after meetings at wells (discussed below) and in Song of Songs:

> How sweet is our love, my sister, my bride!
> . . . a garden fountain, a well of living water,
>   and flowing streams from Lebanon. (Song 4:10, 15)

Especially important for an event in which the woman receives the water that Jesus gives through his words is the connection with speech and wisdom:

> The words of the mouth are deep waters;
>   The fountain of wisdom a gushing stream. (Prov. 18:4)

> She will feed him with the bread of learning,
>   and give him the water of wisdom to drink. (Sir. 15:3)

3. The mention in 7:39 of "glorified," which in John is especially connected with the death of Jesus, also alerts us to resonances with the crucifixion: Jesus as he dies handing over *to pneuma* ("the spirit/Spirit, breath" [19:30]; see discussion on John 19), water flowing from the side of the dead Jesus, and later in chap. 4 Jesus speaking of "the hour" (vv. 21, 23) and of his mission "to complete his [the Father's] work" (v. 34).

4. Daly-Denton, *David in the Fourth Gospel*, 287. See further below on John 7:38, where Ps. 78:16 is quoted, and Daly-Denton's perceptive discussion on pp. 144–63.

So there are several dimensions of meaning here. Within the story, Jesus is opening up the woman's imagination to something beyond her own Scriptures, as well as to himself. The reader's image of water, as shaped by earlier chapters, is being further enriched, with associations rippling out through the Jewish Scriptures, other Christian Scriptures,[5] and the wider resonances of water as something essential to all people, animals, and plants. And the rereader of John is led deeper into the meaning of the Spirit, the death of Jesus, and who he is.

Beyond the Impasse: The Woman's Marriages and Jesus as Prophet (4:16–19)

> 16 Jesus said to her, "Go, call your husband, and come back." 17 The woman answered him, "I have no husband." Jesus said to her, "You are right in saying, 'I have no husband'; 18 for you have had five husbands, and the one you have now is not your husband. What you have said is true!" 19 The woman said to him, "Sir, I see that you are a prophet."

The impasse already noted is broken through by Jesus speaking with insight into the woman's marital life. It is an abrupt shift in the conversation and is read very differently by interpreters.

A common, fruitful approach is to see it taking up the marriage theme as a variation on several biblical betrothal scenes set at wells. That was where Abraham's servant found Rebecca for Isaac (Gen. 24), where Jacob met Rachel (Gen. 29:1–14), and where Moses met Zipporah (Exod. 2:15–22). This approach is reinforced by the wedding at Cana in John 2 and by John the Baptist calling Jesus "the bridegroom" in John 3:29. That connects with another layer of meaning through the theme of God's covenant relationship with Israel being seen in terms of bridegroom/husband and bride/wife. And that in turn lets us understand how the next topic of conversation between Jesus and the Samaritan woman, that of worship, follows on naturally—Israel's worship of other gods, for example, is often seen as adultery.[6] Worship has already been connected with Jesus both through the way the prologue refers to him as God and through the identification of his body with the temple in John 2.

So there are a number of links—a man meets a woman at a well, the marriage theme, and the worship theme—and since these themes have already been associated with Jesus as bridegroom and temple, the embracing concern is who Jesus is.

5. See especially Rev. 7:17; 21:6; 22:1, 17.
6. See, e.g., Jer. 3:8–9; Ezek. 23:37; Hosea 1–3.

Within that understanding, one major surprise is in the identity of the "bride": not Israel or a Jew but a Samaritan woman who has had many husbands. That opens up many questions, and the woman raises one of them, the relation of Jewish and Samaritan worship, which will be discussed below. For now, what about the woman's history with men?

The unexpected introduction of the marriage theme stimulates rereading the earlier part of the encounter with this in mind. Harold Attridge, alert to the long history of literary and visual representation of this scene, presents the whole story as a dramatic script, with notes for its director about the issues to be faced.[7] Is the erotic potential to be played up or down? Does the woman approach the well provocatively or nonchalantly? Does she project shame, modesty, or sexual availability? What tone of voice does she first use to Jesus—polite, ironic, flirtatious? Does she understand Jesus's request for water as a sexual advance? Is her response to Jesus's offer of "living water" one of genuine astonishment and openness, ironic dismissal, or wistful longing?

The surprise change of subject by Jesus telling her to bring her husband is, Attridge suggests, "the pivot on which the whole dialogue turns. . . . Flirtation ends when Jesus indicates his knowledge of her unavailability, yet at the same time her attraction to him becomes more serious."[8]

What about her five marriages? There is a possible allegorical meaning, identifying them with the five books of Moses accepted by the Samaritans or with the five gods of the ancient Samaritans. There is also a traditional reading of her as immoral, intensified by her now living in an extramarital relationship. Yet there is no explicit suggestion in the story of her being immoral or ashamed, and a wave of recent interpretations give alternative explanations. She could have married young, had five husbands who died, and now be living with a male relative. She could have been divorced five times—and it was possible for husbands to divorce for relatively trivial reasons. There could have been a mixture of divorces and bereavements. *Yet, whatever the truth, a life shot through with disappointment, pain, and grief is suggested. The way through the impasse is her recognition of who Jesus is.*

Steven Hunt has written imaginatively on what all this might have meant in her context and community. He concludes by speculating whether, when the people from her city came to Jesus and believed, her present man was among them; and whether, when "they asked him to stay with them; and he stayed there two days" (4:40), Jesus might have stayed in their home; and whether,

7. Attridge, "The Samaritan Woman."
8. Attridge, "The Samaritan Woman," 276.

"in short, the man came to know Jesus as the Savior of the world because of the woman with whom he cohabited."[9]

Brendan Byrne also sees this switch in the conversation from water to marriage as pivotal. He suggests that it is "something familiar to all engaged in spiritual direction. The woman cannot enter into a deeper appreciation of who Jesus is and the gift he has to offer her until she has transcended her own immediate needs and come to recognize her 'thirst' at this deeper level. She cannot move from the literal to the symbolic level until she has explored her own personal situation more profoundly."[10] It is then that a key insight into who Jesus is comes to her: **"Sir** [*kyrios*, which also means "Lord"], **I see that you are a prophet."** Such testimony, able to say "I see," is central to John's Gospel, beginning with "we have seen" in the foundational announcement of the incarnation in 1:14. This woman goes on to become a witness to her whole city, using the words of invitation "Come and see" (4:29), which also go back to the first chapter, where they are said by both Jesus and Philip (1:39, 46).

Beyond Samaritan and Jewish Centers of Worship: "I Am," and Worship in Spirit and Truth (4:20–26)

> 20 "Our ancestors worshiped on this mountain, but you say that the place
> where people must worship is in Jerusalem." 21 Jesus said to her, "Woman,
> believe me, the hour is coming when you will worship the Father neither
> on this mountain nor in Jerusalem. 22 You worship what you do not know;
> we worship what we know, for salvation is from the Jews. 23 But the hour is
> coming, and is now here, when the true worshipers will worship the Father
> in spirit and truth, for the Father seeks such as these to worship him. 24 God
> is spirit, and those who worship him must worship in spirit and truth." 25 The
> woman said to him, "I know that Messiah is coming" (who is called Christ).
> "When he comes, he will proclaim all things to us." 26 Jesus said to her, "I
> am he, the one who is speaking to you."

The woman immediately speaks of a fundamental matter dividing Samaritans from Jews: their different centers of worship—Mount Gerizim (the ruins of the Samaritan temple there may have been within sight of the well where the scene is set) and the temple in Jerusalem (which by the time this Gospel was written had been destroyed by the Romans).

The rest of this conversation can be read in several perspectives.

9. Hunt, "The Men of the Samaritan Woman," 291.
10. Byrne, *Life Abounding*, 83–84.

Within the story, the woman is being invited to believe that a momentous event is happening (**"Believe me, the hour is coming. . . . The hour is coming, and is now here"**), one that changes the basic ideas through which she thinks about salvation and worship. Instead of a false alternative between two central places of worship, there is a combination of statements that together summarize John's Gospel: rooted in Judaism; centered on the person of Jesus and the fatherhood of God; and involving worship, spirit/Spirit, and, inseparable from all those, a particular understanding of truth.

The "third wave" of the conversation with Nicodemus (3:11–21) had provocatively distilled the Gospel for a Jewish teacher and leader in a way that drew on the terms of his tradition—Son of Man, Moses in the wilderness, eternal life, God's love, judgment, darkness and light—but was centered on a new event, God giving "his only Son" in love. Similarly, here the climactic third wave of exchange with the Samaritan woman, after the first two on Jesus as source of the water of eternal life and Jesus as prophet, culminates in an event that is a person: **Jesus said to her, "I am he** [*egō eimi*, "I am"], **the one who is speaking to you."** Typical of John's levels of meaning, this could be an affirmation of the woman's expectation of the Messiah (itself a momentous event); or, in the light of the rest of the Gospel, it could be reread as the first "I am," identifying Jesus with God, and so an even more radical characterization of the person of Jesus than in what was said to Nicodemus.

Other elements here vital to John's Gospel are that there is a particular people and tradition through which God gives this person (**salvation is from the Jews**) and that there is a universal vision of future worship (**true worshipers will worship the Father in spirit and truth**). Again typical of John, the way the story is told overflows its setting and brings in a postresurrection perspective. This is caught in the phrase **the hour is coming, and now is**, and in the future tense of **will worship**. The meaning of that "hour" slowly unfolds through the Gospel after its first mention in 2:4 until the hour arrives in the crucifixion and resurrection. The first-time reader of the Gospel already has a richer perspective than the woman at the well, shaped by the prologue and the first three chapters. Especially relevant to worship of the Father is Jesus calling the temple "my Father's house" and the identification of his body with the temple (2:16, 19–22). But, in John, it is only after the resurrection that the fatherhood of God is extended beyond Jesus to his followers, when he speaks to Mary Magdalene of "my Father and your Father" (20:17), and it is only then that Jesus himself is addressed by Thomas explicitly as "my Lord and my God" (20:28).

From the perspective of the whole Gospel, and its Christian, Jewish, and Hellenistic context, what might be the meaning of **God is spirit** and of worshiping **the Father in spirit and truth**?

God is spirit means that God is life-giving action; God is free to spring surprises; God is as necessary for life as wind or breath or a constant supply of water; God inspires truth seeking, teaching, witnessing, and loving service; and God is generously self-giving through Jesus—"He whom God has sent speaks the words of God, for he gives the Spirit without measure" (3:34). More will be said about spirit and the Holy Spirit later.

God as **Father** is the giver of life in love, the Father of Jesus, on whom the Spirit permanently rests, and one who even shares his own glory—as Jesus says to him, "The glory that you have given me I have given them" (17:22). John is pervaded by references and allusions to the Psalms and their worship. Within that "ecology" of worship—praise, thanks, confession, lament, and petition—John inseparably connects the most embracing act of worship, that of calling on God, with calling on Jesus, as in making requests "in my name" (14:13; 15:16; 16:24; cf. 17:6, 11–12, 26). So, to enter more deeply into worship involves entering more deeply into who Jesus is, the one identified through this name; that means taking part in the relationship of Jesus with his Father; and that in turn is lived out in the intensity of mutual love and "glorifying," which is John's key term for dynamic interaction with and within God (17:1–5, 24).

Spirit likewise is connected as closely as possible with Jesus, from the first mention of the Spirit remaining (abiding) on Jesus (1:32–33) to the climactic giving of the Spirit to the disciples through the risen Jesus breathing on them (20:22). **Truth** too is identified with Jesus: "I am the way, and the truth, and the life" (14:6).

This centering on Jesus in Christian terms does not exclude wider reference. The horizon of "all things" and "all people" opened up in the prologue is the horizon for "worship in spirit and truth" too. This invites the exploration of endlessly rich connections (which may be more or less affirmative, or more or less negative) with the whole of Scripture; with all areas of knowledge, culture,

> The new "sacred site" is the Johannine Jesus, who gives the priceless gift of the Spirit to those who thirst for life, women as well as men, a gift that issues in divine worship in the eschatological now of the incarnation. Water has thus become a full symbol by the end of the narrative. It signifies both the Spirit and the word/revelation/wisdom which Jesus embodies in his own person and gives to those who are thirsty. What the woman seeks and finds is the water of wisdom flowing from the well of the Spirit, implanted in the heart by Jesus. No barrier of race or gender can stand in the way of such a gift.
>
> —Dorothy Lee, *Flesh and Glory*, 76–77

and civilization; and with other religious traditions. The example of Jesus here is of in-depth, one-to-one engagement across the boundary of his own religious tradition with someone from another tradition that has a history of conflict-ridden division from his own. The broadening from Nicodemus at the heart of the Jewish establishment to the Samaritan woman is continued in the next story, that of the royal official.

That broad horizon is the context for a further significant element in what Jesus says here, using the key term *zētein*, meaning "seek, search for, look for, want, desire, ask for": **"The Father seeks such as these to worship him."** This is the first verb that Jesus uses in John, when he addresses his first disciples: "What are you looking for?" (1:38). And the rest of the Gospel uses it more than thirty times in many settings. *This Gospel is a drama of seeking and desiring—by God, Jesus, disciples, friends, and enemies.* At its heart is the desire of God for **true worshipers**, and the attractiveness of a love that says, "I, when I am lifted up from the earth, will draw all people to myself" (12:32).[11] As Dorothy Lee says, Jesus is the new "sacred site" (see the quotation from Lee in the sidebar). And this breadth and universality are the overflow of the sort of worship, mutual desire, and love exemplified in John 17, as Jesus draws his disciples into intimate communion with himself and his Father "so that the world may believe" (17:21).

A Double Shock: Speaking with a Woman! A Woman Witnessing! (4:27–30)

> 27 Just then his disciples came. They were astonished that he was speaking with a woman, but no one said, "What do you want?" or, "Why are you speaking with her?" 28 Then the woman left her water jar and went back to the city. She said to the people, 29 "Come and see a man who told me everything I have ever done! He cannot be the Messiah, can he?" 30 They left the city and were on their way to him.

The note of countercultural surprise now shifts from a Jew meeting with a Samaritan to a man speaking with a woman. The disciples are shocked that **he was speaking with a woman**. This underlines the boundary crossing that is happening, and it prepares for the next surprise: **the woman left her water jar** and witnessed to her own people, and they were attracted to Jesus by what she said. Her leaving her water jar parallels the Synoptic call stories in which

11. The verb for "draw" (*helkein*) is used again, translated as "haul" by the NRSV, in the postresurrection story of the large catch of fish: "They were not able to haul it in," and "Simon Peter . . . hauled the net ashore" (21:6, 11). This resonates with the imagery Jesus uses in the Synoptic Gospels for attracting followers: "Follow me and I will make you fish for people" (Mark 1:17).

disciples leave their nets: it is a decisive act of dedication to a new calling. It is even more radical for a woman than for a man, suggesting a vocation beyond conventional domestic responsibilities. That a marginalized Samaritan woman, who has suffered much, should respond like this, while the senior male leader Nicodemus is left bewildered, is in line with other paradoxes of the Gospel, above all the drama of a salvation centered on a master who washes feet, the Son of God who is crucified.

It is important to note that the disciples do not question Jesus about this: they trust him even when he welcomes someone who is not only different in religious tradition, social standing, and gender, but who also energetically takes on a role of witnessing in an unprecedented setting. *In later church history major developments in inclusivity and boundary crossing have often stretched such trust within the mother community to the breaking point.* Examples include the inclusion of gentiles (non-Jews) in the early church, as told in the book of Acts and Paul's Letters, and more recent disputes over slavery, women's ministry, disciplines surrounding marriage and the Eucharist, charismatic gifts, missionary practices, sexuality, and relations with persons of other religions.

Like Nicodemus, the woman's last words in the story are a question: **"He cannot be the Messiah, can he?"** She witnesses to her own experience and leaves her listeners with a question. They then come to meet Jesus for themselves.

Food, Work, Harvest, and Eternal Life (4:31–38)

> 31 Meanwhile the disciples were urging him, "Rabbi, eat something." 32 But
> he said to them, "I have food to eat that you do not know about." 33 So the
> disciples said to one another, "Surely no one has brought him something
> to eat?" 34 Jesus said to them, "My food is to do the will of him who sent
> me and to complete his work. 35 Do you not say, 'Four months more, then
> comes the harvest'? But I tell you, look around you, and see how the fields are
> ripe for harvesting. 36 The reaper is already receiving wages and is gathering
> fruit for eternal life, so that sower and reaper may rejoice together. 37 For
> here the saying holds true, 'One sows and another reaps.' 38 I sent you to
> reap that for which you did not labor. Others have labored, and you have
> entered into their labor."

In the interlude between the woman's departure and the response of her people in faith is a conversation between the disciples and Jesus that, in different imagery, follows through on the theme of attraction: **gathering fruit for eternal life**. It is triggered by the disciples urging Jesus to eat and him speaking of having **food to eat that you do not know about**, which is doing **the will** (or "desire"—*thelēma* can mean both) of God.

In line with his method of teaching in waves, John here introduces themes that will be taken further later, such as food (especially in chap. 6), the interrelation of Jesus's work and his Father's (especially in chap. 5), and the sending of Jesus's disciples (especially in the Farewell Discourses and resurrection stories, chaps. 13–17 and 20–21), and they will be discussed when we come to those chapters. But here there is a distinctive emphasis on the surprising nature

Amos wrote of days to come "when the one who ploughs shall overtake the one who reaps and the treader of grapes the one who sows the seed" (Amos 9.13–14), but what Jesus says here surpasses even that. Jesus has just spoken of accomplishing (Gk. *teleioō*: fulfil, bring to completion; also used in Jn 19.30 [as Jesus dies]) the work God has sent him to do. For an audience who knows the Scriptures, the echo is loud and clear.

> For as the rain and the snow come down from heaven, and do not return there until they have watered the earth, making it bring forth and sprout, giving seed to the sower and bread to the eater, so shall my word be that goes out from my mouth; it shall not return to me empty, but it shall accomplish that which I purpose, and succeed in the thing for which I sent it. (Isa 55.10–11)

These Samaritan fields are the extraordinary realization of Deuteronomy's vision of Israel as "a land that drinks water by the rain from heaven," and because of this continual expression of the divine care is astonishingly productive (Deut 11.10–12 *RSV*). In Jesus, the Word sent from God has watered the Earth. In fact, the Word runs so swiftly (Ps 147.15 [LXX 147.4]) and with such alacrity that the seasonal rhythms of Earth are accelerated to a point where ordinary times and seasons converge into the one moment of completion and fulfilment. The saying, "I sent you to reap that for which you did not labour" (Jn 4.38), has much in common with the Markan Jesus' parable comparing the *basileia* ["kingdom"] to the way seeds mysteriously sprout and grow while the farmer sleeps (Mk 4.26–29). Again the disciples are challenged by the *epigeia*—the "way" of things on Earth: that without any human intervention the divine watering satisfies the thirsty ground, enabling the crops to grow (Ps 104.13–14). Later in the gospel Jesus will develop this theme from another angle: the death and burial of the grain that is the precondition for the harvest (Jn 12.24).

—Margaret Daly-Denton, *John*, 91–92

of what is happening. Instead of having to wait for harvest after sowing, with the coming of Jesus, the "I am," there is a transformation of time, and eternal life is being tasted now (see the quotation from Daly-Denton in the sidebar).

Culmination: Knowing the Savior of the World (4:39–42)

> [39] Many Samaritans from that city believed in him because of the woman's testimony, "He told me everything I have ever done." [40] So when the Samaritans came to him, they asked him to stay with them; and he stayed there two days. [41] And many more believed because of his word. [42] They said to the woman, "It is no longer because of what you said that we believe, for we have heard for ourselves, and we know that this is truly the Savior of the world."

The Samaritans who believe are not satisfied with what the woman tells them at second hand, and they invite Jesus to stay (*menein*, "abide") with them. The result is both an expansion in numbers and a deepening of faith—**many more believed**—and they come to a recognition that goes beyond what the woman told them: **"We know that this is truly the Savior of the world."** This final surprise of the encounter goes beyond the boundary crossing between Jews and Samaritans, or men and women, to see Jesus as the global healer, boundary crosser, and reconciler. **Savior of the world** (*sōtēr tou kosmou*), later reinforced by Jesus saying that he came "to save the world" (12:47), has, like many other key terms in John, strong associations both with his Bible (where God is the incomparable Savior [Isa. 43:3, 11; 45:15, 21]) and with the surrounding civilization (where the Roman emperor is called savior). Here it shows the Samaritans accepting something that would have been hard for them to swallow, that **salvation is from the Jews**, but in a way that embraces both the Jews and themselves in something bigger than either of them.

Conclusion: Learning to Recognize and Respond to Who Jesus Is

What is happening through this story? The dramatic encounter of Jesus with the Samaritan woman can be read as a learning process for the woman, her community, and the disciples, and therefore for John's readers and rereaders. The horizon for this is the whole world. The learning is ongoing, as the capacious images and concepts—water, eternal life, marriage, worship, salvation, spirit, truth, food, work—take on fuller meaning through experience, reading and rereading John and the rest of the Bible together, and pursuing relevant questions. *And the relationship with Jesus is deepened as those images and concepts both feed into a richer understanding of who he is as human being, Jew, greater than*

Jacob, prophet, Messiah/Christ, "I am," and Savior of the world, and also inspire a life of boundary crossing, witness, and worship.

The Second Sign: Believing and Life (4:43–54)

This is the first healing by Jesus in the Gospel of John, coming relatively late compared to Mark's Gospel, which has many healings in its first chapter. This delay is in line with John's concern to draw readers into mature faith, not based on **signs and wonders**, but above all oriented to who Jesus is—up to this point that has been, as it continues to be, the central concern of this Gospel. Inseparable from this believing and trusting in Jesus is receiving through him life in many forms, one of which is physical health.

> [43] When the two days were over, he went from that place to Galilee [44] (for
> Jesus himself had testified that a prophet has no honor in the prophet's own
> country). [45] When he came to Galilee, the Galileans welcomed him, since
> they had seen all that he had done in Jerusalem at the festival; for they too
> had gone to the festival.

What is Jesus's **own country** (the Greek term is *patris*, from "father")? Scholars differ about whether the reference is to Galilee, which seems less likely because here **the Galileans welcomed him**, or Jerusalem and Judea, where throughout the Gospel of John he meets opposition, and with which he, as a Jew, has just been identified in the conversation with the Samaritan woman. But there is irony in any geographical location of the *patris* of Jesus when his true origin with the Father has been made clear since the prologue. The refusal to give **honor** to Jesus is in line with the prologue's headline statement: "He came to what was his own, and his own people did not accept him" (1:11).

> [46] Then he came again to Cana in Galilee where he had changed the water
> into wine. Now there was a royal official whose son lay ill in Capernaum.
> [47] When he heard that Jesus had come from Judea to Galilee, he went and
> begged him to come down and heal his son, for he was at the point of death.
> [48] Then Jesus said to him, "Unless you see signs and wonders you will not
> believe." [49] The official said to him, "Sir, come down before my little boy
> dies." [50] Jesus said to him, "Go; your son will live." The man believed the
> word that Jesus spoke to him and started on his way. [51] As he was going
> down, his slaves met him and told him that his child was alive. [52] So he asked
> them the hour when he began to recover, and they said to him, "Yesterday

> at one in the afternoon the fever left him." 53 The father realized that this was the hour when Jesus had said to him, "Your son will live." So he himself believed, along with his whole household. 54 Now this was the second sign that Jesus did after coming from Judea to Galilee.

It is not only the mention of Jerusalem that connects with the story of the Samaritan woman. Like that encounter, this one too leads the reader further into the interconnection of two core realities in John: believing in Jesus and life through Jesus. The repetitions underline their centrality: three mentions of believing, three of life, six of Jesus.

Another parallel is the surprising process of learning to believe. Here the surprise is the effectiveness of **the word that Jesus spoke** in healing at a distance. Like the first sign at the wedding in Cana, there is an echo of creation, suggested both by the effect of **the word** of Jesus and by the repetition of **Jesus did** (or "Jesus created," *epoiēsen ho Iēsous*).[12]

The learning process that the **royal official** goes through repeats some elements of the first sign. There is a similar pattern of someone taking the initiative of appealing to Jesus, his initial reluctance, and a refusal (by his mother in the first, by the royal official here) to be put off, leading to Jesus responding far in excess of expectation: a huge amount of the best wine; complete recovery of the son without Jesus even having to **come down** from Cana to Capernaum.

There is a lively two-way interaction with Jesus in both cases, as also with the Samaritan woman. Faith involves a fully reciprocal relationship that is not about being equal with Jesus but that tests the believer, drawing him or her into active response, and allowing for complex growth in trust. As Martin Luther said of this royal official, "Christ allows us to be challenged, so that we might grow in faith."[13] The challenges begin with the first words of Jesus when he questions his first disciples (1:38), and they continue through the Gospel, culminating in his crucifixion, which is followed by an array of further challenges in his postresurrection encounters.

The whole Gospel is written so that "through believing you may have life in his name" (20:31). This brief story brings "believing" and "life" together in a distinctive way, inseparable from "his name," who Jesus is. It also suggests that this believing and life have crossed another boundary, moving beyond Jews and Samaritans to embrace this royal official and **his whole household**.

12. See comments on 1:1; 20:30; 21:25.

13. Martin Luther, "Sermon on Twenty-First Sunday after Pentecost" (1525), quoted in Farmer, *John 1–12*, 154.

Is the royal official also meant to represent the gentiles? Similar stories of healing at a distance in the Synoptic Gospels are about a pagan gentile military officer (Matt. 8:5–13; Luke 7:1–10). Whether gentile or not, the royal official served the regime of Herod Antipas, who collaborated closely with the Romans. "Thus some might picture this royal officer as a pagan, though he could as easily be a Herodian Jew whom John merely allows to stand ambiguously for Hellenism."[14] *Either way, Jesus is attracting to himself a strikingly diverse group of believers: Jewish disciples, Samaritans, and now a family identified with the royal court, the Roman Empire, and Hellenistic civilization.*

14. Keener, *The Gospel of John*, 1:631.

John 5:1–47

Into Controversy

Chapters 1–4 have opened up a horizon of God and all reality for understanding Jesus; there have been multiple beginnings, using the language of creation, birth, baptism, the Spirit, the call to follow Jesus, and marriage; and Jesus has had deep encounters within and beyond his own Jewish community. Now a new phase in the story begins, chapters 5–12, in which a series of Jesus's actions and teachings (often in the context of arguments) come back again and again to the heart of the matter: who Jesus is and the sort of life he gives. Its wave-like presentation treats that basic theme with repetitions and variations, and together these draw readers further and deeper, as conflict intensifies, as Jerusalem becomes the main setting, and as the drama moves toward its climax.

Here in chapter 5 there are three core matters: Jesus does a healing that shows him as the giver of life; his approach to the Sabbath leads into teaching on his relationship with his Father, opening up new dimensions of that; and the astonishing nature of what he does and who he claims to be raises massive truth questions that challenge common assumptions about God, life, Scriptures, glory, and what is possible.

The dynamic intensity of the chapter is sustained by a concentration of some of John's key interrelated verbs: wanting, seeking and finding; seeing and hearing; knowing and believing; doing and working; loving and giving life; judging and testifying; being astonished and rejoicing; saving and abiding; coming and accepting. Each of these verbs could be traced through the first twelve chapters of John's Gospel, having their meaning enriched by the stories and teachings, until, through the Farewell Discourses and later chapters, the reader/hearer is invited not only to enter more deeply into their meaning but also to live them out in fresh ways in the ongoing drama.

"Do You Want to Be Made Well?" A Sign of Full Life (5:1–9a)

> 1 After this there was a festival of the Jews, and Jesus went up to Jerusalem.
> 2 Now in Jerusalem by the Sheep Gate there is a pool, called in Hebrew
> Beth-zatha, which has five porticoes. 3 In these lay many invalids—blind,
> lame, and paralyzed. 5 One man was there who had been ill for thirty-eight
> years. 6 When Jesus saw him lying there and knew that he had been there
> a long time, he said to him, "Do you want to be made well?" 7 The sick man
> answered him, "Sir, I have no one to put me into the pool when the water is
> stirred up; and while I am making my way, someone else steps down ahead
> of me." 8 Jesus said to him, "Stand up, take your mat and walk." 9a At once
> the man was made well, and he took up his mat and began to walk.

Jesus here gives a vivid sign of the life he brings: delivering a lame man from thirty-eight years of illness and disappointment. Jesus does not heal all of the **many invalids—blind, lame, and paralyzed**—whom he finds at the pool. This is a sign, not an instantaneous solution to all health problems, or an alternative to caring for the sick, or something to be always replicated in similar situations, or even a critique of what was going on at **Beth-zatha**. For readers who are sent as Jesus was sent (20:21), what might the meaning of this sign be?

First of all, it is about active compassion for the sick. The previous story of the royal official showed Jesus responding to an urgent cry for help; here he takes the initiative in helping.

Second, such compassion takes each person seriously, alert to his or her particular history and situation: **Jesus saw him lying there and knew that he had been there a long time**.

Third, there is a conversation that respects the dignity, freedom, and desires of the sick person: **"Do you want** [*thelein*, "desire"] **to be made well?"** That question may also hint at the ways in which long illness, addiction, grief, depression, or a dysfunctional habit of relating to ourselves or others can over time become so much part of who we are that we lose the will or desire to be liberated from it. The first words of Jesus in John's Gospel, "What are you looking for?" (1:38), had shown him, from the beginning, opening up in those he meets this area of desire, longing, motivation, and hope.

But, fourth, the rest of the story leads us into further ramifications of meaning. Health is more than physical—"Do not sin any more, so that nothing worse happens to you" (5:14). Full life is nothing less than "eternal life" (5:24). Above all, the sign leads back to who the sign giver is and this in turn into fresh understanding of who God is (5:17–47).

Yet none of these expansions of meaning undermines the value and integrity of the initial act of compassion by Jesus. He did it for its own sake, because it was a good thing to heal the man, and then he "disappeared in the crowd" (5:13). The man "did not know who it was" who had healed him (5:13). The activity of Jesus can be done incognito, as can ours.

God's Sabbath—But Who Is God? What Is Equality? (5:9b–18)

Keeping the Sabbath was a very serious matter indeed for Jews: the death penalty was attached to violating it (Exod. 31:14–15; Num. 15:32–36). In the Synoptic Gospels, as here, controversy about the Sabbath involves fundamental questions of who Jesus is ("For the Son of Man is lord of the sabbath" [Matt. 12:8]) and also threats to his life ("The Pharisees went out and immediately conspired with the Herodians against him, how to destroy him" [Mark 3:6]). Here, in line with John's postresurrection perspective and the horizon set by chapters 1–4, Jesus's response to his opponents goes straight to the heart of the theological issue, provoking them with a claim that his working on the Sabbath is to be identified with God's.

> [9b] Now that day was a sabbath. [10] So the Jews said to the man who had been cured, "It is the sabbath; it is not lawful for you to carry your mat." [11] But he answered them, "The man who made me well said to me, 'Take up your mat and walk.'" [12] They asked him, "Who is the man who said to you, 'Take it up and walk'?" [13] Now the man who had been healed did not know who it was, for Jesus had disappeared in the crowd that was there. [14] Later Jesus found him in the temple and said to him, "See, you have been made well! Do not sin any more, so that nothing worse happens to you." [15] The man went away and told the Jews that it was Jesus who had made him well. [16] Therefore the Jews started persecuting Jesus, because he was doing such things on the sabbath. [17] But Jesus answered them, "My Father is still working, and I also am working." [18] For this reason the Jews were seeking all the more to kill him, because he was not only breaking the sabbath, but was also calling God his own Father, thereby making himself equal to God.

In saying **"Do not sin any more, so that nothing worse happens to you,"** does Jesus imply a connection between sin and illness? Later, in the case of a man born blind, he denies any such connection (9:1–3), but that need not be a general rule. There may be such a connection, and Jesus seems to be making one here, but that too need not be a general rule. It is a matter for particular judgment. *This statement shows Jesus as judge after the healing has shown him as* *life giver.* These are the two activities that Jews of the time generally saw God continuing on the Sabbath, despite resting. On the Sabbath life continues to be sustained by God, and babies are born; and God continues to judge the quality of worship, love, truth seeking, goodness, and of each of our lives, including those who die on the Sabbath. Life and judgment are key elements in the next part of this discourse (5:19–30).

"My Father is still working, and I also am working" is therefore a headline for what follows, covering all the activity of Jesus and his Father, including giving life and executing judgment. The hostile response to this claim is that Jesus was **calling God his own Father, thereby making himself equal to God**. Jesus certainly calls God his own Father, but does he make himself equal to God? Lesslie Newbigin answers no (see the quotation from Newbigin in the sidebar).

> The Jews have used the word "equal." Jesus bypasses this word altogether. The unity of Father and Son is not one of "equality" but of love and obedience. Jesus is utterly dependent upon the Father, and precisely because this is so Jesus is entrusted with the fullness of the Father's power both to give life and to judge—a power which the Father is exercising "till now" and which the Son will therefore exercise in absolute obedience to the Father, and which he is able to exercise because the Father's love is given to him in fullness.
>
> The Jews have understood the words of Jesus to be a claim to equality with God. In his reply Jesus shows that what is being revealed is not equality but unity. The unique intimacy which is conveyed in Jesus's constantly repeated phrase "my Father" implies a perfect unity which is not equality. These are two quite different and even opposed patterns of relation. The ideal of equality (which our culture has espoused from the rationalist element in our pagan heritage) leads on to independence. Those who are in all respects equal do not need to depend on each other but can stand on their own feet. In spite of the fact that paternity appears to be a fact of life, paternalism is condemned as a violation of human dignity because it rests on inequality and involves dependence. Our ideal of human dignity is in fact the very ancient one advocated by the Serpent (Gen. 3:5), needing nothing and independent of any judgment of good and evil other than our own. In total contrast to this vision of equality, Jesus speaks of a relation between himself and his Father in which filial obedience is as complete and total as is paternal love. . . . All ideas about what the word "God" means . . . must be tested by what is to be seen in the words and deeds of this totally humble and obedient man. That we have here the germ of the doctrine of the Trinity will be obvious.
>
> —Lesslie Newbigin, *The Light Has Come*, 66–67

Newbigin's provocative principle of "not equality but unity" grasps well the fundamental concern with interrelationship and mutuality, and also the negation of any idea of equality that leads to autonomous, self-sufficient individualism, or to the sort of independence that denies interdependence and undermines community.

Yet Newbigin's unity of "love and obedience" is not quite true to the rest of this text, in which love is mentioned (the verb in 5:20 is *philein*, referring to love as between friends), but not obedience. Indeed, John never mentions obeying, either by Jesus or his followers. He has many closely related terms (e.g., *tērein*, "keep, observe"; *entolē*, "commandment"; *entellesthai*, "command"; *menein*, "abide, persevere"; *akouein*, "hear"; and *akolouthein*, "follow"), all of which require obedience; and, of course, John's use of *kyrios*, "Lord," and *theos*, "God," imply obedience too. But John's main concern, underlined by him not actually speaking of obedience, is to attract readers into something that is beyond obedience. This is best understood in terms of mutual love, of being friends rather than servants (15:15), of mutual indwelling (17:20–26), and of sharing in the same life and Spirit (20:22).

There is here a sort of equality that avoids what Newbigin is rejecting. *It is the equality of a friendship in love that can embrace many sorts of inequalities, dependencies, and differences.*

Dynamic Divine Unity: Loving, Life Giving, Judging, Honoring, Speaking, Willing (5:19–30)

John has several ways of emphasizing the special importance of certain statements, including repetition with variation and Jesus saying, **"Very truly, I tell you"** (*amēn amēn legō hymin/soi*).[1] Jesus here repeats that phrase twice, and the whole passage repeats with variations the message just given in 5:17: "My Father is still working, and I also am working." The active unity of Father and Son was first headlined in the prologue (1:18), it was indicated in the Nicodemus encounter (3:16) and the teaching after that (3:35), and it was implied in the conversation with the Samaritan woman (4:19–26). *Now this dynamic unity is emphasized as of central importance, and for the first time its meaning is explicitly opened up.*

As usual with John, this is an opening up without closure. Not only do the themes recur through later chapters, but also each key term resonates more widely

1. This is used twenty-five times in John and often indicates connection with the Synoptic Gospels (sometimes direct connection, sometimes contrasting, always worth reflecting upon), where *amēn legō hymin/soi* (John's version has a doubled *amēn*) is also a characteristic phrase of Jesus: thirty in Matthew, thirteen in Mark, and six in Luke.

through the Septuagint and the Synoptic Gospels, so readers are invited to deepen and expand their understanding continually. But the invitation is into more than understanding; as has already been vividly indicated in a variety of ways, it is also about wholehearted, life-transforming participation—being born into a family (1:12–13; cf. 3:1–10), believing and trusting (1:12; 2:11; 3:15–16; 4:42, 50, 53), following (1:43), acting "in God" (3:21), receiving the Spirit without measure (3:34; cf. 3:8; 4:13–14), and worshiping in spirit and in truth (4:23–24). The Farewell Discourses (chaps. 13–17) will be particularly concerned with participation in the dynamics between the Father and the Son that are opened up in the present passage.

> 19 Jesus said to them, "Very truly, I tell you, the Son can do nothing on his
> own, but only what he sees the Father doing; for whatever the Father does,
> the Son does likewise. 20 The Father loves the Son and shows him all that
> he himself is doing; and he will show him greater works than these, so that
> you will be astonished. 21 Indeed, just as the Father raises the dead and gives
> them life, so also the Son gives life to whomever he wishes. 22 The Father
> judges no one but has given all judgment to the Son, 23 so that all may honor
> the Son just as they honor the Father. Anyone who does not honor the Son
> does not honor the Father who sent him. 24 Very truly, I tell you, anyone who
> hears my word and believes him who sent me has eternal life, and does not
> come under judgment, but has passed from death to life.
>
> 25 "Very truly, I tell you, the hour is coming, and is now here, when the
> dead will hear the voice of the Son of God, and those who hear will live.
> 26 For just as the Father has life in himself, so he has granted the Son also to
> have life in himself; 27 and he has given him authority to execute judgment,
> because he is the Son of Man. 28 Do not be astonished at this; for the hour is
> coming when all who are in their graves will hear his voice 29 and will come
> out—those who have done good, to the resurrection of life, and those who
> have done evil, to the resurrection of condemnation.
>
> 30 "I can do nothing on my own. As I hear, I judge; and my judgment is
> just, because I seek to do not my own will but the will of him who sent me."[2]

"This section is one of the most profound in the whole Gospel."[3] "The discourse that follows the healing is one of the most exalted in John."[4]

2. The Greek of "I seek to do not my own will but the will of him who sent me" is *ou zētō to thelēma to emon alla to thelēma tou pempsantos me*—literally, "I do not seek/search for my own will/desire but the will/desire of the one who sent me." The latter, the desire of God, is the encompassing desire in this Gospel of desire.

3. Schnackenburg, *The Gospel according to St. John*, 2:99.

4. R. Brown, *The Gospel according to John*, 1:216.

What is it that the Son **sees the Father doing**? One basic divine activity is creating. The Greek verb translated as "do" (*poiein*) also means "make, create" (as in Gen. 1:1), and from the beginning of his Gospel John has seen Jesus involved in creation and the generation of **life** (1:1–4).

Here, the first thing the Father is mentioned as doing is loving: **The Father loves the Son**. So we are to think of a relationship of mutual love, with the Son loving like the Father. What is the meaning of this love? There is an obvious place to seek it. If **the Son can do nothing on his own, but only what he sees the Father doing; for whatever the Father does, the Son does likewise**, then it follows that the Gospel story of the words and actions of Jesus is an enactment of this love. All that Jesus does and says feeds into the meaning, which therefore is inexhaustibly rich.

Its climax is seen in his crucifixion: "No one has greater love than this, to lay down one's life for one's friends" (15:13). Is that "greater love," seen in his death, to be related to the **greater works than these** that the Father will **show** the Son? If the crucifixion of Jesus is understood, with John, as inseparable from his resurrection, then this goes well with the following statement that **just as the Father raises the dead and gives them life, so also the Son gives life to whomever he wishes**. And the crucifixion and resurrection of Jesus also fit the prediction, **You will be astonished**.

There are other possible identifications of these astonishing **greater works**. They could be the later signs Jesus does, including the raising of Lazarus (John 11). Or they could be the greater works that the disciples are told they will be able to do in the name of Jesus after his death and resurrection: "Very truly, I tell you, the one who believes in me will also do the works that I do and, in fact, will do greater works than these, because I am going to the Father" (14:12). All three readings could be simultaneously possible, with the last two emerging for rereaders, intensifying the astonishment.

How this passage is "profound" and "exalted" can be explored further through other passages where key terms are discussed, including "love," "word," "resurrection," and "voice." For now, the concentration will be on **life in himself** and **judgment**.

God's Life and Self

"For just as the Father has life in himself, so he has granted the Son also to have life in himself." This "as . . . so . . ." challenges thought and imagination to go on being stretched year after year in trying to do some justice to the reality of God.

Who can fathom that "self" of the Father? The attempt to do so never ends, leading through Israel's Scriptures, the Synoptic Gospels, this Gospel, and then through centuries of prayer and worship, theology, philosophy, poetry and other arts, and experience. That need not be an overwhelming and intimidatingly difficult prospect or project, but rather an endlessly attractive one, trusting that little by little (and occasionally in great leaps) understanding can grow, and that no one ever finishes fathoming and being amazed and delighted by who God is. This is an **eternal life** of love, and John 5 gives some of its dynamic elements: doing, creating, and life giving; being astonished; honor and glory; truth; and rejoicing.

Here the emphasis is on free divine self-giving: *this is a "self" that is utterly shared in love.* The living God shares what most essentially characterizes God's very self: life and love—and even, as will emerge in John 17, God's "glory" (see below on vv. 31–47). *But that "what" of the divine self can be fully expressed only in a "who," the self of the Son.* This is at the heart of Christian monotheism. There is a unity of divine life, love, and glory. God is free to give God's self completely. Yet in this self-giving there is no loss of self. Rather, what is revealed is that the self of God is utterly relational. It is a selfhood in which the self of the Father is only the divine self through unity in love with who the Son is—the Son on whom the Spirit abides (1:32–33). This unique unity does not erase distinctiveness: the Father and the Son are different yet inseparably one.

Nor is it a unity that can be inspected or known from the outside, or from any neutral point of view (as will emerge in the next section, vv. 31–47, John does not recognize any neutral standpoint on such fundamental matters—everyone stands somewhere, is committed to some way of life). This "life" can be appreciated only by tasting it and sharing in it, and John's Gospel is written to help this happen—"that through believing you may have life in his name" (20:31). That name, the "who" of Jesus, is utterly relational, inseparable from who the Father is.

What sort of life is this? It is **eternal life** (v. 24). The time of this life is the time of God, and so relates to all times. In a culture where shortage of time is one of the most common problems and where anxiety about the future often spoils life, it is worth meditating on the eternal life of God as the embracing reality. Awareness of God-centered time helps set priorities for our limited time, such as worshiping God for who God is, and loving other people. It also helps with anxiety by focusing on the great truth about the future: this eternal life of love between the Father and the Son.

The deepest insight into what this means is given in the prayer of Jesus in John 17 (where there are many echoes of John 5), which asks for the fullest imaginable participation in this love by others, "so that the love with which you have loved me may be in them, and I in them" (17:26). This is then enacted by Jesus laying down his life in love, after which that prayer for participation is fulfilled through the crucified and resurrected Jesus breathing the Holy Spirit into his disciples (20:22). The verb that John uses for this breathing, *emphysan*, is the same as that used for when God "breathed" the "breath of life" into the first human being, Adam (Gen. 2:7). Just as, in Jesus, God and human life are united together through the Word becoming flesh (1:18), so the ordinary life of creation becomes united with the eternal life of the Holy Spirit.

Judgment and Decision, Death and Life

Alongside life, the other great theme of this passage is **judgment**. It is taken for granted that judgment is a good and necessary thing. Otherwise, how do we know who and what to **honor** and **believe**, and how do we distinguish **good** from **evil**? Without judgments there can be no ethics, no politics, no knowledge or **truth** (v. 33), no worthwhile **life**; and we all make judgments every day of our lives. But whose judgment is most to be trusted in what is most important, in matters of **death** and **life**? The answer of Jesus and his Jewish tradition is clear: God's. God as creator of life and goodness is inseparable from God as judge—hence, for example, the passionate enthusiasm for the judgments of God in the Psalms, above all in Psalm 119.

Here there is a new idea: **"The Father judges no one but has given all judgment to the Son."** God is still judge but is united in agency with Jesus. *So judgment is now defined by who Jesus is.* This judge is one who heals the lame man, but also warns him not to sin. This judge is loved by the Father and **sent** by him in love for the world, so at the heart of judgment is love. (St. Augustine said that he would rather be judged by God than by his own mother.) This judge **gives life to whomever he wishes**, and his wish is to "draw all people to myself" (12:32). The critical issue is whether people will be drawn, whether the love will be returned, whether there will be the listening and trust that are essential to a mutual relationship. **"Very truly, I tell you, anyone who hears my word and believes him who sent me has eternal life, and does not come under judgment, but has passed from death to life."** That is an open "anyone." Eternal life can begin now through hearing, trusting, and loving Jesus.

So what about **the resurrection of life** and **the resurrection of condemnation**? What is sometimes called John's "dualism"[5] never takes for granted that God's love for the world is completely successful in getting its desired response. The possibility of rejection not only is allowed for but also is dramatically described in the opposition that Jesus faces. More will be said later

5. See Bauckham, *Gospel of Glory*, chap. 6, for a perceptive discussion of the issues; see also Barton, "Johannine Dualism and Contemporary Pluralism," and Volf, "Johannine Dualism and Contemporary Pluralism."

about this conflict. The present passage is illuminated by reading it in terms of Rudolf Bultmann's "dualism of decision." If response to the Gospel had been either predetermined or inevitable, it would have been pointless to write it. The Gospel in fact is an appeal to readers to respond by deciding to believe in Jesus. The repeated "anyone" in this passage underlines that the decision can go either way.

So there is no overview of how the ultimate judgment will go, and no simple affirmation that there will be universal salvation for all no matter how people believe and behave. Rather, there is an ongoing drama, with decisions that have consequences. Each reader who **hears my word** (*logos*) is faced with a decision about whether or not to trust this word—and its speaker.

Testimony, the Problem of Knowing Its Truth, and Seeking God's Glory (5:31–47)

Jesus says, **"I know that his testimony to me is true."** But how do we know that what he claims to know is true?

That is one of the most important questions of all. The dilemma applies to all fundamental, encompassing affirmations about reality. If we affirm an unsurpassable truth, then to claim that some other truth testifies to it adequately seems to make that other truth the encompassing one. Anselm of Canterbury saw God as that "than which none greater can be conceived."[6] To think that God can be shown to be real within any framework of reality apart from God therefore means that something greater than God is being conceived. Beginning with his prologue, John has opened up an unsurpassable, encompassing horizon of God and all reality. Jesus is inseparable from both, and the basic testimony of John and his community is, "We have seen his glory, the glory as of a father's only son, full of grace and truth" (1:14).

Here he faces the problem: How might this comprehensive understanding be verified? He also poses its most radical challenge: to **seek the glory that comes from the one who alone is God**.

> 31 "If I testify about myself, my testimony is not true. 32 There is another who
> testifies on my behalf, and I know that his testimony to me is true. 33 You
> sent messengers to John, and he testified to the truth. 34 Not that I accept
> such human testimony, but I say these things so that you may be saved. 35 He
> was a burning and shining lamp, and you were willing to rejoice for a while

6. Anselm, *Proslogion* 2.

> in his light. 36 But I have a testimony greater than John's. The works that the Father has given me to complete, the very works that I am doing, testify on my behalf that the Father has sent me. 37 And the Father who sent me has himself testified on my behalf. You have never heard his voice or seen his form, 38 and you do not have his word abiding in you, because you do not believe him whom he has sent.
>
> 39 "You search the scriptures because you think that in them you have eternal life; and it is they that testify on my behalf. 40 Yet you refuse to come to me to have life. 41 I do not accept glory from human beings. 42 But I know that you do not have the love of God in you. 43 I have come in my Father's name, and you do not accept me; if another comes in his own name, you will accept him. 44 How can you believe when you accept glory from one another and do not seek the glory that comes from the one who alone is God? 45 Do not think that I will accuse you before the Father; your accuser is Moses, on whom you have set your hope. 46 If you believed Moses, you would believe me, for he wrote about me. 47 But if you do not believe what he wrote, how will you believe what I say?"

The core verification here is pointed to in verse 32, **another who testifies on my behalf**, and then stated clearly in verse 37, **The Father who sent me has himself testified on my behalf**. *God alone is an adequate witness to God.*

This is a deep theme of the prophets. Isaiah 43, for example, is a rich, multifaceted appeal to the people of Israel to be God's witnesses (with many linguistic echoes of John 5 in the Greek of the Septuagint, underlined in the passage following), and their witness is grounded in recognizing who God is and what God does, according to God's own witness:

> 9 Let all the nations gather together,
> and let the peoples assemble.
> Who among them declared this,
> and foretold to us the former things?
> Let them bring their witnesses to justify them,
> and let them hear and say, "It is true."
> 10 You are my witnesses, says the LORD,
> and my servant whom I have chosen,
> so that you may know and believe me
> and understand that I am he.
> Before me no god was formed,
> nor shall there be any after me.
> 11 I, I am the LORD [LXX *theos,* "God"],
> and besides me there is no savior.

12 I declared and saved and proclaimed,
  when there was no strange god among you;
  and you are my witnesses, says the Lord.
13 I am God, and also henceforth I am He;
  there is no one who can deliver from my hand;
  I work and who can hinder it? (Isa. 43:9–13)

One fascinating aspect of the Greek, not reflected in this English translation (which is from the NRSV and based on the Hebrew), is that in both verse 10 and verse 12 the literal translation is, "You (are) my witnesses, and I (am) a witness, says the Lord God." This emphasizes God as the primary witness to who God is and what God does. The whole chapter (and much else in Isa. 40–55) also testifies to the freedom with which God works and the need to be open to astonishing new things that do not fit previous ideas:

18 Do not remember the former things,
  or consider the things of old.
19 I am about to do a new thing;
  now it springs forth, do you not perceive it?
I will make a way in the wilderness
  and rivers in the desert.
20 The wild animals will honor me,
  the jackals and the ostriches;
for I give water in the wilderness,
  rivers in the desert,
to give drink to my chosen people,
  21 the people whom I formed for myself
so that they might declare my praise. (Isa. 43:18–21)

That also connects with the theme of glory and honoring in John 5 (which culminates in the desire of Jesus in John 17 to share the glory fully with others), as well as having the water imagery of John 4.

But what sort of verification is this? The answer leads into two fundamental areas of theological wisdom.

God's Self-Communication: Mediated, Indirect Knowing

The first area is about the way God communicates who God is, what is often called "mediation": *God is known not directly but in a variety of mediations.* These can be words in many forms, oral and written; actions and events; festivals and symbols; animals and people; and more. John has all those, with Jesus as the primary mediation of God. This is the culminating insight of the prologue: "No one has ever seen God. It is God the only Son, who is close to the Father's heart, who has made him known" (1:18). Here in John 5:37–38 this is put negatively: **"You have never heard his voice or seen his form, and you do not have his word abiding in you, because you do not believe him whom he has sent."** There are many ways of trying to understand the reason for this indirectness, the most common in the Bible being one or a combination of the following: that the full reality of God would be completely overwhelming to human capacity; and that human sin, lack of holiness, is the barrier.

The present passage names three forms of mediation that testify to Jesus. These are the testimony of **John** the Baptist, **the works that the Father has given me to complete**, and **the scriptures . . . that testify on my behalf**. Each of these can be helpful in convincing people of **the truth**. Jewish law required more than one witness in support of a claim for it to be valid, and Jesus here goes along with that: **"If I testify about myself, my testimony is not true."**

One classic way of arguing for Christianity, and still perhaps the most effective, has been cumulative. Like a table with more than one leg, the case is supported by several mediations. The ones given here are personal witness, testimony to "the works" that Jesus has done, and "the scriptures." To these can be added many others. Indeed, because Jesus is seen as the one through whom "all things came into being" (1:3) and the Holy Spirit is given to guide "into all the truth" (16:13), the sources of truth in relation to Jesus are unlimited and often surprising.

Yet none of these can produce conclusive proof that wraps up the case decisively. Personal witness and the testimonies to what Jesus did need not be trusted; and the Scriptures can be interpreted in very different ways. Likewise, all the other angles can be understood in conflicting ways. Some of the most intelligent and best-educated people in the world come down on different sides in these arguments, so the issue is not one of intelligence or rationality or education. And nobody is neutral: everyone stands somewhere, has certain assumptions, has been shaped in particular ways, is embedded in a network of relationships and interests.

This is not to give up on argument and discussion, and Jesus engaged in them too. But his confidence in them was limited: **"Not that I accept such human testimony, but I say these things so that you may be saved."** That captures both the limitation and the usefulness of these mediations of truth. On the Scriptures, he offers a challenging rereading, probably especially thinking of Deuteronomy, where God promises Moses, "I will raise up for them a prophet like you from among their own people; I will put my words in the mouth of the prophet, who shall speak to them everything that I command. Anyone who does not heed the words that the prophet shall speak in my name, I myself will hold accountable" (Deut. 18:18–19). Jesus is identifying himself as that prophet, and the refusal to believe him means that **your accuser is Moses**.

Where Jesus does place all his confidence is in his relationship with **the Father**. He speaks from within that in order to attract others too to take part in it. The Father testifies to him through sending him as his Word, his full self-expression and self-giving, giving him both **works** to **complete** and **glory**. There is no conceivable independent proof of the truth of all this, and those faced with Jesus may respond with trust and love or with other responses. John describes a full range—from believing in him completely to betrayal and murderous enmity. *He faces his readers with the decision: With whom do you identify in this drama?* And central to that is deciding whether to enter into relationship with Jesus in the way he wants: recognizing who he is and trusting what he says and does.

Faith Seeking Understanding

This brings us to the second basic theme of theological wisdom: *faith seeking understanding*. This realistically says that nobody's ultimate, comprehensive framework can be verified, because that would mean there is something more ultimate and comprehensive. So the best approach is to take one such framework on trust and try it out from the inside, using all one's capacities of heart, mind, and imagination to understand it, test it, and live by it. Most of us take one on trust from birth, entering into the worldview and way of life of a family, culture, and religion. But the world has many such frameworks and ways of living, and the one we were brought up in can be challenged, in smaller and greater ways. Then we have to decide how to respond.

The opponents of Jesus are being faced with a radical challenge to their understanding of their own religion by a fellow Jew. Jesus is saying and doing things that do not fit their inherited framework. He is claiming here that he has been sent by the God they worship, but they do not believe him: **"You do not have his word abiding in you, because you do not believe him whom he has sent."** God's "word abiding in you" because you "believe": that would have been a position of faith from within which they could have sought understanding. Not being in that position means that they are judging Jesus from within a different framework. John's whole Gospel is an invitation to readers to "believe" that "word" and let it "abide" in them, so that they understand and live from within that truth rather than another.

Unless one has been brought up within the framework, this means a paradigm shift, a new way of understanding reality. But even if one has been brought up within it, the Gospel of John is radically and continually challenging. The process of faith seeking understanding is endless, and being guided into "all the truth" (16:13) by the Spirit of the One who was sent into darkness, humiliated, and crucified can and should lead believers more than once into fundamental rethinking, repentance, and reorientation.

But to see this only in terms of a framework, worldview, paradigm, orientation, or different way of interpreting Scripture does not reach to the heart of the matter. That comes when Jesus says, **"Yet you refuse to come to me to have life."** Encountering Jesus and recognizing him is utterly crucial. John's Gospel aims at enabling that meeting and recognition, and on that basis encouraging a life of faith in Jesus that seeks ever-deeper and fuller understanding. One might think of marriage, which has been one of the main images in the previous chapters, where Jesus is "the bridegroom" and John the Baptist is "the friend of the bridegroom" (3:29). There is an understanding possible in marriage that can come only through years of relating in trust and love. This is the wisdom of faith seeking understanding.

So much in the ongoing drama of our lives turns on who it is we believe in, trust, and love, matters in which there can be many relevant considerations and signs of reliability, but no proof, absolute verification, or certainty. Yet when, for whatever reasons (and there can be inadequate reasons for entering the right relationships!), we do enter into commitments in trust and love, they become the arena of new understanding and truth. *John's Gospel is an invitation to enter and remain in such an arena.*

Seeking Glory from Whom?

The culminating theme of John 5 is **glory**. The dynamics of who gives glory to whom and who honors whom are vital to the Gospel of John, and to the whole Bible—it is no accident that John quotes from Psalms more than any other biblical book. The whole Gospel is testimony to the glory of Jesus, which is inseparable from that of his Father (e.g., 1:14; 12:27–28; 17:1–5). It is a glory revealed through all the signs Jesus does (2:11) and above all through his crucifixion and resurrection. It radically challenges other conceptions of glory, honor, and power, as seen in Jesus washing his disciples' feet (13:1–20). It is closely connected with love (e.g., 13:31–35; 17:20–26).

The character of a person or group becomes clear in their dynamics of honoring, respecting, glorifying, praising, worshiping, delighting, rejoicing, or loving. It is our way of actively showing who and what is most important to us, where our commitments are oriented, what our core values are. Nothing is more important in the Bible: "You shall love the Lord your God with all your heart, and with all your soul, and with all your might" (Deut. 6:5).

Jesus has already introduced this in 5:19–23, where the love of the Father for the Son results in him wanting to share with Jesus the honor due to himself, "so that all may honor the Son just as they honor the Father. Anyone who does not honor the Son does not honor the Father who sent him" (v. 23). Now the theme returns, with three linked accusations: **"I know that you do not have the love of God in you"**; **"You do not accept me"**; and **"You accept glory from one another and do not seek the glory that comes from the one who alone is God."** This amounts to a diagnosis of pathological honoring. Its priority is not loving God; it fails to honor Jesus; and its dominant desire is for honor from other people, not from God.

One might ask: Was it not unreasonable, and even problematic according to the Scriptures that they shared, for Jesus to expect these practicing Jews to accept such radical ideas based on his authority and on that of the signs he has done? Is it not completely understandable that they should reject him?

The postresurrection perspective of John does lead to sharpening the controversies with **the Jews**. As in the Synoptic Gospels, John is clearly referring to the controversies that Jesus had with the religious leaders of his own people in Jerusalem, which were one key element in his eventual execution. But beyond that, it seems likely that John's own Christian community had had a painful break with their parent Jewish synagogue community (scholars have suggested that the references to being expelled from the synagogue in 9:22, 12:42, and 16:2 point to this) and that his writing reflects this trauma and perhaps ongoing persecution.

Yet, beyond both the original controversies of Jesus and those of John's community, there is John's concern for a wider readership across space and time, testified to from the prologue onward. So these accusations, and the whole passage, can also be taken to heart by readers as a further stage in the education of desire that began with the first words of Jesus to his first disciples: "What are you looking for?" (1:38). The verb translated as "look for" or "seek," *zētein*, which is so important for John, is used here in Jesus's accusation that his disputants **do not seek the glory that comes from the one who alone is God**.

There is a challenge to readers to examine ourselves about our dominant desires and practices of honoring, and about what and whom we rely on for our sense of our own worth, dignity, significance, and purpose. Individuals and whole communities can get caught in pathological dynamics of honoring, glorifying, and idolizing what is false, distorted, evil, or just inadequate, and in our time the media allow these to spread with unprecedented rapidity and intensity. Giving divine honor to a man who healed the sick, washed feet, and was crucified does seem unreasonable and scandalous.

Yet in the history of reception of the Gospel of John by Christians there is a terrible irony in relation to "the Jews." Here they are described as refusing to accept Jesus and seeking to kill him because of a fundamental difference in belief. When the situation was reversed in later centuries and Christians had the power to persecute those with different beliefs, they often acted worse than Jesus's opponents did here. There will be more on this when the controversy of Jesus with his opponents reaches its height in John 8, but for now it is worth considering that in reading John it is inadequate to identify "the Jews" only with the opponents of the historical Jesus or with the opponents of John's own community. As readers, we need to take their opposition as a mirror in which to see our own possibilities in any situation of encounter with those who fundamentally challenge our most precious beliefs and practices.

John 6:1–71

Food in Abundance

Three Dramas and Four Courses

John 6 unfolds through three minidramas and four waves of teaching, the latter here called "courses," in line both with the focus on eating and drinking and with stages of learning. The resonances with other parts of John, with the Synoptics (all of which have the stories of the feeding and the walking on water), and with Jesus's and John's Scriptures are especially abundant, and John also has his own distinctive emphases.

The dramatic sign of the feeding of the five thousand with "five barley loaves and two fish" (v. 9) is named later in the chapter as the event of having "eaten the bread after the Lord had given thanks" (v. 23). The Greek verb for giving thanks is *eucharistein,* from which we derive "Eucharist," one of the names of the celebration central to a majority of the world's Christians, also called the Lord's Supper, Holy Communion, and the Mass. Unlike the other three Gospels, John does not describe the institution of the Eucharist by Jesus on the night before he died (this omission is discussed below). But in this chapter John uses the language of Eucharist—thanks, bread, food, distributing, eating and drinking, blood, for your sakes, betrayal, death, and eternal life—to affirm in fresh ways what is most essential for him: who Jesus is, the life Jesus gives, believing in Jesus as the "work of God" in response (v. 29), and mutual indwelling—believers who "abide in me, and I in them" (v. 56).

At the same time, who Jesus is, the life he gives, and the responses to him are all understood through allusions to the exodus, the foundational event of the liberation of the people of Israel from slavery in Egypt, led by Moses.

These allusions are most obvious in mentions of the Passover, crossing a sea, eating manna in the wilderness, complaining, and going up a mountain alone, but there are also many more.[1] The book of Exodus should be read alongside John 6.

First Drama: Feeding Five Thousand and Avoiding Being Made King (6:1–15)

It is worth reading the parallel Synoptic accounts of feedings by Jesus (see Matt. 14:13–21, along with 15:32–39; Mark 6:32–44, along with 8:1–10; Luke 9:10–17) to get a sense of John's message. The core elements in John's and their accounts are the large number of people, Jesus giving thanks over (or blessing) five loaves and two fish in order to feed them so that they are filled, and twelve baskets of leftovers. John's readers who knew the Synoptic feedings would have read of Jesus being motivated by compassion for the crowds (Matt. 14:14; 15:32; Mark 6:34; 8:2) and accompanying the feeding with teaching and healing (Matt. 14:14: "He . . . cured their sick"; Mark 6:34: "He began to teach them many things"; Luke 9:11: "He . . . spoke to them about the kingdom of God, and healed those who needed to be cured"). John keeps the central miracle or sign, and also adds several significant elements.

Jesus Creates Abundance

> 1 After this Jesus went to the other side of the Sea of Galilee, also called the Sea of Tiberias. 2 A large crowd kept following him, because they saw the signs that he was doing for the sick. 3 Jesus went up the mountain and sat down there with his disciples. 4 Now the Passover, the festival of the Jews, was near. 5 When he looked up and saw a large crowd coming toward him, Jesus said to Philip, "Where are we to buy bread for these people to eat?" 6 He said this to test him, for he himself knew what he was going to do. 7 Philip answered him, "Six months' wages would not buy enough bread for each of them to get a little." 8 One of his disciples, Andrew, Simon Peter's brother, said to him, 9 "There is a boy here who has five barley loaves and two fish. But what are they among so many people?" 10 Jesus said, "Make the people sit down." Now there was a great deal of grass in the place; so they sat down, about five thousand in all. 11 Then Jesus took the loaves, and when he had given thanks, he distributed them to those who were seated; so also the fish,

1. For an excellent exploration of the allusions and of the history of how they have been interpreted down through the centuries, see Hylen, *Allusion and Meaning in John 6.*

> as much as they wanted. [12] When they were satisfied, he told his disciples, "Gather up the fragments left over, so that nothing may be lost." [13] So they gathered them up, and from the fragments of the five barley loaves, left by those who had eaten, they filled twelve baskets. [14] When the people saw the sign that he had done, they began to say, "This is indeed the prophet who is to come into the world."

In all four Gospels this feeding, like John's account of water being turned into wine at Cana, is a quiet event without surface drama that happens simply through what Jesus says. What was said on 2:1–11 about the miraculous and God as Creator is especially relevant here.[2] There are, of course, frameworks of meaning within which this feeding is utterly incredible, and there have been attempts to understand it in naturalistic terms—for example, that the boy's willingness to share his five loaves and two fish sparked off a wave of generosity in the crowd, so that they all shared whatever food they had. If each gives from what little he or she has, with God's blessing there will be enough for all; that is a helpful encouragement. But the main theological message of the four accounts is a triple one: *the compassionate love of Jesus; the unique relationship of Jesus with God the Creator, who is free to generate this abundance from very little; and the rich symbolism of bread and eating, resonating with the Eucharist and much else.* John intensifies and deepens each of those teachings in this chapter.

The loving compassion of Jesus in feeding the crowd is later made clear in him giving "life to the world" (v. 33), further understood as giving his own flesh "for the life of the world" (v. 51), and so connecting with his death and with the bread and eating of the Eucharist.

That later discourse also again and again emphasizes the unique relationship of Jesus with his Father (vv. 27, 32, 37–40, 42–47, 57, 65) and the abundance of the feeding, echoing God's generous gift of "manna" (vv. 31, 49) through forty years in the wilderness, pointing to the unending abundance of "eternal life" (vv. 27, 47, 54), "true bread from heaven" (v. 32), "true food" and "true drink" (v. 55), again connecting with the Eucharist.

The reader's imagination is prepared for that abundance by John's intensification of it in his account of the feeding itself. The dialogue with Philip stresses how **little** even six months' wages would provide for each person (they **would not buy enough bread for each of them to get a little**, whereas according to Mark 6:37 such an amount would have been enough), and Andrew's despairing comment about the inadequacy of the boy's food makes a similar point. While Matthew and Mark mention the grass, John says that **there was a great deal**

2. See comments on 2:1–12.

of grass in the place—he evokes the abundance of nature itself in that part of the world in the spring around the time of Passover. And John heightens the crowd's level of satisfaction and its direct relation to Jesus: **he distributed . . . as much as they wanted.**

The relationship to Jesus is further emphasized by John (who as usual is especially concerned with who Jesus is) being the only Gospel writer to speak of the crowd's reaction: **They began to say, "This is indeed the prophet who is to come into the world."** This probably refers to the prophet like Moses promised in Deuteronomy 18:18–19, discussed above on John 5,[3] with whom, as the reader of that chapter will know, Jesus does identify himself.

A Dangerous Surprise: Temptation and Discernment

> [15] When Jesus realized that they were about to come and take him by force to make him king, he withdrew again to the mountain by himself.

Moses was also seen popularly as a leader who combined being a prophet and a king, and he had led his people to liberation in the exodus. The crowd makes the connection, and this leads into a surprise not in the other Gospels: the people **were about to come and take him by force to make him king**. Jesus, however, avoided this and **withdrew again to the mountain by himself**. What is happening here?

This is the second time the title "king" has been applied to Jesus. In 1:49 he was called "King of Israel," and that is associated with God as King of Israel and with God's eternal covenant with David, promising that his descendants would be kings. But the Roman emperor was also called a king, and he appointed lesser kings throughout the empire. Any others claiming kingship were seen as rebels and punished by execution. So for the crowd to "make him king" would be for Jesus to defy Rome and lead an insurrection, seeking the sort of liberation that Moses the prophet-king had achieved.

This opens up the whole matter of the Gospel of John's relationship to the Roman Empire,[4] which comes to a climax in the trial of Jesus before the Roman governor Pontius Pilate in John 18–19, where the question of Jesus as king is central. "King" is just one of several titles for Jesus that are used not only in Jewish Scriptures and traditions but also in the surrounding Hellenistic civilization of the Roman Empire. Others include "shepherd," "Savior of the world," "Son of God," and "Lord and God." *These are directly competitive with the Roman emperor,*

3. See the section "God's Self-Communication: Mediated, Indirect Knowing" in the comments on 5:31–47.

4. On this, see Carter, *John and Empire*.

to whom all of them were also applied. In addition, some of the distinctively Jewish titles, such as "Messiah/Christ" and "Son of Man," have associations with political power and dominion that challenge Roman imperial claims. It is the same with other major matters: "eternal life" when contrasted with Rome as the eternal city; Jesus exercising God's judgment contrasted with the emperor as the supreme judge in the empire; God as the "Father" of Jesus over against the emperor as father of the empire; and Jesus as the "Lord" who, unlike the emperor at the top of a hierarchy, instead washes feet like a slave (13:1–10).

There is clearly a strong, explicit contrast in character between the realms of lordship of Jesus and of the emperor and between the sorts of community shaped by each. John's readers in the Roman Empire would have had to negotiate this tension daily, and later Christians have had a similar task in whatever societies they have lived in. Some interpreters of John have mainly emphasized how he reflects the negotiation and tension with the parent Jewish community, and that is undoubtedly important in ways that continue to be relevant.[5] But both Jews and, even more so, Christians were a small minority in the empire and had to work out how to live within it.

Interpreters differ on how those whom John was addressing were working this out. John's Gospel can be read as being written to confirm a sectarian community in living cut off from both the synagogue and the surrounding society; or it can be read as challenging its Christian community because it is too accommodating to the ways of the empire and needs to distance itself from them. I see something different.

Whether the main tendencies of his readers are toward excessive sectarian introspection and exclusive closure, or excessive accommodation and openness toward the surrounding society, I see an author shaping through long reflection and experience a Gospel seeking to guide them into a mature faith that might enable them to make responsible decisions about boundaries and openness. The encompassing reality is a God who offers abundant life to all, relativizing many boundaries and divisions (e.g., between Jews and Samaritans in 4:1–42). But there are judgments and decisions to be made. The abundance of this life is inseparable from costly love; following Jesus requires trust and perseverance through times of testing, and in such times disciples are faced by Jesus asking, "Do you also wish to go away?" (6:67). John 6 combines confidence in the superabundance given by God with a radical challenge to make wise decisions.

Here the one who is challenged is Jesus: Does he wish to be king? If John 6 is read alongside the accounts of the temptations of Jesus in Matthew 4:1–11

5. This is mainly discussed below on chap. 8, where the conflict between Jesus and "the Jews" is at its most polemical. See also the comments on 2:13–25.

and Luke 4:1–13, there are fascinating parallels and variations, relating to each of the three—about bread, spectacular signs, and authority.

In Matthew and Luke, the connection of the temptations of Jesus with Moses is through the wilderness setting, the forty days and nights of Moses fasting alone on Mount Sinai, and Jesus quoting Moses (Deut. 8:3; 6:13, 16). "One does not live by bread alone but by every word that comes from the mouth of God" (Matt. 4:4; cf. Luke 4:4; Deut. 8:3) might be a text for the whole of John 6, with Jesus himself as both the bread and the word of God, and the repeated emphasis on his relationship to his Father corresponding to the devil's repeated "If you are the Son of God . . ." (Matt. 4:3, 6; Luke 4:3, 9).

When the crowd says to Jesus, "What sign are you going to give us then, so that we may see it and believe you?" (6:30)—a question that seems strange after the feeding, but perhaps emphasizes how quiet, ordinary, and ephemeral it seemed—there is an echo of the temptation to do something impressively dramatic to prove who he is, like throwing himself off the pinnacle of the temple in Jerusalem.

But the explicit temptation in John 6 is to kingship, just as in Matthew and Luke Jesus is offered "authority" over "all the kingdoms of the world" (Matt. 4:8–9; Luke 4:5–6). There will be more about Jesus as king in John 18–19, and that will be prepared for especially in John 13.

Here, Jesus **withdrew** [*anachōrein*] **again to the mountain by himself** [*monos*], again inviting comparison with Moses. In the Septuagint, Moses too is "alone" (*monos*), not only on the mountain for forty days and nights (Exod. 24:2), but also alone in carrying the weight of responsibility for the whole people (Num. 11:14). Matthew and Mark, in their versions of the sea crossing, speak of Jesus being alone, but John emphasizes the parallels with Moses by having the sea crossing at the end of the feeding. It also suggests, as do the temptations in the Synoptics, the importance of solitude.

Thomas Brodie suggests that Jesus sitting on the mountain with his disciples in 6:3 is "carefully coordinated" with Jesus alone on the mountain in 6:15, his solidarity with the community of his disciples, "who had some sense of their weakness," contrasted with his resistance to "strong-arm king-making" attempts to force him to conform to popular expectations.[6] Steven Hunt comments, "Brodie's explanation, while quite unprovable, works well in conjunction with an author like John who superimposes deep spiritual and theological significance on details that would normally be considered mundane and unworthy of careful deliberation."[7]

6. Brodie, *The Gospel according to John*, 264.
7. Hunt, *Rewriting the Feeding of the Five Thousand*, 279.

Hunt's own masterly analysis of John 6:1–15 convincingly bears out this description of John. Hunt shows, in ways far more numerous than can be detailed here, how this passage is worth such "careful deliberation," especially in its resonances with the Septuagint and all the Synoptics. His study concludes that John not only was steeped in the Septuagint but also "had read (and assiduously studied) all three of the Synoptic Gospels. And this is an old-fashioned position indeed."[8] It is a position that the present commentary also takes.

The withdrawal of Jesus here is in line with what Mark Stibbe calls the theme of "the elusive Christ" in John.[9] The verb translated as "withdraw," *anachōrein* (which Matthew uses before the feeding [Matt. 14:12]), is the origin of the word "anchorite." Anchorites (such as the fourteenth-century Mother Julian of Norwich) are part of a tradition of living a largely solitary life, and there are fresh forms of it being lived today in many countries. Such shapes of living raise deep questions about belonging, conformity, and resistance to social and political pressures.

For readers working out how to live in relation simultaneously to the realms of Jesus and of the Roman emperor (or any other political, cultural, and religious setting), there is no specific ethical or political guidance in this chapter. Rather, we find a focus on who Jesus is, an encouragement to fresh reading, thinking, and imagining, an invitation into the abundance, challenges, testing, and growth in discernment involved in following Jesus, and an encouragement to value solitude when under pressure. It is striking that where John does use the word "tempt" or "test" (v. 6: *peirazein*), it is Jesus who is testing his disciple.

Second Drama: Sea Crossing—"It Is I; Do Not Be Afraid" (6:16–21)

It is not clear why the disciples sail away in the dark without Jesus, but once they do, and meet rough weather, Jesus comes to them. His appearance walking on the sea is a terrifying surprise, met by the further surprise of what he says.

> 16 When evening came, his disciples went down to the sea, 17 got into a boat,
> and started across the sea to Capernaum. It was now dark, and Jesus had
> not yet come to them. 18 The sea became rough because a strong wind was
> blowing. 19 When they had rowed about three or four miles, they saw Jesus

8. Hunt, *Rewriting the Feeding of the Five Thousand*, 283.

9. Stibbe sees a shift after the healing on the Sabbath in 5:1–15. The danger of being killed means that "from this point onwards, Jesus is evasive and secretive. His actions and movements are those of the hidden Messiah. His dialogue is characterized by a discontinuity which utterly mystifies his listeners" (*John*, 83).

walking on the sea and coming near the boat, and they were terrified. [20] But he said to them, "It is I; do not be afraid." [21] Then they wanted to take him into the boat, and immediately the boat reached the land toward which they were going.

Whereas Moses led his people through the Red Sea on dry land, Jesus brings his disciples to **the land toward which they were going** by walking on water—something that the Scriptures reserve for God alone. The Septuagint version of Job 9:8 has God walking on the sea, using the same Greek words as here. Isaiah 51, a passage promising a second exodus, affirming God's mastery of the sea and its storms and promising deliverance from fear, speaks of God as the one "who made the depths of the sea a way for the redeemed to cross over" (v. 10), and then reassures the people with a repeated "I am, I am the one who comforts you" (LXX v. 12: *egō eimi egō eimi ho parakalōn se* [the Greek for "comforts" is later taken up by John as a term for the Holy Spirit]).[10] As with Jesus's reply to the Samaritan woman, "I am he" (4:26), the same words, *egō eimi*, here translated as **"It is I,"** can mean that, or can be the self-identification of God, as in Exodus 3:14 and many passages in Isaiah. John takes up the Synoptic use of it in the sea crossing but makes clearer than they do that this is identifying Jesus with God. In this chapter it recurs in the "I am" statements by Jesus (6:35, 48, 51).

So Jesus here is acting with the freedom of God, just as after his resurrection he appears in spite of locked doors. He is also acting with the compassion of God, bringing comfort. Yet there is, too, as with the quantity and quality of wine at Cana and the twelve baskets left over after the feeding, a sense of something more than necessary. There has been no indication of the boat being in danger of sinking—the fear is a response to seeing Jesus walking on the water. This sign is gratuitous, an intimate revelation to the disciples of who Jesus is. They are not in control, Jesus is free to go (as he had been in going up the mountain) and come in his own surprising ways, and the vital truth, however dark and unsettled the situation and whether he is physically absent or present, is who he is.

The discourse that follows goes deeper into this. The response of the disciples to the words of Jesus is that **they wanted to take him into the boat**. This gives the crucial clue to their later receptivity to the "difficult teaching" (v. 60) that Jesus gives. The verb for "take" (*lambanein*) is a favorite of John for receiving and believing in Jesus, beginning with 1:12 and 1:16,[11] and their openness to him

10. See comments on 14:15–17.

11. See also especially 13:20; 20:22.

is shown in their desire, what they "wanted." *The sign has achieved its purpose in surprising them, arousing their desire, and further opening them up to who Jesus is.*

First Course: Believing in Jesus Is the One Basic Work God Wants (6:22–29)

The crowd, by contrast, is **looking for Jesus**, but he sees them as fixated on their desire for **food that perishes**. Jesus's concern for the education of desire began with his opening words to the first disciples, "What are you looking for?" (1:38).

This chapter continues that education and also pursues further the other two related seminal questions that John 1 places at the heart of the learning community around Jesus: "Who are you?" and "Where are you staying/abiding?"[12] The "courses" of teaching that follow in verses 25–58 advance in stages and are best understood as a dialogue sermon, as suggested by verse 59: "He said these things while he was teaching in the synagogue at Capernaum." Synagogue services at the time had readings from Torah (the first five books of the Bible) and the Prophets and prayer through Psalms. Here the Torah text, from Exodus 16:4, 15, is given by the crowd: "He gave them bread from heaven to eat" (John 6:31); Isaiah 54:9–55:5 is the text from the Prophets, which is quoted in John 6:45 (Isa. 54:13) and also alluded to several times; and in addition Psalm 78:24 is echoed.[13] So, growing out of the feeding and the sea crossing, which themselves have many scriptural echoes and also improvise on all three Synoptic Gospels, this discourse is a rich interweaving of Torah, Prophets, and Psalms, together with further Synoptic allusions, all combined in surprising teaching in dialogue with the crowd. It is teaching that encourages reflective rereading of many texts, while still, as will emerge, having a pivotal center in verse 35: "Jesus said to them, 'I am the bread of life. Whoever comes to me will never be hungry, and whoever believes in me will never be thirsty.'"

This first course is on the basic requirement for learners who are open to Jesus, are willing to undergo a reorientation and deepening of desire, and are ready for a permanent commitment. All those elements are embraced in John's use of *pisteuein*—listening to Jesus, believing in him, trusting him, and long-term involvement with him.

> 22 The next day the crowd that had stayed on the other side of the sea saw that there had been only one boat there. They also saw that Jesus had not

12. See comments on 1:19–51.

13. For a fuller account of how synagogue practice is reflected here, see Lincoln, *The Gospel according to Saint John*, 223–25.

got into the boat with his disciples, but that his disciples had gone away alone. [23] Then some boats from Tiberias came near the place where they had eaten the bread after the Lord had given thanks. [24] So when the crowd saw that neither Jesus nor his disciples were there, they themselves got into the boats and went to Capernaum looking for Jesus.

[25] When they found him on the other side of the sea, they said to him, "Rabbi, when did you come here?" [26] Jesus answered them, "Very truly, I tell you, you are looking for me, not because you saw signs, but because you ate your fill of the loaves. [27] Do not work for the food that perishes, but for the food that endures for eternal life, which the Son of Man will give you. For it is on him that God the Father has set his seal." [28] Then they said to him, "What must we do to perform the works of God?" [29] Jesus answered them, "This is the work of God, that you believe in him whom he has sent."

Jesus answers his own core question, "What are you looking for?" (1:38), not their question. He says that they had seen the feeding not as a sign but simply as satisfying their hunger. Where should their energies be focused? Jesus tells them, **"Do not work for the food that perishes, but for the food that endures for eternal life, which the Son of Man will give you. For it is on him that God the Father has set his seal."** That is a minisummary of John's Gospel through the imagery of food. It includes answers to the three seminal questions in John 1: what to desire and work for;[14] what abides/endures/remains/stays;[15] and who Jesus is, "the Son of Man," the only title Jesus gives himself in John 1. The future tense here, "will give," points ahead to the climactic self-giving of Jesus in his death, in line with the later future tense: "The bread that I will give for the life of the world is my flesh" (v. 51).

This concentrated verse 27 also evokes, through the imagery of sealing—"on him . . . God the Father has set his seal"—the climactic affirmation of the prologue: "the only Son, who is close to the Father's heart" (1:18). A seal was a mark of authority, validating something or someone as trustworthy, authentic, to be believed.

Then comes the basic question, **"What must we do to perform the works of God?"** and the surprising answer, **"This is the work of God, that you believe in him whom he has sent."** The relationship between faith and works was very controversial in the early church, as reflected in Paul's Letters, and disputes

14. Later, in the pivotal v. 35, another basic food-related image of desire, being "thirsty," is introduced.

15. The verb translated as "endures" in v. 27 is *menein* in Greek, which is translated in 1:32, 33 as "remain," in 1:38 as "stay," and elsewhere, including in v. 56 below and in the parable of the vine (or vineyard) in John 15, as "abide."

about it have often recurred, above all in the Reformation. The issues at stake go to the heart of Christian faith and life. Here Jesus refuses any simple distinction, let alone competition, between faith and works. He redefines faith as the one basic "work of God." The phrase can mean either "the work God wants done" or "the work God himself does." That is a noncompetitive double meaning typical of John.

It is also profound theology. It resists putting divine action and human action on the same level. It recognizes the radical initiative of God, who sent Jesus. He is a gift of abundant grace to whom the only appropriate response is radical receptivity: "From his fullness we have all received, grace upon grace" (1:16). Believing in him is therefore a "passive action," well symbolized by being given food to eat. Believers have had no part to play in sending Jesus, any more than they have been in any way responsible for their own creation or birth. There is a mystery about why some believe and others do not (see further below), but it is not solved by giving autonomous agency, independent of God, to the believer. Believers know that the response to God's grace is sheer gratitude, without any claim to having done anything to deserve it, again, any more than they did anything to bring about their own creation or birth. Yet God's initiative does not do away with human freedom, but rather intensifies it. Human freedom increases in direct proportion to human involvement with God in trust and love, because God created freedom, and it is fulfilled through trust in its Creator.

So John's response to the controversy about faith and works is the radical priority of faith, that relationship of trust through which are received the grace, freedom, energy, inspiration, truth, love, and superabundant life, which of course overflow in works of many sorts, above all works of love. The deepest secret of this union of faith and works is union with Jesus in the mutual indwelling/abiding that is first introduced in John 6 and most profoundly opened up in John 13–17.

Second Course: "I Am the Bread of Life" (6:30–40)

Now comes the second course, centered on the pivotal verse of the whole sermon dialogue: **Jesus said to them, "I am the bread of life. Whoever comes to me will never be hungry, and whoever believes in me will never be thirsty."**[16] That reaches back to the bread of the feeding, to the "I am" of the sea crossing,

16. For a perceptive analysis of how this verse is pivotal with regard to vocabulary, style, literary structure, intertextuality, imagery, and theology, see Maritz and Van Belle, "The Imagery of Eating and Drinking in John 6:35." Their study, together with other literary and theological approaches, shows the coherence of John 6 in ways that avoid the need to ascribe its elements to various authors or editors with different theologies. As Maritz and Van Belle say, "The chapter . . . is composed creatively to form an impressive unit" (p. 334).

and to the first course's food that endures for eternal life and the work of God as believing in Jesus. It reaches forward to the reiterated themes of believing, bread, life, and Jesus in the third and fourth courses, and to the addition of drinking to eating, which intensifies the concentration on desire, being hungry reinforced by being thirsty.

> [30] So they said to him, "What sign are you going to give us then, so that we may see it and believe you? What work are you performing? [31] Our ancestors ate the manna in the wilderness; as it is written, 'He gave them bread from heaven to eat.'" [32] Then Jesus said to them, "Very truly, I tell you, it was not Moses who gave you the bread from heaven, but it is my Father who gives you the true bread from heaven. [33] For the bread of God is that which comes down from heaven and gives life to the world." [34] They said to him, "Sir, give us this bread always."
>
> [35] Jesus said to them, "I am the bread of life. Whoever comes to me will never be hungry, and whoever believes in me will never be thirsty. [36] But I said to you that you have seen me and yet do not believe. [37] Everything that the Father gives me will come to me, and anyone who comes to me I will never drive away; [38] for I have come down from heaven, not to do my own will, but the will of him who sent me. [39] And this is the will of him who sent me, that I should lose nothing of all that he has given me, but raise it up on the last day. [40] This is indeed the will of my Father, that all who see the Son and believe in him may have eternal life; and I will raise them up on the last day."

The crowd asks for a sign in line with the gift of manna to the people of Israel in the wilderness, which was given not just once but continually over forty years. First, Jesus interprets the text given by the crowd by emphasizing who gave the manna, **my Father**; and he then identifies what is given as **the true bread from heaven** and **the bread of God . . . which comes down from heaven and gives life to the world**. There was a long tradition of seeing both wisdom and Torah (the law, and the associated way of living and worshiping before God within a covenantal relationship) as bread, food, life-giving nourishment, a feast given by God.

So Jesus has broadened the significance of **manna** and **bread**, opening up the horizon of God and all God gives, within which to introduce the pivotal verse 35. The crowd fails to pick up on the wider reference and asks for a continual supply of manna. This closely parallels the misunderstanding of the Samaritan woman when, after Jesus has spoken of giving "a spring of water gushing up to eternal life," she says, "Sir, give me this water, so that I may never be thirsty or have to keep coming here to draw water" (4:14–15). John is teaching his readers to imagine, think, and desire at different levels simultaneously, uniting **heaven** and **the world** as Jesus does.

That union is then dramatically expressed by Jesus: **"I am the bread of life."** This is the "I am" of God, in line with the prologue. *This is not only ultimate reality but the One who is to be desired utterly.* He relativizes all other realities and desires. There is no necessary conflict or competition with them, as this chapter shows: Jesus does literally feed people; but they do not live by bread alone. The abundance of the feeding both is good in itself and points to the permanent abundance of eternal life. The reality of Jesus and what he gives is to be desired above all.

There is a deep resonance here with the teaching of Jesus in the Synoptic Gospels on desire: "Therefore I tell you, do not worry about your life, what you will eat, or about your body, what you will wear. For life is more than food, and the body more than clothing. . . . And do not keep striving for what you are to eat and what you are to drink, and do not keep worrying. For it is the nations of the world that strive after all these things, and your Father knows that you need them. Instead, strive for his kingdom, and these things will be given to you as well" (Luke 12:22–23, 29–31 [cf. Matt. 6:25–34]). The Greek here for "strive" is *zētein*—also one of John's key words—meaning "seek, desire, search for, look for, want, expect, examine, investigate." John 6 has those Synoptic themes of not being afraid, eating and drinking, the noncompetition between desire for the things of God and other natural desires, and the overwhelming priority of God.

But John does two distinctive further things. The "I am" focuses on who Jesus is; and (as John has taught readers through the story of Nicodemus) the kingdom is understood in terms of life. Jesus refuses to be made king and presents himself and the life he gives as the goal of desire.

There is a further, vital dimension of desire here too: the desire of Jesus himself, in line with the desire of his Father. Jesus longs for people to come to him and trust him. His ministry is centrally one of attraction, drawing people to himself through giving signs of abundant life. Rejection of him leads to the ultimate sign of his attractive love, his crucifixion: "I, when I am lifted up from the earth, will draw all people to myself" (12:32). In all this he is sent by his Father in love for the world (3:16) and is at one with his Father in speaking, willing, doing the truth, giving life, and loving.

In this second course, the mystery of who responds and who does not is raised sharply. This has been a matter of great controversy within Christianity. Does the present passage suggest that, on the one hand, the Father chooses some for salvation and **gives** them to Jesus, who works and dies to make sure none of them is lost; but that, on the other hand, there are those whom the Father does not choose for salvation? That deterministic view of God's activity, classically called "double predestination"—God consigning some to salvation, some to damnation—has been held by many Christians and has also been energetically rejected by many, and John has been used to back both positions. The question is discussed further elsewhere in this commentary,[17] but as regards this passage two points can be made.

First, the thrust of this chapter is that of a promise with an appeal to respond. Verse 35 is a promise to anyone who gets hungry or thirsty that Jesus can satisfy their desires beyond their wildest dreams. There is, as often in John, an openness in the **whoever . . . whoever . . . anyone . . . all who**. Yet, second, there is nothing inevitable about the response, there is a radical challenge involved, and the chapter culminates with Jesus asking even his closest followers, the Twelve, "Do you also wish to go away?" (v. 67).

As always, one has to think of this being written for readers who also face such challenges. There would be little point in writing the Gospel if all were predetermined. Instead, the ongoing drama of God's love for the world, and of the world's response, is still being played out. We are given no overview of the outcome. Rather, we are invited to stay with Jesus and not "go away," and there is much we are not given knowledge about—we are even encouraged to be agnostic about a great deal, especially the relationship of Jesus to others (e.g., 21:20–23).

Third Course: All Taught by God; "My Flesh" Given for the Life of the World (6:41–51)

What Francis Moloney calls "an intensifying concentration on the person of Jesus" continues.[18] The complaining of the people recalls not only their complaints about nothing to drink in Exodus 15, nothing to eat in Exodus 16, and again nothing to drink in Exodus 17, but also the God-centered lesson, "Your complaining is not against us [Moses and Aaron] but against the Lord" (Exod. 16:8), the basic question being, "Is the Lord among us or not?" (Exod. 17:7). This course emphatically repeats key elements of the first two and ends with a surprise further "dish."

> 41 Then the Jews began to complain about him because he said, "I am the
> bread that came down from heaven." 42 They were saying, "Is not this Jesus,
> the son of Joseph, whose father and mother we know? How can he now
> say, 'I have come down from heaven'?" 43 Jesus answered them, "Do not

17. Briefly on John 3 above; more fully below on John 9.
18. Moloney, *The Gospel of John*, 219.

> complain among yourselves. 44 No one can come to me unless drawn by the
> Father who sent me; and I will raise that person up on the last day. 45 It is
> written in the prophets, 'And they shall all be taught by God.' Everyone who
> has heard and learned from the Father comes to me. 46 Not that anyone has
> seen the Father except the one who is from God; he has seen the Father.
> 47 Very truly, I tell you, whoever believes has eternal life. 48 I am the bread
> of life. 49 Your ancestors ate the manna in the wilderness, and they died.
> 50 This is the bread that comes down from heaven, so that one may eat of it
> and not die. 51 I am the living bread that came down from heaven. Whoever
> eats of this bread will live forever; and the bread that I will give for the life
> of the world is my flesh."

The rejection of Jesus based on familiarity with his family origins (also a Synoptic theme: Matt. 13:53–58; Mark 6:1–6) leads Jesus to talk of his ultimate origin, his Father. There is no more a contradiction between his human and divine origins, since God is free to express himself in human form, than there is between the freedom of those who **come to me** and the fact that they are also being **drawn by the Father who sent me**. This divine initiative enabling a human response is then further understood through the relationship of teacher and taught: **And they shall all be taught by God**. This refers to Isaiah 54:13, and, beyond that, "allusions to the larger context of Isaiah 54–55 seem to be presupposed in the rest of the discourse."[19] Isaiah is making a passionate appeal for the people to respond. He has confidence that the abundance of God's mercy, together with the mystery of God's thoughts and ways being higher than those of the people, will mean that, like rain and snow making the earth fruitful, so with "my word that goes out from my mouth; . . . it shall accomplish that which I purpose, and succeed in the thing for which I sent it" (Isa. 55:11).

"Everyone who has heard and learned from the Father comes to me." As in Isaiah, Jesus's whole purpose is for God to be listened to, learned from, trusted, and believed; and John's Gospel serves this pedagogy, above all through the drama of the person of the Word of God made flesh (1:14). It is that flesh which is now introduced in a surprising promise.

"Whoever eats of this bread will live forever; and the bread that I will give for the life of the world is my flesh." This introduces the identification of bread with flesh that is intensified to the point of shocking scandal in the

19. Keener, *The Gospel of John*, 1:686. He goes on to comment: "That Jesus appears as the 'teacher' from God par excellence in this Gospel is significant (3:2; 6:59; 7:14, 28, 35; 8:20; 18:20); Jesus learned from the Father (8:28; cf. 7:15–17; cf. 8:26, 40) and the Spirit would continue Jesus's ministry (14:26; cf. Luke 12:12; 1 Cor 2:13)."

following section. Some commentators have seen this as a later addition, inserted to connect with the church's eucharistic practice but not fitting well with the rest of the discourse. *I am more convinced by those who see the whole chapter carefully crafted, not only to connect with that core practice but also to broaden and deepen it.*

Assuming that John knew the Synoptic Gospels, we might wonder why he omitted the institution of the Eucharist at the Last Supper, to which he gives far more space in John 13–17 than do the Synoptic Gospels. There are many plausible reasons, best illustrated by the effects of what he does.

John 6 connects eucharistic language, so familiar to his readers, with his own core themes: who Jesus is; the gift of abundant, eternal life; and believing and abiding in Jesus. In particular, he sharpens and deepens the prologue's central affirmation that the Word became flesh. John 6 does this, not in the Last Supper context of a small group of disciples (though that is where this chapter culminates, explicitly looking ahead to that meal by mentioning the betrayal by Judas) but through the event of feeding many thousands of people abundantly. So the horizon of this eucharistic practice is an open "whoever . . . "; its orientation is toward "the life of the world" that needs both literal bread and the Word of God.

At the same time, the replacement of the institution of the Eucharist by Jesus washing his disciples' feet in John 13 sets up a continually fruitful twin focus. It stimulates those who know the Synoptics to reflect repeatedly on how Eucharist and footwashing relate to each other. *How might sharing in the bread and wine of the Eucharist be related to practical, loving service? How might a community of practical service be rooted in remembering Jesus through worship, celebration, and teaching? In that community, does the exercise of power and authority ring true with Jesus washing feet?* These and many other rich questions are inspired by John setting the footwashing alongside the Synoptic institution of the Last Supper; and John 6, where there is the most complete convergence between the Synoptics and John, offers in its discourse a theology that holds the two together through their focus on the person of Jesus and the event of the crucifixion in which his "flesh" is given "for the life of the world."

Fourth Course: True Food, True Drink, and Mutual Abiding (6:52–59)

This is a shocking text. The identification just made, of the "flesh" of Jesus with "the living bread that came down from heaven" that must be eaten in order to have life, is uncompromisingly repeated and intensified through the addition of drinking his blood. The crowd (called "the Jews" since v. 41) asks the obvious question about how this might happen. Is it cannibalism? Not only does the crowd find this hard to take, but, as the following section shows, so do many of his disciples (v. 60). As always, John's primary concern is with readers and rereaders: What might this mean for them?

> 52 The Jews then disputed among themselves, saying, "How can this man
> give us his flesh to eat?" 53 So Jesus said to them, "Very truly, I tell you, un-
> less you eat the flesh of the Son of Man and drink his blood, you have no
> life in you. 54 Those who eat my flesh and drink my blood have eternal life,
> and I will raise them up on the last day; 55 for my flesh is true food and my
> blood is true drink. 56 Those who eat my flesh and drink my blood abide in
> me, and I in them. 57 Just as the living Father sent me, and I live because of
> the Father, so whoever eats me will live because of me. 58 This is the bread
> that came down from heaven, not like that which your ancestors ate, and
> they died. But the one who eats this bread will live forever." 59 He said these
> things while he was teaching in the synagogue at Capernaum.

For readers and rereaders, John gives vital indicators of how to come to terms with the scandalous talk of **whoever eats me**. But coming to terms with it does not lessen the mind-blowing, shocking magnitude of what is being said. On the contrary, the **true** meaning is about taking part in a reality that goes beyond normal conceptions even more comprehensively than cannibalism violates social and religious norms. Later, in the pivotal verses 61–63, the full horizon of meaning will be laid out, within which "the flesh" alone "is useless"—but the scandal will remain: "Many of his disciples turned back" (v. 66).

There are no less than four key indicators here of other levels of meaning. First is the eating and drinking of the Eucharist. There is dispute among commentators on this, but the connection is obvious for those who think that John knew the Synoptic Gospels. That does not end the disputes, which became especially sharp at the time of the Reformation. Is the bread and wine of the Mass "really" transubstantiated into the body and blood of Christ? At the other extreme, are the bread and wine simply signs to stimulate remembering him in faith through the Spirit? Much hangs on how verse 63 is understood, but John cannot adjudicate such later issues. His contribution is to focus on who Jesus Christ is, whatever the understanding of the bread and wine. The "I am" of Jesus, affirming him to be present as God is present, is a reminder of what most of the Protestant, Anglican, and Catholic positions shared: *despite their differences over the "real presence" of Jesus Christ in the Eucharist, none affirmed his "real absence."* Another shared focus in the Eucharist is on death and resurrection, and both are also concerns of this discourse.

Second, **My flesh is true food and my blood is true drink** parallels other uses of "true" and "truth" in John. Relevant here are his later statements, "I am the way, and the truth, and the life" (14:6), and "I am the true vine" (15:1). These again open up meanings beyond the literal and point to who Jesus is. In particular, the nonliteral understanding of food has been encouraged by Jesus: "My food is to do the will of him who sent me and to complete his work" (4:34). Such a meaning of "true food" prepares the sensitive reader for verse 63.

The third indicator is that this is the first time a key idea is introduced: **"Those who eat my flesh and drink my blood abide in me, and I in them."** "Abide" is one of John's most important words, and he has already used it, but not so far to speak of mutual indwelling. This use will climax in John 15, the parable of the vine, where its meaning is explained by "My words abide in you" and "Abide in my love" (15:7, 9). This again prepares for verse 63.

Fourth, there is the most comprehensive statement of all: **"Just as the living Father sent me, and I live because of the Father, so whoever eats me will live because of me."** The sending of Jesus by the Father covers the whole of Jesus's life, death, and resurrection, and then, by a parallel "as . . . so . . ." statement, covers the whole ongoing drama in which disciples live in the Spirit: "'As the Father sent me, so I send you.' When he had said this, he breathed on them and said to them, 'Receive the Holy Spirit'" (20:21–22). This is yet another pointer to verse 63. And as Birger Olsson says, the description of God as "the

> One particular Johannine description of God that is unique both in the Bible and in contemporary Judaism as we now know it is the saying "the living Father." . . . The word "Father" in a Johannine context directs the reader's thoughts immediately to the Son. According to this verse, the divine life permeates the Father and the Son and the one who is united with the Son. Jesus gives the believer a part in God's own life. We might formulate a new Johannine statement about God, "God is life," and exposit it in the same way as "God is light," "God is spirit," and "God is love." This would provide an understanding of the unusual Johannine expression, "the living Father." The underlying expression "the living God" recalls the personal God of the Old Testament who is active in human life. The word "Father" points to the consequences of the incarnation in the Johannine view of God. The end of 1 John maintains God's transcendence, speaking of "the true God," but casts the spotlight rather on the Son and says, "He is true God and eternal life." The one who believes in his name has eternal life here and now. God's immanence, not only his transcendence, is maximised in the Johannine writings. *Deus semper maior* (*God always greater*).
>
> —Birger Olsson, "*Deus semper maior?*," 170–71

living Father" is unique in the Bible and the Judaism of John's time (see the quotation from Olsson in the sidebar).

Third Drama: Difficult *Logos*; Words, Spirit, and Life; Desertion and Betrayal (6:60–71)

All the drama between Jesus and others in John's Gospel is framed by a wider, postresurrection perspective. This perspective begins with the prologue, continues with 2:22, and is explicit or implied at many other points. Here, faced with complaints from his disciples, the perspective is given by Jesus: **"Then what if you were to see the Son of Man ascending to where he was before?"** From this vantage point (which readers are invited to share), Jesus speaks the pivotal verse 63.

> [60] When many of his disciples heard it, they said, "This teaching is difficult; who can accept it?" [61] But Jesus, being aware that his disciples were complaining about it, said to them, "Does this offend you? [62] Then what if you were to see the Son of Man ascending to where he was before? [63] It is the spirit that gives life; the flesh is useless. The words that I have spoken to you are spirit and life. [64] But among you there are some who do not believe." For Jesus knew from the first who were the ones that did not believe, and who was the one that would betray him. [65] And he said, "For this reason I have told you that no one can come to me unless it is granted by the Father."
>
> [66] Because of this many of his disciples turned back and no longer went about with him. [67] So Jesus asked the twelve, "Do you also wish to go away?" [68] Simon Peter answered him, "Lord, to whom can we go? You have the words of eternal life. [69] We have come to believe and know that you are the Holy One of God." [70] Jesus answered them, "Did I not choose you, the twelve? Yet one of you is a devil." [71] He was speaking of Judas son of Simon Iscariot, for he, though one of the twelve, was going to betray him.

The theological culmination of the chapter is verse 63. This is underlined by its association with believing: **Among you there are some who do not believe** (see also the rest of that verse); and by Peter repeating its key elements (**the words** of Jesus and **life**), before making a fundamental declaration of believing in who Jesus is: **"You are the Holy One of God."** "For the first time in the narrative a character has expressed faith in Jesus for the right reason, *his origins*. The holiness of Jesus comes from the fact that he is *of God*."[20]

20. Moloney, *The Gospel of John*, 229 (italics original).

For readers of the prologue, and rereaders of the whole Gospel, to speak of the difficulty of **this teaching** (the Greek for "teaching" being *logos*, as in 1:1, 14) and then to speak of **flesh** is to acknowledge the difficulty of who Jesus is, the astonishing "teaching" that he is "the Word of God" who "became flesh and lived among us," and of the whole Gospel about him, above all his crucifixion and resurrection. For readers of the Synoptics, there is a clear parallel with the climactic acknowledgment of Jesus by Peter at Caesarea Philippi, followed soon after by the difficult teaching (there resisted by Peter) about the suffering, rejection, death, and resurrection of Jesus (Matt. 16:13–23; Mark 8:27–33; Luke 9:18–22).

It is the spirit that gives life; the flesh is useless could be taken as contradicting, or at least in tension with, the earlier imperative of eating the flesh of Jesus in order to have life. It is better understood as graphic insistence on the need to hold together the different levels, the flesh *alone* being useless. The multileveled understanding is if anything more surprising, and it can be appreciated only from the later standpoint of the resurrection and the giving by Jesus of the Holy Spirit. I am taking it that in responding to his own question, **"Does this offend you?"** with the further question, **"Then what if you were to see the Son of Man ascending to where he was before?"** Jesus is suggesting that the offense would be increased.

That would match the Synoptic stress, not only on Peter being offended at the suffering, rejection, death, and resurrection of Jesus, but also on the different levels ("For you are setting your mind not on divine things but on human things" [Mark 8:33]) and on seeing "the Son of Man" in the future ("Those who are ashamed of me and of my words in this adulterous and sinful generation, of them the Son of Man will also be ashamed when he comes in the glory of his Father with the holy angels" [Mark 8:38]).

The decisive statement is, **"The words that I have spoken to you are spirit and life."** That gives a vital insight into the whole Gospel of John and the purpose for which its author wrote it. It brings together the "I" of Jesus with three deeply interrelated realities: words, spirit (or Spirit), and life. They have already come together earlier: "He whom God has sent speaks the words of God, for he gives the Spirit without measure. . . . Whoever believes in the Son has eternal life" (3:34–36). The Farewell Discourses bring together in even richer ways the words of Jesus, the Spirit, and life, and will be opened up later.

For now, it is worth reflecting on what might be happening through reading this Gospel. In receiving through this text the words of Jesus, readers can receive what gives spirit (Spirit) and life. The measurelessness of the Spirit and the abundance of life are here identified with the richness of meaning; and these are embodied in Jesus, who invites those who trust in him to share in all three, receiving "from his fullness . . . grace upon grace" (1:16). *So access to that abundance of meaning, Spirit, and life is opened up by reading this text.*

Whatever the larger perspective, John never loses a sense of the fallibility and fragility of human life and the possibility that even those apparently most fully committed and reliable might disappoint. For rereaders, the strong statement by Peter ironically contrasts with his later denial of Jesus. For first-time readers, the desertion of Jesus by many disciples and the prediction of betrayal by Judas heighten the drama of decision-making in the face of Jesus, as dark clouds gather. And there is a vulnerability in Jesus's question: **"Do you also wish to go away?"**

John 7:1–52

Danger and Division, Identity and Desire

The scene now shifts from Galilee to Jerusalem, where Jesus is in increasing danger and at the center of controversy. When he decides the time is right, during the festival of Booths, he gives astonishing teaching and cries out his message in the temple. He polarizes people: Is he a "good man," or is he "deceiving the crowd" (v. 12)? Antagonism intensifies: "'You have a demon!'" (v. 20); "The chief priests and Pharisees sent temple police to arrest him" (v. 32). But some are on his side: "Many in the crowd believed in him. . . . 'This is really the prophet.' . . . 'This is the Messiah'" (vv. 31, 40, 41). Even the authorities and their agents are not united in opposing him: the temple police are unexpectedly impressed—"Never has anyone spoken like this!" (v. 46)—and Nicodemus stands up for due legal process.

At the heart of the drama is the question of the identity of Jesus and the life he gives, provoking diverse responses and especially challenging those he encounters about what they really want. The language of desire—wishing, wanting, looking for, trying to, seeking, resolving, and searching—reaches its climax in this chapter. One of John's favorite words, *zētein*, which was first used in the first words of Jesus in 1:38, occurs in verses 1, 4, 11, 18 (twice), 19, 20, 25, 30, 34, and 36. In addition, *thelein* is in verses 1 ("wish"), 17 ("resolve"), and 44 ("want"), and *eraunan* is in verse 52, meaning "search, examine, inquire, try to find out." Above all, there is the cry of Jesus, using a key Johannine image of desire: "Let anyone who is thirsty come to me, and let the one who believes in me drink" (vv. 37–38).

That cry, uniting belief in Jesus with reference to the Spirit to be given later, distills the double thrust of the desire of Jesus according to this Gospel: that readers might trust and know who he is and might live glorifying God, inspired by the Spirit. It is a desire that culminates in his own cry on the cross, "I am thirsty!" (19:28).

In John 7 that desire is in dramatic contrast and conflict with a range of others, all of them still powerful today. There is the desire of Jesus's brothers for popularity and public success, concerned with what Jesus should do if he "wants to be widely known" (v. 4), and the associated conflict for Jesus between pleasing his family and pleasing God. There is the conflict between seeking God's glory and one's own. Jesus provokes revealing responses, showing what people most value: educational background ("He has never been taught" [v. 15]); "appearances" (v. 24); family or geographical origin (vv. 27, 41–42); or being part of a higher class or an inner circle that feels superior to "this crowd, which does not know the law—they are accursed" (v. 49).

This continuing education of desire is further enriched by reminders of earlier chapters and anticipations of later ones and also by the continuing parallels and contrasts with Moses. And the setting is very important: Jesus, who has already been identified with the temple (2:19–22) and with quenching thirst (4:7–15; 6:35), is in the temple, that focus of Israel's desire for God and worship of God, taking part in a festival of great joy, whose central imagery is of water and light (the light is to come soon in John 8).

Jesus, His Brothers, and the Festival of Booths (7:1–13)

From 7:1 until 10:21 the celebration of the Feast of Tabernacles, or **festival of Booths**, now often known by its Hebrew name, Succoth or Sukkot (meaning "booths" or "shelters"), is the background of John's story. This was the most popular and joyful of the three feasts that brought pilgrims to Jerusalem. It was associated with harvest and also with the exodus from Egypt: "Now, the fifteenth day of the seventh month,[1] when you have gathered in the produce of the land, you shall keep the festival of the Lord, lasting seven days; a complete rest on the first day, and a complete rest on the eighth day. On the first day you shall take the fruit of majestic trees, branches of palm trees, boughs of leafy trees, and willows of the brook; and you shall rejoice before the Lord your God for seven days. . . . You shall live in booths for seven days . . . so that your generations may know that I made the people of Israel live in booths when I brought

1. This was in September-October.

them out of the land of Egypt: I am the Lord your God" (Lev. 23:39–43). It included a water-pouring ceremony with singing and trumpet blasts and prayer for abundant rain, and by the time of Jesus the water was associated with the gift of Torah, the law and way of living given through Moses. There was also a ceremony of light with dancing, lasting most of the night for seven nights, the light also being associated with Torah. And at dawn each day the priests, after processing to the east gate of the temple area, faced away from the rising sun toward the temple and proclaimed that, while some of their ancestors had worshiped the sun (see Ezek. 8:16), "our eyes are turned towards the Lord."[2]

> 1 After this Jesus went about in Galilee. He did not wish to go about in
> Judea because the Jews were looking for an opportunity to kill him. 2 Now
> the Jewish festival of Booths was near. 3 So his brothers said to him, "Leave
> here and go to Judea so that your disciples also may see the works you
> are doing; 4 for no one who wants to be widely known acts in secret. If you
> do these things, show yourself to the world." 5 (For not even his brothers
> believed in him.) 6 Jesus said to them, "My time has not yet come, but your
> time is always here. 7 The world cannot hate you, but it hates me because I
> testify against it that its works are evil. 8 Go to the festival yourselves. I am
> not going to this festival, for my time has not yet fully come." 9 After saying
> this, he remained in Galilee.
>
> 10 But after his brothers had gone to the festival, then he also went, not
> publicly but as it were in secret. 11 The Jews were looking for him at the
> festival and saying, "Where is he?" 12 And there was considerable complain-
> ing about him among the crowds. While some were saying, "He is a good
> man," others were saying, "No, he is deceiving the crowd." 13 Yet no one
> would speak openly about him for fear of the Jews.

There are some puzzling aspects of this passage, such as Jesus's apparent change of mind. Yet three things seem clear.

One is the climate of danger, threat, division, fear, and hatred, contrasting with the atmosphere of the festival. This continues through the following chapters.

Another is the freedom of Jesus, and therefore often his elusiveness and unpredictability, and alternations between openness and hiddenness. He has his own agenda, timing, and priorities, a mission that is about good confronting evil. He reveals the truth about a world gone wrong, he provokes murderous hatred in those exposed by the light of his message, and he polarizes the

2. See Moloney, *The Gospel of John*, 232–36.

commentators. Time can, on the one hand, be seen as part of a God-centered drama heading to a significant future, with urgencies, critical turning points, and vital decisions en route; or, on the other hand, it can be undifferentiated, without fundamental meaning or purpose, just more of the same—**your time** [*kairos*] **is always here.** Jesus freely takes initiatives to advance the drama.

The third point is the relationship with his brothers. They had appeared briefly in 2:12 after the wedding at Cana. There they accompanied his mother and his disciples, both of whom believed in Jesus, but nothing was said about the brothers. Now a contrast is drawn: they are described negatively, as not believing in him, and as being on the side of **the world.** It is a theme in the Synoptics too: being in Jesus's natural family is no guarantee of being with him in his mission. There is a wider implication for John's readers: it may be necessary to resist the pressures exerted by your family if you are to follow Jesus. You have a new, primary, God-centered, "family" identity. As the prologue says, "To all who received him, who believed in his name, he gave power to become children of God, who were born, not of blood or of the will of the flesh or of the will of man, but of God" (1:12–13). The problem with his brothers seems to be that they are tempting him to be successful through spectacular signs, without the basic, essential element of recognizing and believing in who Jesus is.

In verses 11–13 the conflicting verdicts on Jesus set up alternatives for readers' responses too, and the atmosphere of intimidation and threats probably rang true for many of John's first readers, as it has for many more since.

Beyond Appearances: God's Teaching, God's Glory, the Whole Person Made Healthy (7:14–24)

Midway through the festival Jesus goes public with astonishing teaching. We are not told what the teaching is—the Synoptics give plenty of examples of surprising teaching by Jesus, as does John elsewhere, but here John goes behind the teaching to its source in God. **Do not judge by appearances, but judge with right judgment** is a fundamental concern of John. He takes a postresurrection standpoint, as announced in his first two chapters, in order to draw readers into underlying truth. Key elements in that truth are given here: **God** as the source of the **teaching** of Jesus; the connection between recognizing this and being committed to doing **the will of God**—some sorts of knowing can happen only through trusting and being in a committed relationship; Jesus as **the one who . . . is true** because he **seeks the glory of him who sent him**; and (in an important statement whose meaning is not caught by the NRSV translation here) the sign of this glory is a **whole** person made fully alive. *The latter two* *elements, desiring to glorify God and desiring the full flourishing of people, are the secret of healthy desire.*

> [14] About the middle of the festival Jesus went up into the temple and began to teach. [15] The Jews were astonished at it, saying, "How does this man have such learning, when he has never been taught?" [16] Then Jesus answered them, "My teaching is not mine but his who sent me. [17] Anyone who resolves to do the will of God will know whether the teaching is from God or whether I am speaking on my own. [18] Those who speak on their own seek their own glory; but the one who seeks the glory of him who sent him is true, and there is nothing false in him.
>
> [19] "Did not Moses give you the law? Yet none of you keeps the law. Why are you looking for an opportunity to kill me?" [20] The crowd answered, "You have a demon! Who is trying to kill you?" [21] Jesus answered them, "I performed one work, and all of you are astonished. [22] Moses gave you circumcision (it is, of course, not from Moses, but from the patriarchs), and you circumcise a man on the sabbath. [23] If a man receives circumcision on the sabbath in order that the law of Moses may not be broken, are you angry with me because I healed a man's whole body on the sabbath? [24] Do not judge by appearances, but judge with right judgment."

Jesus moves from speaking of himself seeking God's glory to reflecting on the earlier healing of the lame man on the Sabbath in John 5. The connection between **glory** and **sign** is suggested by John's programmatic statement after the wedding in Cana: "Jesus did this, the first of his signs, in Cana of Galilee, and revealed his glory" (2:11).[3] But now, in relation to the lame man, there is a further dimension. The glory of Jesus and, inseparably, the glory of God are seen in what happened in that healing. A literal translation of the last part of verse 23 is "because I made [or "created," *epoiēsa*][4] a whole person [or "human being"] healthy [*holon anthrōpon hygiē*] on the sabbath." The NRSV is misleading in using **man**, because *anthrōpos* embraces man and woman,[5] and it is even more misleading to speak of **body** when this is about the whole human being.

3. See the section "The Drama: The Puzzle, the Sign/Miracle, and Two Lessons" in the comments on 2:1–12.

4. The verb is the one used in the Septuagint in Gen. 1:1, 7, 16, 21, 25, and, of special significance, 26 and 27, where it is about the creation of the human being (*anthrōpos*) in the image and likeness of God.

5. Though it can also mean, as in v. 22, a "male"—that here makes the NRSV translation understandable.

Anthrōpos, "human being," is a key word in John, used over fifty times. Like some other words, such as "seek" (*zētein*), "stay/abide" (*menein*), or "make/do/create" (*poiein*), it can be used both in ordinary ways and also filled with John's special meaning, with further meaning emerging through rereading not only John but also the Septuagint and the rest of the New Testament. Here, the resonances reach back to creation (including the Sabbath), through all the signs Jesus does, and forward to his trial, crucifixion, and resurrection. For John, it is Jesus who is the true *anthrōpos*: the whole human being, the bread of life, the resurrection and the life, the source of living water, and more.[6]

The Double Cry: "I Am from Him!" "Come and Drink!" (7:25–52)

The focus moves on from the origin of Jesus's teaching to the origin and identity of Jesus himself. Who is Jesus? Amid speculation about the geographical origins of the Messiah (or Christ), and whether Jesus is the Messiah, **Jesus cried out as he was teaching in the temple.** His core statement identifying himself points to his origin in God. *The answer to the question about where he is from is who he is from: **"The one who sent me is true. . . . I am from him."***

As with his origin, so with his future: the vital issue is not geographical destination—**"Does he intend to go to the Dispersion among the Greeks and teach the Greeks?"**—rather, it is the "who" question, **"I am going to him who sent me."** The problem is, **"You will search for me, but you will not find me; and where I am, you cannot come."**

The response to that comes on the **last day of the festival, the great day,** when Jesus again **cried out.** It is an invitation to a person-to-person encounter in receptivity and trust: **"Let anyone who is thirsty come to me, and let the one who believes in me drink."** But this invitation is given a new dimension by the evangelist's postresurrection perspective. He looks ahead to the giving of **the Spirit**, opening up the horizon of an ongoing dynamic of superabundant, generously shared life: **"Out of the believer's heart shall flow rivers of living water."**

Yet the natural imagery of overflowing abundance is immediately given a reality check: **There was a division in the crowd because of him.** The rest of the chapter describes conflicting responses to him, contradictory interpretations of Scripture, and hardening hostility toward him by the authorities.

6. *Anthrōpos* in the singular is, crucially, used both of every created human being (1:9) and of Jesus himself. He is the *ho huios tou anthrōpou*, usually translated as "the Son of Man," but literally as "the Son of the Human Being" (1:51; 3:13–14; 5:27; 6:27, 53, 62; 8:28; 9:35; 12:23–34; 13:31), and this title is often used in relation to his crucifixion, which John especially associates with glory. Jesus is also simply called an *anthrōpos* (4:29; 9:11; 10:33; 11:47, 50; 18:14, 17, 29); and, climactically, Pilate proclaims, "Here is the man!" (19:5: *ide anthrōpos*).

25 Now some of the people of Jerusalem were saying, "Is not this the man whom they are trying to kill? 26 And here he is, speaking openly, but they say nothing to him! Can it be that the authorities really know that this is the Messiah? 27 Yet we know where this man is from; but when the Messiah comes, no one will know where he is from." 28 Then Jesus cried out as he was teaching in the temple, "You know me, and you know where I am from. I have not come on my own. But the one who sent me is true, and you do not know him. 29 I know him, because I am from him, and he sent me." 30 Then they tried to arrest him, but no one laid hands on him, because his hour had not yet come. 31 Yet many in the crowd believed in him and were saying, "When the Messiah comes, will he do more signs than this man has done?"

32 The Pharisees heard the crowd muttering such things about him, and the chief priests and Pharisees sent temple police to arrest him. 33 Jesus then said, "I will be with you a little while longer, and then I am going to him who sent me. 34 You will search for me, but you will not find me; and where I am, you cannot come." 35 The Jews said to one another, "Where does this man intend to go that we will not find him? Does he intend to go to the Dispersion among the Greeks and teach the Greeks? 36 What does he mean by saying, 'You will search for me and you will not find me' and 'Where I am, you cannot come'?"

37 On the last day of the festival, the great day, while Jesus was standing there, he cried out, "Let anyone who is thirsty come to me, 38 and let the one who believes in me drink. As the scripture has said, 'Out of the believer's heart shall flow rivers of living water.'" 39 Now he said this about the Spirit, which believers in him were to receive; for as yet there was no Spirit, because Jesus was not yet glorified.

40 When they heard these words, some in the crowd said, "This is really the prophet." 41 Others said, "This is the Messiah." But some asked, "Surely the Messiah does not come from Galilee, does he? 42 Has not the scripture said that the Messiah is descended from David and comes from Bethlehem, the village where David lived?" 43 So there was a division in the crowd because of him. 44 Some of them wanted to arrest him, but no one laid hands on him.

45 Then the temple police went back to the chief priests and Pharisees, who asked them, "Why did you not arrest him?" 46 The police answered, "Never has anyone spoken like this!" 47 Then the Pharisees replied, "Surely you have not been deceived too, have you? 48 Has any one of the authorities or of the Pharisees believed in him? 49 But this crowd, which does not know the law—they are accursed." 50 Nicodemus, who had gone to Jesus before, and who was one of them, asked, 51 "Our law does not judge people without first giving them a hearing to find out what they are doing, does it?" 52 They

> replied, "Surely you are not also from Galilee, are you? Search and you will see that no prophet is to arise from Galilee."

The two cries of Jesus carry us further into answering the two questions in John 1: "Who are you?" and "What are you looking for?" They correspond in classical Christian theology to the double concern with the "person" and "work" of Jesus Christ. John opens up one dimension after another of who Jesus is, and one dimension after another of his work in shaping and fulfilling people's deepest desires, his coming so that "they may have life, and have it abundantly" (10:10).

Here, as the darkness deepens—signaled by confusion and **division**, threats to **kill** Jesus and attempts **to arrest him**, false or misleading claims to knowledge, conflicting desires and values, and riddling speech of Jesus that can be understood only retrospectively—themes of earlier chapters are repeated in the new situation and so take on fresh meaning. Besides further answering those two key questions of John 1, in John 7 the prologue's statement that "the world did not know him" and "his own people did not accept him" is being played out further, as are its concerns with life, glory, believing, truth, Moses, and the relationship of Father and Son.

Within that horizon, John 7 is a fresh interweaving of themes from John 2–6: the drinking at Cana, followed by the Jerusalem festival, the temple, and the postresurrection perspective of chapter 2; chapter 3 on Nicodemus, water and Spirit, astonishing teaching, eternal life, and judgment; chapter 4 on thirst, drinking, water, eternal life, healing, and believing; chapter 5 on healing, the Father-Son relationship, searching the Scriptures, glory, and Moses; and chapter 6 on signs, Moses, the origins of Jesus, drinking, teaching, believing, and eternal life. John is continuing to teach in waves, both using repetition, which allows attentive readers to be grasped more fully by earlier themes, and introducing fresh dimensions of those themes as new events happen.

Likewise, John 7 anticipates later developments, with the continuing enrichment of those themes already mentioned, and above all looking ahead to the climactic **hour** of the arrest, trial, death ("I am thirsty" [19:28]), and resurrection of Jesus, and his handing over (19:30) and breathing (20:22) of the Spirit.

The deepening here is through the interplay of at least four elements: Jesus and his Father; the Festival of Booths in the temple; seeking/searching/desiring; and the giving of the Spirit as living water to believers.

So, first, the reader's world of meaning is being centered, as it is repeatedly through the Gospel, in the reality that culminates the prologue: "God the only Son, who is close to the Father's heart." Here there is an emphasis on the knowledge of Jesus within that relationship: **"I know him, because I am from**

him, and he sent me." Knowing is a fascinating, multidimensional theme in this Gospel, whose pedagogy is aimed at drawing readers into an ongoing process of knowing as Jesus knows. It is a knowing inseparable from loving, as Jesus says in the Farewell Discourses: "I do not call you servants any longer, because the servant does not know what the master is doing; but I have called you friends, because I have made known to you everything that I have heard from my Father" (15:15).

Second, the drama of the life of Jesus is being interwoven with the festivals, the Scriptures, and the central building of his people in their relationship with God. The understanding of readers is therefore being shaped and reshaped through learning what the temple, the Scriptures, and the festivals mean, and through exploring further dimensions of that meaning in relation to Jesus.

For example, one rich source of meaning (among very many others) that resonates deeply with the temple and the Festival of Booths is Ezekiel 47. This has already been evoked by the references to water, worship, and Spirit in John 4. The present passage stimulates rereading Ezekiel 47. There the water flowing from the temple gets deeper and deeper: "ankle-deep . . . knee-deep . . . up to the waist . . . deep enough to swim in" (vv. 3–5); it brings abundant life: "a great many trees . . . very many fish . . . of a great many kinds . . . all kinds of trees for food. Their leaves will not wither nor their fruit fail, but they will bear fresh fruit every month, because the water for them flows from the sanctuary" (vv. 7–12); and this brings health and wholeness: "their leaves for healing" (v. 12 [in the Septuagint the Greek word for "healing" is *hygieia*, like *hygiē* in John 7:23, referring back to 5:6, 9, 11, 14, 15]). Once Jesus is identified with the temple, and the water with the Spirit, this vision of abundance takes on new dimensions, and in the New Testament these culminate in the book of Revelation's vision of the new Jerusalem, where Jesus is on the throne and promises, "To the thirsty I will give water as a gift from the spring of the water of life" (Rev. 21:6). The final scene improvises on the Ezekiel vision: "Then the angel showed me the river of the water of life, bright as crystal, flowing from the throne of God and of the Lamb through the middle of the street of the city. On either side of the river is the tree of life with its twelve kinds of fruit, producing its fruit each month; and the leaves of the tree are for the healing of the nations" (Rev. 22:1–2).

Third, readers are being drawn into the complex dynamics of that drama and encouraged to ask questions, face alternatives, and reorient their core desires. Entering into this drama, which is lived within a horizon of God (who is inseparable from Jesus the Lamb of God) and the healing of the nations, can become a continuing exercise in searching for Jesus, coming to know him better, swimming in the river of the water of life, and tasting the abundance of life with its twelve kinds of fruit. The Scriptures of Israel and the rest of the New Testament are the first place to search. If John is writing for readers who know the Synoptic Gospels, the Acts of the Apostles, and Paul's Letters, the present passage will stimulate further reflection on his origins, his birth in Bethlehem, his messiahship, and the later mission to the Greeks and other gentiles.

Fourth, the ongoing postresurrection drama of following Jesus opens up a future in which Jesus gives and believers receive **the Spirit**. The second cry of Jesus, **"Let anyone who is thirsty come to me, and let the one who believes in me drink. As the scripture has said, 'Out of the believer's heart shall flow rivers of living water,'"** is a scholarly challenge. There is no Scripture exactly matching the quotation, and the Greek literally says, "out of his belly shall flow," which could refer to Jesus rather than the believer. If forced to choose, I would, with the NRSV, take it as referring to the believer—the more surprising meaning.

But why choose? The vagueness (of both the quotation and "his") invites the reader to think down more than one path of meaning, and these are not mutually exclusive. The quotation seems like a composite of more than one text, or a midrash on one or more. Possibilities include: Nehemiah 9:15, 20; Psalms 78:16, 20; 114:8; Isaiah 12:3; 43:20; 44:3; 58:11; Ezekiel 47:1–2; Joel 2:28; 3:18; Zechariah 14:8–9.

If the water flows from Jesus, that connects with him being the source of the Spirit and water flowing from his side after his death. If it flows from the believer, that connects with what has already been said in 4:14: "The water that I will give will become in them a spring of water gushing up to eternal life." That in fact contains both possible meanings of 7:38b: Jesus giving the water and believers becoming, in turn, a source. This strong, daring idea of believers in succession to Jesus receiving his Spirit, so as to carry on doing what he did, is in line with the promises of the Farewell Discourses in John 13–17 and with the commissioning of the disciples as they receive the Holy Spirit: "As the Father has sent me, so I send you" (20:21). And for believers there is the fundamental simplicity of thirsting, wanting, desiring (see the quotation from Bruner in the sidebar).

> Christ himself, and all alone, offered this sacrifice, and so he can rightly offer his gift to whomever he wants, and we learn from this text that simply *wanting* the gift, "*thirsting*" for it, is all that Jesus asks in requirement.
>
> —Frederick Dale Bruner, *The Gospel of John*, 491

Conclusion

This chapter has been a maelstrom of desires and values in conflict around the identity of Jesus, with life-or-death implications for him. His hearers and John's readers are being faced with a radical challenge, which the next chapter will intensify.

John 8:1–59

A Drama of Bitterly Contested Identities

The drama moves forward into even more bitter dispute, leading to the verge of violence: "So they picked up stones to throw at him" (v. 59).

The central issue is the identity of Jesus: "Who are you?" (v. 25); "Who do you claim to be?" (v. 53). This is heightened by a series of further "I am" statements by Jesus, relating who he is to light: "I am the light of the world" (v. 12); to sin and believing: "You will die in your sins unless you believe that I am he" (v. 24); to his own death: "When you have lifted up the Son of Man, then you will realize that I am he" (v. 28); and finally to Abraham, an astonishing move that sets the drama within the horizon of God and God's time and provokes violence: "Very truly, I tell you, before Abraham was, I am" (v. 58).

Throughout, who Jesus is is inseparable from his Father: "It is not I alone who judge, but I and the Father who sent me" (v. 16; cf. vv. 18–19); "The one who sent me is true, and I declare to the world what I have heard from him. . . . And the one who sent me is with me" (vv. 26, 29); "I declare what I have seen in the Father's presence" (v. 38). *So the identity of Jesus is utterly relational, both with God and through involvement with the world and its people to the point of death.*

For readers who know the postresurrection perspective of the prologue, chapter 8 enriches key themes of light, darkness, life, testimony, the relationship of Father and Son, believing, truth, children, seeing, sending, glory, word, knowing, and time in relation to God.[1] The enrichment for the readers comes

1. "Before Abraham was, I am" could be read as filling out the statement by John the Baptist in the prologue when he says, "He who comes after me ranks ahead of me because he was before me" (1:15).

particularly through the interplay in them of believing in Jesus, being made free by knowing the truth, loving Jesus, and keeping his word.

But, perhaps most of all, this chapter dramatizes the prologue's statement, "He came to what was his own, and his own people did not accept him" (1:11). The climax of that rejection is to come in chapters 18 and 19 in the arrest, trial, and condemnation of Jesus. Chapter 8 is the rhetorical climax. It is theological polemics at its most intense, with Jesus telling his opponents, "You are from your father the devil" (v. 44) and "You are not from God" (v. 47), and them replying, "Now we know that you have a demon" (v. 52). *It raises acute questions both about Jesus and what it means to "accept him," and also about the appalling historical aftermath of such polemics in Christian treatment and persecution of Jews.* The discussion that follows will try not only to be open to the light of what is being taught to readers about Jesus and life lived following him but also to find some way through the darkness of theological polemics fueling violence.

But before plunging into the controversy, we must first look at the story of Jesus and the woman caught in adultery.

A Woman Caught in Adultery; All Caught in Sin; Hope and Challenge for All (7:53–8:11)

This story is not in the most reliable early manuscripts of the Gospel of John, and very likely was not part of the Gospel as read during at least the first century of its transmission. It is also found in some manuscripts of the Gospel of Luke after Luke 21:38, and its Greek style is more like Luke's than John's. John 7:52 connects very well with John 8:12, and this story interrupts the flow. Yet, as C. K. Barrett says, "It is probably ancient," and "It represents the character and method of Jesus as they are revealed elsewhere."[2] There is also a theological connection with 8:15, where Jesus says, "I judge no one." E. C. Hoskyns and F. N. Davey conclude, "The story was current in very early days, as an authentic episode in the ministry of Jesus. . . . Consequently this episode requires serious attention and a careful commentary."[3]

> [7:53] Then each of them went home, [1] while Jesus went to the Mount of Olives.
> [8:2] Early in the morning he came again to the temple. All the people came
> to him and he sat down and began to teach them. [3] The scribes and the
> Pharisees brought a woman who had been caught in adultery; and making
> her stand before all of them, [4] they said to him, "Teacher, this woman was

2. Barrett, *The Gospel according to St. John*, 589–90.
3. Hoskyns and Davey, *The Fourth Gospel*, 566.

> caught in the very act of committing adultery. [5] Now in the law Moses commanded us to stone such women. Now what do you say?" [6] They said this to test him, so that they might have some charge to bring against him. Jesus bent down and wrote with his finger on the ground. [7] When they kept on questioning him, he straightened up and said to them, "Let anyone among you who is without sin be the first to throw a stone at her." [8] And once again he bent down and wrote on the ground. [9] When they heard it, they went away, one by one, beginning with the elders; and Jesus was left alone with the woman standing before him. [10] Jesus straightened up and said to her, "Woman, where are they? Has no one condemned you?" [11] She said, "No one, sir." And Jesus said, "Neither do I condemn you. Go your way, and from now on do not sin again."

This is an attempt to test and trap Jesus, not a genuine inquiry. The dilemma in which he is placed is either to agree the woman should be stoned or to teach that the law should be broken. But the dilemma may be even sharper. Under Roman rule, only the Romans could exercise the death sentence, so Jesus might be being asked to agree to oppose the Romans or oppose the law of Moses. It is a dilemma similar to that in the Gospel of Mark about whether or not to pay taxes to Caesar (Mark 12:13–17). As in that case, Jesus acts so as to move the issue to another level, changing the terms of the engagement and posing a dilemma to his interrogators. *Questioning Jesus leads to the questioners being questioned in a way that transforms the very terms of inquiry.*

Jesus first pauses the exchange by bending down and writing on the ground. There is much speculation about what he might have been writing, just as there is about other aspects of this story, such as why there is no mention of the man with whom the woman was committing adultery. But the story gives no hint of answers. Jesus takes charge of the pace of the drama, slowing it down, refusing to play it the way his opponents want, his silence allowing tension to build.

When they persist in questioning, his response tests them: **"Let anyone among you who is without sin be the first to throw a stone at her."** That not only strikes at the heart of their purpose in bringing her to him; it challenges all of them and readers to radical self-examination as regards habits of blame, judgment, condemnation, and punishment. Its impact is like Jesus's sayings in the Sermon on the Mount: "Do not judge, so that you may not be judged. For with the judgment you make you will be judged, and the measure you give will be the measure you get. Why do you see the speck in your neighbor's eye, but do not notice the log in your own eye? Or how can you say to your neighbor, 'Let me take the speck out of your eye,' while the log is in your own eye? You hypocrite, first take the log out of your own eye, and then you will see clearly to take the speck out of your neighbor's eye" (Matt. 7:1–5). Hypocrisy is exactly what is at stake here: concern for justice as a cover for trapping Jesus. There can be no "us-them" divide when it comes to sin: all are caught in it, and accusing others of it without recognizing our solidarity in sin leads us deeper into it.

But what is the solution? Jesus condemns neither the woman's accusers nor the woman herself. He sets the accusers on the challenging path of self-examination—truth is always essential in any serious attempt to deal with sin.

Then, in a second dramatic pause, he bends down again and writes. When they withdraw, he goes further with the woman.[4] The fact and seriousness of her adultery are taken for granted, but a challenging alternative to condemnation and death is opened up: **"Go your way, and from now on do not sin again."** She is given a fresh start, freed from her past to begin again. But is this a realistic command—not to sin again? What is her way likely to be? And, most fundamentally of all, who is Jesus to release her from condemnation and tell her not to sin again?

Such questions lead beyond this story. If it is read in the context of the rest of the Gospel of John, the headline statement about sin is that of John the Baptist about Jesus in chapter 1: "Here is the Lamb of God who takes away the sin of the world!" (1:29). The right question is not *what* but *who* is the solution to sin; and "the world," as the scene of the sin that is taken away, embraces here both the accusers and the woman. The rest of chapter 8, in line with the core thrust of the whole Gospel of John, intensifies concentration on the "who" of Jesus.

John also intensifies, more than the Synoptic Gospels do, the importance of Jesus encountering, "who to who," each individual—as in the fresh start of new birth into which Nicodemus is invited in chapter 3, the water of eternal life given to the Samaritan woman in chapter 4, and the meeting with Peter in chapter 21 when, after Peter's denial of him, the risen Jesus reestablishes a relationship of love with Peter and gives him a challenging command and forecast. For any individual's future with regard to sin, the essentials are continuing trust in Jesus, abiding in Jesus, following Jesus, receiving from him the Holy Spirit who animates continuing discernment regarding sin and forgiveness in the community (20:22), and ever-renewed obedience to the new commandment to love as Jesus has loved (13:34). Each person's sin—rather than leading to broken relationships with God, other people, and oneself, to

4. The NRSV says **Jesus was left alone with the woman standing before him**, but the Greek for "before him" is *en mesō* (literally, "in middle"), the same phrase translated in v. 3 as "before all of them." The more likely meaning is that Jesus was left alone without the accusers but with the woman, and the crowd still there as audience of this drama—there would be no reason for them to go away and every reason to stay till the end.

guilt, shame, fear, addiction, loss of meaning and purpose, or worse—can be faced with Jesus.

Recognition of the need for repeated self-examination, confession, and forgiveness in a community whose embracing reality is abiding "in the Son and in the Father" (1 John 2:24) is clear in the First Letter of John. With many scholars, I see this letter addressing a community that is trying to live according to the Gospel of John, meets the inevitable problem of repeated sin, and affirms both that "the blood of Jesus his Son cleanses us from all sin" and that "if we say that we have no sin, we deceive ourselves, and the truth is not in us. If we confess our sins, he who is faithful and just will forgive us our sins and cleanse us from all unrighteousness. . . . My little children, I am writing these things to you so that you may not sin. But if anyone does sin, we have an advocate with the Father, Jesus Christ the righteous; and he is the atoning sacrifice for our sins, and not for ours only but also for the sins of the whole world. Now by this we may be sure that we know him, if we obey his commandments" (1 John 1:7–2:3).

There we find the same combination of truthfully facing sin, a challenging summons to trust and obey Jesus, and the embracing reality of who Jesus is and what he has done for "the whole world."

Light and Darkness: To the Heart of the Gospel and the Heart of Darkness (8:12–59)

> 12 Again Jesus spoke to them, saying, "I am the light of the world. Whoever
> follows me will never walk in darkness but will have the light of life." 13 Then
> the Pharisees said to him, "You are testifying on your own behalf; your testi-
> mony is not valid." 14 Jesus answered, "Even if I testify on my own behalf, my
> testimony is valid because I know where I have come from and where I am
> going, but you do not know where I come from or where I am going. 15 You
> judge by human standards; I judge no one. 16 Yet even if I do judge, my judg-
> ment is valid; for it is not I alone who judge, but I and the Father who sent
> me. 17 In your law it is written that the testimony of two witnesses is valid.
> 18 I testify on my own behalf, and the Father who sent me testifies on my
> behalf." 19 Then they said to him, "Where is your Father?" Jesus answered,
> "You know neither me nor my Father. If you knew me, you would know my
> Father also." 20 He spoke these words while he was teaching in the treasury
> of the temple, but no one arrested him, because his hour had not yet come.
>
> 21 Again he said to them, "I am going away, and you will search for me,
> but you will die in your sin. Where I am going, you cannot come." 22 Then
> the Jews said, "Is he going to kill himself? Is that what he means by saying,

'Where I am going, you cannot come'?" 23 He said to them, "You are from below, I am from above; you are of this world, I am not of this world. 24 I told you that you would die in your sins, for you will die in your sins unless you believe that I am he." 25 They said to him, "Who are you?" Jesus said to them, "Why do I speak to you at all? 26 I have much to say about you and much to condemn; but the one who sent me is true, and I declare to the world what I have heard from him." 27 They did not understand that he was speaking to them about the Father. 28 So Jesus said, "When you have lifted up the Son of Man, then you will realize that I am he, and that I do nothing on my own, but I speak these things as the Father instructed me. 29 And the one who sent me is with me; he has not left me alone, for I always do what is pleasing to him." 30 As he was saying these things, many believed in him.

31 Then Jesus said to the Jews who had believed in him, "If you continue in my word, you are truly my disciples; 32 and you will know the truth, and the truth will make you free." 33 They answered him, "We are descendants of Abraham and have never been slaves to anyone. What do you mean by saying, 'You will be made free'?"

34 Jesus answered them, "Very truly, I tell you, everyone who commits sin is a slave to sin. 35 The slave does not have a permanent place in the household; the son has a place there forever. 36 So if the Son makes you free, you will be free indeed. 37 I know that you are descendants of Abraham; yet you look for an opportunity to kill me, because there is no place in you for my word. 38 I declare what I have seen in the Father's presence; as for you, you should do what you have heard from the Father."

39 They answered him, "Abraham is our father." Jesus said to them, "If you were Abraham's children, you would be doing what Abraham did, 40 but now you are trying to kill me, a man who has told you the truth that I heard from God. This is not what Abraham did. 41 You are indeed doing what your father does." They said to him, "We are not illegitimate children; we have one father, God himself." 42 Jesus said to them, "If God were your Father, you would love me, for I came from God and now I am here. I did not come on my own, but he sent me. 43 Why do you not understand what I say? It is because you cannot accept my word. 44 You are from your father the devil, and you choose to do your father's desires. He was a murderer from the beginning and does not stand in the truth, because there is no truth in him. When he lies, he speaks according to his own nature, for he is a liar and the father of lies. 45 But because I tell the truth, you do not believe me. 46 Which of you convicts me of sin? If I tell the truth, why do you not believe me? 47 Whoever is from God hears the words of God. The reason you do not hear them is that you are not from God."

[48] The Jews answered him, "Are we not right in saying that you are a
Samaritan and have a demon?" [49] Jesus answered, "I do not have a demon;
but I honor my Father, and you dishonor me. [50] Yet I do not seek my own
glory; there is one who seeks it and he is the judge. [51] Very truly, I tell you,
whoever keeps my word will never see death." [52] The Jews said to him, "Now
we know that you have a demon. Abraham died, and so did the prophets;
yet you say, 'Whoever keeps my word will never taste death.' [53] Are you
greater than our father Abraham, who died? The prophets also died. Who
do you claim to be?" [54] Jesus answered, "If I glorify myself, my glory is nothing. It is my Father who glorifies me, he of whom you say, 'He is our God,'
[55] though you do not know him. But I know him; if I would say that I do not
know him, I would be a liar like you. But I do know him and I keep his word.
[56] Your ancestor Abraham rejoiced that he would see my day; he saw it and
was glad." [57] Then the Jews said to him, "You are not yet fifty years old, and
have you seen Abraham?" [58] Jesus said to them, "Very truly, I tell you, before
Abraham was, I am." [59] So they picked up stones to throw at him, but Jesus
hid himself and went out of the temple.

extraordinary discomfort
messiness
darkness
death
hiddenness
blindness and self-deception
difficulty
exclusion
extreme provocation
immense obstinacy
destructive argument
pessimism about humanity
the grimness of the world
handling dynamite
painful judgment
murderous hatred
demonizing the other
religious violence

This is just a selection of the language I once jotted down during a symposium on John 8:12–59. Yet at the same time there was the language of light, life, love, freedom, truth, goodness, glory, and joy.

I will take two journeys in what follows: the first tries to be open to the intensity of a light that is vital to knowing and living the journey that John wants his readers to take; the second attempts to face the darkness of the journey that many readers have actually taken, as seen in the way this text has been used by Christians against Jews. Then will come the crucial question: How do we respond to all this now?

The First Journey: Following Jesus, the Light of the World

The journey into the light is partly about meaning, seeing, knowing, and truth, but overwhelmingly about living in freedom, following, loving, and actually keeping the word of Jesus. *Those two dimensions, meaning and living, or cognition and action, are interwoven all through the chapter and are integrated through believing, trusting, and rejoicing in Jesus.*

The keynote is given by Jesus: **"I am the light of the world. Whoever follows me will never walk in darkness but will have the light of life."** The sun is the literal light of the world, a symbol that unites perfectly both dimensions: we need it to see and we need it to live. It is also unique, a singularity in our experience that also relates to the whole world. Jesus is claiming such singularity and universality. That has radical consequences both for our world of meaning and for our living, and this chapter provocatively poses the challenge to both, as the next two sections explore. But first it is worth reflecting on Jesus as "the light of the world."

Jesus here is still taking part in the Festival of Booths, with its celebration of light and its ritual of turning away from the sun in order to affirm worship of the God of Israel.[5] In the festival, both light and water were identified with Torah, Israel's whole God-given way of life. So for Jesus to say "I am the light of the world" identifies him both with God and with Torah and the rest of Scripture. Within the rest of John's Gospel, where this "I am" is supplemented by others, the identification is intensified: the absolute "I am" points directly to God, as in 8:58, and the others, such as "I am the bread of life" (6:35) or "I am the way, and the truth, and the life" (14:6), point to the personal embodiment of Torah and God's Word.

When this declaration is read alongside the Synoptic Gospels, the most striking parallel is with the story of the transfiguration of Jesus, where Matthew even says, "And he was transfigured before them, and his face shone like the sun, and his clothes became dazzling white" (Matt. 17:2). There Jesus speaks with Moses, representing Torah, and Elijah, representing the word of God through the prophets, and is affirmed by the divine voice: "This is my Son, the Beloved; with him I am well pleased; listen to him!" (Matt. 17:5). Within the Orthodox Christian tradition, where the transfiguration—in icons, liturgy, theology, and practices of prayer—is especially celebrated, the biblical Festival of Booths is identified with the Feast of the Transfiguration, so bringing John and the Synoptics into interplay. One practice of contemplative prayer, hesychasm, centers on the uncreated light, the light of the transfiguration. The Johannine tradition, on light as on love, draws out the theological implications of the Synoptics with

5. Discussed above on John 7:1–13.

a decisive directness. The Gospel of John's "I am the light of the world" is followed through, in the First Letter of John, with "God is light and in him is no darkness at all" (1 John 1:5).

Light is an endlessly rich symbol, both in the Bible and in most cultures and religions, and it is also fascinating scientifically. Just as John's use of *logos*, "Word," in the prologue, connects Jesus with all of Scripture and with the whole of created reality,[6] so his use of "light," both in the prologue and here, has the same scope of Jesus in relation to God, Scripture, all life, and all things. Theology, spirituality, and the arts continue to revel in the abundance of insights into Jesus as light and the connections that these can generate across fields of discourse, cultures, and religions. But one does not have to think on that scale. Reflecting on light in our ordinary lives gives rich material for understanding how Jesus can be our light: locating where we are; keeping things in perspective; seeing people and situations in the light of love; recognizing dangers and ways forward; moving with confidence; finding our way; enjoying beauty; delighting in people; and much else.[7]

In John's terms, the results of both ordinary and more sophisticated thinking and imagining through the symbol of light can be found, through appropriate discernment, to be examples of being led further into truth (16:13). John 8 lays down the basic guideline for that process of discernment: that the primary emphasis is on the "I am" of Jesus. This means that both meaning and action are to be continually reflected upon in the light of who Jesus is, and the result for both is radical challenge.[8]

The Challenge to Common Sense and Worldviews. As we begin to trace the challenge to common sense meaning, the first shock is to the imagination, trying to conceive a person who is **the light of the world . . . the light of life**. The reader has been prepared for the shock since the very beginning through the most comprehensive meaning statement of all, "The Word was God" (1:1), followed soon after by "In him was life" that "was the light of all people" (1:4). Later chapters continue to stretch the imagination, as, for example, when Jesus speaks of his body as the temple (2:21) and of being "born" of a wind or Spirit that "blows where it chooses" (3:8), when he offers the Samaritan woman "a spring of water gushing up to eternal life" (4:14), and when he identifies himself as "the bread of life" (6:35). All this cannot fit within ordinary imagery and

6. See comments on 1:1–4.

7. But one must be careful not to imply that literal light and sight are necessary for all this—the blind, too, can follow Jesus.

8. A commentary on John that, as its title suggests, is especially concerned with this theme and prophetically poses the challenge of this Gospel to modern readers is that of Newbigin, *The Light Has Come*.

symbols; they are stretched to contain the uncontainable, the ultimate union of singularity and universality—the "Word" of God that "became flesh" (1:14).

But the characters in the drama of chapter 8 have not read the prologue. As so often in John, the meaning is given by Jesus saying things that make sense in terms of the prologue but are almost bound to be misunderstood by his interlocutors. The contrast sets up a learning situation for John's readers, and especially his rereaders. We, the rereaders, know how the story ends in crucifixion and resurrection, the giving of the Holy Spirit, and Thomas's "My Lord and my God!" (20:28). But we, like the characters in the drama, are also part of a world where such things are countercultural, shocking, and surprising. Our minds and imaginations need to be continually challenged, stretched, defamiliarized, reeducated, reopened to a reality that is endlessly rich and always surprising. It is about genuinely new news, something that can be known only through **testimony** (8:13, 14, 17). But our common sense—our habits of mind and the assumptions, beliefs, and ideas that have shaped us, what is here called judging **by human standards** (8:15) and later described with **There is no place in you for my word** (8:37)—inclines us to suspect, resist, distrust, and dismiss the news and its implications. *If the surprise does not fit within our framework, then either our framework changes or the surprise is rejected. Chapter 8 is a drama of rejection whose primary purpose is to confront readers with that decision.*

The decision is posed through a powerful set of images. First, there is *the natural imagery of light and darkness.* Then there is *the courtroom imagery of believing or not believing testimony.* Then comes the *theological and cosmic imagery of below and above*: **He said to them, "You are from below, I am from above; you are of this world, I am not of this world"** (8:23). Finally, there is the household and family imagery of being either a slave or a child in the family.

That accumulation of strong images, drawing on nature, law, cosmology, and blood relations, is interwoven with cognitive theological concepts that emphasize the decision facing readers. There is knowledge of the origin and destiny of Jesus: **"I know where I have come from and where I am going, but you do not know where I come from or where I am going"** (8:14). And there is knowledge of Jesus in relation to his Father: **"It is not I alone who judge, but I and the Father who sent me. . . . If you knew me, you would know my Father also. . . . I speak these things as the Father instructed me. . . . The one who sent me is with me. . . . I declare what I have seen in the Father's presence. . . . It is my Father who glorifies me, he of whom you say, 'He is our God'"** (8:16, 19, 28, 29, 38, 54).

Inseparable from that relationship are the "I am" statements of Jesus. The framework that is needed to comprehend these is nothing less than the God who is known in and through Jesus, together with not only the whole of created reality (**"I am the light of the world"**) and the whole Gospel story with its climax in the crucifixion (**"When you have lifted up the Son of Man, then you will realize that I am he"**)[9] but also the divine temporal horizon of time and eternity (**"Very truly, I tell you, before Abraham was, I am"**). That "then you will realize" acknowledges the postresurrection perspective that is needed to realize the scope of the identity of Jesus in relation to God, and also suggests that rereaders of the whole Gospel are the primary target of such statements. Any worldview that is not centered on this understanding of God will inevitably be challenged, and chapter 8 intensifies the cognitive challenge posed in the beginning by the prologue. Indeed, it can be read as a dramatic enactment of the interplay of elements of the prologue, including the rejection of Jesus by his own people and the final affirmation in 1:18 of the mind-blowing mystery. To know this mystery of "God the only Son, who is close to the Father's heart" is to recognize that we cannot comprehend it: "No one has ever seen God"; yet we need always to be open to more and more light, knowledge, and understanding: "From his fullness we have all received, grace upon grace" (1:16). Jesus as "the light of the world" offers that abundance to all, and the paradoxical challenge is that he seems too good, generous, and loving to be true.

The Challenge to a Way of Life and to Core Identity. So John tells his story in such a way that there is a radical cognitive challenge to common sense and worldview; there is also, inseparably, a radical practical challenge to any way of life and activity.

The imagery here includes following, walking, living as a free member of a household, dying in sin, honoring, and dishonoring. Those blend with concepts such as testifying, judging, doing what pleases God, continuing (abiding, remaining) in Jesus's word, loving, and seeking or giving glory. These are all filled out by later chapters, especially by the Farewell Discourses (chaps. 13–17), and that is where they will be explored further.

There is a progressive integration of knowing and living in this chapter. The early part, up to 8:20, majors on knowing; after that, knowing and living are interwoven. And at the heart of the integration is the question of identity. Here, as throughout the Gospel of John, who Jesus is, in his being ("I am") and also in his relationship to his Father and to the world, is the most radical challenge of all. *It is a challenge to any reader's worldview, way of living, and core identity in relation to God and other people.*

But a distinctive thing about chapter 8 is that here the focus is on the Jewish identity in which Jesus was brought up and the confrontation between him and

9. The language of glorifying in John also refers to the crucifixion and resurrection—see 12:27–28; 13:31–32; 17:1–5.

some fellow Jews. It has the hallmarks of a bitter family dispute exacerbated by religion, and it has had tragic consequences. How is it to be understood?

The Second Journey: Into Darkness, Slavery, Sin, Death, Dishonor, Lies, Murder—Jesus, the Jews, and the Believing Jews

What about the other side of this chapter, the language of darkness, slavery to sin, death, dishonor, lies, and murder? There has been considerable scholarly debate about whether John, above all in this chapter, is anti-Semitic (meaning hostility to Jews simply for being Jews) or anti-Jewish (meaning hostility to Jewish religion and religious Jews). Ruth Edwards surveys the literature and comes to what I find to be a well-supported set of conclusions.[10] The Jewish scholar Adele Reinhartz goes further in her analysis (and accompanies it with a helpful summary of the huge amount of literature on

> The Gospel's appropriation of Jewish symbols, ideas, and practices does not make the Gospel pro-Jewish or anti-Jewish. This move, however, can account for a pattern according to which the Gospel's fundamental framework is familiar to—because it is taken over from—Jewish practices and values at the same time as it promotes a separation from the group called the *ioudaioi*. . . . On one point there is general agreement: however one might read John's hostile comments about the *ioudaioi*, the Gospel is not anti-Semitic on "racial" or genealogical grounds. Rather, what is at stake is belief or non-belief in Jesus as the Messiah. Furthermore, the Gospel cannot be held responsible for later interpretations of passages such as 8:44, which became foundational for Christian anti-Semitism. At the same time, it is reasonable to assume that the rhetorical force of the Gospel would have encouraged audiences to view Jews and non-Christ-confessing Judaism in a negative light; the generally anti-Jewish readings of John by the church fathers attest to that rhetorical effect. As I have noted, the Gospel engages in an elaborate rhetoric of affiliation and disaffiliation, which encourages its audience to align themselves with Jesus and the disciples, and distance themselves from the *ioudaioi*. While such distancing may be interpreted as theological, the history of Christian anti-Semitism shows that it was often read also as a sociological imperative.
>
> —Adele Reinhartz, "The Jews of the Fourth Gospel," 133–34

10. R. Edwards, *Discovering John*. On her conclusions, see the section "Further Reflections: Does Jesus Replace the Temple? Is John Supersessionist?—John and the Challenge of Jewish-Christian Relations" in the comments on 2:1–25.

the subject) and is especially illuminating on what she calls "an elaborate rhetoric of affiliation and disaffiliation," which in my terms translates into John's desire to face readers with a fundamental decision (see the quotation from Reinhartz in the sidebar).

John uses the term "the Jews" far more than the Synoptics do, often negatively. Yet many of the negative references refer to the religious authorities, and Edwards concludes, with others, that "John did not intend to denote the whole Jewish people as opponents of Jesus, which must surely clear him of the charge of 'anti-Semitism.'"[11] Likewise, "John does not depict all Jews as ignorant, deceitful and unbelieving" or associate them all with darkness or "the world."[12] Indeed, John represents Jews in a wide variety of ways, some positive, and, of course, Jesus himself and the Beloved Disciple are Jews. As regards John's portrayal of the confrontational Jesus in debates and Jesus associating "the Jews" whom he addresses in chapter 8 with the devil, many features of these debates are also found in Jesus's Scriptures, especially in God's accusations against his people and in hyperbolic prophetic denunciations, and they also conform to the polemical religious rhetoric practiced within Judaism at the time. As Edwards says, "It is unlikely that John's Jewish contemporaries would have perceived John 8 as constituting uniquely bitter invective."[13]

The overall verdict is that there was clearly a history of hostility and conflict in the time both of Jesus and of the Johannine community, but that it is not appropriate to speak of anti-Semitism or anti-Judaism. Rather, this is the language of family quarreling between Jews and later between Jews and Jewish Christians.[14] The context is a ruthless empire and a province with deep divisions and endemic instability, violence, exploitation, and bitter intra-Jewish conflict. Chapter 8 is set some decades before the traumatic Jewish revolt against the Romans, leading to the destruction of the second temple in 70 CE. The Gospel was most likely written in its aftermath, possibly for readers who included some Jewish Christians who had had to leave their homeland because of the revolt and had hostile relationships with fellow Jews in synagogue communities. It might even be that the main context is among Jewish Christians themselves. It is striking that the strongest language is directed **to the Jews who had believed in** Jesus (v. 31). They are being challenged to a decision in a situation where Jesus is the one running the risk of violence. He is appealing to them to go much further in their recognition of who he is, in line with the horizon already set out in the prologue. He affirms the central thrust of the prologue in the final,

11. R. Edwards, *Discovering John*, 133.
12. R. Edwards, *Discovering John*, 134.
13. R. Edwards, *Discovering John*, 140.
14. For more on this, see above on 2:13–25.

provocative statement: **"Before Abraham was, I am."** The move to violence that follows is a measure of how fundamentally he has threatened and shaken the identity of his attackers.

Facing the Terrible Aftermath

But when the context changes and the language of John 8, now carrying the authority of Scripture, is used in situations where Christians have the power to persecute Jews, the results can be horrendous. Church fathers, Martin Luther, Nazis, and now neo-Nazis, have been among the many who have kindled, with the help of this text, contempt for Jews and murderous hostility against them. The continuing history of using John polemically against Jews means that it is not enough to ask about the original meaning of the text and its context. Something that has played such a role in nearly two thousand years of Jewish-Christian interaction cries out for a thorough response, including, if possible, a reading of John for today that faces the appalling history to which this text has contributed and that helps to shape a different history.

Two elements in that response, in line with the journey along the first path taken above, are suggested. The first is to renounce supersessionism, or "replacement theology," as already proposed above in the discussion of 2:13–25. The second is for Christians to reread their Scriptures with Jews, as also recommended in that discussion.[15] Christians need the help of Jews and others to diagnose and treat what has gone so tragically wrong over so long a period. Especially since the Holocaust, this has been happening in many ways, a process that is often painful for both sides. The best way to heal the wounds of history is to shape a better history, and, in this case, since an influential text is at issue, there is unlikely to be healing without reading together.

Yet it is also clear that Christian faith involves a decision about who Jesus is that does distinguish Christians from others, including most Jews today. John's Gospel, with its postresurrection perspective, is more interested in putting this decision before its readers than it is in the polemics between Jesus and his contemporaries. In this it echoes repeated calls to decision in Israel's Scriptures. The culmination of Torah in the book of Deuteronomy is a radical challenge by Moses: "I call heaven and earth to witness against you today that I have set before you life and death, blessings and curses. Choose life so that you and your descendants may live" (Deut. 30:19). One prophet after another

15. In my reading of the New Testament I am indebted to reading it repeatedly with Jews and Muslims during the whole period of working on this commentary. On John 8 I am especially grateful to Professor Peter Ochs for studying it with me over a three-week period while he was delivering his Hulsean Lectures at Cambridge University.

calls to decision in graphic terms, and in the Wisdom literature the ways of wisdom and foolishness radically diverge.

Jesus is in that tradition of Torah, prophecy, and wisdom, in all three of which the word of God, life, and light are inseparable, and he, like they, calls for decisive response. Rabbinic Judaism is in that same tradition and calls for a different response. This is a deep pluralism. For both Jews and Christians it involves whole shapes of living, with their modes of worshiping, praying, knowing, imagining, interpreting, and acting; their individual and communal habits; their inner and outer conflicts; and their ways of forming and sustaining complex identities. John 8 leaves no doubt about the seriousness and dimensions of such difference.

Invitation to Undertake the First Journey

Is it possible for those today who are Jewish and those who are Christian to have a present and future together that is better than their past? That is a challenge for both.

For those of us who are Christians, rereading the Gospel of John must be part of our response. John 8 invites us to undertake what is above described as the first journey: a progressive integration of knowing and living, centered on fuller and deeper recognition of and response to who Jesus is and what he desires. Can we see ourselves, our communities, and our world in the light of Jesus? Can we be open to wave after wave of reeducation of our desires, imaginations, minds, and habits? What changes are needed in our common sense and our worldviews? If **the truth will make you free**, how can that freedom come not only from the truth of who Jesus is but also from the often painful truth of our history, both communal and personal? Can our daily lives be more and more fully shaped by inhabiting God-centered, love-centered reality?

The chapter has strong encouragement for the journey.

"I am the light of the world. Whoever follows me will never walk in darkness but will have the light of life." This encourages constantly renewed attention to who Jesus is and the way of life he desires.

"If you continue [abide] **in my word, you are truly my disciples** [learners]; **and you will know the truth, and the truth will make you free."** This inspires lifelong learning, leading into more and more truth and the freedom to act on it.

"The slave does not have a permanent place in the household; the son has a place there forever. So if the Son makes you free, you will be free indeed." This is an assurance of a new family life, on both sides of death, where there can be the freedom of mutual understanding, love, joy, and friendship—"I do not call you servants any longer" (15:15).

"Very truly, I tell you, whoever keeps my word will never see death." This relativizes death in relation to Jesus, who sees death, is raised to eternal life, and in this way transforms the reality and meaning of death. To trust the word of Jesus is to see not death as it was, but death through his crucifixion and resurrection.

"Very truly, I tell you, before Abraham was, I am." This is perhaps the most surprising, comprehensive, and mysterious encouragement of all. The timescale for this journey reaches back before Abraham and into all eternity—it is the timescale of God. The good surprises and promises given to Abraham and to so many others on the Abrahamic journey are from a God who has not ceased to spring good surprises and fulfill promises—to Jews, to Christians, and to all who will receive them.

John 9:1–41

"He Opened My Eyes"

Here, in seven scenes, is the drama of a man born blind whose eyes are opened and of the controversy that results. Key themes reappear: Jesus doing a life-giving sign and accompanying it with teaching; who Jesus is, as "the light of the world," "the man," "a prophet," "the Messiah," "from God," "Son of Man," and "Lord"; conflict with Jewish leaders; Moses and Jesus; the giving and testing of testimony; and knowing and not knowing, seeing and not, believing and not, keeping the Sabbath and not, sinning and not.

This is a classic example of how John writes: simple language, well-crafted drama, a combination of action and teaching, many contrasts, earlier themes repeated with variations, the centrality of who Jesus is, and many levels of meaning. There is, as Gail O'Day describes, a tragic clash between comfort, with accompanying closed mindset and ideas, and risk, with an openness to life-changing truth (see the quotation from O'Day in the sidebar).

And something is happening beyond previous chapters, and this is shown in both direct and subtle ways. A surprise, traced below, is the way this man born blind corresponds to Jesus himself, with one parallel after another, and uniquely is given center stage for so much of the drama. He emerges as exemplary, a model believer, who is somehow both innocent and wise and learns well. There is also a repeated emphasis on the fact that he was "blind from birth" (see vv. 1, 2, 3 [although, as discussed below, the Greek text of v. 3 does not state his blindness], 19, 20, 32).

Then there is the massive theological question of sin: "Who sinned, this man or his parents, that he was born blind?" and perhaps most challenging of all: "I came . . . so that . . . those who do see might become blind."

> John 9:1–41 is a dramatic embodiment of the clash between comfort and risk, between closed categories and open possibilities in the encounter with Jesus. The man born blind, in even more basic ways than the Samaritan woman, has nothing to lose in the encounter with Jesus and so is open to who Jesus is and what Jesus has to offer. The Pharisees, in contrast, have much to lose and therefore much to protect, and they, even more intensely than Nicodemus, fight to maintain their known world. In order to communicate the power and poignancy of this clash, this rich text must not be reduced to a series of propositions along the lines of: "The blind man stands for . . . ," "The Pharisees stand for . . . ," "The moral of the story is . . ." John 9:1–41 is a long and intricate text, and only by staying with this story from beginning to end will we be able to speak of what it means to know and see.
>
> —Gail O'Day, *The Word Disclosed*, 54–55

Do the Works of God While We Can! (9:1–5)

> [1] As he walked along, he saw a man blind from birth. [2] His disciples asked him,
> "Rabbi, who sinned, this man or his parents, that he was born blind?" [3] Jesus
> answered, "Neither this man nor his parents sinned; he was born blind so
> that God's works might be revealed in him. [4] We must work the works of
> him who sent me while it is day; night is coming when no one can work. [5] As
> long as I am in the world, I am the light of the world."

The disciples assume conventional wisdom about the man, that his blindness was the result of sin. That Jesus declares both him and his parents innocent at the beginning of the story is important later, when they face opponents of Jesus and choose different courses—the man becomes a courageous witness, while his parents are dominated by fear. This chapter makes many of its points by such contrasts: the neighbors and the Pharisees as questioners; the Pharisees and the man born blind; the Pharisees and Jesus. But all are in the service of the man born blind coming to believe in and worship Jesus, and, in the process, the comparison of him with Jesus.

What of the positive teaching of Jesus here? The Greek translated as **He was born blind so that God's works might be revealed in him** emphasizes God's involvement in the man's birth less than the translation does: it reads literally, "Neither this man nor his parents sinned; *but* so that God's works might be revealed in him." The stress is on what God brings out of the situation, and what is **revealed in him**, as will appear, requires the man's response. This issue of divine action and human action will be raised more acutely by this chapter's final scene and will be explored then. But the conclusion there regarding God's initiative and human response is anticipated here: both are needed, and the "we" in **We must work the works** implies a responsive community, just as **of him who sent me** implies a unique divine initiative in Jesus. The **I am** of Jesus, who is the Word of God and **the light of the world**, is this Gospel's embracing answer to the question of origins and of orientations. Both images—word and light—help us to understand the noncompetitive relationship between divine initiative and human response: this Word is utterly God's and comes to creatures created free to respond to it;[1] this light is utterly God's and illuminates the "dualism of decision" that faces each person (on which more will be said below).

How might John want his readers to respond to this statement of Jesus? As always, his concern is for knowledge of Jesus that turns into active discipleship, and this chapter gives a vivid example of the making of a disciple. *The imperative for those who are sent as Jesus is sent is to seize every opportunity that arises to do "the works" of God—here combining active compassion with testimony centered on Jesus.* But there are times when **night** comes and **no one can work**, just as the time of Jesus doing signs in his ministry comes to an end.

Smeared, Sent, Washed, Then Able to See (9:6–7)

> [6] When he had said this, he spat on the ground and made mud with the saliva and spread the mud on the man's eyes, [7] saying to him, "Go, wash in the pool of Siloam" (which means Sent). Then he went and washed and came back able to see.

The miracle itself is described very briefly. In requiring cleansing, it echoes other biblical miracles such as the healing of Naaman (2 Kings 5:1–19) by the prophet Elisha. If the man was aware of this, it might explain his willingness later to describe Jesus as a prophet. The washing may also be intended to recall baptism, and this would be in line with the man's exemplary role. The stress on the meaning of the pool, **Sent**, takes up the earlier words of Jesus about "the works of him who sent me" and is the first of several parallels between Jesus and this man. The "work" of spitting and smearing (perhaps together with that of traveling to the pool and washing) means that later there can be an accusation against Jesus of breaking the Sabbath.

1. When a word causes something to happen, it involves response, and light too enables things to happen by noncoercively illuminating.

"I Am"; "I Do Not Know" (9:8–12)

> [8] The neighbors and those who had seen him before as a beggar began to ask, "Is this not the man who used to sit and beg?" [9] Some were saying, "It is he." Others were saying, "No, but it is someone like him." He kept saying, "I am the man." [10] But they kept asking him, "Then how were your eyes opened?" [11] He answered, "The man called Jesus made mud, spread it on my eyes, and said to me, 'Go to Siloam and wash.' Then I went and washed and received my sight." [12] They said to him, "Where is he?" He said, "I do not know."

Somewhat surprisingly, the man stays center stage while Jesus disappears from the story till verse 35. The man continues to be described in ways that recall Jesus: being interrogated, the dispute about his identity, the need to give testimony about himself, and especially the key identity statement, **"I am the man"** (*egō eimi*, "I am"). But he is also described as at the beginning of a learning process, as he says, **"I do not know."**

From God? Yes (9:13–17)

> [13] They brought to the Pharisees the man who had formerly been blind. [14] Now it was a sabbath day when Jesus made the mud and opened his eyes. [15] Then the Pharisees also began to ask him how he had received his sight. He said to them, "He put mud on my eyes. Then I washed, and now I see." [16] Some of the Pharisees said, "This man is not from God, for he does not observe the sabbath." But others said, "How can a man who is a sinner perform such signs?" And they were divided. [17] So they said again to the blind man, "What do you say about him? It was your eyes he opened." He said, "He is a prophet."

Bringing the man to the Pharisees may have been a hostile act (the Greek verb for **they brought** is the same as that used in 8:3 for the Pharisees bringing the woman taken in adultery to Jesus), especially in the light of the news in verse 14 that **it was a sabbath day**. Under interrogation, the man gives clear testimony, which divides the Pharisees in their verdicts on Jesus: Is he **from God** or not? One side voices the question that this sign provokes: **"How can a man who is a sinner perform such signs?"** *The division shows a basic truth of this Gospel: even spectacular signs do not compel faith.* The vital thing is the one who is doing the signs; and the man, showing increasing insight, courageously testifies of Jesus: **"He is a prophet."** This can be taken to mean that he is someone close to God or sent by God.

Blind from Birth? Yes (9:18–23)

> [18] The Jews did not believe that he had been blind and had received his sight until they called the parents of the man who had received his sight [19] and asked them, "Is this your son, who you say was born blind? How then does he now see?" [20] His parents answered, "We know that this is our son, and that he was born blind; [21] but we do not know how it is that now he sees, nor do we know who opened his eyes. Ask him; he is of age. He will speak for himself." [22] His parents said this because they were afraid of the Jews; for the Jews had already agreed that anyone who confessed Jesus to be the Messiah would be put out of the synagogue. [23] Therefore his parents said, "He is of age; ask him."

The emphasis on the amazing element of this drama being that the man had been blind from birth is increased still further by this scene.

The man's parents give reluctant, limited, but clear testimony that he had been born blind. The author's comments on them explain the limitation as due to intimidation. Many scholars see this passage (with 12:42 and 16:2) reflecting a later situation, that of the Christian community in John's day that had been **put out of the synagogue**. Whatever the truth of that, *the postresurrection concern of John for the long-term ongoing drama of the church would make the present story relevant to many situations of hostility and exclusion that called for witness and even martyrdom.* Here, the parents' fear brings out their son's courage. And there might be a further parallel with Jesus, who was not able to trust some of those close to him.

Astonishing! "Never Since the World Began . . ." (9:24–34)

> [24] So for the second time they called the man who had been blind, and they said to him, "Give glory to God! We know that this man is a sinner." [25] He answered, "I do not know whether he is a sinner. One thing I do know, that though I was blind, now I see." [26] They said to him, "What did he do to you? How did he open your eyes?" [27] He answered them, "I have told you already, and you would not listen. Why do you want to hear it again? Do you also want to become his disciples?" [28] Then they reviled him, saying, "You are his disciple, but we are disciples of Moses. [29] We know that God has spoken to Moses, but as for this man, we do not know where he comes from." [30] The man answered, "Here is an astonishing thing! You do not know where he comes from, and yet he opened my eyes. [31] We know that God does not listen to sinners, but he does listen to one who worships him and obeys his

> will. [32] Never since the world began has it been heard that anyone opened the eyes of a person born blind. [33] If this man were not from God, he could do nothing." [34] They answered him, "You were born entirely in sins, and are you trying to teach us?" And they drove him out.

The character and insight of the man born blind continues to develop in the face of hostile interrogation. He stands firm in his testimony and counterattacks, even ironically asking, **"Do you also want to become his disciples?"** As often in John, there is a clash of basic concepts: **his disciple** versus **disciples of Moses**; **"We know that God has spoken to Moses"** versus **"We do not know where he comes from"**; **"You do not know where he comes from"** versus **"He opened my eyes"**; **"We know that God does not listen to sinners"** versus **"He does listen to one who worships him and obeys his will."** The reader has since the prologue been instructed in the true concepts of discipleship, the origins of Jesus, worship, and the will of God, but here we see the man beginning to enter into their truth.

The man's main argument is simple: **"Never since the world began has it been heard that anyone opened the eyes of a person born blind."** It corresponds exactly to what Jesus says later: "Believe the works" (10:38); "Believe me because of the works themselves" (14:11). And as the man—a former beggar—learns, he develops as a character, his earlier innocent directness growing in courage, in discernment, in argumentative skill, and, above all, in understanding Jesus. *This is a transformative discipleship course in a tough school,* with the most painful lessons again paralleling Jesus: **Then they reviled him. . . . And they drove him out**. The seventh and final scene completes the learning process in one-to-one conversation with Jesus.

"I Believe"; "Your Sin Remains": An Intractable Problem? (9:35–41)

> [35] Jesus heard that they had driven him out, and when he found him, he said, "Do you believe in the Son of Man?" [36] He answered, "And who is he, sir? Tell me, so that I may believe in him." [37] Jesus said to him, "You have seen him, and the one speaking with you is he." [38] He said, "Lord, I believe." And he worshiped him. [39] Jesus said, "I came into this world for judgment so that those who do not see may see, and those who do see may become blind." [40] Some of the Pharisees near him heard this and said to him, "Surely we are not blind, are we?" [41] Jesus said to them, "If you were blind, you would not have sin. But now that you say, 'We see,' your sin remains."

Jesus . . . found him. John's Gospel is very open about how or when or where or why people might find or be found by Jesus. The embracing truth is that there is a love that is meant for all, enacted above all on the cross: "And I, when I am lifted up from the earth, will draw all people to myself" (12:32). As the Word of God, through whom all things and people were created, Jesus already is in relationship with everyone. *But, if it is to be a relationship of trust, understanding, and love, it must be two-way.* The Word becoming flesh and living among us (1:14) is a radical appeal, with its climax on the cross, for mutuality, for response in trust and love. It is an imperative invitation into nothing less than friendship and the life of a new family, as embodied in the new community formed by Jesus when, on the cross, he brought his mother and the disciple he loved together in one household (19:25–27). The cross is the supreme sign of the seriousness of evil, sin, suffering, and death—everything John includes in "darkness" and "blindness." It is in line with the rest of biblical history in its realism about what can go wrong. John is also realistic about the continuing darkness: the disciples will be hated, Peter will glorify God by his death, and so on. Darkness and blindness continue in each person, in each family and community, whether Christian or other,[2] and in every society, sphere of life, and religion. Who would claim to lead lives of perfect light, truth, wisdom, holiness, patience, self-giving, and love for all?

John's Gospel has as its central aim to draw people into trust, belief, love, and shared life with Jesus and other people—though it never gives any overall account of those mysterious "many dwelling places" that are "in my Father's house" (14:2), let alone the list of their occupants or the timetable for their occupation. But John is passionately clear about the importance of the ongoing life of love in a world where so much militates against love. He does not believe that that life can be lived in isolation: the new family life is essential. Above all, he believes that at the heart of that life, embodying it and sharing it, is Jesus, crucified and risen, sharing his Spirit "without measure" (3:34). And one of its most distinctive emphases is on the importance of each person's belief, trust, and love, and of the decisions that need to be taken in order to live that life.[3]

Many modern commentators have noted this "dualism of decision" in John. *He writes in order to help people take vital decisions, both to begin to trust, follow, and love Jesus, and to continue and deepen that life in the long term.* And he does not pretend that all is easy or straightforward. His very way of writing opens

2. The First Letter of John shows the Johannine community itself learning the painful lessons of recognizing and dealing with sin in each person and in the church as well as in the world.

3. On John and the individual, see Bauckham, *Gospel of Glory*, chap. 1.

up depths, and, with them, areas of uncertainty, ambiguity, and complexity, mysteries of both light and darkness.

The ending of John 9 is one place where those mysteries are intensified. The core dualism of decision in the Gospel is vividly laid out.

On the one hand, the man born blind meets with Jesus, and the light-giving sign of his restored sight is fulfilled by finding the answer to the "who" question about Jesus, seeing Jesus, believing in Jesus, and worshiping him. There is no more complete example of believing in Jesus till Thomas cries out to the resurrected Jesus, "My Lord and my God!" (20:28). It completes the learning that the man born blind has been doing through the chapter and also crowns the way he has been described in terms associated with Jesus: it is a model "who to who" relationship.

Both Thomas and the man born blind also emphasize the importance of seeing that leads into worship. The climax of Dante's *Divine Comedy*, in which Dante in the poem is given the gift of such seeing, is one of the most moving testimonies to it (see the quotation from Dante in the sidebar). Dante distills into poetry a biblical wisdom of seeing and not seeing, resonant with John's testimony in the prologue, "We have seen his glory. . . . No one has ever seen God" (1:14, 18), and the *Divine Comedy* draws on more than a millennium of theology and prayer, culminating in Bernard of Clairvaux, Thomas Aquinas, and Bonaventure. Also resonating with the prologue is Dante's vision of all creation, and even of the incarnation—"our human form"—riveting his sight as he is overwhelmed by a vision of God that exceeds his sight's capacity and finds "my will and my desire were turned, / as wheels that move in equilibrium, / by love that moves the sun and other stars." This is a glimpse of the sort of vision hinted at in the desire of Jesus in his prayer in John 17:24: "Father, I desire that those also, whom you have given me, may be with me where I am, to see my glory, which you have given me because you loved me before the foundation of the world."

On the other hand, there is the shocking statement by Jesus: **"I came into this world for judgment so that those who do not see may see, and those who do see may become blind."** Does that final statement mean that Jesus is sent by his Father to make some people blind, to ensure a negative judgment on them and their divine rejection?

It is worth reinforcing the question by adding other similar statements, such as, "No one can come to me unless it is granted by the Father" (6:65); "And so they could not believe, because Isaiah also said, 'He has blinded their eyes and hardened their heart, so that they might not look with their eyes, and understand with their heart and turn—and I would heal them'" (12:39–40); "You did not choose me but I chose you" (15:16).

So, is the human dualism of decision determined by a divine dualism of decision?

And drawing nearer, as I had to now,
the end of all desires, in my own self
I ended all the ardour of desire. . . .

My sight, becoming pure and wholly free,
entered still more, then more, along the ray
of that one light which, of itself, is true. . . .

Grace, in all plenitude, you dared me set
my seeing eyes on that eternal light
so that all seeing there achieved its end.

Within its depths, this light, I saw, contained,
bound up and gathered in a single book,
the leaves that scatter through the universe—

beings and accidents and modes of life. . . .

And so my mind, held high above itself,
looked on, intent and still, in wondering awe
and, lit by wonder, always flared anew.

We all become, as that light strikes us, such
we cannot (this would be impossible)
consent to turn and seek some other face.

For good—the only object of our will—
is gathered up entire in that one light.
Outside it, all is flawed that's perfect there. . . .

Within that being—lucid, bright and deep—
of that high brilliance, there appeared to me
three circling spheres, three-coloured, one in span.

And one, it seemed, was mirrored by the next
twin rainbows, arc to arc. The third seemed fire,
and breathed to first and second equally. . . .

Eternal light, you sojourn in yourself alone.
Alone, you know yourself. Known to yourself,
you, knowing, love and smile on your own being.[a]

An inter-circulation, thus conceived,
appears in you like mirrored brilliancy.
But when a while my eyes had looked this round,

deep in itself, it seemed—as painted now,
in those same hues—to show our human form.
At which, my sight was set entirely there. . . .

But mine were wings that could not rise to that,
save that, with this, my mind was stricken through
by sudden lightning bringing what it wished.

All powers of high imagining here failed.
But now my will and my desire were turned,
as wheels that move in equilibrium,

by love that moves the sun and other stars.[b]

—Dante Alighieri, *The Divine Comedy 3: Paradiso*, canto 33, lines 46–48, 52–54, 82–88, 97–105, 115–20, 124–32, 139–45

a. Dante's theology of the smile is imaginatively and profoundly explored in Hawkins, "All Smiles: Poetry and Theology in Dante's *Commedia*."

b. For a contemporary long poem that engages with the developments of modernity, yet has much in common with Dante's *Divine Comedy*, culminating in a vision of God in the final canto, see O'Siadhail, *The Five Quintets*. For more on Micheal O'Siadhail and *The Five Quintets*, see below, in the epilogue, the section "God and All Reality."

As the quotation from Isaiah in John 12:39–40 shows, the question arises in the Jewish Scriptures too, and it is also raised elsewhere in the New Testament. It has also run through Christian history, with some of the weightiest teachers supporting what came to be called "double predestination"—God deciding that some are to be saved and others damned. There has also been strong dissent from this (see the sidebar for a passionate view by the seventeenth-century English Anglican priest Thomas Traherne, who was wrestling with Calvinist views of the time), and most mainstream Christian theologians of the past century have sided with Karl Barth, who rejected his own Calvinist tradition of double predestination, and Karl Rahner, who rejected the Catholic version of it. In commentaries on the Gospel of John, the Lutheran Rudolf Bultmann has argued passionately for a dualism of undetermined human decision, and the Catholic Rudolf Schnackenburg has argued a nuanced case leading in the same direction.

I suggest that the most helpful reflections, which are of considerable importance to the interpretation of this Gospel, have been as follows.

First, there is no necessary competition between divine and human decision and action, since they are not on the same level. The philosophical and theological arguments in favor of this position are helpful, though not directly taken from John.[4] But the radical difference between divine and human time, knowing, speech, action, and reality is indicated by John, and leads to the next point.

Second, human beings do not have a divine overview of reality, and so there can be no neat solution to how divine and human decision and action relate to each other—this is bound to be mysterious. One problem with double predestination is that it is too neat and all-knowing. Human views are from within the drama of living, facing situations and decisions as they come. Further, that drama includes evil, darkness, blindness, sin of many sorts, suffering, falsehood, bias, slavish addiction, ambiguity and ambivalence, self-deception, misinterpretation, and multiple tragic dimensions. So the mystery intensifies, as individual and social limitation, darkness and blindness combine.

Third, John's Gospel is testimony to there being a way out of this darkness, seeing a way forward, and is written to offer the possibility of walking in the light, following Jesus, having abundant life. It would make no sense at all to write it if the fate of everyone were already predetermined by God. Nor would it make sense if a God who created all and loves all were to predestine some to damnation. So it has one overwhelming aim: to draw people to Jesus and

> For indeed it is impossible, that he [God] by determining their Wills, should make them the Authors of Righteous Actions, which of all things in the World he most desired. There is as much Difference between a Willing Act of the Soul it self, and an Action forced on the Will, determined by another, as there is between a man that is dragged to the Altar, whether he will or no, and the man that comes with all his Heart with music and Dancing to offer sacrifice. There is a Joy, and Honour, and Love in the one, fear and constraint, and shame in the other. That GOD should not be able to deserve our Love, unless he himself made us to Love him by violence, is the Greatest dishonour to him in the World: Nor is it any Glory or Reputation for us, who are such sorry Stewards, that we cannot be entrusted with a little Liberty, but we must needs abuse it. GOD adventured the possibility of sinning into our hands, which he infinitely hated, that he might have the Possibility of Righteous Actions, which he infinitely Loved.[a]
>
> —Thomas Traherne
>
> a. Quotation in Inge, *Happiness and Holiness: Thomas Traherne and His Writings*, 204.

4. One of the best discussions of this is Tanner, *God and Creation in Christian Theology*.

help them stay with him. It is written for readers immersed in the drama of living in order to face them with a decision regarding Jesus. It is not written in order to give information by describing the eternal fate of the Jewish leaders or anyone else who does not follow Jesus. The sharp contrasts and dualisms are set forth in order to break through resistance, and they have an element of hyperbole and shock treatment—as seen in many of Israel's prophets and in the Synoptic Gospels. It would be worth challenging the resistance only if the outcome were not already decided.

Fourth, how do you explain all those Christians who conceive of God being so completely in control that this includes determining all decisions both for and against God? There is a range of possible reasons. Partly, it can concern the priority of the "who" question in relation to God. If this is central in the way this commentary has found it to be in John and God is identified through Jesus, then the character of God, as embodied in Jesus, theologically outweighs the apparent logic of divine omnipotence and omniscience that is often used to support double predestination. Partly, too, it can come from them deciding not to give priority to the "all" in statements about the will of God for salvation and the death of Jesus and, instead of utterly good news, offering what Karl Barth calls bad news as well as good news. Partly, it can be about taking Scripture's rhetoric out of its dramatic settings and using it as an overview giving objective information. Partly, it can be a reinforcement of group identity and the decisions that those in the group have already made. But perhaps the most sympathetic partial explanation is to follow the logic of gratitude to God, the "insider view" of salvation.

Those who come into faith, who find or are found by Jesus and decide for him, who come to abide in him and he in them, who receive his Spirit and light and love, who find in him "life in all its abundance," living water "welling up to eternal life," a new community of love and friendship, joy, fulfillment, and a vocation following him—or however their Christian life is described—they usually are deeply grateful. The gratitude does not apportion some credit to Jesus and some to themselves; the whole event is ascribed to Jesus, all thanks are given to him, all glory to God. Just as creation is a divine initiative, so too is salvation. The insider view is of an utterly free, gracious gift, for which the only adequate response is unqualified thanks, acknowledging God's complete responsibility for all that has happened. It is a short step to see God as completely responsible for everyone else's destiny too.

But gratitude is retrospective. In relation to the present and future, even grateful believers must act as if they are free and responsible. In the midst of the drama of living, with all its darkness and blindness, there are decisions to be taken. John is a realist about this situation of needing to risk acting despite unclarity, complexity, sin, evil, and death. He does not take an easy way out by trying to give detailed instructions. Instead, he expects believers to become mature and make their own decisions. His ethics is a summons to "love one another as I have loved you," with an open "as" sending the disciples back to reflect on who Jesus is and on the story of his life. They are meant to be the very opposite of automata who have been predetermined by their maker: they breathe in the Spirit of Jesus and are sent as he was sent, as his friends, with freedom and responsibility analogous to his. This indicates not a God of detailed predetermination but one who shares the divine life so deeply that those in this mutual relationship (as evoked by John 17) are empowered with the freedom of divine love. It is a mature relationship of trust in which who God is, who Jesus is, matters most, and there is frank realism about the way the world is: a difficult place to live well in, with much darkness and blindness, and serious possibilities of going wrong.

So, fifth, John's Gospel is crafted to help people find their way in this world, and the purpose of its difficult language, as at the end of John 9, is to refuse to allow readers to ignore the continuing darkness and blindness. John's Gospel is sometimes seen as the antithesis of tragedy. But the way John stimulates his readers to wrestle with the relation of light and darkness, sight and blindness, without giving any simple resolution, has something of the quality of Greek or Shakespearean tragedy. There are similar notes of intractability, character development through testing and conflict, self-deception and recognition, dramatic irony, multiple meanings, questions without neat answers, the precariousness of human life, moral flaws, and imperfect understanding. Indeed, dramatic literature has been of increasing interest to scholars of John, and some have gone far in exploring the resonances between them.[5] The scandalous nature of the suggestion that Jesus has come so that **those who do see may become blind** leads us into the sphere of tragedy, with its insistence that **sin remains**, darkness remains. Yet the point of this is not determinism. The final words to the Pharisee bystanders are a tragic pronouncement: **Jesus said to them, "If you were blind, you would not have sin. But now that you say, 'We see,' your sin remains."** Within the drama of the story, they are stuck in their blindness. For the reader, the message is to be like the man born blind, not the Pharisees—this text is presenting you with that choice.

Sixth, and finally, this text is presenting Jesus. John's Gospel is not simply tragic, or simply anything else. It is testimony to Jesus, who is utterly identified with humanity in its tragic and other dimensions, and with God. He is the light

5. The most illuminating for me have been Brant, *John*, and Parsenios, *Departure and Consolation*.

shining in a darkness that does not master it, but yet the darkness continues till now. His followers, too, continue to be sent into darkness, and their main comfort is knowing who is with them in it: **Jesus said to him, "You have seen him, and the one speaking with you is he." He said, "Lord, I believe." And he worshiped him.**

John 10:1–42

Wonderful Shepherd, Abundant Life, Father and Son

Jesus now expands on the contrast between how he and the Pharisees have related to the blind man. He takes the shepherd—a classic model of leadership in Israel's Scriptures, in the other Gospels, and in the surrounding Roman Empire—and develops it in new ways.

Compared with those models, there is heightened mutual relationship with each individual sheep: "He calls his own sheep by name. . . . And the sheep follow him because they know his voice" (vv. 3–4). There is a fresh dramatic intensity of love: this is a shepherd who "lays down his life for the sheep" (v. 11). There is enriched theology, crucially uniting human and divine shepherding: "I am the gate. . . . I am the good shepherd. . . . I know my own and my own know me, just as the Father knows me and I know the Father. . . . The Father and I are one. . . . The Father is in me and I am in the Father" (vv. 7, 11, 14–15, 30). There is an expectation of increasing in the future, as the flock expands: "I have other sheep that do not belong to this fold" (v. 16).

Running through all these dimensions is the multifaceted theme "life." Jesus sums up his vocation: "I came that they may have life, and have it abundantly" (v. 10). The abundant life is seen in the intimate knowing of sheep "by name" (v. 3), in the promise that the sheep "will come in and go out and find pasture" (v. 9), in the shepherd who "lays down his life" (v. 11), in the embracing reality of the divine life and love, and in the astonishing statement by Jesus: "I lay down my life in order to take it up again" (v. 17).

There is also mobile, multifaceted imagery. Besides shepherds and sheep, there are also a thief and a bandit, a gate and a gatekeeper, a stranger, a hired hand, a wolf, and other elements. These, as well as the central shepherd/sheep image, encourage readers now to continue to exercise our imaginations, not least on the interplay of all this with the rest of John's Gospel, with other Scriptures, and with models of leadership beyond the Scriptures. Practically, we are encouraged to connect our reading with the ongoing drama of following this shepherd and attending to his voice in the face of conflict, danger, and life-shaping decisions.

Overall, we are given a dynamic image that can draw readers deeper into the rest of the Bible, deeper into relationship with God and Jesus, deeper into life in community with whomever Jesus calls by name, deeper into a vocation of trust, love, and compassion that shares in the eternal, abundant life of the Father and the Son, and further into a world in need of such abundant life.

Jesus the wonderful shepherd, as described here, fits in ideally with this Gospel's theology: "shepherd" is used of God and also of key human representatives of God, and so is well suited to symbolizing the self-expression and self-giving of God in a particular person; the shepherd is utterly vital to the life of the sheep, both individually and as a flock; and there is endless scope for enriching and improvising on the imagery through connecting with other passages in both John and the rest of Scripture, through reflecting on the surrounding society and its uses of the shepherd image for its leaders, and through relating to new situations in the ongoing drama.

Knowing His Voice (10:1–6)

> 1 "Very truly, I tell you, anyone who does not enter the sheepfold by the gate
> but climbs in by another way is a thief and a bandit. 2 The one who enters
> by the gate is the shepherd of the sheep. 3 The gatekeeper opens the gate
> for him, and the sheep hear his voice. He calls his own sheep by name and
> leads them out. 4 When he has brought out all his own, he goes ahead of
> them, and the sheep follow him because they know his voice. 5 They will not
> follow a stranger, but they will run from him because they do not know the
> voice of strangers." 6 Jesus used this figure of speech with them, but they
> did not understand what he was saying to them.

To whom should we listen? Who is to be trusted? Who should be followed? At the heart of those interrelated decisions is the "who to who" relationship, already seen in the encounters of Jesus in earlier chapters, with yet more to come in the rest of his story. Now this is summed up in a new variation on the shepherd/sheep image: **He calls his own sheep by name**. But for the relationship to work there must be recognition and response: **The sheep follow him because they know his voice**. The Gospel of John is written to enable readers to know, through its testimony, who their true shepherd is, to learn to recognize his voice through attending to his teachings and conversations, to trust him because of who he is and what he does, and to follow him. Reading and rereading what John writes, together with following through John's allusions to the rest of Scripture, is a vital way to stay attuned to the voice of the Word made flesh.

In a culture with innumerable other voices coming through many media, what are the habits of listening, attention, reading, rereading, meditation, reflection, and communication through those many media that can best nurture what is desired, the abundant life that Jesus now says he came to enable (10:10)?

One essential element in these habits is an alert, discerning, adventurous imagination. In all four Gospels Jesus uses one **figure of speech** after another, and often the result is that **they did not understand what he was saying to them**. Perhaps more than any of the other Gospels, John's is crafted in order to teach, shape, and challenge the imaginations of his readers, and this chapter is one of its masterpieces. For rereaders, its importance is reinforced by the resurrected Jesus in conversation with Peter in 21:15–19, when the themes of naming, loving, knowing, leadership, nurture, conflict, following, and laying down life recur. There the emphasis is on Peter, who is called by name to be a shepherd in the spirit of Jesus, his pastoral imagination and practice rooted in the love between him and Jesus.

Abundant Life (10:7–10)

> [7] So again Jesus said to them, "Very truly, I tell you, I am the gate for the
> sheep. [8] All who came before me are thieves and bandits; but the sheep did
> not listen to them. [9] I am the gate. Whoever enters by me will be saved, and
> will come in and go out and find pasture. [10] The thief comes only to steal
> and kill and destroy. I came that they may have life, and have it abundantly."

The opening verses invited readers to imagine a nighttime scenario, in which a gatekeeper recognizes the shepherd and the sheep in the fold need to distinguish the voice of the shepherd in the dark. Now there is a surprise twist, as a new, repeated "I am" saying, introduced by the strongly emphatic **"Very truly, I tell you,"** shifts the focus to who Jesus is: **"I am the gate for the sheep."** The "who to who" is being intensified still further. At the same time the scope is expanded to include **whoever enters by me** and to embrace salvation and abundant **life**—the whole purpose of Jesus is being summed up.

The contrast with **thieves and bandits**, those who come **only to steal and kill and destroy**, is also intensified. **All who came before me** in the context includes the Jewish leaders of recent times and his own times, but who else? It is not clear how far back to go or how many spheres of leadership to include, but the point for the reader is clear: there is a decision to be made between Jesus and others who claim the right to be listened to. The image of **the gate** is extended beyond entry to include ongoing life: those who enter **will come in and go out and find pasture**. This is in line with John's double concern for both coming to Jesus and following him; both being born again (or from above) and continuing to learn and mature; both entering into a relationship of trust and love and abiding in it. *All of that is summed up in his mission:* ***that they may have life, and have it abundantly.***

This summary is very important. It resonates through the whole of John's Gospel, beginning with the prologue: "What has come into being in him was life, and the life was the light of all people" (1:3–4). Jesus does signs of abundant life for all: wine at a wedding, healing, feeding, raising Lazarus. His dying, soon to be identified as the most distinctive mark of his shepherding, is for the sake of life and bearing "much fruit" (12:24). His very person is identified with "the resurrection and the life" (11:25; cf. 14:6).

It also resonates through many other texts in Scripture. Here, where the key issue is who the sheep should attend to and be led by, among the many intertexts perhaps the most relevant is Ezekiel 34, especially its first sixteen and last nine verses.[1] Note there the echoes of John 10: denunciation of the leaders of Israel as shepherds who are in fact enemies of their flock; the noncompetitive harmony

1. Here is the text of Ezek. 34:1–16, 23–31:

The word of the Lord came to me: Mortal, prophesy against the shepherds of Israel: prophesy, and say to them—to the shepherds: Thus says the Lord God: Ah, you shepherds of Israel who have been feeding yourselves! Should not shepherds feed the sheep? You eat the fat, you clothe yourselves with the wool, you slaughter the fatlings; but you do not feed the sheep. You have not strengthened the weak, you have not healed the sick, you have not bound up the injured, you have not brought back the strayed, you have not sought the lost, but with force and harshness you have ruled them. So they were scattered, because there was no shepherd; and scattered, they became food for all the wild animals. My sheep were scattered, they wandered over all the mountains and on every high hill; my sheep were scattered over all the face of the earth, with no one to search or seek for them.

Therefore, you shepherds, hear the word of the Lord: As I live, says the Lord God, because my sheep have become a prey, and my sheep have become food for all the wild animals, since there was no shepherd; and because my shepherds have not searched for my sheep, but the shepherds have fed themselves, and have not fed my sheep; therefore, you shepherds, hear the word of the Lord: Thus says the Lord God, I am against the shepherds; and I will demand my sheep at their hand, and put a stop to their feeding the sheep; no

of shepherding both by God ("I myself will be the shepherd of my sheep" [34:15]) and by a human leader ("I will set up over them one shepherd, my servant David" [34:23]); and themes such as "the word of the Lord" (34:1, 7, 9), "rescue" (34:10, 12), "good pasture" (34:14), and divine-human mutuality: "You are my sheep, the sheep of my pasture and I am your God, says the Lord God" (34:31).

Note, too, in Ezekiel 34 the scope for further developing John's message through reflection on justice and the use and abuse of power; covenant; fear; special attention to the weak, injured, and lost; and (of particular relevance to the twenty-first century) the importance for abundant life of including animals and the material creation in any God-centered image of peace, justice, and blessing. Margaret Daly-Denton acutely appreciates the relevance of **All who came before me are thieves and bandits** to the exploitation and abuse of power by the priestly elite in Jerusalem, by the Roman imperial rulers and their agents, and by their many successors today. She also draws out the ecological wisdom of John 10 and its intertexts such as Ezekiel 34, while connecting them with the theme of sight and blindness in John 9 (see the quotation from Daly-Denton in the sidebar).

---

longer shall the shepherds feed themselves. I will rescue my sheep from their mouths, so that they may not be food for them.

For thus says the Lord God: I myself will search for my sheep, and will seek them out. As shepherds seek out their flocks when they are among their scattered sheep, so I will seek out my sheep. I will rescue them from all the places to which they have been scattered on a day of clouds and thick darkness. I will bring them out from the peoples and gather them from the countries, and will bring them into their own land; and I will feed them on the mountains of Israel, by the watercourses, and in all the inhabited parts of the land. I will feed them with good pasture, and the mountain heights of Israel shall be their pasture; there they shall lie down in good grazing land, and they shall feed on rich pasture on the mountains of Israel. I myself will be the shepherd of my sheep, and I will make them lie down, says the Lord God. I will seek the lost, and I will bring back the strayed, and I will bind up the injured, and I will strengthen the weak, but the fat and the strong I will destroy. I will feed them with justice. . . .

I will set up over them one shepherd, my servant David, and he shall feed them: he shall feed them and be their shepherd. And I, the Lord, will be their God, and my servant David shall be prince among them; I, the Lord, have spoken.

I will make with them a covenant of peace and banish wild animals from the land, so that they may live in the wild and sleep in the woods securely. I will make them and the region around my hill a blessing; and I will send down the showers in their season; they shall be showers of blessing. The trees of the field shall yield their fruit, and the earth shall yield its increase. They shall be secure on their soil; and they shall know that I am the Lord, when I break the bars of their yoke, and save them from the hands of those who enslaved them. They shall no more be plunder for the nations, nor shall the animals of the land devour them; they shall live in safety, and no one shall make them afraid. I will provide for them a splendid vegetation so that they shall no more be consumed with hunger in the land, and no longer suffer the insults of the nations. They shall know that I, the Lord their God, am with them, and that they, the house of Israel, are my people, says the Lord God. You are my sheep, the sheep of my pasture and I am your God, says the Lord God.

> “Believing in(to) Jesus” should be a dynamic, ongoing process of being brought from blindness to sight—insight into the ways of the life-loving energy of Wisdom at work in the creation, vision for the work of repairing the damage we have done in our ignorance of Wisdom’s “way” and foresight that will help us to avoid such damage in the future. . . . Jesus’ disciples are to be pastoral people, carers who seek the flourishing of creation and not predatory thieves who “constantly consume and destroy, while others are not yet able to live in a way worthy of their human dignity.”[a]
>
> —Margaret Daly-Denton, *John*, 145
>
> a. Here Daly-Denton is quoting from Pope Francis’s 2015 encyclical letter *Laudato Si’*, par. 193.

Core Theology: The Wonderful Shepherd and His Own, the Loving Father and His Son (10:11–21)

> 11 “I am the good shepherd. The good shepherd lays down his life for the sheep. 12 The hired hand, who is not the shepherd and does not own the sheep, sees the wolf coming and leaves the sheep and runs away—and the wolf snatches them and scatters them. 13 The hired hand runs away because a hired hand does not care for the sheep. 14 I am the good shepherd. I know my own and my own know me, 15 just as the Father knows me and I know the Father. And I lay down my life for the sheep. 16 I have other sheep that do not belong to this fold. I must bring them also, and they will listen to my voice. So there will be one flock, one shepherd. 17 For this reason the Father loves me, because I lay down my life in order to take it up again. 18 No one takes it from me, but I lay it down of my own accord. I have power to lay it down, and I have power to take it up again. I have received this command from my Father.”
>
> 19 Again the Jews were divided because of these words. 20 Many of them were saying, “He has a demon and is out of his mind. Why listen to him?” 21 Others were saying, “These are not the words of one who has a demon. Can a demon open the eyes of the blind?”

“I am the good shepherd.” Here the Greek word for “good” is *kalos*, which can mean “noble, beautiful, fine, precious, right, proper, fitting, good.” “Model shepherd” works well here; “wonderful shepherd” is a way of indicating how Jesus in this chapter is divine and human, transcending the usual categories in remarkable ways.

There is now a shift from **"I am the gate"** back to the chapter's opening theme of the shepherd "who enters by the gate" (v. 2) and forward to the deepest secret of that abundant life that Jesus brings through his death. Here is the open secret of this Gospel, the heart of reality, headlined at the end of the prologue: "the only Son, who is close to the Father's heart" (1:18). Here Jesus states the theological core of the Gospel: **"I know my own and my own know me, just as the Father knows me and I know the Father. And I lay down my life for the sheep . . . in order to take it up again."**

It is a core of relationships, the loving relationship of the Father and the Son embodied historically in his death and resurrection, generating—amazingly—a similar relationship in "my own." The pivotal "just as" encourages continual theological questioning, imagining, and conceptualizing, as seen in the Farewell Discourses and through the history of Christian thought. Inseparably, it encourages continual meditation, prayer, and worship, as seen in John 17 and through the history of Christian devotion. But, inseparably from both thought and prayer, above all it encourages wholehearted participation in the ongoing drama of loving, as seen in John 20 and 21 and through the history of Christian discipleship.

What might be the truth of how **the Father knows me**? How does the Father know Jesus? It is by name; in utter love and wisdom; with joy and delight; with complete understanding; as no one else does; with a desire for complete mutuality in knowledge; in line with who the Father is and who Jesus is. The exploration could continue indefinitely.

If that is on the right track, then the truth of "I know my own," how Jesus knows his friends, and potentially all for whom he lays down his life, is that his friends can trust in being known by name by Jesus; being loved wisely, with joy and delight; being understood completely; and having their wholehearted response desired so that there can be complete mutuality, as between Jesus and his Father; and more.

What might be the truth of how **I know the Father**? How does Jesus know the Father? It is by name; in utter love and wisdom; with joy and delight; with complete understanding; as no one else does; with a desire for complete mutuality in knowledge; in line with who the Father is and who Jesus is; through prayer and mutual glorifying, in a union of mutual indwelling; and through perfect obedience to the point of laying down his life and taking it up again: **"I have power to lay it down, and I have power to take it up again. I have received this command from my Father."**

If that is on the right track, then the truth of how **my own know me**, how we might know Jesus, is analogous with each of those. But here any straightforward similarity, between us knowing Jesus and him knowing his Father, does not quite work. The analogies are more distant. Yes, we can know Jesus by name;

in love and wisdom; with joy and delight; with understanding; with a desire for complete mutuality in knowledge, as with a friend. We can know Jesus in line with how we identify him and his Father through Scripture; through prayer and worship, in a union of mutual indwelling; and through doing what he desires.

But all of that is the knowing of disciples, learners. The power of John's habitual use of "just as" or "as" is its capacity to accommodate the more distant as well as the closer analogies, and then to inspire growth into closeness, into a knowing that is nearer to utter love and wisdom, moving into more complete understanding and mutuality in knowledge, into fuller obedience to the command of love, into ever-deeper mutual indwelling and joy. Here in 10:14–15 the main emphasis is on the knowing between Father and Son in analogy with the knowing between Jesus and us; elsewhere emphasis is on the analogy of mutual abiding or indwelling in love (17:20–26), or the analogy of being sent by Jesus as Jesus was sent by the Father (20:21). Growing knowledge and understanding, deepening love, and expanding mission might be seen as examples of the prologue's testimony to the inexhaustible abundance given through Jesus: "From his fullness we have all received, grace upon grace" (1:16). John writes his Gospel to enable such receiving continually—more and more and more.

The image of shepherd and sheep is transcended by this sort of mutuality in knowing. It is also stretched by the idea of the shepherd laying down his life for the sheep. Indeed, the associated image from John that comes forcefully to mind is of John the Baptist's cry: "Here is the Lamb of God who takes away the sin of the world!" (1:29). Jesus dies at the time when the Passover lambs are killed (chap. 19). The diverse pastoral images of Jesus as lamb, gate of the sheepfold, and shepherd not only make the exercise of the imagination essential and literalist understanding impossible; they also direct readers back to the scriptural sources and parallels for each image, as was done on 1:29 in relation to the sacrifice of Isaac, the Passover lamb, and the Suffering Servant in Isaiah, and they encourage further imaginative improvisation, such as that of Denise Levertov's poem on the Lamb of God.[2] The theological poetry on shepherding that has perhaps been most influential is Psalm 23, and to read it intertextually with John 10 is a fruitful exercise.[3]

The image is stretched in a further direction by Jesus saying, **"I have other sheep that do not belong to this fold. I must bring them also, and they will listen to my voice. So there will be one flock, one shepherd."** This apparent reference to inclusion of non-Jews in the Christian community will be taken up later in commenting on John 12 and 14.

2. See comments on 1:29–34.

3. Daly-Denton does this perceptively in *David in the Fourth Gospel*, 258–64.

This section begins with further polemics against bad leaders, this time under the label of the **hired hand**, and ends with division among **the Jews** about whether Jesus **has a demon**. Both passages reinforce the message to the reader: Decide for Jesus! The rest of the chapter further heightens the division and conflict around Jesus to the verge of violence.

Intensification: "The Father and I Are One"—Blasphemy! (10:22–42)

Here, a couple of months later, at a different festival but in the same temple setting, the same questions surrounding who Jesus is, his relationship to God, what he does, and how to respond to him generate a fresh intensity of conflict. The key issues—what Jesus did, Jesus as Messiah and Son of God, believing in Jesus, and having eternal life—are exactly those that sum up the whole purpose of the Gospel (20:30–31) and have been present from the opening chapter.

But there are new elements here. Jesus as shepherd gives utter security to his followers and makes a provocative statement of the reason for this: "The Father and I are one." The accusation of blasphemy against Jesus is made explicit for the first time. Jesus gives a new argument from Scripture to back up his claim to be God's Son. In line with the Festival of Dedication, Jesus calls himself "the one whom the Father has sanctified," suggesting his identification with the rededicated altar of the temple, and gives the theological purpose of his works: "so that you may know and understand that the Father is in me and I am in the Father." Jesus then has to escape from attempts to stone him and arrest him.

There is a sense of summary and closure about this section. The series of conflictual exchanges that began in chapter 5 comes to a conclusion, setting the scene for the climactic sign of the raising of Lazarus in chapter 11 and the climactic final entry into Jerusalem in chapter 12. There is a summary of the core reality, the relationship of Jesus and his Father, in relation to the key titles "Messiah" and "Son of God," and these in turn point to the reasons why he was eventually killed. There are condensed statements of issues running all through the Book of Signs: **"The works that I do in my Father's name testify to me,"** and **"Even though you do not believe me, believe the works."** And Jesus's ministry has come full circle back to where it began, "across the Jordan," and to John the Baptist, the first witness to him.

But, just as it has many beginnings,[4] *so this Gospel has successive waves of endings.* Yet to come is a series of them: the concluding sign in the public ministry of Jesus (chap. 11); the teaching summary in 12:44–50; the Farewell Discourses in

4. Elements of beginning are found not only in 1:1–18 but also in 1:19–51; 2:1–12, 13–25; 3:1–36.

chapters 13–17; the final words of Jesus, "It is finished" (19:30); the piercing of the side of the dead Jesus (19:31–37); his burial (19:38–42); the summary purpose of the Gospel given at the end of chapter 20, sometimes called by scholars "the first ending" (20:30–31)—but in fact, I am suggesting, one of several; and the epilogue's conclusion, suggesting that there can be no end to telling the story of Jesus. So, after all these endings, the final one opens into endless further testimony, truth, and writings in abundance: "I suppose the world itself could not contain the books that would be written" (21:25).

> 22 At that time the festival of the Dedication took place in Jerusalem. It was winter, 23 and Jesus was walking in the temple, in the portico of Solomon. 24 So the Jews gathered around him and said to him, "How long will you keep us in suspense? If you are the Messiah, tell us plainly." 25 Jesus answered, "I have told you, and you do not believe. The works that I do in my Father's name testify to me; 26 but you do not believe, because you do not belong to my sheep. 27 My sheep hear my voice. I know them, and they follow me. 28 I give them eternal life, and they will never perish. No one will snatch them out of my hand. 29 What my Father has given me is greater than all else, and no one can snatch it out of the Father's hand. 30 The Father and I are one."
>
> 31 The Jews took up stones again to stone him. 32 Jesus replied, "I have shown you many good works from the Father. For which of these are you going to stone me?" 33 The Jews answered, "It is not for a good work that we are going to stone you, but for blasphemy, because you, though only a human being, are making yourself God." 34 Jesus answered, "Is it not written in your law, 'I said, you are gods'? 35 If those to whom the word of God came were called 'gods'—and the scripture cannot be annulled—36 can you say that the one whom the Father has sanctified and sent into the world is blaspheming because I said, 'I am God's Son'? 37 If I am not doing the works of my Father, then do not believe me. 38 But if I do them, even though you do not believe me, believe the works, so that you may know and understand that the Father is in me and I am in the Father." 39 Then they tried to arrest him again, but he escaped from their hands.
>
> 40 He went away again across the Jordan to the place where John had been baptizing earlier, and he remained there. 41 Many came to him, and they were saying, "John performed no sign, but everything that John said about this man was true." 42 And many believed in him there.

The **festival of the Dedication** (Hanukkah) celebrated the reconsecration of the temple after Jerusalem was liberated by the Maccabees from the Syrian king Antiochus Epiphanes in 165 BCE. Antiochus had desecrated it by offering sacrifices to his gods on its altar. So for Jesus to describe himself, in a concept he has not used before, as **the one whom the Father has sanctified** is to identify himself further with the temple. Already in John's Gospel he has been seen as "the Lamb of God" (1:29, 36), his body has been identified with the sanctuary of the temple (2:21), and he has declared himself as the source of the true water and light associated with the Festival of Tabernacles (chap. 7–9). Now, at the Festival of Dedication, as he approaches his death, he is also associated with the consecrated altar in the temple.

All these associations invite readers into further reflection (potentially limitless) on the mutual illumination, through one text after another and one festival after another, of the temple and Jesus. As his death approaches, perhaps the richest temple connections that John opens up are with the presence of God ("I am") and God's glory,[5] and with sacrifice—in John, Jesus dies at the time of the killing of the Passover lambs.

Jesus is surrounded by **the Jews**, presumably the religious leaders, and their question, **"How long will you keep us in suspense?"** is hostile. The Greek literally means, "How long are you taking away our life?" and probably is better translated, "How long will you keep annoying us?"[6] The reply of Jesus, as so often, both serves to advance the story, provoking his opponents into picking up stones to throw at him, and also speaks to John's readers in later situations.[7] Readers are encouraged in following Jesus, offered the ultimate reassurance, **"I give them eternal life, and they will never perish. No one will snatch them out of my hand,"** and given the ultimate theological grounding, **"The Father and I are one."**

"One" in that statement is neuter, meaning "a union," "united"—not "one person." In the immediate context, it could mean simply "united in purpose and agency." But the opponents take it to mean more than that, indeed to be **blasphemy, because you, though only a human being, are making yourself God.** And certainly, in the light of the rest of the Gospel of John, it can mean more than that. John presents, in narrative, figural, and conceptual terms, a unique form of union between Jesus and his Father. *It is a union that by no*

5. On glory, see Ford, "'To See My Glory'"; Ford, "Ultimate Desire"; see also comments on 1:14; 2:11; 11:4, 40; 12:28; 13:31–32; 17:1–5, 20–26; 21:19.

6. Lincoln, *The Gospel according to Saint John*, 304.

7. Jesus's statement **"You do not believe, because you do not belong to my sheep"** raises the issue of human freedom and divine freedom again, and whether, in view of the fact that, as he says later, "You did not choose me, but I chose you" (15:16), believing is simply the result of divine predetermination. My reading of such statements is that they are best understood as a "dualism of decision," as strong appeals to readers to make sure that they decide, or continue to decide, for Jesus. They try to make the alternative unthinkable for oneself. A determinist reading makes nonsense of John's purpose in writing the Gospel. See comments on John 9:35–41.

means compromises the unity of God but does lead to rethinking it, a task that still continues.[8] And one of this Gospel's most important theological features is its insistence (culminating in chap. 17) that this union is not exclusive but capaciously hospitable. Part of the uniqueness of the union of Father and Son is that it can be both incomparable, unparalleled, and distinctive, with all the uniqueness of God and God's name, and also at the same time hospitable in welcoming others into this loving union: "I made your name known to them, and I will make it known, so that the love with which you have loved me may be in them, and I in them" (17:26).

In the next stage of the confrontation, Jesus quotes Psalm 82:6: **"I said, you are gods."** In line with Jewish exegetical argument from lesser to greater, he is saying that, if those addressed by God in the psalm are called "gods," how much more might he **whom the Father has sanctified and sent into the world** be called **God's Son**? He then moves on to argue from his works: **"Even though you do not believe me, believe the works, so that you may know and understand that the Father is in me and I am in the Father."** This further wave of theology expands on the unity between Father and Son by the concept of mutual indwelling. That is to be central in the theology of the ongoing drama, especially as developed in the Farewell Discourses.

In this dramatic moment, it provokes an attempt to **arrest him again**. Jesus **escaped** and then went back to where his ministry began. The witness of John the Baptist to Jesus is reaffirmed: **"Everything that John said about this man was true."** And it is emphasized that Jesus does not have opponents only: **Many believed in him there**. There is a community awaiting those who decide for him.

8. For a profound reflection on "the One God," see Sonderegger, *The Doctrine of God*, part 1, worked out further through the rest of the volume in relation to God's omnipresence, omnipotence, and omniscience.

John 11:1–57

"The Dead Man Came Out"

Now comes the climax of the public ministry of Jesus, and the most dramatic of his signs. They began with a wedding; they end with a funeral.

All through the Gospel, since John the Baptist's enigmatic acclamation, "Here is the Lamb of God who takes away the sin of the world!" (1:29), and Jesus's similarly enigmatic announcement, "Destroy this temple, and in three days I will raise it up" (2:19), there have been pointers to the death and resurrection of Jesus. Now, the anticipation intensifies, the plot thickens, and the meaning deepens.

Jesus walks into acute danger and does something that provokes the Jewish authorities to decide on his death. His behavior is at the same time vulnerable and authoritative, as he not only weeps and is deeply disturbed but also says, "I am the resurrection and the life" (11:25), and summons Lazarus back to life from the tomb. This is humanity and divinity vividly and seemingly paradoxically together in one person. The intensity and significance are emphasized in several ways.

Some ways are familiar from earlier in the Gospel: the sign is associated with God's glory; there are positive and negative responses; there is imagery of light and darkness, life and death; Jesus is Messiah/Christ and Son of God; there is an "I am" saying; and among "the Jews" there are both believers and enemies.

But there are also new elements. The most obvious is the sign itself, whose distinctiveness is underlined—a dead man is raised; Lazarus is named, unlike earlier subjects of miracles by Jesus; there is a uniquely long buildup to him being raised, including a tension-raising delay by Jesus; the feelings of Jesus are shown in unprecedented ways; the deadness of Lazarus is graphically evoked through imagining the stench of decomposition after four days; Jesus prays for the first time in this Gospel; and the culminating loud, imperative cry by Jesus, "Lazarus, come out!" (11:43), contrasts with the relative quietness of his other miracles in John, as if they have been kept lower in volume in order to let this have greater impact. In addition, the love between Jesus and Lazarus, Martha, and Mary is repeatedly stressed—this is the first time Jesus is said to love any particular people; the confession of faith by Martha is the first to anticipate in full what is later said to be the purpose of the whole Gospel, "But these are written so that you may come to believe [or "continue to believe"] that Jesus is the Messiah, the Son of God, and that through believing you may have life in his name" (20:31); and the whole plot of the Gospel is carried a decisive step further by the reaction to the miracle: "So from that day on they planned to put him to death" (11:53)

Within the narrative, the plot advances toward an imminent climax in Jerusalem, with religion and politics intertwined. At the same time, readers are not only led further into who Jesus is, both in his relationship with his Father through prayer and in the depth of his emotion as he engages with friends, enemies, danger, grief, and death. They are also helped, through Jesus, to deepen their relationship with God in the face of death and grief. And rereaders are invited to reflect on the meaning of this event in relation to the rest of the story, as Jesus loves his friends "to the end" (13:1), opens up to them his relationship to his Father (chap. 17), dies, and is raised to a life that relativizes all death: "Those who believe in me, even though they die, will live, and everyone who lives and believes in me will never die" (11:25–26).

The ongoing community is being taught how to respond in faith, through trusting in Jesus as "the resurrection and the life," to the continuing reality of death and grief.

Love and Delay, Death and Glory, John and Other Gospels (11:1–6)

> [1] Now a certain man was ill, Lazarus of Bethany, the village of Mary and her sister Martha. [2] Mary was the one who anointed the Lord with perfume and wiped his feet with her hair; her brother Lazarus was ill. [3] So the sisters sent a message to Jesus, "Lord, he whom you love is ill." [4] But when Jesus heard it, he said, "This illness does not lead to death; rather it is for God's glory, so that the Son of God may be glorified through it." [5] Accordingly, though Jesus loved Martha and her sister and Lazarus, [6] after having heard that Lazarus was ill, he stayed two days longer in the place where he was.

Readers are here introduced to three new characters, Lazarus, Mary, and Martha, the first in this Gospel who are said to be loved by Jesus—his friends, living in a household where he is clearly at home.[1]

The mention here of Mary as **the one who anointed the Lord with perfume and wiped his feet with her hair**, before this is told in 12:1–8, has much significance. It shows the love is mutual. It sets the whole story in the context of Jesus's own death (12:7) and what leads up to it and follows it, and rereaders can find more and more resonances between the two, beginning here with the love of Jesus for his friends (see especially 15:13), and the theme of **God's glory** and the glorifying of Jesus (see especially 12:28; 13:31–32; 17:1–5, 22; 21:19).

It also may suggest that the author expects readers to be familiar already with the anointing, which appears in various forms in the other Gospels. But the raising of Lazarus does not appear elsewhere. There is speculation about whether this story is related to the only other Gospel story naming a Lazarus, Luke's parable about a rich man and a poor man, in which Jesus concludes, "If they do not listen to Moses and the prophets, neither will they be convinced even if someone rises from the dead" (Luke 16:31). Might Luke have inspired John's story, or vice versa? Another recurring question is how likely it was that such a startling event as the raising of Lazarus could have been omitted by the Synoptic Gospels. Yet the raising of the son of the widow of Nain is unique to Luke (7:11–17), and there might have been reasons for the earlier Gospels omitting a story associated with Lazarus: the threat to his life (John 12:9–11) might still have been current when they were being written. The factual question of the return to life of a man four days in the tomb is so bound up with assumptions about God's agency and freedom in relation to the world that it is undecidable by historical investigation.[2] As so often, John here has a story that resonates with various Synoptic stories and sayings but has been crafted to bring out his deepest concerns: who Jesus is; believing in Jesus; going deeper into the life, death, and resurrection of Jesus; and enabling ongoing life in his name.

1. This is a key element in the study by Esler and Piper, *Lazarus, Mary and Martha*. "Through the figures of Lazarus and his sisters, we have suggested that an understanding of Christian existence in the world was set out. Here is a Christianity that is not so much dogmatically based as relationally based. Above all, Christians are characterised by friendship, love and examples of devotion. The kinship group provides the 'natural' context for depicting such an ethos" (pp. 156–57). While disagreeing with the apparent binary contrast of the cognitive (rather slightingly described as dogmatic) and the relational, which I see as opposed by John's emphasis on the Word, knowing, and truth, this focus on relationships rings true with the present work. Esler and Piper also make illuminating connections with John 14:2–3 and 19:26–27.

2. See comments on 2:1–12 and on the resurrection in John 20. On the literary, historical, and theological issues raised by John 11, see Lincoln, "The Lazarus Story"; Thompson, "The Raising of Lazarus in John 11"; Torrance, "The Lazarus Narrative."

Much is made of Jesus delaying to come in response to the message of the sisters. Jesus puts it in the largest possible context, “God’s glory,” and later says, “For your sake I am glad I was not there, so that you may believe” (v. 15). Both Martha and Mary say, “Lord, if you had been here, my brother would not have died” (vv. 21, 32), and the onlookers say, “Could not he who opened the eyes of the blind man have kept this man from dying?” (v. 37). This is facing one of the great problems of those who believe in a life-giving God of love who yet lets people die. *The thrust of this chapter’s response to that problem is to face the harsh facts of illness, death, and decomposition, and do justice to the realities of loss, grief, and anger, while trusting that they do not have the last word. The relationship with the living Jesus in love and trust is more fundamental and embracing. Living in that trust and love can begin now, and the relationship with Jesus is not destroyed by physical death. Jesus himself does not avoid grief, danger, suffering, and death, but offers a life that has come through them and sustains others through them.*

Danger and Death (11:7–16)

> 7 Then after this he said to the disciples, “Let us go to Judea again.” 8 The
> disciples said to him, “Rabbi, the Jews were just now trying to stone you, and
> are you going there again?” 9 Jesus answered, “Are there not twelve hours of
> daylight? Those who walk during the day do not stumble, because they see
> the light of this world. 10 But those who walk at night stumble, because the
> light is not in them.” 11 After saying this, he told them, “Our friend Lazarus
> has fallen asleep, but I am going there to awaken him.” 12 The disciples said
> to him, “Lord, if he has fallen asleep, he will be all right.” 13 Jesus, however,
> had been speaking about his death, but they thought that he was referring
> merely to sleep. 14 Then Jesus told them plainly, “Lazarus is dead. 15 For your
> sake I am glad I was not there, so that you may believe. But let us go to him.”
> 16 Thomas, who was called the Twin, said to his fellow disciples, “Let us also
> go, that we may die with him.”

The decision of Jesus to return, for the sake of **our friend Lazarus**, to Judea, the place of maximum danger for him, in order to do a life-giving act that in fact leads to Jesus being condemned to death gives this sign its climactic significance. It is doing what Jesus later says: “No one has greater love than this, to lay down one’s life for one’s friends” (15:13).

The response of Jesus to the warning given by his disciples is a parable about acting while there is still light, echoing what he said earlier: “We must work the works of him who sent me while it is day; night is coming when no one can work" (9:4). But the rest of that saying is also implied: "As long as I am in the world, I am the light of the world" (9:5). *Light, life, love, and friendship converge in this sign, and in the person of Jesus. But they, like Jesus, are not general, ideal, or abstract qualities or ideas or principles. They are first of all embodied in a person in a drama of encounters, relationships, passionate feelings, decisions, and actions.* In this drama, timing really matters. Jesus is using the time remaining before his "hour" comes in order to "work the works of him who sent me," and his actions move the drama to its climax. The danger that the disciples see is real, but the more profound danger is not that they **die** but that they **stumble**. In the "hour" (13:1) and "night" (13:30) that are to come there will be much stumbling, and one disciple will betray Jesus and another will deny him.

The relativizing of physical death that is such a mark of this sign is imaginatively prepared for by first introducing it as sleep: **"Our friend Lazarus has fallen asleep, but I am going there to awaken him."** The disciples' misunderstanding of the metaphor leads them, in a typical case of Johannine irony, to speak the truth: **"He will be all right"** (*sōthēsetai*; literally, "He will be saved" or "He will recover"). Death is not a full stop to life and is not the worst thing that can happen to someone: it is like sleep.

Jesus then speaks **plainly, "Lazarus is dead."** The deadness of Lazarus is emphasized in several ways in the course of this story, including the expected stench and in referring to him as **the dead man** even while he is walking alive out of the tomb. There is no evading the grim, sad fact of death—not just that of Lazarus, but also of believers (v. 25). But it is not the last word: **"For your sake I am glad I was not there, so that you may believe."** Death can be, and often is, the occasion of coming to deeper faith. Jesus's words, **"But let us go to him,"** are misunderstood by Thomas. His response, **"Let us also go, that we may die with him,"** is in line with his character as it emerges in this Gospel (see also 14:5; 20:24–29). He both trusts Jesus and is a realist who wants certainty and a clear way forward.

"I Am the Resurrection and the Life" (11:17–27)

> [17] When Jesus arrived, he found that Lazarus had already been in the tomb
> four days. [18] Now Bethany was near Jerusalem, some two miles away, [19] and
> many of the Jews had come to Martha and Mary to console them about their
> brother. [20] When Martha heard that Jesus was coming, she went and met
> him, while Mary stayed at home. [21] Martha said to Jesus, "Lord, if you had
> been here, my brother would not have died. [22] But even now I know that God
> will give you whatever you ask of him." [23] Jesus said to her, "Your brother

> will rise again." [24] Martha said to him, "I know that he will rise again in the
> resurrection on the last day." [25] Jesus said to her, "I am the resurrection
> and the life. Those who believe in me, even though they die, will live, [26] and
> everyone who lives and believes in me will never die. Do you believe this?"
> [27] She said to him, "Yes, Lord, I believe that you are the Messiah, the Son of
> God, the one coming into the world."

Usually in John, the theological meaning of a sign is given after Jesus does it. But, when it comes to the most important matters, John prefers to give the meaning—scriptural references and allusions, and the categories, ideas, and images for understanding and interpretation—in advance. So, the prologue is given before the whole story begins, and the Farewell Discourses (chaps. 13–17) come before the death and resurrection of Jesus. The importance of this sign is emphasized by its meaning being opened up in advance of the raising of Lazarus. This happens in a triple way: first through the words of Jesus in conversation with Martha; then in the emotional response of Jesus to the grief of Mary and her companion Jews, leading him to weep; and, finally, through the prayer of Jesus. *It is a meaning that unites the person of Jesus and the depths of human trust, grief, and love with God and God's purposes.*

Martha reaches out in trust to Jesus through her disappointment and grief: **"But even now I know that God will give you whatever you ask of him."** She takes his first response, **"Your brother will rise again,"** as a distant future prospect of **the resurrection on the last day**. But then Jesus makes the core statement: **"I am the resurrection and the life."**

This gains content from previous "I am" statements, where the theme of life is especially strong. In conversation with the Samaritan woman at the well (4:1–42), Jesus had spoken of giving "water gushing up to eternal life" and confessed, in the words "I am," to being the Messiah/Christ. After the feeding of the five thousand, Jesus says, "I am the bread of life. . . . This is indeed the will of my Father, that all who see the Son and believe in him may have eternal life; and I will raise them up on the last day" (6:35, 40). The absolute statement that provokes an attempt to stone him, "Before Abraham was, I am" (8:58), takes us out of linear time that heads for **the last day** and sets the person of Jesus in relationship to past, present, and future, therefore transcending death. So, being in relationship with this person is the key to life that is not dominated or ended by death. The Jesus who says "I am the good shepherd" lays down his life for his sheep and does so "of my own accord. I have power to lay it down, and I have power to take it up again" (10:18). Moreover, he calls his own sheep by name (10:3), the most dramatic instance of which is in this story: "Lazarus, come out!" (11:43).

This death-transcending relationship is then explained further: **"Those who believe in me, even though they die, will live, and everyone who lives and believes in me will never die."** Physical death happens, but it is relativized by Jesus who is **the resurrection and the life**. In the light of Jesus, there is a distinction between the ordinary sense of life, together with the death that ends it, and the eternal life of one who says "I am."

Yet the distinction is by no means a separation. Rather, Jesus fully affirms ordinary life and weeps over ordinary death—even, as will shortly occur, becoming angry at death and the cost of experiencing it. What he offers is full immersion in ordinary life and exposure to ordinary death—in his own case, in extremely painful form—together with confidence in resurrection and a quality of life, love, and relationship with himself that can begin now. It is a realism, expressed in his person, of both the ordinary and the extraordinary together; but the extraordinary is for him the divine ordinariness of life in union with his Father, as articulated in his prayer at the tomb of Lazarus. And this "extraordinary ordinary" is available to anyone who responds to him in trust, to **everyone who lives and believes in me**. The trust is essential because the life is in relationship with him and inseparable from mutual love. Its fullest articulation is in his prayer in John 17. Its fullest realization is in the ongoing drama beginning in John 20 with the encounter of the resurrected Jesus with Mary Magdalene, as he says, "Mary!"

For readers experiencing the death of loved ones or facing death themselves, this Jesus-centered realism of the "extraordinary ordinary" is "good news," testimony that can be trusted—or not.[3] John's whole purpose is to encourage, enable, and deepen that trust, as summarized at the end of John 20. Martha now anticipates that summary, combining its titles, **the Messiah** and **the Son of God**, which also come in John 1,[4] with one from John 1:9 and the feeding of the five thousand (6:14), **the one coming into the world**. Her (and any other believer's) understanding of them could no doubt be further enriched, expanded, and deepened, but in John's terms she has the basic template right.

3. There will be fuller reassurance later in the Farewell Discourses, especially in 14:1–7, where the John 11 themes of troubled hearts, believing and trusting, Thomas, the Father, life, and, above all, the "I am" of Jesus as the comprehensive truth are repeated:

> "Do not let your hearts be troubled. Believe in God, believe also in me. In my Father's house there are many dwelling places. If it were not so, would I have told you that I go to prepare a place for you? And if I go and prepare a place for you, I will come again and will take you to myself, so that where I am, there you may be also. And you know the way to the place where I am going." Thomas said to him, "Lord, we do not know where you are going. How can we know the way?" Jesus said to him, "I am the way, and the truth, and the life. No one comes to the Father except through me. If you know me, you will know my Father also. From now on you do know him and have seen him."

4. So, for rereaders, her affirmation embraces the whole Gospel.

Jesus, Greatly Disturbed and Deeply Moved, Weeps (11:28–37)

> 28 When she had said this, she went back and called her sister Mary, and
> told her privately, "The Teacher is here and is calling for you." 29 And when
> she heard it, she got up quickly and went to him. 30 Now Jesus had not yet
> come to the village, but was still at the place where Martha had met him.
> 31 The Jews who were with her in the house, consoling her, saw Mary get up
> quickly and go out. They followed her because they thought that she was
> going to the tomb to weep there. 32 When Mary came where Jesus was and
> saw him, she knelt at his feet and said to him, "Lord, if you had been here,
> my brother would not have died." 33 When Jesus saw her weeping, and the
> Jews who came with her also weeping, he was greatly disturbed in spirit
> and deeply moved. 34 He said, "Where have you laid him?" They said to him,
> "Lord, come and see." 35 Jesus began to weep. 36 So the Jews said, "See how
> he loved him!" 37 But some of them said, "Could not he who opened the eyes
> of the blind man have kept this man from dying?"

Now comes the second wave of meaning in advance of the sign itself. With Martha, Jesus shared meaning in words. With Mary, Jesus is meaning incarnate. The Word is vulnerable flesh, is **greatly disturbed in spirit and deeply moved**, and weeps. This is the response by Jesus to seeing both Mary **weeping** and **the Jews who came with her also weeping**. He is in solidarity with them and shares their grief. More than that, he is moved as a friend of Lazarus: "**See how he loved him!**"

But there is more even than that. The unusual Greek verb translated as **greatly disturbed**, *embrimaomai*, whose importance is reinforced by being repeated a few verses later when **Jesus, again greatly disturbed, came to the tomb** (v. 38), is in other cases used to convey deep emotion with an element of anger. Commentators have identified many possible targets of the anger of Jesus, ranging from Mary and the Jewish onlookers, and the pressure on him to perform a miracle, to his own danger and approaching death, and even death itself.

John is perhaps deliberately not specific. He has chosen a rare, capacious word to describe the intense emotional state of Jesus at this culminating point of his ministry and doing signs. That ministry has engaged with friends and enemies, weddings and sickness, misunderstanding and hunger, light and darkness—all of which have emotional implications. *Now, on the verge of entering the ultimate darkness of his own death, Jesus faces the death of Lazarus and enters into the emotions surrounding death, including love, blame, grief, and anger.* Whereas in the Synoptic Gospels the most graphic account of the emotion of Jesus in the face of death is in his agony in prayer just before he is arrested in the garden of Gethsemane (Matt. 26:36–46; Mark 14:32–42; Luke 22:39–46), John here shows the emotion of Jesus when faced with the death of his friend. John does not have the scene in Gethsemane. He has echoes of it elsewhere (12:27; 13:21; both of those use *tarassein*, the verb translated here as "deeply moved"), but it is here that he concentrates most attention on Jesus gripped and shaken by emotion. It is worth reflecting on two often ignored aspects of this scene.

The first is the range of the solidarity of Jesus: both with **Mary**, who stands for those to whom he is closest in mutual love, and with **the Jews**, who in John's Gospel cover a wide range of reactions to Jesus, including rejection and hatred.[5] Soon, John will describe the purpose of the death of Jesus being "to die for the nation, and not for the nation only, but to gather into one the dispersed children of God" (11:51–52); and in the next chapter Jesus will speak of the consequence of his death being to "draw all people to myself" (12:32). Here, there is a foretaste of all that, as the death of Lazarus gathers a varied group, and Jesus enters into solidarity with them all, including those who turn out to be skeptics or informers. This solidarity does not exclude anger.

The second is to note that Jesus's great disturbance is **in spirit** (*tō pneumati*; literally, "in the spirit/Spirit"). This can simply mean "in himself," but John's habit of multileveled communication invites finding further meaning. Right at the start of the Gospel, John the Baptist testified, "I saw the Spirit [*to pneuma*] descending from heaven like a dove, and it remained on him" (1:32). The Spirit (or spirit [the original manuscripts do not differentiate]) is far more prominent through the rest of John's Gospel than in the Synoptics, and of special relevance here are the accounts of the death of Jesus when he "gave up his spirit" (19:30; literally, "the spirit/Spirit," *to pneuma*); and of the resurrected Jesus when he "breathed" (the Greek verb is the one used in the Septuagint account of God breathing the breath of life into Adam at creation [Gen. 2:7]) his spirit/Spirit into his disciples: "Receive the Holy Spirit" (20:22). The Holy Spirit and the human spirit of Jesus are inextricably united, in line with the Word of God becoming human flesh, and this has profound implications for his disciples. *As they unite with him and one another, they are being drawn into the sort of passionate solidarity with others, and especially suffering others, that Jesus demonstrates with Mary and the Jews.*

Yet readers are not allowed to forget the dramatic context here: **But some of them said, "Could not he who opened the eyes of the blind man have kept this**

5. For more on Jesus and the Jews see above on John 2 and 8. See also Bieringer, Pollefeyt, and Vandecasteele-Vanneuville, *Anti-Judaism and the Fourth Gospel*; Frey, "'Die Juden' im Johanesevangelium."

man from dying?" John is yet again showing the possibility of very different responses to Jesus.

"Lazarus, Come Out!" "Unbind Him, and Let Him Go" (11:38–44)

> 38 Then Jesus, again greatly disturbed, came to the tomb. It was a cave, and
> a stone was lying against it. 39 Jesus said, "Take away the stone." Martha, the
> sister of the dead man, said to him, "Lord, already there is a stench because
> he has been dead four days." 40 Jesus said to her, "Did I not tell you that if you
> believed, you would see the glory of God?" 41 So they took away the stone.
> And Jesus looked upward and said, "Father, I thank you for having heard
> me. 42 I knew that you always hear me, but I have said this for the sake of the
> crowd standing here, so that they may believe that you sent me." 43 When
> he had said this, he cried with a loud voice, "Lazarus, come out!" 44 The
> dead man came out, his hands and feet bound with strips of cloth, and his
> face wrapped in a cloth. Jesus said to them, "Unbind him, and let him go."

Finally, on the verge of the actual raising of Lazarus, comes the third and greatest wave of meaning. Teaching and weeping are followed by prayer that goes to the heart of the theological reality of this Gospel: the relationship of Jesus with his Father.

Before the prayer, there is a striking contrast between **stench** and **glory**. Martha warns of the stench after the body has been decomposing for four days; Jesus responds, **"Did I not tell you that if you believed, you would see the glory of God?"** This echoes Jesus's opening statement to his disciples about the illness of Lazarus, "It is for God's glory, so that the Son of God may be glorified through it" (11:4). The idea of divine glory, and the content given to it by Jesus, is central to John's theology, beginning with the prologue: "We have seen his glory, the glory as of a father's only son, full of grace and truth" (1:14). The first sign, water turned into wine, was said to have "revealed his glory; and his disciples believed in him" (2:11); and now this climactic sign begins and ends with reference to seeing **the glory of God**.

The meaning of glory will be further enriched by John 12–21.[6] John's key move is to see the glory of God in the whole of Jesus's life, work, death, and resurrection. One way of seeing this is that the glory and the light focused in the transfiguration of Jesus—a pivotal event in each of the Synoptic Gospels,[7] in which the face and clothes of Jesus become radiant—are in John distributed

6. See comments on 13:31–32; 17:1–5, 20–26; 21:19.
7. See Matt. 17:1–13; Mark 9:2–13; Luke 9:28–36.

throughout the Gospel, beginning with the prologue. As noted above, something similar happens with the agony of Jesus in the garden of Gethsemane on the night before his death: Jesus being "deeply moved / troubled" is spread through three occasions (11:33; 12:27; 13:21). A comparable distribution of a Synoptic event through more than one Johannine narrative also occurs with the trial and condemnation of Jesus, one part of which, the verdict of the Sanhedrin, occurs in this chapter.

John also sometimes concentrates several Synoptic stories into one,[8] as will be seen in John 12, when Mary anointed Jesus's feet with costly "pure nard," and "the house was filled with the fragrance of the perfume" (12:3). That act, which Jesus connects with "my burial" (12:7), might be understood as a symbol of God's glory in scent, letting the reader imagine that instead of the stench of the body of Lazarus. Just as God's glory frames this sign, so does reference to Mary, who "anointed the Lord with perfume and wiped his feet with her hair" (11:2 [see 12:1–8]). All the senses are brought into play at this point: seeing, hearing, smelling, touching, and (in the dinner Martha serves at Bethany [12:2]) tasting. And each of them gives an invitation to meditate on it as a sign, which is both fully physical and yet has layers of further meaning. **"Did I not tell you that if you believed, you would see the glory of God?"** What sort of seeing is that, inseparable from believing? Clearly, not all who saw the dead Lazarus coming out of the tomb alive also saw the glory of God.

John's Gospel has been a constant inspiration to the rich tradition of the "spiritual senses," through which depths of significance are found (or missed) in drinking water or wine, eating bread or fish, breathing *pneuma* (breath, wind, spirit/Spirit), walking in light or darkness, anointing or washing feet, smelling a stench or a scent, or hearing one's name called. The depth is often indicated by the note of abundance—gallons of wine, water welling up, baskets of bread left over, an enormous catch of fish, *pneuma* given without measure, light for the whole world, scent filling a house. *Incarnation for John means bringing all the senses into play, both literally and imaginatively, for the sake of abundant life.*

Next, after the stone is taken away from the entrance to the tomb, **Jesus looked upward and said, "Father, I thank you for having heard me. I knew that you always hear me, but I have said this for the sake of the crowd standing here, so that they may believe that you sent me."** This is a prayer of utter communion between Jesus and his Father, coming from "the only Son, who is close to the Father's heart" (1:18). This communion in love and trust is the

8. The effect of John's reworking of material shared with the Synoptics should not be to replace them but rather to stimulate rereading them, and John, afresh. See below, in the present section, on the loud cry of Jesus.

most embracing context for the raising of Lazarus, and points forward to the long prayer of Jesus in John 17. That prayer is prefaced by "He looked up to heaven" and opens, "Father, the hour has come; glorify your Son so that the Son may glorify you," and it says of the disciples, "They have believed that you sent me," before opening up further depths and heights.[9] Here, what Jesus is about to do has been related not only to key elements of the prologue (flesh, seeing glory, believing, communion between Father and Son) but also to that culminating prayer of Jesus's life.

And now, finally, resonating with the culminating events of Jesus's story, his death and resurrection, the sign happens—quickly and simply, but authoritatively, loudly, visibly, and decisively.

Jesus **cried with a loud voice**. In the Synoptic Gospels, Jesus cries "with a loud voice" on the cross before he dies (Matt. 27:50; Mark 15:37; Luke 23:46). By moving this powerful, memorable phrase to here, John associates it with death and resurrection together. *After John, the Synoptic loud cries from the cross cannot be heard without also hearing this cry to Lazarus.* The effect is not to supersede the Synoptics but to relate them to John's theology of glory seen through crucifixion and resurrection together, and to let us hear the "It is finished" of John's crucifixion scene (19:30) as a victorious verdict, in line with the cry "I have conquered the world!" (16:33).

"Lazarus, come out!" The shepherd whose voice is recognized by his sheep, who calls them by name, and who lays down his life for them so that they may have life in abundance (10:3, 10, 15), now calls Lazarus by name, and **the dead man came out**. This is the authority of a love that is willing to die.

What follows, as the **hands and feet** of Lazarus need to be unbound, signals that this is resuscitation, not resurrection like that of Jesus. In John's account of the resurrection of Jesus, a good deal is made of how the grave clothes of Jesus were lying in the tomb, as was "the cloth that had been on Jesus' head, not lying with the linen wrappings but rolled up in a place by itself" (20:5–7). Both Peter and the Beloved Disciple saw these, but only the Beloved Disciple "saw and believed" (20:5–8). Again, there is seeing—and seeing.

"Unbind him, and let him go." The command is clear and practical. It also bursts with further meaning. *The astonishing, life-giving event has occurred; now others are needed to join in making it effective.* Even after coming to believe, having been "born . . . of God" (1:13), "born of water and Spirit" (3:5), or having heard the voice of the shepherd calling us by name (10:3–5), we may still need to be liberated from beliefs, attitudes, habits, addictions, constrictions, traumatic experiences, self-images, or whatever else hinders full living, keeping us bound

9. See especially the comments on 17:20–26.

> The raising of Lazarus is the centrepiece of the Fourth Gospel, bringing to a climax the themes and symbols of the first half of the Gospel. It contains the greatest of the "I am" sayings (11:25–26), has its centre in the major Johannine theme of life (*zōē aiōnios*, e.g., 1:4; 3:15–18; 5:21–29; 10:10b), and completes the "signs" of the ministry of Jesus, where the divine glory is made manifest in the flesh through his symbolic words and works. At the same time, if the sequence is seen to include the plot to kill Jesus (11:45–53), the raising of Lazarus sets in motion the second half of the Gospel, where the divine glory is again manifest in the flesh, this time through the cross. . . . The decision of the Sanhedrin leads in a straight line to Jesus' arrest, conviction, and death (11:55–57). . . . On a deeper level, the narrative reveals the evangelical purpose of Jesus' coming, and therefore, the Father's sending: to give life to believers at the cost of Jesus' death (3:16). In this program, the anointing plays a key symbolic role, signifying, on the one hand, the interplay of life and death and the triumph of the one over the other and, on the other hand, the intimacy that holds the community together in the Father's love.
>
> —Dorothy Lee, *Flesh and Glory*, 200

up in things that smell of death and deprive us of freedom; and that liberation usually needs the attentive help of other people. "Unbind him, and let him go" is a watchword for love in action.

How this event and the rest of this chapter leading into the anointing of Jesus by Mary in John 12 are pivotal in John's Gospel is summed up by Dorothy Lee (see the quotation from Lee in the sidebar).

Dying in Order to Gather the Dispersed Children (11:45–54)

> 45 Many of the Jews therefore, who had come with Mary and had seen what
> Jesus did, believed in him. 46 But some of them went to the Pharisees and
> told them what he had done. 47 So the chief priests and the Pharisees called
> a meeting of the council, and said, "What are we to do? This man is per-
> forming many signs. 48 If we let him go on like this, everyone will believe in
> him, and the Romans will come and destroy both our holy place and our
> nation." 49 But one of them, Caiaphas, who was high priest that year, said to
> them, "You know nothing at all! 50 You do not understand that it is better
> for you to have one man die for the people than to have the whole nation
> destroyed." 51 He did not say this on his own, but being high priest that year
> he prophesied that Jesus was about to die for the nation, 52 and not for the

nation only, but to gather into one the dispersed children of God. [53] So from that day on they planned to put him to death.

[54] Jesus therefore no longer walked about openly among the Jews, but went from there to a town called Ephraim in the region near the wilderness; and he remained there with the disciples.

In the immediate aftermath of the miracle, there is a divided response. **Many of the Jews . . . believed in him**, and noting this is important for John's complex portrayal of the Jews. **But some of them** acted as informers, and this led to **the chief priests and the Pharisees** deciding **to put him to death**. *Jesus is caught between the fear-driven politics of his own people and the ruthless Roman Empire—and the trial of Jesus will show Rome's power is also dominated by fear,* with Pilate becoming "more afraid than ever" during the process (19:8). Jesus's **performing many signs** and attracting popular belief in himself causes the Jewish leaders justifiably to fear that he will lead to the destruction of **both our holy place and our nation**. There is great irony in the high priest's prudential reasoning that **it is better for you to have one man die for the people**, and the author underlines this. The irony is not only that Jesus is to die for others in a different sense—as "the Lamb of God who takes away the sin of the world" (1:29), as the one who gives his flesh "for the life of the world" (6:51), as the shepherd who lays down his life for his sheep, as the one who gives his life for friends such as Lazarus, and who, "when I am lifted up from the earth, will draw all people to myself" (12:32). The irony is also that, as was clear by the time this Gospel was being read, all the efforts to save "our holy place and our nation" from the Romans failed.

The author's comment reaches into that future: **Jesus was about to die for the nation, and not for the nation only, but to gather into one the dispersed children of God**. That unity into which Jesus is to gather people is what he prays to his Father for in 17:20–26. It is desire for a family oriented toward attracting others through their dynamic unity in love, with God and one another, "so that the world may know that you have sent me and have loved them even as you have loved me" (17:23). How to be such a community has continued to be a central challenge and task for followers of Jesus. There have always been massive forces—religious, political, economic, and cultural—that militate against it, and fear has continued to be a core motive. The sign of the raising of Lazarus shows Jesus acting in love despite the danger he was in and suffering the consequences. The stark contrast is between being driven by love and by desire for the glory of the God of love, or by the religion, politics, economics, and culture of fear. Religious, political, business, ethnic, familial, and other communities are still asked regularly to make decisions that require discerning whether love or fear is primary. John's Gospel does not give detailed guidelines for such decision-making but promises the Jesus-breathed Spirit, who draws on the witness to him and guides "into all the truth" (16:13). And John is crystal clear that no one can follow this way alone: we need to be gathered **into one**.

Back to the immediate drama: Jesus **went from there** into hiding, biding his time with his disciples until Passover.

Will He Come to This Passover? (11:55–57)

> 55 Now the Passover of the Jews was near, and many went up from the
> country to Jerusalem before the Passover to purify themselves. 56 They were
> looking for Jesus and were asking one another as they stood in the temple,
> "What do you think? Surely he will not come to the festival, will he?" 57 Now
> the chief priests and the Pharisees had given orders that anyone who knew
> where Jesus was should let them know, so that they might arrest him.

This is the third Passover in John, and each of the previous two was accompanied by conflict (2:13–24; 6:4–71). Now the conflict is approaching its climax, and the suspense is increased by speculation about whether Jesus will **come to the festival** and by the issuing of a warrant for his **arrest**.

John 12:1–50

"The Hour Has Come"

Ultimate Glory, Attraction, and Decision

The aftermath of the raising of Lazarus continues into the final scene of the public ministry of Jesus. The theme of death deepens and broadens, expressed as betrayal and greed, burial, death plots, a seed in the ground, Jesus's troubled soul, self-judgment, darkness, unbelief, blindness, hardheartedness, fear, and rejection. The countertheme of abundant life, expressed as house-filling fragrance, generosity, serving, blessing, testifying, raising the dead, glorifying, fruitfulness, attraction, healing, light, believing, and eternal life, more than matches death. Yet death and life are not simple opposites. Like a seed that, "if it dies, . . . bears much fruit" (12:24), the death of Jesus will be the secret of his glory and his attractive power, and also the secret of the lives of service lived by his followers. Even rejection of Jesus is set alongside his expectation that, from the cross, "I . . . will draw all people [or, perhaps better, "all things"] to myself" (12:32), and God's healing purposes are not necessarily defeated by unbelief, blindness, and hard-heartedness.

Jesus makes the momentous announcement, anticipated since his first sign (see 2:4): "The hour has come for the Son of Man to be glorified" (12:23). His triumphant entry into Jerusalem as a humble king on a donkey inaugurates, in a powerful yet subversive way, the final act. This is set in the royal, holy city, at the time of the great feast of Passover, with Roman military power as the dominant political context. The rest of John 12 acts both as a conclusion to the Book of Signs (chaps. 2–12) and as a preparation for the rest of the Gospel.

The Greeks who ask to see Jesus represent the whole world beyond Judaism, and other elements in the chapter reinforce this global horizon: "Look, the world has gone after him" (v. 19); "Now is the judgment of this world; now the ruler of this world will be driven out. And I, when I am lifted up from the earth, will draw all people [or "all things"] to myself" (vv. 31–32); "I have come as light into the world, so that everyone who believes in me should not remain in the darkness. I do not judge anyone who hears my words and does not keep them, for I came not to judge the world, but to save the world" (vv. 46–47).

This is the broad context for three profound challenges. First, there is *the ultimate statement on glory*, given by the Father himself, the only time in the Gospel of John that a "voice . . . from heaven" is heard. Centrally, there is *the ultimate image of attraction*, Jesus lifted up from the earth on the cross. Finally, there is *the ultimate decision*, between walking in the light and walking in darkness, or between believing/trusting in Jesus and rejecting him. The meaning of each of those—glory, the crucifixion, and believing—will be intensified, deepened, and expanded by the chapters that follow.

Scented Sign (12:1–8)

> 1 Six days before the Passover Jesus came to Bethany, the home of Lazarus, whom he had raised from the dead. 2 There they gave a dinner for him. Martha served, and Lazarus was one of those at the table with him. 3 Mary took a pound of costly perfume made of pure nard, anointed Jesus' feet, and wiped them with her hair. The house was filled with the fragrance of the perfume. 4 But Judas Iscariot, one of his disciples (the one who was about to betray him), said, 5 "Why was this perfume not sold for three hundred denarii and the money given to the poor?" 6 (He said this not because he cared about the poor, but because he was a thief; he kept the common purse and used to steal what was put into it.) 7 Jesus said, "Leave her alone. She bought it so that she might keep it for the day of my burial. 8 You always have the poor with you, but you do not always have me."

As the countdown to Passover begins, Jesus comes out of retreat and nearer to Jerusalem, to a dinner in his honor in Bethany. Lazarus, **raised from the dead** by Jesus, remains prominent, but largely passive. He never speaks, in contrast to his sisters.

Martha served. The same verb is repeated later in the chapter when Jesus says, "Whoever serves me must follow me, and where I am, there will my servant be also. Whoever serves me, the Father will honor" (12:26). Martha earlier showed exemplary faith, now she gives exemplary service—both are centered on Jesus. The classic contrast of Martha the activist and Mary the contemplative (Luke 10:38–42) is not in John, where both are portrayed as model friends of Jesus. In Luke's story, set long in advance of the final entry of Jesus into Jerusalem, Martha was "distracted by her many tasks" and complained about Mary sitting at the feet of Jesus and not helping her. In John, just before the entry into Jerusalem, we see Martha serving and Mary at the feet of Jesus, paying him intense, extravagant attention, but there is no sign of tension between the sisters. It is as if, in John's version, the grief and joy around Lazarus and the approaching death of Jesus relativize any such complaints or comparisons. Death can have such a unifying effect, allowing the essentials to be seen more clearly, in particular the importance of key relationships.

The essentials in John 11 and 12 include being loved by Jesus, loving and trusting Jesus, recognizing who Jesus is, a heart open to the suffering of others, prayer, service, life-giving signs, extravagant attention and generosity, and playing different parts in the drama of friendship with Jesus. John has portrayed a model community of disciples as friends of Jesus, and this meal in Bethany is set **six days before the Passover** on a Sunday, the first day of the week, when the later community met to worship and share a meal together in the name and presence of Jesus.

Martha was the more prominent sister in John 11. Gail O'Day's perceptive analysis of her role there concludes that "the narrator's comments about Martha help to bring the domestic intensity of death to the forefront. But death is also more than personal in John 11. . . . Her words to Jesus are not simply personal complaint, lament, or petition, but mirror and embody the faithful speech of her religious community,"[1] especially that of the lament psalms that voice her community's movement through complaint and petition to confidence and confession. Not only does Martha's confession fulfill the purpose of the whole Gospel as stated in 20:31; she even gives it before she sees Lazarus raised from death, and so fulfills the beatitude announced by Jesus just before this: "Blessed are those who have not seen and yet have come to believe" (20:29). Here in 12:2 the brief reference to Martha's service completes the picture of a model friend of Jesus: *loved, loving, believing, and now active in a practical way.*

But the more prominent sister here in John 12 is Mary. In John 11, she sat weeping at Jesus's feet, joined in grief by her Jewish community and by Jesus. Now she interrupts the celebratory meal with a daring, surprising act (see the quotation from Chartres in the sidebar).

1. O'Day, "Martha: Seeing the Glory of God," 502–3.

This "scent event," countering the imagined stench of the decomposing Lazarus, is a recognition of who Jesus is as the anointed one, of his unique presence, and of him laying down his life. In line with the promise of Jesus that his crucifixion would "draw all people to myself," scent is also powerfully attractive. Like the air that carries it, fragrance also evokes the Spirit: encompassing and edgeless; spreading unpredictably and crossing boundaries; connecting with potent memories and deep relationships.

As often in John, Song of Songs comes to mind:

> For your love is better than wine,
> your anointing oils are fragrant,
> your name is perfume poured out;
> therefore the maidens love you. . . .
> While the king was on his couch,
> my nard gave forth its fragrance. (Song 1:2–3, 12)
>
> Awake, O north wind,
> and come, O south wind!
> Blow upon my garden
> that its fragrance may be wafted abroad.
> Let my beloved come to his garden,
> and eat its choicest fruits. (Song 4:16)

> Mary went over the top. Her prefiguring of the foot-washing in John 13 is not only an extravagant gesture, and as such expresses one of the leading themes of the Gospel, the abundant generosity and even extravagance of God; there is also a disturbing erotic dimension as she uses her hair instead of a towel. Yet it is desire taken up into honouring Jesus as the Christ, anointing the Anointed One. Jesus gives the authoritative interpretation of it: "She bought it so that she might keep it for the day of my burial. You always have the poor with you, but you do not always have me." Nard was the main ingredient of the perfume that was used in making the consecrated incense, the Ketoret. This was the incense offered on the altar of the First and Second Temples. John had already spoken of the body of crucified and resurrected Jesus as the Temple (2:21). Now, in the aftermath of the climactic sign of Lazarus dying and being raised, Mary anticipates Jesus dying and being raised by filling the house in Bethany with the odour of the fragrance that evoked Temple worship. To "have me" is the height of mutual desire, later enacted in the crucified and risen Jesus in encounter with another Mary (20:16).
>
> —Richard Chartres (in a personal communication, April 2016)

As in Song of Songs, here in Bethany there are fragrance, food, and utter mutuality in love. Jesus, in a climactic sign, has put his life on the line for those he loves and is now sharing a meal with them; Mary responds, in an act of daring self-involvement, love, and devotion, with the only sign that is done to him, rather than by him. "Mary's loosened long hair could be understood both as a sign of intimacy and as a customary indication of mourning. As she wipes Jesus's feet with her hair, she too becomes an anointed one who exudes and spreads the *pistikē* fragrance that symbolizes faith."[2]

Judas objects. In contrast to Matthew, where it is the disciples who angrily object (Matt. 26:8), and to Mark, who says that "some were there who said to one another in anger, 'Why was the ointment wasted in this way? For this ointment could have been sold for more than three hundred denarii, and the money given to the poor'" (Mark 14:4–5), John names the objector. This sharpens the moment and connects it directly to the coming betrayal and death of Jesus. John also sees in Judas a motive of greed and theft, resonating with Synoptic accounts (lacking in John) of Judas being paid to betray Jesus.

The response of Jesus in Mark's account is fuller than John's and helps to avoid misinterpretation of John: "But Jesus said, 'Let her alone; why do you trouble her? She has performed a good service [*kalos ergos*; literally, 'a beautiful work'] for me. For you always have the poor with you, and you can show kindness to them whenever you wish; but you will not always have me. She has done what she could; she has anointed my body beforehand for its burial. Truly I tell you, wherever the good news is proclaimed in the whole world, what she has done will be told in remembrance of her'" (Mark 14:6–9). *This is one of many cases where reading John alongside the Synoptics enhances the meaning of both.* John's emphasis on fragrance enriches the aesthetics of Mark's "beautiful work"; his naming of Judas heightens the drama; his naming of Mary (in Mark the anointing is done by "a woman" [14:3]), as one loved by Jesus, intensifies the mutuality and brings out her action's relevance to the ongoing community; and placing this in relation to the climactic sign of raising Lazarus deepens the meaning of the action. Mary is both expressing gratitude for her brother's life and recognizing what the action of Jesus will cost him. Mark's account explains more fully that this is by no means intended to discourage people from showing "kindness" to the poor, and the horizon

2. Daly-Denton, *John*, 156. *Pistikē*, translated in the NRSV as "pure," is cognate with *pisteuein* ("believe, trust, have faith"). Comparisons with analogous stories in the Synoptic Gospels (Matt. 26:6–13; Mark 14:3–9; Luke 7:36–50; 10:38–42) give much food for further intertextual reflection. Through them, John's story is enriched with themes of global dissemination, forgiveness, and "great love" (Luke 7:47), and they are in turn oriented more toward themes of abundance and community.

of "the whole world" is taken up by John in what follows in chapter 12. The two agree on the imperative of Jesus: "Let her alone" in Mark, **"Leave her alone"** in John.[3] To how many critical responses to women's actions through Christian history might this be applied? This story has been effectively used in support of the roles, ministries, and vocations of women within and beyond the church.

Enmity, Mutuality, and Death (12:9–11)

> 9 When the great crowd of the Jews learned that he was there, they came
> not only because of Jesus but also to see Lazarus, whom he had raised from
> the dead. 10 So the chief priests planned to put Lazarus to death as well,
> 11 since it was on account of him that many of the Jews were deserting and
> were believing in Jesus.

There could have been no more effective way of undoing the final public sign of Jesus and of contradicting the life-giving character of all his signs than to **put Lazarus to death as well** as Jesus. These verses not only heighten the "dualism of decision" between the enemies of Jesus and those who believe in him; they also complete the picture of the model community of his friends: loved, loving, believing, serving, daringly and generously self-involved—and now, in the person of Lazarus, attracting public attention and risking death.

Not only that, the mutuality between Jesus and his friends is filled out. Martha had evoked from Jesus his self-identification, "I am the resurrection and the life," and she in turn had decisively acknowledged him (11:27) and served him (12:2). Jesus had wept in response to Mary's grief (11:35), and at the meal in Bethany the two were united by scent, touch, and the prospect of his death. Jesus had shown love for his friends in risking his life for Lazarus, and now he and Lazarus are joined both in attracting the crowds and in having their deaths **planned**. Each member of this little family community has prompted Jesus to reveal himself in a different way, through a drama that is also a model for the ongoing drama of his followers. *John's way of telling it helps readers, and especially rereaders, to figure themselves into it, to be prepared for grief and danger as well as family life and celebration, and to improvise further, and daringly, in line with who Jesus is and what he does and suffers.*

3. The Greek verb is the same in both; Mark's is plural because the objectors are several, John's singular is addressed to Judas.

Enter the King of Israel on a Little Donkey (12:12–19)

> 12 The next day the great crowd that had come to the festival heard that
> Jesus was coming to Jerusalem. 13 So they took branches of palm trees and
> went out to meet him, shouting,
>
> "Hosanna!
> Blessed is the one who comes in the name of the Lord—
> the King of Israel!"
>
> 14 Jesus found a young donkey and sat on it; as it is written:
>
> 15 "Do not be afraid, daughter of Zion.
> Look, your king is coming,
> sitting on a donkey's colt!"
>
> 16 His disciples did not understand these things at first; but when Jesus was
> glorified, then they remembered that these things had been written of him
> and had been done to him. 17 So the crowd that had been with him when
> he called Lazarus out of the tomb and raised him from the dead continued
> to testify. 18 It was also because they heard that he had performed this sign
> that the crowd went to meet him. 19 The Pharisees then said to one another,
> "You see, you can do nothing. Look, the world has gone after him!"

Jesus enters Jerusalem to acclamation and blessing from **the great crowd that had come to the festival**. All four Gospels tell of this, and it is worth reading the other three alongside John.

They all agree on the crowd welcoming Jesus in the words of Psalm 118, John's version being **"Hosanna! Blessed is the one who comes in the name of the Lord!"** This was how pilgrims to Jerusalem were greeted, and reading the full psalm gives a rich theological context for the whole of John 11 and 12, with themes of love, compassion, not fearing, rulers, salvation, victory, death and life, entering, rejection, light, and the altar of the temple.

But John is the only one to add **"the King of Israel!"** to their shout.[4] This recalls Nathanael's cry at the very beginning of Jesus's ministry, "Rabbi, you are the Son of God! You are the King of Israel!" and the promise of Jesus to him, "You will see greater things" (1:49–50). Here, it sharpens the messianic political edge, and the mention (also only by John) of **branches of palm trees** makes the edge sharper still, because palm branches were associated with the Jewish nationalism of the Maccabees: in 141 BCE they were carried in Simon Maccabee's triumphal procession into the Jerusalem citadel. The title also looks ahead to the trial and crucifixion of Jesus, in which the nature of his kingship will be central.

4. Luke simply says "the king" (19:38).

All four Gospels also agree on Jesus riding in, but John is the only one to call the animal an *onarion*, which the NRSV translates as **a young donkey**, giving only one aspect of its meaning. It is a diminutive that can also mean "little donkey," and that seems appropriate here. Having emphasized the messianic power politics of the crowd, expecting someone like Simon Maccabee and his victorious army, John at once undermines it with this little donkey. For rereaders, that Jesus **sat on it** is an added reference forward to a key, multileveled moment in Jesus's trial (19:13),[5] in which the subversion and transformation of worldly power are also at issue.

There may be another reference forward to the trial, in which Pilate's fear and Jesus's lack of fear are emphasized, in the quotation **"Do not be afraid, daughter of Zion. Look, your king is coming, sitting on a donkey's colt!"** John has here added to a text from Zechariah 9:9 (which Matthew also uses in 21:5), "Do not be afraid," which probably is a reference to Zephaniah 3:16. Alone of the Gospels, John adds a retrospective reflection about the event: **His disciples did not understand these things at first; but when Jesus was glorified, then they remembered that these things had been written of him and had been done to him.**

What specifically are the "things" that "had been written"? If, as the quotations suggest, they include at a minimum Zechariah 9:9–17 and Zephaniah 3, then we have a set of illuminating intertexts for this event and the rest of John 12. Zechariah has the king coming "humble and riding on a donkey" (9:9), which Matthew quotes and which reinforces the undermining of militant messianism. Also in Zechariah 9 are a global horizon ("He shall command peace to the nations" [v. 10]), reference to "the blood of my covenant with you" (v. 11); promises of restoration and salvation ("Today I declare that I will restore to you double" [v. 12], and "On that day the Lord their God will save them for they are the flock of his people" [v. 16]); and images of abundant life ("For what goodness and beauty are his! Grain shall make the young men flourish, and new wine the young women" [v. 17]). Zephaniah 3 opens with denunciation of the wickedness of Jerusalem, especially its religious leaders. Then God announces, "My decision is to gather nations" (v. 8) so that "all of them may call on the name of the Lord and serve him with one accord" (v. 9). Finally comes a crescendo of exultation in what the king of Israel, the Lord, is about to do, with a focus on Jerusalem and a global horizon:

> Sing aloud, O daughter Zion;
> shout, O Israel!

5. On this as a classic case of Johannine ambiguity, see comments on 19:13–16a.

> Rejoice and exult with all your heart,
> O daughter of Jerusalem! . . .
>
> The king of Israel, the Lord, is in your midst. . . .
>
> Do not fear, O Zion. . . .
>
> The Lord, your God, is in your midst,
> a warrior who gives victory;
> he will rejoice over you with gladness,
> he will renew you in his love. . . .
>
> I will make you renowned and praised
> among all the peoples of the earth. (Zeph. 3:14–20)

John, in this also alone among the Gospels, both ties the event back into the raising of Lazarus, as the crowd of eyewitnesses **continued to testify**, and also gives the response of the Pharisees, **"You see, you can do nothing. Look, the world has gone after him!"** This anticipates the coming of "some Greeks" (12:20) and the prophecy of Jesus that he would "draw all people to myself" (12:32), and introduces the global orientation that continues through this chapter.

"The Hour Has Come": Glorification, Death and Life, Ultimate Attraction (12:20–36a)

> [20] Now among those who went up to worship at the festival were some Greeks. [21] They came to Philip, who was from Bethsaida in Galilee, and said to him, "Sir, we wish to see Jesus." [22] Philip went and told Andrew; then Andrew and Philip went and told Jesus. [23] Jesus answered them, "The hour has come for the Son of Man to be glorified. [24] Very truly, I tell you, unless a grain of wheat falls into the earth and dies, it remains just a single grain; but if it dies, it bears much fruit. [25] Those who love their life lose it, and those who hate their life in this world will keep it for eternal life. [26] Whoever serves me must follow me, and where I am, there will my servant be also. Whoever serves me, the Father will honor.
>
> [27] "Now my soul is troubled. And what should I say—'Father, save me from this hour'? No, it is for this reason that I have come to this hour. [28] Father, glorify your name." Then a voice came from heaven, "I have glorified it, and I will glorify it again." [29] The crowd standing there heard it and said that it was thunder. Others said, "An angel has spoken to him." [30] Jesus answered, "This voice has come for your sake, not for mine. [31] Now is the judgment of this world; now the ruler of this world will be driven out. [32] And I, when

I am lifted up from the earth, will draw all people to myself." [33] He said this to indicate the kind of death he was to die. [34] The crowd answered him, "We have heard from the law that the Messiah remains forever. How can you say that the Son of Man must be lifted up? Who is this Son of Man?" [35] Jesus said to them, "The light is with you for a little longer. Walk while you have the light, so that the darkness may not overtake you. If you walk in the darkness, you do not know where you are going. [36a] While you have the light, believe in the light, so that you may become children of light."

The way of life and worship of Jews, centered in the magnificent temple, was deeply attractive to some beyond Judaism, and non-Jewish "God-fearers" were welcome to worship in the Court of the Gentiles in the temple. The Synoptic story of the cleansing of the temple comes at this point in their narratives, and one of its main points is that the buying and selling that was happening in the Court of the Gentiles stopped it being a place of prayer. Jesus there quotes Isaiah, the prophet who is cited at length later in this chapter (and also has so many other echoes throughout John's Gospel), saying, "My house shall be called a house of prayer for all the nations" (Mark 11:17; cf. Matt. 21:13; Luke 19:46).

Isaiah had his vision of God's glory in the temple:

> Holy, holy, holy is the Lord of hosts;
> the whole earth is full of his glory. (Isa. 6:3)

That global horizon of glory is later embodied in the figure of "my servant, Israel, in whom I will be glorified" (Isa. 49:3), who is told:

> It is too light a thing that you should be my servant
> to raise up the tribes of Jacob
> and to restore the survivors of Israel;
> I will give you as a light to the nations,
> that my salvation may reach to the end of the earth. (Isa. 49:6)

Here, the desire of **some Greeks** drawn to the festival is **to see Jesus**, and they approach Andrew and Philip (Jews with Greek names, so probably Greek-speaking). The whole passage should be read alongside John 1:35–51, where the first Jewish disciples are drawn to Jesus, with similar themes of one telling another, seeing Jesus, and Jesus as the Son of Man, all following on from John the Baptist calling Jesus "the Lamb of God," the first indication of his death.[6]

6. See comments on 1:29, 35.

The parallels here indicate the beginning of a new phase: Jesus as **light** for **the world** (12:35–36, 46–47) and the gathering of disciples from among the Greeks and other nations.

But the response to the Greeks' desire is not that they are introduced to Jesus now. The response will be the event that enables that global reach. *More precisely, it will be the person at the heart of that event:* ***"And I, when I am lifted up from the earth, will draw all people to myself."***

There is yet another deep resonance with Isaiah here. It is one that has given rise to some of the most profound theology, poetry, music, and spirituality down through the centuries, centering on the Suffering Servant, whose description gave Christians language to make sense of Jesus. The key passage, later quoted from in verse 38, is Isaiah 52:13–53:12 (to which I have added notes on some significant echoes between it, in its Septuagint Greek version that John knew, and John 12—there are also a great many other echoes of it, throughout John and in the rest of the New Testament, that are well worth exploring):

> 52:13 See, my servant shall prosper;
> he shall be exalted and lifted up,
> and shall be very high.[7]
> 14 Just as there were many who were astonished at him
> —so marred[8] was his appearance, beyond human semblance,
> and his form[9] beyond that of mortals—
> 15 so he shall startle many nations;[10]
> kings shall shut their mouths because of him;
> for that which had not been told them they shall see,[11]
> and that which they had not heard they shall contemplate.
> 53:1 Who has believed[12] what we have heard?
> And to whom has the arm of the LORD been revealed?[13]
> 2 For he grew up before him like a young plant,
> and like a root out of dry ground;

7. The Greek verbs in the Septuagint are *hypsōthēsetai* ("lifted up," the same verb used in John 12:32 and underlined by being repeated in 12:34) and *doxasthēsetai* ("glorified," the same verb used in 12:16, 23, and three times in 12:28).

8. The Greek is *adoxēsei* (literally, "deprived of glory, deprived of good appearance").

9. The Greek is *doxa* ("glory"), which in 12:41 occurs in relation to Isaiah seeing the glory of Jesus, soon after quoting in 12:38 from the Suffering Servant passage, Isa. 53:1.

10. Note the global horizon, which pervades John 12 from v. 19 onward.

11. The same Greek verb is used of the Greeks wanting to see Jesus in John 12:21, in the quotation attributed to Isaiah in 12:40, and in 12:41 about Isaiah seeing the glory of Jesus.

12. This verb, *pisteuein* ("believe, trust, have faith"), is a key one throughout John, and in chap. 12 appears in vv. 11, 36, 37, 38, 39, 42, 44, 46.

13. This whole verse is quoted in John 12:38.

he had no form or majesty[14] that we should look[15] at him,
nothing in his appearance that we should desire him.
3 He was despised and rejected by others;[16]
a man of suffering and acquainted with infirmity;
and as one from whom others hide their faces
he was despised, and we held him of no account.

4 Surely he has borne our infirmities
and carried our diseases;
yet we accounted him stricken,
struck down by God, and afflicted.
5 But he was wounded for our transgressions,
crushed for our iniquities;
upon him was the punishment that made us whole,
and by his bruises we are healed.
6 All we like sheep have gone astray;
we have all turned to our own way,
and the Lord has laid on him
the iniquity of us all.

7 He was oppressed, and he was afflicted,
yet he did not open his mouth;
like a lamb that is led to the slaughter,
and like a sheep that before its shearers is silent,
so he did not open his mouth.
8 By a perversion of justice[17] he was taken away.
Who could have imagined his future?
For he was cut off from the land of the living,
stricken[18] for the transgression of my people.

14. The Greek word is *doxa* ("glory") again.

15. The Greek verb is the same as that translated as "see" in 52:15 and in John 12:21, 40, 41.

16. The Septuagint Greek here is *pantas anthrōpous* ("all human beings"), and this word "all" is an important part of the global horizon of John 12, used in the key verse 32. Of particular interest in 12:32 is a strongly attested variant reading. Instead of "draw all people [*pantas*]," Papyrus 66 and some other manuscripts have "draw all things [*panta*]," which embraces the whole of creation, and echoes John 1:3, "All things came into being through him."

17. The Greek word is *krisis* ("judgment, condemnation, punishment, justice"), and it comes in John 12:31: **Now is the judgment of this world**. This describes **the hour**, the most important time and event of the whole Gospel: **The hour has come for the Son of Man to be glorified** (12:23). *Krinein* ("judge, condemn, punish"), the verb from *krisis*, is then used four times in the final summary statement by Jesus, 12:47–48.

18. The Greek means "he was done to death" and uses here, in the next verse, and in v. 12 the word *thanatos* ("death"). John 12 is full of references to death, some indirect but many direct (vv. 1, 7, 9, 10, 17, 24, 33). The first reference to the death of Jesus, in 12:7, echoes Isa. 53:9 by referring to his burial (John, *entaphiasmos*; Isaiah, *taphē*); the final one, in 12:33, **He said this to indicate the kind of death he was to die**, echoes Isa. 53:8, 9, 12 by using *thanatos*.

9 They made his grave with the wicked
and his tomb with the rich,
although he had done no violence,
and there was no deceit in his mouth.

10 Yet it was the will of the Lord to crush him with pain.
When you make his life an offering for sin,
he shall see his offspring, and shall prolong his days;
through him the will of the Lord shall prosper.
11 Out of his anguish he shall see light;[19]
he shall find satisfaction through his knowledge.
The righteous one, my servant, shall make many righteous,
and he shall bear their iniquities.
12 Therefore I will allot him a portion with the great,
and he shall divide the spoil with the strong;
because he poured out himself to death,
and was numbered with the transgressors;
yet he bore the sin of many,
and made intercession for the transgressors.

The multiple resonances of that passage, including the reimagining of glory through one who suffers on behalf of others (as the notes show, this is much clearer in the Greek that John echoes), are only one dimension of the extraordinarily rich meaning of verses 20–36a.

The desire of the Greeks triggers the pivotal announcement by Jesus: **"The hour has come for the Son of Man to be glorified."** This "hour" has been anticipated since Jesus said to his mother, "My hour has not yet come" (2:4) before he did "the first of his signs . . . and revealed his glory" (2:11). Now "the hour has come," the culmination of the drama is beginning to happen, and it is first of all about who Jesus is and what happens to him. The title on the lips of Jesus here is "the Son of Man." In earlier usage (e.g., Dan. 7:13–14) and in the Synoptic Gospels it was associated with the glory of an apocalyptic figure uniting heaven and earth. John's use keeps the glory and the uniting of heaven and earth (see especially below on John 17), but in addition uniquely emphasizes not only the Son of Man as the one from God who is made flesh, and whose glory is seen in human form (1:14), but also that that glory is seen in the humiliation of the crucifixion. There is a transformation of the concept of glory by identifying it with the full incarnation, crucifixion, and resurrection of Jesus.[20]

19. The Greek *phōs* ("light") is a key word throughout John, and in John 12 occurs in vv. 35 (twice), 36 (thrice), 46.

20. An excellent account of this is in Bauckham, *Gospel of Glory*, especially chap. 3.

There follows a series of moves that together make up the fullest reflection in the Gospel of John on the meaning of the death of Jesus. Just as in his prologue John gives some of the key concepts needed to understand the whole Gospel, so in John 12 he prepares the mind and imagination of readers for the remaining chapters. *The sequence here has three steps, each vital for this Gospel's sounding of the depths of the crucified Jesus.*

First, there is a parable, whose importance is emphasized by its opening words, **"Very truly, I tell you."** The message for the Greeks is that the fruitfulness to come from Jesus, reaching beyond his own people, depends on his death. The vivid phrase **It remains just a single grain** (*autos monos menei*; literally, "it/he remains/abides alone") uses one of John's richest verbs, *menein*, in strong contrast with its use elsewhere for mutual indwelling in the fullest possible community of love (e.g., 15:1–17).[21] *It is an indicator of the relational, love-centered understanding of the death of Jesus.* It has already been suggested by John 10 on Jesus as the good shepherd who lays down his life for his sheep, and by John 11 on Jesus exposing himself to death by raising his friend Lazarus. The Farewell Discourses will go further with this, as we will see in the footwashing, in Jesus saying "No one has greater love than this, to lay down one's life for one's friends" (15:13), and in his final prayer in John 17. That prepares for two events, one on either side of the death of Jesus, that are only in this Gospel: Jesus on the cross actually forms a new community of those closest to him, his mother and the disciple he loved (19:25–27); and, when his dead body is pierced by a soldier's spear, "at once blood and water came out" (19:34), those symbols of the life and the Spirit given to his followers through his death.[22]

The parable of the seed dying is immediately connected to how the followers of Jesus are to be inspired by him to live: not fearing death; free to risk their lives for the sake of love; trusting in Jesus; living in service to him; and being **where I am**. Where is that? The words are said by Jesus again in his final prayer, expressing his great desire as he goes to his death, bringing together his glory and the love he shares with his Father, in both of which his followers can participate.[23] "Where I am" is in a union of love with his Father and with those who trust and love him, and this love embraces the whole world, as the global horizon of this chapter shows. "Where I am" is also where there is need

21. On *menein* see comments on 1:38 and 15:1–17.

22. See 6:47–59 on giving his life and drinking his blood; 4:7–26 and 7:37–39 on the "'rivers of living water' . . . which believers in him were to receive; for as yet there was no Spirit, because Jesus was not yet glorified."

23. "Father, I desire that those also, whom you have given me, may be with me where I am, to see my glory, which you have given me because you have loved me before the foundation of the world. . . . I have made your name known . . . , so that the love with which you have loved me may be in them, and I in them" (17:24, 26).

for life-giving signs or where feet are being washed. This love does not shy away from radically rejecting, to the point of hating, the negative side of **life in this world** that is turned in on itself and is closed to God, to the free generosity of self-giving love, and to the reality of **eternal life**—the life that is present on both sides of physical death, wherever "I am." *So, being "where I am" means that followers, like Jesus, can be utterly committed to God and to a life of love in the world, whatever the cost.*

Second, there is an extraordinary exchange between Jesus and his Father. In the Synoptic Gospels, the voice of the Father is heard in absolute affirmation of Jesus at both his baptism and his transfiguration. Neither of those is described by John; nor is the agony of Jesus in the garden of Gethsemane. John, with striking brevity, combines key elements of all three. He unites testimony to Jesus being shaken and disturbed, **"Now my soul is troubled,"** and to him facing the possibility of avoiding his death, **"And what should I say—'Father, save me from this hour'? No, it is for this reason that I have come to this hour,"** with a prayer of acceptance, **"Father, glorify your name,"** and direct affirmation by his Father, **Then a voice came from heaven, "I have glorified it, and I will glorify it again."** These two verses should be read in conversation with the three Synoptic stories.

But John's distillation adds something that is essential to his framework for understanding the death of Jesus. *The death of Jesus goes to the heart of who God is.* The name of God, who God is in God's own being, is glorified through this hour, central to which is the death of Jesus. This, the only instance of the Father's voice sounding in John's Gospel, unites the death of Jesus inextricably with the glory of God's name, the most comprehensive way of identifying the reality, character, and mystery of God. And the way this happens is through an exchange between Jesus and his Father about the ultimate test of their relationship. *So, at the heart of this relational, love-centered understanding of the death of Jesus is the trust and love between the Father and the Son.*

There now comes a third vital dimension of the meaning of the death of Jesus. In addition to its centrality for the community of followers and its revelation of who God is, there is its relevance to **the crowd** and, beyond them, to **this world** and **all people** (a variant reading says "all things") in it. The crowd reacts to the voice with a divided opinion, though both speculations, about **thunder** and **an angel**, could suggest the involvement of God. Jesus responds with a triple statement in which each element resonates down through the centuries in Christian ways of trying to do justice to the dimensions of his death.

First, the meaning of **this hour** is given in judicial language: **"Now is the judgment** [*krisis*] **of this world."** The theme of judgment, which pervades John's Gospel, will culminate, appropriately, in the trial and condemnation of Jesus and will be discussed further there. Here, the connection is with the voice of the Father, giving a God-centered framework for understanding all that is to come. The events that are unfolding are to be taken as the ultimate judgment on "this world," the decisive truth that should orient all thought and action. Further, this judgment is not just a pronouncement; it is the Word made flesh, a person—the exchange with the crowd soon turns on the central question of the Gospel of John, the "who" question: **"Who is this Son of Man?"** Theologies of the death of Jesus have developed, stretched, and sometimes distorted judicial metaphors in many ways. The Gospel of John never lets them dominate, but rather stimulates continual reimagining and rethinking in the light of Jesus and the drama of his encounters, signs, relationships, death, and resurrection.

Second, the element of conflict in that drama is essential to it: **"Now the ruler of this world will be driven out."** There are no exorcisms in the Gospel of John; it is as if the only driving out that really matters is the one that happens "now," in "this hour." This figure, "the ruler of this world," appears again in the Farewell Discourses (14:30; 16:11) and probably is identical to the devil, or Satan (e.g., 8:44; 13:2, 27). There is no independent interest in this figure's person, origins, or future, and John says less about him than the Synoptics do (e.g., no temptation narrative). He represents powers beyond the human individual, dynamics of evil, falsehood, and death that are, so to speak, systemic and can take hold of and shape human lives, communities, values, and powerful global forces (religious and secular, economic, political, military, judicial, racial, sexual, scientific, ideological) in devastating, hate-filled, malicious, horrifying, and destructive ways. Speaking of evil is always a very sensitive, even dangerous, matter. Especially when personified, evil can become fascinating and dominate the imagination in pathological ways. *The wisdom of the Gospel of John on this is to let Jesus be the fascinating one; so do not fear these powers, because they are not ultimate, they have already been defeated and need not dominate us, and they attain power only if they are feared, if their falsehoods are believed and trusted, and if they are obeyed.* The message is summed up in the Farewell Discourses: "I have said this to you, so that in me you may have peace. In the world you face persecution. But take courage; I have conquered the world!" (16:33). This imagery of victory over Satan, evil, and the negative dynamics of "the world" has been central to one of the main ways of expressing the meaning of the death of Jesus, the Christus Victor approach.[24]

Third, the **I** of Jesus, **the kind of death** he suffered, and his reaching out in love to **all people** come together in one of the most important statements of the Gospel: **"And I, when I am lifted up from the earth, will draw all people to**

24. See Aulén, *Christus Victor*.

myself." *This is the climactic pointer to the meaning of his death. John's Gospel is about this strange attraction.* The first words of Jesus to his first disciples focus on their desire: "What are you looking for?" (1:38). He opens up his own deepest desire in prayer to his Father as he prepares for his death: "Father, I desire that those also, whom you have given me, may be with me where I am, to see my glory" (17:24). That prayer gives a fresh triple wave of meaning to his death, corresponding exactly (though in a different order) to the three dimensions of its meaning given here in John 12: first, there is the glorifying between Father and Son, and with an emphasis on God's name (17:1–5); then there is a focus on the community of disciples (17:6–19); and finally the horizon opens out to the purpose of the community, "so that the world may believe" (17:20–26). The glory that Jesus desires to be seen is clearest when he is lifted up on the cross.

Yet when the desire of Jesus meets the desires of others, there can be many results: rejection, hatred, misunderstanding, and confusion, as well as many sorts and strengths of trust, faith, and love. The Gospel of John again and again appeals to us as readers not only to believe, trust, and love Jesus for the first time, but also to deepen and live more fully whatever life of faith and love we might have already begun. The rest of this chapter is a passionate, almost desperate appeal to readers in three stages, beginning here with the crowd. The imagery is of deciding between **light** and **darkness**, not just in a one-off way but so as to live in the light, to **walk** [in] **the light** and not **walk in the darkness**. It is not just about individuals: the goal is the life of a family, **so that you may become children of light**. And there is an urgency: **now** has been insistently repeated in this passage (vv. 27, 31 [twice]). So seize the moment now: **"While you have the light, believe in the light."**

Who Has Believed? (12:36b–43)

36b After Jesus had said this, he departed and hid from them. 37 Although he
had performed so many signs in their presence, they did not believe in him.
38 This was to fulfill the word spoken by the prophet Isaiah:

> "Lord, who has believed our message,
> and to whom has the arm of the Lord been revealed?"

39 And so they could not believe, because Isaiah also said,

> 40 "He has blinded their eyes
> and hardened their heart,
> so that they might not look with their eyes,
> and understand with their heart and turn—
> and I would heal them."

> [41] Isaiah said this because he saw his glory and spoke about him. [42] Nevertheless many, even of the authorities, believed in him. But because of the Pharisees they did not confess it, for fear that they would be put out of the synagogue; [43] for they loved human glory more than the glory that comes from God.

The second wave of appeal for a positive response is the author's Scripture-led reflection on not believing and believing. It can be read as a sort of shock therapy.

First, there is a quotation from Isaiah 53:1, asking an open question, **"Lord, who has believed our message . . . ?"** That passage about the Suffering Servant has already been discussed as essential background to John 12 on glory revealed through someone being "lifted up," suffering, and dying for the sake of others. Who can believe in such a paradoxical, unattractive figure?

Then there is the shock of Isaiah saying that the reason for people not believing is that God **has blinded their eyes and hardened their heart, so that they might not look with their eyes, and understand with their heart and turn—and I would heal them**. Does God really blind eyes and harden hearts in order deliberately to stop people from believing, repenting, and being healed? It is the sort of extreme statement that might drive people to despair. Indeed, Martin Luther saw this and other similar texts in Scripture as aiming to do just that, so that the only response is to cry out in despair, at which point the free grace and mercy of God is given. In other words, our despair acknowledges the truth that we can do nothing at all to win the grace of God, only cry out for it.

That is one version of what I am calling shock therapy. Why does Isaiah or John even bother to give hearers such a message if God has already determined the result? *I see it as a sharp, paradoxical, hyperbolic wake-up call. Hearing this is meant to stimulate a decision*. And, in fact, readers are at once given the chance to see themselves as not included in any divine determinism: **Nevertheless many, even of the authorities, believed in him**. If even "many" from a group that was plotting the death of Jesus avoided this blindness, then surely it can be avoided by readers now. So the way is opened by the least likely believers for readers to respond to John's message.

But readers are not to stop there. Those believers were still ruled by fear of "coming out" and risking their membership in the synagogue.[25] John's diagnosis of their behavior is that **they loved human glory more than the glory that comes from God**. That rounds off the theme of glory in John 12 and suggests questions

25. This is one of the places in John where many scholars see him reflecting the situation of the Christian community in his own time, which may well be true. In that case, he is urging Jewish Christian readers to stand up and be counted.

for self-examination by any believer: Am I motivated more by fear about my social standing, peer-group respect, public image, reputation, authority, influence, popularity, or acceptability in certain groups or organizations than by desire to please God as met in Jesus? John, as usual, is wanting to draw readers into deeper faith, life, truth, and love, by encouraging them to respond more and more fully in trust, without fear, to the one who says, "I, when I am lifted up from the earth, will draw all people to myself" (12:32).

Jesus Cries Aloud: Divine Sending, Ultimate Decision (12:44–50)

> 44 Then Jesus cried aloud: "Whoever believes in me believes not in me but in
> him who sent me. 45 And whoever sees me sees him who sent me. 46 I have
> come as light into the world, so that everyone who believes in me should not
> remain in the darkness. 47 I do not judge anyone who hears my words and does
> not keep them, for I came not to judge the world, but to save the world. 48 The
> one who rejects me and does not receive my word has a judge; on the last day
> the word that I have spoken will serve as judge, 49 for I have not spoken on
> my own, but the Father who sent me has himself given me a commandment
> about what to say and what to speak. 50 And I know that his commandment is
> eternal life. What I speak, therefore, I speak just as the Father has told me."

Having moved through two appeals for faith—first, Jesus addressing the crowd, and then the author reflecting on Scripture—now there is a loud cry by Jesus that seems to jump out of the context[26] and address the reader directly. It concludes the Book of Signs (chaps. 2–12), and distills some of its main truths. It acts as the first of several "conclusions"—yet to come are John 17, concluding the Farewell Discourses; the final words of Jesus at the end of his life, "It is finished," followed by the piercing of Jesus's side and his burial, concluding the story of his passion and death (19:30–42); the summary of the Gospel's purpose at the end of John 20; and the ending of the epilogue, with the author's "signature," in John 21. All are complementary and can fruitfully be read together.

This ending of John 12 also echoes (as does each of the other conclusions in different ways) John's prologue. Shared themes include believing in Jesus and seeing him; Jesus coming **as light into the world**, contrasted with **the darkness**; rejection of Jesus; **the word**, *logos* (here, where the Word of the prologue is speaking in person, it is **the *logos* that I have spoken**); the Father in relation to the Son; and **eternal life** given through the Son.

26. According to 12:36b, Jesus is in hiding.

Yet there are two distinctive emphases, each very important for the whole Gospel and for ongoing Christian thinking and living.

First, there is the repeated stress on the initiative of **the Father**, in sending Jesus (vv. 44, 45, 49) and in commanding Jesus, telling him what to say (vv. 49, 50). This has consequences for believers: **"Whoever believes in me believes not in me but in him who sent me. And whoever sees me sees him who sent me."** Clearly, this does not mean that they do not believe in Jesus; rather, it is an emphatic way of insisting that believers do not stop at Jesus, but always reach through him toward the Father, and always seek the Father in what they see in him. There are forms of faith in Jesus (including quite widespread ones, heard in popular songs, and in some spiritualities) that absolutize Jesus, ignoring his most important relationship.

This sort of "Jesuolatry" can easily be encouraged by selective quotations from the Gospel of John, not least from the prologue and the "I am" statements of Jesus. The dominant impression reading the first twelve chapters of the Gospel is of Jesus filling the horizon, and that is indeed the central testimony and "good news." But by his emphasis here at the conclusion of John 12, the author is, as it were, directing the reader to both reread and rethink the Gospel so far, this time being especially alert to how the Father is being revealed through Jesus, and then carrying this balanced theology into the rest of the Gospel.[27] The multidimensional richness of John's theology is such that it can be taken in only with the help of constant rereading, rethinking, rebalancing, and deepening—and by taking all of this into prayer. It makes sense to concentrate at first primarily on Jesus in his encounters and signs, as did the Synoptic Gospels; but then it is wise to go back over those stories, and through them begin to enter, thoughtfully and prayerfully, into the relationship of Jesus with his Father that they open up, and, through that, to learn to believe in and see **him who sent me.** In relation to the theology of God, the most important sources for this are John's own Scriptures, especially Genesis, Exodus, Deuteronomy, Isaiah, Jeremiah, Ezekiel, Song of Songs, and, perhaps above all, Psalms, together with the later tradition's trinitarian wisdom. Perhaps the single most helpful guide to this whole tradition of engagement with God is the prayer of Jesus in John 17, with its full orientation toward the Father, the one who sent Jesus, and its concluding, repeated emphasis on who God is and on the love that originates with him: "I made your name known to them, and I will make it known, so that the love with which you have loved me may be in them, and I in them" (17:26).

27. Especially strong on the theocentricity of the Gospel of John and the theological wisdom of reading with this in mind, is Thompson, *The God of the Gospel of John*. For a contemporary theology of God in line with this, see Sonderegger, *The Doctrine of God* and *The Doctrine of the Holy Trinity*.

Second, there is the striking idea of what might be called "self-judgment." **"The one who rejects me and does not receive my word has a judge; on the last day the word that I have spoken will serve as judge."** We are judged by how we respond to a word that comes to us from the one through whom all things came into being (1:3), who knows us more intimately than we know ourselves, who loves us more than we can ever imagine, and who longs to draw us to himself. It is not wise to speculate about how others have responded, are responding, or might respond, or what anyone else's future is in relation to this love—a reverent agnosticism is in order, as Jesus says to Peter about the disciple he loved, "What is it to you if . . ." (21:20–23). Jesus **came not to judge the world, but to save the world**, and he does that saving lovingly, person by person, with all eternity at his disposal, and the capacity to spring endless surprises (not least for prominent Christians such as Peter).

This passage, as so often in John, is about the singular, the one to one, the individual and Jesus: **"Whoever** [singular, *ho*] **believes in me . . . Whoever** [singular, *ho*] **sees me . . . Everyone who** [singular, *pas ho*] **believes in me . . . I do not judge anyone who** [singular, *tis*] **. . . The one who** [singular, *ho*] **rejects me . . ."** That "one" is each individual. The thinker who has grasped this most profoundly in recent centuries is Søren Kierkegaard, with his passionate insight into the importance of the individual. It is no accident that, having been virtually ignored for decades, he was rediscovered in the twentieth century, as people grappled with the totalitarianisms of communists, fascists, and Nazis, and also with mass consumer capitalism and forms of mass or totalitarian religion. Each has bid to be a "ruler of this world" (centered on class, race, money, or—perhaps the most powerful of all, whether for good or evil—faith in God); each is radically challenged by Jesus; and its defeat happens individual by individual, each called by name. This by no means leads to individualism, but into the new community of love[28] and mutual indwelling with God and one another. The Farewell Discourses are about to introduce this new sort of family, and the crucifixion of Jesus will inaugurate it, beginning with his mother and his Beloved Disciple.

This final cry in the ministry of Jesus, as he faces crucifixion, is a call to each reader to make the most important decision he or she is ever faced with, the ultimate decision by which each is judged, showing who each really is when faced with Jesus.

28. See Kierkegaard's profound meditation on love, *Works of Love*; see also Kierkegaard, *Practice in Christianity*, 147–262.

John 13:1–38

Love like Jesus—Utterly, Intimately, Vulnerably, Mutually

Now begin what are usually called the Farewell Discourses of Jesus, John 13–17, though this is a unique form of farewell, mainly oriented to future discipleship after the resurrection of Jesus—"Farewell, Hello Again, and Welcome to Life Together Always." Frederick Dale Bruner's title, "Jesus's Discipleship Course,"[1] indicates the content better: after John 2–12, in which the main emphasis is on Jesus in engagement with those who are not his disciples, now the focus shifts to them. These chapters are unique to John's Gospel, and yet (as will be shown) intricately related to the Synoptic Gospels throughout, with which they are mutually illuminating; and the final prayer in John 17 resonates deeply with the Lord's Prayer, which Matthew sets in the exact center of his summary of the teaching of Jesus on discipleship in the Sermon on the Mount. The setting here is the night before Jesus is crucified, at the intimate gathering of Jesus with his disciples.

The Farewell Discourses: Waves of Love, Comfort, Spirit, and Prayer

First, in John 13, there is the drama of Jesus washing his disciples' feet, telling them to do likewise, predicting both his betrayal by Judas and his denial by Peter, and giving "a new commandment, that you love one another. Just as I have loved you, you also should love one another." In the course of this, a new

1. Bruner, *The Gospel of John*, 747.

major character, to whom the testimony of this Gospel is attributed in John 21:24, is introduced,[2] "one of his disciples—the one whom Jesus loved."

John 13 gives the main "headline" for the rest of the discourses. The primary, encompassing theme is Jesus's love "to the end" for "his own." *Love is the repeated, core concern throughout the discourses, progressing in three waves through the loving service of footwashing, then friendship with Jesus, and finally culminating in "the summit of love" in his prayer in John 17.*

The footwashing reveals who Jesus is through a paradigmatic act of prophetic love. It is at the same time intimately personal, one to one with each disciple; thoroughly communal, inspiring mutual love and service in a community ("You also ought to wash one another's feet" [v. 14]); and radically challenging to the hierarchies of power in church and society, then and now. It is also oriented both to his imminent betrayal and death—"Jesus knew that his hour had come to depart from this world and go to the Father" (v. 1)—and, beyond that, to the ongoing drama of his followers: "But later you will understand" (v. 7). Within the overarching concern with love, these are the two leading themes of John 13–17: the meaning of the approaching death of Jesus and bereavement of the disciples; and offering the teaching, example, commandment, prayer, and promises (above all of sending the Holy Spirit, the Paraclete—the Comforter, Encourager, Advocate, Helper) that can shape the ongoing community of the followers of Jesus.

John 14 speaks to the troubled hearts of the disciples, the first of several waves of comfort in the face of the imminent bereavement, above all given through the promise of the Holy Spirit, the Comforter. Jesus encourages trust and belief in God, and in himself as "the way, and the truth, and the life" (v. 6). He predicts that in his name they will "do greater works" than he has done and invites them to pray with daring and receive the gift of the Spirit: "I will do whatever you ask in my name. . . . And I will ask the Father, and he will give you another Advocate, to be with you forever. . . . And he will be in you" (vv. 13–17). The love theme is developed through mutual indwelling—"On that day you will know that I am in my Father, and you in me, and I in you"—understood through mutual love: "They who have my commandments and keep them are those who love me; and those who love me will be loved by my Father, and I will love them and reveal myself to them. . . . And we will come to them and make our home with them" (vv. 20–23).

In the parable of Jesus as the "true vine," John 15 gives a key image of mutual love in relation to Jesus: "As the Father has loved me, so I have loved you; abide

2. Though he may have been introduced without this description in 1:35–42 as one of the first two disciples of Jesus, only one of whom, Andrew, is named.

in my love" (v. 9), leading to abundant fruitfulness and joy. This is directly connected with his death understood as an act of love for his friends, which in turn enables them to love one another and come through the world's hatred. There are further waves of prayer (vv. 7, 16) and the Spirit (v. 26).

John 16 has more waves of comfort in the face of future persecution and the pain of imminent bereavement (vv. 4, 6–7, 12, 20–22, 28, 33), of teaching on the promised coming of the Holy Spirit (vv. 7–15), and of prayer (vv. 23–24, 26). Yet again, all is grounded in mutual loving: "The Father himself loves you, because you have loved me" (v. 27).

Then comes "the summit of love" in John 17, which is also the summit of prayer and comfort. Beginning from the ultimate loving relationship of Jesus and his Father, this intimate mutuality is opened up first to the disciples, and then beyond them to embrace "those who will believe in me through their word" (v. 20), an overflow of love to which no limit is set. Most of the key themes of the Gospel of John, and especially of the Farewell Discourses, are woven together here: Jesus and his Father; glorifying; eternal life; knowing and believing; truth and word; receiving, giving, and sending; the disciples and the world; joy and hatred; mutual indwelling; desire and seeing; and "I am" (v. 24). And implicitly other vital elements are there too, especially the Spirit, who has been inseparable from Jesus since the beginning, as testified by John the Baptist in 1:32–33. The culminating practical purpose is "so that the love with which you have loved me may be in them, and I in them" (v. 26).

So love is the conclusion as well as the opening of the Farewell Discourses, and it is the utterly central reality of Jesus, of God, of discipleship, of life.

Love and Betrayal, One to One (13:1–11)

> 1 Now before the festival of the Passover, Jesus knew that his hour had come
> to depart from this world and go to the Father. Having loved his own who
> were in the world, he loved them to the end. 2 The devil had already put it
> into the heart of Judas son of Simon Iscariot to betray him. And during sup-
> per 3 Jesus, knowing that the Father had given all things into his hands, and
> that he had come from God and was going to God, 4 got up from the table,
> took off his outer robe, and tied a towel around himself. 5 Then he poured
> water into a basin and began to wash the disciples' feet and to wipe them
> with the towel that was tied around him. 6 He came to Simon Peter, who
> said to him, "Lord, are you going to wash my feet?" 7 Jesus answered, "You
> do not know now what I am doing, but later you will understand." 8 Peter
> said to him, "You will never wash my feet." Jesus answered, "Unless I wash

> you, you have no share with me." [9] Simon Peter said to him, "Lord, not my feet only but also my hands and my head!" [10] Jesus said to him, "One who has bathed does not need to wash, except for the feet, but is entirely clean. And you are clean, though not all of you." [11] For he knew who was to betray him; for this reason he said, "Not all of you are clean."

The opening verse gives a context rich with historical, theological, and dramatic meaning. First, there is **the festival of the Passover**, the annual Jewish celebration of the exodus, the key event in Israel's history, in which the liberation of the people from slavery in Egypt was reenacted. In what follows, Jesus performs the service of a slave.

Next, there is the divine context of the **hour**, the climax of the whole Gospel, centered on the relationship of **Jesus** and **the Father**. Now is the time **to depart from this world**, echoing the exodus language of departure from Egypt in the Passover celebration.[3] The death of Jesus has been anticipated throughout the Gospel, indirectly and directly, since John the Baptist announced, "Here is the Lamb of God who takes away the sin of the world!" (1:29). In John, Jesus dies at the time of the sacrifice of the Passover lambs, central to the meal commemorating the final night of the people of Israel in Egypt.[4]

Then there is a vital key to the interpretation of the footwashing, the Farewell Discourses, and the life, death, and resurrection of Jesus: **Having loved his own who were in the world, he loved them to the end**. The story so far can now be reread as showing the love of Jesus, and it is well worth doing this in preparation for what is to come—one way of doing so is to reflect on how leading themes of John 2–12, such as light and abundant life, relate to love. We have also been given a clue to understanding the rest of the story: it is about Jesus loving **to the end** (*eis telos*). This means both "utterly, completely, perfectly" and "to the point of death." Later, when Jesus is on the cross, the Greek verb *telein* (from

3. Luke actually calls this climactic time of Jesus's life his "departure" (*exodos*, "exodus"): in Luke's account of the transfiguration, Jesus, Moses, and Elijah "appeared in glory and were speaking of his departure, which he was about to accomplish at Jerusalem" (Luke 9:31).

4. Exodus 12–15, on "the hour" of the first Passover and the exodus, has many resonances with John's account of the final evening of Jesus and of his passion, death, and resurrection, such as the festival, night, lambs, hyssop, the glory of God, knowledge, fearing and not fearing, holiness, and several verbal echoes that are not apparent without reading the Septuagint—e.g., "In your steadfast love you led your people whom you redeemed; you guided [*parakaleō*, the verb related to John's term for the Holy Spirit in the Farewell Discourses, *paraklētos*] them by your strength to your holy abode" (15:13). But perhaps the key element is the connection between the sacrifice of the lambs and the consecration of every firstborn male (Jesus being called the only Son of the Father from the beginning in the prologue of John [1:14, 18]), which also connects both Exodus and John with the near sacrifice of Isaac, Abraham and Sarah's only son, in Gen. 22. On the Lamb of God, see comments on 1:29–34.

telos, "end"), meaning "end, finish, perfect, complete, accomplish, fulfill," is used twice in three verses, culminating in the last word of Jesus, *tetelestai*, "It is finished" (19:30). And the conclusion of that verse is that Jesus *paredōken to pneuma*—literally, "handed over[5] the spirit/Spirit." This will be explored further on John 19, but for now it is important to note that this "loving to the uttermost" on the cross can, as in the Farewell Discourses, be associated with the giving of the Spirit: this is a perfection of loving that, through death, becomes even more fruitful.

Immediately, in verse 2, the love of Jesus is set alongside the betrayal of Judas, attributed to the devil. This will be discussed when it comes to a head later in the chapter. Here it draws attention to the tragic reality of resistance to love, to the vulnerability of Jesus in his loving, and to the fallible, flawed, and sinful character of his community. Some have denied that Jesus would have washed the feet of Judas, but everything points to Judas being included—and as regards sharing bread later, he is the only one named as receiving it from Jesus. In the context, this might be seen as John showing Jesus fulfilling the Synoptic command to love one's enemies.

The lead-in to the footwashing both reaffirms the origin and destiny of Jesus in God and also describes him as **knowing that the Father had given all things into his hands**. Who Jesus is, therefore, is central to the meaning of what follows. If the hands that wash the disciples' feet (and are later nailed to the cross) are the hands into which "all things" have been committed by God, then this footwashing reveals who Jesus is, who God is, and what their love is like.

Jesus **began to wash the disciples' feet**. There is no parallel in ancient sources to a person of authority doing such servile work. Jean Vanier[6] captures its radical challenge to our world as well as to that of Jesus in the Roman Empire, its prophetic meaning, and its connection with love and who God is (see the quotation from Vanier in the sidebar).

That also goes to the heart of Peter's problem, which parallels Mark's description of Peter's resistance to Jesus suffering and dying (Mark 8:31–33): Peter simply cannot conceive of Jesus, his Lord, either washing feet like a slave or being crucified like a slave. The whole New Testament stretches its conceptuality, imagery, and scriptural and other resources as it tries to express adequately the scandal, and the reversal of expectations and values, of the crucifixion of Jesus, the Son of God. John is unique in approaching it through Jesus washing the feet of his disciples, including those of Judas, of the Beloved Disciple, and of Peter.

5. The verb also means "betray" and is used in 13:2 of Judas betraying Jesus. Judas hands over Jesus; Jesus hands over the Spirit.

6. For more on Jean Vanier see the section "Ongoing Drama" in the epilogue.

Washing feet happens, like love, one to one. It is a gentle, tender act of touching. Jesus has already had his own feet anointed with precious perfume (12:1–8) and will soon have them nailed to the cross. Here, in response to Peter's resistance, Jesus first says, **"You do not know now what I am doing, but later you will understand."** This action can be adequately grasped only in the context of the whole event of the death and resurrection of Jesus and the sharing of the

All groups, all societies, are built on the model of a pyramid:
at the top are the powerful, the rich, the intelligent.
They are called to govern and guide.
At the bottom are the immigrants, the slaves, the servants,
people who are out of work, or who have a mental illness
or different forms of disabilities.
They are excluded, marginalized.
Here, Jesus is taking the place of a person at the bottom,
the last place,
the place of a slave.
For Peter this is impossible.
Little does he realize that Jesus came to transform
the model of a society
from a pyramid to a body,
where each and every person has a place,
whatever their abilities or disabilities. . . .
The gospel message is the world upside down. . . .
[Peter] does not understand that Jesus' answer
shows that the washing of the feet
is not a new ritual that we can follow or not
or that we should accomplish at certain moments.
It is an essential part of his message of love.
It is the revelation that in order to enter into the kingdom
we have to become like little children;
we need to be "born" from on high
to discover who God is
and who we are called to be.
It is only if we receive the Spirit of God
that we can understand and live
this message of littleness, humility and service to others.

—Jean Vanier, *Drawn into the Mystery of Jesus*, 227–29

Holy Spirit. John's Gospel repeatedly insists on this (beginning in 2:22) and is written explicitly from a postresurrection standpoint.

Then, when Peter says, **"You will never wash my feet,"** Jesus makes the decisive statement, **"Unless I wash you, you have no share with me."** The "you" is singular. This is a one-to-one statement embodied in a one-to-one action, "I wash you." *Then comes the core meaning: "you" can "share with me."* It is hard to imagine any fuller sharing than what the Farewell Discourses speak of, culminating in the prayer of Jesus in John 17. To have a "share with me" is to share in the love between the Father and the Son, in their dynamic of mutual glorifying, in their truth, and in joy. It is also to become part of a community called to the "summit of love"—love for God, for one other, and for the world—in order to "become completely one" (17:23).[7] But to "share with me" also includes opposition, hatred, suffering, and possibly death, as the Farewell Discourses frequently insist. As Jesus says later about footwashing, "Very truly, I tell you, servants are not greater than their master, nor are messengers greater than the one who sent them" (13:16). The ongoing drama of loving draws disciples as deeply as Jesus into engagement with the world and its dark forces and provokes powerful resistance.

The resistance of Peter to having his feet washed by Jesus is later compounded by his denial of Jesus. Then in John 21 he does finally show what is meant by "Later you will understand." In line with the footwashing, that final conversation is about one-to-one love ("Simon son of John, do you love me?") and service in community ("Feed my lambs"), with an indication of "the kind of death by which he would glorify God" (21:15–19). Peter is a paradigm of a disciple who goes terribly wrong but repents and goes right.

Judas, whose decisive one-to-one moment with Jesus comes a little later in this meal, is now referred to again as the one **who was to betray him**. He is a paradigm of one who, so far as is known,[8] goes wrong and does not repent. And "the one whom Jesus loved," soon to appear in his first one-to-one encounter with Jesus (13:23), is yet another sort of paradigm, a model disciple. John, as often, is letting readers encounter a set of exemplary characters and is clearly indicating with whom we should choose to identify: the core invitation of his Gospel is to be with the Beloved Disciple on the bosom of Jesus, as Jesus is

7. The Greek here is *teteleiōmenoi eis hen*—literally, "completed/perfected/fulfilled/matured into one." The verb *teleioun* (from *telos*, "end") is used of Jesus's thirst on the cross being "to fulfill" Scripture (19:28), and the closely related verb *telein* is used twice in reference to his work being "finished" in his crucifixion (19:28, 30). See also the introductory remarks in the comments on 19:1–42.

8. This is an important qualification, as with Jesus telling Peter not to presume to know the future of the Beloved Disciple (21:20–23). Karl Barth mounted a strong theological argument from Scripture for the possibility of salvation even for Judas (*Church Dogmatics* II/2, §35.4, "The Determination of the Rejected").

on the bosom of the Father (1:18), and this is reinforced at the very end of the Gospel when this incident is recalled (21:20–23).[9]

When Peter swings to the other extreme and says, **"Lord, not my feet only but also my hands and my head!"** the reply of Jesus is, **"One who has bathed does not need to wash, except for the feet, but is entirely clean. And you are clean, though not all of you."**[10] This seems to mean that having their feet washed is not something that should be put on the level of their whole relationship with Jesus and his word—as Jesus says later in the Farewell Discourses, "You have already been cleansed by the word that I have spoken to you" (15:3). Rather, it is a further dimension, a deepening, focusing, and enacting, of the relationship with Jesus. *It translates the relationship and the drama of his life, death, and resurrection into an ethos and an ethic.* Yet it is not that this way of acting toward others is at all secondary; rather, the two are inseparable: if the relationship with Jesus is important, then, to be true to him, acting like this is vital. There is a seamless union between being loved by him, having one's feet washed by him, knowing him, believing in him, trusting him, loving him, and imitating him in doing things like footwashing. All this is summed up as participation in him—having, or not having, a "share with me." That is made clearer in the teaching Jesus now gives about it.

A Multiply Reinforced Imperative (13:12–20)

> 12 After he had washed their feet, had put on his robe, and had returned to
> the table, he said to them, "Do you know what I have done to you? 13 You
> call me Teacher and Lord—and you are right, for that is what I am. 14 So if I,
> your Lord and Teacher, have washed your feet, you also ought to wash one
> another's feet. 15 For I have set you an example, that you also should do as I
> have done to you. 16 Very truly, I tell you, servants are not greater than their
> master, nor are messengers greater than the one who sent them. 17 If you
> know these things, you are blessed if you do them. 18 I am not speaking of
> all of you; I know whom I have chosen. But it is to fulfill the scripture, 'The
> one who ate my bread has lifted his heel against me.' 19 I tell you this now,
> before it occurs, so that when it does occur, you may believe that I am he.
> 20 Very truly, I tell you, whoever receives one whom I send receives me; and
> whoever receives me receives him who sent me."

9. See the section "Intimacy at the Heart of Reality" in the comments on 1:1–18.

10. There are differences among the best manuscripts here, some omitting the phrase "except for the feet." I am following the NRSV, which includes it.

The extreme importance of the example of footwashing is now made clear by a remarkable series of emphatic statements. *Nothing else in the Gospel of John is insisted upon like this.* It is all the more forceful by contrast with the lack of such imperatives connected with earlier actions of Jesus, beginning with the first sign of turning water into wine. The one exception, the feeding of the five thousand, is very significant: "Very truly, I tell you, unless you eat the flesh of the Son of Man and drink his blood, you have no life in you. Those who eat my flesh and drink my blood have eternal life, and I will raise them up on the last day; for my flesh is true food and my blood is true drink. Those who eat my flesh and drink my blood abide in me, and I in them" (6:53–56). That is where John has his equivalent of the imperative that Luke's Gospel connects with the Last Supper: "This is my body which is given for you. Do this in remembrance of me" (Luke 22:19).[11]

This raises the fascinating question of why John does not have the institution of the Eucharist at the Last Supper.[12] Luke gives a vital clue. In his account of the Last Supper he has a verbal equivalent of John's footwashing. Jesus teaches about greatness and authority, concluding, "For who is greater, the one who is at the table or the one who serves? Is it not the one at the table? But I am among you as one who serves" (Luke 22:27). John's account highlights this teaching through the footwashing and also highlights the eucharistic imperative by setting it in the context of the feeding of the five thousand, which is resonantly connected with the giving of manna, bread from heaven, during the exodus desert journey. John's separation of the two elements in Luke's account allows him to emphasize each of them even more than does Luke, while keeping the exodus echoes. And omitting the institution of the Eucharist increases the emphasis on the footwashing. If, as I think, John expects his readers to know Luke, he may also be sending a message to the churches of his time: *Beware of becoming so caught up in worship, in the celebration of the Eucharist, and in communion with Jesus, that you fail to follow it through in lives of service to one another, and in building communities where authority is a form of humble, loving service. Communion with Jesus happens through both celebrating the Eucharist and improvising on the footwashing.*

11. See comments on 6:52–59.

12. Speculations abound on this. Is John anti-sacramental? Is he deeply sacramental, expecting readers to be led further into the Eucharist by the footwashing combined with John 6? Is he simply assuming that all his readers know the Synoptics and complementing them? Does John trace the Eucharist back to the feeding of the five thousand? Was there a "secret discipline" in John's community that avoided writing about the Eucharist, its most sacred practice? Did an editor move an original account of the Eucharist from John 13 to John 6? For some initial thoughts on these matters, see comments on 6:41–51.

It is worth noting the ways in which John's account cumulatively amounts to saying, *This is of the utmost importance.* No other instruction in the Gospel of John has anything like this weight of emphasis:

- *The timing is climactic.* It is not only the major festival of Passover but also the "hour," the time of the culminating events of the Gospel, and key players in those events are woven into the story of the footwashing: Judas, Peter, the disciple Jesus loved, and the other disciples.
- As the first act that Jesus does immediately after we have been told that "he loved them to the end," it is clearly intended to be understood as *an exemplary act of love,* with feet being washed by the "hands" into which "the Father had given all things." No action could have higher authority.
- The action points to the fundamental theme of *participation in Jesus,* having a "share with me" (see above), and combines the one to one with mutual service in the community.
- *Jesus explicitly claims authority* as **Teacher and Lord . . . , for that is what I am** (*eimi*), and that echo of the repeated "I am" (*egō eimi*) in John's Gospel is reinforced later in verse 19: **so that . . . you may believe that I am he** (*egō eimi*). So the footwashing is twice associated with this Gospel's distinctive way of affirming the divinity of Jesus.
- There is *an explicit command* directly flowing from the claim to authority: **"So if I, your Lord and Teacher, have washed your feet, you also ought to wash one another's feet."** The "you ought" (*hymeis opheilete*) is very strong, implying what is owed to one another.[13]
- Jesus says he is giving ***an example*** *to be followed* and setting a challenge to improvise further, inspired by what he has done: **"You also should do as I have done to you."** This is the capacious Johannine "as," which elsewhere too opens the way for creativity in thought, imagination, and action.[14] "Example" does not imply exact repetition, but rather suggests the possibility of continual variations, in innumerable other situations, in the spirit of what Jesus has done.
- The significance is further intensified by the formula **"Very truly, I tell you,"** which is repeated later in verse 20, the final, summary statement

13. The verb *opheilein* and related nouns, associated with debt, are used in the Lord's Prayer (Matt. 6:12: *opheilēma* and *opheiletēs*; Luke 11:4: *opheilein*) about mutual forgiveness, and this is in line with the language of John 13 about washing and the exchange between Jesus and Peter about being clean.

14. See comments on 1:14, the section "'As . . . So . . .': A Daring Theological Imagination" in the comments on 3:11–21, and comments on 10:11–21; 13:31–35; 17:18; 20:21.

of the section. The theme here in verse 16 is greatness, closely allied to importance, power, authority, and God: **"Servants are not greater than their master, nor are messengers greater than the one who sent them."** God's power and authority are surprisingly different from most conceptions, and *their truth is revealed in slave-like service,* done in love.

- *There is even a beatitude,*[15] the first of only two in John. This one is about the basic connection of knowing and doing: **"If you know these things, you are blessed if you do them."**[16]
- *The authority of Scripture* is also invoked: **"It is to fulfill the scripture."**
- Finally, after the divine "I am" and introduced by the second "Very truly, I tell you" comes a culminating statement about receiving or welcoming, which is one of the key actions in this Gospel:[17] **"Whoever receives one whom I send receives me; and whoever receives me receives him who sent me."** Receiving, or welcoming, Jesus, his Father, whomever they send, and whatever they give might be a summary of the main purpose of this Gospel, expressed elsewhere through the language of believing/trusting, mutual indwelling/abiding, and mutual love. So this final, emphatic intensification of the imperative of footwashing integrates it with the dynamics of mutual receptivity that are at the heart of the Gospel. *The tender, touching act of washing one another's feet is a sign of welcoming one another in love.*

Enter the Disciple Jesus Loved; Exit the Betrayer, Refusing and Violating Love (13:21–30)

> 21 After saying this Jesus was troubled in spirit, and declared, "Very truly, I tell you, one of you will betray me." 22 The disciples looked at one another, uncertain of whom he was speaking. 23 One of his disciples—the one whom Jesus loved—was reclining next to him; 24 Simon Peter therefore motioned

15. When the footwashing and the Beatitudes in the Sermon on the Mount (Matt. 5:3–12) are read alongside each other, they are mutually illuminating, especially the first three: "Blessed are the poor in spirit, . . . Blessed are those who mourn, . . . Blessed are the meek/gentle, . . ."

16. The second is about the connection of seeing and believing: "Blessed are those who have not seen and yet have come to believe" (20:29).

17. The Greek verb translated as "receives" is *lambanein,* which can mean "receive, welcome, accept, take, put on," and more. Like many other key words in John, it can be used in quite ordinary ways, but it can also go to the heart of John's message, as in 1:12, 16; 3:11, 32, 33; 5:43; 10:18; 12:48; 14:17; 20:22. These are about receiving Jesus himself, grace upon grace, vital testimony, the Father's command, the word of Jesus, and the Holy Spirit. In John 13 *lambanein* is first used of Jesus putting on a towel (v. 4) and later his robe (v. 12); next about receiving people, Jesus, and his Father (v. 20); and then about Judas receiving bread from Jesus (v. 30).

> to him to ask Jesus of whom he was speaking. 25 So while reclining next to
> Jesus, he asked him, "Lord, who is it?" 26 Jesus answered, "It is the one to
> whom I give this piece of bread when I have dipped it in the dish." So when
> he had dipped the piece of bread, he gave it to Judas son of Simon Iscariot.
> 27 After he received the piece of bread, Satan entered into him. Jesus said
> to him, "Do quickly what you are going to do." 28 Now no one at the table
> knew why he said this to him. 29 Some thought that, because Judas had the
> common purse, Jesus was telling him, "Buy what we need for the festival";
> or, that he should give something to the poor. 30 So, after receiving the piece
> of bread, he immediately went out. And it was night.

This is the third time John describes Jesus as **troubled in spirit**. What in the Synoptics is concentrated in the agony of Jesus in Gethsemane, in John is distributed across three events, each of them pointing to the meaning of his crucifixion. First, as he faced the death of Lazarus, whom he loved (11:3, 5, 36) and for whom he was about to put his own life on the line by raising him to life, Jesus "was greatly disturbed in spirit and deeply moved" (11:33). Second, when Greeks wanted to see him and he proclaimed that "the hour has come for the Son of Man to be glorified" (12:23) and connected his own death by crucifixion with fruitfulness for "all people" (12:32), he was shaken by what he was facing: "Now is my soul troubled" (12:27). Here, as "the hour" intensifies, he faces the most radical refusal and violation of love and trust: betrayal by Judas, one of his closest followers.

Everything converges on the violation of love. Already, the headline "Having loved his own who were in the world, [Jesus] loved them to the end" (13:1) has been immediately followed by "The devil had already put it into the heart of Judas son of Simon Iscariot to betray him" (13:2). Judas is one of Jesus's "own." He lovingly washes the feet of Judas, in full awareness that "not all of you are clean" (13:11). He quotes Psalm 41:9 about betrayal by an intimate friend, "The one who ate my bread has lifted his heel against me" (13:18), and then, **when he had dipped the piece of bread, he gave it to Judas son of Simon Iscariot**. The tension has been building toward this moment, and the awareness and superior knowledge of Jesus only serve to intensify his agony, shaking him more deeply. Given who Jesus is, he has full awareness of the horror of the violation of intimacy, love, and trust and yet is committed to entering it fully, with no holding back. We will see later how the solidarity of Jesus both with God and with humanity at its worst is consummated on the cross.[18]

18. See especially Denise Levertov's poem "On a Theme from Julian's Chapter XX" in the comments on 19:28–29.

And now, at this crucial point, the great contrast figure to Judas enters the drama. He is characterized only as being **loved** by Jesus. He is also described as **reclining next to him** and then again as **reclining next to Jesus**. This NRSV translation is poor and does not allow readers in English to grasp John's point. The first "reclining" (v. 23) is literally "seated at table in/on the bosom of Jesus" (*anakeimenos . . . en tō kolpō tou Iēsou*). The other use of "bosom" by John is in the culminating verse of the prologue (1:18), about Jesus as the only Son, which is far better translated by the NRSV as "close to the Father's heart" (literally, "into the bosom of the Father"). So "bosom" is there used to describe the ultimate intimacy of love. In John 13 the second "reclining" (v. 25) is literally "leaning back onto the breast of Jesus" (*anapesōn . . . epi to stēthos tou Iēsou*), and this is the form that is recalled in 21:20. John therefore gives remarkable prominence to this image of intimacy, at the beginning of his Gospel, at its end, and at this climactic moment. That the disciple **whom Jesus loved** is the subject here and at the end, after which he is revealed as the source of this Gospel's true "testimony" (21:24), emphasizes the significance of this moment and its key point: Judas violates the love of Jesus, which, in the love between him and his Father, is at the heart of all reality, and which is also, through being loved and loving, at the heart of human fulfillment.

After he received the piece of bread, Satan entered into him. As with other major events in his Gospel—above all, the rejection and crucifixion of Jesus, his resurrection, and the giving of the Holy Spirit—John has prepared us for this. After Jesus fed the five thousand and taught about giving his flesh for the life of the world and about the importance of eating his flesh and drinking his blood, he said, "'Did I not choose you, the twelve? Yet one of you is a devil.' He was speaking of Judas son of Simon Iscariot, for he, though one of the twelve, was going to betray him" (6:70–71). When Judas objects to Mary anointing Jesus's feet with costly perfume, he is described as "the one who was about to betray him" (12:4). In John 13 Judas is repeatedly brought to the reader's attention. First, he is again associated with the devil: "The devil had already put it into the heart of Judas son of Simon Iscariot to betray him" (13:2). Then he is anonymously referred to as a betrayer, as unclean, and as an intimate friend who "has lifted his heel against me" (13:18).

Profound questions about the devil (or Satan), Judas, and the responsibility of Judas for what he does are raised by all this. Is Judas really responsible for betraying Jesus? Does it not appear that this was his unavoidable fate, with the devil or Satan as the agent responsible? Judas is sometimes seen in that way, but in the context of the Gospel of John and the rest of the Bible, that is a terrible misunderstanding. Instead, the way the story is told allows for a multiple realism: about Judas and his responsibility; about the devil, or Satan, and evil that goes beyond individual responsibility; and about Jesus and his love. *This does not give theoretical solutions to problems such as the mystery of evil and sin or the interrelationship of divine freedom and human freedom but rather describes a reality in which all three elements are combined and to be taken seriously: individual human responsibility, evil beyond the individual, and the love of Jesus.* The main effect in John is practical: the reader is challenged to respond to the love of Jesus and invited to take part in the ongoing drama of loving, identifying not with Judas or with the forces represented by Satan but with the disciple Jesus loved.

Judas in this Gospel is dishonest about money and hypocritical in responding to Mary's action in anointing the feet of Jesus with precious perfume (12:1–8). But above all he is the intimate enemy, the one close to Jesus who violates trust and love. He is given one opportunity after another to respond differently. Mary's anointing is an act of extravagant love that Judas sees as a missed opportunity to increase the amount of money available for him to steal. Jesus's footwashing is an act of humble, tender love for Judas in person. Then Jesus shares bread with him in a final act of intimate sharing. Judas fails to respond to either initiative.

No excuses are made for Judas, but he is also set in a larger context of evil. His betrayal is seen as inspired by Satan, he himself is called a devil, and after he received the piece of bread, **Satan entered into him**. This is the only direct action by Satan described in this Gospel. Earlier, Jesus has described the devil as "a murderer from the beginning" and "a liar and the father of lies" (8:44), the opposite of Jesus himself as identified with life and truth. He is also called by Jesus "the ruler of this world" (12:31; 14:30; 16:11), always in the context of his defeat: "driven out" (12:31); "no power over me" (14:30); "condemned" (16:11). There is no independent interest in him at all. Evil is personified in Satan, but he is not a full character in the drama. He represents murder, lies, betrayal, and the violation of trust and love. Those powerful dynamics in "this world" exert such huge pressure on individuals that it is unrealistic to see people simply as free agents who are able to choose from a position of neutrality. More recent theologians have identified these forces (which in Judas also includes the desire for money) as structural or systemic evil and sin. It is possible to be gripped by them and to contribute one's own agency to these powerful forces. The focus here is not on Satan but on Judas, whose inspiration by Satan is not seen as reducing his responsibility. Judas has already succumbed to the temptation to steal and deceive and so has alienated himself from Jesus and the other disciples. Now he decisively confirms that alienation.

It is Jesus, however, not Satan or Judas, who is the primary agent in this scene. His agency is that of love. This is straightforward in the case of **one of his disciples—the one whom Jesus loved**, with whom the reader is being invited to identify, resting on the bosom of Jesus in mutual warmth. But, as already shown, the love of Jesus embraces this whole scene and all the disciples, including Judas and Peter. This is love "to the end" (13:1), with Jesus washing feet like a slave and vulnerable to betrayal and denial. The priority of Jesus is emphasized by him saying to Judas, "Do quickly what you are going to do." *This is the third realism, that of Jesus and his love, confident that neither the betrayal of Judas nor the forces of death and falsehood identified with Satan will have the last word.*

Judas **immediately went out. And it was night.** The darkness into which Judas goes is then at once contrasted with the glorification of Jesus.

Glory, Searching, and a New Commandment: "Love as I Have Loved" (13:31–35)

> 31 When he had gone out, Jesus said, "Now the Son of Man has been glorified,
> and God has been glorified in him. 32 If God has been glorified in him, God
> will also glorify him in himself and will glorify him at once. 33 Little children,
> I am with you only a little longer. You will look for me; and as I said to the
> Jews so now I say to you, 'Where I am going, you cannot come.' 34 I give you
> a new commandment, that you love one another. Just as I have loved you,
> you also should love one another. 35 By this everyone will know that you are
> my disciples, if you have love for one another."

The exit of Judas allows a new level of openness and mutuality, the beginning of the main discourses. These verses are a fresh introduction, an overture that combines four key themes to follow.

First come the dynamics of glorification, which by the end of the discourses have embraced not only Jesus and his Father but also the disciples: "The glory you have given me I have given them, so that they may be one, as we are one" (17:22). This is the largest horizon conceivable, resonating all through the Bible and seen in Jesus (John 1:14). *It reaches to the heart of who Jesus is, who God is, and who the "little children" are. The dynamics of glorification might be seen as the ultimate ecology.* Glory, the overflowing radiance, intensity, and energy of divine life and holiness, is redefined by this "hour" through Jesus and his footwashing, discourses, crucifixion, and resurrection. These are deeply disorientating, not least as regards time. The indicators of time in these verses seem odd and contradictory: **Now . . . has been . . . has been . . . has been . . . will . . . will . . . a little longer . . . will.** This springs not only from John's postresurrection perspective but also from his horizon of divine time. This has been glimpsed at various points, beginning with the prologue's "In the beginning . . ." and

"He who comes after me ranks ahead of me because he was before me" (1:1, 15) and is above all indicated by the "I am" sayings and the prayer in John 17. Jesus requires us to reimagine time—past, present, future, and eternal—with him as its deepest, enduring meaning.

Next comes the separation of bereavement: **"Little children, I am with you only a little longer."** The intimacy and intensity of relationship is underlined by the unique address, which might be translated as "dear little children" This in turn underlines the pain of separation, as does the picture of searching for the lost one: **"You will look for me."**

Third comes **a new commandment**. At the core of the redefinition and intensification of glory is the love of Jesus embodying the love of God. This has already been demonstrated in the footwashing and the accompanying imperatives. So washing feet is the immediate content of the "as" in **"Just as I have loved you, you also should love one another."** But the "as" is far wider than that and encourages reflection on the whole Gospel. To obey this command, readers need to reread the Gospel asking two leading questions: How is Jesus loving here? and How might this inspire our loving now? Not only that, the stories of Jesus speaking and acting are set in a broad framework, first outlined in the prologue and climaxing in his prayer in John 17. This opens up the horizon of our loving toward the whole world. *So the ethics being taught here is triply imaginative: entering as deeply as possible into the story, together with its actions, characters, conversations, and imagery; entering as deeply as possible into contemporary situations and challenges, searching for ways of loving that echo the loving of Jesus; and doing all this within a horizon of thinking, imagining, and praying that relates to God, all people, and all creation.* But, as will be seen in John 15:12–17, there is yet more to come on this commandment. "So the love-command to be obeyed is actually the whole story of Jesus, calling for a 'see-and-do-likewise' response."[19]

Finally, that global horizon is tied to this loving in a most challenging way: **"By this everyone will know that you are my disciples, if you have love for one another."** Love among the "little children," in the Christian family, is to be the primary sign that we really are disciples of Jesus—in other words, that we are learning from him, imitating him, following him, being inspired by him. The mission of the church is inseparable from the sort of community the church is. That is a key theme of the Farewell Discourses, and it reaches a crescendo in John 17: "As you, Father, are in me and I am in you, may they also be in us, so that the world may believe that you have sent me. The glory that you have given me I have given them, so that they may be one, as we are one, I in them

19. Daly-Denton, *John*, 180.

and you in me, that they may become completely one, so that the world may know that you have sent me and have loved them even as you have loved me" (17:21–23). Such unity in love, with God and one another, is the deepest desire of Jesus (17:24).

Following and Denial (13:36–38)

> [36] Simon Peter said to him, "Lord, where are you going?" Jesus answered,
> "Where I am going, you cannot follow me now; but you will follow afterward."
> [37] Peter said to him, "Lord, why can I not follow you now? I will lay down my
> life for you." [38] Jesus answered, "Will you lay down your life for me? Very
> truly, I tell you, before the cock crows, you will have denied me three times."

It might seem that Peter ignores the new commandment just given, but in fact he focuses on the most important new element in it, Jesus as Lord, and what he does: **"Lord, where are you going?"**

Jesus answers the question by redefining, with reference to what is about to happen, what it means to follow him. The disciples have, of course, been following Jesus (1:40, 43), but this "hour" in which he will die and be raised to life is a radical break, a unique, pivotal event of love for all, which creates a profound distinction between **now** and **afterward**. "Afterward," the crucified and risen Jesus will breathe his Spirit into his disciples, send them as he was sent, and summon them to follow in this new mode—and Peter will be the main example of this (chaps. 20–21).

But "now" that is not yet possible. Peter does not understand, and the misunderstanding of the disciples is emphasized repeatedly as the discourses go on. But how could they understand at this point? This sort of misunderstanding seems inseparable from the overwhelming reality of this "hour" and of who Jesus is. John's whole Gospel is told from a postresurrection perspective that assumes adequate understanding can only be retrospective. But Peter's misunderstanding here is of a special sort: it fundamentally confuses what he can do and what Jesus is doing. He says, **"I will lay down my life for you."** Jesus asks, **"Will you lay down your life for me?"** The exact reverse is the case: Jesus is to lay down his life for Peter.

Then Jesus emphatically—**"Very truly, I tell you"**—predicts that Peter will deny him. This, on top of himself being "troubled in spirit" and his emphatic "Very truly, I tell you" prediction that "one of you will betray me" (13:21), makes for a deeply troubled group and prepares for his repeated words in John 14, "Do not let your hearts be troubled."

By the end of this chapter, readers have not only been given the most important imperative of the Gospel (to love like Jesus as exemplified in his washing feet) and two models of discipleship (Judas, violating that love, and Peter, eager to pursue it but unable to wait and follow the timing of Jesus). We have also been offered the quiet, anonymous figure of "the one whom Jesus loved" (13:23) lying on his bosom, awaiting what is to come.

John 14:1–31

Comfort and More

Trusting, Dwelling, Praying, and Loving

Faced with his deeply troubled disciples, Jesus gives them comfort and something far beyond it. The comfort reassures them that they can trust him and his Father for the future: "Believe in God, believe also in me. . . . Where I am, there you may be also. . . . I will not leave you orphaned. . . . Peace I leave with you; my peace I give to you" (vv. 1, 3, 18, 27). But this comfort has extraordinary dimensions.

It is not just about the future but also about the continual presence of Jesus, who is "the way, and the truth, and the life" (v. 6). That involves a new way of knowing God: "If you know me, you will know my Father also. . . . Whoever has seen me has seen the Father" (vv. 7, 9). Even more than this, it involves being embraced in the dynamic, loving relationship between Jesus and his Father: "I am in the Father and the Father is in me. . . . I am in my Father, and you in me, and I in you. . . . Those who love me will keep my word, and my Father will love them, and we will come to them and make our home with them" (vv. 11, 20, 23).

So those who give themselves to this continuing interrelationship in trust, understanding, and love have an utterly secure home. But that is not all. This home gives a base from which to act in unprecedented, daring ways: "Very truly, I tell you, the one who believes in me will also do the works that I do and, in fact, will do greater works than these, because I am going to the Father" (v. 12). That is one of the most astonishing promises conceivable and will be explored below. It is inseparable from the equally astonishing promise that follows it: "I will do whatever you ask in my name, so that the Father may be glorified in the Son" (v. 13). *Daring prayer and daring action are two sides of the same coin.* They are both to be in line with who Jesus is, to be done "in my name." They are also both to be done for God's sake, "so that the Father may be glorified in the Son." Later, in chapter 17, as Jesus himself prays for the perfecting of mutual indwelling in trust and love, he sees the disciples too sharing in that glory: "The glory that you have given me I have given them, so that they may be one, as we are one" (17:22).

But even that is not all. Here there is a new element in this mutual indwelling: "I will ask the Father, and he will give you another Advocate, to be with you forever. This is the Spirit of truth" (v. 16). The commentary explores this more fully. For now, the vital point is that Jesus here, together with verse 26, adds "the Advocate, the Holy Spirit" as a third, permanent presence, "with you forever," to that of the Father and the Son. The Spirit too is indwelling: "You know him, because he abides with you, and he will be in you" (v. 17); and the Holy Spirit connects disciples with the Father, Jesus, and one another through truth, teaching, and remembering.

The Holy Spirit as the Paraclete—Advocate, Encourager, Comforter, Helper—is the massive new element in John 14, just as the footwashing was the distinctive new element of John 13. Readers are led deeper into the life, love, and glory of God as their true home and at the same time inspired to pray and love daringly in the ongoing drama in the name of Jesus.

Yet this is only the first wave of these discourses. All its key elements—Father, Son, and Encourager; trust and believing; dwelling and abiding; life; truth; love; glory; prayer; action; and who Jesus is—are also part of further waves to come.

"A Place for You Where I Am" (14:1–3)

> [1] "Do not let your hearts be troubled. Believe in God, believe also in me. [2] In my Father's house there are many dwelling places. If it were not so, would I have told you that I go to prepare a place for you? [3] And if I go and prepare a place for you, I will come again and will take you to myself, so that where I am, there you may be also."

The first, basic encouragement given by Jesus in the face of deep disturbance is to trust in God and in himself. The whole Gospel is pervaded by the invitation to believe, trust, have faith. It is "written so that you may come to believe that Jesus is the Messiah, the Son of God, and that through believing you may have life in his name" (20:31), and the Farewell Discourses open up the depths of what it means to trust **in God**, and, inseparably, **in me**.

Dwelling is central to this. Where is our true home? Where are we utterly loved? Where can we feel comprehensively safe? The answers shift the focus of those questions from "where" to "who." Whose is our true home? By whom are we utterly loved? With whom can we feel comprehensively safe? The key to all of them is **where I am** (a phrase repeated at crucial points such as 12:26 and 17:24).[1] But being where Jesus is is not just a matter of physical proximity—his enemies as well as his friends had that. It is about the basic condition for being truly at home, for love that is mutual, for comprehensive safety: well-founded trust. Therefore, **"Believe in God, believe also in me."**

Here, the main emphasis of the "dwelling" is on the future: **"If I go and prepare a place for you, I will come again and will take you to myself."** It connects with the Synoptic Gospels and Paul's Letters about the future return of Jesus. But the "where I am" embraces the present too, and the rest of the chapter adds further dimensions to this dwelling:

- "I am in the Father and the Father is in me." To be where Jesus is is to be with his Father.
- "The Spirit of truth . . . abides with you, and he will be in you." To be with Jesus is to have the indwelling Spirit.
- "Those who love me will keep my word, and my Father will love them, and we will come to them and make our home with them." To trust and love Jesus, and keep his word, is to be at home in God's family.

The rest of the discourses open up further dimensions of inhabiting this ecology of truth, trust, and love, culminating in John 17, where the language of dwelling and abiding is condensed into a multiply repeated "in" (17:17, 19, 21, 23, 26).

"In my Father's house there are many dwelling places." What are these? One pointer to the meaning of "my Father's house" is 2:13–22, where Jesus uses it to describe the temple, and then, when Jesus speaks of it being destroyed and raised up in three days, the evangelist says that "he was speaking of the temple of his body," which was understood by the disciples only after his resurrection. So we can associate "my Father's house" not only with the multiple meanings of the temple—as the place of God's presence and special closeness to God,

1. Like many key words and phrases in John (e.g., "word," "life," "dwell/remain/abide/stay," "seek/want/search," "as"), those referring to the whereabouts of Jesus can have a spectrum of meanings, ranging (in this case) from very ordinary geographical location to the mutual indwelling of Jesus with the Father, the Spirit, and believers. This spectrum might be seen as a verbal indicator of incarnation, that the Word is both ordinary flesh and divinely deep—what I have called the "deep plain sense" of this Gospel.

as a microcosm symbolizing the entire creation, and as the focus of the whole community's covenantal bond with God and with one another, expressed above all in worship, sacrifice, and feasting, as a foretaste of heaven—but also with the postresurrection community in its intimate, familial, mutually indwelling relationship with God through Jesus and the Spirit in the ongoing drama.[2]

But why "many"? Interpretations vary greatly, and that may be what John intended. Two lines are especially fruitful.

Perhaps the most obvious is that "my Father's house" is wherever Jesus dwells, "where I am." That embraces the whole of the past of Jesus with God (e.g., 1:1, "In the beginning was the Word, and the Word was with God, and the Word was God"; 8:58, "Before Abraham was, I am"), including the temple, as well as the present and the future. Jesus, in his mutual indwelling relationship with the Father, is the embracing location for the "many dwelling places." In John 14 the plurality of this dwelling is most simply and vividly expressed in the plurality of those who love Jesus: "Those who love me will keep my word, and my Father will love them, and we will come to them and make our home [*monē*, "dwelling," the singular of "dwelling places" in v. 2] with them" (v. 23) (these are the only two occurrences of the word in the New Testament). *Our divine home, the home of Jesus and his Father, is in these many places of mutual love.*

Another line affirms the first and also insists on being open to divine surprises. We have no overview of the "where I am" of the one through whom all things were made, whose Spirit blows where it will, who promises to draw all people (and even all people and things) to himself,[3] and who sets no time limits on his work. One set of "dwelling places" in relationship with God need not exclude another very different set. *"My Father's house" might be unimaginably capacious, and even those most at home there might meet many surprises—especially other people they do not expect, but also dimensions of truth and life.* This can have radical implications not only for Christian relations to those not in their own faith community (see below on v. 6b) but also for many of the ways Christians are divided from one another. The last word of this Gospel on these matters is a twice-repeated warning to the Christian community about claiming, or even wanting, to know too much about this future dwelling and what will happen to other people: "If it is my will that he remain [*menein*, "abide, live on, dwell"]

2. Another pointer is 8:35–36, where Jesus is speaking of slavery to sin: "The slave does not have a permanent place in the household [*ou menei en tē oikia eis ton aiōna*, "does not abide/remain/dwell in the house forever / for eternity"]. The son has a place there forever [*menei eis ton aiōna*, "abides/remains/dwells forever / for eternity"]. So if the son makes you free, you will be free indeed." The Greek for "dwelling place," *monē*, is the noun from *menein*, the verb for "abide/remain/dwell."

3. See comments on 12:32.

until I come, what is that to you?" (21:22–23). Yet there is a sort of knowledge that is utterly vital.

Knowing the Way Is Knowing Jesus as the Way, the Truth, and the Life (14:4–6a)

> [4] "And you know the way to the place where I am going." [5] Thomas said to him, "Lord, we do not know where you are going. How can we know the way?" [6a] Jesus said to him, "I am the way, and the truth, and the life."

The place—"my Father's house" (14:2), the ultimate family home, where Jesus is—could not be more important. But the "how" question posed by Thomas about the way to it misses the key point, which is also the key point of this Gospel: the central question is always, "Who?"

Just as "where" questions about "my Father's house" had to be reoriented as "who" questions to do justice to the "where I am" of Jesus, so too here the "how" question has to be answered in "who" terms. The answer is the most comprehensive of all the "I am" statements of Jesus in John: **"I am the way, and the truth, and the life."** This has immense implications. Just four dimensions are explored here; many others are explored in commenting on other parts of the Gospel.

First, there is the basic "who" statement: **"I am."** *The most vital thing is to meet this person, listen to this person, get to know this person, trust this person, follow this person, converse with this person, relate continually to this person, be loved by and love this person. All else flows from this. And the most fundamental thing to know is that Jesus is as God is.* He is the "I am" of God: God's self-giving in life and love, God's self-expression in Word and truth, embodied in a person living among us. The whole of John's Gospel testifies to this in concepts, images, and above all stories of encounters with Jesus, seeking to do justice to someone who stretches to the breaking point even biblical categories. The meaning of God, humanity, time, and place are being transformed through this person.

Here in John 14, where the emphasis has initially been on the future, the "I am" insists that Jesus is present as God is present, relating to every "now," whether past, present, or future. *The unique and unsurpassable concept, who Jesus is, is about to be given its climactic content through the crucifixion and resurrection of Jesus.* This exchange between Jesus and Thomas, like all the Farewell Discourses, is written with two perspectives in interplay: the approaching crucifixion and the ongoing drama of life with the crucified and risen Jesus. The "I am" spans those events. Jesus, like his Father, is present on both sides of death, and so death itself is relativized for those who trust him. "Where" and "what" questions—such as Thomas's **where you are going**, or What is beyond death?—give way to the "who" question and its answer: "I am." The mystery of death is met by the greater mystery of this person who has been through it and who offers now the reality of eternal life and love.

One of the ways in which John 14 indicates this reality of the presence of Jesus both beyond death and now is by first imagining the "many dwelling places" being prepared "in my Father's house" for the future and then immediately emphasizing the present reality through the "I am." This presence is to be realized in new ways after the resurrection of Jesus through the indwelling of the Spirit, who "will be in you" (v. 17), and of the Father and Son, who "will make our home" with those who love them (v. 23). There is a surprise reversal of direction between "I go to prepare a place for you" (v. 3) and "We will come to them and make our home with them" (v. 23). The massive emphasis of the Farewell Discourses is on the latter, the postresurrection abiding and mutual indwelling in the ongoing drama, as vividly pictured in the metaphor of the vine in 15:1–11 and ardently prayed for in 17:20–26.

Second, **the way** is the leading term of the three, with the others explaining it: the way as "the truth" and as "the life." "Way" is another capacious Johannine image and has innumerable resonances within and beyond the Bible. Like "word" (vv. 23–24),[4] it can be understood further through all parts of Israel's Scriptures, including Genesis,[5] Exodus,[6] Deuteronomy,[7] the prophets from Samuel[8] through Isaiah (who is quoted as a headline for all four Gospels, associating Jesus with John the Baptist's cry, "Prepare / Make straight the way

4. See comments on 1:1.

5. After the expulsion of Adam and Eve from the garden of Eden, God places cherubim with a flaming, turning sword "to guard the way to the tree of life" (Gen. 3:24). This combination of "way" and "life" is especially relevant to John, whose intertexts with the early chapters of Genesis are numerous. Jesus is the way to this abundant life.

6. The exodus from Egypt is often described as a way (Hebrew *derek*, Greek *hodos*)—e.g., Exod. 13:17–21; cf. Neh. 9:19 and the next note.

7. To live in line with the teaching of Torah is to follow a way (e.g., Deut. 5:33). Of special relevance to John 14 and the comforting of the disciples is what Moses says in Deut. 1:29–33: "I said to you, 'Have no dread or fear of them. The Lord your God, who goes before you, is the one who will fight for you, just as he did for you in Egypt before your very eyes, and in the wilderness, where you saw how the Lord your God carried you, just as one carries a child, all the way [*hodon*] that you traveled [*eporeuthēte*] until you reached this place [*topon*]. But in spite of this, you have no trust in [*enepisteusate*] the Lord your God, who goes before you [*proporeuetai*] on the way [*hodō*] to seek out a place [*topon hodēgōn*] for you to camp, in fire by night, and in the cloud by day, to show you the route [*hodon*] you should take [*poreuesthe*].'" The brackets show words, or closely related words, in the Septuagint version that also occur in John 14:1–7, echoing the latter's scenario of the Lord going ahead to prepare a place.

8. E.g., "This God—his way is perfect; the promise of the Lord proves true" (2 Sam. 22:31).

of the Lord" [Matt. 3:3; Mark 1:3; Luke 3:4; John 1:23]), Jeremiah,[9] Ezekiel,[10] the Wisdom literature,[11] and Psalms.[12] The New Testament also has many uses of "way," and John 14:6 reads like a reflective summary of the significance suggested by John the Baptist's opening cry that identifies Jesus with "the way of the Lord." A similar distilled summary of how Jesus in person is inseparable from the way that he opens up is given in the Letter to the Hebrews' description of "the new and living way that he opened for us through the curtain (that is, through his flesh)" (10:20).

Coming here, just after the reassuring glimpse ahead beyond death, the impact of "I am the way" is to refocus on the main concern of these discourses, the ongoing drama of life as followers of Jesus after his crucifixion and resurrection. Jesus is the way to God, as the rest of the verse makes clear: "No one comes to the Father except through me" (v. 6b). But he is the way to God through becoming human, living his life of teaching and doing signs of abundant life, going the way of the cross, being raised to life, and sending his disciples into the world as he was sent. In the immediate context of these discourses, his way is that of footwashing and loving to the extent of giving his life. But his followers cannot go this way independently of relationship with him: the "I am" unites those who follow his way with him himself, in an intimacy that John 15 calls mutual indwelling and friendship and John 17 calls the perfection of union in eternal life, glory, truth, and love.

Third, there is "I am the way" as **the truth**. In the Septuagint and the New Testament the Greek word *alētheia* ("truth") not only means what corresponds

9. Of many instances, one of special relevance to John is the promise, "I will give them one heart and one way, that they may fear me for all time. . . . I will make an everlasting covenant with them" (Jer. 32:39–40).

10. Again, out of a great many examples (even more than in Isaiah or Jeremiah), Ezek. 18 has a dialogue between God and Israel about "the way of the Lord" versus Israel's ways, in which, as in John 14:6, both truth ("Therefore I will judge you, O house of Israel, all of you according to your ways" [v. 30]) and life itself ("Turn, then, and live" [v. 32]) are at stake. Ezekiel is especially concerned to pose the radical choice between the two ways, as in John's "dualism of decision."

11. Here "way" is a core, pervasive image, with dozens of instances. In Job, of special relevance are the huge questions posed to Job by God in chaps. 38–41, resonating simultaneously with Johannine themes of dwelling, truth, life, and the priority of the "who" question—in Job 38 alone, for example, "Who . . . ?" "Who . . . ?" "Who . . . ?" "Where is the way to the dwelling of light. . . ?" "What is the way to the place where the light is distributed. . . ?" "Who . . . ?" "Who . . . ?" "Who . . . ?" "Who . . . ?" (vv. 2, 5, 8, 19, 24, 25, 36, 37, 41). In Proverbs there are repeated appeals to choose between the ways of wisdom, goodness, innocence, uprightness, or understanding and the ways of foolishness, evil, darkness, or wickedness. Teaching and learning the ways of wisdom are vital.

12. The headline in Ps. 1 lays out the basic divide, and its life-or-death importance: "For the Lord watches over the way of the righteous, but the way of the wicked will perish" (v. 6). The classic instance is Ps. 119, where the "way" imagery is introduced in v. 1 and then runs right through this longest of psalms, constantly connecting with Johannine themes such as keeping commandments, seeking, word, life, desire, teaching, faithfulness, love, trust, truth, comfort, the name, eternity, remembering, light, salvation, judgment, and joy.

to fact but also carries the content of the Hebrew *'emet*. This has a broader sense of what, and especially who, is reliable and to be trusted. It is as much about what is done as what is known or believed—belief, cognition, and behavior are interwoven, as in the truth of a promise. Above all, truth is an attribute of God, as in Exodus 34, where the divine name (the twice-repeated four-letter Tetragrammaton, "YHWH," articulated as "the LORD") is explained to Moses by God:

> The LORD, the LORD,
> a God merciful and gracious,
> slow to anger,
> and abounding in steadfast love and faithfulness,
> keeping steadfast love for the thousandth generation,
> forgiving iniquity and transgression and sin,
> yet by no means clearing the guilty. (Exod. 34:6–7)

"Faithfulness" there is *'emet* in Hebrew and *alēthinos* in Greek in the Septuagint.

Moving through the first twelve chapters of the Gospel, John shows that Jesus is "full of grace and truth" (1:14); "God is true" (3:33); the truth is to be done (3:21); the Father is to be worshiped "in spirit and in truth" (4:24); John the Baptist "testified to the truth" (5:33); the judgment of Jesus is true (8:16); abiding in the word of Jesus brings knowledge of the truth, and this "truth will make you free" (8:32). So truth is about Jesus, God, action, worship, trusting testimony, judgment, abiding, the word, knowledge, and freedom. In short, *this truth is the reality of God and Jesus that can become the reality of believers. It is about recognition of, and participation in, God-centered reality.* Then in the Farewell Discourses the focus on truth intensifies, beginning here in John 14 with "I am . . . the truth" and followed soon by the promise of "the Spirit of truth." Truth continues as a theme in John 15, 16, and 17 and then is decisively at issue in the trial of Jesus in John 18.

John's Gospel is written to draw readers deeper and deeper into this truth, not only through related concepts such as those just listed, but also through the whole narrative and through rich imagery, the one most closely associated with truth being that of light (e.g., 1:4–9; 3:19–21; 8:12; 9:5; 11:9–10; 12:35–36, 46). This ever-deepening, ever-broadening way of truth is walked within the horizon of God and all reality, as outlined at the beginning of the Gospel. The prologue is immediately followed by a description of the formation of a community of disciples/learners gripped by such core questions as "Who are you?" (1:19) and "What are you looking for?" (1:38), to which answers are always incomplete.[13] The Farewell Discourses make it clear that the desire for more and more truth

13. See comments on 1:19–51.

is also essential to the postresurrection ongoing drama. The intrinsic connection between "the way" and "the truth" means that learning is ongoing, a dynamic process that never ends because of the superabundant truth of God, and especially because that truth is embodied in a living, continually creative person and his Spirit, whom he shares with others. We will explore this further when discussing the promise in 16:13, "When the Spirit of truth comes, he will guide you into all the truth."

So the importance of reading "the truth" as closely connected to "the way" should not obscure the fact that it is also identified with Jesus in person. "I am . . . the truth" has many implications for our conception of truth. *There can be no more inclusive framework or overview of truth that can claim priority over this person.* Yet Christians, too, cannot claim to have the ultimate framework or overview; we simply testify to Jesus and seek in his light to understand more and more truth, while acknowledging how little we know and that he alone has the overview. More will be said on this in the next section. One important general lesson to learn from Jesus as the truth in person is that, without at all ignoring or reducing the significance of other forms of truth—whether factual or fictional; conceptual or narrative; quantitative or qualitative; scientific, moral or artistic; intellectual, emotional, or practical—if Jesus as a particular human being is "the truth," then *the basic category for truth, to which all those others should be related, is this: each human person in deep relationship with God, with other people, with ongoing history, and with the whole of creation.*

Fourth, "I am the way" as **the life** introduces yet another multidimensional reality. "Life" has already been a leading concept in the first twelve chapters.[14] The Farewell Discourses shift the main emphasis to love, but this statement should have the effect of encouraging a rereading of all those passages and making more connections between this life and love. What emerges is that the Father, in love for the world, sends Jesus to give abundant life, above all the very life of God, eternal life, life from heaven. *Its signs of life are signs of love,* including water becoming wine, healing, teaching, feeding thousands, and raising the dead to life. The latter two are especially illuminating for the Farewell Discourses.

John 6 is where John does his version of what the Synoptic Gospels do in their accounts of the Last Supper and the institution of the Eucharist, and the teaching there is the fullest, richest, and most astonishing until the Farewell Discourses. "I am . . . the life" invites us to read into John's account of the Last Supper the teaching given in John 6. Jesus and life are the central thrust of that earlier passage. There Jesus speaks of "the food that endures [*menousan,*

14. See above on 1:4; 3:15; 4:14; 5:24–40; 6:25–71; 8:12; 10:10; 11:25; 12:25, 50.

"abides"] for eternal life" (v. 27) and says, "I am the bread of life. . . . Very truly, I tell you, whoever believes has eternal life. I am the bread of life. . . . I am the living bread that came down from heaven. Whoever eats this bread will live forever; and the bread that I will give for the life of the world is my flesh. . . . Very truly, I tell you, unless you eat the flesh of the Son of Man and drink his blood, you have no life in you. Those who eat my flesh and drink my blood have eternal life, and I will raise them up on the last day. . . . Just as the living Father sent me, and I live because of the Father, so whoever eats me will live because of me. . . . The one who eats this bread will live forever" (vv. 35, 47–48, 51, 53–54, 57–58).

That concentrates together key elements of the Farewell Discourses, such as "I am," eternal life, believing, the world, the death of Jesus, resurrection, and the living Father sending the Son. But in John's account of the Last Supper there is no mention of anyone except Judas eating or drinking.[15] What is happening?

It is a classic case of the priority of the "who" question.[16] John 6 makes a journey of intensification into the imagery of bread, eating, and drinking, in line with the sign of the feeding of the five thousand. Its intimate connection with 14:6 is in the repeated "I am" of Jesus, the repeated theme of eternal life, and the repeated "true" (*alēthēs*) in "my flesh is true food and my blood is true drink" (v. 55), linking life with truth. It further anticipates the Farewell Discourses by teaching about mutual indwelling for the first time: "Those who eat my flesh and drink my blood abide in me, and I in them" (v. 56). John 6 even prepares readers for a shift in imagery. When the disciples complain, "This teaching [*logos*] is difficult; who can accept it?" (v. 60), Jesus first opens up the horizon of resurrection and ascension, as in the Farewell Discourses: "Then what if you were to see the Son of Man ascending to where he was before?" (v. 62). Then he springs a surprise, anticipating the Paraclete: "It is the Spirit that gives life; the flesh is useless. The words that I have spoken to you are spirit and life" (v. 63). By the end of the Farewell Discourses those "words" have included both the radical eucharistic language of Jesus earlier in John 6 and the radical teaching of Jesus on footwashing, love, prayer, and the Spirit. Both are integrated through the crucified, risen, and ascended Son of Man and his comprehensively radical "I am."[17]

The raising of Lazarus in John 11 gives further content to "I am . . . the life." It is the climactic sign in the Book of Signs and includes the climactic "I am" saying of Jesus before the Farewell Discourses: "I am the resurrection and the

15. Significantly, 6:64, 70–71 has the first mention of the betrayal by Judas.

16. It is other things too, especially a way of highlighting the massive importance of the command to follow the example of Jesus in footwashing.

17. See comments on 6:35–51.

life. Those who believe in me, even though they die, will live" (11:25). It is said to Martha about her brother Lazarus; with their sister Mary, they are the first individuals in John's Gospel said to be loved by Jesus. In John 11, as in John 6, Jesus does a sign, Jesus interprets it (in John 11, as in the Farewell Discourses, the interpretation comes before the main event), life on both sides of death is at issue, and the key integrating truth is who Jesus is—"I am."

Knowing and Seeing Jesus Is Knowing and Seeing His Father (14:6b–11)

> 6b "No one comes to the Father except through me. 7 If you know me, you will
> know my Father also. From now on you do know him and have seen him."
> 8 Philip said to him, "Lord, show us the Father, and we will be satisfied."
> 9 Jesus said to him, "Have I been with you all this time, Philip, and you still do
> not know me? Whoever has seen me has seen the Father. How can you say,
> 'Show us the Father'? 10 Do you not believe that I am in the Father and the
> Father is in me? The words that I say to you I do not speak on my own; but
> the Father who dwells in me does his works. 11 Believe me that I am in the
> Father and the Father is in me; but if you do not, then believe me because
> of the works themselves."

There is a fifth, all-embracing dimension to Jesus as "the way, and the truth, and the life": the relationship of Jesus to **the Father**. Elsewhere there is a discussion of some key issues about the centrality of the Father-Son relationship in the Gospel of John, such as male, female, and other language for God, and the potential of John to oppose and offer alternatives to top-down patriarchy and other hierarchies by seeing this Father-Son relationship as one of open, welcoming intimacy, vulnerable power, and love that inspires footwashing, friendship, and community gathered by the humiliated, crucified Jesus. Here, the two main issues are the exclusiveness of **"No one comes to the Father except through me"** and deepening knowledge of the Father by seeing and believing Jesus.

The way that this exclusive "no one . . . except . . ." is understood depends largely, as so often in John, on how the "who" question is answered: Who is this "me"? If this is, as the prologue says, the Word through whom "all things" have been created, whose "life" is "the light of all people," and who "enlightens everyone," then he is already in deep relationship with everyone, and "no one" is excluded from that. In addition, there are assurances such as Jesus saying that, through his crucifixion, "I will draw all people to myself" (12:32). What all this means for their ultimate relationship to God as Father is mostly a mystery. *We have no overview of it, no timescale for it, just glimpses of it from time to time, and these can come through people of all religions and none, and through experiences labeled "religious" or not. Jesus is free to relate to all in both open and hidden ways.* Within this broad, inclusive horizon, John's Gospel is concerned to introduce readers to Jesus so that he can be trusted as the way to the Father and to lead those who begin to trust him deeper into this relationship and truth. Each personal drama matters, and each has vital decisions to make, above all about trusting and loving in response to being loved. In this God-centered, eternal perspective no one comes to the Father without encountering the one sent by the Father to embody the love at the heart of reality and to draw all people into that love. However and whenever that encounter happens for each person, its inside story is a mystery known only to God—and usually, perhaps, only very partially understood by the person who has the encounter.

This exchange with Philip is one of the multiple deepenings of the Farewell Discourses, and what Jesus says allows for understanding at different levels. **"Whoever has seen me has seen the Father"** reaches beyond empirical, surface seeing to something deeper, as suggested by Jesus's question, **"Do you not believe that I am in the Father and the Father is in me?"** This seeing involves hearing and believing: **"The words that I say to you I do not speak on my own; but the Father who dwells in me does his works."** There are many responses to Jesus that understand his words and works in disconnection from God.

Yet even among those who do make the connection there can be levels of understanding in their faith: **"Believe me that I am in the Father and the Father is in me; but if you do not, then believe me because of the works themselves."** Following the story of what Jesus does and says is a good way into believing in him; but there is more and more and more to be entered into, here expressed through recognizing the deeper reality of who Jesus is in relation to his Father—their life of mutual indwelling in love. The Farewell Discourses are heading for the richest and most comprehensive deepening of this in John 17.

The Depth of Action Is Prayer in the Name of Jesus (14:12–14)

> 12 "Very truly, I tell you, the one who believes in me will also do the works
> that I do and, in fact, will do greater works than these, because I am going to
> the Father. 13 I will do whatever you ask in my name, so that the Father may
> be glorified in the Son. 14 If in my name you ask me for anything, I will do it."

The emphatic (**"Very truly, I tell you"**) promise that **the one who believes in me will also do the works that I do and, in fact, will do greater works than these** is astounding. Does this mean that believers in Jesus can expect to turn water into wine, heal the sick, give sight to the blind, feed thousands, and raise the dead to life? Such surprises are not ruled out, but the setting of this promise in the Farewell Discourses suggests something that is perhaps even more surprising and challenging. None of those "works" of Jesus done as signs in John 2–11 carries with it instructions to disciples to imitate it or do similar things. The only action of Jesus to be set as an example to his followers is washing their feet. That was given overwhelming, commanding weight in John 13. So what is "greater" than washing feet? The very meaning of "greater" is transformed by such an action: to surpass it in humility, in loving service.

Thinking along that line, as in imagining variations on the example of footwashing, is a necessary beginning. Many commentators understand "greater" as quantitative rather than qualitative: followers of Jesus over the centuries and around the world can imitate him on a far-greater scale than anything he was able to do in his short life in one place. But there is far more than that here. The quality, too, is sustained and heightened by direct connection with the risen Jesus and his Father: **"Because I am going to the Father."** *The ongoing drama of loving service is inspired and empowered from the center of creative love.* That is not something one-off or occasional. For it to happen as a way of life, the followers need to be participating in that love—hence the pervasive emphasis on mutual indwelling, abiding (see especially John 15), and love, culminating in the prayer of Jesus in 17:26: "so that the love with which you have loved me may be in them, and I in them."

This dynamic synergy happens through prayer: **"I will do whatever you ask in my name, so that the Father may be glorified in the Son. If in my name you ask me for anything, I will do it."** There can be superficial and self-centered ways of taking this astonishing promise, but the repeated "in my name" points to the character and depth of such prayer: it is inspired by who Jesus is. *The depth of action, its authority and glory, and the measure of its quality lie in who Jesus is, and the action that needs to accompany all other action is prayer that is inspired by who Jesus is. So the depth of action is prayer in the name of Jesus.*

One practical implication of this is that readers who trust this promise are drawn to enter ever more deeply into the meaning of this Gospel, whose central question is, Who is Jesus? Who Jesus is is the inspiration of prayer and action together: both are always to be done in his presence, in communication with him, in imitation of him, in loving response to his love, and "so that the Father may be glorified in the Son." And knowing who Jesus is comes not only through this Gospel but also through the other Gospels, through their many intertexts, and through people and events encountered in the ongoing drama, all of which send us back to reread John, enrich our understanding of Jesus, and deepen our relationship with him.

Further light on the meaning of "greater" is later shed in John 15:13 when Jesus says, "No one has greater love than this, to lay down one's life for one's friends." *The depth of both prayer and action is love.* The supreme, incomparable action, springing from the heart of God as opened up in the prayer in John 17, is Jesus laying down his life in love on the cross. *The crucifixion of Jesus is the event through which greatness, love, life, glory, family, and even who God is are redefined and transformatively revealed.*

Yet further light on "greater" is shone later in John 14 when Jesus says, "If you loved me, you would rejoice that I am going to the Father, because the Father is greater than I" (v. 28). In a context where greatness is being defined through humble acts of loving service and where the relationship between the Father and Son is seen in terms of mutual indwelling, it makes no sense to understand this as being about somehow separating the Father from the Son and comparing their quantitative greatness. Their relationship is better conceived through their eternal life of mutual love, rejoicing, and glorification, the mutual "magnifying" of each by the other in love and delight. If one does want to insist on a differentiation between the two in terms of greatness, a thought from the tradition of trinitarian thinking may help: the Father is the "begetter" and sender of the Son, his origin from all eternity, and the Son is "God from God, light from light, true God from true God"; and this means that in God there is differentiation and an ordering of relationship that give priority to the Father as eternal begetter and sender of the eternal Son. This is consistent with John's prologue and John 17.

But speculation about the inner logic of God's being is far from 14:28. Its concern is to comfort the disciples by encouraging them to trust that there is a better future for Jesus beyond death, one to be celebrated in love and joy, and dependent on the one who will resurrect Jesus. From the standpoint of the human Jesus approaching death, "the Father is greater than I" and is the ultimate source of comfort. But the paradox of greatness in the littleness and humility of footwashing and in the humiliation and love of the crucifixion means that the greatness of the Father is at one with this strange, radically challenging greatness and glory of the Son, whom he glorifies (13:31–32; 17:1–5).

The Ultimate Gift (14:15–17)

> [15] "If you love me, you will keep my commandments. [16] And I will ask the Father, and he will give you another Advocate, to be with you forever. [17] This is the Spirit of truth, whom the world cannot receive, because it neither

> sees him nor knows him. You know him, because he abides with you, and he will be in you."

Now there is a simple, practical summary of the ongoing life of prayer and action, both deepening and daring, inspired by who Jesus is, by what he does and says, and by love for him: **"If you love me, you will keep my commandments." "And . . ."**—there is more: *the crowning, ultimate gift is promised for living this life.* **"I will ask the Father, and he will give you . . ."**—this gift comes from the heart of God, the Father in relationship with the Son (cf. 1:18). The gift is **another Advocate . . . the Spirit of truth**, soon also called "the Holy Spirit" (14:26).

All through John's Gospel the Spirit has been anticipated, beginning in chapter 1. There has been a Spirit-studded path to the Farewell Discourses, highlighting the Holy Spirit abiding on Jesus (1:32–33), the need to be born of the Spirit (3:1–10), the Spirit being given without measure (3:34), God as spirit/Spirit, God to be worshiped in spirit/Spirit and truth (4:23–24), the words of Jesus as spirit/Spirit and life (6:63), the Spirit as rivers of living water (7:37–39), and Jesus being troubled in spirit (11:33; 13:21). Here, five points are especially important.

First, Jesus says, **"I will ask the Father."** This personal promise by Jesus, even more directly related to the Father than the prayer of the disciples, who are promised that they will receive whatever they ask in the name of Jesus, is even more astonishing. It is about being given a share in the very life of the God who "is Spirit" (4:24).

Second, **"He will give you another Advocate"** (*paraklētos*). The otherness of the Holy Spirit, the Spirit's differentiation from both the Father and Jesus (who, as 1 John 2:1 says, is also a *paraklētos*), goes with the personification of the Spirit as Advocate, Encourager, Comforter, Helper. John's insistence that the Spirit could not be given to the disciples until after the death of Jesus, together with the strong identification of Jesus with the Spirit, suggests that the most straightforward way of understanding the Spirit is as the shared, distributed, indwelling presence of the crucified and risen Jesus, who is also at one with the Father. The full reality of Jesus, and therefore of God, is given in the Spirit, and the Spirit's description as **the Spirit of truth** carries this sense of reality as well as cognition.

Third, the Holy Spirit is **another Advocate, to be with you forever**. The differentiation of the Spirit from the Father and the Son is permanent, "forever." This is emphasized by the combined language of abiding and indwelling, which are also used of the Father and the Son: **"He abides with you, and he will be in you."** The same language is extended in the Farewell Discourses to embrace believers in and lovers of Jesus. That embrace begins here with the eternal indwelling of the Spirit, and the meaning is then enriched, intensified, and expanded—first, later in this chapter, with the promise that both Father and Son "will come to them and make our home with them" (14:23), then still more in John 15, 16, and 17. Wave after wave of indwelling imagery invites readers to live in this amazing home.

Fourth, there is not only a differentiation between Spirit, Son, and Father in their mutual indwelling; there is also a strong, contrasting differentiation between all of them and "the world." Here, the "Spirit of truth" is one **whom the world cannot receive, because it neither sees him nor knows him**. The ongoing drama is again anticipated, with its inescapably conflictual reality, involving fundamental decisions, oppositions, and hatreds, which will be emphasized even more as these discourses proceed.

Fifth, as the second wave of discourse about "the Spirit of truth" says, "the Advocate, the Holy Spirit, whom the Father will send in my name, will teach you everything, and remind you of all that I have said to you" (14:26). *Receiving truth, being taught, and remembering are how disciples are indwelt by the Spirit.* And this learning, and being reminded, is not limited; it is about "everything," about "all that I have said to you" (14:26), and so it is ongoing. The first wave focused briefly on the Spirit in distinction from Father and Son; in this second wave the Spirit is in a more usual, self-effacing mode on behalf of Jesus and the Father.

The Open Secret: Loved and Loving, Hearing and Keeping (14:18–26)

> 18 "I will not leave you orphaned; I am coming to you. 19 In a little while the world will no longer see me, but you will see me; because I live, you also will live. 20 On that day you will know that I am in my Father, and you in me, and I in you. 21 They who have my commandments and keep them are those who love me; and those who love me will be loved by my Father, and I will love them and reveal myself to them." 22 Judas (not Iscariot) said to him, "Lord, how is it that you will reveal yourself to us, and not to the world?" 23 Jesus answered him, "Those who love me will keep my word, and my Father will love them, and we will come to them and make our home with them. 24 Whoever does not love me does not keep my words; and the word that you hear is not mine, but is from the Father who sent me.
>
> 25 "I have said these things to you while I am still with you. 26 But the Advocate, the Holy Spirit, whom the Father will send in my name, will teach you everything, and remind you of all that I have said to you."

In between those two waves of teaching about the Encourager, Jesus himself exemplifies the Spirit's activity through a further wave of encouragement and reassurance for his disciples: **"I will not leave you orphaned; I am coming to you."** There is repetition of previous teaching on seeing him, receiving life from him, keeping his commandments, and loving him, but these waves reach further. Not only is Jesus **"in my Father,"** but also **"you** [are] **in me and I in you."** It is not only that **"those who love me will be loved by my Father, and I will love them and reveal myself to them,"** but also that both Father and Son **"will come to them and make our home with them."**

These truths are completely involved with a particular person and his ongoing history: **"I am coming to you. In a little while the world will no longer see me, but you will see me; because I live, you also will live. On that day you will know that I am in my Father, and you in me, and I in you."** The followers are to live through the crucifixion and resurrection of Jesus as the way into new life, knowledge, and indwelling. These events, and their central character, hold the open secret of the ongoing drama. It seems a strange way, hidden from most people, as the question of **Judas (not Iscariot)** expresses: **"Lord, how is it that you will reveal yourself to us, and not to the world?"**

The answer by Jesus seems to avoid the point of the question, but in fact addresses it indirectly, in line with the thrust of the Gospel. **"Those who love me will keep my word, and my Father will love them, and we will come to them and make our home with them."** *What is given to "the world" is a God-centered family community, loved by God and loving God, its life shaped by "my word."* Just as God, whom "no one has even seen" (1:18), has been given to the world through the medium of Jesus, "the Word," who "became flesh and lived among us" (1:1, 14) and then, in shocking, paradoxical indirectness, is humiliated and crucified and **no longer** seen by **the world**, so too the family of his followers witnesses to his resurrection and life-through-death (**"You will see me; . . . you also will live"**) and to their participation in him (**"you in me, and I in you"**) by being at home with him and his Father and keeping his word. *Their primary communication to the world is indirect: as Jesus has been an embodied message of God's love, so his followers, through being loved and keeping the command to love as Jesus has loved them, are called to be an embodied message of God's love.* And just as the crucifixion intensifies the indirectness of revelation in Jesus, transforming ideas of who God is and what love is, so the command of Jesus to his followers to make his act of footwashing paradigmatic confronts the world with a strange, challenging, indirect sign, lived out by the fragile community of his fallible friends.

The Farewell Discourses insist on such indirect communication through the character of the community, beginning immediately after the footwashing in 13:35: "By this everyone will know that you are my disciples, if you have love for one another." It culminates in John 17, where first Jesus says, "I am not asking on behalf of the world, but on behalf of those whom you gave me" (v. 9), and later prays to the Father "that they may be one, as we are one, I in them and you in me, that they may become completely one, so that the world may know that you have sent me and have loved them even as you have loved me" (vv. 22–23). Here too, in John 14, Judas's "not to the world" is later complemented by Jesus saying "so that the world may know that I love the Father" (v. 31).

Throughout this passage, and throughout the Gospel, being loved and loving is inseparable from being taught and learning. This is a community that continually loves and learns, and the learning includes hearing, searching, questioning, seeing, believing, understanding, remembering, and knowing. Jesus gives commandments and speaks words for a limited time: **"I have said these things to you while I am still with you."** And the learning is ongoing: **"But the Advocate, the Holy Spirit, whom the Father will send in my name, will teach you everything, and remind you of all that I have said to you"** (see the quotation from Ecclestone in the sidebar).

One implication of this is that the text that witnesses to the words of Jesus and to Jesus as the Word is vital for the community in the ongoing drama. The importance of the Gospel of Jesus's own testimony is underlined in 14:18–26 by

To pray the Fourth Gospel means above all other things to pray in and for the guidance of the Holy Spirit. It means praying with a concern as wide as life itself. The Holy Spirit was confessed to be Lord and giver of life in the Nicene Creed. The task set to the Christian church was then, now and as it was at the beginning, to learn what believing in such a Spirit does mean in terms of living. This Gospel was written to help in the process of learning, to throw as much light as possible on the venture of faithful living to which John and his readers were committed. . . . They were still learning now, years later, though he had gone to the death that he had told them would come. The learning process had had to go on with the help of the Holy Spirit. That help Jesus had promised them also. They would find out for themselves, he had said, that they could do the things they had learnt from him and even do more. This too had proved to be true. So when John writes of the things that took place in those years long past when Jesus had worked among them, it is not their pastness that concerns him but the illumination they give to what the Holy Spirit is teaching them now.[a]

—Alan Ecclestone, *The Scaffolding of Spirit*, 114–15

a. Ecclestone's profound and sadly neglected book (subtitled *Reflections on the Gospel of St John*) has been a key inspiration for this commentary. Ecclestone offers the sort of wise and prophetic spirituality, through reading and praying the Gospel of John in the Spirit, that is well suited to being at the heart of any Johannine renaissance today.

words and phrases such as “my commandments,” “reveal myself,” “my word,” “my words,” “the word,” “I have said these things,” and “all that I have said.” The encouragement undergirding the whole Gospel is to read and reread this Gospel; *through it the Holy Spirit will let you trust that you are loved by the Father and the Son, will inspire your learning and loving, and will guide you deeper and deeper into an inexhaustible divine abundance of truth and love.* As the First Letter of John (which in so many ways illuminates this Gospel from the vantage point of a later stage in the ongoing drama, with all its problems and pathologies) graphically sums up this double reality, “God is light” and “God is love” (1 John 1:5; 4:8, 16).

The Depth of Peace, Joy, and Trust (14:27–29)

> [27] “Peace I leave with you; my peace I give to you. I do not give to you as the world gives. Do not let your hearts be troubled, and do not let them be afraid. [28] You heard me say to you, ‘I am going away, and I am coming to you.’ If you loved me, you would rejoice that I am going to the Father, because the Father is greater than I. [29] And now I have told you this before it occurs, so that when it does occur, you may believe.”

The encouragement intensifies. The multiple deepenings of mutual indwelling and “I am,” of action with prayer, and of loving and learning are now joined by **peace** with rejoicing, comforting **hearts** that are **troubled** and **afraid**. We are back **now** firmly **before** the crucifixion **occurs**, but oriented beyond it: **so that when it does occur.** And the opening invitation to trust, “Believe in God, believe also in me” (14:1), is repeated, but now **you may believe** has the further content of those multiple depths.

Crunch Time (14:30–31)

> [30] “I will no longer talk much with you, for the ruler of this world is coming. He has no power over me; [31] but I do as the Father has commanded me, so that the world may know that I love the Father. Rise, let us be on our way.”

The crunch time is approaching: **The ruler of this world is coming**. The hostile dynamics of “this world” are converging on Jesus in his ultimate test. **“He has no power over me”** is literally, “In me he has nothing at all,” an emphatic intensified negative. So who does have something “in” Jesus? Who does fill him so completely that there is no room for the ruler of this world? Jesus expresses the imperative force of his vocation and mission, **"I do as the Father has commanded me"**; he affirms its deepest truth, **"I love the Father"**; and he proclaims its purpose, **"so that the world may know"** this love.

"Rise, let us be on our way" is rather puzzling, since it seems like a signal to leave where they are gathered, but in fact the discourses continue. Scholars have suggested many solutions, but readers can be grateful that these extraordinary discourses do continue with further waves of teaching. The ongoing drama is poised at a moment of permanent significance, and John 15, 16, and 17 open up that significance more fully. Indeed, Mary Coloe suggests that what follows in John 15:1–17 is a rereading and rewriting of John 14 done in order to develop further its key themes, such as the indwelling love of the Father and Jesus, the glorification of the Father, asking in the name of Jesus, and keeping the commandments of love. The questions in John 14 raised by Thomas, Philip, and Judas are to be explored even more deeply.[18]

18. Coloe, *Dwelling in the Household of God*, 145–58.

John 15:1–27

"Abide in Me"

A new image is suddenly introduced: "I am the true vine, and my Father is the vinegrower" (v. 1). It is placed exactly halfway through John 13–16, and, as Chrys Caragounis says, this "tends to confirm that the parable of the vineyard occupies the center of the last discourse both literally and theologically."[1]

"I am" immediately sounds the often repeated and most profound note of the Gospel. This is the seventh and, with its companion saying, "I am the vine, you are the branches" (v. 5), the final such "I am."[2] Who Jesus is has been central since the beginning of the Gospel; now this image of vine, vinegrower, and branches unites who Jesus is both with who "my Father is" and with who "you are"—*the triple "who" relationship of love and mutual indwelling into which this Gospel wants to draw its readers.* If, as will be suggested below, a better translation is, "I am the true vineyard, and my Father is the vinegrower," and "I am the vineyard, you are the vines," the core triple interrelationship still stands, now with different nuances.

As the vine(yard) figure helps to reimagine the core triple interrelationship of this Gospel, so *it also faces readers with the core, sharp challenge of this Gospel.* Are you going to be a branch or vine that the Father removes because it "bears no fruit" (v. 2), that is "thrown away . . . and withers," to be "gathered, thrown into the fire, and burned" (v. 7)? Or are you going to be one that the Father "prunes to make it bear more fruit" (v. 2), one who has "been cleansed by the word" (v. 3), who abides in Jesus and in his love, in whom the words of Jesus abide, by whose fruit bearing "my Father is glorified" (v. 8), and who is oriented

1. Caragounis, "'Abide in Me,'" 259.

2. There are other "I am" statements, but no more with predicates.

toward the ultimate delight: “so that my joy may be in you, and that your joy may be complete” (v. 11)?

Already the horticultural and plant imagery was being stretched to breaking point by weaving into it the interpersonal language of word and words, asking, glorifying, and love. This language then takes over in a further wave of the love commandment that was first taught in 13:34. *The new thing in this wave is friendship.* “No one has greater love than this, to lay down one’s life for one’s friends. You are my friends if you do what I command you” (vv. 13–14). It is a friendship that includes service but goes beyond it in shared knowledge and understanding: “I have made known to you everything that I have heard from my Father” (v. 15). It is mutual, but completely the initiative of Jesus: “You did not choose me but I chose you” (v. 16).

It is also the key relationship to be sustained in the ongoing drama of discipleship. Bearing fruit in that drama is what “I appointed you” to do (v. 16). Yet there is a realistic facing of what belonging to Jesus and not to the world means in practice: being hated without a cause, persecuted, and sinned against. In the face of all that, Jesus repeats the promise of the Advocate, the Encourager, this time with a fresh emphasis on testifying: “He will testify on my behalf. You also are to testify” (vv. 26–27).

Abiding (15:1–8)

> 1 “I am the true vine, and my Father is the vinegrower. 2 He removes every branch in me that bears no fruit. Every branch that bears fruit he prunes to make it bear more fruit. 3 You have already been cleansed by the word that I have spoken to you. 4 Abide in me as I abide in you. Just as the branch cannot bear fruit by itself unless it abides in the vine, neither can you unless you abide in me. 5 I am the vine, you are the branches. Those who abide in me and I in them bear much fruit, because apart from me you can do nothing. 6 Whoever does not abide in me is thrown away like a branch and withers; such branches are gathered, thrown into the fire, and burned. 7 If you abide in me, and my words abide in you, ask for whatever you wish, and it will be done for you. 8 My Father is glorified by this, that you bear much fruit and become my disciples.”

It is rare that a major, familiar New Testament text has to be rethought because it is discovered that key words have been mistranslated, but that has happened with the Greek words *ampelos*, translated here by the NRSV as “vine,” and *klēma*, translated as “branch.” There now seems to be overwhelming evidence that these words began by meaning what the NRSV says they do, but that they shifted their meanings over time. As Chrys Caragounis, the scholar who has done the most to gather the evidence, summarizes his findings about the change, which had happened before John was written and is especially clear in popular, demotic texts, "Ἄμπελος [*ampelos*] was no longer the plant *vitis vinifera* but the plot of land on which the vines had been planted, the vineyard; and κλῆμα [*klēma*] was no longer merely the branch or twig but the whole plant, the vine itself."[3]

So a better translation of the two "I am" sayings here is, **"I am the true vineyard, and my Father is the vinegrower"** and **"I am the vineyard, you are the vines."** It makes better sense to translate verse 2 as **"He removes every vine in me that bears no fruit"**—the verb for "removes" in Greek is awkward when applied to pruning. Even more important, pruning is applied not to branches but to the vine itself. It does not make good sense here to say that Jesus is being pruned, so the second half of verse 2 is better translated as **"Every vine that bears fruit he prunes to make it bear more fruit."**[4] The translation of verse 4 is now, **"Just as the vine cannot bear fruit by itself unless it abides in the vineyard, neither can you unless you abide in me."**[5] Perhaps most important is verse 6, now translated as **"Whoever does not abide in me is cast out like a vine and withers; such vines are gathered, thrown into the fire, and burned."** The words translated as "cast out" (*eblēthē exō*) evoke the image of uprooting, and are better suited to a vine than a branch.

"I am the vine, you are the branches" has been interpreted with rich theological fruitfulness down through the centuries, and this continues. **"I am the vineyard, you are the vines"** has a comparable richness of potential meaning, and not only does it fit better with the detail of the other language used in 15:1–6, as already discussed, but also it goes well with two other marked features of the Farewell Discourses.

The first is John's characteristic emphasis on each person and on particular individuals. Here this is brought home by the repetition of the singular *klēma*: **every vine . . . every vine . . . the vine . . . like a vine . . .** To speak of a "vine"

3. Caragounis, "'Abide in Me,'" 251. That essay also gives references to other articles by Caragounis that present the full case for the semantic shift and argue convincingly for John 15:5 making better literary and theological sense if translated as "I am the vineyard, you are the vines."

4. This is reinforced by a play on the Greek words *airei* ("removes") and *kathairei* ("prunes"), the latter meaning also "cleanses" or "purifies" (origin of the English word "cathartic") and not a usual word for pruning.

5. Caragounis says on v. 4, "This exhortation would be unnatural and superfluous if it were directed to a branch, in as much as the branch is an integral part of the vine, but it would be quite natural if directed to a vine, which is not a natural or integral part of the soil (of the vineyard) in which it is planted. And a vine that does not have its roots in the soil (of the vineyard) cannot bear fruit." "'Abide in Me,'" 254.

rather than a "branch" is more in line with John's focus on individuals. This is not at all in tension with these individuals being completely part of a community and inseparable from their relationships with Jesus, with his Father, and with one another; and the language alternates between singular and plural. Here, the community is imagined as the individual vines together in a vineyard. That balances the relationship of individuals and community better than does the organic image of branches of one plant, which is open to more collectivist understandings by overemphasizing the communal and endangering the distinct identity of each person.

The second feature is closely connected with the first. The language of abiding is that of home, dwelling, and habitation, where individuals are in long-term relationships with one another. It is soon to be expanded by Jesus calling his disciples "friends." All this goes well with the Father's vineyard as the home of the vines, a place where individual vines are rooted and flourish together, but also can be pruned or even uprooted. This plant cultivation imagery of vinegrower, vineyard, and vines has many parallels with that of shepherd, sheepfold, and sheep in John 10, where the individualizing is especially vivid: "He calls his own sheep by name" (10:3).

It is even conceivable that the author of this text was aware of the shift in meaning from "vine" to "vineyard" and "branch" to "vine" and left his own language deliberately ambiguous, able to generate fresh interpretations according to different intertexts and contexts. It is striking that the most important and relevant set of intertexts with John for vine and vineyard imagery, which come in Psalms, Isaiah, Jeremiah, and Ezekiel, above all identify it with Israel and imagine Israel sometimes as a vine and sometimes as a vineyard.

In Jeremiah, Israel is "a choice vine" (2:21), which in the Septuagint is translated as *ampelos alēthinē*, a "true vine," as in John 15:1. In Isaiah, "The vineyard of the Lord of hosts is the house of Israel, and the people of Judah are his pleasant planting" (5:7), and here there is explicit emphasis on the relationship of love and on fruit bearing, destruction, and pruning: "Let me sing for my beloved my love-song concerning his vineyard: My beloved had a vineyard on a very fertile hill. . . . He expected it to yield grapes, but it yielded wild grapes. . . . I will remove its hedge, and it shall be devoured; . . . it shall not be pruned or hoed" (5:1–6). Psalm 80 begins with God as "Shepherd of Israel" and then imagines him as a vinegrower, and Israel as a vine: "You brought a vine out of Egypt; you drove out the nations and planted it" (v. 8). But, before returning later to the vine image, the psalm shifts to Israel as a vineyard: "Why then have you broken down its walls?" (v. 12).

John's text resonates with these intertexts and more, but their ramifications are characteristically focused on who Jesus is, who his Father is, and who believers are. And, for the believers, there is the challenge and invitation, already issued in so many ways earlier in the Gospel, to be true to Jesus. There is the terrible possibility of being a vine that is uprooted, withers, and is burned. There is also the challenge of growth that can be painful: **"Every branch that bears fruit he prunes to make it bear more fruit."**[6]

"More fruit" introduces yet another Johannine image of abundance, reaching back through "greater works" (14:12), the blessing attached to footwashing (13:17), "much fruit" coming from a single grain that dies (12:24), a house "filled with the fragrance of the perfume" (12:3), Jesus coming "that they may have life, and have it abundantly" (10:10), "rivers of living water" (7:38), Jesus having "the words of eternal life" (6:68), the hunger of five thousand satisfied with five barley loaves and two fish and the twelve baskets of leftovers (6:4–14), "a spring of water gushing up to eternal life" (4:14), Jesus giving "the Spirit without measure" (3:34), back to the very first sign, which is especially associated with the vine, when Jesus turns a huge amount of water into wine (2:1–11).

That wine and this vine have both been associated with the Eucharist. In Mark's Gospel, Jesus at the Last Supper "took a cup, and after giving thanks he gave it to them, and all of them drank from it. He said to them, 'This is my blood of the covenant, which is poured out for many. Truly I tell you, I will never again drink of the fruit of the vine until that day when I drink it new in the kingdom of God'" (Mark 14:23–25). John 6 connects that blood drinking with abiding: "Those who eat my flesh and drink my blood abide in me, and I in them" (6:56); but here, in John's Last Supper, the massive emphasis is on "abiding"—the verb *menein* is used eleven times in 15:1–17. The fundamental reality is mutual indwelling. As so often, John takes a key term or image and intensifies it, expands it, and deepens it, leaving his readers to make further rich connections, both within his own Gospel and in its intertexts.

Another instructive example of this is "covenant." Mark (together with Matt. 26:28 and Luke 22:20) suggests covenant as a key to the meaning of the Last Supper and the death of Jesus. John never mentions the word, but abiding in love goes to the heart of it: a permanent, living bond of trust, long-term faithfulness, and utter commitment to God and other people. God as the vinegrower irresistibly evokes Israel as the vine or vineyard and the covenant between them.[7] Jesus, in saying "I am the vine/vineyard," signals a new covenantal reality,

6. See further below on pruning lesser joys.

7. The whole Gospel of John can fruitfully be read in relation to covenant, culminating in the mutual belonging of the Father, Jesus, and believers in chap. 17: "All mine are yours, and yours are mine" (v. 10). Other key terms not mentioned in John but implicit through the Gospel include "hope," "repentance," "church," and "wisdom." Some, such as "grace" and "kingdom of God," are mentioned early, only to be replaced later by other terms.

fulfilling the prophets' and the psalmists' longing for a true, fruitful vineyard, God and God's beloved people deeply bonded in the joy of a good marriage.

So John's account of the Last Supper omits Eucharist and covenant, yet through this figure of the vine/vineyard, together with the image of abiding, it offers readers a way of understanding, deepening, and living both Eucharist and covenant, centered on who Jesus is and the call to abide in him.

"Abide in me as I abide in you" is as much a longing and an invitation as it is a command.[8] In this passage one key to its meaning is the later variation, **"If you abide in me, and my words abide in you."** To receive and digest the words of Jesus, taking them to heart and giving them constant attention, learning from him—that is to have him abiding in us. The earlier statement **"You have already been cleansed by the word that I have spoken to you"** recalls the exchange between Jesus and Peter about the footwashing (13:6–11). To be cleansed by Jesus is to be forgiven and to have a fresh start like the woman caught in adultery (8:1–11) and like Peter himself (21:15–19). The "words" in this relationship go both ways, with prayer vital to the disciples' part: **"Ask for whatever you wish, and it will be done for you."** The repetition of this astonishing promise (see discussion on 14:13–14) goes with a reminder of who and what is to inspire and orient "whatever you wish": the desire to glorify God through bearing **much fruit** and becoming **disciples** of Jesus—learners who receive his **words** and **abide in** him.

What might we ask for to fulfill that desire? All of John's Gospel, but the Farewell Discourses most of all, cries out to be turned into prayer by the readers. Petitions in line with this short passage alone might include to be led deeper into who Jesus is as the true vine/vineyard, including eucharistic practice and covenantal living; to abide more fully in Jesus, becoming more open to him and his words; and to be willing to face the truth about ourselves and be pruned and cleansed of whatever prevents bearing the fruit of love.

Dynamics of Abiding: "My Love . . . My Commandments . . . My Father . . . My Joy . . . My Friends . . . My Name" (15:9–17)

> [9] "As the Father has loved me, so I have loved you; abide in my love. [10] If you keep my commandments, you will abide in my love, just as I have kept my

8. In the first words he speaks in this Gospel Jesus asks his first disciples what they desire, and when they ask him where he is staying/abiding he invites them, "Come and see" (1:38–39); and in the prayer that culminates the Farewell Discourses Jesus longs for their mutual indwelling and unity in love with him, his Father, and one another, and he prays, "Father, I desire that those also, whom you have given me, may be with me where I am, to see my glory, which you have given me because you loved me before the foundation of the world" (17:24).

Father's commandments and abide in his love. [11] I have said these things to you so that my joy may be in you, and that your joy may be complete.

[12] "This is my commandment, that you love one another as I have loved you. [13] No one has greater love than this, to lay down one's life for one's friends. [14] You are my friends if you do what I command you. [15] I do not call you servants any longer, because the servant does not know what the master is doing; but I have called you friends, because I have made known to you everything that I have heard from my Father. [16] You did not choose me but I chose you. And I appointed you to go and bear fruit, fruit that will last, so that the Father will give you whatever you ask him in my name. [17] I am giving you these commands so that you may love one another."

The imaginative "vine" language is now complemented by some rich concepts, including a major new one: friendship between Jesus and his disciples.

Understanding what it means to abide begins here with a mind- and heart-stretching "as . . . so . . ." analogy linked with a command that, like verse 4a, is also a longing and invitation: **"As the Father has loved me, so I have loved you; abide in my love."** How has the Father loved Jesus? Who can ever fathom that? What content is to be given to that capacious "as . . . so . . ."? John's Gospel offers a text that, through constant rereading, intertextual engagement, rethinking, praying, conversation, and living a life of love and service (together with learning from the distilled wisdom of those experienced in such things in the past and around the world today), can lead slowly to understanding more and more of the truth of this central mystery that the prologue calls "the Son, who is close to the Father's heart" (1:18).

Here are just two of the many lines opened up for further thought, prayer, and action by thinking, in the context of the rest of John's Gospel, of how the Father has loved Jesus:

- The Father has loved Jesus since before the world existed (17:5, 24), in utterly mutual honoring, delight, knowledge, and intimacy. This is love "who to who," for the sake of who each is in themselves, the ultimate reality of interpersonal love. It is a love in which each is completely at home, abiding eternally. This is the deepest source of speech and action. The stupendous implication of "so I have loved you; abide in my love" is that we too are loved like that, welcomed into this home, able to speak and act from within this eternal relationship and perspective, welcoming others into this love as Jesus does.
- *The Father has loved Jesus by completely involving him in the whole of creation for the sake of its life and full flourishing* (e.g., 1:3–5; 5:26; 6:33; 10:10;

> 11:25). To be loved by Jesus is to be drawn with him into that involvement, called to be continually attentive and inventive in loving, and to do signs of abundant life and love for the sake of all creation and all people. "All things came into being through him" (1:3). What more might come into being through abiding in him?

Just as the Father-Son relationship gives fuller content to abiding in love, so it transforms what it means to be commanded and to keep commandments. Jesus says that he himself has **"kept my Father's commandments and abide in his love."** *These are commandments inseparable from deep trust, mutual love, and delight.* Such commandments are not alien impositions but a recipe for the further fulfillment of love and joy. They are commandments that can be trusted as directed entirely toward one's own good and flourishing and the flourishing of all creation. This is the wisdom of the law, of Torah, that is at the heart of Judaism, summed up in the Shema: "Hear, O Israel: The Lord is our God, the Lord alone. You shall love the Lord your God with all your heart, and with all your soul, and with all your might. Keep these words that I am commanding you today in your heart. Recite them to your children and talk about them when you are at home and when you are away, and when you lie down and when you rise. Bind them as a sign on your hand, fix them as an emblem on your forehead, and write them on the doorposts of your house and on your gates" (Deut. 6:4–9). That ties inseparably together the keeping of commandments, love, and daily abiding. This is reaffirmed and celebrated time and again in Torah,[9] in the Prophets, in the Wisdom writings, and in the Psalms, perhaps most powerfully in Psalm 119. **"If you keep my commandments, you will abide in my love"** is not the laying down of some external condition for abiding in the love of Jesus but is revealing the secret of that life of love: *not keeping the commandments means that the love cannot be mutual and, as the next verse says, joyful.*

"I have said these things to you so that my joy may be in you, and that your joy may be complete." What is "my joy"? The obvious basic meaning is the joy of being loved by the Father. One can also reread the whole Gospel through this lens, hearing "these things" that "I have said" as being said for our joy, "so that my joy may be in you." This includes the difficult sayings, such as the one a few verses earlier: "Every branch/vine that bears fruit he prunes to make it bear more fruit" (15:2). What are the things that need pruning? Sometimes they are serious forms of disobedience or blindness—desires, orientations, or behaviors that radically hinder love of God and of one another. But there are also things that distract from our core vocation of love, that fill hearts, minds,

9. Consider the commands to feast for days on end and to enjoy rest on the Sabbath.

and lives with lesser things that squeeze out greater things. *Often the need is to prune lesser joys that distract from "my joy."* John's Gospel can be read as an education in desire for that complete joy, most fully expressed in the desire of Jesus in prayer to his Father: "But now I am coming to you, and I speak these things in the world so that they may have my joy complete in themselves" (17:13).

The repetition of the commandment **"Love one another as I have loved you"** invites further reflection on how Jesus has loved his disciples, to which the whole Gospel story is relevant, but now especially invites reflection on his death: **"No one has greater love than this, to lay down one's life for one's friends."** In John 12, as discussed already, two actions and three concepts are given to help in understanding the death of Jesus. The headline, the "scent event" pointing to his burial, is the anointing of the feet of Jesus with costly perfume by his friend Mary, an act of extravagant love that filled the house with fragrance. After this, Jesus enters Jerusalem humbly on a little donkey. Then, in his meeting with some Greeks (12:20–26), come three core concepts. First, Jesus says that "the hour" that includes his death is one of glorification, and he describes the fruitfulness of his death and of his servants, through the image of a grain of wheat that dies in order to bear "much fruit." Second, an exchange between Jesus and his Father (12:27–28) roots this glorification in the heart of their relationship. Third, the significance of his death in relation to his Father and to his committed servants is expanded by the promise that through his death, he says, "I . . . will draw all people [or "all things"] to myself" (12:32). After this, in John 13 Jesus expresses his love for his disciples and points to the meaning of his death through washing their feet, the action of a slave. Now a further wave of teaching on his death moves beyond the language of servants and service into that of friendship. There is no denial of the continuing importance of service, any more than there is a denial of the massive imperatives attached to the footwashing. But there is something new here (see the quotation from Thomas Aquinas in the sidebar).

One striking feature is the inclusive range and multiple depths of the language of love and friendship. *Agapē*, the word for "love" (verb *agapan*), is the key word for love in the Septuagint translation of Israel's Scriptures, used for love of God, love of other people, and the love between the lovers in Song of Songs. But it is extremely rare in classical Greek and Hellenistic civilization. So *agapē* directs attention to the depths and heights of Scripture. *Philoi*, the word for "friends" (singular *philos*, verb *philein*), is also present in Scripture and is especially common in the Wisdom literature that is in the most extensive engagement with the surrounding culture. And in that culture there is a very rich conception of friendship, including laying down one's life for a friend. Aristotle, for example, wrote, "To a noble man there applies the true saying that

> Gregory: But when all our Lord's sacred discourses are full of his commandments, why does he give this special commandment respecting love, if it is not that every commandment teaches love, and all precepts are one? Love and love only is the fulfilment of every thing that is enjoined. As all the boughs of a tree proceed from one root, so all the virtues are produced from one love: nor has the branch, i.e., the good work, any life, except it abide in the root of love. . . . The highest, the only proof of love, is to love our adversary; as did the Truth himself, who while he suffered on the cross showed his love for his persecutors: "Father, forgive them, for they know not what they do" (Luke 23:24). Of which love the consummation is given in the next words, "Greater love has no one than this, to lay down one's life for one's friends." Our Lord came to die for his enemies, but he says that he is going to lay down his life for his friends, to show that by loving we are able to gain over our enemies, so that they who persecute us are by anticipation our friends.
>
> —Thomas Aquinas, *Catena Aurea*, 4:284

he does all things for the sake of his friends . . . and, if need be, he gives his life for them";[10] and many other writers in both Greek and Latin agreed. So this saying resonates simultaneously with Scripture and the surrounding culture, just as does the headline concept of the whole Gospel, that of the Word, *logos*.[11] It both draws upon and challenges that culture.

The scriptural resonance of "friends" includes friendship with God. This is an especially prominent concept in a remarkable intertext with the Gospel of John, Wisdom of Solomon.[12] There the figure of Wisdom acts like Jesus in John,

10. Aristotle, *Nicomachean Ethics* 1169a, quoted in Lincoln, *The Gospel according to Saint John*, 406, where other references are also given.

11. See comments on 1:1.

12. Wisdom of Solomon was written in Greek in Alexandria in the second or first century BCE and is recognized as part of the canonical Bible by some Christians but not others, so that some Bibles sadly omit it. Many for whom it is not canonical have yet strongly recommended that this profound, powerful text be read widely. Its influence can be detected in many New Testament writings, especially the Gospels of Luke and John. It is especially fruitful to read it alongside John 15. The themes and thoughts in common include bearing fruit, branches cut off, word and words, abiding, God as Father, spirit, judgment, love, commandments, joy, glorifying, knowledge and truth, prayer, being chosen, the hatred and persecution of enemies, and oppression by the surrounding world. Wisdom of Solomon 6–9 are particularly relevant chapters to John 15:1–17; and the themes of enmity, persecution, and hatred in John 15:18–25 are resonant with Wisd. 1–5 and 10–19. The central concern of that whole book is "wisdom," one of the great missing words (along with "covenant" and "hope") in John. But, as with covenant and hope, John is deeply concerned with the reality of wisdom. In John *logos*, above all, embraces the meaning of wisdom; but other expressions, such as spirit/Spirit, creating, listening, receiving, love, desire, friendship, learning, knowledge, truth, understanding, light, seeing, glory, fullness, way, following, life, commandment,

as one who shares the Spirit of God, embodies God's glory and light, relates to all creation, indwells those who love her, and makes them "friends of God":

> For she [Wisdom] is a breath of the power of God,
> and a pure emanation of the glory of the Almighty;
> therefore nothing defiled gains entrance into her.
> For she is a reflection of eternal light,
> a spotless mirror of the working of God,
> and an image of his goodness.
> Although she is but one, she can do all things,
> and while remaining[13] in herself, she renews all things;
> in every generation she passes into holy souls
> and makes them friends of God, and prophets;
> for God loves nothing so much as the person who lives with wisdom.
> (Wisd. 7:25–28)

Both Wisdom of Solomon and the Gospel of John resound with echoes of the exodus and of Moses, who was called a friend of God: "Thus the Lord used to speak to Moses face to face, as one speaks to a friend" (Exod. 33:11). Moses was the unsurpassed embodiment of this friendship: "Never since has there arisen a prophet in Israel like Moses, whom the Lord knew face to face" (Deut. 34:10). In John, from the prologue onward, Jesus is seen as more intimate with God than Moses was and drawing believers into that intimacy in ways that Moses could not. So the love the Father has for Jesus is to be imagined as at least as deep, intimate, and mutual as that shown in God's friendship with Moses. Since Jesus loves the disciples as the Father has loved him, they too can, in the light of what Jesus is about to say about friendship, be friends of God. What that means in practice can be grasped partly through the sort of immersion in the Scriptures about Moses that John draws on to testify to Jesus at many points, perhaps above all in the discourse about the bread of life. There, the death of Jesus sums up what he gives to the world: "The bread that I will give for the life of the world is my flesh" (6:51); and this leads to the mutual indwelling of Jesus and his disciples (6:56). *In John 6, life is the key concept; in John 15, love; both are transformed by the death of Jesus.*

"You are my friends if you do what I command you. I do not call you servants any longer, because the servant does not know what the master is doing; but I have called you friends, because I have made known to you everything that I

judgment, cleansing, dwelling, praying, joy, eating, drinking, healing, fragrance, and celebrating also convey aspects of its multifaceted scriptural meaning.

13. The verb in Greek is *menein*, "remain, abide."

have heard from my Father." After reaffirming the importance to this unique friendship of doing what Jesus commands (see above on v. 10), the key element of friendship that is emphasized is the sharing of knowledge. To be entrusted with a friend's deepest and most intimate thoughts, motivations, intentions, and truth—that is a knowledge far beyond a master-servant relationship. This is yet another stupendous statement. What is the content of "everything that I have heard from my Father"? There are two lines of thought on this that might be followed:

- First, it is to be understood through knowing "what the master is doing." The verb *poiein* has a wide range of meaning: "do, make, cause, effect, bring about, produce, yield, bear, give, prepare, celebrate (of feasts), claim, show (mercy), work, be active, spend, stay (of time), exercise (of authority), execute (judgment), give (alms), and create (of God)." It is one of the most important words in John. In two summary statements the Gospel itself is described as giving only a selection of what "Jesus did" (*epoiēsen ho Iēsous* [20:30, 21:25]). So because, as Jesus says, "I have kept my Father's commandments" (v. 10), we can understand what "I have heard from my Father" through reading and rereading the testimony to what he did.
- But John gives much more than a plain narrative account. He seeks to draw the reader deeper and deeper into the meaning of the events, and above all into truth embodied in his central character, Jesus. He himself is the Word, the self-expression of the Father; he embodies what is to be "heard from my Father." To know him as our friend is to know a love than which none greater (v. 13) can be conceived. We abide in this love by listening as Jesus listened, loving as Jesus loved, and being free to ask in prayer (vv. 9–10, 12–13, 16), as Jesus does in John 17, and to testify, inspired by the Advocate, the Spirit of truth (vv. 26–27).

"You did not choose me but I chose you." Disciples no more choose and call themselves than they create themselves. Our being chosen and called by name is sheer gift, utter grace. It is a mystery: Why us? Why here? Why now? Why not so many others like us, here and now? It requires the strange combination of single-minded following of Jesus with not knowing about the choosing and calling of others, as shown in the final story of this Gospel (21:20–23).

"And I appointed you to go and bear fruit, fruit that will last [*menein*, "abide"], **so that the Father will give you whatever you ask him in my name."** Love is "fruit that will last"; prayer is ongoing communication in love shaped by knowing who Jesus is and what he desires. "My name"—who Jesus is—is the culminating "my . . ." after "my love . . . my commandments . . . my Father . . . my joy . . . my friends." All these belong to Jesus, but all are also completely shared by Jesus.

This belonging and sharing will be summed up in the prayer of Jesus at the end of the Farewell Discourses, where the hatred and not belonging, which are yet to come in John 15, are also emphasized: "All mine are yours, and yours are mine. . . . The world has hated them because they do not belong to the world, just as I do not belong to the world" (17:10, 14).

"I am giving you these commands so that you may love one another." The strength of love in the community is a vital resource in the face of the hatred about to be described.

Hated without Cause (15:18–25)

> [18] "If the world hates you, be aware that it hated me before it hated you. [19] If you belonged to the world, the world would love you as its own. Because you do not belong to the world, but I have chosen you out of the world—therefore the world hates you. [20] Remember the word that I said to you, 'Servants are not greater than their master.' If they persecuted me, they will persecute you; if they kept my word, they will keep yours also. [21] But they will do all these things to you on account of my name, because they do not know him who sent me. [22] If I had not come and spoken to them, they would not have sin; but now they have no excuse for their sin. [23] Whoever hates me hates my Father also. [24] If I had not done among them the works that no one else did, they would not have sin. But now they have seen and hated both me and my Father. [25] It was to fulfill the word that is written in their law, 'They hated me without a cause.'"

Here the triple "who" relationship of love and mutual indwelling between the Father, the Son, and the friends indwelt by the Holy Spirit, which is the "home" in which this Gospel above all wants its readers to abide, is faced with its most testing challenge. There is a decision between belonging in this home and belonging to **the world**. The world's ways are so radically challenged by Jesus and his **works** that he is **hated**; *those who belong with him will arouse the same sort of hatred and persecution and will often need to distance themselves from the desires, values, practices, and enthusiasms of the groups, institutions, and societies to which, in some sense (that must constantly be discerned), they belong.*

"Remember the word that I said to you, 'Servants are not greater than their master.'" He said this in 13:16, just after telling his disciples, "So if I, your Lord and Teacher, have washed your feet, you also ought to wash one another's feet.

For I have set you an example, that you also should do as I have done to you" (13:14–15). So Jesus is reminding his disciples of that instruction, which is the most emphatic command in the whole of this Gospel. Its unique importance was reinforced by being a paradigmatic act of love (cf. 13:1: "He loved them to the end") done by Jesus at this climactic hour, and by many other signals of its significance. These include the introduction, "Jesus, knowing that his Father had given all things into his hands, and that he had come from God and was going to God"; the beatitude, "If you know these things, you are blessed if you do them"; and the follow-through into the first giving of his distinctive love command, "I give you a new commandment, that you love one another. Just as I have loved you, you also should love one another" (13:3, 17, 34).[14] Now, in John 15, there is not only a further wave of teaching on the love command, but there is also a reaffirmation of the sort of loving service at its heart. And footwashing is such a radical, loving alternative to the deeply rooted ways of the world that it provokes resistance (as Peter showed) and rejection (as Judas showed).

"If they persecuted me, they will persecute you." The whole New Testament is clear about the inevitability of persecution if Christians are being faithful, and John is here strongly in agreement with the Synoptics (Matt. 10:16–42; 24:9–14; Mark 13:9–13; Luke 21:12–15). The past century has seen more Christians killed for their faith than any previous one.

"But they will do all these things to you on account of my name, because they do not know him who sent me." As always in this Gospel, the core issue is the "who": "my name," "him who sent me." Hatred, as well as love, reaches its greatest intensity when focused on particular persons.

"If I had not come and spoken to them, they would not have sin; but now they have no excuse for their sin. . . . If I had not done among them the works that no one else did, they would not have sin. But now they have seen and hated both me and my Father." Genuinely to encounter Jesus, his message, and his actions is to meet someone and something new, acting like "no one else." It puts those who meet him in a new situation of decision: Do I trust him? In John the basic sin is not to trust Jesus. In between a complete trust and a complete rejection that can be described as "They have seen and hated both me and my Father," there are many forms of trust/faith/believing and their opposites described in John's Gospel, often exemplified in particular characters.[15] Think, for example, of John the Baptist; the diversity among the disciples (the Beloved Disciple, Peter, Thomas, Philip, Judas); Nathanael; the mother of Jesus; Nicodemus;

14. For more, see comments on John 13.

15. Rudolf Bultmann's tendency to portray Johannine faith in Jesus as an either/or binary decision has been convincingly critiqued by more recent scholarship—e.g., all through O'Day and Hylen, *John*.

the Samaritan woman at the well; the men healed in chapters 5 and 9; various groups of Jews who have very different responses; Mary, Martha, and Lazarus in their diverse responses; Pontius Pilate; and Mary Magdalene.[16] John's pedagogy of trusting and believing gives many models, some to be imitated and others definitely not, while always inviting readers further toward the ideal of being loved and loving, as best represented by the Beloved Disciple reclining on Jesus's breast (13:23–25), sharing his home with the mother of Jesus (19:27), believing (20:8), following (21:20), and abiding (21:22–23).

"It was to fulfill the word that is written in their law, 'They hated me without a cause.'" The Greek word for "without a cause" is *dōrean* (literally, "as a gift"), and is an important term. When Jesus in Matthew's Gospel sends out his disciples, he tells them, "Proclaim the good news, 'The kingdom of heaven has come near.' Cure the sick, raise the dead, cleanse the lepers, cast out demons. You received without payment [*dōrean*]; give without payment [*dōrean*]" (Matt. 10:7–8). Paul uses the word in summarizing his core message of grace.[17] The book of Revelation uses it to describe the ultimate gift of "the water of life."[18] Those are all profoundly positive uses, trying to do justice to what Jesus gives: good news, human flourishing, his own life. In the Septuagint the meaning is often more negative. Here, John probably is quoting the Septuagint translation of Psalm 69:4 (LXX 68:5), though the same phrase occurs in Psalm 35:19 (LXX 34:19). Psalm 69, which is often quoted in the New Testament, is a cry of anguish in the midst of pitiless enmity, hatred, false accusations, humiliation, insults, gossip, ridicule, and poisoning, which yet also cries out in praise, thanks, and trust in God. It ends with confidence in what John 15 would call a place of abiding and loving centered on who God is: "and those who love his name shall live in it" (Ps. 69:36; LXX 68:37). Psalm 35 (where *dōrean* is used twice, vv. 7, 19 [LXX 34:7, 19]) is a cry of anguish in the midst of murderous

16. For all these characters and more, see Hunt, Tolmie, and Zimmermann, *Character Studies in the Fourth Gospel*, which has sixty-two essays on both named and anonymous characters; Skinner, *Character and Characterization in the Gospel of John*, which in particular has fascinatingly different readings of John the Baptist, Nicodemus, the Samaritan woman, Martha, Mary, the disciple whom Jesus loved, and Pilate.

17. "But now, apart from law, the righteousness of God has been disclosed, and is attested by the law and the prophets, the righteousness of God through faith in Jesus Christ for all who believe. For there is no distinction, since all have sinned and fall short of the glory of God; they are now justified by his grace as a gift [*dōrean*], through the redemption that is in Christ Jesus, whom God put forward as a sacrifice of atonement by his blood, effective through faith" (Rom. 3:21–25). Cf. 2 Cor. 11:7.

18. "Then he said to me, 'It is done! I am the Alpha and the Omega, the beginning and the end. To the thirsty I will give water as a gift [*dōrean*] from the spring of the water of life" (Rev. 21:6); "The Spirit and the Bride say, 'Come.' And let everyone who hears say, 'Come.' And let everyone who is thirsty come. Let everyone who wishes take the water of life as a gift [*dōrean*]" (22:17).

enmity, hatred, plotting, entrapment, malice, false testimony, mockery, deceit, and treachery, which yet also cries out to God in prayer, joy, and praise.

Perhaps the most fascinating use of *dōrean* to set alongside "They hated me without a cause" is Job 1:8–11:

> The Lord said to Satan [or "the Accuser"], "Have you considered my servant Job? There is no one like him on the earth, a blameless and upright [*alēthinos*, "true"] man who fears God and turns away from evil." Then Satan [or "the Accuser"] answered the Lord, "Does Job fear God for nothing [*dōrean*]? Have you not put a fence around him and his house and all he has, on every side? You have blessed the work of his hands, and his possessions have increased in the land. But stretch out your hand now, and touch all that he has, and he will curse you to your face."

That question "Does Job fear God for nothing [*dōrean*]?" can be seen as the key to the whole book of Job.[19] Does Job's relationship of worship, awe, honoring, glorifying, trusting, and fearing God depend on the good things he has been given and how he has been blessed, or is it given *dōrean*, as a gift, freely, without such causes, for God's sake, for the sake of who God is, for what Psalm 69 calls love of God's name?[20] The rest of the book of Job shows him being stripped of children, wealth, health, social standing, dignity, religious comfort, and the support of friends but still refusing to curse God, crying out and arguing but still believing: "Though he slay me, yet I will trust in him" (Job 13:15 KJV).

In the uses of dōrean *the dark mystery of hatred, evil, enmity, and malice, which can never be adequately explained, meets the bright mystery of love, given freely for the sake of the other; and that meeting is at the heart of the drama of Jesus.*

"He Will Testify. . . . You Also Are to Testify" (15:26–27)

> 26 "When the Advocate comes, whom I will send to you from the Father, the Spirit of truth who comes from the Father, he will testify on my behalf.
> 27 You also are to testify because you have been with me from the beginning."

This further wave of teaching about the Paraclete, **the Advocate . . . the Spirit of truth**, adds a new dimension to his work, **"He will testify on my behalf,"** which is also to become a vital dimension of the calling of the disciples, **"You also**

19. See Ticciati, *Job and the Disruption of Identity*.

20. For a wider theological discussion of this, see Ford, *Christian Wisdom*, chaps. 3 ("Job!") and 4 ("Job and Post-Holocaust Wisdom").

are to testify." And the immense importance of eyewitnesses in testimony to Jesus is emphasized by **"because you have been with me from the beginning."**

This passage, with its interrelating of Jesus, **the Father**, and **the Spirit**, and the personifying of the Spirit as **who**, helps to appreciate further the movement in Christian thought toward the understanding of God as the Trinity of Father, Son, and Holy Spirit.

Testifying "on my behalf," being led by "the Spirit of truth," and reaching back to an even more original "beginning" (1:1) than that at which the eyewitnesses were present describe what John's Gospel is doing too. In John 15, as in chapter 14, the immediate practical implication of the insistent emphasis on "the word that I have spoken to you," "if . . . my words abide in you," "if you keep my commandments," "I have said these things to you," "what I command you," "everything that I have heard from my Father," "I am giving you these commands," "Remember the word that I said to you," "if they kept my word," "if I had not come and spoken to them" (15:3, 7, 10, 11, 14, 15, 17, 20, 22) is that ongoing testifying, living, and loving are to be resourced by ongoing engagement with this text, where those words and commands are written. John gives "words" that are to "abide" in readers, to be remembered, to be kept, and to be shared in testimony.

John 16:1–33

The Final Realism and Encouragement

Now come more waves of teaching and encouragement, taking further themes already opened up in John 13–15: suffering and persecution; grief about the departure of Jesus; his parting gift of the Spirit of truth; the relationship of the Spirit to the world, to the ongoing community, and to the Father and the Son; sin and judgment; trusting and believing; glorifying and asking in prayer; peace and, above all, joy.

In this final part of the Farewell Discourses, before the climactic prayer in John 17, there is a sense of crisp, realistic summary of basic truths in preparation for the death and resurrection of Jesus and for the ongoing drama of life beyond that. The pain of persecution and the prospect of martyrdom; the trauma of bereavement; a world gone wrong, prone to religion-related violence, and unable to recognize or trust Jesus; the failure of the disciples, soon to be evident when they abandon Jesus—all these are faced squarely.

Yet there is no balance between these negatives and the positives. The main thrust is radical encouragement. Jesus tells his disciples that it is actually "to your advantage that I go away" (v. 7), because the Advocate and Encourager, the Spirit of truth, will be sent and will inspire a new relationship with Jesus (summed up as "He will glorify me" [v. 14]), lead into more truth, and give fresh confidence in the face of all the negatives, grounded in the most embracing love of all: "The Father himself loves you" (v. 27). The final imbalance is a complete assurance that all will be well: "I have said this to you, so that in me you may have peace. In the world you face persecution. But take courage; I have conquered the world!" (v. 33).

The crisp directness and confident orientation are not, however, marks of closure. This is no neat, conclusive package that allows believers to feel proudly that they have mastered the truth or can claim a superior overview. At every point readers are reminded of two vital truths.

First, we are immersed in life in a divided, violent world, and we are unavoidably vulnerable to sin, evil, suffering, misperception, disorientation, falsehood, and failure.

Second, there is always *more,* a multidimensional abundance: more suffering to come, more truth to be led into, more glorifying, more rejoicing, more praying, more peace, more courage, more life, and, most important of all, more loving and trusting—"For the Father himself loves you, because you have loved me and have believed that I came from God" (v. 27).

This summary finale is oriented to realistic, humble, faithful, vulnerable, and joyful participation together in the ongoing drama of being loved and loving.

Preparation for Trauma (16:1–4a)

> [1] "I have said these things to you to keep you from stumbling. [2] They will put you out of the synagogues. Indeed, an hour is coming when those who kill you will think that by doing so they are offering worship to God. [3] And they will do this because they have not known the Father or me. [4a] But I have said these things to you so that when their hour comes you may remember that I told you about them."

Shock events are less traumatizing and disabling if we have some way of making sense of them. This preparation for persecution predicts expulsion from the Jewish community and violence to the point of being killed. Many scholars think that this resonates with the experience of John's community as a small group in conflict with the much larger Jewish community and that the division had all the passionate intensity of a family quarrel, since the author and many of his group were Jews.[1]

The verb for **stumbling**, *skandalizein,* has the extended meaning of falling away, lapsing from the faith, or falling into or being led into sin. It points to the negative aim of the Farewell Discourses, why **"I have said these things,"** what Jesus wants to **"keep you from."** Their purpose is to help the ongoing

1. On John and the Jews see comments on John 2, 8.

community avoid what is seen as the most serious error of all: failing to keep the faith, not persevering in trusting and following Jesus—betraying him, denying him, abandoning him, not abiding in him. This is a crucial matter for this small group under great pressure.

In the other Gospels, too, this verb and its related noun, *skandalon*, "stumbling block, cause or occasion for sin, rock of offense," are used of what causes people to reject or miss out on what is most important. Above all, it is applied to Jesus and his call: "Blessed is anyone who takes no offense [*skandalisthē*] at me" (Matt. 11:6). The one other use of it in John is in chapter 6, which is a companion discourse to John 13–17, especially on who Jesus is, on the Eucharist, and on mutual indwelling. After hearing "difficult teaching" about Jesus as the bread of life and mutual abiding through eating his flesh and drinking his blood, the disciples have a crisis of faith, and Jesus asks them, "Does this offend [*skandalizei*] you?" (6:61). And in fact "many of his disciples turned back and no longer went about with him" (6:66).

That is just one of many places in John where the key issue is about who Jesus is and whether he is to be trusted to the point of following him. The Farewell Discourses concentrate mainly on teaching and encouraging those who do trust him and follow him and who will have that commitment tested in extreme ways in the years to come. The realism of this preparation here faces the profound seriousness of those who oppose them. The enemies are deeply committed believers in God, doing violence in God's name, and with sincere motives: by killing the followers of Jesus they think that **they are offering worship to God**. There is a fundamental issue of ignorance of the truth: **"They will do this because they have not known the Father or me."** John's account of the trial of Jesus will highlight the issue of truth. Here in the Farewell Discourses the concern is to draw the disciples as deeply as possible into Jesus as the truth and into his relationship with his Father and to prepare them for the gift of the Spirit of truth. Their ability to be faithful to him and to persevere in following him will require not only the sort of trust and love they have now but also being led further into all dimensions of the truth and deeper into trusting and loving Jesus.

A vital resource for such maturing in faith and love are the words of this Gospel: **"But I have said these things to you so that when their hour comes you may remember that I told you about them."** And inseparable from what Jesus has said are his death and resurrection. *This encouragement in the face of martyrdom is effective only if death is not the worst thing that can happen to us: ongoing relationship with the One who has been resurrected from the dead relativizes our own death and makes it clear that losing that relationship is incomparably worse than being killed for the sake of it.*

The Secret of Succession in the Spirit: "It Is to Your Advantage That I Go Away" (16:4b–7)

> [4b] "I did not say these things to you from the beginning, because I was with you. [5] But now I am going to him who sent me; yet none of you asks me, 'Where are you going?' [6] But because I have said these things to you, sorrow has filled your hearts. [7] Nevertheless I tell you the truth: it is to your advantage that I go away, for if I do not go away, the Advocate will not come to you; but if I go, I will send him to you."

Reference to **the beginning** reminds readers of the opening verses of the prologue of the Gospel, with its summary big picture, culminating in Jesus being "close to the Father's heart" (1:18), being *with* **him who sent me**; and this is about to be illuminated further when John 17 gives a glimpse of what goes on in that ultimate and intimate "with" relationship. But here, within the story, the reference is to the beginning of when **"I was with you,"** the disciples, going back to when Jesus began to gather them later in John 1.

The disciples had, uncomprehendingly, asked earlier, "Where are you going?" (Peter in 13:36; cf. Thomas in 14:5), but here Jesus says, **"None of you asks me** [i.e., "is asking me now"], **'Where are you going?'"** and offers a reason that suggests they are understanding more now: **"Because I have said these things to you, sorrow has filled your hearts."** As Andrew Lincoln says, "Drawing attention to their silence at this point is a means of highlighting their profound sadness, with which Jesus will attempt to deal in the rest of the discourse."[2]

This leads into a decisive statement, underlined emphatically by the words introducing it, **"I tell you the truth."** This is a pivotal truth: **"It is to your advantage that I go away."** It has many dimensions, of which three will be explored here.

These first disciples will receive the Holy Spirit, their Advocate, Encourager, and Helper—a new form of the presence of Jesus after his resurrection. Their depression will be followed by joy, and the paralysis and de-energizing of grief will be followed by the Spirit reenergizing them in a renewed relationship with Jesus and with one another. He will no longer be physically present in just one place, but available as God, who "is Spirit" (4:24), is available. This is "to your advantage."

Second, for John's first readers, too, that presence of Jesus in the Spirit is utterly vital. John's Gospel is "written so that you may come to believe [or "continue to believe"] that Jesus is the Messiah, the Son of God, and that through believing you may have life in his name" (20:31), a life that had just

2. Lincoln, *The Gospel according to Saint John*, 418.

been breathed into the disciples (20:22) in fulfillment of the promise in the Farewell Discourses. But, whereas the critical transition that the first disciples had gone through was the death and resurrection of Jesus, John's first readers not only were faced by testimony to that (and also, presumably, had gone through immersion in it by baptism), but as 21:23 makes clear, they also had to cope with the transition, years later, beyond the death of those who had led their community from the beginning and who were eyewitnesses to Jesus and those events. *This is about something every long-lasting community, organization, or movement faces: the challenge of succession. How do we make the critical transition to the next generation? John's whole Gospel can be read as a response to this question. It is written for those who have not seen Jesus, in order to enable them to meet him and receive his Spirit.* The transition beyond the original eyewitnesses is to be made by reading and rereading this Gospel, trusting this testimony (1:7, 14; 20:31; 21:24), receiving these words ("The words that I have spoken to you are spirit [or "Spirit"] and life [6:63b]), and being guided by the Spirit into more truth (16:13). "Blessed are those who have not seen and yet have come to believe" (20:29).

In such transitions from early leaders to their successors there are many dangers and acute anxieties. The fear is that the leadership will prove irreplaceable and that the community will regress, decline, lose impetus and direction. Yet here Jesus himself says, "It is to your advantage that I go away." Not only is decline not envisaged; instead, there is confidence that the community will flourish even more after his departure. *The Holy Spirit, inseparable from the ongoing presence of the crucified and risen Jesus and from his words that are "Spirit and life" (6:63), is the secret of succession.*

Third, all this, as already suggested, continues to be relevant beyond the first disciples and the community of the first readers. It is yet another dimension of John's wisdom of abundance, in line with the promise of Jesus that "he gives the Spirit without measure" (3:34). Perhaps there can be no greater resource for a Christian wisdom of succession than to reread and go deeper into the Gospel of John. Perhaps every leader needs to come to the point of being able to discern when it is right to say, "It is to your advantage that I go away"; and any community going through a succession transition can gain from reflecting together on the Gospel of John, open to further truth and confident that the God of abundance can give a better future.

"For if I do not go away, the Advocate will not come to you; but if I go, I will send him to you." This is about completion without closure. John insists that there is a completeness about the life, death, resurrection, and ascension of Jesus (e.g., 13:1; 16:33; 17:4; 19:30). *But it is the completeness of a person who, after "finishing the work that you gave me to do" (17:4), is more alive than ever, no less* *present and active, but in a new and surprising mode, generating through the Spirit a continuing life of rejoicing, praying, truth seeking, serving, and loving.* The pivotal moment of this union of completion with continuing, overflowing life is the death of Jesus, when "he said, 'It is finished.' Then he bowed his head and gave up his spirit" (19:30). The Greek actually says "gave up the spirit [*to pneuma*]," and, since the manuscript did not capitalize words as we do in modern English, we can also write "gave up the Spirit." Such levels of meaning are typical of John. The death of Jesus and the giving of the Spirit are here inseparable.[3] The finishing of his life's work is followed by a greater generativity, as he inspires "greater works than these, because I am going to the Father" (14:12).

Exposed: The Truth about a World Gone Wrong (16:8–11)

> [8] "And when he comes, he will prove the world wrong about sin and righteousness and judgment: [9] about sin, because they do not believe in me; [10] about righteousness, because I am going to the Father and you will see me no longer; [11] about judgment, because the ruler of this world has been condemned."

Now come two waves of condensed teaching about the Spirit, verses 8–11 and verses 12–15.

This first wave is about how the Spirit exposes, in three ways, the reality of a world gone wrong. The word translated as **prove . . . wrong** is *elenchein*. It has a rich, multifaceted meaning, covering examining, proving, blaming, convincing, convicting, exposing, shaming. It is what the prosecution does in a trial, and through John's Gospel the imagery of a trial and associated judgment recur, until it climaxes in the literal trial of Jesus before Pilate in chapters 18–19. The irony is that the One on trial is the ultimate judge, revealing the truth of others in his light. Such conviction can be public, but also more inward—being convinced in one's conscience.

The promise is that the Spirit will enable a probing, in-depth examination of how the world can go wrong on the fundamental matters of **sin and righteousness and judgment**. *Together, these three amount to whatever makes for evil and good, injustice and justice, falsehood and truth, misery and joy, hatred and love, distrust and trust, hard-heartedness and compassion, violence and peace, despair and hope, meaninglessness and meaning.* In the light of the rest of this Gospel, three points are worth making about this activity of the Spirit.

3. See comments on 19:30.

First, it is an ongoing activity, with no timescale given. It is still happening, and all who are moved by the Spirit of truth are participants in it, daily challenged to live in the light of the Spirit of Jesus.

Second, this is the Spirit whose truth is that of the Word in whom "was life, and the life was the light of all people . . . which enlightens everyone" (1:4, 9); and this is the Spirit that has all the freedom of God, and "blows where it chooses" (3:8). The Spirit can therefore work in surprising ways, through surprising people and events, drawing on unexpected sources. Jesus is free, through the Spirit, to work invisibly (**"You will see me no longer"**), and we have no overview of that work. Disciples of Jesus should be especially alert to truth wherever it is found and to the moving of the Spirit both in public and in the hiddenness of consciences, and both within and beyond their own communities.

Third, one lesson of the Gospel of John and of subsequent history is that Christians, and whole communities of Christians, are not immune to going tragically wrong, and that there is in the church much of the wrongness of what Jesus calls **the world**. Awareness of this makes it all the more important for the followers of Jesus not only to be open to the truth wherever it is found, but also to enter as fully as possible into the truth found right here in this Gospel. This is the truth indicated in summary form in the next three verses, 16:9–11.

Being wrong **about sin, because they do not believe in me** goes to the heart of truth in John: "me," Jesus. The "who" question runs all through the Gospel, with the answer given not only by the whole story but also in a series of "I am" statements that include "I am the light of the world" (8:12) and "I am the way, and the truth, and the life" (14:6).

Why is not believing in Jesus seen as at the root of sin? It is because the "me" who is to be believed in is one who embodies the truth and love of God, and participation in such personal truth and love can happen only through a relationship of trust, of faith and faithfulness. *There is no healthy mutual love without trust and truth.* Sin happens when this really does become clear but then is rejected; when there is a genuine, illuminating encounter with Jesus, but one turns away; when the Spirit of truth somehow exposes convincingly the wrongness of the world's hostility to Jesus, but yet one sides with the world.

This sin is not about honest doubt, or an unbelief that has never had a convincing encounter with Jesus or his Spirit of truth. There is terrible potential for misunderstanding and betrayal of the Spirit here. That potential has in fact often been fulfilled, in ways ranging from persecution of Jews and heretics, through manipulative or threatening forms of Christian upbringing, teaching, and preaching ("If you do not believe what I say, you will be damned"), to all sorts of other failures by Christians to be true to who Jesus is in their living and witnessing. These words are addressed to those who *have* had a completely convincing encounter with Jesus. They are being prepared to endure massive pressure from those who have not had such an encounter, who "have not known the Father or me" (16:3). For such disciples, the basic sin would be to break faith with Jesus, to betray or deny him; and being right about sin is to know him, to believe in, to trust in, and to be faithful to him.

Being wrong **about righteousness, because I am going to the Father and you will see me no longer** looks, from a standpoint at the end of the story, at the vital matter of righteousness, which in the Bible embraces right relationship with God, with other people, and with creation. It is defined by and centered on who God is and on responding to who God is and what God desires. In John, from the opening of the prologue, these right relationships are embodied, revealed, and modeled in the relationship of Jesus with his Father. As the prologue says, this relationship involves "all things," all "life," "the light of all people"; it is about "the glory as of a father's only son, full of grace and truth"; Torah, "the law" and its righteousness, which was "given through Moses," came in person in "grace and truth . . . through Jesus Christ." The invisibility of God remains: "No one has ever seen God." Jesus has "lived among us" and "made him known." But Jesus does not stay visible and local. He is "God the only Son, who is close to the Father's heart," and he has returned into the bosom of the Father.[4] And so now he is invisible: "You will see me no longer."

This is where the Farewell Discourses are oriented: "Now I am going to him who sent me" (16:5); "Now I am coming to you" (17:13). The central truth at the heart of all reality and embracing all reality is this love in this relationship. It is about to be realized in history in a new way, when Jesus dies, is raised from the dead, and ascends "to my Father and your Father, to my God and your God" (20:17). The Farewell Discourses give their inner meaning, most fully in the prayer of Jesus in John 17. *That meaning is nothing less than the desire of Jesus to open up this relationship to all who trust and love him and for this love to overflow through the world (17:20–26)*. Any idea or practice of right living and right relationship that falls short of this is "wrong . . . about righteousness."[5] But followers of Jesus need to note that it is the Advocate, not necessarily anything they say or do, who convicts the world of being wrong and so opens the way for the truth.[6]

4. On the quotations in this paragraph, see comments on 1:1–18, including John McHugh's translation of 1:18 in the section "Intimacy at the Heart of Reality."

5. Paul, especially in his Letter to the Romans, gives the most thorough attention in the New Testament to righteousness in relation to Jesus and the gospel.

6. As Lesslie Newbigin says, "Once more we see that the Spirit is not the domesticated auxiliary of the Church; he is the powerful advocate who goes before the Church to bring the world under conviction" (*The Light Has Come*, 211).

Being wrong **about judgment, because the ruler of this world has been condemned** imagines a trial that produces a verdict of final, global significance. This will be enacted in the trial of Jesus, and here the disciples and readers are given its inner meaning in advance. As Lesslie Newbigin says, "The 'going' of Jesus by way of the cross is that final judgment. It is judgment in a unique sense, because in it the 'ruler of the world'—represented by the combined authority of law, state, religion, temple, and public opinion—passed judgment on Jesus and yet in that act of judgment sentence was passed on the judge."[7]

It might seem that "the ruler of this world" has won; but, in fact, there is a radical reversal. The One who washes feet, who lays down his life in love, and who is humiliated on the cross—he is the victor. *For the disciples before the crucifixion; for John's first readers, against whom all that "combined authority" was still being exercised; and for readers through history and around the world now, who have found themselves under massive pressure from systems and forces involving coercive power, manipulation, falsehood, love of money, comfort (or other attractive temptations), humiliation, hard-heartedness, and injustice, this is a liberating message of encouragement.*

One practical effect of confidence in the decisive defeat of the personified "ruler of this world" is that he can cease to be a focus of interest. The message is that this is a figure, whoever or whatever he may be or represent, who is best understood to be rejected and defeated; so do not be attracted or distracted by him and all he represents, but instead turn to the true judge and ruler of the world, and be guided by his Spirit. The next verses, 16:12–15, give to this positive turning a content that is full and gripping enough to counter any such attraction or distraction.

"He Will Guide You into All the Truth"; "He Will Glorify Me" (16:12–15)

> 12 "I still have many things to say to you, but you cannot bear them now.
> 13 When the Spirit of truth comes, he will guide you into all the truth; for
> he will not speak on his own, but will speak whatever he hears, and he will
> declare to you the things that are to come. 14 He will glorify me, because he
> will take what is mine and declare it to you. 15 All that the Father has is mine.
> For this reason I said that he will take what is mine and declare it to you."

This amazing multiple promise opens with a basic statement about the sort of truth Jesus is and gives. There is more and more of it, and he will share it:

7. Newbigin, *The Light Has Come*, 210–11.

"I still have many things to say to you." But it cannot be taken in all at once, only over time, after going through further experience: **"You cannot bear them now."** What sort of experience?

The Greek word for "bear," *bastazein*, has fascinating connections. *Most important, in John it is used for Jesus bearing the cross (19:17).* In Luke's Gospel, it is used both for the mother of Jesus bearing him ("Blessed is the womb that bore you" [11:27]) and for the disciples of Jesus having to carry the cross ("Whoever does not carry the cross and follow me cannot be my disciple" [14:27]). Paul used it for members of the church being urged to "bear one another's burdens" (Gal. 6:2) and to "put up with the failings of the weak" (Rom. 15:1), and he describes his own sufferings: "I carry [*bastazein*] the marks of Jesus branded on my body" (Gal. 6:17). In the Acts of the Apostles, Ananias is told by the Lord in a vision that Paul is to "bring [*bastazein*] my name before Gentiles and kings and before the people of Israel; I myself will show him how much he must suffer for the sake of my name" (9:15–16).

So this is experience that involves suffering, and especially suffering that comes through following the example of Jesus, who is here preparing, on the last night of his life, to lay down his life in love. *Some truths can be taken in only after the space for them has been hollowed out by suffering in love and service.*

This is reinforced and deepened by some Septuagint uses of *bastazein*, especially in Isaiah, which has such a rich intertextual relationship with John.[8] And, given the focus of this passage on understanding and truth, one of the most illuminating parallels is in the Wisdom literature, whose language is also often echoed in John. In the book of Sirach (Ecclesiasticus), just after a strong

8. For example, in Isa. 40:11 the Septuagint, translated literally in one of its versions, says, "He will tend his flock like a shepherd, and gather lambs with his arm, and bear them in his bosom [*en tō kolpō autou bastasei*], and comfort [*parakalēsei*] those that are with young." In one of Isaiah's Servant Songs, which were very important to early Christians (see comments on 1:29–34), the servant "will bear [*bastasei* in the Aquila text] their sins" (Isa. 53:11). In the climactic chapter, Isa. 66, whose language is echoed at so many points in John 16 that it is clear this final part of the Farewell Discourses is meant to be read alongside Isaiah (both speak of sin, judgment, suffering, joy, glory, comfort, and love, and have a vivid image of the pain and joy of giving birth), there is a powerful prophecy of joy after mourning: "Rejoice with Jerusalem, and be glad for her, all you who love her; rejoice with her in joy, all you who mourn over her—that you may nurse and be satisfied from her consoling breast; that you may drink deeply with delight from her glorious bosom. For thus says the Lord: . . . you shall nurse and be carried [*bastazein* is the verb in the Aquila text] on her arm, and dandled on her knees. As a mother comforts her child, so I will comfort you; you shall be comforted in Jerusalem" (66:10–13). Very striking in the Septuagint is the use of the words for "comfort," the noun *paraklēsis* and the verb *parakalein*, five times in three verses (vv. 11–13), paralleling John's use of *paraklētos*—"comforter, encourager, advocate"—for the Holy Spirit. This parallel is part of the case for not translating *paraklētos* only by the legal term "advocate."

affirmation of the importance of friendship,[9] the readers are urged passionately to make the search for wisdom central to their lives: "Put your feet into her fetters, and your neck into her collar. Bend your shoulders and carry [*bastazein*] her, and do not fret under her bonds. Come to her with all your soul, and keep her ways with all your might. Search out and seek, and she will become known to you; and when you get hold of her, do not let her go. For at last you will find the rest she gives, and she will be changed into joy for you. Then her fetters will become for you a strong defense, and her collar a glorious robe" (Sir. 6:24–29). That combination of love, friendship, suffering, joy, glory, and the disciplining and stretching of one's whole being in the search for wisdom and understanding prepares well for the promise, in the next three verses, of abundant truth through Jesus and his Spirit.

This second wave of teaching on the Spirit gives an extraordinarily comprehensive promise: **"When the Spirit of truth comes, he will guide you into all the truth."** How comprehensive? There have been many attempts to limit it.

Some limit the "you" to the first apostles or to their successors as leaders in the church. But the thrust of the Farewell Discourses is to embrace not only the first hearers but also all later believers: "I ask not only on behalf of these, but also on behalf of those who will believe in me through their word" (17:20).

Some limit "all the truth" to truth about the person of Jesus, or truth directly relevant to the teaching of the church, or truth explicitly given in Scripture, and rule out wider concerns and inquiries. But if Jesus is identified with the Word of God, and "all things came into being through him, and without him not one thing came into being" (1:3), then the horizon for "all the truth" must be God and the whole of created reality. The Wisdom literature, the Gospel of John, and other Scriptures encourage readers to seek truth continually wherever it is to be found.

Such attempts at narrowing the promise, whether to particular people or to specific "religious" topics and texts, reveal strong impulses of control and some of the fears and anxieties associated with truth, knowledge, understanding, questioning, and authority. Individuals, groups, and whole traditions can seek the security and certainty of a neatly defined package of meaning. The Gospel of John above all resists such packaging and closure, with its abundance of grace, light, and truth, its association of truth and liberation ("The truth will make you free" [8:32]), its Spirit given "without measure" (3:34), and its daring promise of being guided "into all the truth." Here, the broad, God-centered

9. "Faithful friends [*philos pistos*] are a sturdy shelter: whoever finds one has found a treasure. Faithful friends are beyond price; no amount can balance their worth. Faithful friends are life-saving medicine; and those who fear the Lord will find them. Those who fear the Lord direct their friendship aright, for as they are, so are their neighbors also" (Sir. 6:14–17).

comprehensiveness of the horizon of meaning is reinforced by what follows: **"He will take what is mine and declare it to you. All that the Father has is mine."** What are the limits to what "the Father has"?

Yet this Gospel is also very clear that truth is inseparable from action. The truth is above all to be done: "Those who do what is true come to the light, so that it may be clearly seen that their deeds have been done in God" (3:21). In 16:13 the Greek for "he will guide," *hodēgēsei*,[10] and even the reference to "all truth" and to glory, reflect language about the practice of wisdom: "For she knows and understands all things, and she will guide me [*hodēgēsei*] wisely in my actions and guard me with her glory" (Wisd. 9:11).[11]

The conclusion is that the horizon of the truth into which the Spirit can guide is unlimited, but the central focus is on Jesus and learning to live wisely together (the sixfold "you" in 16:12–15 is plural) in his light.

"He will glorify me" can mean, within this horizon, not only living in line with who Jesus is and what he has commanded—which in the Farewell Discourses especially means following the example of his footwashing and of his love, even to the point of dying for others (the final mention of glorifying in this Gospel is Peter glorifying God by dying [21:19]). It can also mean asking such questions as, Does this science and technology glorify Jesus? Does this way of treating the earth glorify Jesus? Does this politics, economics, law, or culture glorify Jesus? And, whatever the answers, what is the Spirit inspiring in response?

The promise **"He will declare to you the things that are to come"** does not seem, in this context, to be about detailed prophecy of future events. The Farewell Discourses do prepare readers for **things that are to come**, especially the death and resurrection of Jesus, the sufferings and joys of discipleship, and above all the giving of the Holy Spirit, bringing truth that cannot yet be borne; but the conclusion of the Gospel questions a specific prediction in the community about the death of the Beloved Disciple and the return of Jesus: "If it is my will that he should remain until I come, what is that to you?" (21:23). *"Until I come" points to the key to the "things that are to come": the person of Jesus.*[12] Hence the statement of 16:13 is followed at once by 16:14: "He will glorify me."

These verses encourage the disciples/learners continually to seek more truth. The first imperative is to listen or read attentively—reinforced by the threefold repetition, **declare to you . . . declare it to you . . . declare it to you**. At the center,

10. The first part of this verb is from *hodos*, "way, path," as in 1:23, "Make straight the way of the Lord," and 14:6, "I am the way, and the truth, and the life."

11. See also Pss. 25:5 (guidance and truth), 86:11 (guidance and truth), 143:10 (God's Spirit guiding), all of which in the Septuagint translation use the same Greek word for "guide" (*hodēgein*).

12. See comments on 14:1–6; 21:20–23.

in intimate relationship with **the Spirit** and **the Father** is Jesus, again underlined by a threefold repetition, **is mine . . . is mine . . . is mine**. And **what is mine**, to be shared with learners, is **all that the Father has**—an unlimited superabundance of truth. John 17 will intensify this dedication to truth: "Sanctify them in the truth; your word is truth. As you have sent me into the world, so I have sent them into the world. And for their sakes I sanctify myself, so that they also may be sanctified in truth" (17:17–19).

The Most Important "Little While" in History (16:16–24)

> 16 "A little while, and you will no longer see me, and again a little while, and
> you will see me." 17 Then some of his disciples said to one another, "What
> does he mean by saying to us, 'A little while, and you will no longer see me,
> and again a little while, and you will see me'; and 'Because I am going to the
> Father'?" 18 They said, "What does he mean by this 'a little while'? We do
> not know what he is talking about." 19 Jesus knew that they wanted to ask
> him, so he said to them, "Are you discussing among yourselves what I meant
> when I said, 'A little while, and you will no longer see me, and again a little
> while, and you will see me'? 20 Very truly, I tell you, you will weep and mourn,
> but the world will rejoice; you will have pain, but your pain will turn into joy.
> 21 When a woman is in labor, she has pain, because her hour has come. But
> when her child is born, she no longer remembers the anguish because of
> the joy of having brought a human being into the world. 22 So you have pain
> now; but I will see you again, and your hearts will rejoice, and no one will
> take your joy from you. 23 On that day you will ask nothing of me. Very truly,
> I tell you, if you ask anything of the Father in my name, he will give it to you.
> 24 Until now you have not asked for anything in my name. Ask and you will
> receive, so that your joy may be complete."

This is about the most important time in history, the **little while** during which Jesus is crucified, is dead and seen **no longer**, is resurrected and seen **again**, and goes **to the Father** to begin a new time, **that day** of utter **joy**, embracing those sharing his Spirit in an intimacy that can **ask anything of the Father in my name**.

The importance is emphasized, and the key elements underlined, by multiple repetitions: **a little while** (7x); **see** (two Greek words) (7x); **Jesus** and pronouns for him, **I**, **me**, **my**, **he**, **him** (19x); **disciples** and pronouns for them, **you**, **your**, **one another**, **we**, **us**, **they**, **them** (31x); **rejoice**, **joy** (6x); **pain** (reinforced by **weep**, **mourn**, **anguish**) (4x); **ask** (two Greek words) (4x); **the Father** and the associated pronoun **he** (3x); **very truly** (the phrase in Greek is itself a repetition, *amēn amēn*) (2x); **in my name** (2x).

The depth and intensity are brought home by the **pain** and **joy** of the **woman in labor**. Childbirth is an irreversible, unrepeatable event of immense meaning, risk, and consequence. John has already imagined it as repeatable in spiritual terms (3:3, 5, 14–17).[13] Now, on the night before his death, Jesus prepares the hearts and imaginations of his disciples for the coming days by evoking the agony and joy of childbirth.

But this is not only preparation for the coming days. Scholars rightly question what this "little while" is referring to. Might it not also point to the time between the ascension of Jesus and his coming again? That begins with Jesus **going to the Father**—"ascending to my Father and your Father, to my God and your God" (20:17); for the disciples it will be a time of pain and joy; and it will culminate in **that day**, the ultimate face-to-face encounter with Jesus when **"I will see you again,"** and in **joy** that is **complete**. *As often in John, the alternatives need not exclude each other*. The disciples discuss the meaning of what Jesus has said, and they raise questions. Jesus gives not a direct answer but a vivid image, the dramatic metaphor of a woman's labor and childbirth. This can apply to several deeply interconnected realities: what he himself is about to go through; the grief and joy of the disciples at his crucifixion and resurrection; the baptism his followers undergo ("born of water and Spirit" [3:5]); their suffering and joy in following him later, learning truth that they "cannot bear now" (16:12), that they are to be sent as he was sent, which includes being sent into darkness and suffering; their mutual abiding in Jesus and Jesus in them (6:56; 15:1–12); and the ultimate, eternal abiding as family with Jesus—the "where I am" of "my Father's house" (14:2–4) and the "where I am" of the summit of love and union, with God and with one another, that is about to be prayed for in 17:20–26.

All of those dimensions are also present in Dante's *Divine Comedy*. As the three chief characters of the poem are together at a critical moment of transition from purgatory, a place of pain for the sake of joy, to paradise, the place of joy and utter love for God and other people, this passage from John is quoted (see the quotation from Dante in the sidebar).

Literal, physical seeing is a key activity in the Gospel of John. It is vital to the testimony that shapes the whole Gospel. But human seeing has its limitations, as statements early and late in the Gospel affirm: "No one has ever seen God" (1:18); and, when Jesus is no longer visible in the flesh, "Blessed are those who have not seen and yet have come to believe" (20:29). Here, the key verse has the final mention by Jesus of seeing: **"So you have pain now; but I will see you**

13. See comments on John 3.

Weeping, the women then began—now three,
now four, alternately—to psalm gently,
"Deus venerunt gentes";[a] and at this,

sighing and full of pity, Beatrice
was changed; she listened, grieving little less
than Mary when, beneath the Cross, she wept.

But when the seven virgins had completed
their psalm, and she was free to speak, erect,
her coloring like ardent fire, she answered:

"Modicum, et non videbitis me
et iterum, sisters delightful to me,
modicum, et vos videbitis me."[b]

Then she set all the seven nymphs in front
of her and signaled me, the lady, and
the sage who had remained, to move behind her.

So she advanced; and I do not believe
that she had taken her tenth step upon
the ground before her eyes had struck my eyes

and gazing tranquilly, "Pray, come more quickly,"
she said to me. . . .

"Brother, why not try,
since now you're at my side, to query me?" . . .

If, reader, I had ampler space in which
to write, I'd sing—though incompletely—that
sweet draught for which my thirst was limitless."

—Dante Alighieri, *The Divine Comedy: Purgatorio*,
canto 33, lines 1–20, 23–24, 136–38

a. The Latin is the opening of Ps. 79, "O God, the heathen have come," which laments the destruction of the Jerusalem temple, resonating with the death of Jesus, which is referred to three lines later.

b. The Latin translates John 16:16, "A little while, and you will no longer see me, and again a little while, and you will see me." There are multiple resonances in this canto with John 16—the death of Jesus; love, pain, and joy; question and answer; facing great fear; deep puzzlement; forgetting and remembering; seeing and not seeing; and the pervasive importance of will and desire: "my thirst was limitless." But Dante has daringly put the words of Jesus in the mouth of Beatrice, who is central to Dante's education of desire through hell, purgatory, and paradise; and in addition he has identified Beatrice also with Mary, the mother of Jesus. The *Divine Comedy* can be read not only as an intertext with the Bible but also as claiming something of the authority of the Bible. For a perceptive discussion of Dante and Scripture, with a particular focus on the Gospel of John, see Hawkins, *Dante's Testaments*, chap. 3, "John Is with Me." Some of Hawkins's description of Dante could be applied to the author of the Gospel of John, especially his union of faithfulness and daring: "Dante manages simultaneously to be both the obedient scribe and the radically independent genius. . . . [His] stakes are no less high than the *mysterium evangelii* itself. He knows he is playing with sacred fire. . . . One cannot stop marvelling at the sureness of his [tightrope-walker's] footing, the careful measure of each bold step forward, the confident way he holds on to the air" (pp. 69, 71).

again, and your hearts will rejoice, and no one will take your joy from you." Note the emphasis: not "You will see me again," but "I will see you again." Being seen by Jesus is the permanent reality, and trusting in this in "your hearts" gives the joy that cannot be taken away. The rest of the chapter moves away from the visual into the language of telling and saying (vv. 23, 25, 26, 29, 33), asking (vv. 23, 24, 26, 30), and believing and trusting (vv. 27, 30, 31).

At the heart of that saying, asking, and believing is what E. C. Hoskyns calls "the new economy of prayer,"[14] prayer in the name of Jesus. **"On that day you will ask nothing of me. Very truly, I tell you, if you ask anything of the Father in my name, he will give it to you. Until now you have not asked for anything in my name. Ask and you will receive, so that your joy may be complete."** That is the final wave of teaching on prayer in the Farewell Discourses, before Jesus actually prays in John 17. There, he will model the sort of prayer that his disciples are here urged to imitate—not only its intimacy and mutuality, but also its daring expectation for both the church and the world.

Two Coming Hours and Now: Complete Love, Full Believing, Daring Prayer; Being Scattered, Leaving Jesus; and Imperfect Believing Now (16:25–32a)

> 25 "I have said these things to you in figures of speech. The hour is coming when I will no longer speak to you in figures, but will tell you plainly of the Father. 26 On that day you will ask in my name. I do not say to you that I will ask the Father on your behalf; 27 for the Father himself loves you, because you have loved me and have believed that I came from God. 28 I came from the Father and have come into the world; again, I am leaving the world and am going to the Father."
>
> 29 His disciples said, "Yes, now you are speaking plainly, not in any figure of speech! 30 Now we know that you know all things, and do not need to have anyone question you; by this we believe that you came from God." 31 Jesus answered them, "Do you now believe? 32a The hour is coming, indeed it has come, when you will be scattered, each one to his home, and you will leave me alone."

As the Farewell Discourses move to their end, Jesus speaks of two coming "hours," one of fulfillment, the other of failure. The lesson for disciples **now** is clear, but imperfectly grasped: their believing, trusting, and loving are vital.

14. Hoskyns and Davey, *The Fourth Gospel*, 487, 489.

The first **hour** is also a **day**, a time of understanding, trusting, and loving that this whole Gospel is written to draw readers into, further and deeper. The prologue (1:1–18) had first laid out the embracing reality of what this involves: God, the Word, all things, light, life, glory, grace and truth, and God the only Son, who is close to the Father's heart, making known the invisible God. The Farewell Discourses have drawn us further and deeper in many ways, and now there is a short summary of what fills this time: clearer understanding of God, the new economy of prayer, and **the Father** loving those who love and trust Jesus as the Son sent by God. The overarching narrative framework within which this happens is then summed up in a single sentence: **"I came from the Father and have come into the world; again, I am leaving the world and am going to the Father."** Jesus comes, dies, and goes in love for both the world and the Father, and his followers are to be part of that same loving.

When is "the hour," "that day," spoken of here? A good deal points to it being the time beyond the death and resurrection of Jesus and the giving of the Holy Spirit. It may perhaps best be understood as the "now" of any reader of this Gospel, who is invited to believe in, trust, and love Jesus within the horizon of reality opened up from the prologue onward.

There are two somewhat puzzling negatives in these verses. **"I will no longer speak to you in figures, but will tell you plainly of the Father"** may refer to the figures used in the earlier part of the Gospel (in 10:6 *paroimia* is used to describe the imagery of the good shepherd, which is then explained) and in the Farewell Discourses, most recently that of the woman in labor. The Greek word for **figures of speech**, **figures**, and **figure of speech** (vv. 25, 29) is *paroimia*. In the Septuagint both this word and *parabolē* ("parable") are used to translate the Hebrew *māšāl*, and the meaning can include various forms of comparison and puzzling language, including parables, allegories, proverbs, and riddles (in this chapter, "a little while" would fit). The early church was left by Jesus with many parables, images, and puzzling actions and sayings. The Synoptic Gospels tried to interpret and explain them in various ways; John, at a later stage, seeks to interpret and explain more, and he omits the Synoptic parables but often takes up their meaning in other forms. The negative **no longer . . . in figures** probably should be seen as actually meaning "no longer *only* in figures," given John's own abundant use of figures of speech, and the negative serves to emphasize the positive statement that follows.

But what is the meaning of that positive statement, **"I . . . will tell you plainly of the Father"**? The Greek word *parrhēsia* is not adequately translated by "plainly"; indeed, that gives the wrong impression of a simple contrast between lack of clarity in figures of speech and clarity in later speech without figures. Rather, the meaning of *parrhēsia* that fits here, and with the whole of John's way of writing and teaching, is that of *free, confident, abundant speech.* So it is better to translate, "The hour is coming when I will no longer speak to you (only) in figures, but will tell you freely, confidently, and abundantly of the Father." This is the sort of speech that the Holy Spirit inspires in prayer, worship, preaching, and teaching, in line with the prologue's testimony that "we have seen his glory, the glory as of a father's only son, full of grace and truth" (1:14), and "from his fullness we have all received, grace upon grace" (1:16), together with all the other expressions of abundance throughout the Gospel. *This* parrhēsia *is speech corresponding to the Spirit that is given "without measure" (3:34) and that "will guide you into all the truth" (16:13).* The Farewell Discourses give the supreme example of such speech in the prayer of Jesus in John 17. That prayer is largely in nonfigurative language, but it also shows how figures of speech earlier in John can generate further language that says even more about the Father and his relationship with the Son and with believers (e.g., the imagery of being in the vine in John 15, as it is taken further in 17:20–26).

The other puzzling negative is, **"I do not say to you that I will ask the Father on your behalf."** The reason given is, **"For the Father himself loves you, because you have loved me and have believed that I came from God."** This too is illuminated by John 17. It is not that Jesus ceases to be in intimate relationship and communication both with the Father and with those who love and trust him. The Father, the Son, and believers are in such a close mutual relationship, each with the others, that the new economy of prayer and intimacy does not set the disciples at a remove from the Father, while being closer and more in communication with Jesus. *The attentive, listening love of the Father and of the Son are joint and simultaneous.*

The second "hour" is one, Jesus says, that **"is coming, indeed it has come, when you will be scattered, each one to his home, and you will leave me alone."** The first "hour" was one of open duration, a "day" filled with a sustained life of believing, praying, understanding, and loving. This second hour is an event that is on the verge of happening on this evening: the arrest of Jesus, the scattering of his disciples, and Jesus left alone in the face of betrayal, violence, humiliation, denial, false accusation, condemnation, and crucifixion. The language echoes Zechariah, "Strike the shepherd, that the sheep may be scattered" (13:7), which is quoted also in Matthew 26:31 and Mark 14:27 in regard to the abandonment of Jesus by his disciples. But there is, as so often, a further element in John. In his telling, there is in fact one disciple at the foot of the cross of Jesus, "the disciple whom he loved" (19:26), and there is an echo of this verse: "to his home" in 16:32 is the same Greek phrase (*eis ta idia*) as "into his own home" in 19:27 about the Beloved Disciple taking the mother of Jesus to live with him. C. K. Barrett suggests that the Synoptic refusal to admit any exceptions among the disciples is "almost certainly better history, and better theology too."[15] But, whatever about the history (and there could well be a distinct strand of testimony feeding into John's account), the theology might be that the aloneness of Jesus on the cross is not just a matter of physical abandonment. *He is alone in the face of betrayal, violence, humiliation, denial, false accusation, political expediency, religious manipulation, condemnation, and crucifixion—an overwhelming combination of sin, evil, suffering, and death.* The physical presence of the disciple he loved and of his mother might, if anything, intensify the weight of all that and the experience of dying. Barrett says that "a formal contradiction is avoided"[16] by the use of the same phrase, *eis ta idia*, but both the literary craft and the theological richness of John suggest that there may be something more here than an attempt to avoid formal contradiction.

That suggestion is strengthened by two further elements. First, the only other use of *eis ta idia* in John is in the prologue: "He came to what was his own [*eis ta idia*], and his own people did not accept him" (1:11); and its repetition, first in relation to his own disciples and then again in relation to the two people in the Gospel who do accept him most fully, intensifies his human aloneness in death. Second, there is the contrast with his lack of abandonment by his Father in 16:32b: "Yet I am not alone because the Father is with me"—the utter human isolation, bearing death and "the sin of the world" (1:29), goes with his fundamental knowledge and trust. But does this contradict the Synoptic cry of abandonment by Jesus from the cross (Matt. 27:46; Mark 15:34)? We will come to that question soon.

In between those two "hours" are three "nows." The first two "nows" come in a confident statement by disciples: **"Yes, now you are speaking plainly, not in any figure of speech! Now we know that you know all things, and do not need to have anyone question you; by this we believe that you came from God."** The disciples claim to understand clearly, to see and believe, and what they claim to know is doctrinally correct, in line with what the Gospel affirms. But the third now of Jesus is deeply skeptical: **Jesus answered them, "Do you now believe?"** This echoes what he has said earlier in response to Peter's claim that he would lay down his life for Jesus: "Will you lay down your life for me? Very truly, I tell you, before the cock crows, you will have denied me three times" (13:38). As then, Jesus adds a prediction of what will actually happen. This will show that their believing now is radically inadequate because it will be falsified by their actions. It fails the most crucial test of all.

This whole Gospel is about believing, which comes in many forms. The aim is a depth and maturity of believing, a permanent relationship of trusting,

15. Barrett, *The Gospel according to St. John*, 498.
16. Barrett, *The Gospel according to St. John*, 497.

knowing, and loving that overflows into action—and if the action is not there, the believing is suspect. The First Letter of John, coming at a later stage of the community's history, after a bitter experience of the reality of how believing can be disconnected from love, repeatedly insists on this imperative connection between faith and action. The Farewell Discourses began with the many-layered imperative to imitate the action of Jesus in washing feet, followed through with the command to love as Jesus has loved, which was then further reinforced and deepened. "Now," as the Farewell Discourses are about to turn into a prayer that is the summit of believing and loving in John's Gospel, every reader is faced by Jesus with the key question for every "now": "Do you now believe?"

The Final Encouragement: The Father with Me, You in Me, I Win My Sort of Victory (16:32b–33)

> 32b "Yet I am not alone because the Father is with me. 33 I have said this to you, so that in me you may have peace. In the world you face persecution. But take courage; I have conquered the world!"

The human isolation of Jesus in what he is going through, perhaps even to be intensified by the physical presence at his crucifixion of his mother and the disciple he loved, has just been emphasized: "You will leave me alone" (16:32a). But Jesus utterly trusts in his unbroken relationship with his Father: **"Yet I am not alone because the Father is with me."** This trust is sustained all through the following two chapters, during his trial, passion, and death. There is no wobble in the Johannine Jesus on this score. Is this in tension with the Synoptic Gospels? There has been massive theological pressure to see Jesus as authentically in solidarity with humanity only if his union with his Father is shaken on the cross, summed up in the pivotal importance that can be given to the cry, "My God, my God, why have you forsaken me?" (Matt. 27:46; Mark 15:34).[17] But John's account (which, here as so often, takes a postresurrection standpoint) might be read as a corrective to that conclusion.

That cry of Jesus quotes the opening words of Psalm 22, and John can be understood as siding with the many interpreters who hear Jesus as implying the whole psalm. The psalmist's opening cry is not his last word. That anguish, deepened in the following verses, is followed, as here in John, by a "yet" that contrasts human isolation with trust in divine help: "Yet it was you who took me from the womb; you kept me safe on my mother's breast. On you I was

17. Perhaps most radically by Moltmann, *The Crucified God.*

cast from my birth, and since my mother bore me you have been my God. Do not be far from me, for trouble is near and there is no one to help" (vv. 9–11). Increasing suffering then alternates with cries to God for help, until the cries turn into praise and gratitude: "You who fear the Lord, praise him! All you offspring of Jacob, glorify him; stand in awe of him, all you offspring of Israel! For he did not despise or abhor the affliction of the afflicted; he did not hide his face from me, but heard when I cried to him" (vv. 23–24). There is even an overflow of response in faith by others who know of this: "All the ends of the earth shall remember and turn to the Lord; and all the families of the nations shall worship before him. For dominion belongs to the Lord, and he rules over the nations. . . . And I shall live for him" (vv. 27–29). *This realism of anguish and suffering, combined with trust in God but not in balance with it, goes to the heart of the mystery of the crucifixion and resurrection of Jesus.*

That imbalance, coming down decisively and triumphantly on the side of trust in God, is the final note of this final teaching of Jesus. **"I have said this to you"** emphasizes the continuing importance of the Farewell Discourses and the words of this Gospel. The drama continues, together with the relevance of what "I have said," because **"in the world you face persecution"** and will be shaken. But persecution, evil, suffering, sin, failure, and death do not have the last word. The ultimate Word is a person, "me," and **"in me you may have peace."** When the risen Jesus appears to them, he will bring this peace, "Peace be with you. . . . Peace be with you" (20:19, 21), and will send them as he has been sent, as bringers of peace.

"But take courage; I have conquered the world!" This confidence in victory rings through the Gospel of John and the later Johannine community. In the First Letter of John it is the message to the rising generation: "I am writing to you, young people, because you have conquered the evil one. . . . I write to you, young people, because you are strong and the word of God abides in you, and you have overcome the evil one. . . . Little children, you are from God, and have conquered them; for the one who is in you is greater than the one who is in the world" (1 John 2:13–14; 4:4). It is a victory that is inseparable from love and faith: "For the love of God is this, that we obey his commandments. And his commandments are not burdensome, for whatever is born of God conquers the world. And this is the victory that conquers the world, our faith. Who is it that conquers the world but the one who believes that Jesus is the Son of God?" (1 John 5:3–5).

What sort of victory is this? It turns most types of triumphalism upside down. In the Farewell Discourses it is symbolized by footwashing and humble service in love. In the chapters following, the victor is arrested, condemned, humiliated, tortured, and killed; he carries in his resurrected body the marks of nails and spear (20:20, 27); and he sends Peter to fulfill a similar vocation that will result in him being coerced and killed (21:18–19).

Peter is a sign of this victory. He was turned from his resistance to having his feet washed, and from his overconfident dedication to Jesus, and his eventual denial of being a disciple of Jesus, to sharing breakfast with Jesus, affirming his love of Jesus, taking on responsibility for the community of Jesus's followers, and then following Jesus to the point of dying. *In short, Peter is transformed by love to live and die in faith and loving service.* But it does not happen until after the victory of Jesus on the cross.

John 17:1–26

The Summit of Love

Now, in the words of Jesus to his Father, there is a culmination not only of the Farewell Discourses but also of the most important and profound themes in the Gospel. Is there any chapter in the Bible richer in meaning than this?[1]

The three-part prayer, spoken at the climactic time, "the hour" of the passion, death, and resurrection of Jesus, begins in the ultimate intimacy between Jesus and his Father and the intensity of their mutual "glorifying." This is connected with the extensity of their "authority over all people," their giving of "eternal life," the completion of "the work" of Jesus, and his communication of who God is ("your name") and of the meaning God wants them to receive ("your word . . . the words that you gave to me . . . they . . . know in truth" [vv. 6–7]) to those who "have believed that you sent me" (v. 8). At the heart of it all is the desire of Jesus "now": "Father, glorify me in your own presence with the glory that I had in your presence before the world existed" (v. 5).

All time and all creation are embraced and transcended by this divine presence and glory. The standpoint of the prayer is, as so often in John, simultaneously both preresurrection and postresurrection. Here the preresurrection stretches back to before the world existed, and the postresurrection stretches forward not only to later generations of believers, "those who will believe in me through their word" (v. 20), but also, most comprehensively of all, to eternal life in the immediate presence of Jesus, when those for whom Jesus prays "may be with me where I am, to see my glory" (v. 24). By the end of the prayer this glory has been further described as love that is not only at the origin of all

1. For a discussion of this chapter with special reference to Christian prayer, see Ford, "Ultimate Desire"; for a discussion of 17:20–26, see Ford, "Mature Ecumenism's Daring Future."

creation—"my glory, which you have given me because you loved me before the foundation of the world" (v. 24)—but is also to be shared, utterly and intimately: "So that the love with which you have loved me may be in them, and I in them" (v. 26).

The second part (vv. 9–19) is the prayer of Jesus for his disciples as they approach his death and resurrection and, beyond that, enter the ongoing drama that will result from them being sent as Jesus was sent: "As you have sent me into the world, so I have sent them into the world" (v. 18). They will face hatred as Jesus did, because their core belonging, like that of Jesus, is not to the world. Jesus prays both for their protection and for them to be sanctified (consecrated, dedicated, committed, purified, made holy, and focused on what matters most) through immersion in the purest, deepest, most gripping, and most embracing meaning: "Sanctify them in the truth; your word [*logos*] is truth" (v. 17). He himself embodies this truth and utter dedication: "For their sakes I sanctify myself" (v. 19). And the promise, through all the hatred and purification, is "that they may have my joy made complete in themselves" (v. 13).

The final part (vv. 20–26) opens toward the unsurpassable vision of union with God in love and participation with others in the glorious intensity of this love. There is an extraordinary combination of definitive ultimacy and intimacy ("as you, Father, are in me and I am in you," "that they may become completely one," "with me where I am [*eimi egō*]," "I in them" [vv. 21, 23, 24, 26]), together with the invitation into an infinitely capacious abundance of meaning and life, signaled especially by multiple repetitions of those important little words into which John has been pouring fresh meaning since the prologue: "in" and "as."

"I desire . . ." (v. 24). Could any desire be more daring than this desire of Jesus for those for whom he prays? *Here the inner dynamic of believing and trusting in Jesus is shown to be the desire for union in love.*

For those who have taken to heart the first words he says in this Gospel, "What are you looking for?" (1:38), this is his invitation to desire what (actually, who)[2] is most fulfilling. Could anything be more imperative, gripping, or challenging than this desire accompanied by the petition for unity? This prayer of Jesus, together with the desire that shapes it, becomes the encompassing priority and primary orientation, in relation to which other desires, purposes, and goals are to be oriented. *The desire of Jesus is for the intimacy and intensity of God's own life to be opened up for wholehearted, trusting participation through the ongoing drama of being loved and loving.* And the desire of Jesus, who is at one with God, amounts to a promise.

2. This question will be repeated with reference to Jesus himself, with "who" instead of "what," in 18:4, 7; 20:15.

The prayer concludes with a renewed emphasis on who God is. There is a fresh address, “Righteous Father” (v. 25), with resonances throughout the Bible. There is the reality of not knowing God and the mission of Jesus (now shared with his followers) to share his knowledge: “I made your name known to them, and I will make it known” (v. 26). And there is, finally, the desired purpose of all this: “So that the love with which you have loved me may be in them, and I in them” (v. 26).

That summit of love is a place from where we can look back and see paths of meaning converging: not only the Farewell Discourses and the rest of the Gospel of John, but also the Synoptic Gospels (especially the Lord’s Prayer) and the rest of the New Testament, the Old Testament / Hebrew Bible, and whatever else illuminates God, creation, and human life. It is also a place from which to look ahead, not only from the vantage point of when it was written, and then across the centuries during which it has been continually generative, but also ahead from today, as it continues to shape thought, imagination, prayer, and life in the twenty-first century. The vistas opened up by looking back and looking ahead through this text raise profound questions of many sorts, and the combination of multileveled depth and multidirectional openness (well exemplified by those endlessly rich words “in” and “as”) invites readers into daring responses in their thinking, imagining, praying, and living.

Glorifying, on Earth as in Heaven: Ultimate Intimacy, Unlimited Extensity (17:1–8)

> 1 After Jesus had spoken these words, he looked up to heaven and said, “Father, the hour has come; glorify your Son so that the Son may glorify you, 2 since you have given him authority over all people [*sarx*, “flesh”], to give eternal life to all whom you have given him. 3 And this is eternal life, that they may know you, the only true God, and Jesus Christ whom you have sent. 4 I glorified you on earth by finishing the work that you gave me to do. 5 So now, Father, glorify me in your own presence with the glory that I had in your presence before the world existed.
>
> 6 I have made your name known to those whom you gave me from the world. They were yours, and you gave them to me, and they have kept your word. 7 Now they know that everything you have given me is from you; 8 for the words that you gave to me I have given to them, and they have received them and know in truth that I came from you; and they have believed that you sent me.”

After Jesus had spoken these words, he . . . said . . . This is a minimal introduction, without any reference to the setting or to those with Jesus, unlike the Synoptic accounts of the prayer of Jesus in the garden of Gethsemane. John has already conveyed the Gethsemane-like anguish of Jesus in three earlier chapters (11:33, 35, 38; 12:27; 13:21). This prayer fits the situation of "the hour" of the Last Supper but also includes a postresurrection perspective. Both John's Jewish Scriptures and other literature of his Greek-speaking culture have conventions of distilling meaning into a prayer or into a speech that combines testimony to what someone said in many settings with later reflection on what that means. A particularly illuminating intertext for John 17 in the context of the Farewell Discourses is the long farewell of Moses in Deuteronomy 32–33.[3]

Lesslie Newbigin says about John 17, "The prayer is not a free invention of the evangelist; nor is it a tape recording of the words of Jesus. It is a representation of what Jesus was doing when he prayed in the presence of his disciples during the supper, a re-presentation which rests upon the authority of the Beloved Disciple guided by the Holy Spirit in and through the continuous experience[4] of the community which gathers week by week to rehearse again

3. The Greek of the Septuagint in Deut. 32–33 has many echoes in John 17: heaven; earth; name; words; true; works; God as father, righteous, and holy; eternal; guarding; love; one; I am; life; all; sanctify; truth; and glorify.

4. In *The Gospel of John and Christian Origins*, John Ashton, a leading historical-critical scholar of John (and sharply polemical against many literary approaches to the Gospel, as well as against what he describes as postmodern "cultural studies"), goes beyond his earlier work in making the category of "experience" central to his interpretation of how the author comes to write as he does. He centers this on the experience of the glory of the risen Jesus in a charismatic Johannine community in which prophetic gifts are exercised. This culminates in John 17. While I differ from Ashton on a number of points (notably, his denial of the tragic human dimension in John's testimony to Jesus), his affirmation of "the continuing presence in their midst of the Glorified One" (p. 198) is also central to my understanding, as is John 17. One striking element in Ashton's reading of John is his appreciation (pp. 195–97), along with Rudolph Bultmann (and myself), of Robert Browning's poem about the Fourth Evangelist, "A Death in the Desert," in which John says,

> Since much that at the first, in deed and word,
> Lay simply and sufficiently exposed,
> Had grown . . .
> Of new significance and fresh result;
> What first were guessed as points, I now knew stars,
> And named them in the Gospel I have writ. (lines 169–75)

Ashton comments, "It is worth asking ourselves whether Browning, himself a poet of considerable power, may not have displayed real insight when he attributed the evangelist's ability to form stars from points to his poetic and/or his religious genius. For many great poets and writers do just that: looking back on, reimagining, and reliving their experiences, they realise that these have grown 'of new significance and fresh result.' . . . I venture to suggest that Robert Browning, equipped with none of the gleaming tools of scholarly exegesis, and with only his poet's imagination and a tentative faith to assist him, realized, as scholars have never quite managed to do, that to account for the Fourth Gospel we have to accord to its author a quite exceptional *vision*. For the object of

the words and action of Jesus on that night when he was betrayed."[5] In other words, it is testimony distilled and enriched by the Spirit, who, as Jesus in the previous chapter says, "will guide you into all the truth . . . and . . . will glorify me, because he will take from what is mine and declare it to you" (16:13–14).

One effect of minimal introduction is to draw readers apart for a while, somewhat like the disciples in the Synoptic accounts of the transfiguration of Jesus,[6] and give us a mountaintop experience, inviting us to be present as Jesus prays, drawing us into his relationships, first with his Father, then with his first disciples, and finally with his ongoing community. This opens up a horizon of trust, life, and love—on earth as in heaven—centered on the relationship of Father and Son.

The text itself, as often in John, indirectly underlines its own significance. To say, **"They have kept your word** [*logos*]. . . . **The words** [*rhēmata*] **that you gave to me I have given to them, and they have received them,"** means, *You, the readers, are now able to receive this "word," the* logos *that since the prologue has been identified with Jesus, through these "words" you are reading.* This is reaffirmed in verse 14, "I have given them your word [*logos*]." Then readers are explicitly prayed for in verse 20: "I ask not only on behalf of these, but also on behalf of those who will believe in me through their word [*logos*]."

"Father" and "Our Father": John 17 and the Lord's Prayer

He looked up to heaven and said, "Father." A rich intertext for this chapter, as many commentators and worshipers down through the centuries have discovered, is the Lord's Prayer or "Our Father." Each illuminates the other, and following through the interplay between them has transformed my daily praying of the Lord's Prayer. Taking the Gospel of Matthew's version in the Sermon on the Mount (Matt. 6:9–13), we see some obvious verbal parallels: "Father"; "heaven"; "glorified, sanctified" (// hallowed); "name"; "on earth"; "gave, given, give"; "protect them from the evil one."

Others are less obvious but convincing. The "kingdom" of the Lord's Prayer refers to the kingdom of heaven (or, in Mark and Luke, the kingdom of God). In John there is a switch in terminology (indicated in John 3 and discussed above

---

that vision Browning chose the word *stars*. The evangelist's word was *glory*" (pp. 196–97). The image of the "points" of the words and deeds of the historical Jesus turning into "stars" through, in the Gospel's terms, many years of being led further into the truth by the Holy Spirit, is in line with what Newbigin says about this prayer.

5. Newbigin, *The Light Has Come*, 224.

6. It is illuminating to read the accounts of the transfiguration as intertexts with John 17, especially that of Luke, with his emphasis on Jesus praying, on glory, and on Jesus heading for his death in Jerusalem (Luke 9:28–36).

in relation to that)[7] from "kingdom of God" to "eternal life" as John's equivalent from then on. In 17:2 the association of **eternal life** with the kingship of God is strengthened by the mention of **authority over all people** (*sarx*, "flesh"). Doing the will of God is also present in John 17. The will is done by Jesus: **finishing the work that you gave me to do**; and by the disciples: **They have kept your word**. Since the main imperative of the will of God is to love, the emphasis on love later in the prayer is another rich resonance. And the Greek word for "will" (*thelēma* [Matt. 6:10]) is echoed by Jesus about himself in 17:24, "I desire [*thelō*]." Forgiveness is not explicit in John 17 but is surely implied by the vision of unity with God and one another. The "daily bread" of the Lord's Prayer might be read in the light both of Jesus saying, "My food is to do the will of him who sent me and to complete his work" (4:34), and of Jesus himself as "the bread from heaven" and "the bread of life" (6:22–71).

Perhaps the most embracing parallel from the Lord's Prayer is "on earth as it is in heaven." Indeed, that might be a suitable headline for a good deal in the Gospel of John. John's heaven is relationship-centered, with the love between the Father and the Son opening up to those who trust and love Jesus. One key image for it is a family home with a variety of spaces: "In my Father's house there are many dwelling places" (14:2).[8] Yet the dwelling, or abiding, can begin now, because the relationship can happen now: encountering Jesus, being loved by him and friends with him, receiving his Spirit through his words, loving as he loved, being sent as he was sent. There is a future dimension to heaven, but primarily (as throughout the Bible) it is, as here, simultaneous with earth. It is the sphere of God's intimate and intense presence (expressed in John 17 by terms such as "glorify," "eternal life," and "love"), and the purpose of Jesus being sent is to attract people into full participation in it, above all through the events of this "hour": "And I, when I am lifted up from the earth, will draw all people [or "all things"] to myself" (12:32). In John 17 the focus is simultaneously and inseparably on the Father in heaven and on life on earth: the Father is addressed in every verse; "world" occurs no less than sixteen times.[9]

The prayer now unfolds in a rhythm of petitions alongside basic truths.

7. See the section "The Kingdom of God" in the comments on 3:1–36.

8. See comments on 14:1–3.

9. A further very rich reflection is inspired by the parallel between the position of the Lord's Prayer at the exact center of Matthew's most substantial block of teaching, the Sermon on the Mount, and John 17 at the culmination of John's most substantial block of teaching, the Farewell Discourses. Each not only distills into prayer the body of teaching in which it is set (so that the most illuminating commentary on the Lord's Prayer is the Sermon on the Mount, as are the Farewell Discourses on John 17), but also invites readers to interrelate the bodies of teaching. They are mutually illuminating in profound and challenging ways.

Glory: Encompassing Reality

The first petition is **"Glorify your Son so that the Son may glorify you,"** soon expanded as **"So now, Father, glorify me in your own presence with the glory that I had in your presence before the world existed."** Glory is as much the encompassing reality of this Gospel as love is, and the two need to be thought together. John indicates the embracing quality of glory by emphasizing it first in the prologue (1:14); then at the beginning and end of the Book of Signs, associating it with the first sign (2:11) and the last sign (11:4, 40), and with the conclusion of that book (12:28, 43); then again at the beginning and conclusion of the Farewell Discourses (13:31–32; 17:24), and, within this concluding prayer of John 17, here at its beginning as well as at its end; and finally in the final chapter (21:19).

To speak of glory "before the world existed" is to see it as all-embracing and God-centered; and to ask "Glorify me in your own presence" is to center it in an eternal relationship of mutual love. It is the radiant, attractive intensity of who the Father and the Son are together. *Participation in this glory and love realizes the fullest connectivity between earth and heaven.* That connectivity is embodied in Jesus and is underlined by repeating six times that he was sent by the Father (vv. 3, 8, 18, 21, 23, 25) and three times that he is going back to the Father (vv. 5, 11, 13). The unity with which the prayer culminates in verses 20–26 has as its ecology this God-centered dynamic interaction of earth and heaven.

Authority over Flesh

The first basic affirmation in support of the petition is, **"Since you have given him authority over all people** [*sarx*, "flesh"], **to give eternal life to all whom you have given him."** The word for "authority," *exousia*, is a headline word in the prologue: "But to all who received him, who believed in his name, he gave power [*exousia*] to become children of God" (1:12). What is this authority? This Gospel, beginning with the prologue and all through to the end, offers a challenging, transformative understanding of "authority" in relation to "flesh."

John 1:12 says that *exousia*, in the fundamental matter of identity as "children of God," is a gift of the Word of God, through whom all things came into being. It is the gift above all of a person, who needs to be "received," "believed in," and trusted. Our *exousia* is rooted in who we are in this relationship. Verse 12 continues into 1:13: "who were born, not of blood or of the will of the flesh or of the will of man, but of God." This is not negative about "flesh" but is clear about the priority of God. Who we are is rooted in God. This identity relativizes all others, whether to do with human family, race, tribe, culture, gender, ability or disability, and so on.

Then 1:13 continues into 1:14: "And the Word became flesh and lived among us." So the one who has been given "authority over all flesh" himself "became flesh," a model of authority from God. *To follow what this Gospel says about Jesus is to be challenged to receive and exercise authority in line with who he is and what he does and says.* That involves learning from the variety of ways Jesus relates to flesh. It is worth reflecting on some examples relating to celebrating a marriage, compassion for the sick and hungry, physical meetings, responding to a friend's death, washing feet, his own physical suffering and crucifixion, and the vocation of his followers after his resurrection.

In his first sign he exercises authority over the matter of creation in order to provide wine to celebrate a marriage, in which husband and wife "become one flesh" (Gen. 2:24).

In his healings and the feeding of the five thousand he exercises his authority over flesh and matter in compassion for the flesh of others.

In his physical, face-to-face encounters with people in his ministry, as he "lived among us," he exercises authority through listening, conversation, and confrontation.

Before he calls his friend Lazarus back to life, he is in anguish and weeps, his authority over death inseparable from the solidarity in love that is soon to lead to his own death.

In his "face-to-feet" engagement with his disciples, touching their flesh, he makes footwashing the paradigm of loving service that can transform practices of authority.

Following this prayer in John 17, his trial, flogging, and crucifixion demonstrate the cost to his own flesh of the "authority over all flesh" that he has been given.

This cost will be imprinted on his risen body. Immediately before authoritatively sharing the Holy Spirit by breathing on his disciples and then sending them as the Father has sent him, "he showed them his hands and his side" (20:20).

It is a cost that his disciples too need to be willing to pay. The authority of Peter to be a leader and pastor, tending and feeding the lambs and sheep of Jesus, is accompanied by a prediction of the cost to Peter in physical constraint and suffering to the point of death (21:18–19). It is also clear that at the heart of this exercise of authority is the mutual knowledge and love between Jesus and Peter, and Peter's willingness to "glorify God" by his death as well as his life.

Eternal Life

That conversation between the risen Jesus and Peter is as good an illustration as any of what Jesus goes on to pray about the purpose of his authority: **"To give**

eternal life to all whom you have given him. And this is eternal life, that they may know you, the only true God, and Jesus Christ whom you have sent. I glorified you on earth by finishing the work that you gave me to do."

Earlier, at a critical juncture in the ministry of Jesus, when many disciples left him because of his difficult teaching,[10] Peter had responded with a parallel combination of Jesus, eternal life, God, and knowledge: "Lord, to whom can we go? You have the words of eternal life. We have come to believe and know that you are the Holy One of God" (6:68–69). Peter failed to be true to this faith when under pressure during the trial of Jesus (18:15–18, 25–27), while Jesus himself, in the words of John 17, was glorifying God "on earth by finishing the work that you gave me to do." Peter's culminating encounter with Jesus in 21:1–23 combines vital elements of what "eternal life" means: acknowledgment of Jesus ("It is the Lord!"); amazing abundance (the net "full of large fish, a hundred fifty-three of them"); sharing food together ("Come and have breakfast"); being repeatedly called by name ("Simon son of John" [three times]); being asked by Jesus about love for him ("Do you love me?" [three times]); affirming that love, and the mutual knowledge that goes with it ("Yes, Lord, you know that I love you" [twice]; then "Lord, you know everything; you know that I love you"); being part of a community and given work to do for it ("Feed my lambs. . . . Tend my sheep. . . . Feed my sheep"); being willing to go against one's own desires and be taken "where you do not wish to go," even to the point of glorifying God by dying; all summed up by "Follow me." *It is about being known and loved, knowing and loving*—participating in what Frederick Dale Bruner calls "deep, lasting life."

Who receives eternal life? Who is meant by **all whom you have given him**? In the immediate context, it is those disciples who are present, and the question of who are meant beyond these disciples will be dealt with later (on vv. 20–26). The key thought here is about disciples being given to Jesus by his Father, which is repeated three times: here in verse 6, **"I have made your name known to those whom you gave me from the world"**; later in verse 9, "those whom you gave me"; and later again in the prayer, referring to all later disciples too, "those also, whom you have given me" (v. 24). So it is important. It raises again the profound theological question of the relationship between divine initiative and human response. In this context of prayer by Jesus to his Father the main emphasis is on the initiative of the Father and it being inseparable from the Son, as intensified by the language of mutual belonging: "They are yours. All mine are yours, and yours are mine" (vv. 9–10). But there is also strong emphasis on

10. John 6:60: "This teaching [*logos*] is difficult." The teaching of this discourse in John 6 has multiple resonances with John 17 and should be considered alongside it.

the need for human response: **"They have kept your word. Now they know. . . . They have received them and know in truth . . . ; and they have believed."**

There can be no outside overview of this relationship. From the human perspective of being inside it, having received and believed the word, and now trying to keep it, it is utterly due to the initiative of God, and it would make no sense to try to distinguish divine from human agency. "From his fullness we have all received, grace upon grace" (1:16): just as creation is not at all due to human initiative, so neither is this grace—believers are receivers. Yet there is still the mystery of receiving and not receiving, and John's Gospel has, as has been seen frequently already, repeated appeals to believe and trust. Writing the Gospel would make no sense if all was predetermined by God. Its own stated purpose is "that you may come to believe [or "continue to believe"] that Jesus is the Messiah, the Son of God, and that believing you may have life in his name" (20:31). *I have read the whole Gospel as an invitation to enter into a relationship of trusting Jesus, with continuing "life in his name" involving an ongoing drama of desiring, learning, praying, and loving in community, for the sake of God's love for the world.* The teaching of the Gospel and also the way its story is told are a sustained challenge not only to believe but also continually to go deeper and

John believed in the transcendent, in the self-transcendence which is, in Viktor Frankl's words, the essence of existence.[a] He wanted to make room in his Gospel for human imagination to be free and fearless enough to transcend all those titles of Messianism that people were accustomed to using. He sought to awaken them to spiritual response such as no one as yet had discerned. His own task as a poet was not just to make the words that were familiar mean more than most people had ever guessed but to call on his fellow-Christians to make the imaginative leap that loving inspires. . . . He remembered the difficulties that so many people had voiced: could messiah be like this? Do the authorities believe him to be the Messiah? Could a Galilean be the Messiah? He could not have stopped them from asking such questions but he wanted to lift them right out of that kind of thinking and to focus their eyes anew on Jesus. "This is life eternal, to know you, the only God, and Jesus Christ whom you have sent." John knew that the sending never stopped; so neither could the learning to know him. It must go on now. We must be continually asking, what is Jesus Christ for us today?

—Alan Ecclestone, *The Scaffolding of Spirit*, 106

a. Frankl, *The Doctor and the Soul*. Frankl's experience of surviving Auschwitz led to him beginning the influential practice of logotherapy, whose meaning-centered approach to psychotherapy has many resonances with John's *logos*-centered worldview.

further. Each chapter gives an existential, practical challenge to each reader and community. The point is not to receive an overview of how God deals with others (the repeated "What is that to you?") but to "Follow me" (21:19–23). John 17 is perhaps the most challenging chapter of all (see the quotation from Ecclestone in the sidebar).

Belonging to God in the World: Protection and Joy; Hated, Sanctified, and Sent (17:9–19)

> 9 "I am asking on their behalf; I am not asking on behalf of the world, but on
> behalf of those whom you gave me, because they are yours. 10 All mine are
> yours, and yours are mine; and I have been glorified in them. 11 And now I
> am no longer in the world, but they are in the world, and I am coming to
> you. Holy Father, protect them in your name that you have given me, so
> that they may be one, as we are one. 12 While I was with them, I protected
> them in your name that you have given me. I guarded them, and not one of
> them was lost except the one destined to be lost, so that the scripture might
> be fulfilled. 13 But now I am coming to you, and I speak these things in the
> world so that they may have my joy made complete in themselves. 14 I have
> given them your word, and the world has hated them because they do not
> belong to the world, just as I do not belong to the world. 15 I am not asking
> you to take them out of the world, but I ask you to protect them from the
> evil one. 16 They do not belong to the world, just as I do not belong to the
> world. 17 Sanctify them in the truth; your word is truth. 18 As you have sent
> me into the world, so I have sent them into the world. 19 And for their sakes
> I sanctify myself, so that they also may be sanctified in truth."

The next petition is **"Holy Father, protect them in your name that you have given me, so that they may be one, as we are one,"** and this plea for protection is repeated: **"I ask you to protect them from the evil one."** These petitions are preceded and followed by basic affirmations, before a further petition, **"Sanctify them in the truth,"** which is filled out by further affirmations. *Together, the petitions and affirmations give a way of belonging to God in the world.* Fundamental is what the prayer itself models: **"I am asking."** The Farewell Discourses have repeatedly, in wave after wave, encouraged confident, daring prayer (14:13–14; 15:7; 16:23–24). Now Jesus, in a final wave, a towering breaker of direct prayer, performs what he has taught. *Part of being sent into the world as Jesus was sent is to pray as he prayed. The practice of prayer is at the heart of belonging to God in the world.*

"I am not asking on behalf of the world" probably should be understood as Jesus not asking on behalf of the world "yet" or "at this point," because later the world is prayed for: "so that the world may believe . . ."; "so that the world may know . . ." (vv. 21, 23). An alternative interpretation is that of C. K. Barrett: "To pray for the *kosmos* would be almost an absurdity, since the hope for the *kosmos* is that it should cease to be the *kosmos*." But Barrett also guards against any suggestion (which many scholars who follow his interpretation have made) of an inward-turned sectarian community cut off from the world: "John, having stated (3.16) the love of God for the κόσμος [*kosmos*], does not withdraw from that position in favor of a narrow affection for the pious. It is clear (see especially v. 18) that in this chapter also there is in mind a mission of the apostolic church to the world in which others will be converted and attached to the community of Jesus."[11]

Mine, Yours, and Identity

"All mine are yours, and yours are mine." Just as authority is exercised by Jesus in radically transformative ways, so possession and belonging are modeled by Jesus in relation to his Father in ways that will profoundly change any sense of self and identity that is shaped by him.[12] So there are radical implications for all concepts of "mine" and "yours," divine and human.[13] The Greek, *kai ta ema panta sa estin kai ta sa ema*, suggests this broadening: "all," "mine," and "yours" are neuter plurals—literally, "and my things all your things are and your things my things." The word order suggests inseparable union.

11. Barrett, *The Gospel according to St. John*, 506. The spatial imagery of John 17 does imply a rich interiority of trusting, knowing, and loving in each believer, together with a corresponding richness of internal community life in unity with God and one another, but these are set within the comprehensive upward and outward imagery of Jesus looking "up to heaven," his "authority over all flesh," and sixteen mentions of "the world." The temporal imagery, such as "before the world existed" and "eternal life," likewise resists any sense of being inward-turned or narrow.

12. This prayer is the culmination of a formation beginning with the gathering of a community of learners in John 1, then moving through a wide range of formative experiences (events, conversations, conflicts, challenges, transformative insights) into the Farewell Discourses for the committed disciples—and even now the climactic events and experiences are yet to come. This Gospel, through key terms such as "abide" and "eternal life," recognizes the long-term character of identity formation and the need for loving, gentle relationships in communities that are, like that formed by Jesus, vulnerable and fragile.

13. Some of the most fruitful intertexts for this verse, and for the other references to mutual belonging in this prayer, are the many Old and New Testament references to covenant. Jeremiah's combination of interiority and mutual possession, all set within a wider concern for the ethical and political implications of covenantal belonging, is especially resonant: "But this is the covenant that I will make with the house of Israel after those days, says the Lord: I will put my law within them, and I will write it on their hearts; and I will be their God, and they shall be my people" (Jer. 31:33).

Further, "them" at the end of the sentence, **and I have been glorified in them**, could refer back to the disciples in the previous verse, or it could refer to "my things" and "your things." John has several such open double meanings, where either makes appropriate sense and both together may well be intended,[14] one effect of which is to stimulate rereading and further thinking. Here "glorified in them" can mean that the life, light, and love of Jesus are radiated by "them," his followers; or it can mean that the followers are included in "them," a far-wider reality (indeed, the whole of creation, the "all things" that have come into being through the Word [1:3]) that belongs inseparably to both the Father and the Son and is the sphere of divine glory—"The whole earth is full of his glory" (Isa. 6:3).

This can have far-reaching practical consequences—for example, in how we regard our responsibility within creation and therefore our environmental ethics and politics. If we belong as fully to the Father as to the Son, this helps to correct any imbalance in our understanding of our own identity (e.g., any narrowness of horizon in our idea of what being a follower of Jesus means) and in our conception of Christian vocation (e.g., that it is about personal holiness and love, and witness to Jesus, but not also about public service and care for creation).

"Who to Who to Who": Between Two Attractors

"And now I am no longer in the world." This is taking a postresurrection perspective, as does the phrase a little later, **while I was with them**. The tenses of this prayer interweave past, present, and future, all with reference to a life, glory, and love that are eternal. Above all, there is the presence of the Father to the Son, who is involved in yet transcends the linear time of creation. At the beginning and the end of the prayer this temporal transcendence is signaled: "the glory that I had in your presence before the world existed"; "my glory, which you have given me because you loved me before the foundation of the world" (vv. 5, 24). What time and eternity are, and how they might be related, has been an ongoing challenge to thinkers in Christian and other traditions. John's distinctive emphasis is to stress "who" questions over "what" and "how" questions. This leaves room for many ways of conceptualizing time and eternity, so long as each does justice to the "who to who to who" relationship in love of the Father, the Son, and those who belong to them.[15]

14. Perhaps the best-known one is "born *anōthen*," meaning either "born from above" or "born again." See above on 3:3, 7.

15. The Johannine concept of time (covering topics such as past, present, and future, eternity/eternal life, preexistence and "time" before creation, eschatology and apocalyptic, preresurrection and postresurrection perspectives, the fusion of temporal horizons, the "hour" of Jesus, the

It is for this precious interrelationship that the petition asks for protection: **"Holy Father, protect them in your name that you have given me, so that they may be one, as we are one."** "Holy [*hagie*] Father" prepares for the climax in verses 18–19 of this second part of the prayer, with its thrice-repeated verb *hagiazein* ("sanctify, hallow, make holy"). It recalls such peak moments of adoration as in the vision of Isaiah, quoted above: "Holy, holy, holy is the LORD of hosts; the whole earth is full of his glory" (Isa. 6:3).

But above all it recalls the holy of holies,[16] the innermost sanctuary of the temple (e.g., 2 Chron. 5:7) and, before that, of the tent of meeting (e.g., Exod. 26:33–34). This was the most sacred of all places for Jews, the place of God's special, invisible, glorious presence—and it had been destroyed in 70 CE. There are references and allusions to the temple and its festivals all through the Gospel of John,[17] the most relevant here being the identification of the temple with the body of Jesus (2:21) and the conversation about holy places between Jesus and the Samaritan woman, leading to Jesus's statement, "But the hour is coming, and is now here, when the true worshipers will worship the Father in spirit and truth" (4:23). Now in John 17 is "the hour" in which Jesus (who has in chaps. 14–16 spoken about himself as the truth and at length about the Spirit) prays to his Father, opening up to those who trust and love him the "true" holy of holies, his own communion with his Father, **so that they may be one, as we are one**. Naming God as holy, praying for the sanctifying of the disciples, and sanctifying himself are the preparation (somewhat as the people of Israel were sanctified before the giving of the law at Mount Sinai, or the high priest was sanctified before entering the holy of holies in the temple) for the climax of the prayer in verses 20–26. This holy of holies, the place of mutual glorifying, indwelling, and loving in utter joy, is, says Jesus, **"where I am"** (see the quotation from Traherne in the sidebar).

---

maturing of faith, the narrative shaping of time, time and ethics, and the relationship to time of the person of Jesus and the Holy Spirit) has been the subject of much fruitful scholarship and theological reflection, well summarized and assessed by Zimmermann, "Eschatology and Time in the Gospel of John," and Williams, "Faith, Eternal Life, and the Spirit in the Gospel of John." Zimmermann analyzes this Gospel's "carefully thought out concept of time" and its "highly reflective and intentional processing of the past" (pp. 292–93) and describes something important throughout the present work, how "the Gospel itself thus becomes a medium for opening up the future" (p. 297), and why the temporality of this "turbulent text" eludes complete understanding (p. 304). Williams perceptively reflects on two further key elements of the present work: the relational aspect of both faith and eternal life; and their many dimensions, "embracing the material and the spiritual, the human and the divine, the present and the future" (p. 354).

16. In the Septuagint, *to hagion tōn hagiōn*, literally translating the Hebrew superlative "holy of holies" (cf. "song of songs"), meaning "most holy." The resonances of God as the Holy One and the sanctifying of people, things, food, times, and places pervade the Scriptures of Jesus (especially prominent in the books of Exodus, Leviticus, Numbers, 2 Chronicles, Isaiah, and Ezekiel) and offer many illuminating intertexts with John.

17. See Schuchard, "Temple, Festivals, and Scripture in the Gospel of John."

> Those Things are most Holy which are most Agreeable with Gods Glory. Whose Glory is that he is Infinit Lov.[a]
>
> —Thomas Traherne
>
> a. Quotation in Inge, *Happiness and Holiness: Thomas Traherne and His Writings*, 141.

Within the Gospel of John and in the rest of the New Testament, "Holy Father" recalls the Holy Spirit, as does much else in this prayer. Jesus, who is looking up to heaven and praying, is the one of whom John the Baptist testified, "I saw the Spirit descending from heaven like a dove, and it remained on him" (1:32). So, throughout the Gospel, Jesus and the Spirit are always assumed to be inseparable. The Spirit's self-effacing role is above all to focus attention on the Son and the Father, as in this prayer in which the Spirit is not mentioned.

Protect [*tērēson*] **them** has a broad meaning. The verb *tērein* includes "guard, keep, pay attention to," and, when applied to people, is strongly associated with keeping God's word or commandments, as above in verse 6.[18] The primary meaning here is, "Keep my disciples holy—in the sort of relationship with you and me that involves them keeping the commandment of love," and so being **one, as we are one**. It is more comprehensive than physical protection; indeed, given what is to happen to Jesus and Peter, that is not a necessary part of God's protection. What is essential is the lasting relationship of mutual trust and love, on both sides of death. The essential protection is therefore against **the evil one** (as prayed for here in the companion petition), representing the negation, disruption, and death of that relationship.

Your name is the "who" of God, utterly shared with the Son in love, and their "who to who" communion is the origin and analogy of the disciples' communion—primarily with God, but also with one another. What is the literal **name that you have given me**? This probably is a reference to what is called the Tetragrammaton, the four letters YHWH, revealed to Moses at the burning bush in Exodus 3. It was never pronounced, except by the high priest in the holy of holies, and the Septuagint substituted for it *kyrios ho theos*, "the Lord God" (as in Exod. 3:15). There are many ways in which John identifies Jesus as having received this name that is never spoken, including above all the title "Lord"[19] and the "I am" statements.[20]

18. Elsewhere in John, see 8:51–55; 14:15, 21, 23–24; 15:10, 20.
19. First used identifying Jesus with God in 1:23.
20. See Soulen, *Distinguishing the Voices*.

The affirmations supporting this petition and the companion one to "protect them from the evil one" speak of tragic loss, complete joy, and being hated. The critical issue is belonging or not belonging to "the world." The prayer faces the worst but does not let it have the last word.

The worst is the negation of the relationship of trust and love by Judas. **The one destined to be lost** is literally "the son of loss/destruction/ruin," imagining a radically alternative, tragic family, belonging to which has no good future. The tragedy is especially that of betrayal by someone close, as in Psalm 41:9, already quoted with regard to Judas in 13:18.[21] The existential force of this worst of destinies is to confront the reader with the shocking alternative to trust and love.[22]

The best destiny is **my joy made complete in themselves**. As 15:10–11 has said, the joy of Jesus springs from abiding in love.[23] That is inseparable from his teaching and prayer: "If you abide in me and my words abide in you, ask for whatever you wish, and it will be done for you" (15:7). Here, too, the joy is connected with keeping his teaching, **"I have given them your word,"** and prayer is the context.

So disciples are placed between two attractors, one deadly (in 8:44 identified as "a murderer" and "a liar and the father of lies") and the other having the words and joy of eternal life. The two come together in life "in the world," the ongoing drama toward which this prayer is oriented. Readers too are attracted in both directions, with the added disincentive of the hatred attracted by the community of disciples, and are challenged to decide where they belong. The next petition, **"Sanctify them in the truth; your word is truth,"** asks for what is needed if their belonging and vocations are to be faithful and fruitful.

Being Sent and "As . . . So . . ." Improvisation

Corresponding to the holiness of God is the holiness of those who belong to him. This is about being single-minded and single-hearted in dedication to what and to who matters most. **The truth** is defined as **your word**. This brings us back to the beginning of the Gospel and the range of meaning discovered there—embracing all the Scriptures, truth relating to "all things" (1:3), and, above all, the "light" and meaning embodied in Jesus, the self-expression and

21. See comments on 13:21–30, especially in regard to Judas and evil.

22. For a powerful philosophical account of betrayal as the most serious sin, see Royce, *The Problem of Christianity*, vol. 1, *The Christian Doctrine of Life*, lecture 5, "Time and Guilt." For a classic poetic description making a similar point, see Dante Alighieri, *The Divine Comedy 1: Inferno*, canto 34, where the deepest circle of hell has the traitors, represented by Judas, Brutus, and Cassius.

23. For other examples of the importance of joy in this Gospel, see 3:29; 15:11; 16:20–24; 20:20.

self-giving of God—meaning further developed through the Gospel and culminating in the Farewell Discourses: "I am the way, and the truth, and the life" (14:6).

Here, in 17:18, the emphasis is on the vocation of disciples as like that of Jesus: **"As you have sent me into the world, so I have sent them into the world."** This again points beyond the resurrection, when the risen Jesus appears to his disciples, gives them their basic orientation in the ongoing drama—"As the Father has sent me, so I send you"—and then breathes on them to give the Holy Spirit (20:21–22). The giving or sending of Jesus by the Father is of the greatest importance in this Gospel and is stated in each of the three parts of this prayer. The giving and the sending are first combined in the summary of the Gospel in 3:16–17: "For God so loved the world that he gave his only Son, so that everyone who believes in him may not perish but may have eternal life. Indeed, God did not send his Son into the world to condemn the world, but in order that the world might be saved through him." *For disciples to be sent as Jesus was sent is for them to have a vocation of life-giving love for the world.*

The "as . . . so . . ." commissioning encourages two things that together are vital to this vocation. First, there needs to be continual reflection on how Jesus has been sent into the world. The commentary above on his "authority over all people/flesh" (17:2) gives several pointers and suggests the value of thinking through the whole Gospel with this question in mind. The sending of Jesus, and therefore the sending of his followers, involves things such as being steeped in the Scriptures, forming a learning community, teaching, doing signs of abundant life for those beyond his immediate circle (wine for a wedding celebration, healing, feeding, and more), repeated face-to-face encounters, washing feet, and praying. Jesus is also sent into darkness, conflict, suffering, and death, yet without them being the last word. Now the inner secret of sustaining such a vocation is given as Jesus prays for his disciples: **"Sanctify them. . . . For their sakes I sanctify myself."** The secret is being utterly for God and utterly for the disciples. As 3:16–17 and the third part of this prayer indicate, being dedicated to the God who loves the world also means being utterly for the world that God loves. The extent of what that will involve is to unfold in chapters 18 and 19. Most commentators agree that "I sanctify myself" is primarily a reference to his death "for their sakes," offering himself sacrificially, as animals about to be sacrificed were consecrated.

Second, the openness of the "as . . . so . . . ," which has already been explored (e.g., in relation to the mutual knowledge of Father and Son on 10:14–15, to footwashing on 13:14–15, and to loving on 13:34; 15:12), invites ever-new discernment and improvisation in new situations. What does it mean to be sent like Jesus now? John's massive emphasis is, *above all, get to know who the living*

Jesus is. The "what" question will not be answered well if the "who" of Jesus is not known, trusted, and loved. And, since knowing, trusting, and loving Jesus are inseparable from his relationship with his Father, the "who to who to who" relationship that this prayer opens up is the deepest reality of all—or, to change the spatial metaphor, this is the summit of divine and human love. The "what" and "how" questions about living now are then answered from within this relationship. There are many sources of wisdom that can help with the answers, but the central criterion is whether an action rings true with who Jesus is. "I am . . . the truth" (14:6) is perhaps the most illuminating intertext for each clause of verses 17–19: "Sanctify them in the truth; your word is truth. As you have sent me into the world, so I have sent them into the world. And for their sakes I sanctify myself, so that they also may be sanctified in truth."

Completely One in Love (17:20–26)

> 20 "I ask not only on behalf of these, but also on behalf of those who will believe in me through their word, 21 that they may all be one. As you, Father, are in me and I am in you, may they also be in us, so that the world may believe that you have sent me. 22 The glory that you have given me I have given them, so that they may be one, as we are one, 23 I in them and you in me, that they may become completely one, so that the world may know that you have sent me and have loved them even as you have loved me. 24 Father, I desire that those also, whom you have given me, may be with me where I am, to see my glory, which you have given me because you loved me before the foundation of the world.
>
> 25 "Righteous Father, the world does not know you, but I know you; and these know that you have sent me. 26 I made your name known to them, and I will make it known, so that the love with which you have loved me may be in them, and I in them."

This third part of the prayer is the culmination of culminations.

It is the culmination of this whole prayer. Key elements in the first two parts, simple words with resonances throughout the Bible, are enriched and deepened: "ask," "believe," "word," "all," "one," "as," "Father," "in," "world," "sent," "glory," "given," "before the foundation of the world," "know," "name." The scope of the prayer now broadens to embrace not only "those who will believe in me through their word" but also "the world." The orientation of the prayer is still toward the ongoing drama in the world, but it also reaches beyond that, toward being "with me where I am, to see my glory."

It is the culmination of the Farewell Discourses, which themselves are the culmination of the teaching of Jesus. Not only does their repeated emphasis on the importance of prayer reach a climax, but also "love" enters this prayer for the first time here in its third part. Inseparable from that, participation in mutual indwelling, whose earlier waves in the Farewell Discourses had been most vividly expressed in the parable of the vine, is articulated with unprecedented directness and comprehensiveness. The central theological and practical pattern of analogical thinking and action, signaled by "as," also reaches its greatest intensity here.

It is also the culmination of the first twelve chapters of John's Gospel. The simple words just listed run through those chapters too, and the meanings given to them there need to be recalled here through rereading, reflection, and prayer. The culmination of the prologue in "God the only Son, who is close to the Father's heart" (1:18) is here enacted most fully, through heart-to-heart communication in "desire" and "love." Other earlier streams of meaning flow together here, and it is worth specially mentioning how in John 10 there is a parallel convergence of elements found in 17:20–26: hearing "the voice" of Jesus (10:3–4); "I am" sayings (10:7, 11, 14); anticipation of the death and resurrection of Jesus (10:11, 15, 17, 18); mutual knowledge between Jesus and his followers ("just as the Father knows me and I know the Father" [10:15]); anticipation of future believers and emphasis on their unity ("I have other sheep that do not belong to this fold. I must bring them also, and they will listen to my voice. So there will be one flock, one shepherd" [10:16]); and the unity and mutual indwelling of Jesus and his Father ("The Father and I are one. . . . The Father is in me and I am in the Father" [10:30, 38]).

It can also be read as the culmination of strands in the Synoptic Gospels, such as Jesus in relation to his Father, the commandments of love, and prayer. The "as" and "in" of "on earth as in heaven" in the Lord's Prayer are echoed multiple times.

Likewise, if *the Letter to the Ephesians is taken as a culminating point in the Pauline tradition,* these verses not only echo the prayer at the heart of that letter in Ephesians 3:14–21: "Father," "name," "glory," "indwell," "faith," multidimensional "love," "knowledge," "all generations," "forever and ever." They also embrace the massive emphasis on unity in love that both precedes and follows it: "For he is our peace; in his flesh he has made both groups into one and has broken down the dividing wall, that is, the hostility between us" (Eph. 2:14); ". . . bearing with one another in love, making every effort to maintain the unity of the Spirit in the bond of peace. There is one body and one Spirit, just as you were called to the one hope of your calling, one Lord, one faith, one baptism, one God and Father of all, who is above all and through all and in all" (Eph. 4:2–6).

Further, *the echoes resound through all of the Scriptures of Israel: this is their culmination too.* If the covenant between God and Israel is central to their relationship, its reality of mutual belonging in love reaches its Johannine climax here, interwoven with the scriptural themes of "word," "Father," "desire," "I am," creation, righteousness/justice, and knowledge of God's "name."

These verses are also a culmination of preparation for the death and resurrection of Jesus, which runs all through the earlier chapters, beginning with John the Baptist's cry, "Here is the Lamb of God who takes away the sin of the world!" (1:29). And just as the prologue gave categories, concepts, and images through which the later chapters (perhaps especially John 17) can be understood more and more fully; and as John 6 introduced the mutual indwelling of Jesus and those who trust him, interwoven with strong eucharistic/communion language in association with the death of Jesus and the eternal life he gives (also especially related to John 17); and as John 12 likewise prepared readers to grasp the Farewell Discourses and the death and resurrection of Jesus;[24] so this third part of John 17 is the climax of the key Johannine terms through which the death and resurrection of Jesus are interpreted: "glory," "love," the mission of Jesus, and, above all, the relationship of Jesus and his Father.

These and Those: May They All Be One

The next petition is not only for **these**, the disciples present, but also for **those who will believe in me through their word** [*logos*], **that they may all be one**. A strong interpretation of this (in recent centuries especially advocated by Søren Kierkegaard)[25] is that later generations can have as full a relationship of trust in Jesus as the first eyewitness disciples did. *There is no disadvantage in coming later.* The later disciples are one with the earlier. Indeed, there is a special blessing for those who have not been eyewitnesses: "Blessed are those who have not seen and yet have come to believe" (20:29). That blessing is immediately followed by a direct address to readers saying that the purpose of writing this Gospel is "so that you may come to believe that Jesus is the Messiah, the Son of God, and that through believing you may have life in his name" (20:31). So, the "word" that enables later believing is exemplified by this Gospel: reading, understanding, and trusting this writing opens readers toward knowing and following Jesus together. *"All" can "be one," across generations and within each generation.*

A further implication is that the meaning found in this "word" by previous generations, and now being found by those of our own time around the world,

24. See comments on 12:20–50.
25. See especially Kierkegaard, *Philosophical Fragments.*

is intrinsic to being part of one community. The learning and the communication of such meaning are essential: this is a community of listeners and readers, disciples who are always learners.

This third part of John 17 has given perhaps the main biblical impetus to the ecumenical movement within Christianity, seeking ways to be one church together. Since the early twentieth century that movement has achieved things probably never before seen in religious history: Christian bodies with hundreds of millions of members have turned from confrontation and sometimes conflict toward conversation, frequently with collaboration, and in some cases have joined one another in full mutual recognition and sometimes even institutional unity.

Yet at the same time there have also been innumerable splits, divisions, and conflicts. The Johannine community itself suffered from these (as the Letters of John show), and the ongoing drama of church history repeatedly confronts Christians with multiple temptations to be alienated or divided from one another. Seen through the lens of this prayer, what might some key elements of Johannine wisdom be? Three stand out.[26]

First, if this is the unqualified, ultimate desire of Jesus at the climactic moment of his mission, then all who trust and follow Jesus should join with him in desiring it, praying for it, and orienting our lives and communities toward it. Serving others, as in washing feet, and being friends of Jesus and one another (even to the point of laying down our lives) are very good. But there is also this summit of love. Any desire, word, or action that draws us or others away from it is to be repented of. Of course, in many cases there are complex issues of discernment, judgment, and decision, and there is always the possibility that any one of us and any community might betray, deny, or ignore Jesus. But he is the patient educator of our desires, longing for wholehearted participation in his love and truth, inviting us above all to **be with me where I am**. So one element is recognizing the radical desire of Jesus in this **I ask** and letting his petition and desire become ours.

Ultimate Mutuality and Intimacy

A second element is given in the second wave of this petition: **"As you, Father, are in me and I am in you, may they also be in us."** The unity has an ultimate basis, a generative source, and an embracing reality: the mutual indwelling of the Father and the Son.

26. All three of these are explored at greater length Tom Greggs's theology of the church. His first volume of *Dogmatic Ecclesiology, The Priestly Catholicity of the Church,* also sketches what is to come in the further two planned volumes. Especially relevant to the prayer of Jesus for unity is the conclusion to that volume: "Coda: The Church as One" (451–59).

How are we to imagine and think of this mutuality, the Father being "in" the Son and the Son "in" the Father? Within this chapter, key pointers along paths of imagination and thought include *mutual glorifying, mutual belonging, and mutual love*. These are further enriched by other shared divine realities, such as joy, truth, and holiness. All these can gather further content from earlier chapters and the rest of the Bible, and also from the coming chapters and the later history of worship, theology, and creativity in song and music, art, architecture, and literature. Perhaps they are illuminated most of all by lives of love and holiness, truth seeking, joy, and worship—in other words, by people and communities that embody at least partial answers to this prayer and are signs of the abundant eternal life of God.

This prior divine relationality means that unity is more fundamentally a gift than it is a task. It is to be received from God, entered into as a reality already and always happening in God. To take the spatial imagery of "in us" seriously, there is a family home where we are fully welcome, a place to live in intimacy with the Father and the Son, somewhere to abide permanently in mutual honoring, belonging, and love. The basic task is to trust the gift and its giver. The core dynamic of unity is a life of worship and love, fed by shared communication, understanding, and truth. Those we love and know well indwell us, and we them.

Ultimate Orientation: The Spread of Trust

A third element is the outward orientation of this dynamic unity. Just as the Father's relationship with the Son led to the sending of Jesus, so the Son's gathering of a community is oriented beyond the community, **so that the world may believe that you have sent me**. The world is both loved by God and the limit case of resistance to trusting God. In the coming of Jesus, that love meets that resistance. The community is called to embody a love and trust that look beyond the resistance and to act as a sign of God's love in sending Jesus.

The petition "that the world may believe" sets no limits. It is conceivable that the whole world might come to know and trust that Jesus comes to it in utter love, from the heart of God. There is no timescale for the spread of such trust in God, and the forms it might take are inconceivable in advance, just as Jesus springs many surprises (not least on his closest followers) and the Spirit "blows where it chooses" (3:8). Yet the orientation is clear, as is the core imperative: to be united in a love and trust that are rooted in the life and love of the God who sent Jesus.

Ultimate Gift: Glory Shared

The greatest intensity and most abundant overflow of that life and love can be summed up as the unsurpassable **glory that you have given me**. *This is the ultimate gift of God, and here Jesus amazingly says that this is what* ***"I have given them."***

We have seen that glory is one of the fundamental realities of this Gospel,[27] heading for its climactic realization in the crucifixion and resurrection of Jesus. Here, taking a postresurrection standpoint, Jesus says that it has already been given to his disciples.

Ultimate Unity and Orientation in Love: God, Community, and World with All Creation

Then Jesus reaffirms all three of the key elements: the unity of the disciples, its grounding in his own union with the Father, and its orientation toward the world: **"So that they may be one, as we are one, I in them and you in me, that they may become completely one, so that the world may know that you have sent me and have loved them even as you have loved me."** Yet that is not just repetition; it is a wave that does cover the same ground but also goes further, in two ways.

First, there is the ultimacy of the word "completely," whose underlying Greek term can also be translated as "perfectly." This Greek verb, *teleioun*, was used in 4:34, 5:36, and 17:4 about Jesus completing the work or works the Father had given him to do. Its related noun *telos* ("end") was used in the headline for the Last Supper, the footwashing, and the Farewell Discourses: "Having loved his own who were in the world, he loved them to the end" (13:1). And a related verb, *telein*, will be the last word that Jesus speaks on the cross before dying, "It is finished" (19:30). *So it is about a completion or perfection that interconnects Jesus doing the will of God, loving his disciples, and laying down his life. That is his enactment of perfect unity.*

Second, there is the first explicit mention of love in this prayer, **and have loved them even as you have loved me**, signaling that we have arrived at the summit of love. *Not only is the glory of God shared; so also is the love of God.* And the love that is shared is the ultimate, unsurpassable love of the Father for the Son.

Who is meant by "them"? Scholars are divided on whether those who are loved as Jesus is loved are the disciples or the world. The majority I have read favor the disciples, but the world could be intended. And there is also the pos-

27. See Ford, "'To See My Glory'"; Ford, "Ultimate Desire"; see also comments on 1:14; 2:11; 11:4, 40; 12:28; 13:31–32.

sibility, which I favor, of this being yet another double meaning. The boundary between the disciples and the world is, as 3:16 says, crossed by the love of God. Here the vision is of a shifting, expanding boundary, with more and more people recognizing Jesus as one sent to share the love of God with them. Again, no limits are set, in time, space, numbers, or forms, to the spread of knowledge of God's gift of love through Jesus.

And we have to be extremely careful, especially in a time of global environmental crisis, not to limit the process of becoming "completely/perfectly one" to human beings. This God loves the whole of creation. This Jesus, the Word of God, is the one through whom "all things came into being . . . , and without him not one thing came into being" (1:3). Has he stopped caring for creation—animal, vegetable, and mineral? How could God's love for the world not embrace all creatures? How could the destiny of human beings be separate from that of the rest of creation? All through this commentary there have been pointers to ways in which this Gospel can help us to be more creation conscious and earth friendly. These culminate now in its vision of an ultimate unity that does not make sense without involving the whole of creation, simply because at the heart of this unity is the One through whom all things were made.

God's glory shining in the whole earth is vital to God's desire and will being done on earth as in heaven. An acidic ocean, the extinction of whole species, deforestation and desertification, polluted air, and climate changes that are disastrous for ecosystems, plants, and animals as well as for billions of people—those, as well as relationships gone wrong with God and between people, contradict this vision of perfect unity and peace and should inspire passionate desire, prayer, communion, and action in the service of abundant life, love, and peace with God, one another, and creation.[28]

Ultimate Desire: Glory, Love, and Being with Jesus

"Father, I desire that those also, whom you have given me, may be with me where I am, to see my glory, which you have given me because you loved me before the foundation of the world" (see the quotation from Traherne in the sidebar).

The first words of Jesus in this Gospel, addressed to his first disciples, were, "What are you looking for?" (1:38). In response to their question, "Rabbi, where are you staying [*menein*, "abide"]?" his first imperative was an invitation, "Come and see" (1:39). The reader had already been told in the prologue where his

28. For a comprehensive, prophetic reading of John in relation to these matters, see Daly-Denton, *John*.

ultimate home is, "close to the Father's heart" (1:18). Now Jesus, in the presence of those same disciples, expresses his ultimate **desire** for them, directing their desiring toward finding their ultimate home **where I am** and their seeing toward the vision of **my glory**, grounding everything in the relationship of love that generated and still sustains all creation.

So this prayer, which here breaks out of the mode of asking into the authoritative *thelō*, **I desire that**, having the force of "My will is that . . ." (and so can be taken as a promise), takes earlier questions, earlier affirmations (especially the series of "I am" statements by Jesus and all he says about his relationship with his Father), earlier symbols and ideas of what is to be desired (such as wine, water, bread, light, abundant life, joy, peace, love), and earlier imperatives (beginning with "Come and see" and culminating in the instructions to follow his example in washing feet and to love as he did in laying down his life for his friends) *up to this summit of love: utter unity and communion in love with God and with one another, akin to that of the Father with the Son.*

This is most obviously about the ultimate future, eternal life beyond death, eschatological fulfillment. But it need by no means be limited to that. The "I am" of Jesus is at one with the "I am" of God in omnipresence, and his glory is seen in many signs of abundant life and sacrificial love, above all in his crucifixion and resurrection, to which the coming chapters will testify. Any separation between the ultimate future beyond death and present life now is relativized by the "I am" of who Jesus is, now and always, on earth as in heaven.

Infinit Wants Satisfied Produce infinit Joys; And, in the Possession of those Joys, are infinit Joys themselves. The Desire Satisfied is a Tree of Life.[a] Desire imports som thing absent: and a Need of what is Absent. GOD was never without this Tree of Life. He did Desire infinitly; yet he was never without the Fruits of this Tree, which are the Joys it produced. I must lead you out of this, into another World, to learn your Wants. For till you find them you will never be Happy. Wants themselves being sacred Occasions and means of Felicitie.[b]

—Thomas Traherne

a. Prov. 13:12.

b. Quotation in Inge, *Happiness and Holiness: Thomas Traherne and His Writings*, 128. Traherne is an eloquent and profound theologian of desire, as demonstrated in Inge, *Wanting like a God: Desire and Freedom in the Work of Thomas Traherne*.

Ultimate Meaning, Promise and Intimacy: The God of Justice and Love; Knowing Who God Is; Jesus Christ in Us

"Righteous Father, the world does not know you, but I know you; and these know that you have sent me. I made your name known to them, and I will make it known, so that the love with which you have loved me may be in them, and I in them."

Now in conclusion God is addressed for a sixth time, now as **Righteous Father**. "Righteous" (*dikaios*) is a term that runs through the whole Bible. Of God, it especially indicates divine justice and judgment, and the comprehensive importance of Torah, wisdom, and the message of the prophets. Here, with the words that follow, **The world does not know you**, it draws readers back into the ongoing drama, both that of Jesus, as he approaches his trial and its judgments on him and on those who judge him, and that of his later followers who will be faced with incomprehension, opposition, trials, and critical decisions that test their faithfulness. Righteousness in people is both personal and public, covering both individual lives lived in ways that please God and also the conduct of legal, social, political, and international affairs in line with God's justice—which includes care for the poor, the weak, the refugee, and the immigrant.

This closing concern for his followers is confident that they know both the key truth about Jesus, **that you have sent me**, and also the key truth of who God is, **your name.** Such knowledge is not one-off, grasped once and for all time. It is ongoing, developing, open to more truth and love, and given through a continuing, lively relationship. Jesus promises that his side of the relationship will be sustained: **"And I will make it known."** It is a personal knowledge whose goal is the quality of love that the Father has for the Son: "So that the love with which you have loved me may be in them."

Here the identity of God, "your name," inseparable from Jesus, is shared in love and trust, and any other identity not centered on God is relativized.

Finally, **I in them**: *Jesus in us is our core identity, knowing and known, intimately loving and loved, breathing his Spirit into us, uniting us in community, sending us as he was sent, and praying like this.*

John 18:1–40

Arrest and Trial

The long preparation for the dramatic climax has ended.

Jesus and his disciples go to a garden where they were used to gathering. Judas knows to bring a detachment of soldiers and police there to arrest Jesus. When Jesus identifies himself, they fall to the ground. Peter violently resists by cutting off the ear of the high priest's slave, but he is rebuked by Jesus. Jesus is bound and taken first to the house of Annas, the father-in-law of the high priest, Caiaphas, where he is interrogated. Next, he is taken to Caiaphas, and then on to the headquarters of Pilate, the Roman governor. Meanwhile, Peter has been challenged three times about being a disciple of Jesus and has denied it each time. Pilate fails to persuade the Jewish leaders to try Jesus themselves, and he begins his own examination by asking Jesus whether he is the king of the Jews. Jesus transforms the title, saying that his kingdom is "not from this world" (v. 36) and that he "came into the world to testify to the truth" (v. 37). Pilate finds no case against Jesus and proposes releasing him in accordance with a Passover custom, but "the Jews" shout that they want the bandit Barabbas to be released, not Jesus.

Those are the bare events of this chapter, but the way the story is told makes it dense with the meaning that previous chapters have been building up. John 17 was the "culmination of culminations" of that meaning in the mode of prayer, preparing for the narrative culmination in the events of John 18–21. Those concluding four chapters of the Gospel can be read as the final dramatic enactment of the identity and mission of Jesus. They give definitive content to key elements of earlier chapters—words, concepts, symbols, signs, encounters, and events. At the same time, they shape and inspire an ongoing drama in which later disciples, who have breathed in the Spirit of Jesus through attending to this meaning, can find further truth and do greater works. In John 18 there is a dramatic enactment, through event, action, and dialogue, of several of those key elements.

Who Jesus is runs through the chapter and is explicit during his arrest in the triple "I am," in the relationship with his Father that leads him "to drink the cup that the Father has given me" (v. 11), in his negative description of "my kingdom" as "not from this world" (v. 36), and in his positive self-description, "For this I was born, and for this I came into the world, to testify to the truth" (v. 37). This question of core identity is also there in Peter's repeated "I am not" (v. 25) and in Pilate's "I am not a Jew, am I?" (v. 35).

Jesus as *the gatherer of disciples* into a fragile and fallible community also pervades the chapter. He brings them to a familiar garden, is the "good shepherd" (10:11) who does "not lose a single one of those whom you gave me" (18:9), is betrayed by one disciple, and is denied by another.

The purpose of Jesus reaching *beyond his disciples* to the rest of the world is also clear. It is suggested ironically by quoting Caiaphas saying that "it was better to have one person die for the people" (v. 14). It is affirmed directly in what Jesus says to the high priest, "I have spoken openly to the world" (v. 20), and to Pilate, "For this I came into the world" (v. 37).

Inseparable from that purpose of Jesus is the *opposition* to him, which has been building since the beginning of his public ministry. It now moves toward its deadly climax: the armed detachment comes to arrest and bind him; the Jewish and Roman authorities come together (the next chapter will take this collaboration further); Pilate focuses on the decisive religiopolitical issue, whether Jesus is "the King of the Jews" (v. 33; this will also be intensified in the next chapter); and his Jewish opponents make it clear that they want nothing less than the death penalty.[1] In short, the portrayal of Jesus over against the world, represented in its negative sense by both Jews and Romans, is sharpened; and at the same time the negativity of betrayal and denial among his own disciples reaches its greatest intensity.

Other important elements from earlier chapters that enter into John 18 include Passover, truth, listening to the voice of Jesus, and, above all, judgment. The whole trial is, of course, about judgment. John's distinctive approach to it, in which the one who is being judged is both the true witness and the true judge, is set up in this chapter and followed through in the next. But, more broadly, the theme of judgment has run through many earlier chapters: this

1. Death is mentioned three times in this chapter and is implied by the final demand for the release of Barabbas, not Jesus.

whole Gospel can be read as a trial centered on Jesus, and readers are being judged by whether they trust or reject him.

Integrating these elements are two complementary emphases: early on, the triple "I am," and later, Jesus's summary of his whole mission, "For this I was born, and for this I came into the world, to testify to the truth. Everyone who belongs to the truth listens to my voice" (v. 37). *John shapes his account around who Jesus is and the meaning of his coming.*

In telling this story John agrees with the essentials told by the Synoptic Gospels: Jesus was arrested; Judas betrayed him; Peter denied him; he was examined before Jewish authorities; he was tried before Pilate; Barabbas was released instead of him; and a key issue was his kingship. There are numerous differences among the four and a wide range of explanations for these in terms of sources, influences, editing, attempts to reconstruct what might have happened, and literary and theological interests. I see John wanting both to give reliable testimony to events and also to open up the theological depth that comes through ongoing, Spirit-led, postresurrection relationship with Jesus. In doing this he, like other ancient biblical and nonbiblical authors, often shapes the details to make the fuller meaning clearer, testifying to both pre- and postresurrection truth.[2]

The Arrest: "I Am / I Am He" (18:1–12)

> 1 After Jesus had spoken these words, he went out with his disciples across
> the Kidron valley to a place where there was a garden, which he and his dis-
> ciples entered. 2 Now Judas, who betrayed him, also knew the place, because
> Jesus often met there with his disciples. 3 So Judas brought a detachment of
> soldiers together with police from the chief priests and the Pharisees, and
> they came there with lanterns and torches and weapons. 4 Then Jesus, know-
> ing all that was to happen to him, came forward and asked them, "Whom
> are you looking for?" 5 They answered, "Jesus of Nazareth." Jesus replied,
> "I am he." Judas, who betrayed him, was standing with them. 6 When Jesus
> said to them, "I am he," they stepped back and fell to the ground. 7 Again he
> asked them, "Whom are you looking for?" And they said, "Jesus of Nazareth."
> 8 Jesus answered, "I told you that I am he. So if you are looking for me, let

2. Rudolf Schnackenburg captures something of this intention: "The whole section, Jn 18:12–27, is informative about the evangelist's relationship to the tradition. It takes it over, reflects it and uses it in a sovereign way so as to draw his picture of Christ. He is not concerned with exact historical reproduction, but with theological interpretation; but neither does he speculate freely; rather, he holds to what supports his tradition, because for him the Christ of faith is none other than the historical Jesus" (*The Gospel according to St. John*, 3:240).

> these men go." [9] This was to fulfill the word that he had spoken, "I did not lose a single one of those whom you gave me." [10] Then Simon Peter, who had a sword, drew it, struck the high priest's slave, and cut off his right ear. The slave's name was Malchus. [11] Jesus said to Peter, "Put your sword back into its sheath. Am I not to drink the cup that the Father has given me?" [12] So the soldiers, their officer, and the Jewish police arrested Jesus and bound him.

After Jesus had spoken these words, he went out. This transition from words to action—from teaching and prayer to suffering, death, resurrection, and sending his disciples—is of great theological significance. Some commentators have seen John 17 as a culmination that cannot be surpassed, and they downplay the importance of the following four chapters. But, in line with the Word becoming flesh and with the fact that most of the Gospel is in narrative form, the theology of John is seriously misunderstood if it is not seen to culminate in the drama of "the hour" of the crucifixion and resurrection of Jesus, followed immediately by the ongoing drama of his disciples being sent as he was sent.

So, this Gospel does not arrive at the summit of love and prayer in John 17 in order to stay there. It immediately comes down into the world of betrayal, violence, denial, falsehood, injustice, religion-related power politics, torture, and execution of the innocent. The love, prayer, and mutual indwelling of John 17 are to be enacted in such a world, and the whole Gospel is in the service of inspiring and deepening such a way of following Jesus. John 17 is especially the culmination of preparation for what is about to happen now, and its theology is empty or escapist if it is separated from these events and the ongoing drama of the followers of the crucified and risen Jesus.

John's account of the arrest of Jesus has several differences from the Synoptic Gospels. For example, he omits elements included by one or more of the Synoptics, such as Judas kissing Jesus, the desertion of Jesus by all the disciples, a meeting of the Sanhedrin at daybreak, and an examination of Jesus before Herod.

But theologically the main difference is the emphasis on the *egō eimi*, **I am** or **I am he** (vv. 5, 6, 8). This, in its first translation, can be seen as a postresurrection headline for the final four chapters, pointing to the most important reality of this hour, who Jesus is. In postresurrection perspective, Jesus is described as **knowing all that was to happen to him**, and the author's wish to signal to the reader the deeper meaning of the threefold "I am" (which, as the second translation, "I am he," says, can be a straightforward self-identification, meaning simply "I am indeed Jesus of Nazareth") is indicated by a surprising touch: **They stepped back and fell to the ground**. This is a classic response to divine revelation. To read John alongside the Synoptics is to be forcefully faced with his theological message about Jesus, summed up in the double meaning of the *egō eimi*: the human **Jesus of Nazareth**, at one with the **I am** of God.[3]

That is only one of the initiatives Jesus takes, even while being arrested, bound, and put on trial. He also steps forward to address those who come to arrest him; he instructs them to **let these men go**,[4] and he has the ability not to **lose a single one of those whom you gave me**. His question rebuking Peter, **"Am I not to drink the cup that the Father has given me?"** echoes the Synoptic accounts of Jesus in the garden of Gethsemane, but in a less anguished mode.[5] Readers are being given the concepts and images through which to come to theological terms with the arrest and what follows, and this question to Peter points to a core theological truth in this Gospel: the relationship of mutual trust and unity between Jesus and his Father.

Peter's violent defense of Jesus fails to understand the purpose of God and how it is to be worked out, just as did his initial resistance to having his feet washed (13:8). Does this rebuke suggest a critique of all armed violence in the cause of Jesus? John's ethics work more by inviting reflection on the narrative in the circumstances of the readers than by issuing direct commands for all circumstances, but *the thrust of this story does strongly inhibit any resort to violence in the name of Jesus*. This conclusion is reinforced later before Pilate by Jesus's statement, "If my kingdom were from this world, my followers would be fighting" (18:36).

The actual arrest underlines the cooperation between Roman soldiers and Jewish police: **So the soldiers, their officer, and the Jewish police arrested Jesus and bound him**. This is collaboration between the greatest military power in that world and those in charge of security at the temple, the place of God's special presence in Israel. *The outcome of their engagement with Jesus will be a judgment on both*.

Peter's Denial: "I Am Not" (18:13–18)

> [13] First they took him to Annas, who was the father-in-law of Caiaphas, the high priest that year. [14] Caiaphas was the one who had advised the Jews that it was better to have one person die for the people.

3. The emphasis on the "who" question is underlined by recalling the opening words of Jesus to his first disciples in this Gospel in 1:38, "What are you looking for?" The same question using the same verb is now repeated, but with "whom" instead of "what": **"Whom are you looking for?"** The resurrected Jesus later asks the same question of Mary Magdalene, "Whom are you looking for?" (20:15). John's repetition of it suggests that it is the core question of his Gospel.

4. This is Passover, as John reminds readers more than once, and this recalls the repeated appeal of Moses leading to the exodus, "Let my people go" (Exod. 5:1; 7:16; 8:20; 9:1, 13; 10:3).

5. John testifies to the anguish earlier; see comments on 11:33, 35, 38; 12:27; 13:21.

> 15 Simon Peter and another disciple followed Jesus. Since that disciple
> was known to the high priest, he went with Jesus into the courtyard of
> the high priest, 16 but Peter was standing outside at the gate. So the other
> disciple, who was known to the high priest, went out, spoke to the woman
> who guarded the gate, and brought Peter in. 17 The woman said to Peter,
> "You are not also one of this man's disciples, are you?" He said, "I am not."
> 18 Now the slaves and the police had made a charcoal fire because it was
> cold, and they were standing around it and warming themselves. Peter also
> was standing with them and warming himself.

Annas had been deposed as high priest by the Romans, but he and his family remained in power, in collaboration with the Romans, and he could still be called high priest (v. 22). The advice of Caiaphas **that it was better to have one person die for the people** had been given during a meeting of the Sanhedrin that had decided Jesus should be put to death (11:47–53) and was interpreted by the evangelist as an unintended prophecy "that Jesus was about to die for the nation, and not for the nation only, but to gather into one the dispersed children of God" (11:51–52). That is in line with the prayer of Jesus for unity in John 17 and, like that, also pushes the scope wider than Israel. This earlier "trial" in John 11 lets the author now bypass the Synoptic accounts of a formal trial before the Sanhedrin and also explains the assumption (18:31) that the aim was to put him to death.

Who was **another disciple** who knew the high priest and enabled Peter to access the courtyard? Speculation has ranged from the Beloved Disciple to Judas. If it was the Beloved Disciple, it fits with the eyewitness source for this Gospel having a special concern with the temple, its festivals, and those in and around Jerusalem, such as Mary, Martha, and Lazarus. It would also be another example, as in John 13, 20, and 21, of Peter being paired with the Beloved Disciple to the advantage of the latter—here, Peter denies Jesus and disappears, but the Beloved Disciple follows Jesus to the cross. Yet the vagueness of John may deliberately allow for alternative interpretations, and the main point may be the one that is twice repeated, that this disciple **was known to the high priest**, explaining how Peter was able to be there at all.

The triple "I am" of Jesus at his arrest is further emphasized by way of contrast through the **"I am not"** in Peter's threefold denial of being a disciple of Jesus (vv. 17, 25, 27). For the rereader, this in turn is contrasted with the later threefold exchange between the risen Jesus and Peter, "Simon son of John, do you love me?" (21:15–19).

The denials of Peter are also emphasized by being set on either side of the interrogation of Jesus by Annas: Peter lies, takes the comfortable, selfish option (**warming himself** is repeated twice [vv. 18, 25]), is **standing with** those who had arrested Jesus, and refuses to take responsibility for his attack on Malchus (vv. 26–27); Jesus, by contrast, takes full responsibility for his open, public ministry and sets out on his path toward the extremity of discomfort by being struck on the face and bound. Yet Peter had also courageously followed Jesus into the courtyard and had earlier risked defending Jesus, even if mistakenly.

Under Interrogation: "I Have Spoken Openly to the World" (18:19–24)

> 19 Then the high priest questioned Jesus about his disciples and about his teaching. 20 Jesus answered, "I have spoken openly to the world; I have always taught in synagogues and in the temple, where all the Jews come together. I have said nothing in secret. 21 Why do you ask me? Ask those who heard what I said to them; they know what I said." 22 When he had said this, one of the police standing nearby struck Jesus on the face, saying, "Is that how you answer the high priest?" 23 Jesus answered, "If I have spoken wrongly, testify to the wrong. But if I have spoken rightly, why do you strike me?" 24 Then Annas sent him bound to Caiaphas the high priest.

The high priest questioned Jesus about his disciples and about his teaching, but Jesus answers about himself and his teaching. The Greek stresses the "I" of Jesus by twice using *egō*, **"*I* have spoken openly to the world; *I* have always taught in synagogues and in the temple,"** and then again using *egō* in the emphatic final position as the last word of Jesus's reply, **"They know what I said"**—the Greek translated literally as "They know what said *I*."

The openness (*parrhēsia*—public availability, frankness, confident and free communication) to the world of Jesus and his teaching is in line with the open horizon of this Gospel. In the prologue Jesus is identified with the unlimited communication of "the Word" of God, through whom "all things came into being," including the "life" that "was the light of all people" (1:3–4). *When the Word becomes vulnerable flesh, this open communication happens vulnerably.* It has to appeal for a hearing and can be questioned and tested, corroborated or refuted, welcomed or rejected.

Here Jesus appeals for the corroboration of witnesses to his teaching. His confident reversal of the examination by interrogating the high priest provokes **one of the police** to strike him **on the face**. He then appeals for justice, but his question is unanswered.

Jesus is **sent . . . bound to Caiaphas the high priest**. John seems to assume that his readers can find out about what happened there from other sources, because it is passed over in order to concentrate (at greater length than the Synoptics) on the trial before Pilate.

Peter Again: "I Am Not" (18:25–27)

> [25] Now Simon Peter was standing and warming himself. They asked him, "You are not also one of his disciples, are you?" He denied it and said, "I am not." [26] One of the slaves of the high priest, a relative of the man whose ear Peter had cut off, asked, "Did I not see you in the garden with him?" [27] Again Peter denied it, and at that moment the cock crowed.

Peter again denies his association with Jesus, even in the face of a witness to what he did during the arrest in the garden. The prediction by Jesus, "Very truly, I tell you, before the cock crows, you will have denied me three times" (13:38), is fulfilled.

Peter is a complex and ambivalent character. During the arrest he showed courage and misunderstanding; here he has shown courage in following Jesus, but then it fails under pressure. Earlier, when he first became a disciple, Jesus gave him the symbolic name "Rock" (1:42), and after the feeding of the five thousand, when other disciples are abandoning Jesus, Peter stands firm. On behalf of those disciples who stay loyal, he makes a fundamental confession of faith in Jesus (6:66–69). At the Last Supper he first resists Jesus washing his feet, then overcompensates for it and elicits some basic teaching from Jesus. Then, when Jesus hints at his own imminent death, Peter promises to lay down his life for Jesus, who responds by predicting the three denials. "Full of courage and also full of failure" is how one study of Peter describes him.[6]

How are readers to take him? He and other complex characters (perhaps especially Nicodemus, the Samaritan woman at the well, and Thomas) can help inspire the development of a mature faith that recognizes the complexity of discipleship and the need for continual searching reflection on its many forms, pitfalls, and challenges. Peter's own restoration in John 21 will take the form of repeated interrogation by Jesus about love, a call to ongoing responsibility, and a prediction of further testing to the point of martyrdom. By offering a diverse set of stories and characters in interaction with Jesus, John resists not only any simplistic "one size fits all" practice of faith but also any idealization of it.

6. Labahn, "Simon Peter," 167.

Outside (1): Pilate, the Jews, and the Handing Over of Jesus (18:28–32)

> 28 Then they took Jesus from Caiaphas to Pilate's headquarters. It was early in the morning. They themselves did not enter the headquarters, so as to avoid ritual defilement and to be able to eat the Passover. 29 So Pilate went out to them and said, "What accusation do you bring against this man?" 30 They answered, "If this man were not a criminal, we would not have handed him over to you." 31 Pilate said to them, "Take him yourselves and judge him according to your law." The Jews replied, "We are not permitted to put anyone to death." 32 (This was to fulfill what Jesus had said when he indicated the kind of death he was to die.)

By emphasizing the time, **early in the morning** on the day the lambs were killed for the celebration of **Passover** (further emphasized at 19:14, 31, 42), and reinforcing this by spatial separation **so as to avoid ritual defilement**, John both puts what is happening in the context of the most important event of Israel's history and also sets the stage for the complex relationship between the Jewish and the Roman authorities. The trial is structured around the movement back and forth between outside and inside **Pilate's headquarters**.

Pilate asks about the **accusation** against Jesus, who is called **this man** (*anthrōpos*), the term for a human being, which Pilate uses again in 19:5, "Here is the man!" His accusers respond, **"If this man** [*houtos*, "this one"—the Greek is the masculine of "this" and does not have *anthrōpos*] **were not a criminal, we would not have handed him over to you."** This seems to assume previous communication about Jesus (which would chime with the presence of Roman soldiers at the arrest), some of which emerges in Pilate's first question to Jesus, showing that he knows the accusation that Jesus is "King of the Jews" (v. 33). But, more than communication between Jewish and Roman authorities, the present response may hint at their habitual collaboration. As the rest of the trial shows, they have a common interest in maintaining the status quo in which they hold power together, even if the balance of military and political power is in Pilate's favor. Here, there is a confidence in the relationship that assumes that Pilate will trust their judgment, a confidence that grounds their later exercise of pressure on him, even to the extent of threatening him (19:12–15).

But the limits of their power are also immediately made clear. Pilate's reply, **"Take him yourselves and judge him according to your law,"** tries to let him avoid the whole affair. It also exposes the nonnegotiable prior decision to put Jesus to death (11:47–53), and this in turn shows why the accusers need Pilate: **"We are not permitted to put anyone to death."**

The trial has now been set up in terms of Jewish and Roman power and collaboration; but *John typically will not let these categories be the only ones. The authorial comment, with its postresurrection perspective, sets up Jesus and what he says as the decisive framework of meaning*: **This was to fulfill what Jesus had said when he indicated the kind of death he was to die.** During the trial, as during the arrest, this framework is repeatedly reinforced.

Inside (1): Jesus and Pilate on Kingship and Truth (18:33–38a)

> [33] Then Pilate entered the headquarters again, summoned Jesus, and asked him, "Are you the King of the Jews?" [34] Jesus answered, "Do you ask this on your own, or did others tell you about me?" [35] Pilate replied, "I am not a Jew, am I? Your own nation and the chief priests have handed you over to me. What have you done?" [36] Jesus answered, "My kingdom is not from this world. If my kingdom were from this world, my followers would be fighting to keep me from being handed over to the Jews. But as it is, my kingdom is not from here." [37] Pilate asked him, "So you are a king?" Jesus answered, "You say that I am a king. For this I was born, and for this I came into the world, to testify to the truth. Everyone who belongs to the truth listens to my voice." [38a] Pilate asked him, "What is truth?"

Inside his headquarters Pilate focuses on the key issue for the Roman Empire: **"Are you the King of the Jews?"** "King" (*basileus*) was what Romans called the local rulers, such as Herod, through whom they often ruled their provinces. To claim to be a king without being appointed by Rome was seen as sedition, treason, rebellion. And the top king was the Roman emperor (19:15). So this is a life-or-death question for Jesus.

Jesus replies by interrogating Pilate, as he had Annas. His question probes the sensitive relationship between the Jewish and Roman authorities: **"Do you ask this on your own, or did others tell you about me?"**

Pilate's **"I am not"** points to one key identity in the present drama, that of the Roman Empire. This is alongside the "I am" of Jesus, the "I am not" of Peter the disciple, and the conflicted identity of the Jewish authorities—religiously observing the Passover, convinced that the protection of their people and the temple requires the elimination of Jesus, and eventually, in the culminating moment of the trial, explicitly declaring for Rome and against not only Jesus but also the kingship of their God, "We have no king but the emperor" (19:15). *Who Jesus is is the key issue of the trial, as it is of the rest of the Gospel, and other identities and commitments are tested and judged in responding to him.* Rome, the Jewish authorities, and Peter are all judged during this trial, and the final verdict on them is the resurrection of Jesus, revealing who Jesus is (e.g., "My Lord and my God!" [20:28]) and the secret of his nonviolent power and authority (e.g., "Peace be with you. . . . He showed them his hands and his side. . . . Receive the Holy Spirit. If you forgive . . ." [20:19–23]; "Do you love me?" [three times in 21:15–17]).

*The reply of Jesus emphatically claims kingship—**my kingdom** is repeated three times—and at the same time transforms its meaning.* It is **not from this world . . . not from here**. That has sometimes been understood to mean that the kingship of Jesus is otherworldly, or "spiritual," as opposed to being involved with such "worldly" matters as political or economic power; or private and inward rather than being exercised in the public sphere; or religious as distinguished from political. None of those is true. The kingdom of Jesus is from a God who is deeply concerned with political and economic power, with the public as well as the private, and with the political as well as the religious. One of the first series of headline titles given to Jesus in John 1 was "King of Israel," set alongside "Son of God" (1:49); his first public action was against turning the temple into a marketplace, and he claimed this greatest of Israel's religious and political centers as "my Father's house" (2:16); and he entered Jerusalem to cries of "Hosanna! Blessed is the one who comes in the name of the Lord—the King of Israel" (12:13). All those point to the kingship of God, which pervades Israel's Scriptures. This is about what the Synoptics (and John in chap. 3) call the "kingdom of God" or the "kingdom of heaven." John's transposition of this terminology into that of life and love[7] has the exactly opposite meaning to otherworldliness or separating private from public, or religion from politics. It also resists any understanding of the kingship as being only future. That Jesus has come from his Father, that the Word of God, through whom all things have come into being, has become flesh, and that his disciples are sent into the world as he was sent mean that worldly power, such as that of the Roman and Jewish authorities (both of which were inseparably political, economic, judicial, and religious), is being directly and radically challenged in this world now by a Lord who has washed his disciples' feet and is about to undergo humiliation, torture, and crucifixion for love.

The character of the power of Jesus is further described as nonviolent: **"If my kingdom were from this world, my followers would be fighting to keep me from being handed over to the Jews."** Pilate's verdict in verse 38b, "I find no case against him," shows that he believes that there is no violent threat from Jesus.

7. See above on 3:1–21, where the first two waves in kingdom language culminate in the third wave in terms of life and love (as condensed in 3:16).

"So you are a king?" is an obvious follow-up question. Jesus does not simply accept the category as understood by Pilate but fills it with his own meaning. He **was born** as a human being and he **came into the world** from God in order **to testify to the truth.** This is a very emphatic mission statement, at least as strong as earlier ones in which he said that he came to bring both abundant life and light.[8] "Truth" has been a recurrent theme through this Gospel from the beginning: Jesus is "full of grace and truth" (1:14; cf. 1:17); it is a perfection of God ("God is true" [3:33; cf. 8:26]); God is to be worshiped "in spirit and truth" (4:23–24); and truth is liberating ("The truth will make you free" [8:32]). This culminates in the Farewell Discourses, where the person of Jesus is identified with the truth: "I am the way, and the truth, and the life" (14:6); and the disciples are promised "the Spirit of truth" (14:17), who, Jesus says, "will testify on my behalf. You also are to testify" (15:26–27). Their whole mission is conceived in terms of their dedication to the truth that is inseparable from the mission and person of Jesus: "Sanctify them in the truth; your word is truth. As you have sent me into the world, so I have sent them into the world. And for their sakes I sanctify myself, so that they also may be sanctified in truth" (17:17–19).

When references to truth are understood in their context in this Gospel, connecting with key themes such as word and Spirit, trusting and believing, seeing and knowing, light and life, creation and salvation, testifying and judging, and peace and love, and also resonating throughout the Septuagint, *this final occurrence of "truth" is seen to bring together the deep reality of who God is, who Jesus is, and who disciples are, together with the mission of Jesus and of his disciples.* The resonances of truth with trustworthiness, with faithful belonging, and with

> I see full well that human intellect
> can never be content unless that truth
> beyond which no truth soars shines down on it.
>
> When once they come to it, as come they may,
> minds couch in truth as beasts do in their lairs.
> Were that not so, then all desire would fail.[a]
>
> —Dante Alighieri, *The Divine Comedy 3: Paradiso*, canto 4, lines 124–29
>
> a. For a set of rich discussions of how Dante understands truth and theology, see Montemaggi, *Reading Dante's* Commedia *as Theology*, especially chaps. 1 and 2. There are numerous analogies and mutual illuminations that come through relating the encounters in John to those in Dante.

8. E.g., 10:10, "I came that they may have life, and have it abundantly"; 12:46, "I have come as light into the world, so that everyone who believes in me should not remain in the darkness."

utterly reliable and authoritative testimony are especially present here. And, of course, the author is also implicitly saying that *this truth is what (and who) you readers are now being given.*

But this truth is here embodied in someone who has been arrested, bound, slapped in the face, and put on trial, with worse to come. Jesus acknowledges his kingship only when the circumstances make it clear how fundamentally he is challenging most ideas of power, domination, and authority.

"Everyone who belongs to the truth [*ho ōn ek tēs alētheias*; literally, "the one who is from the truth," giving the positive content of the earlier "is not from this world," *ouk estin ek tou kosmou toutou*] **listens to my voice."** What does it mean for this sort of truth to be dominant? It is an invitation into a belonging and core identity that is continually attentive to Jesus. John's Gospel is written to convey this invitation, which is also a challenge to decide. To whom, among all the voices that attract us, is it most worth listening?

Pilate asked him, "What is truth?" There have been many interpretations of this question. Is it a genuine one? Is it philosophical? Is it skeptical or even cynical, despairing of any possibility of finding truth? Is it sarcastic dismissal? Is it a moment of reflection in which Pilate comes to the true verdict that he delivers later in the verse?

It may be misleading to focus on Pilate's motive and better to notice how this question works in the context. Within the drama of the trial, it is clear that, whatever Pilate's motive or tone of voice, the moment does not lead to an outcome in line with the truth. Truth and the politics of empire do not go together. For the reader, who has heard Jesus say "I am . . . the truth" (14:6), the irony is that Pilate, faced with "the truth" in person, is asking a "what" instead of a "who" question. For the rereader, the question asked by Jesus during his arrest and by the risen Jesus with reference to himself, "Whom are you looking for?" (18:4, 7; 20:15), suggests the right question: *"Who is truth?"*

Outside (2): "Not This Man, but Barabbas!" (18:38b–40)

> [38b] After he had said this, he went out to the Jews again and told them, "I find no case against him. [39] But you have a custom that I release someone for you at the Passover. Do you want me to release for you the King of the Jews?" [40] They shouted in reply, "Not this man, but Barabbas!" Now Barabbas was a bandit.

Pilate delivers a verdict in legal language: **"I find no case** [*aitia*, "guilt, reason, valid accusation"] **against him."** From this moment, it is clear that any outcome other than acquittal will be unjust. The importance of the verdict is highlighted through being delivered by Pilate three times (see also 19:4, 6).

But—Pilate does not end the trial there. He offers to release Jesus according to a **custom . . . at the Passover**. Is he playing with **the Jews**? Is he mocking them? Is it a genuine offer? Does he expect them to accept the offer to release Jesus after they have made plain their intention to have him executed? Is he offering a face-saving compromise? Again, focusing on Pilate's motives may miss the main point. This Gospel's way of telling the story of the release of Barabbas differs from the three Synoptic Gospels in several ways, and its much shorter version (it does not even include the outcome, the release of Barabbas) seems to have as its main point *a "who versus who" stark contrast: **the King of the Jews / this man** versus **Barabbas/bandit**.* How John tells it clarifies both the determination of Jesus's own people to reject his kingship and the injustice of Pilate in even offering the choice. In the process there are several ironies: the fact that the offer and the choice combine to show that the trial is not about justice; the name "Barabbas," meaning "son of the father"; and the substitution of a "bandit" (*lēstēs*—the only other occurrences in this Gospel are in 10:1, 8, where the bandit is contrasted with Jesus as the good shepherd)[9] for Jesus. The act of substituting one life for another is rich with multiple connections: with the lambs killed at Passover and with Jesus as "the Lamb of God who takes away the sin of the world" (1:29), as well as Jesus as the good shepherd who "lays down his life for the sheep" (10:11); with Jesus as "the living bread that came down from heaven. . . . The bread that I will give for the life of the world is my flesh" (6:51); with the whole tradition of sacrifice and atonement; with having "one person die for the people" (11:50; 18:14); and with laying "down one's life for one's friends" (15:13).

9. In John 10 a key theme is hearing the voice of Jesus, the good shepherd, as in 18:37.

John 19:1–42

Condemnation and Crucifixion

Now comes the dramatic climax. Readers have been prepared for it since the opening chapter[1] and all through the Gospel, but there is more to be taken in here: the stark event of the death of Jesus, and further pointers to his transformative significance.

Jesus himself continues to be the main focus, now strongly emphasized by exclamations and visual language: "Hail, King of the Jews!" (v. 3); "Look [*ide*,

1. Rereading John 1 is especially helpful as a preparation for this chapter. Note especially in John 1 the following: (1) *exclamations and testimonies focused on Jesus* ("John testified to him and cried out, 'This was he'" [v. 15]; "He saw Jesus coming toward him and declared, 'Here is [*ide*, 'see'] the Lamb of God who takes away the sin of the world!'" [v. 29; cf. *ide* in v. 36]; "And John testified, 'I saw the Spirit descending from heaven like a dove, and it remained on him. I myself did not know him but the one who sent me to baptize with water said to me, "He on whom you see the Spirit descend and remain is the one who baptizes with the Holy Spirit." And I myself have seen and have testified that this is the Son of God'" [vv. 32–33]; "We have found the Messiah" [v. 41]; "We have found him about whom Moses in the law and also the prophets wrote, Jesus son of Joseph from Nazareth" [v. 45]; "Rabbi, you are the Son of God! You are the King of Israel!" [v. 49]); (2) *fundamental, inexhaustible questions* ("Who are you?" [vv. 19, 22]; "What are you looking for?" [v. 38]; "Where are you staying?" [v. 38]); (3) *visual language*, that of witnesses and of Jesus himself ("We have seen his glory" [v. 14; also vv. 29, 32, 33, 36, 38, already referred to above]; "Jesus turned and saw them following" [v. 38]; "Come and see" [vv. 39, 46]; "They came and saw" [v. 39]; "He brought Simon to Jesus, who looked at him" [v. 42]; "When Jesus saw Nathanael . . ." [v. 47]; "I saw you. . . . You will see greater things than these. . . . You will see heaven opened" [vv. 48, 50–51]); and all of this within (4) *the comprehensive horizon* opened up by the prologue, centered on "the Word of God," who "became flesh and lived among us" (v. 14). The vulnerability and mortality of that flesh; the meaning of glory, Lamb of God, the Spirit, Messiah, Son of God, King of Israel, and greater; the way Jesus is seen and sees; the importance of testimony; and, above all, who Jesus is—all these elements of John 1 are at issue in the culminating drama of John 19, and readers are drawn further into them in ways only hinted at in John 1.

"see"]. . . . Here is [*idou*, "see, behold"] the man!" (vv. 4–5); "Crucify him! Crucify him!" (v. 6); "Here is [*ide*] your King!" (v. 14); "Away with him! Away with him! Crucify him!" (v. 15). The controversy about the inscription on the cross, "Jesus of Nazareth, the King of the Jews" (v. 19), carries on this focus. As Jesus hangs on the cross, there is a shift to what he himself is focusing on: "When Jesus saw his mother and the disciple whom he loved . . ."; "Here is [*ide*] your son. . . . Here is [*ide*] your mother" (vv. 26–27). Then the final threefold concentration is on his thirst; his last word, "It is finished"; and his last action, "Then he bowed his head and gave up his [literally, "the"] spirit [or "Spirit"]" (v. 30). "Spirit" is the final word of the death scene.

Even in death, his pierced body pours out "blood and water" (v. 34), and there is an extraordinary emphasis on this being seen by a reliable eyewitness and confirmed by Scripture. And "Jesus" is the last word of the Greek text of John 19.

But what sort of king? Who is this man? What is the significance of his death? What about his spirit/Spirit? What sort of seeing is needed?

The theological meaning of the final scenes in the trial pivots around kingship and power. Here, in the region's center of imperial power, there is a demonstration of a different sort of power, embodied in someone who is flogged, mocked, hit in the face, condemned to death, stripped, and crucified. Pilate, the emperor's representative, is "afraid" (v. 8), and his power is radically relativized: "You would have no power over me unless it had been given you from above" (v. 11). The hatred and religiopolitical aims of the Jewish leaders lead them, in the terms of their own Scriptures, to idolatry and blasphemy: "We have no king but the emperor" (v. 15). Pilate's fear leads him to give in to the hatred and go against his own judgment: "I find no case against him. . . . I find no case against him" (vv. 4, 6). So, "he handed him over to them to be crucified" (v. 16).

Jesus carries his cross to Golgotha, and "there they crucified him" (v. 18). The controversy about the inscription placed on the cross underlines the scandal of a crucified king. The division of his clothes by the soldiers is crucially understood through Psalm 22, and his thirst through Psalm 69.

In John's account of the crucifixion a key, distinctive event happens between Jesus, his mother, and the disciple whom he loved. *It is about the love, desire, and seeing of Jesus.* He "saw" them there together (v. 26) and united them in a new "home"-based community, beginning from "that hour" (v. 27).

The climactic finality of the death of Jesus is emphasized by the double use of the verb *telein*, meaning "finish, complete, fulfill, come to an end": "Jesus knew that all was now finished. . . . He said, 'It is finished'" (vv. 28, 30). This is reinforced by the related verb *teleioun*, meaning "fulfill, make perfect, make complete": "He said (in order to fulfill the scripture), 'I am thirsty'" (v. 28). This short scene resonates with earlier Scripture, the Synoptic Gospels, and the earlier chapters of John. "Then he bowed his head and gave up his spirit [or "Spirit"]" (v. 30). This description of the death of Jesus allows for it being a giving of the Holy Spirit.

In the aftermath of the death of Jesus, the most distinctive event in John's account is the soldier piercing "his side with a spear, and at once blood and water came out" (v. 34). This piercing, the unbroken bones, and the blood and water open up depths of meaning, as do Jesus's kingship and power, his mother and the disciple whom he loved, his thirst, and the breathing out of the spirit/Spirit.

The burial of Jesus by Joseph of Arimathea and Nicodemus is the final indication of kingship: the massive amount of myrrh and aloes suggests royalty through yet another sign of abundance. The last verse gives yet another reminder of the Passover setting, so crucial to John's narrative and theology.

Inside (2): Jesus Flogged, Mocked, and Struck in the Face (19:1–3)

> [1] Then Pilate took Jesus and had him flogged. [2] And the soldiers wove a
> crown of thorns and put it on his head, and they dressed him in a purple
> robe. [3] They kept coming up to him, saying, "Hail, King of the Jews!" and
> striking him on the face.

Jesus is **flogged**, a brutal form of torture, here exacerbated by **thorns** pressed into Jesus's head and a **purple robe** placed on top of the lacerations. The sustained mockery ironically intensifies the kingship theme, with hints of coronation and investiture. And by making Jesus look ridiculous and impotent, Pilate is both showing that he is no political threat and mocking the seriousness with which the Jewish leaders take him.

Outside (3): "Here Is the Man!" "He Has Claimed to Be the Son of God" (19:4–8)

> [4] Pilate went out again and said to them, "Look [*ide*], I am bringing him out
> to you to let you know that I find no case against him." [5] So Jesus came
> out, wearing the crown of thorns and the purple robe. Pilate said to them,
> "Here [*idou*] is the man!" [6] When the chief priests and the police saw him,
> they shouted, "Crucify him! Crucify him!" Pilate said to them, "Take him
> yourselves and crucify him; I find no case against him." [7] The Jews answered
> him, "We have a law, and according to that law he ought to die because he
> has claimed to be the Son of God."
>
> [8] Now when Pilate heard this, he was more afraid than ever.

Pilate reaffirms the innocence of Jesus, backed up by showing him to his accusers as a mock king. **"Here is** [*idou*, "behold, see, look"] **the man** [*anthrōpos*, "human being"]**!"** can be heard in several ways. For Pilate, this man is someone in his power, demonstrably insignificant and unthreatening. For **the chief priests and the police**, this man threatens their religiopolitical power **because he has claimed to be the Son of God**. For readers of earlier chapters, Jesus has since the opening chapter been both "Son of God" (1:34, 49) and "Son of Man [*anthrōpos*]" (1:51). His humanity, his divinity, and their interrelation have been given content through events, actions, encounters, discourses, intertexts, and authorial comment, and there have been many pointers to this "hour" as the decisive enactment of who Jesus is. *What is being described now therefore adds content to that surprising, unique identity*. For rereaders, this is the man who will die breathing out the Spirit and will be resurrected and called "My Lord and my God!" (20:28). For readers who know the Synoptics, this is one of several unique features of John's much longer trial before Pilate and an invitation to reread the Synoptic accounts seeing Jesus as a representative human being, and in particular identified with those who suffer humiliation. For readers who know the Septuagint, of many resonances (such as Gen. 3:22 or Dan. 7:13) the clearest is Samuel hearing the Lord identify Saul as the first king of Israel, "*Here is the man*[2] of whom I spoke to you. He it is who shall rule over my people" (1 Sam. 9:17), leading eventually to Saul's tragic end. For those who know Christian art, this is an iconic moment that has inspired many paintings.

Within the story, Pilate is threatening to bring to nothing the long-standing plans of the accusers of Jesus and is taunting them—he knows that in fact they have no power to do as he says, **"Take him yourselves and crucify him."** So, for their part, Pilate must be persuaded to have Jesus crucified.

Shouting having failed, they come out with their own fundamental accusation, **"We have a law, and according to that law he ought to die"**—probably Leviticus 24:16, which says, "One who blasphemes the name of the Lord shall be put to death." This plays the religious card, but it is also political—both for themselves, since their religious and political power are inseparable, and also for Pilate, in a world where Roman emperors can claim divine status. **Now when Pilate heard this, he was more afraid than ever.** Pilate's fear may be inspired not only by recognizing the wider implications for himself if the chief priests, his allies in ruling this province, vehemently persist in staking their whole law-centered identity and their relationship with himself on this demand. His fear may also be due to the impact of the presence of Jesus before him. Jesus has

2. In the LXX, this is *idou ho anthrōpos*, the same phrase Pilate uses in John 19:5; the phrase appears nowhere else in the LXX or New Testament.

already challenged Pilate's attempt to categorize him and has suggested that his secret lies in having a kingdom "not from this world" (18:36) and an identity and mission to do with a transcendent reality and origin: "For this I was born, and for this I came into the world, to testify to the truth" (18:37). That was left by Pilate as an open question, "What is truth?" (18:38). Now Pilate returns to the question of origins.

Inside (3): Whence Jesus? Whence Power? From Above! (19:9–12)

> 9 He entered his headquarters again and asked Jesus, "Where are you from?" But Jesus gave him no answer. 10 Pilate therefore said to him, "Do you refuse to speak to me? Do you not know that I have power to release you, and power to crucify you?" 11 Jesus answered him, "You would have no power over me unless it had been given you from above; therefore the one who handed me over to you is guilty of a greater sin." 12 From then on Pilate tried to release him, but the Jews cried out, "If you release this man, you are no friend of the emperor. Everyone who claims to be a king sets himself against the emperor."

"Where are you from?" is a fundamental question about Jesus throughout the Gospel of John, sometimes explicitly (7:27–28; 8:14; 9:29), but more often by reference to him being "from above" or sent by his Father. So readers know the answer, and Jesus has already said enough to give Pilate the answer too, had he been open to it. The silence of Jesus provokes Pilate to assert his **power** (*exousia*, "power, authority"). Jesus does not dispute this, but again affirms the larger, God-centered reality: **"You would have no power over me unless it had been given you from above."** Theologically, this yet again opens up the issue of the relationship of divine to human action and responsibility. Here, it is clear not only that people are held to account for what they do with what God gives them, but also that there are more and less serious sins: **"Therefore the one who handed me over to you is guilty of a greater sin."** Who is meant? The singular "one" might suggest Judas, Caiaphas, or Annas, but the phrase could also refer to a collective agency, in this context the Jewish leadership; and the vagueness may be deliberate. *But what is most striking is that Jesus, the accused, is delivering a judgment "from above" on both his judge, Pilate, and on all those responsible for bringing him before Pilate.*

From then on Pilate tried to release him. It is not explained why he did this. One possibility is that what Jesus said had an impact, and Pilate decides that the answer to "Where are you from?" carries no political threat.

But then the accusers play their trump card: **"If you release this man, you are no friend of the emperor. Everyone who claims to be a king sets himself against the emperor."** This changes the focus from relations between Pilate and the Jewish leaders to relations between Pilate and the Roman emperor, and from provincial to imperial politics. "Friend of the emperor" may even have been an official title held by Pilate; but, even if it was not, the threat of "these words" (19:13)—an accusation of disloyalty to the emperor and of failing to eliminate a direct challenge to the emperor's authority—proves decisive in persuading Pilate to have Jesus executed.

Outside (4): "Here Is Your King!" "Away with Him! Crucify Him!" (19:13–16a)

> 13 When Pilate heard these words, he brought Jesus outside and sat on the
> judge's bench at a place called The Stone Pavement, or in Hebrew Gabbatha.
> 14 Now it was the day of Preparation for the Passover; and it was about noon.
> He said to the Jews, "Here is your King!" 15 They cried out, "Away with him!
> Away with him! Crucify him!" Pilate asked them, "Shall I crucify your King?"
> The chief priests answered, "We have no king but the emperor." 16a Then he
> handed him over to them to be crucified.

The move **outside** to **the judge's bench** signals Pilate's readiness to pronounce his verdict. There is a fascinating ambiguity in the Greek for **sat**: it could mean that Pilate himself sat, but it could also mean that Pilate sat Jesus on the judge's bench, a double meaning that suggests how in this trial Jesus is both judged and judge.

The decisiveness of this moment is signaled by precisely naming the **place** in two languages, **The Stone Pavement, or in Hebrew Gabbatha**, and by giving the time: **Now it was the day of Preparation for the Passover; and it was about noon** (*hōra ēn hōs hektē*; literally, "it was about the sixth hour"). The place is the seat of Roman power, the time is one of the holiest of the Jewish year. On this "day" at about "noon" (the Greek uses the key term "hour") the Passover lambs are being killed.

He said to the Jews, "Here is [*ide*, "see"] **your King!"** Again, there are multiple meanings. Pilate seems to be taunting and humiliating the Jews by proclaiming this pathetic, humiliated figure as their king. In response, **They cried out, "Away with** [*aron*] **him! Away with** [*aron*] **him! Crucify him!"** vehemently rejecting being identified with "him . . . him . . . him." The reader is taken back to the first, headline acclamation of Jesus by his first witness, John the Baptist: "Here is [*ide*, "see"] the Lamb of God who takes away [*airōn*] the sin of the world!" (1:29). At this time when the Passover lambs are being killed, the same verb, *airein* (which through John's Gospel is often associated with life and death),[3] is used for doing away with Jesus as it has been for doing away with sin. For the reader of the Synoptics, where the kingship theme is mainly presented as the inauguration of the kingdom of God or the kingdom of heaven, Pilate's acclamation and the violent response to it intensify the emphasis on the kingship and person of Jesus and the connection of his distinctive authority with his crucifixion. For the reader of the Septuagint, the verb *airein* is just one of multiple pointers to a key passage through which the crucifixion of Jesus has been understood both in the New Testament and down through the centuries: the Suffering Servant passage in Isaiah 52:13–53:12.[4]

Pilate's final question, **"Shall I crucify your King?"** brings together crucifixion and kingship and is the final provocation to **the chief priests**. Their answer, **"We have no king but the emperor,"** is their final rejection, not only of Jesus, but of the very belief in a messianic king or in God as king. In their moment of victory in persuading Pilate to crucify Jesus, they also capitulate to him and the emperor he represents.

Then he handed him over [*paredōken*] **to them to be crucified.** Handing over, *paradidonai*, has been a key action in this story, a marker of critical events advancing the story. It is used of the betrayal by Judas (6:64, 71; 12:4; 13:2, 11, 21; 18:2, 5; possibly 19:11; and 21:20), of the chief priests handing Jesus over to Pilate (18:30, 35), of Jesus being handed over to them (18:36), and now of Pilate

3. The basic meaning of the verb translated in 19:15 as "away with," *airein*, is "take, take up, take away, remove," and its association with life and death in John is seen, e.g., in "I lay down my life in order to take it up again. . . . I have power to lay it down, and I have power to take it up again" (10:17–18); at the tomb of Lazarus Jesus says, "Take away the stone" (11:39), and later Mary Magdalene finds that the stone at Jesus's tomb "had been removed" (20:1), and then she says to Jesus, "They have taken away my Lord. . . . I will take him away" (20:13, 15); after the raising of Lazarus, the chief priests and the Pharisees fear that "the Romans will come and destroy [*airein*, "take away"] both our holy place and our nation" (11:48); and Joseph of Arimathea asked permission to "take away the body of Jesus" and later "removed" it (19:38). In the Synoptics it is used for disciples taking up the cross (Matt. 16:24; Mark 8:34; Luke 9:23); for the cry of the crowd at the trial, "Away with this fellow!" (Luke 23:18); and for Simon of Cyrene helping Jesus to carry his cross (Matt. 27:32; Mark 15:21).

4. This major intertext has already been discussed above (see comments on 12:20–36a). Of special significance here are the opening acclamation, "See [*idou*]"; the themes of lifting up, glorification, kings, believing, thirst, judgment, injustice, death and burial; the servant as a human being (*anthrōpos*) who suffers violent beating, humiliation, rejection, and death; the servant compared to a lamb led to the slaughter; the threefold use of the verb *paradidonai* ("hand over, deliver up, betray" [discussed below in this section]); and the emphasis throughout on the servant's suffering on behalf of others and their sins. The verb *airein* occurs twice in Isa. 53:8: "In humiliation his justice was *taken away*; who will tell of his posterity? For his life was *taken away* from the earth, and he was led to death as a result of the transgressions of my people" (my literal translation of the LXX).

handing Jesus over to be crucified. The most important handing over of all is yet to come: the giving of "his spirit [or "Spirit"]" in 19:30.

Who is meant by **to them**? There is a perhaps deliberate ambiguity: the grammar points to the chief priests, and the account that follows points to the Roman soldiers.

The Crucifixion (19:16b–18)

> [16b] So they took Jesus; [17] and carrying the cross by himself, he went out to what is called The Place of the Skull, which in Hebrew is called Golgotha. [18] There they crucified him, and with him two others, one on either side, with Jesus between them.

So they took Jesus. Being taken has also happened to him at his arrest (18:12), in being sent bound to Caiaphas (18:24), in being taken to Pilate (18:28), and in Pilate having him flogged (19:1) and then brought to the judge's bench (19:13). Yet this passivity of Jesus is alongside his active initiatives, as at his arrest and during his appearances before both Annas and Pilate. Here, he is **carrying the cross by himself**,[5] in contrast to the Synoptic accounts of Simon of Cyrene helping him (Matt. 27:32; Mark 15:21; Luke 23:26). The importance of the crucifixion is underlined by naming its location in two languages.

There they crucified him. In all four Gospels the actual crucifying of Jesus is simply stated, with no further description.

And with him two others, one on either side, with Jesus between them. B. F. Westcott comments on the centrality of Jesus, "Even in suffering Christ appears as a King."[6]

The Inscription (19:19–22)

> [19] Pilate also had an inscription [*titlos*] written and put on the cross. It read, "Jesus of Nazareth [*ho Nazōraios*], the King of the Jews." [20] Many of the Jews read this inscription, because the place where Jesus was crucified was near the city; and it was written in Hebrew, in Latin, and in Greek. [21] Then the chief priests of the Jews said to Pilate, "Do not write, 'The King of the Jews,' but, 'This man said, I am King of the Jews.'" [22] Pilate answered, "What I have written I have written."

5. For the verb "carry, bear" (*bastazein*), see comments on 16:12–15.

6. Westcott, *The Gospel according to St. John*, 274.

The **inscription** (the usual Greek for this is *epigraphē*, as used by Mark 15:26 and Luke 23:38 at this point) is actually called a *titlos* ("title"), borrowing a Latin term, *titulus*. This could be significant, since *ho Nazōraios* ("the Nazarene") might well have been a royal messianic title associated with rebuilding the temple, in line with John's association of the death and resurrection of Jesus with the destruction and rebuilding of the temple (in 2:13–25, during this Gospel's first Passover in Jerusalem).[7] If so, it serves to emphasize still further not only the kingship of Jesus but also the identification of Jesus with the temple (see further below). The use of **Hebrew**, **Latin**, and **Greek** signals the relevance of what is happening to the whole world of the Roman Empire.

In his dispute with **the chief priests** Pilate refuses to change the title, which meant one thing to him, another to the chief priests, and another to the author, who turns Pilate's **"What I have written I have written"** into Scripture.

Dividing Jesus's Clothes and the Fulfillment of Psalm 22 (19:23–25a)

> [23] When the soldiers had crucified Jesus, they took his clothes and divided
> them into four parts, one for each soldier. They also took his tunic; now the
> tunic was seamless, woven in one piece from the top. [24] So they said to one
> another, "Let us not tear it, but cast lots for it to see who will get it." This
> was to fulfill what the scripture says,
>
> "They divided my clothes among themselves,
> and for my clothing they cast lots."
>
> [25a] And that is what the soldiers did.

When the soldiers had crucified Jesus, he was naked, but no attention is drawn to this. Instead, the focus is on what the soldiers do with **his clothes**, and the whole scene is "covered" by Scripture. The quotation is from Psalm 22:18 (LXX 21:19). In that psalm, which has already been discussed in relation to 16:32 above, the psalmist begins with a cry to God of abandonment by God, "My God, my God, why have you forsaken me?" Then he alternates between past, present, and future. He looks to the past, gratefully remembering ("It was you who took me from the womb; you kept me safe on my mother's breast"). He also looks to the present, lamenting in anguish his vividly described present humiliation and suffering (he is despised; "All who see me mock at me"; "I am poured out like water"; "My mouth is dried up like a potsherd, and my tongue sticks to my jaws; you lay me in the dust of death"; "A company of evildoers encircles me") and crying out for help. He also looks confidently to

7. Mary Coloe makes the case for this in "The Nazarene King."

the future, anticipating being rescued by God, along with others who are poor and afflicted, and being able to praise God along with all the people of Israel; exhibiting an even more expansive confidence that "all the ends of the earth shall remember and turn to the Lord; and all the families of the nations shall worship before him"; celebrating the kingship of God over the nations; trusting that those "who go down to the dust," including himself, will live to God; and finally envisioning future generations serving God and proclaiming "his deliverance to a people yet unborn, saying that he has done it."

All four Gospels quote from this psalm in their crucifixion scenes, with different emphases. Mark and Matthew focus on the opening cry, as well as on Jesus being mocked and stripped of clothing. Luke focuses on the mockery. John alone quotes directly the division of clothing. But, as often, his allusions go far wider. To read Psalm 22 alongside the crucifixion accounts of John and the Synoptics is to be especially struck by John's omission of the cry of abandonment, by his greater emphasis than the Synoptics on the kingship theme and on power "from above" the nations, and by the resonances with three of his distinctive events, involving the mother of Jesus, the cry of thirst, and water pouring from the side of Jesus's dead body. John's account has the marks of long immersion in Psalms and in the Synoptic Gospels, inviting his readers to reread all three in the light of one another. That is an endless process (and can be enriched still further by adding other intertexts), but I will engage here with just one frequently asked question: How is John's omission of the cry of abandonment, present in Psalm 22, Mark, and Matthew, to be understood?

The first issue is whether John does omit it. Might it not be implied by the quotation from the middle of the same psalm? There is a debate among scholars as to whether one should take a scriptural quotation as implying the rest of the passage it comes from. Whatever the general answer (there probably is none that fits all cases, but a sensible general rule is to read the quotation in context, as one presumes the author did), with Psalm 22 and the Gospel passion narratives the case seems to be very strong for assuming that the whole psalm is meant, since all accounts quote it and there are so many echoes beyond the quotations.

Yet, the choice of what to focus on explicitly is still significant. I assume that John and John's first readers knew the Synoptics,[8] so they will have faced Mark's testimony, repeated by Matthew, to Jesus's raw, loud cry of forsakenness, followed by another loud cry as he died. They will also know that Luke omitted that cry and instead included a quotation from Psalm 31:5, "Father, into your hands I commend my spirit" (Luke 23:46). We will come to John's distinctive words from the cross below. But what is the impact of his omission of the cry

8. And even if they did not, we do.

of forsakenness? It is not that he ignores the anguish of Jesus—besides Jesus being "greatly disturbed in spirit and deeply moved" to the point of tears at the tomb of Lazarus (11:33–35), he also cries out in prayer, "Now my soul is troubled" (12:27), is "troubled in spirit" as he faces betrayal (13:21), and says "I am thirsty" on the cross (19:28). The initial impact of the omission is to stimulate readers to move beyond the first verse of Psalm 22 and be open to other elements in it, such as the division of clothing, the mother, the thirst, and being poured out like water. But in addition there is the wider horizon of this psalm, with its fundamental confidence in God and God's kingship over the whole earth. This is easily missed if the cry of forsakenness fills the whole horizon, as it sometimes does—and probably does for everyone at certain times. John's is a postresurrection perspective that is also realistic about both preresurrection and postresurrection suffering, hatred, mockery, injustice, and all the other things suffered by the psalmist, by Jesus, and by so many others. In omitting the cry of forsakenness and instead focusing where he does, John is affirming that such sufferings and evils do not have the last word. That lies with the One to whom the cry of forsakenness is addressed.[9]

That Jesus's **clothes** were **divided** by the soldiers is a vivid detail, introduced by the mention that these soldiers had **crucified Jesus**, and is a reminder of the indignity and humiliation that crucifixion was meant to inflict. Humiliation, already inflicted through the flogging, the mockery, and hanging nailed and naked on the cross, is theologically crucial to what immediately follows.

"Woman, Here Is Your Son"; "Here Is Your Mother" (19:25b–27)

> [25b] Meanwhile, standing near the cross of Jesus were his mother, and his mother's sister, Mary the wife of Clopas, and Mary Magdalene. [26] When Jesus saw his mother and the disciple whom he loved standing beside her, he said to his mother, "Woman, here is [*ide*, "see"] your son." [27] Then he said to the disciple, "Here is [*ide*, "see"] your mother." And from that hour the disciple took her into his own home.

Four women and one man are close to the crucified Jesus.[10] It may well be that **Clopas** is the same person as Cleopas in Luke's account of the risen

9. E. C. Hoskyns concludes his discussion of Jesus's last words as follows: "The Matthean-Marcan word, *My God, my God, why has thou forsaken me*, and the Johannine, *It is finished*, have therefore the same significance; the former cites the first words of the Psalm, and in so doing involves the whole; the latter sums up its meaning, and is less open to misunderstanding" (*The Fourth Gospel*, 531).

10. There is scholarly debate about how many women are intended. I favor four.

Jesus joining two disciples on the road to Emmaus; and **Mary the wife of Clopas** may well have been the second of those two (Luke 24:13–35). **Mary Magdalene**, who first appears here in this Gospel, later plays a key role in the resurrection accounts in John 20. So these two women are witnesses of the momentous words between **Jesus** and **his mother and the disciple whom he loved**.

How and why momentous?

- It happens in **that hour** for which John has been preparing readers ever since Jesus said to his mother before he did "the first of his signs" (2:11), "My hour has not yet come" (2:4). *Jesus crucified is the supreme sign.*[11] This is indicated all through the Gospel, beginning in the first chapter (see above, note 1).
- Jesus being "lifted up" on the cross is essential to the core message of the Gospel about the love of God for the world and his only Son being given for the salvation of the world (3:14–17); it is also the decisive revelation of who Jesus is ("Then you will realize that I am [*egō eimi*]" [8:28]); and it is the secret of how he attracts people to himself ("And I, when I am lifted up from the earth, will draw all people to myself" [12:32]). Now that lifting up has finally happened, these first words Jesus speaks from that position unite a new community those drawn to the cross.
- Above all, the Farewell Discourses go to the heart of the meaning of the forthcoming death of Jesus: *love*. They begin, "Jesus knew that his hour had come to depart from this world and go to the Father. Having loved his own [*tous idious*] who were in the world he loved them to the end" (13:1). It is hard to think of anyone more "his own" than "his mother" and "the disciple whom he loved," who first appears later in that chapter reclining

11. There has been an avalanche of scholarly work on the death of Jesus in the Gospel of John, with an impressive agreement among many that, as R. H. Lightfoot wrote many years ago, "the crucifixion was to St John doubtless the greatest sign of all." This is quoted in the magisterial paper by Gilbert Van Belle, "The Death of Jesus and the Literary Unity of the Fourth Gospel" (p. 13), in which he advances scholarly discussion of this theme (showing how the summary statement in John 20:30–31 about the signs that Jesus did should be taken to include his crucifixion and resurrection, and that indeed there should be affirmative answers to such questions as, "Can one accept that the cross is *the* sign *par excellence* in John's gospel? Is one correct in speaking of 'the sign of the cross' with respect to John's gospel?") (p. 14). He also includes an appendix helpfully surveying "The Death of Jesus According to John in Recent Research" (pp. 43–64). The same massive volume includes what I have found to be the single most helpful writing on the meaning of the death of Jesus in John by a New Testament scholar, Jörg Frey, "Edler Tod—wirksamer Tod—stellvertretender Tod—heilschaffender Tod" (a translation of the article's full title: "Noble Death—Effective Death—Vicarious Death—Atoning/Expiatory Death: On the Narrative and Theological Meaning of the Death of Jesus in the Gospel of John") (pp. 65–94).

on the breast of Jesus; and the Greek here for **into his own home** uses a related term, *eis ta idia*.[12]

- In John 13, Jesus washing his disciples' feet like a slave is a sign of the sign of the cross, on which he is now suffering a humiliating death that the Romans especially inflicted on slaves. And the final sentence of the footwashing is, "Very truly, I tell you, whoever receives [*lambanōn*] one whom I send receives [*lambanei*] me; and whoever receives [*lambanōn*] me receives [*lambanei*] him who sent me" (13:20). To read that alongside this scene at the cross is to glimpse a deeper meaning in the mother of Jesus receiving the disciple Jesus loved and him receiving her—**the disciple took** [*elaben*, "received"] **her into his own home** uses the same verb, *lambanein*.[13] The event at the cross is the creation of a new sort of family through mutual receiving within a joint loving relationship with Jesus and therefore also with his Father.[14]
- In the Farewell Discourses loving service is then deepened further into friendship to the point of dying for the other: "No one has greater love than this, to lay down one's life for one's friends" (15:13). The Beloved Disciple is the representative friend at the cross.
- Then the culmination of deepening and heightening comes in Jesus's prayer in John 17, as he anticipates his death the next day. That has an unsurpassable affirmation of mutual belonging between Jesus, his Father, and those who love and trust them: "All mine are yours, and yours are mine; and I have been glorified in them" (17:10). It also desires the ultimate union in face-to-face vision, glory, and love: "Father, I desire that those also, whom you have given me, may be with me where I am, to see my glory, which you have given me because you have loved me before the foundation of the world" (17:24). Here at the cross that desire is being fulfilled: two who have been given to him, his mother and his Beloved Disciple, see his glory on the cross, rooted in God's love, resulting in the intimate mutual belonging of "your son" and "your mother."

12. Both terms are also used in the prologue: "He came to what was his own [or "his own home," *ta idia*], and his own people [*hoi idioi*] did not accept him" (1:11).

13. Receiving, like sending and giving, is a key activity in John, and all three first occur in the prologue, where the use of *lambanein* and the language of family and beyond family, as children "born . . . of God," are especially important for what happens here at the cross: "But to all who received [*lambanein*] him, who believed in his name, he gave power to become children of God, who were born, not of blood or of the will of the flesh or of the will of man, but of God" (1:12–13).

14. See also below, in the comments on 20:11–18, on Mary Magdalene being told for the first time by the risen Jesus that God is "my Father and your Father" (20:17).

At the beginning of that chapter, Jesus is humiliated—he is flogged, a crown of thorns is pressed into his head, he is mocked, and slapped in the face.

The people with learning disabilities in our communities have been humiliated too. They have been seen as of no worth, having no dignity. They have been marginal to what other people really value and centre their lives on: knowledge, education, and work; sex, marriage, family life, and friendship; health, sport, and beauty; power, wealth, and fame.

Then Jesus is nailed to the cross, and what does he do from there?—He forms a community! When he sees his mother and the disciple he loved at the foot of the cross, he says to his mother, "Woman, here is your son," and to the disciple, "Here is your mother." Then John says that the disciple took her into his home. So, out of the depths of humiliation Jesus creates a community. At the heart, the root, of this community is the humiliated one.

—Jean Vanier

But what is the importance of Jesus saying this *from the cross*? I once asked Jean Vanier, founder of the international federation of L'Arche communities, in which people with and without serious learning disabilities live together in family-like households, about this.[15] He spoke about its connection with the L'Arche communities (see the quotation from Vanier in the sidebar).

"I Am Thirsty" (19:28–29)

> 28 After this, when Jesus knew that all was now finished, he said (in order to fulfill the scripture), "I am thirsty." 29 A jar full of sour wine was standing there. So they put a sponge full of the wine on a branch of hyssop and held it to his mouth.

At this agonized moment of the crucifixion, there is a concern, as throughout John 18 and 19, to remember who Jesus is, one with his Father, here seen in him knowing **that all was now finished**. Jean Vanier's insight is how John's testimony to the crucifixion of Jesus can inspire communities of love and solidarity with the most humiliated; the insight of Julian of Norwich, as developed by Denise Levertov (see Levertov's poem in the sidebar), is focused on the uniqueness of

15. The occasion was a celebration in London of the award to Vanier of the Templeton Prize in 2015. For more on Vanier see the section "Ongoing Drama" in the epilogue.

who Jesus is, and therefore on the unrepeatable, once-for-all, comprehensive, "finished" character of what is happening here.

Levertov's Johannine insistence on "the oneing with the Godhead," the "flood of knowledge," incarnation, the comprehensive horizon of "the pain of all minds, all bodies . . . from first beginning / to last day," "seeing it whole," and the kinship of Jesus with "*every sorrow and desolation*" is a testimony (as is much else in her later poetry) to *both the singularity and the universal solidarity of Jesus*, inseparable from either his divinity or his humanity, and challenging many ideas of both.

"I am thirsty." This cry connects with the themes of drinking, wine, and water that run right through this Gospel. They culminate in this chapter's references to Psalm 22, this thirst, the **sour wine**, Jesus handing over the Spirit, and the piercing of the body of the dead Jesus leading to an outflow of blood and water. All are about life and death, and all are concentrated on the body of Jesus, as in Levertov's poem. Here in this person, through this one death, a transformation is happening, utterly identified with humanity, life, and the matter of creation, and also utterly identified (at this time of Passover) with God and God's liberating love.

For what does Jesus thirst? Obviously for a drink, as raging thirst torments him. This shows his vulnerability, mortality, and solidarity with those in physical pain and with all life. Hydration is essential for plant, animal, and human life. But he is also immersed in the psalms, where thirst is both for drink and for God. "As a deer longs for flowing streams, so my soul longs for you, O God. My soul thirst for God, for the living God. When shall I come and behold the face of God?" (Ps. 42:1–2); "O God, you are my God, I seek you, my soul thirsts for you; my flesh faints for you, as in a dry and weary land where there is no water. . . . Your steadfast love is better than life" (Ps. 63:1, 3); "I stretch out my hands to you; my soul thirsts for you like a parched land" (Ps. 143:6). At his arrest Jesus said, "Am I not to drink the cup that the Father has given me?" (18:11). This thirst is a desire for the desire and will of his Father to be done, in line with what he said earlier to his disciples, "My food is to do the will of him who sent me and to complete his work" (4:34). So he is simultaneously at one with created life and with God. A further question to ask about this saying, through and beyond the question "For what does Jesus thirst?" is, "For whom does he thirst?" *"I am thirsty" is the words "I desire" (17:24) made flesh.*

The one who earlier said he was the source of "living water," so that "those who drink of the water that I will give them will never be thirsty" (4:10–15; see also 7:37–39), now says, "I am thirsty." The one whose glory was seen in the first of his signs through turning water into "good wine" (2:10–11) is now himself given "sour wine." There is great irony in this, but there is more. *This is tragic irony.* John is sometimes said to be the least tragic of the Gospels. Arguably,

"On a Theme from Julian's Chapter XX"

Six hours outstretched in the sun, yes,
hot wood, the nails, blood trickling
into the eyes, yes—
but the thieves on their neighbor crosses
survived till after the soldiers
had come to fracture their legs, or longer.
Why single out the agony? What's
a mere six hours?
Torture then, torture now,
the same, the pain's the same,
immemorial branding iron,
electric prod.
Hasn't a child
dazed in the hospital ward they reserve
for the most abused, known worse?
This air we're breathing,
these very clouds, ephemeral billows
languid upon the sky's
moody ocean, we share
with women and men who've held out
days and weeks on the rack—
and in the ancient dust of the world
what particles
of the long tormented,
what ashes.

But Julian's lucid spirit leapt
to the difference:
perceived why no awe could measure
that brief day's endless length,
why among all the tortured
One only is "King of Grief."

The oneing, she saw, *the oneing*
with the Godhead opened Him utterly
to the pain of all minds, all bodies
—sands of the sea, of the desert—
from first beginning
to last day. The great wonder is
that the human cells of His flesh and bone
didn't explode

when utmost Imagination rose
in that flood of knowledge. Unique
in agony, Infinite strength, Incarnate,
empowered Him to endure
inside of history,
through those hours when he took to Himself
the sum total of anguish and drank
even the lees of that cup:

within the mesh of the web, Himself
woven within it, yet seeing it,
seeing it whole. *Every sorrow and desolation*
He saw, and sorrowed in kinship.

—Denise Levertov, *Breathing the Water*, 68–69

the opposite is true. Right from the start, there is realism about darkness, sin, suffering, death, falsehood, and evil—not only in "the world" but also in religion, in Jesus's own disciples, and in each person. "The light shines in the darkness, and the darkness did not overcome it" (1:5)—this does not say that the darkness ceases. As Donald MacKinnon, a profound interpreter of the Gospel of John and tragedy, wrote, "The darkness remains."[16] It remains in the immediate aftermath of the crucifixion and resurrection of Jesus and also, as the letters 1 John, 2 John, and 3 John testify, in the Johannine community; and it remains down through the centuries and persists around the world today. The whole Gospel is a cry of thirst in this situation and an invitation to drink. It is a drinking that unites the drinkers with Jesus: "Those who eat my flesh and drink my blood abide in me, and I in them" (6:56). And this means uniting with the thirst of Jesus too.[17] His is a continuing thirst, in the ongoing drama of desire expressed by the prayer in John 17.

So they put a sponge full of the wine on a branch of hyssop and held it to his mouth. The mention of hyssop (odd, because its stems are not strong enough to bear a sponge) seems to be an echo of the hyssop used in the exodus from

16. MacKinnon, "Order and Evil in the Gospel," in *Borderlands of Theology*, 92.

17. Giles Waller has spoken of how John here conveys the reality of tragedy, turning the positive, celebratory symbol of wine in John 2 into an ironic tragic symbol of the bitterness of suffering in John 19. Glory and desolation coinhere in this sign (personal communication; see also Taylor and Waller, *Christian Theology and Tragedy*, especially Waller's essay "Freedom, Fate and Sin in Donald MacKinnon's Use of Tragedy," 101–18).

Egypt to sprinkle the blood of the Passover lambs on the doors of the Israelites' homes to avoid death (Exod. 12:22).

"It Is Finished" (19:30a)

> 30a When Jesus had received the wine, he said, "It is finished."

"It is finished" is something that any dying person could say. But the verbs related to finishing, completing, and fulfilling also take up what Jesus has said about the completion of his mission. In "It is finished" (*tetelestai*) the "finishing" (*teleiōsas*) of "the work that you gave me to do" (17:4; see also 4:34) is being completed in the death of Jesus. What is completed is to be understood through the coming of Jesus, his whole story, his relationship with his Father and with "all things" (*panta* [1:3]), and his relationship with his followers by loving them "to the end" (*eis telos* [13:1]), which is now. So the horizon of these final words of Jesus is, as the author has just said, "Jesus knew that all [*panta*] was now finished [*tetelestai*]" (19:28). That verb is a passive, inviting the question, "Finished by whom?" The answer is clear: by Jesus. The whole Gospel has made him central and has led up to this "hour." Within this hour this moment of death is the most extreme, intensive moment of concentration. What happens in this unprecedented, culminating, unsurpassable moment?

Jesus Hands Over His Spirit / the Spirit (19:30b)

> 30b Then he bowed his head and gave up [*paredōken*] his spirit [*to pneuma*, "the spirit/Spirit"].

What happens is, simultaneously, the death of Jesus and a new beginning, the handing over of "the spirit/Spirit." Both have been prepared for since the opening chapter. Sometimes the death has been the main focus,[18] sometimes

18. Illuminating passages on the death of Jesus worth rereading at this point include the identification of the body of Jesus with the temple, and his death and resurrection with its destruction and rebuilding (2:13–22); the start of plotting to kill Jesus, followed by his discourse on judgment, death, resurrection, eternal life, the love of God, Scripture, and glory (chap. 5); the connection of the "lifting up" of the Son of Man and of overcoming death with his self-description as "I am" (8:28, 58); Jesus as the good shepherd who lays down his life for his sheep, with power to lay down and take up his life (10:11–18); the raising of Lazarus, with its messages about death and resurrection, its consequence of the decision to have him killed, and the unintended prophecy of Caiaphas "that Jesus was about to die for the nation, and not for the nation only, but to gather into one the dispersed children of God" (chap. 11); the anointing of the feet of Jesus by Mary in

the Spirit.[19] Most illuminating here are the passages in which both come together.

In John 1 John the Baptist announces Jesus as "the Lamb of God who takes away the sin of the world" and also as the one on whom the Spirit comes from heaven and remains/abides and who "baptizes with the Holy Spirit" (1:29, 32, 33). This is the first tying together of the Spirit with Jesus's death, through the physical imagery of a lamb dying and a dove descending and resting on him. Because of this abiding presence, therefore, everything to do with Jesus—mission, words, actions, relationships, identity as "I am," trial and death—is to be understood as, at the same time and inseparably, having to do with the Spirit on and in him.

In John 3 the exchange with Nicodemus draws on new imagery to interrelate the death of Jesus and the Spirit: on the death, the Son of Man being "lifted up" leads to eternal life for believers in him, all set in the context of God's love for the world and giving "his only Son" (3:16); on the Spirit, there is the need to "enter the kingdom of God" through being "born of water and Spirit" (3:5), and this Spirit is a wind that "blows where it chooses" (3:8). Then at the end of the chapter comes a headline statement about the Spirit: "He whom God has sent speaks the words of God, for he gives the Spirit without measure" (3:34). That connects the Spirit with the Father and with the person of Jesus, and also with the theme of abundance in the rest of the Gospel—abundance of life, light, truth, love, water, food. There is also a message about the significance and authority of the record of those "words of God" in John's Gospel (3:34).

In John 6 there is yet another way of interrelating the death of Jesus and the Spirit. Jesus says both that "the bread that I will give for the life of the world is my flesh" and that "it is the spirit [or "Spirit"] that gives life; the flesh is useless. The words that I have spoken to you are spirit [or "Spirit"] and life" (6:51, 63). The death of Jesus is his self-giving for the life of the world; but it is not the death itself that gives life, it is "the spirit/Spirit." And again there is a message about "the words that I have spoken," attaching the authority of the Spirit to the text that testifies through "the words."

---

anticipation of "my burial" (12:1–8); and the meaning of his death understood through a grain of wheat dying and bearing fruit and through the glorification of being "lifted up" and drawing "all people to myself" (12:20–36).

19. Illuminating passages on the Spirit worth rereading at this point include "From his fullness we have all received, grace upon grace" (1:16), which retrospectively must be understood through the giving of the Spirit; the meeting with the woman of Samaria, including the "living water" given by Jesus, "a spring of water gushing up to eternal life," the worship of the Father "in spirit and truth," and "God is spirit" (4:1–26); and passages on the symbolism of light that can be read in relation to the Spirit as the Spirit of truth (1:4–9; 3:19–21; 8:12; 12:36).

The passage perhaps most directly linked to the present one is in the following chapter: "On the last day of the festival, the great day, while Jesus was standing there, he cried out, 'Let anyone who is thirsty come to me, and let the one who believes in me drink. As the scripture has said, "Out of the believer's heart shall flow rivers of living water."' Now he said this about the Spirit, which believers in him were to receive; for as yet there was no Spirit, because Jesus was not yet glorified" (7:37–39). That combines thirst, the giving of the Spirit, and the death of Jesus.[20]

The culmination of teaching that prepares for this quiet event, in which Jesus simultaneously both dies and hands over the Spirit, comes in the Farewell Discourses. There the departure of Jesus in death and the promise of the Holy Spirit are inseparable, as already discussed in the commentary on John 13–17. Now, the Spirit of the crucified Jesus, bearing his life, truth, and love, and his relationships with his Father, with humanity, and with creation as summed up in his prayer in John 17, is handed over. To whom first?

Then he bowed his head and gave up his spirit. Many commentators have seen this as Jesus breathing the Spirit down on his mother and his Beloved Disciple at the foot of the cross. That rings true. Few mention the other two women with them, but that, too, rings true, especially in view of Mary Magdalene's role after the resurrection of Jesus and the possible role of the wife of Clopas (see comments on 19:25b).

But why stop there? The horizon that John has already opened up for what happens when Jesus is lifted up on the cross is of drawing "all people to myself" (12:32). The second giving of the Spirit, in 20:22, is to his disciples and is given with explicit directions. But here there is a more open, less defined giving of a less defined spirit/Spirit. Like the wind (*pneuma*, "breath") that "blows where it chooses" (3:8), there is a freedom in how the crucified Jesus

20. See comments on 7:37–39. Jesus crying out then is strikingly different from John's account of the death of Jesus, which, unlike the other Gospels, has no loud cries and no spectacular portents (such as the sun darkened or the veil of the temple torn). The dying of Jesus in John is quiet, unspectacular, and understated, without noise, and its most distinctive incident is an intimate communication with his mother and his Beloved Disciple. Jesus "cried with a loud voice" (11:43) at the tomb of his friend Lazarus; cries during his own crucifixion are not mentioned. Likewise, John's two accounts of the Spirit being given, here in 19:30 and later in 20:22, are quiet. The first need not even be read as a giving of the Spirit, and translators differ over "his spirit" versus "the Spirit." Unlike the Synoptics and Acts, John noticeably avoids the association of the Holy Spirit with fire. Yet his surface quietness covers multiple depths that open up through the sort of rereading and intertextual reading that is being done here. John's account of the Spirit and of the death of Jesus could be designed to complement that of the Synoptics and Acts, emphasizing the ongoing quiet drama of abiding, praying, learning, and loving, as suggested by his final portrayal in John 21 of the Beloved Disciple, who might well "remain/abide until I come" (21:22–23), hidden in home life with the mother of Jesus.

relates to people, not only among but also beyond his followers.[21] *There is here a hint of quiet, unspectacular, anonymous relating, as invisible as breath, but also as vital. It may even be that this mostly hidden spread of the Spirit of the crucified Jesus is primary, pervasive, as embracing and as available as the air we breathe from the atmosphere encompassing the earth, and able to cross boundaries and inspire people, groups, traditions, communities, nations, and movements in repeatedly surprising ways.*

In what immediately follows there is a suggestion of that freedom of the Spirit to spring surprises through unlikely people, in unlikely places, and in unexpected forms: One of those at the foot of the cross, as Jesus breathes out the Spirit, is the Roman soldier who has just crucified Jesus, has gambled for his tunic, and is soon to pierce his side. That action is given extraordinary weight. Might he too have received the Spirit?[22]

But the final comment on the death of Jesus should return to the obvious plain sense of the text, having explored some of its deeper meaning. Just as the last words of Jesus, "It is finished" (19:30a), could have been said by any dying person, so the last action of Jesus, he "gave up his spirit," is that of every dying person: Jesus stopped breathing and died.

The Pierced Side: Blood and Water, No Bones Broken, Eyewitness Testimony (19:31–37)

> [31] Since it was the day of Preparation, the Jews did not want the bodies left on the cross during the sabbath, especially because that sabbath was a day of great solemnity. So they asked Pilate to have the legs of the crucified men broken and the bodies removed. [32] Then the soldiers came and broke the legs of the first and of the other who had been crucified with him. [33] But when they came to Jesus and saw that he was already dead, they did not break his legs. [34] Instead, one of the soldiers pierced his side with a spear, and at once blood and water came out. [35] (He who saw this has testified so that you also may believe. His testimony is true, and he knows that he tells the truth.) [36] These things occurred so that the scripture might be fulfilled, "None of

21. There are recurrent efforts in Christian theology and by Christian churches to define the action of the Holy Spirit and to draw clear boundaries around what and who can be authentically identified as inspired by the Spirit of God or the Spirit of Jesus. Throughout this commentary I have read John as resistant to such efforts at human control: the edge of this wind cannot be seen, the Spirit given "without measure" overflows all our containers, and there are continual surprises. The focus of John is on who is central, not on any boundaries around the light, life, love, and free presence of Jesus in the Spirit.

22. In Luke there is an analogy in the Roman centurion at the cross: "When the centurion saw what had taken place, he praised God and said, 'Certainly this man was innocent'" (Luke 23:47).

his bones shall be broken." [37] And again another passage of scripture says, "They will look on the one whom they have pierced."

Since it was the day of Preparation . . . that sabbath was a day of great solemnity. We are reminded yet again of the special Passover time. This is later reinforced by quoting **"None of his bones shall be broken,"** which connects with both Exodus 12:46 (parallel to Num. 9:12) about not breaking the bones of the Passover lamb and with Psalm 34:20, a psalm of deliverance.

The soldiers **came to Jesus and saw that he was already dead.** The basic message, supported by the testimony to him giving up his spirit and to the piercing of his side, is that *Jesus really died.* John's emphasis on Jesus in union with his Father and giving eternal life could easily lead to thinking that he could not die. But John is just as emphatic that Jesus is mortal flesh. Jesus is a new, unprecedented reality: God's free self-expression and self-giving in this particular mortal person. It leads to rethinking both God and humanity, but not to denying either the divinity or the mortal humanity of Jesus. Christian theology was to wrestle for hundreds of years to find ways of expressing this adequately, and John's Gospel was the main biblical shaper of its thinking. The reality of the death of Jesus was nonnegotiable for the mainstream church.

So, the plain first sense of the testimony that **one of the soldiers pierced his side with a spear, and at once blood and water came out** is that Jesus really was dead.

But the plain sense in John often goes with levels of meaning—what I have called the deep plain sense. This has already been seen in the description of the actual death of Jesus, in which the phrase "gave up his spirit / the Spirit" (19:30) can simply mean "expired, died," and also much more. So, besides confirming death, what might it mean that "at once blood and water came out"? The remarkable highlighting of this event in the following verses invites further reflection on it, and commentaries are full of suggestions. They converge on three main complementary interpretations to do with life and death, with baptism and Eucharist, and (the least recognized by commentators) with the temple.

First, and most important, both blood and water mean life. The death of Jesus—indeed, the person of Jesus, represented in death by his body—is a source of life, and this event is testimony to that. How is this life received? It is through faith in, trust in, belief in Jesus, incarnate, crucified, and risen; and his death is essential to who he is. The purpose of witnessing to this event of the piercing of his dead body, the next verse says to readers, is "so that you also may believe." The summary of the whole Gospel's purpose in 20:31 repeats this and adds "and that through believing you may have life in his name." The rest of John's Gospel gives clear pointers to what is meant by blood and water separately, converging on the person of Jesus giving eternal life. On blood, the key passage to reread is John 6, especially verses 53–56: "So Jesus said to them, 'Very truly, I tell you, unless you eat the flesh of the Son of Man and drink his blood, you will have no life in you. Those who eat my flesh and drink my blood have eternal life, and I will raise them up on the last day; for my flesh is true food and my blood is true drink. Those who eat my flesh and drink my blood abide in me, and I in them.'" On water, key passages include those just mentioned: 3:5–16, connecting water, the Spirit, birth, the love of God, and eternal life; 4:7–15, connecting "living water" with thirst and eternal life; and 7:37–39, connecting thirst, believing, "living water," the Spirit, and Jesus being glorified.

Second, there are strong associations with baptism (water) and Eucharist / Holy Communion / Lord's Supper (blood), signifying both the beginning and the sustaining of new life in Jesus. Together, these are fundamental to the identity and life of a majority of the world's Christians, and the piercing powerfully connects baptism and Eucharist with each other and with the death of Jesus. A convincing further association of the blood is with martyrdom.

Third, blood and water come together in the temple. Blood is strongly associated with the temple and its sacrifices throughout the Old Testament / Hebrew Bible, and John has Jesus dying as the Passover lambs are being killed in the temple and their blood sprinkled. This Gospel's first mention of the body of Jesus in relation to his death and resurrection compares it to the destruction and rebuilding of the temple and says that "he was speaking of the temple of his body" (2:21). The promise by Jesus to the Samaritan woman of "a spring of water gushing up to eternal life" leads into Jesus looking to a coming "hour" when worship will not be centered on the temple, and this is associated with himself as the Messiah (4:7–26). The climactic water cry in 7:37–39 takes place in the temple on "the great day"[23] of the water-related Festival of Booths, and the commentary on that has linked it with the vision of water flowing from the temple in Ezekiel 47:1–12.[24] That passage is again relevant here. So, here blood and water flow from the body that has been identified with the temple the place most closely identified with the presence of God.

There is more to this. Jesus also called the temple "my Father's house" (*ton oikon tou patros mou* [2:16]). In his Farewell Discourses he said, "In my Father's house [*en tē oikia tou patros mou*] there are many dwelling places" (14:2),[25] and

23. The same Greek words have just been used in 19:31, there translated as "day of great solemnity."

24. See comments on 7:25–52.

25. In this phrase the word for house, *oikia*, overlaps in meaning with *oikos* in 2:16 but implies more emphasis on the house with the people in it, as in "household."

the theme of dwelling/abiding in John 13–17 involves the mutual indwelling of Jesus and believers, the indwelling of the Spirit, those who trust Jesus abiding in his love, the word of Jesus abiding in those who trust him, and, in John 17, the ultimate loving union of God, Jesus, and the community of faith. So the main emphasis has moved from the temple building in John 2 to the family household of people in John 14, and then to a vision of "the summit of love" in John 17.[26] At the cross, Jesus has already formed a new household of his mother and the disciple he loved.[27] Now that is set alongside a vivid image of the life-giving body of Jesus. The new household and the life-giving flow of blood[28] and water have united the imagery of family and beyond family, temple and beyond temple.

(He who saw this has testified so that you also may believe. His testimony is true, and he knows that he tells the truth.) "He who saw this" could be either the soldier who pierced the side of Jesus or the Beloved Disciple, to whom the testimony of the whole Gospel is attributed in similar terms in 21:24. With most commentators, I favor the Beloved Disciple; but, either way, there is an insistence on the vital importance of both eyewitness testimony and believing it. There is also an insistence on the testimony being true, on the witness knowing the truth. Truth embraces both eyewitness testimony and what is believed. It is about going deeper than facts and moving beyond describing the surface of events that have been seen. In John, it is above all about learning who Jesus is and endlessly receiving from his "fullness" (1:16). In this incident, the reader is drawn through description into truth by being connected with deep meanings of temple, Passover, slaughtered lambs, blood, water, and the body of the dead Jesus, and then with texts of Scripture.

What is it that this eyewitness (understood as the Beloved Disciple) has seen in the piercing that he wants the readers to believe? The answer is, as throughout the Gospel, who Jesus is. But, specifically in relation to this incident, it is illuminating to hear afresh an earlier cry and a summary statement about the death of Jesus.

The cry is that of John the Baptist: "Here is the Lamb of God who takes away the sin of the world" (1:29). In this Gospel the core sin is unbelief, lack of the

26. See comments on John 17, esp. on vv. 20–26.

27. Mary Coloe sums up the development: "The personalising of the temple, begun in the transfer of temple imagery to Jesus, then continued with the promise of the divine indwellings in the community of believers constituting them as 'my Father's Household,' is completed in this scene." "The Nazarene King," 847.

28. The first reference to blood, in 1:12–13, also refers to a new family beyond the bloodline of ordinary family: "But to all who received him, who believed in his name, he gave power to become children of God, who were born, not of blood or of the will of the flesh or of the will of man, but of God."

sort of trust and faith in Jesus that make mutual love possible. To believe is to have this sin taken away.

The summary statement is John 3:14–16, about receiving eternal life through believing in the Son of Man "lifted up," and this being due to the love of God giving his only Son. The pouring out of blood and water is the last thing that happens while Jesus is lifted up on the cross, and it can be seen as the self-emptying love of God, pouring out life, and inviting those drawn to him into trust, thanks, and love in response.

They will look on the one whom they have pierced vividly frames the dead Jesus in a prophecy from Zechariah about the death of the good shepherd: "And I will pour out a spirit of compassion and supplication on the house of David and the inhabitants of Jerusalem, so that, when they look on the one whom they have pierced, they shall mourn for him, as one mourns for an only child [LXX *agapētos*, "beloved"] and weep bitterly over him, as one weeps over a first-born. . . . On that day a fountain shall be opened for the house of David and the inhabitants of Jerusalem, to cleanse them from sin and impurity" (Zech. 12:10; 13:1).[29] Around the piercing, that passage weaves together a beloved person, his death, his family, his nation, and a flow of water that takes away sin.

A Royal Burial (19:38–42)

> 38 After these things, Joseph of Arimathea, who was a disciple of Jesus,
> though a secret one because of his fear of the Jews, asked Pilate to let him
> take away the body of Jesus. Pilate gave him permission; so he came and
> removed his body. 39 Nicodemus, who had at first come to Jesus by night,
> also came, bringing a mixture of myrrh and aloes, weighing about a hundred
> pounds. 40 They took the body of Jesus and wrapped it with the spices in
> linen cloths, according to the burial custom of the Jews. 41 Now there was
> a garden in the place where he was crucified, and in the garden there was a
> new tomb in which no one had ever been laid. 42 And so, because it was the
> Jewish day of Preparation, and the tomb was nearby, they laid Jesus there.

This is a proper Jewish burial, **according to the burial custom of the Jews**, but it is also unusual in the vast quantity of **myrrh and aloes, weighing about a hundred pounds**—a hundred times more than what Mary had used in 12:3. This, together with the tomb being in a **garden**, as royal tombs often were, and

29. Zechariah 9–14 acts as an echo chamber for the accounts of the passion and death of Jesus in all four Gospels, beginning with the king entering Jerusalem on a donkey (Zech. 9:9). John has intensified Zechariah's themes of kingship, shepherd, glory, living water, and the Festival of Booths.

besides being a further example of the theme of abundance, is also the final reference to the kingship theme that has been so important during and after the trial of Jesus. Commentators have found other symbolic meanings in the spices, the cloths, the garden, and the fact that it was **a new tomb**, and there has been much discussion of sources and differences in detail between John and the Synoptics. All four agree on the initiative of **Joseph of Arimathea** and the fact of burial.

John's distinctive emphasis is on Joseph as **a disciple of Jesus, though a secret one because of his fear of the Jews** and on the participation of **Nicodemus, who had at first come to Jesus by night.** It is as if the circle of those drawn to Jesus in his death is widening, now attracting those who have been fearful or undecided in the past. In going to Pilate, Joseph "comes out" as a follower of Jesus. In accompanying Joseph and contributing so generously, Nicodemus too seems to be openly committing himself. His last words to Jesus in his first conversation were an open question, "How can these things be?" (3:9). Later, when he intervened to demand a legal hearing for Jesus from the authorities, he was described as being "one of them" (7:50). But now he commits himself visibly through a most expensive donation of spices and joint action with Joseph. Readers are encouraged by the backward reference to reread his first encounter with Jesus, with its themes of kingdom of God, birth, spirit/Spirit, water, testimony, lifting up, love, eternal life, salvation, judgment, and believing. What he is doing seems to be presented here as a good deed, fitting the final statement about "those who believe in him" (3:18) in that discourse of Jesus: "But those who do what is true come to the light, so that it may be clearly seen that their deeds have been done in God" (3:21).

John's final sentence before the resurrection is yet another reminder of the Passover setting, as Jerusalem gets ready for its most important feast by killing the Passover lambs: **It was the Jewish day of Preparation**.

John 20:1–31

"Mary!"—The Free, Surprising Presence of the Crucified and Risen Jesus

At the end of John 19 the body of the dead Jesus was laid in the tomb. Now, "early on the first day of the week" (v. 1), the third day after the crucifixion, Mary Magdalene discovers that the stone sealing the tomb has been removed. This is the beginning of the first of four carefully crafted scenes dense with meaning.

In the first scene, Mary runs and tells Simon Peter and the Beloved Disciple that the body of Jesus has been taken from the tomb. They run to the tomb and find the body gone but the linen wrappings still there and the headcloth rolled up in a place by itself. The Beloved Disciple "saw and believed" (v. 8). What did he believe? What is the significance of this in a chapter in which seeing and believing are fundamental? And how does it relate to what follows: "For as yet they did not understand the scripture, that he must rise from the dead" (v. 9)?

Next, in the second scene, Mary, who is weeping outside the tomb, looks into it, sees two angels, and tells them that "my Lord" has been taken (v. 13). She turns, and there is a deeply moving recognition scene. Her passionate search for him is met by the risen Jesus calling her by name, "Mary!" and her responding, "Rabbouni!" (v. 16). Then come the mysterious, much-discussed words of Jesus, "Do not hold on to me, because I have not yet ascended to the Father" (v. 17). And he sends her to the other disciples, called for the first time "my brothers," with the message that he is "ascending to my Father and your Father, to my God and your God" (v. 17). So Jesus affirms his followers as children of God, embracing them within his own family relationship to God as Father. She goes and announces, "I have seen the Lord" (v. 18).

The third scene is pivotal for the chapter. Mary's message to the disciples prepares for it; the fourth scene, with Thomas, arises from it. This third scene takes place on the evening of the same day, as the disciples are gathered in fear behind locked doors, and "Jesus came and stood among them" (v. 19). The previous one-to-one scene with Mary Magdalene has meant that the disciples have already heard her message. Now the risen Jesus himself not only confirms her news ("I have seen the Lord" [v. 18]), this time with the added confirmation that he is the crucified Jesus ("He showed them his hands and his side" [v. 20]); he also fulfills key promises of the Farewell Discourses: of peace (twice saying "Peace be with you" [vv. 19, 21]),[1] of joy ("The disciples rejoiced when they saw the Lord" [v. 20]),[2] of sending into the ongoing drama ("As the Father has sent me, so I send you" [v. 21]),[3] and of the Holy Spirit ("Receive the Holy Spirit" [v. 22]).[4] And there is the authority to forgive. *The family community now shares in Jesus's peace, joy, life breath, and authority to forgive, in order to follow a way of living and a mission in line with his.*

In the fourth scene, Thomas refuses to believe that the others have "seen the Lord" (v. 25) unless he can see and touch the signs of crucifixion and death in the body of Jesus. A week later, he gets the chance when he and the others are gathered and again "Jesus came and stood among them and said, 'Peace be with you'" (v. 26). Jesus tells him to use finger, eyes, and hand, and invites him, "Do not doubt but believe" (v. 27). Thomas's response goes far beyond anything that can be touched or seen: "My Lord and my God!" (v. 28). *This is the ultimate theological affirmation of the Gospel.* Jesus's response blesses readers who accept his invitation to believe and trust, as Thomas has been invited, but who, unlike Thomas, are not among the original eyewitnesses: "Blessed are those who have not seen and yet have come to believe/trust" (v. 29).

Then readers are addressed directly. This Gospel is only a selection of the signs that Jesus did "in the presence of his disciples" (v. 30). The purpose in writing is "that you may come to believe" who Jesus is, "the Messiah, the Son of God, and that through believing you may have life in his name" (v. 31).

1. Cf. 14:27; 16:33.
2. Cf. 15:11; 16:19–22.
3. Cf. 17:18.
4. Cf. 14:16–17, 26; 15:26; 16:7, 12–15.

Stone Removed, Body Gone, Headcloth Folded: Seeing, Believing, Not Understanding (20:1–10)

> 1 Early on the first day of the week, while it was still dark, Mary Magdalene
> came to the tomb and saw that the stone had been removed from the tomb.
> 2 So she ran and went to Simon Peter and the other disciple, the one whom
> Jesus loved, and said to them, "They have taken the Lord out of the tomb,
> and we do not know where they have laid him." 3 Then Peter and the other
> disciple set out and went toward the tomb. 4 The two were running together,
> but the other disciple outran Peter and reached the tomb first. 5 He bent
> down to look in and saw the linen wrappings lying there, but he did not go
> in. 6 Then Simon Peter came, following him, and went into the tomb. He
> saw the linen wrappings lying there, 7 and the cloth that had been on Jesus'
> head, not lying with the linen wrappings but rolled up in a place by itself.
> 8 Then the other disciple, who reached the tomb first, also went in, and he
> saw and believed; 9 for as yet they did not understand the scripture, that
> he must rise from the dead. 10 Then the disciples returned to their homes.

There is complete silence about the time (including what the church came to call Holy Saturday) between the burial of Jesus and the discovery of the empty tomb. The last word in the Greek text of John 19 is "Jesus." Now John 20 has a series of material signs and, accompanying them, the progressive discovery and realization of the meaning of what turns out to be a God-sized event centered on Jesus. *His person, who he is,* embraces both discontinuity (real death and burial; and a transformation of his body that is not the result of resuscitation and that allows him to be freely present while also harder to recognize) and continuity (signified by recognition of his voice and of the marks of the nails and the spear in his body). *There is testimony to a new reality: Jesus dead becomes Jesus risen from the dead, who is identified with God—"My Lord and my God!"*

Testimonies to the resurrection in the Gospels might be heard as stuttering in amazement at this unique, God-sized event. *Accounts differ in details* (and there is no consensus among scholars about how to understand their interrelationships) *but converge on two essentials: the empty tomb and encounters with the risen Jesus.* John's first two scenes, in 20:1–10 and 20:11–18, affirm each essential in succession.

The first material sign is the stone removed from the tomb, which Mary Magdalene, **while it was still dark**, misunderstands as unknown people (**they**) having **taken the Lord out of the tomb** to somewhere else. So her initial response is to think of graverobbers.

Simon Peter and the other disciple, the one whom Jesus loved, respond to her message by running to the tomb and seeing the second material sign: the **linen wrappings lying there** and **the cloth that had been on Jesus' head . . . rolled up in a place by itself**. The Beloved Disciple leaps to a conclusion: **he saw and believed**. An obvious reason for him coming to a different conclusion than Mary's is that graverobbers would hardly have gone to the trouble of unwrapping the body and rolling up the headcloth. Looking back to John 11, we see also the contrast with what followed the raising of Lazarus: "The dead man came out, his hands and feet bound with strips of cloth, and his face wrapped in a cloth. Jesus said to them, 'Unbind him, and let him go'" (11:44). The difference hints that what has happened here is not, as with Lazarus, a resuscitation, but something else.

What did the Beloved Disciple believe? One answer is that the body of Jesus was indeed gone—he believed that part of Mary's message. That is true, and by no means trivial. To take in the fact that not only was he bereaved of Jesus but also that the body of Jesus was gone was a considerable challenge. The absence of a body is an anguish that relatives of "the disappeared" in many situations know too well, and coming to terms with it is very hard.

Yet the absolute "believed" carries more weight than that, and here the Beloved Disciple is being differentiated from Peter, who has seen the same things. The Beloved Disciple's believing (like that of Thomas later) is more than taking in what he has seen. He is the first to believe after the resurrection, which is the first time that full believing in Jesus is possible. What he is doing is what Jesus blesses in his exchange with Thomas: "Blessed are those who have not seen and yet have come to believe" (20:29). He has not yet seen the risen Jesus, yet he believes. Such a dawn of believing in a questioning mind is described by the poet R. S. Thomas (see Thomas's poem in the sidebar).

But what is the content of a believing that goes beyond seeing that the body was gone? It seems to be something decisively important. Yet, in view of the next verse, **for as yet they did not understand the scripture, that he must rise from the dead**, it does not seem to be resurrection from the dead.[5] It probably is believing that Jesus, as he had said he would, has returned to his Father. The Beloved Disciple has believed that Jesus is not held by death but is with his Father. He, with Peter and the other disciples, will "understand the scripture" when they meet the risen Jesus. The return to his Father ("I am ascending to

5. Of the several texts that this could refer to, the one that most commentators agree on (partly because it is also used twice in relation to the resurrection of Jesus by Luke in Acts 2:24–28 and 13:35) is Psalm 16:10–11: "For you do not give me up to Sheol, or let your faithful one see the Pit. You show me the path of life, in your presence there is fullness of joy; in your right hand are pleasures forevermore."

Excerpt from "The Answer"

There have been times
when, after long on my knees
in a cold chancel, a stone has rolled
from my mind, and I have looked
in and seen the old questions lie
folded and in a place
by themselves, like the piled
graveclothes of love's risen body.[a]

—R. S. Thomas, *Collected Poems: 1945–1990*, 359

a. Thomas Gardner comments on this poem, "John called this belief—that moment of recognition, below the level of words, when the looming questions, as familiar and nearby as one's own body, simply dissolve and are replaced with what we can only call life, or love. . . . The mystery of the body has not been solved, the problem still remains, but its death-like grip has been set aside, replaced with life and breathing. Thoughts come later. This is as precise an account of the way belief occurs as I know" (*John in the Company of the Poets*, 181–82).

my Father" [20:17]) will not happen without surprising, far-reaching encounters which mean he is risen from the dead and can be met.

So, believing because of the signs of the empty tomb and the graveclothes is, for the Beloved Disciple, the beginning of a new understanding, which will later combine with meeting Jesus and rereading Scripture. *It is the sort of understanding that has shaped this whole Gospel, in which testimony to Jesus is deepened by multiple intertexts that lead into further truth, and readers are invited to share in the process.*

"I Have Seen the Lord!" Mary Meets Jesus and Is Sent (20:11–18)

> [11] But Mary stood weeping outside the tomb. As she wept, she bent over to
> look into the tomb; [12] and she saw two angels in white, sitting where the body
> of Jesus had been lying, one at the head and the other at the feet. [13] They
> said to her, "Woman, why are you weeping?" She said to them, "They have
> taken away my Lord, and I do not know where they have laid him." [14] When
> she had said this, she turned around and saw Jesus standing there, but she
> did not know that it was Jesus. [15] Jesus said to her, "Woman, why are you
> weeping? Whom are you looking for?" Supposing him to be the gardener,
> she said to him, "Sir, if you have carried him away, tell me where you have

> laid him, and I will take him away." 16 Jesus said to her, "Mary!" She turned and said to him in Hebrew, "Rabbouni!" (which means Teacher). 17 Jesus said to her, "Do not hold on to me, because I have not yet ascended to the Father. But go to my brothers and say to them, 'I am ascending to my Father and your Father, to my God and your God.'" 18 Mary Magdalene went and announced to the disciples, "I have seen the Lord"; and she told them that he had said these things to her.

Mary seems traumatized and distracted by grief. She has seen Jesus nailed to the cross and dead. Now there is the further shock of his missing body. She repeats her agonized cry of loss again and again—to the disciples, to the angels, to Jesus. She weeps, as Jesus had wept at the tomb of Lazarus. It is sustained **weeping**, interrupted only by giving the reason for it to the two angels and to Jesus, whom she supposes to be the gardener. She hardly seems to register the significance of the angels[6] and turns away from them without waiting for an answer. She seems already to have turned away from Jesus before he speaks her name. That is the decisive turning point. The good shepherd calls her by name. As Jesus had "cried with a loud voice, 'Lazarus, come out!'" (11:43), here he quietly **said to her, "Mary!"**[7] She is freed from distraction and centered on him: **She turned and said to him in Hebrew, "Rabbouni!" (which means Teacher).**

She had seen him and not recognized him—**she did not know that it was Jesus**. Then she heard his word, turned to him, and responded. She had been calling him "the Lord" (v. 2) and "my Lord" (v. 13), and later she tells the other disciples, "I have seen the Lord" (v. 18). But now her response to his word to her, to her name, is to call him "Teacher." This is the **Lord** who has been seen and mistaken for **the gardener**, but then heard and recognized as the **Teacher**. Just as the Beloved Disciple's seeing and believing would need Scripture to understand the resurrection, so Mary's seeing needs the word of Jesus to understand who he is—and who she is.

Some commentators see "Teacher" as a lesser title than "Lord," or than Thomas's "my God," and suggest that when Jesus says, "Do not hold on to me," he is distancing himself from Mary treating him only as a human teacher.

6. What is their significance? For readers, they suggest something surprising and beyond the ordinary, pointing to an event that carries a message from God. It has also been suggested that the two angels **sitting where the body of Jesus had been lying, one at the head and the other at the feet** are a reminder of the cherubim in the holy of holies in the tent of meeting and later in the temple (see Exod. 25:17–22; 37:6–9; 2 Chron. 3:10–14; 5:7–10; Pss. 80:1; 99:1). The invisible presence of God in the holy of holies is represented by the empty space between the cherubim, as the risen body of Jesus is indicated by the space between these angels.

7. Here Jesus is both himself and identified with Lazarus as the one who had been buried, intensifying both the parallel and the contrast of the two.

That sort of distinction and hierarchy of titles does not ring true: "Teacher" and "Lord" are completely at one.[8] I will come soon to the meaning of not holding on to him, but for now "Teacher" needs to be understood in relation to what has come earlier in this Gospel.

Rereading John 1 is especially illuminating. In the prologue, Jesus as one who teaches, communicating understanding and truth, is emphasized from the start in the title "Word." This Word is set within a horizon of God and all reality, is "the light of all people," "enlightens everyone," and "became flesh," embodying "grace and truth" (1:4, 9, 14). Especially important for this meeting with Mary, and for the whole of John 20, is the culmination of the prologue: "No one has ever seen God. It is God the only Son, who is close to the Father's heart, who has made him known" (1:18).[9]

Mary has been passionately searching for the body of Jesus, pursuing her anguished question of **where** it is (vv. 2, 13, 15). In doing this she is being a model disciple, a learner who is being taught by Jesus the ultimate answer to where he is "located," in line with the prologue's "in the beginning with God" and its ending, "close to the Father's heart," and with his final prayer, "But now I am coming to you" (17:13). He teaches her, and through her the rest of his family: **"I am ascending to my Father and your Father, to my God and your God."** *It is a "place" of permanent relationship with God and with others in love.*

Mary's meeting with Jesus has key elements of his encounter with his first disciples in 1:35–42: hearing, turning, seeing, Jesus as Teacher, the "where" question, brothers, naming, finding Jesus. But there are two significant differences.

The first words of Jesus (his first in the Gospel) to those disciples are a question: "What are you looking for?" (1:38). To Mary he says, **"Whom are you looking for?"**[10] This "who" question has been central to the whole Gospel. *Mary had been looking for a dead "what"; she is questioned and surprised by a living "who."*

Second, the first words of the disciples in response are a "where" question: "Rabbi . . . , where are you staying?" to which Jesus replies, "Come and see," and, at about four o'clock in the afternoon, he takes them for the rest of the day to where he is staying (1:38–39). The answer to Mary's "where" question, that Jesus is ascending to his Father, transcends any temporary earthly location and is centered on the answer to the "who" question: the risen Jesus in his relationships. *This is a "place" from which he can freely relate to all places, all times, and all people.*

8. Cf. 13:13.

9. Cf. the NRSV's rendering of *ho ōn eis ton kolpon tou patros*, "who is close to the Father's heart," with John McHugh's translation: "who is now returned into the bosom of the Father" (*John 1–4*, 49).

10. This is also his repeated question at his arrest (18:4, 7). See note 3 in the comments on 18:1–12.

This encounter of Mary with Jesus brings readers back not only to the beginning of this Gospel but also (as do the Gospel's opening words) to the beginning of the Bible. Here again are a man and a woman in a garden. Further hints are given. The supposed "gardener" here recalls Adam being given "the garden of Eden to till it and keep it," and Adam calls his wife "Woman," and names her (Gen. 2:15, 23; 3:20). There is a sending out from this garden too, not into enmity, pain, hard labor, and death (Gen. 3:14–24), but with a message of life in a new family. Commentators down through the centuries have found many other resonances with the early chapters of Genesis, here and throughout John's last two chapters, and some will be noted as we come to them. The basic message is to read and reread the two texts together and to conceive of the resurrection of Jesus as a new creation, a fresh start for life and relationships—not least with the earth and everything else that figures in the creation accounts of Genesis.

As often in John, there are yet other intertextual dimensions, and here one has been of particular interest, Song of Songs. There, too, are a man and a woman in a deep relationship of mutual belonging, the voice and sight of the beloved are crucial, there is much passionate searching, there is abundant garden imagery, and the trust is that "love is strong as death" (Song 8:6). John gives no support to later nonbiblical traditions about Mary Magdalene as a former prostitute in an amorous relationship with Jesus, but he does shape an account of the two that resonates with Genesis, with Song of Songs, and also with the covenantal bonding of God and Israel that is often compared to a marriage.[11]

In the light of all this, what about Jesus's words, **"Do not hold on to me** [*mē mou haptou*] **because I have not yet ascended to the Father"**?[12] There is for Mary *a new form of relationship with Jesus,* no longer based on physical contact and seeing him in the flesh. Instead, there will be an ongoing, permanent relationship with him in his relationship with his Father. The message she is given to deliver **to my brothers** (the first time they have been called this) is the best possible news for them, for her, and for anyone else who trusts it: **"I am ascending to my Father and your Father, to my God and your God."** This is a further "lifting up" of Jesus, beyond the crucifixion and resurrection. The Farewell Discourses culminated with a glimpse inside this relationship, and opened up a complete sharing of its glory and its intimacy: "The glory that you have given me I have given them, so that they may be one, as we are one, I in them and you in me, that they may become completely one, so that the world

11. For a discerning account of Mary Magdalene and the resurrection, including discussion of the later traditions about her, see Lee, *Flesh and Glory*, 220–32.

12. For a survey of scholarly translations and interpretations of these words and of the whole meeting of Jesus with Mary Magdalene, see Bieringer, "'I Am Ascending to My Father and Your Father.'"

may know that you have sent me and have loved them even as you have loved me"; ". . . so that the love with which you have loved me may be in them, and I in them" (17:22–23, 26). So the negative "Do not hold on to me"[13] is a prelude to the greater, fuller intimacy of mutual indwelling in love. The "who to who" of "Mary!" to "Rabbouni!" can be uninterrupted, abiding. Likewise for the reader.

Further, *it comes with a new family*. The answer to Mary's repeated "where" question is not only that Jesus is with his Father in heaven (perhaps best understood as the eternal sphere of God's immediate, transcendent presence, where the desire of Jesus in 17:24 is fulfilled), but also that both he and his Father are present in a mutual indwelling relationship with those who trust and love them. The "your" in "your Father . . . your God" is plural, meaning the new family. It can embrace the reader too.

Even further, *it comes with a new purpose in ongoing history*. Mary is the first apostle, sent to announce the good news: **"Go . . . say . . ." . . . Mary Magdalene went and announced to the disciples . . . ; and she told them that he had said these things to her;** They hear not only the words of Jesus but also her personal testimony, **"I have seen the Lord."** The theme of seeing and its meaning for readers will reach its climax when Thomas meets Jesus a week later. But first comes a decisive, generative community event that will show a further dimension of why "Do not hold on to me" is good news, in line with what Jesus said in the Farewell Discourses: "I tell you the truth: it is to your advantage that I go away, for if I do not go away, the Advocate will not come to you" (16:7).

The Crucified Jesus among Them: Peace, Joy, Sending, the Holy Spirit, Forgiveness (20:19–23)

> [19] When it was evening on that day, the first day of the week, and the doors of the house where the disciples had met were locked for fear of the Jews, Jesus came and stood among them and said, "Peace be with you." [20] After he said this, he showed them his hands and his side. Then the disciples rejoiced when they saw the Lord. [21] Jesus said to them again, "Peace be with you. As the Father has sent me, so I send you." [22] When he had said this, he breathed on them and said to them, "Receive the Holy Spirit. [23] If you forgive the sins of any, they are forgiven them; if you retain the sins of any, they are retained."

13. The verb *haptein* is also sometimes used in the Septuagint in relation to not touching what is holy (e.g., Lev. 12:4; Num. 4:15), and this would reinforce the identification of Jesus in his death and resurrection with the temple (2:1–12). For a rich literary and theological feast centered on these words, see Cefalu, *The Johannine Renaissance*, chap. 2, "*Noli Me Tangere* and the Reception of Mary Magdalene in Early Modern England" (pp. 97–130).

This scene, central between two where the focus is one to one, Jesus with Mary Magdalene and later with Thomas, is the vital formative and transformative event for the family of **the disciples**. Who was present? The number and names are not given, but there is no suggestion that it was limited to members of the Twelve; and we later learn that at least one of those, Thomas, was not present.

The time is **evening on that day, the first day of the week**. Sunday was the day on which the first Christians used to gather to celebrate the Eucharist. Mary Coloe finds echoes of early Christian worship throughout John 20, concluding that "the household scene of John 20 opens out to the household gatherings of future believers, asking them to see the signs and believe."[14]

"Opening" is a good description of what Jesus does here. The disciples are locked in and afraid. Jesus opens them up to himself, crucified and risen, and to his peace and joy in place of fear. He opens them out toward the future and toward the whole world by sending them as he was sent. He opens his mouth to speak and to breathe into them as God breathed life into Adam (Gen. 2:7), and to share **the Holy Spirit**. He gives authority to open up the past to a new future through forgiveness. And there is no closure to the scene, no departure of Jesus.[15]

Jesus brings a double "peace." His first greeting, **"Peace be with you,"** meets the disciples' **fear of the Jews**. The fear of enemies and threats rings true not only with the situation of the disciples immediately after the execution of Jesus,[16] and with the situation of John's community after painfully breaking with the synagogue, but also with one situation after another down through the centuries and around the world today.[17]

How does Jesus deal with their fear? **He showed them his hands and his side.** These are the signs of a peace that can cope with fear. Suffering and death do not have the last word. *Whatever the fear, even if it is of people or events that really can cause suffering and death, there is a peace that is greater.* "Peace I leave with you; my peace I give to you. I do not give to you as the world gives. Do not let your hearts be troubled, and do not let them be afraid" (14:27). Now, that peace is embodied in Jesus, crucified and risen, it is freely given as a blessing

14. Coloe, *Dwelling in the Household of God*, 188.

15. The resurrection account in Luke, which is the nearest to John's, explicitly makes opening a theme: "Their eyes were opened" (24:31); "while he was opening the scriptures to us" (24:32); "Then he opened their minds to understand the scriptures" (24:45).

16. They may have had their fear increased by the news that Mary had seen the Lord but that she had first suspected graverobbers—his disciples were the obvious suspects.

17. Alongside the persecution of Christians, there has also been the terrible history of the persecution of Jews by Christians and many others. In many places and times Jews have been gathered behind locked doors for fear of Christians.

in greeting, and the Spirit, who rested on him and led him to the cross, is about to be shared with his disciples.

His presence, his blessing, and the sight of his hands and his side succeed in dealing with their grief as well as their fear: **Then the disciples rejoiced when they saw the Lord.** He had promised that "your pain will turn to joy" (16:20).

Then **Jesus said to them again, "Peace be with you."** He not only meets needs and helps to cope with negatives—fear, grief, doubt, sin, or other problems. *He also wants to shape the lives of individuals and communities (the "you" is plural), give deep meaning and purpose, open up vocations, inspire visions, and bring abundant life.* His presence and peace are a home from which to go out in witness, love, and service. What is desired is not only problem-solving but also a peace that has the marks of the Hebrew *shalom*: peace with God, with ourselves and our past, with other people, and with all creation—as in the prayer of Jesus for multifaceted unity in John 17.[18]

So Jesus gives his most comprehensive direction to his followers: **"As the Father has sent me, so I send you."** Using the "as . . . so . . ." form of some of his most important statements in this Gospel,[19] *this opens up a stupendous calling.* It echoes his prayer in 17:18, where being sent as he was sent was seen as receiving a vocation of life-giving love for the world.

On the one hand, this involves the elements seen in Jesus's own mission, such as being steeped in the Scriptures, forming a learning community, teaching, doing signs of abundant life for those beyond his immediate circle, face-to-face encounters, serving, praying, and being sent into darkness, conflict, suffering, and death.

On the other hand, the capacious "as . . . so . . ." invites ever-new discernment and improvisation in new situations. The "as" goes beyond exact repetition of words or actions into imaginative variation, creative analogy, daring innovation, and a capacity to surprise. Yet, without deepening appreciation of who Jesus is, and of what he said and did, the newness risks being shallow, inappropriate, unfruitful, or unfaithful. To ring true it needs to be inspired as Jesus was inspired. This is the essential: the Holy Spirit.

When he had said this, he breathed on them and said to them, "Receive the Holy Spirit."[20] This not only fulfills the promises made in the Farewell

18. The classic New Testament expression of this peace is in the Letter to the Ephesians, especially chap. 2, leading into the multifaceted unity of chap. 4 via the love-centered prayer in chap. 3.

19. See comments on 3:14; 10:11–21; 13:15, 31–35; 17:18; 20:21.

20. The Greek does not have "the," but simply *pneuma hagion*, which can be translated as "holy spirit." But there are no capital letters in the Greek manuscripts, and most commentators agree with the NRSV translation. "Spirit" is used both with and without "the" in 7:39, which looks forward to this event and also includes the same verb for "receive" (*lambanein*).

Discourses;[21] it also recalls other mentions of the Spirit (e.g., 1:32–33; 7:37–39) and in particular the wind/spirit imagery of 3:3–10, which also echoes the wind/spirit of God in Genesis 1:2.

In yet another echo of Genesis, the word for "breathed" is *enephysēsen*,[22] which is the same used in the Septuagint translation of Genesis 2:7: "Then the Lord God formed man [*anthrōpos*, "human being"] from the dust of the ground, and breathed [*enephysēsen*] into his nostrils the breath of life; and the man [*anthrōpos*] became a living being." This breath of Jesus is new life from God, echoing the prologue's echoes of Genesis and its association of the Word with life and light. *Here the breathing in of life is inseparable from words of peace, sending, receiving, and forgiveness*. The disciples receive the Spirit of the crucified and risen Jesus, infusing them with the reality of his life, death, and resurrection, inspiring them to be sent as he was sent. Perhaps most important, this is the Spirit of Jesus the Son who is "close to the Father's heart" (1:18), intimately in union with him. This intimacy is embodied now in face-to-face speaking and breathing.

Further, this is a gift to a community, and it recalls the same rare verb for "breathe" being used in Ezekiel's prophecy of life being given to dry bones: "Thus says the Lord God: Come from the four winds, O breath, and breathe upon these slain, that they may live" (Ezek. 37:9). That is a prophecy for "the whole house of Israel" (v. 11), and it goes on to say, "I will put my spirit within you, and you shall live" (v. 14). That prophecy follows one in the previous chapter promising the gift of "a new heart . . . a new spirit . . . my spirit," when "you shall be my people, and I will be your God" (36:26–28). It matches Jeremiah's prophecy of the gift of "a new covenant with the house of Israel" to be written on their hearts, and that concludes, as does this scene in John, with forgiveness: "For I will forgive their iniquity, and remember their sin no more" (Jer. 31:31, 34). Both Scriptures were favorites of New Testament authors, expressing *the experience of God-centered continuity with newness* that they found in Jesus's life, death, resurrection, and gift of the Holy Spirit.[23]

21. See 14:16–17, 26; 15:26; 16:13–15.

22. The verb could also be translated as "blew into," as one breathes into a wind instrument such as a flute.

23. The major New Testament intertext for the giving of the Holy Spirit is the account of the outpouring of the Holy Spirit at Pentecost in Acts 2. Some commentators see them as two separate events and explain their relationship in a variety of ways. A majority of modern commentators see them as two ways of witnessing to the one experience of the gift of the Spirit—John integrating it with the Farewell Discourses, crucifixion, resurrection, and ascension, all centered on Jesus; and Luke-Acts describing these in a linear sequence of events ending at Pentecost. In line with the account of the crucifixion as interpreted above, John's account of the giving of the Spirit is quiet, intimate, centered on who Jesus is and what he has done ("as . . . so . . ."), and enacts what has been promised in the Farewell Discourses. Acts is noisy, dramatic, and has an immediate public impact. Likewise, the main scriptural intertexts are different: John's with creation in Genesis and

"Receive" is a key verb, used forty-six times in John, often with reference to receiving Jesus himself or receiving from him (beginning in the prologue [1:12, 16]). Here it is as much an invitation as a command and assumes openness to receiving. Yet neither invitation nor command is quite adequate to this. They are already rejoicing, elated; they have received his double "Peace . . ." and a mission like that of Jesus, and now Jesus gives the ultimate gift. It is more like the announcement of news so good that it is bound to be welcome. So Frederick Dale Bruner translates, "Welcome the Holy Spirit!"[24]

The whole Gospel since the first chapter has prepared for this moment, which opens up a new future, centered on intimacy with Jesus and mission in community. It also enables a new relationship with the past: **"If you forgive the sins of any, they are forgiven them; if you retain the sins of any, they are retained."** The peace that Jesus brings requires facing the reality of sin. The Spirit is the *Holy* Spirit. If the desire of Jesus, for a community of peace, trust, unity, truth, and love (expressed above all in John 17) is to be fulfilled, forgiveness is crucial. Yet this is the first mention of forgiveness in this Gospel. Its introduction here has maximum impact, coming immediately after the disciples meet the risen Jesus, are sent on their mission, and receive the promised Holy Spirit. Forgiveness is clearly essential to their mission.

But, granted the vital importance of forgiveness, what does this verse mean? There are at least three key questions.

First, who are "you"? Obviously, they are the disciples gathered there, but are they to be seen as the whole community or just its leaders, understood as the Twelve? John does not make clear whether it is only members of the Twelve (who would, without Judas and Thomas, actually number ten) who are present, and above I have sided with those who are open to it being a wider group. So I agree with those who understand the authority to forgive sins being given to everyone in that community and to their successors in the later community. Yet this need not rule out a wide range of ways of structuring and using this authority in different communities, and John's vagueness allows for diverse interpretations.

Second, what sort of authority is given by "if you forgive the sins of any, they are forgiven them"? The awesomeness of authority to forgive sins is set

with the prophets Ezekiel, Jeremiah, and Isaiah; Luke's with the tower of Babel in Genesis and the prophet Joel. The contrast, and often tension, between the two (further complicated by the teaching of Paul, whose letters predate both) has continued down through the centuries in different Christian traditions and has been especially marked in the past century since the rise of the Pentecostal movement. I see John writing with awareness of both Pauline and Lukan streams, offering an account and theology that can affirm and deepen each of them by his emphases on the centrality of Jesus and his desire for unity in love expressed in John 17.

24. Bruner, *The Gospel of John*, 1164.

within the divine passive, "they are forgiven"—that is, forgiven by God, by Jesus. The relationship of divine action and human action has been an issue at many points in the Gospel, always setting human agency within the encompassing priority of God's.[25] *Authority in the name of Jesus is not autonomous but is responsible to him, and, like prayer in his name, is genuine only if it springs from the intimacy of mutual indwelling, from continuing his revolution in authority (as demonstrated in washing feet), and from being led into more and more truth—in short, from welcoming his Spirit.*

Third, what is the meaning of "if you retain the sins of any, they are retained"? There are two sharply differing translations of the Greek, *an tinōn kratēte kekratēntai.*

This NRSV rendering assumes that "the sins," which do not appear in the Greek, carry over from the first part of the sentence. This means that the granting of forgiveness in the first part is balanced by the withholding of forgiveness in the second.[26] That is in line with this Gospel's emphasis on judgment, on making a decision when faced with Jesus, and on the possibility of wrong decision. The core sin in John's Gospel is rejecting Jesus, failing to believe in and trust him; the corresponding positive requirement is, "This is the work of God, that you believe in him whom he has sent" (6:29). In this light, one aspect of what is meant by the forgiving and retaining of sins may be what happens at the threshold of the community of disciples when someone wants to enter it. That is a point at which the genuineness of faith in Jesus is acutely at issue. Who may and may not be part of the community? Will they repent of sins to follow Jesus? These are major questions, and answers can go either way. As Jesus says to the Pharisees who opposed his healing on the Sabbath of a man born blind, "Your sin remains" (9:41).

The openness of this promise suggests a wider application, beyond entry, to the ongoing life of the community. There are extremely complex issues here, some obvious (such as sexual and other forms of abuse, misuse of authority, or violence) and some not so obvious (such as distortions of the truth, hardheartedness, sloth, or pride). The maxim "The corruption of the best is the worst" applies to forgiveness as well as most other good things. Clearly, the Johannine community itself had to learn some hard lessons in this area—the First Letter of John is shot through with issues of sin and forgiveness. There are few areas where the meaning of disciple, "learner," is more important than in seeking a wisdom of how to cope with sin in oneself, in one's community, and in the wider world. It is an area where the exercise

25. For example, see comments on 2:1–12; 9:35–41; 10:26.

26. Parallels are often drawn with Matt. 16:19; 18:18.

of Christian authority has often been questionable to the point of being itself sinful. And "if you retain" might even be intended as a warning of the misery and devastated lives and of the threat to the unity of the community that can result from refusing forgiveness.

The alternative, minority translation is, "Whoever you hold fast, they have been held fast." This is not, like the NRSV translation, a contrast with the first part, but a reinforcement of it. It means that if you enable the forgiveness of sins by introducing them to Jesus, "the Lamb of God who takes away the sin of the world" (1:29), and embracing them in a loving community, and if you then sustain them in the community, you will find that you are doing what God desires—they are "held fast" by God, by Jesus. This is in line with the repeated insistence of Jesus that he holds fast onto those he receives: "No one will snatch them out of my hand. What my Father has given me is greater than all else, and no one can snatch it out of the Father's hand. The Father and I are one" (10:28–30 [see also 17:12; 18:9]). This avoids a rather downbeat ending to the scene and fits better with its overall thrust of peace, joy, receiving the Spirit, and forgiveness. But, as often in John, there is wisdom in both lines of interpretation.

"My Lord and My God!" Hearing, Seeing, Not Seeing, and Believing (20:24–29)

> 24 But Thomas (who was called the Twin), one of the twelve, was not with
> them when Jesus came. 25 So the other disciples told him, "We have seen
> the Lord." But he said to them, "Unless I see the mark of the nails in his hands, and put my finger in the mark of the nails and my hand in his side, I will not believe."
>
> 26 A week later his disciples were again in the house, and Thomas was with them. Although the doors were shut, Jesus came and stood among them and
> said, "Peace be with you." 27 Then he said to Thomas, "Put your finger here and see my hands. Reach out your hand and put it in my side. Do not doubt
> but believe." 28 Thomas answered him, "My Lord and my God!" 29 Jesus said
> to him, "Have you believed because you have seen me? Blessed are those who have not seen and yet have come to believe."

On the night before Jesus died, Thomas had said to him, "Lord, we do not know where you are going. How can we know the way?" and Jesus had answered, "I am the way, and the truth, and the life. No one comes to the Father except through me. If you know me, you will know my Father also. From now on you do know him and have seen him" (14:5–7). Then, in response to Philip, Jesus had said, "Whoever has seen me has seen the Father. . . . Believe me that I am in the Father and the Father is in me; but if you do not, then believe me because of the works themselves" (14:9, 11). That combination of seeing and believing, in which what is believed goes beyond what is seen, amounts to knowing, and all pivots around who Jesus is in his relationship with the Father—that is now actualized for Thomas. In the opening words of the prologue the reader has been told that Jesus is divine; now, finally, a character in the story says it directly, after the completion of the climactic works of Jesus, laying down and taking up his life: **"My Lord and my God!"**

The theology of the Gospel is complete at this point; but, since it is a theology centered on Jesus, who gives "from his fullness . . . grace upon grace . . . grace and truth" (1:16–17), and "gives the Spirit without measure" (3:34), the Spirit of truth who "will guide you into all the truth" (16:13), it should not be too surprising that there is an overflow into a further chapter after this, which in turn imagines innumerable further books (21:25).

Thomas refused to trust the word of the other disciples, **"We have seen the Lord."** One lesson of this scene is that their testimony is to be trusted. What he does not believe is the identity of whoever they had seen—that this is in fact the same crucified Jesus. When he is convinced of this (it is not said that he actually does touch the wounds—the sight and word of Jesus might have been enough), there is a further lesson: the climactic insight of his faith (and, Jesus implies, the faith of anyone else too), beyond what can be seen or touched, is that Jesus is "My Lord and my God!" Jesus in conclusion speaks into the future: **"Blessed are those who have not seen and yet have come to believe."** *This both accepts Thomas's worshiping cry and blesses all who come to this faith with the help of the testimony of others.*

The theological essence of the resurrection and of the whole Gospel is encapsulated here, involving the body of Jesus, God, and faith. First, there is the question of the body of the risen Jesus. That has been an issue all through the chapter: Mary Magdalene's cry about not knowing where it is, after finding the stone removed; the discovery by Peter and the Beloved Disciple of the linen wrappings and folded headcloth; Mary's recognition of Jesus not by sight but by his voice and then his instruction, "Do not hold on to me"; his presence to the disciples twice despite locked doors; the showing of his hands and side and his breathing on the disciples; and now, finally, the even stronger emphasis on the marks of the nails in his hands and the wound in his side. What sort of body is this? There is no attempt to say directly, but the main concern is clear: this is not a resuscitation, as with Lazarus, but *an event centered on who Jesus is*—as seen in Mary exclaiming, "Rabbouni!" and announcing, "I have seen the Lord"; in

Jesus speaking of his ascension to his Father and his own sending; in Jesus giving the Holy Spirit; and in Thomas culminating the Gospel's long series of confessions of who Jesus is with "My Lord and my God!"[27]

It is in the light of that final statement that all the others are to be understood. This is a God-sized event, centered on one who is in a unique relationship with "my Father . . . my God," and also became an embodied human being who could suffer and die. It is not suggested that there is any prior category adequate to this unique event and person—the new category is *Jesus Christ, incarnate, crucified, risen, ascended to his Father, and breathing his Spirit.* The event is new, surprising, and unprecedented, and the many echoes of the Genesis creation stories in this chapter point to the main analogy for his resurrection, with which this Gospel also opens: creation by God's word—also new, surprising, and unprecedented. Both are events to which God's unique freedom, wisdom, initiative, power, and love are intrinsic and essential; they are unthinkable without God. Yet both are also inseparable from physical, material, bodily reality. The difference with the resurrection is the issue of continuity and discontinuity between the Jesus who was crucified and died and the Jesus who now appears to Mary and his other disciples. The main concern of this chapter is to affirm both continuity of identity, signaled by physical marks and personal recognition, and also newness, signaled by the freedom of Jesus to appear despite locked doors and, above all, by him ascending to his Father. This is something new: one who continues to have a body and is also one with God.[28] More radically, *it is this one person, who has been crucified, who is identified with God.*

So, because of the importance of the continuity of the identity of Jesus, testimony to the empty tomb and the appearances of the crucified Jesus are part of resurrection faith. The resurrection of Jesus is genuinely news: "I have seen the Lord!" And, like all news, it can be disbelieved, doubted, suspected, or faked. **"Do not doubt but believe"** (*mē ginou apistos alla pistos*; literally, "Do not become one who is not believing/trusting/faithful/trustworthy but one who is believing/trusting/faithful/trustworthy"). The Synoptic Gospels also tell of doubt, confusion, fear, disbelief, and the desire for tangible confirmation—the nearest to the Thomas story is in Luke 24:36–43. Apart from being present, there is no way to confirm an encounter with someone in the past other than

27. It is worth rereading some of these confessions: 1:15, 29, 34, 49 (this encounter with Nathanael is especially close to that with Thomas, but it culminates in a promise of new seeing [see further below]); 4:42; 6:69; 9:38; 11:27; 16:30; 20:16.

28. When Paul wrestles with the nature of the resurrected body in 1 Cor. 15:35–57, he reaches back to creation for an analogy and suggests the idea of a "spiritual body," which likewise combines continuity and newness.

by trusting witnesses.[29] This is the dimension of resurrection faith that is to do with the body of Jesus and one-off past encounters with him that were had by a few people but did not continue. When Jesus says, "Blessed are those who have not seen and yet have come to believe," one element in what he is saying is that you will find that it is utterly right to trust the witnesses to my resurrection. The church is a community of those who trust these witnesses.[30]

Yet testimony is only one element of three, and the resurrection is misunderstood if it is taken as sufficient. As a God-sized event centered on Jesus, there are two other essential dimensions, both present in Thomas's cry, "My Lord and my God."

The second is Jesus in union with his Father as God. In the resurrection, God acts and Jesus appears, and Thomas's cry sums up this new revelation of God and humanity together. This insight into who Jesus is exceeds anything that can be seen or heard or touched, and it is a theme that runs all through the Gospel. Testimony to what could be seen or heard or touched is vital ("The Word became flesh and lived among us" [1:14]: anyone could witness this), but not enough ("We have seen his glory, the glory as of a father's only son, full of grace and truth" [1:14]: not all witnessed this). Visible signs can be interpreted in very different ways. *Openness to God, and to the surprises God springs, is even more important than actually being a witness.* The ideal for those who come later is to trust witnesses to the signs and be open to what they are saying about who God is and what these surprises mean.

But there is also the third essential element, summed up in the repeated "My . . . my . . ." of Thomas, corresponding to the "my Lord" of Mary Magdalene (20:16), to the "your Father . . . your God" of Jesus (20:17), and the next chapter's one-to-one, thrice-repeated questioning of Peter by Jesus: "Simon son of John, do you love me?" (21:15–17). *This is the mystery of personal response, which also runs all through this Gospel.* There is no overview of this: each one faces God. It is the mysterious event of divine freedom and human freedom coming together in trust and love. Some testimonies to it emphasize God's free, loving initiative more; some emphasize human free, trusting, and loving response more. John has not only an unlimited, open "anyone," "everyone," and "all people," but also

29. Today, recording technologies, whether video or audio, have not done away with the need for trust—in their case, trust that the technologies, which are open to multiple forms of manipulation, have been honestly used.

30. Witnesses can, of course, be cross-examined and their testimony subjected to rigorous interrogation, and that has happened continually with the accounts of the resurrection. As often in a court of law, in the end the jury is still faced with the decision to believe or not to believe particular witnesses. For a rich and rigorous discussion of resurrection belief, see Carnley, *Resurrection in Retrospect.* Among that book's strengths are how it does justice to the Gospel of John and its emphasis on continuing experience of Jesus through the Spirit.

the tragic possibility of wrong decision, of refusal to believe and trust, of being judged, and of remaining in darkness. In John 20 divine and human freedom come together most clearly in what I have described as the imperative invitation or announcement of Jesus: "Welcome the Holy Spirit!"

So the threefold essence of the resurrection is that God acts, Jesus appears, and the Holy Spirit is given and received.[31] These three essential elements—who God is and what God does, testimony to Jesus, and the mystery of divine initiative and human response—pervade the Gospel and culminate in this chapter, which itself culminates in the confession by Thomas.

Many other rich theological insights have come through this passage over the centuries. I offer just four.

- *Dominus et Deus Noster*, "Our Lord and God," were titles that were part of the imperial cult of the Roman Empire. The emperor Domitian first claimed them, and they had become popular. So for the first readers, the cry of Thomas was also a radical challenge to the most powerful person in their world. *It continues to challenge anything that claims overarching importance in personal, political, or other spheres—whether a person, a relationship, a family, a country, an ideology, an aspect of identity, a system, a way of life, a problem, a vision, or a desire.*
- Thomas missed out on meeting Jesus and on the promised peace and joy, the sending as a community, and the giving of the Holy Spirit because he was not with the other disciples on that first Sunday. Then, when he is present with them the following Sunday, he meets Jesus, receives peace, has his doubts graciously met, and comes to faith. The message is clear: *be fully part of the fragile, fallible community of fellow disciples/learners*—and don't miss Sunday gatherings!
- There are only two beatitudes in John, compared with many in the Synoptics (the best-known being Matt. 5:1–12). The first is about footwashing: "If you know these things, you are blessed if you do them" (13:17). The second is about faith/belief/trust in line with Thomas's confession: "Blessed are those who have not seen and yet have come to believe." These two beatitudes together are one way of summing up the message of this Gospel: *trust Jesus and serve in love as he did.* And the upside-down message of the footwashing about power, authority, and community is

31. This account of the resurrection is convincingly described, analyzed, and justified in Frei, *The Identity of Jesus Christ*. This may well be the past century's most important single book on how to understand the gospel. The foreword by Mike Higton, in the revised and enlarged edition, gives a most helpful summary of the argument and its significance.

> As with the other Easter stories taken up by him [John the Evangelist], he is concerned to lead the believers to the risen one himself who, for him, is a permanent living reality. Presumably on this account, he does not have a farewell scene; he can do without it all the more because, in his case, the earthly Jesus had already spoken in the supper-room about his departure, his return and his constant fellowship with those who belong to him.
>
> —Rudolf Schnackenburg, *The Gospel according to St. John*, 3:335

the practical outworking of the truth that Jesus, not the Roman emperor or anyone or anything else, is "Lord" and "God."

- Here, as in all John's accounts of the resurrection appearances of Jesus, there is no mention of him departing. He can ascend to his Father, but he is also free to be present as he chooses. His knowledge of what Thomas said in his apparent absence suggests that he is present in a different way. Rudolf Schnackenburg speaks of John here indicating "the permanent living reality" and "constant fellowship" of Jesus (see the quotation from Schnackenburg in the sidebar). And this in turn inspires a rethinking of Jesus breathing his Spirit into his disciples. In line with the mutual indwelling of Jesus and his disciples as expressed in the Farewell Discourses and especially in John 15 and 17, *surely the image of Jesus breathing like this is meant never to stop*. This way of giving the Spirit is not meant to be one-off. Is the risen Jesus to be imagined as ceasing to breathe out the Spirit as he indwells his followers, and they him? If not, then this minute-by-minute, intimate, face-to-face sharing of the Spirit, accompanied by hearing the words of Jesus, reaches to the heart of ordinary Christian life.

The Purpose of This Text: Signs Done by Jesus Inspire Trusting Who He Is and Sharing His Life (20:30–31)

> [30] Now Jesus did many other signs in the presence of his disciples, which are not written in this book. [31] But these are written so that you may come to believe that Jesus is the Messiah, the Son of God, and that through believing you may have life in his name.

At the end of the public ministry of Jesus the author had said, "Although he had performed so many signs in their presence, they did not believe him" (12:37).

Now, after the further signs of the crucifixion and resurrection,[32] culminating in the appearances of the risen Jesus **in the presence of his disciples**, the readers are told that there is an abundance of other testimony, among which the selection that John chose has a specific purpose.[33]

The phrase **Jesus did** (*epoiēsen ho Iēsous*) is another echo of the creation account in Genesis, which in the Septuagint begins, *en archē epoiēsen ho theos* ("in the beginning God made/created" [Gen. 1:1]), and the substitution of "Jesus" for "God" is in line with John 1:1 and the confession by Thomas.[34]

The reference to **many other signs . . . not written in this book** implies other books where those signs are written. The current scholarly consensus favors John knowing the Synoptic Gospels, or at least many of their sources and traditions, and that has been assumed in this commentary. Indeed, John often seems to assume that readers will know them too. Whatever the case, his text makes fuller sense if read with the Synoptics as intertexts. Both the Synoptics and John are part of the transition from eyewitnesses testifying to one-off signs to books testifying in durable, written signs that can be read again and again. As Margaret Daly-Denton says, "This is a text that calls for re, re and re-readers," and she quotes Ingrid Kitzberger, who links this verse with the previous verse's beatitude: "Blessed are those who read and re-read the gospel and believe."[35]

The purpose of the Gospel given in verse 31 sheds much light on why John has made his particular selection. His distinctive double focus is on *who Jesus is* and *the life received by those who trust and believe in him*.

The message is not primarily about ideas or instructions but about this unique person, **Jesus**, who **is the Messiah, the Son of God**. He can also be described in many other ways, beginning with "Word," which from the beginning suggests the appropriateness of testimony in writing.

But these are written so that you may come to believe (*pisteusēte*). Other manuscripts have *pisteuēte*, which means "that you may continue to believe." Is the purpose of this Gospel to draw people into believing or to feed and strengthen those who already believe? If forced, I would choose the second, but I agree with the conclusion of Susan Hylen and Gail O'Day: "The supposed opposition between coming to faith and continuing in faith misreads John's own presentation of faith within the Gospel itself. As we have noted repeatedly, faith

32. These were early on introduced as the climactic sign in 2:18–22.

33. The scope of "signs" has sometimes been narrowed to acts that are in some way miraculous, but there are stronger arguments for seeing them as embracing the whole mission of Jesus, including his other actions, his sufferings, and his words. A related term is "work/works," which can also be used to mean his whole mission (4:34; 17:4). See Lincoln, *The Gospel according to Saint John*, 505–6.

34. See footnote 3 in the comments on 1:1.

35. Daly-Denton, *John*, 10.

is not a one-time event, but a process. Many believe in Jesus only to later reject him; others have a tenuous belief that competes with their fear; even those who do believe do not fully understand. The Gospel offers its invitation to any who would begin to believe, or continue to believe, that Jesus is the Messiah, the Son of God."[36] I would even more strongly affirm that one of the remarkable things about this Gospel is its way of simultaneously combining accessibility to newcomers with the ability to go on feeding those with a more mature faith.

Finally, **through believing** [or "trusting"] **you may have life in his name** again brings together the person of Jesus and the response of faith, this time emphasizing life with Jesus. That is life attending to his words and signs, breathing his Spirit, and actualizing the sort of unity in love, peace, and joy with the Father, with other people, and with the whole creation that has been opened up by the Farewell Discourses. It is also a life of prayer "in his name."[37]

36. O'Day and Hylen, *John*, 197–98.

37. Much more could be said about the selection made in this Gospel. One suggestion that makes good sense in line with this commentary, which sees the theological climax coming in John 17 with its emphasis on unity, is that John is writing for a Christian community experiencing conflict and disunity. John therefore focuses on essentials of Christian faith and practice, such as the horizon of God and all reality, who Jesus is, receiving the Holy Spirit, following Jesus in the ongoing drama, and a few basic ethical orientations to do with serving and loving. "It is as if there is a recognition that, as the church grows and meets different situations and practical challenges, faithful Christians and whole communities can come to profoundly different practical conclusions, and that these need not be church-dividing so long as they can be seen as faithful to who Jesus is. John can be read as the ecumenical Gospel, summoning readers into deeper and deeper relationship with Jesus and his Father in the Spirit, while refusing to insist on things not essential to that relationship." Ford, "Mature Ecumenism's Daring Future."

John 21:1–25

The Ongoing Drama

This final chapter is an epilogue matching the prologue. The prologue began with the Word of God and creation; the epilogue points to a future oriented toward Jesus, "until I come" (vv. 22, 23). Jesus and testifying to Jesus are central to both, and in both there are notes of abundance, glory, and love. The centrality of Jesus also means the centrality of God (1:1, 2, 6, 12, 13, 14, 18), here suggested by repeatedly calling Jesus "the Lord" (21:7, 12, 15, 16, 17, 20), and explicit in the death by which Peter "would glorify God" (21:19). The prologue introduced the drama of the life, death, and resurrection of Jesus by telling of the Word becoming flesh in Jesus, living "among us" (1:14), and making God known. *The epilogue introduces the ongoing drama of the family of disciples as they breathe his Spirit, love him, follow him, take responsibility for continuing his work, and are willing to live or die for him.* It concludes by revealing the author who has made these things known, selecting them from "many other things that Jesus did."

Besides further reflection on the prologue, the chapter invites into deeper understanding and practical implications, especially by connecting with earlier chapters in mutually illuminating ways. The abundance of fish adds to the other signs, symbols, and teachings of abundance that are one of the most striking features of this Gospel, including gallons of water changed into wine, the Spirit given without measure, water welling up to eternal life, five thousand fed and twelve baskets of leftovers, light for the whole world, life in all its fullness, a house filled with fragrance, a fruitful vine, and incomparable glory, love, and joy. The haul of fish also invites into rereading Synoptic stories, such as Jesus helping to catch fish and telling Peter that he "will be catching people" (Luke 5:1–11), just as the recognition of the risen Jesus through a meal recalls the two disciples meeting him on the road to Emmaus (Luke 24:13–35). The gathering of a learning community, and the centrality in it of the "who" question from 1:19 onward, is here fulfilled in knowing the risen Jesus: "Now none of the disciples dared to ask him, 'Who are you?' because they knew it was the Lord." The initial invitation, "Come and see" (1:39), is matched by "Come and have breakfast" and the ongoing significance of meals in the community.

Most of all, the final meal on the night before Jesus died, leading into his arrest, trial, and crucifixion, is recalled in two ways. First, there is the failure of Peter as a follower of Jesus: "Will you lay down your life for me? Very truly, I tell you, before the cock crows, you will have denied me three times" (13:38). Peter's threefold denial is matched by his restorative threefold naming, questioning, and commissioning by Jesus. These take up the Farewell Discourses' teachings of service and love into Peter's ongoing vocation as pastor. Then Jesus adds a prophecy of Peter's death, connecting it with his own death by describing it as glorifying God (see 12:27–28; 13:31–32).

Second, the disciple whom Jesus loved, who was first explicitly mentioned at the Last Supper, appears again, with a reminder of his role in that meal. In the meanwhile, he has taken the mother of Jesus into his home (19:27), so that is where we are to imagine him continuing to "remain/abide until I come" (21:22, 23). In him come together not only the Farewell Discourses' key themes of love, abiding, and testifying but also their orientation to a future centered on Jesus.

All this serves the practical thrust of the chapter: shaping the ongoing life of the community around listening to the word of Jesus, meeting him through shared meals, forgiveness and restoration, servant leadership, avoiding distraction (as by fake news in rumors), testifying to Jesus, following Jesus, and being primarily committed to abiding like the Beloved Disciple "until I come" (vv. 22, 23).

Set in Galilee, by the Sea of Tiberias, the overall heading is "Jesus showed himself again to the disciples" (v. 1), emphasized again halfway through: "This was now the third time that Jesus appeared to the disciples after he was raised from the dead" (v. 14). But, as with his other appearances, there is no mention of departure: the risen Jesus is free to appear or not, but he is always present as God is present. The action begins with Simon Peter deciding to go fishing and being joined by six other disciples. The key events of the chapter are the huge catch of fish, breakfast with Jesus, and the two rich, nuanced exchanges between Jesus and Peter—one about Peter himself and the other about the Beloved Disciple. Finally, the Beloved Disciple is identified as the one "who is testifying to these things and has written them," which is immediately complicated by the addition of "and we know that his testimony is true" (v. 24). Who are "we"? And who is the "I" in the final verse?

The final verse of John's Gospel is the closing note of abundance in this Gospel of abundance, first triply signaled in the prologue by "all things came into being through him," by "his glory . . . full of grace and truth," and by "his fullness . . . grace upon grace" (1:3, 14, 16), and shown again in the final chapter by the large catch of fish. Here the emphasis is on the "many other things that Jesus did," which, "if every one of them were written down, . . . the world itself could not contain the books that would be written" (21:25). *It is the ultimate warning against any definitive, conclusive attempt to sum up, wrap up, comprehend, tie down, or write down what Jesus has done, let alone what he continues to do and, above all, who he is.*

"Cast the Net"; "It Is the Lord!" (21:1–8)

> [1] After these things Jesus showed himself again to the disciples by the Sea of
> Tiberias; and he showed himself in this way. [2] Gathered there together were
> Simon Peter, Thomas called the Twin, Nathanael of Cana in Galilee, the sons
> of Zebedee, and two others of his disciples. [3] Simon Peter said to them, "I
> am going fishing." They said to him, "We will go with you." They went out
> and got into the boat, but that night they caught nothing.
> [4] Just after daybreak, Jesus stood on the beach; but the disciples did not
> know that it was Jesus. [5] Jesus said to them, "Children, you have no fish,
> have you?" They answered him, "No." [6] He said to them, "Cast the net to the
> right side of the boat, and you will find some." So they cast it, and now they
> were not able to haul it in because there were so many fish. [7] That disciple
> whom Jesus loved said to Peter, "It is the Lord!" When Simon Peter heard
> that it was the Lord, he put on some clothes, for he was naked, and jumped
> into the sea. [8] But the other disciples came in the boat, dragging the net full
> of fish, for they were not far from the land, only about a hundred yards off.

The opening emphasizes the core focus of this chapter: **Jesus showed himself . . . he showed himself**. The primary concern is with the person of Jesus, his self-revelation, and his freedom to be present, to speak, to serve, and to love. *It is presence within ordinary life, with its necessities of working and eating*. The key reality is given in the statements **It is the Lord** and **It was the Lord**.

Seven disciples gather, led by Simon Peter. They include **Nathanael**, who last appeared in 1:43–51, and whose hometown of **Cana in Galilee** also connects him with the first of Jesus's signs (2:1–11); and **the sons of Zebedee**, who have not appeared before, and mentioning them seems to assume that readers will know the Synoptic Gospels, where they are named as James and John.

Why go **fishing**? The obvious answer is to catch fish in order to make a living. Some scholars speculate that they were failing to follow through on their sending by Jesus in the previous chapter, and it is possible that they demonstrate how even the most intense experiences can soon fade or cease to shape behavior. But there is no hint of a negative judgment on them, and a positive view is that, just as Jesus has been present in the enclosed, special Sunday gatherings in Jerusalem in John 20, so he is present in Galilee as the disciples go to work and carry on ordinary life. There may even be a hint, in the phrase **gathered there together**, of his freedom to be present as much to teams of task-oriented workers contributing to the economy as to gatherings for worship.

Yet this particular work also symbolizes attracting people to follow Jesus, as the Synoptic Gospels make clear, and so the whole passage can be read on two levels. **They caught nothing**—this can therefore be disappointment in work or in mission; but more fundamental is the point made during the Farewell Discourses: "Apart from me you can do nothing" (15:5). What happens is a response to Jesus's instruction, **"Cast the net to the right side of the boat, and you will find some."** The disciples hear and obey: **So they cast it**. Interestingly, the inability to catch fish is followed by an inability to cope with the surprise haul of fish.

That disciple whom Jesus loved said to Peter, "It is the Lord!" As at the tomb in the previous chapter, the Beloved Disciple leaps to the right conclusion, and now Peter trusts him and immediately leaps into the sea and heads for Jesus. The contrast between the two, the one more perceptive and contemplative, the other more enthusiastic and active, continues into the second half of the chapter, with Peter the active pastor and martyr, and the Beloved Disciple the one who abides and writes. They are presented as richly complementary.

The Greek of **It is the Lord** is *ho kyrios estin* and can simply indicate a recognition of who it is. But it literally means "the Lord is" and is repeated exactly in the next sentence when Peter hears and acts on it, translated as **it was the Lord**, and then repeated again in verse 12 when the other disciples recognize Jesus. Given John's series of "I am" statements, and other uses of the verb "to be," "It is the Lord!" can also be understood as a cry acknowledging ongoing divine presence, matching Thomas's cry acknowledging the divine identity of Jesus, "My Lord and my God!" (20:28).

Known at Breakfast: Jesus the Host, Cook, Lord, and Server (21:9–14)

> 9 When they had gone ashore, they saw a charcoal fire there, with fish on it, and bread. 10 Jesus said to them, "Bring some of the fish that you have just caught." 11 So Simon Peter went aboard and hauled the net ashore, full of

large fish, a hundred fifty-three of them; and though there were so many, the net was not torn. 12 Jesus said to them, "Come and have breakfast." Now none of the disciples dared to ask him, "Who are you?" because they knew it was the Lord. 13 Jesus came and took the bread and gave it to them, and did the same with the fish. 14 This was now the third time that Jesus appeared to the disciples after he was raised from the dead.

The **charcoal fire** recalls the one in the courtyard of the high priest at which Peter was warming himself when he denied Jesus three times (18:18). The **fish** and **bread** recall the feeding of the five thousand with bread and fish (6:9–11) and the major discourse that follows it. The parallels with John 6 are so striking that these accounts cry out to be read together: the Sea of Tiberias setting; the meal of bread and fish; the abundance; Jesus serving the food; the mysterious appearance of Jesus (in 6:16–21 Jesus comes walking on the sea and says, "It is I" [*egō eimi*, "I am"]); and Peter's leading role (6:66–70). When they are read together, this little meal is connected with the eucharistic meals celebrated in the ongoing community, with the continuing presence of Jesus, with the gift of eternal life, with the mutual indwelling of Jesus and his disciples (6:56), and with being energized, inspired, and sustained by his words: "The words that I have spoken to you are spirit and life" (6:63).

So Simon Peter went aboard and hauled the net ashore. The Greek verb for "hauled," *helkein*, also means "attract or draw toward" and was used earlier of the attractive power of Jesus through his crucifixion: "And I, when I am lifted up from the earth, will draw all people [or "all things"] to myself" (12:32). This is in line with the second level of meaning in the language of fishing mentioned above, symbolizing attraction into the community. Here, the symbolism suggests the numbers drawn in, the hard work involved, and, through the fact that **the net was not torn**,[1] that the expanded community stays united together—even if under strain. But there may also be another suggestion. Why **a hundred fifty-three**? There have been many proposals, one of which is that this represents the number of kinds of known fish, so that a community with all kinds of people, or even all kinds of creatures, is being envisioned.[2]

1. In Luke 5:6 the nets do begin to tear.

2. Since the early church, an illuminating intertext read with this has been Ezek. 47:1–12. There, the vision is, "People will stand fishing beside the sea from En-gedi to En-eglaim; it will be a place for the spreading of nets; the fish will be of a great many kinds, like the fish of the Great Sea" (v. 10). But there are not just many kinds of fish: "On the banks, on both sides of the river, there will grow all kinds of trees for food. Their leaves will not wither nor their fruit fail, but they will bear fresh fruit every month, because the water for them flows from the sanctuary. Their fruit will be for food, and their leaves for healing" (v. 12).

Jesus plays many parts in this scene. He is the cook who has already begun preparing the food; he asks for a contribution to the meal; he is the host who invites, **"Come and have breakfast"**; and he serves the food: **Jesus came and took the bread and gave it to them, and did the same with the fish.** Yet it is also clear what is most significant: who he is. **Now none of the disciples dared to ask him, "Who are you?" because they knew it was the Lord.**

What kind of knowing is this? *Very importantly, it is not necessarily about seeing Jesus.* John 20 is full of testimony to seeing; here in John 21 there is no "seeing" language referring to Jesus. The nearest to it is the verb used twice in verse 1, *ephanerōsen*: Jesus "showed" himself. But this verb need not involve seeing; it is about disclosure, coming to know or understand, revelation. It is used again in verse 14, this time in the passive voice. It is translated in the NRSV as **Jesus appeared.** A better translation, doing justice to the passive, is in the New American Bible: "Jesus was revealed." This goes with the passive verb in **after he was raised from the dead**, and both can be read as what are called "divine passives": Jesus was "revealed" *by God* and "raised" *by God.*

What is happening here? John 20 was the culmination of eyewitness testimony, initiated by Mary Magdalene: "I have seen the Lord" (20:18). But the final seeing, by Thomas, is followed by a blessing on those who come later and believe without seeing (20:29). *Now John 21 seems to be written as a transition to those later believers.* Clearly, some sort of seeing is implied, but the emphasis is on moving from not knowing in verse 4 ("Jesus stood on the beach; but the disciples did not know that it was Jesus") to knowing in verse 12. It turns out later that they were about "a hundred yards" from the beach (v. 8), too far for seeing a face to be reliable. So the first identification of Jesus by the Beloved Disciple, "It is the Lord!" (v. 7), is not visual. It comes through a cumulative series of events: the words of Jesus questioning and instructing the disciples as a group, their action in obedience to him, and the abundant catch of fish. *All of these are available to later believers, who can receive and follow the directions of Jesus, and can act together to produce signs of the abundance of God.*

The second acknowledgment that "it was the Lord" ("the Lord is"), again in verse 7, comes from Peter in response to the testimony of the Beloved Disciple: *hearing testimony is also available to later believers.*

The third acknowledgment is by the rest of the disciples, after their fish have been given in response to a request by Jesus and they begin to take part in a meal with Jesus: **They knew it was the Lord** ("the Lord is"—exactly the same in Greek as twice before). That "none of the disciples dared to ask him, 'Who are you?' because they knew it was the Lord" seems to indicate that even now, close up, this was not a matter of straightforward visual identification, but rather knowledge based on other things. What then follows, Jesus taking and giving the bread, resonates with eucharistic language elsewhere in the New Testament (Matt. 26:26–29; Mark 14:22–25; Luke 22:15–20; cf. 24:30; 1 Cor. 11:23–26), and the addition of **and did the same with the fish** makes the connection with the eucharistic language in John 6. *So this third wave of recognition points to a communal experience familiar to all later believers: gathering for a meal in which the presence of Jesus is acknowledged.*

But this is not all. The rest of the chapter adds further ways through which who Jesus is is communicated to later believers: *pastoral care in love,* as by Jesus the good shepherd; *following Jesus, even to the extent of martyrdom that glorifies God,* as the death of Jesus did; and *abiding* as the Beloved Disciple did, who rested on the breast of Jesus, just as Jesus himself was in the bosom of his Father, "close to the Father's heart" (1:18).

Finally, there is the way in which all readers of this Gospel are invited to learn who Jesus is and to trust and know him: through written testimony originating with the Beloved Disciple. *This text enables the transition from the eyewitnesses of the first generation to something available to all who come later.* It not only gives a distillation of the essential testimony originating in eyewitnesses, but also, in this final chapter, sums up the main ways in which later disciples of Jesus still come to know him: attending to the words of Jesus and keeping his commandments; doing signs that testify to the abundance of God's life and love; listening to the testimony of other disciples; taking part in community gatherings around meals where the presence of Jesus is acknowledged; being loved and nourished within that community; seeing examples of following Jesus whatever the cost; seeing examples of abiding faithfully in the love of Jesus in ordinary life; and reading and rereading Scripture. This knowing is inseparable from a way of life in community.

Yet this passage and many others in the Gospel of John open up a further question beyond that one about the kind of knowing into which readers are being invited. The deepest question of all, into which all those ways of knowing lead, is, *What kind of being is this?* The threefold repetition of *ho kyrios estin,* "the Lord is," together with numerous affirmations akin to this that have been noted in previous chapters, above all the "I am" sayings of Jesus, point to the central reality of the Gospel, the mysterious depth, breadth, length, and height indicated by the question the disciples did not dare to ask: "Who are you?" The prologue opens it up and gives both the horizon for exploring it and, in 1:18, a pointer to its core mystery. Then in 1:19 the question "Who are you?" becomes a headline for the rest of the Gospel. Each chapter contributes further understanding, culminating in the Farewell Discourses, which in turn culminate in the prayer of Jesus in John 17, where further dimensions are opened up. But the truth of this mystery is above all embodied in the person of Jesus and, climactically, in his crucifixion, resurrection, gift of the Holy Spirit, and ascension. Now in the final chapter, after all that, readers are left with the ongoing question, "Who are you?" All the ways of knowing Jesus into which readers are invited are to be desired and entered into, and they come together in the ongoing drama of following Jesus together.

Now the second half of the chapter, as already mentioned, goes deeper into that following through two exemplary disciples.

"Do You Love Me?"—Peter's Way of Pastoring, Suffering, and Dying (21:15–19)

> [15] When they had finished breakfast, Jesus said to Simon Peter, "Simon son of John, do you love me more than these?" He said to him, "Yes, Lord; you know that I love you." Jesus said to him, "Feed my lambs."
> [16] A second time he said to him, "Simon son of John, do you love me?" He said to him, "Yes, Lord; you know that I love you." Jesus said to him, "Tend my sheep."
> [17] He said to him the third time, "Simon son of John, do you love me?" Peter felt hurt because he said to him the third time, "Do you love me?" And he said to him, "Lord, you know everything; you know that I love you." Jesus said to him, "Feed my sheep.
> [18] Very truly, I tell you, when you were younger, you used to fasten your own belt and to go wherever you wished. But when you grow old, you will stretch out your hands, and someone else will fasten a belt around you and take you where you do not wish to go."
> [19] (He said this to indicate the kind of death by which he would glorify God.) After this he said to him, "Follow me."

"Do you love me?" . . . "I love you." Mutual love like this is the goal of the Gospel. But the relationship between Jesus and Peter has been broken by Peter's threefold denial of Jesus, despite his confidence that he would be willing to lay down his life. Now Jesus takes the initiative and, without explicitly mentioning the past, gives Peter a fresh start. His own love has been demonstrated—as he had said, "No one has greater love than this, to lay down one's life for one's friends" (15:13). Now he asks Peter whether it is mutual. *Peter is examined on love in love.*

The threefold repetition not only more than outweighs the earlier denials, signaling forgiveness, rehabilitation, and mutuality. The need for it also suggests how difficult it is to take it in when we are utterly loved, forgiven, trusted, and welcomed into full mutuality after we have damaged a relationship.

Perhaps, too, repeated self-examination in love in the presence of Jesus is necessary if we are not to repeat patterns that spoil relationships.

But this is not only about a fresh individual start; it is also about a vocation of loving service of others. In line with the commission of Jesus, "As the Father has sent me, so I send you" (20:21), Peter is now commissioned. Jesus has just fed the disciples; likewise, Peter is to **feed my sheep**. Jesus has described himself as the good shepherd, who "came that they may have life, and have it abundantly" and who "lays down his life for the sheep" (10:10–11); likewise Peter.

Each repeated element in the three exchanges between Jesus and Peter is significant. **Simon son of John** (three times) reaches back to the beginning of the Gospel, where this is how Jesus first addresses Peter before giving him the further name Cephas, or Peter, meaning "Rock" (1:42). It suggests a fresh start and also a renewal of identity that yet connects with the past, and especially with family.

"Do you love me?" (twice, vv. 15, 16, with the Greek verb *agapan*) puts love, *agapē*, at the heart of the disciple's relationship with Jesus, as it is at the heart of God's relationship with the world (3:16); the relationship between the Father and the Son (3:35; 10:17; 14:31; 15:9–10; 17:23–24, 26); the relationship of Jesus with his disciples (13:1, 34; 15:9–10, 12); the relationship of the disciples with one another (13:34; 15:12); the relationship of the Father with the disciples of Jesus (14:21, 23; 17:23); and the death of Jesus (15:13). Yet responding in love to the love of Jesus is never taken for granted. Jesus invites it, commands it, and, in John 17, desires and prays for it. But all through the Farewell Discourses there is an acute awareness that there is no assurance that the disciples will love in return: "if you love me" (14:15); "those who love me" (14:23; the Greek has the conditional—literally, "if anyone loves me"); "whoever does not love me" (14:24); "if you loved me" (14:28); "If you keep my commandments, you will abide in my love" (15:10). There is a decision to be made, inseparable from believing in and trusting Jesus. The whole Gospel can be read as an appeal to readers to make this response of trust and love, summed up now in the insistently repeated question of Jesus. Here Peter, after his bitter failure, is given the chance of a fresh start and takes it.

Lord, spoken three times by Peter, by now has all the weight of Thomas's recognition of who Jesus is: "My Lord and my God!" (20:28).

"You know that I love you" (again, spoken three times) deepens the mystery of what is going on in our most important decisions and commitments. Often, it is more like opening our eyes, recognizing a truth, seeing the "elephant in the room" that somehow we had managed to ignore, and in this light our decision is clear. In a relationship of love, we sometimes discover that the other has understood us better than we have understood ourselves and has been waiting for us to wake up to the truth. With God, with Jesus, this is always the case. Jesus patiently waits for us to respond to what he knows will fulfill our deepest desires as well as his desires for us. Jesus has shown this sort of knowledge of Peter before. At the footwashing, Jesus said to him, "You do not know now what I am doing, but later you will understand" (13:7). Later in the Last Supper he said to Peter, "Will you lay down your life for me? Very truly, I tell you, before the cock crows, you will have denied me three times" (13:38). What emerges from the present exchange is that the loving service represented by footwashing is to be done through Peter feeding the sheep; he is indeed to lay down his life, and the wound and shame of denial are healed.

"You know that I love you" raises a further question about the extent to which it is right to call responding to the love of Jesus a decision. That is not wrong, but may sound too proactive. *It is more like being open to receiving a gift, which seems less like a decision and more like a recognition of the character of the gift—and, even more, the character of the giver. Jesus gives himself.* The decision to receive him flows from recognizing who he really is. Peter has received this revelation already, underlined by the threefold "Jesus showed himself / revealed himself" (v. 1 twice, and v. 14), and the threefold "It is/was the Lord" (v. 7 twice, and v. 12). What has happened since Peter's denial of Jesus includes him receiving the Holy Spirit, breathed by Jesus, who had laid down his life in love. Once again, as often in this Gospel, there is the mystery of divine initiative and human response. In Peter's response to Jesus's repeated question, the emphasis is on what Jesus knows, which is that Peter now loves him, a relationship utterly dependent on Peter being loved by Jesus and being receptive to that love. This combination of being loved and known by Jesus will be repeated in the next and final scene, centered on "the disciple whom Jesus loved" (v. 20).

Feed, spoken twice by Jesus, recalls how prominent nourishment is in this Gospel. Jesus himself is identified as closely as possible with food and drink: in his first sign (2:1–11); in the "living water" he gives (4:7–15); in his own mission ("My food is to do the will of him who sent me and to complete his work" [4:34]); in feeding the five thousand and connecting it with himself ("I am the bread of life. Whoever comes to me will never be hungry, and whoever believes in me will never be thirsty" [6:35; on thirst, see also 7:37–39]); in feeding Judas at the Last Supper (13:26–27); and in being cook, host, and server in this final appearance. Whoever comes to me will never be hungry, and whoever believes in me will never be thirsty" (6:35 [on thirst, see also 7:37–39]); in feeding Judas at the Last Supper (13:26–27); and in being cook, host, and server in this final appearance. If Peter is being sent to feed as Jesus fed, then he is to nourish people with literal food as well as life-transforming meaning and can be confident that, given love and willingness to serve, there will be an abundance of both.

My (spoken three times) suggests the primacy of identification with Jesus and the community of those who belong to him. It is a warning to leaders in particular not to be overly possessive of those who belong to someone else, not to cultivate attachment to themselves rather than to Jesus, and not to assume that the boundaries of belonging to their own community are the boundaries of the sheepfold of Jesus. *But it is also an encouragement to be open to continual surprises as to who and what belong to the one through whom all things were made, whose Spirit is given without measure, who longs to draw all people and things together, and who is present as the God of love is present.*

The variations within the repetitions are also significant. Why ask Peter to compare his love with that of other disciples: **"Do you love me more than these?"** This does seem like a hint at Peter's overconfidence before his denial of Jesus. But Peter has learned a lesson, and in reply does not claim any superiority, simply affirming his love for Jesus without any comparison.

Why begin with **lambs** rather than **sheep**? Lambs in the Bible are associated with vulnerability and needing special care and protection (Isa. 40:11; 53:7; Jer. 11:19). The leader is to be particularly attentive to the flourishing of the weak, the young, the marginalized, "the little people."

Why **tend** rather than **feed** in the second of the three commands to Peter? This is a variation that expands the imagery beyond feeding and invites reflection on the broad range of pastoral tasks.

The most discussed variation is in the words that are all translated as **love**. In the first two exchanges, Jesus uses *agapan* and Peter uses *philein*; in the final one, both use *philein*. Most scholars agree that they are being used interchangeably and that no difference in meaning is intended. But that does not mean that there is no significance in the variation. It is striking that the other time the two terms for love are combined is when Jesus speaks of his death as laying down his life in love (*agapē*) for his friends (*philoi*) (15:13). Just as the death of Jesus is about attracting people to respond in trust and love ("I when I am lifted up from the earth will draw all people [or "things"] to myself" [12:32]), so Peter's leadership and pastoring, inspired by loving Jesus, are to form a family community whose unity in love with God and one another is for the sake of "the world" knowing and trusting who he is and why he has come (13:35; 17:21–23). *So both his death and his family life open an unlimited horizon of love.* The conclusion here about the use of *agapan* and *philein* together is the same as earlier on 15:13: *agapan* is a fundamental, distinctively biblical word; *philein* is a rich, deep word from the surrounding Hellenistic civilization that is also used in the Bible. Used together, they encourage each world of meaning and practice to engage with the other in depth; and, used of Jesus and his community, they encourage both learning from the surrounding culture and transforming it.

So, Peter is to love Jesus and pastor Jesus's community of disciples (learners) in love, feeding them in such a way that they learn more and more who

Jesus is and how to love like he does. And as Jesus now goes on to say, Peter himself will give an example of such self-giving love to the point of literally sacrificing his life.

"Very truly, I tell you, when you were younger, you used to fasten your own belt and to go wherever you wished." The importance of this is emphasized by the final "Very truly, I tell you" of this Gospel. Peter is following his love, but that does not mean that he gets all he desires—lesser desires must often be sacrificed for great love, as any parent learns. The education of desire has already been seen in previous chapters to be a key to the pedagogy of this Gospel. It began with the first words of Jesus, questioning his first disciples, "What are you looking for?" (1:38), and is to be completed in the fulfillment of the desire of Jesus, "Father, I desire that those also, whom you have given me, may be with me where I am, to see my glory" (17:24). But it arrives there by way of the cross, by self-denial and willingness to glorify God as Jesus did. The basic teaching on this was given earlier, combining the same themes of glorifying, love, service, God, and following Jesus: "Jesus answered them, 'The hour has come for the Son of Man to be glorified. Very truly, I tell you, unless a grain of wheat falls into the earth and dies, it remains just a single grain; but if it dies, it bears much fruit. Those who love their life lose it, and those who hate their life in this world will keep it for eternal life. Whoever serves me must follow me, and where I am, there will my servant be also. Whoever serves me, the Father will honor'" (12:23–26).

Peter is to follow like that. Jesus's addition, **"Follow me"** (*akolouthei moi*), is repeated even more insistently in the last words of Jesus in this Gospel, again spoken to Peter: "Follow me!" (v. 22).[3] This is the only Gospel in which Jesus gives the invitation and command to follow him after his resurrection. *It has the effect of confirming his continuing presence with his followers in the ongoing drama and the primary importance of that drama of learning and loving in discipleship.*

Another Way of Following: Abiding and Testifying (21:20–25)

The Abundance of Following (21:20–23)

> [20] Peter turned and saw the disciple whom Jesus loved following them; he was the one who had reclined next to Jesus at the supper and had said,

3. The Greek in v. 22 is *sy moi akolouthei*, adding the emphatic *sy* ("you") to the previous command in v. 19 and intensifying the relationship of Jesus with his follower by placing "you" alongside "me"—literally, "You me follow!" This recalls the intimate language of Jesus's prayer in John 17, with the placing of "I" or "me" or "mine" immediately next to "you" or "yours" in vv. 4, 5, 8, 10 (twice), 21, 23, 25. Few of these side-by-side juxtapositions come across in most translations—in the NRSV none of them do; the one in v. 5 does in the King James Version.

> "Lord, who is it that is going to betray you?" [21] When Peter saw him, he said to Jesus, "Lord, what about him?" [22] Jesus said to him, "If it is my will that he remain until I come, what is that to you? Follow me!" [23] So the rumor spread in the community that this disciple would not die. Yet Jesus did not say to him that he would not die, but, "If it is my will that he remain until I come, what is that to you?"

Following is immediately associated also with the disciple whom Jesus loved. The profound themes of this chapter now reach their climax, their inexhaustibility symbolized by the imagery of abundance:

- Knowing Jesus (vv. 4, 7, 12) and being known by him (vv. 15, 16, 17)
- Loving Jesus (vv. 15, 16, 17) and being loved by him (v. 20) (see the quotation from Traherne in the sidebar)
- The ongoing presence of Jesus (vv. 7, 12) and the future oriented toward him (vv. 22, 23)
- Being fed by Jesus (vv. 12–13) and feeding others (vv. 15, 16, 17)
- Following Jesus (vv. 19, 22) and testifying to him (vv. 7, 24)
- The desire of Jesus and abiding (vv. 22, 23)

All these are under the sign of abundance: of provision, of action, and of meaning—and those three speak of love. The provision is signaled by "the net . . . full of large fish" (v. 11), the action by the "things that Jesus did," and the meaning by imagining "the world" overflowing with "the books that would be written" if all possible testimony to Jesus were to be written down (v. 25).

That list reads like an index of key themes, and all the more so if other kindred key themes are included under these headings—for example, word, truth,

> But after all to be Beloved is the Greatest Happiness. All This Glory and all these Treasures, being nothing but the Appendencies, and the ornaments of that person that is our Bride or Friend, prepared all for the Sake of Lov, to commend and sweeten it more unto us . . . for God is Lov. And all this shews his Lov unto my soul. Yea, it Shews indeed that for which I entirely Lov Him, that He is Infinite Lov to every Soul![a]
>
> —Thomas Traherne
>
> a. Quotation in Inge, *Happiness and Holiness: Thomas Traherne and His Writings*, 143.

and light under knowing and testifying; word, trusting, and believing under following; life under love, food, following, and abiding; "I am" under presence and abiding. And Jesus himself is essential to all of them, as well as to the glory that he shares with his Father and with those who trust and love him.

The disciple whom Jesus loved, who was first explicitly introduced on the breast of Jesus at the Last Supper, appears with a reminder of his role in that meal. In the meanwhile, he has taken the mother of Jesus into his home (19:27), so that is where we are to imagine him continuing to **remain** [or "abide"] **until I come**. The contrast with Peter and his up-front leadership is underlined by both mother and Beloved Disciple being anonymous in this Gospel, members of a largely hidden community. In the Beloved Disciple there come together not only key themes of the Farewell Discourses—love, abiding, and testifying—but also their orientation to a future centered on Jesus.

Elsewhere in the New Testament (especially in some of its earliest documents, such as Mark 13 and 1 Thess. 4–5) that future is evoked in imaginative, spectacular language, sometimes including signs of the end and a sense of imminent expectation. Here, probably some decades after the Gospel of Mark was written, the essence of those future expectations has been distilled to focus on a who, not a what or when or how or whether: *the future is Jesus*. Speculation about timing or about what might happen to someone in particular is discouraged. Instead, there is a gentle but firm insistence, underlined by repetition, on the primacy of the desire of Jesus, **my will** (*thelō*, "will/desire"), and on his freedom to act in ways that his followers are not able to anticipate—and indeed they should not see it as their business to try to do so: **"What is that to you?"** Instead of wanting to know such things, the emphatic, Jesus-centered imperative is, **"Follow me!"**[4]

The Final Surprising Abundance: Testifying through Writing (21:24–25)

> 24 This is the disciple who is testifying to these things and has written them, and we know that his testimony is true. 25 But there are also many other things that Jesus did; if every one of them were written down, I suppose that the world itself could not contain the books that would be written.

Then comes the final surprise: the testimony and writing of this Gospel is ascribed to the Beloved Disciple. There could hardly be a more authoritative

4. As we saw in the preceding note, the first "Follow me" to Peter, in v. 19, is simply *akolouthei moi*. The second, in v. 22, is *sy moi akolouthei*—literally, "You me follow," in which the "you" is emphatic, and the relationship with Jesus is stressed by it being placed alongside "me" (compare the discussion above of the personal pronouns in John 17). The effect is to direct Peter back to his own responsibility in his relationship with Jesus.

author. If this is true, and if this is also the last of the four Gospels to be completed, then it has something approaching an ideal combination: eyewitness testimony by someone very close to Jesus; knowledge of other attempts (the other writings implied in 20:30–31 and 21:25) to tell the story and open up its meaning; and many years to reflect on it, learning, testing, and going deeper through participation in the ongoing drama of following Jesus, sharing life with his mother and the rest of the community of friends, and praying in line with the desire of Jesus, "that the love with which you have loved me may be in them, and I in them" (17:26).

Is it true? The complication is evident in the text itself in verses 24–25, where the testimony and writing are ascribed to the Beloved Disciple: **This is the disciple who is testifying to these things and has written them**; yet there is also testimony to his reliability given by others: **We know that his testimony is true**; and then the only authorial "I" comes in the final sentence: **I suppose**. Who are "we"? Who is "I"? And who is "the disciple whom Jesus loved"?

Huge amounts have been written on those questions. My conclusion on what these verses intend to say has several elements.

First, there is eyewitness testimony by a disciple of Jesus at the heart of this Gospel.

Second, both the "we" and the "I" are distinguished from that disciple, and Andrew Lincoln's suggestion rings true, that *grapsas* ("has written") "is best taken loosely in the sense of having instigated or been responsible for the writing of the bulk of the narrative rather than actually having penned it. In 19:19, 22 the verb is also employed in this looser way to describe Pilate's role in writing the inscription on the cross. . . . The Beloved Disciple is being claimed as the authority for the distinctive perspective that has shaped and pervaded the witness of the narrative."[5]

Third, the Beloved Disciple was a leading figure in his community, the "we" who here vouch for the truth of his testimony. He may have died by the time these closing verses were added—hence the concern in the community about false rumors quoting what Jesus said about him (v. 23).

Fourth, the "I" of the final verse seems to be a member of the community of the Beloved Disciple who is responsible for some of the actual writing—it is impossible to say how much.

Fifth, the Beloved Disciple has not been conclusively identified. I agree with those who date the completion of the Gospel of John around 80 CE, two of whom introduce their discussion of its authorship as follows: "In its earliest manuscripts, the Gospel of John was anonymous, as were all the Gospels. Their

5. Lincoln, *The Gospel according to Saint John*, 523.

The "archive of excess," in McCracken's study of John, refers to the claim of 21:25 that the whole world could not contain the books needed to recount all the actions of Jesus, but the phrase aptly characterizes chapter 21 as a whole.[a] This ending deals in excess—the one hundred fifty-three fish, the breakfast waiting even before the fish are hauled to shore, the strength of the nets, the repeated question of Jesus to Peter, the discipleship of Peter and the Beloved Disciple, and, especially, the limitless character of Jesus' deeds. Considered in relation to the Gospel as a whole, the chapter is also a matter of excess, for the Gospel already has an ending in chapter 20. The ending in John 21, however, both recalls a series of scenes throughout the Gospel and signals that this narrative cannot close on a world whose equilibrium is restored or only modestly altered. Following this narrative, nothing can remain unchanged.

—Beverly Roberts Gaventa, "The Archive of Excess," 249

a. Referring to McCracken, *The Scandal of the Gospels*.

titles, which attributed authorship, were added only later. The title added to John was *kata Iōannēn*, 'according to John.' But even those titles do not identify which John (or which Matthew, Mark, or Luke) wrote these works. Christian writers of the second and third centuries attributed this Gospel to John, the son of Zebedee, a disciple of Jesus, but there is little other evidence to support this assertion."[6] Of recent discussions, one that comes to a plausible conclusion is that of Richard Bauckham, who argues for another John, called the Elder, a disciple of Jesus with strong Jerusalem connections.[7] Yet the Gospel's own guarding of the anonymity of the Beloved Disciple should discourage placing too much weight on naming him.

The final verse testifies to **many other things that Jesus did**, using the same phrase, *epoiēsen ho Iēsous* ("Jesus did/made/created"), that was used about the "many other signs" in 20:30, echoing John 1:1 and Genesis 1:1.[8] There is no reason to limit these "many other things" to the time between the birth of Jesus and the appearances recounted in John 20 and 21. His activity in this Gospel spans creation and all of time, and the past tense "did" can be understood to extend up to the minute that sentence was written—and up to every minute since. *This is the ongoing activity of Jesus, who is present as God is present, active in the Spirit, inspiring life-giving signs, work, love, prayer, testimony, and writing.*

6. O'Day and Hylen, *John*, 3.
7. Bauckham, *The Testimony of the Beloved Disciple*.
8. See comments on 20:30 and 1:1.

If every one of them were written down, I suppose that the world itself could not contain the books that would be written. The final image of abundance is of "the world [*ho kosmos*] itself" overflowing with the books that could be written (see the quotation from Gaventa in the sidebar). *It is a world that is being loved by someone whose desire is to unite earth and heaven, to share life in all its fullness, and to address each reader by name.*

Epilogue

The writing of this book has taken twenty years since its conception. It has been interwoven with many other things in my life, and I hope it will help readers understand it better if I give some account of the experience of writing it, and in particular of its companion writings. I will attempt this using the four headings that have proved most helpful in the introduction.

Abundance

The overwhelming experience during these twenty years has been of the abundance of meaning in John. I have been repeatedly amazed at how extraordinarily generative this short text has been and continues to be.

Attempting a commentary on John began as a project for the new millennium. John had long fascinated me, but I had never dared to tackle it directly as a whole. Several elements combined to encourage undertaking it.

The main one was the five years spent with Frances Young (and in conversation with many others, especially Daniel Hardy) reading, translating, teaching, and writing essays on Paul's Second Letter to the Corinthians.[1] Both she and I were classicists (Greek and Latin) by training, after which she had mostly specialized in New Testament and the theology of the early church, while I had largely focused on Christian theology of the past hundred years. What slowly emerged during the five years of collaboration was greater clarity about something I had been groping toward for a long time: how to do justice to the Bible as a book to be understood in its historical context, in relation to many centuries of interpretation, and as a source of meaning and truth for life today.

1. Young and Ford, *Meaning and Truth in 2 Corinthians.*

This approach, combining scholarship, hermeneutics, and contemporary theological and other thinking, was later summed up in a chapter of a book on Christian wisdom.[2] But, before that, it was put into practice in a follow-up book to the work on 2 Corinthians, *Self and Salvation: Being Transformed*, written during the 1990s. The biblical interpretation in that was largely of Paul, the Synoptic Gospels, and the Old Testament / Septuagint / Hebrew Bible, but questions relating to John kept arising. In retrospect, it reminds me of first seeing Mount Everest as our family waited at dawn on a viewing platform near Darjeeling and the rising sun revealed the breathtaking sight. John became for me the Everest of theological understanding.

By the time the new millennium dawned, I regarded John's Gospel as the culminating Christian scriptural text and its author worthy of the Eastern Orthodox title, "The Theologian." I decided to risk the climb.

The basic experience has been that of rereading John continually—and I would be delighted if one effect of this commentary on its readers is to encourage them to develop this habit too. I became convinced that John is both later than the Synoptic Gospels and also written in conversation with them, and probably with the writings of Paul too. After reading many other views (there is an abundance of conflicting scholarly conclusions about John, more than on any of the other Gospels), I still think that is so. It combines eyewitness testimony; selective, reflective, and creative use of other writings; and long-matured thinking about key questions, the main two being, Who is Jesus? and What is essential for those who follow him?

This commentary has especially focused on those questions, within the horizon of God and all reality. While pursuing them and others, one of the most striking things has been what I call the "deep plain sense"—the way John uses carefully chosen ordinary words that turn out to have unfathomable depths, both within this Gospel and through resonating with intertexts and the surrounding culture. I was also intrigued by how the author of John, by showing how he[3] reads his Scriptures, teaches readers to read his text as Scripture. As Scripture, John makes more and more sense through being reread and reread and reread, and after twenty years I have found that it continues to grip me as no other text has. Yet this is by no means competitive with other texts and other bearers of meaning. John generously encourages readers to engage again and again with other texts too, and with meaning and truth wherever it is found.

2. Ford, *Christian Wisdom*, chap. 2, "A Wisdom Interpretation of Scripture."

3. Was the author male? This is one of the many disputed questions about this Gospel. The majority scholarly opinion favors a man, but, as often with such questions, the minority arguments are illuminating, and the involvement of far more than one "author" in the process leading to the text we have now leaves room for a both/and answer.

I am still learning how to read John, and every rereading teaches more. In this process, the blossoming of literary approaches to John, especially during the past thirty years, has been especially helpful. It has illuminated the detailed, imaginative crafting of the text, the use of imagery and metaphor, ambiguity, plot, character, repetition, irony, perspective, time, place, resonance, and levels of meaning. A book such as the present one, short by comparison with many on John, can only sample these feasts of meaning, and otherwise refer to their menus.

Yet the strange thing is that, for all the abundant richness, this is also probably the most immediately and straightforwardly comprehensible of the Gospels:[4] simpler Greek; fewer, well-crafted stories of signs, encounters, and conversations; a few big imperatives (trust, follow, serve, love, abide); and a clear primary focus on who Jesus is. But, once one is gripped by it, every rereading draws one deeper, further, wider, and higher. The Everest imagery of height is true but inadequate and needs those other dimensions—the breadth of continents, the depth and breadth of oceans, and the length of journeys across both.

Imagery of time as well as space is needed. Rereading John year after year, I have found that the adverb that fits best is "slowly." John requires an abundance of time. This project has felt like a task that could not be hurried. It has had its own slow tempo, and whenever I have tried to force the pace, I have ended up having to revise and sometimes completely rewrite. And even when the slow pace has been followed and something has been written, there is no sense of completeness in the interpretation. It is always an interim report.

The slowness with John has, however, been accompanied by other writing that has been quicker. Of the books written and edited during the twenty years while working on John, six have been particularly significant as intertexts for the present book.

Editing three editions of *The Modern Theologians* has been a rich educational experience. The third edition[5] stretched my horizons further than earlier editions in such areas as theology and biological sciences, prayer and spirituality, Christian theology and other faiths, theology and film, pastoral theology, feminist and womanist theologies, theological ethics, postcolonial biblical interpretation, Asian and African theologies, and Pentecostal and Eastern Orthodox theologies. All that richness of theology around the world seemed in line with the horizon opened up by the Gospel of John, especially in its prologue and Farewell Discourses. Indeed, the Johannine horizon, and the Spirit that "leads into all the truth" (16:13), could be seen as essential to the

4. It is often the first one given to new Christians.

5. Ford and Muers, *The Modern Theologians.*

inspiration behind the remarkable flourishing of Christian theology in the past hundred years.

Throughout the past twenty years, besides reading John by myself, with fellow Christians, and with a range of academics, I have also been regularly reading Scriptures with members of other religious traditions in the practice known as Scriptural Reasoning. I took part in the beginnings of this practice in the early 1990s, when it involved Jewish, Christian, and Muslim scriptures. By 2012 it had spread to many countries, and in China been developed to include Confucian, Daoist, and Buddhist scriptures as well as the Abrahamic. In India and elsewhere it is now including Hindu and Sikh scriptures. It also spread beyond the academic settings of its origins into many others—schools, local congregations of the various religions, hospitals, prisons, businesses, armed forces, civil service, civil society organizations, joint leadership training for members of different faiths, and more. Through taking part in Scriptural Reasoning I have often read texts from John with those of other faiths. That has been both enriching and challenging, and the results of this engagement have fed into the commentary at many points, though made explicit only occasionally. Writing on Scriptural Reasoning, while also working on this commentary, has been a further illuminating area of engagement (resulting in the second and third books),[6] and that has helped to reflect further on the mutual illumination (often by improving the understanding of strong disagreements) that can happen between the meanings arising from diverse scriptures.

The fourth and fifth works, *Christian Wisdom: Desiring God and Learning in Love* and *The Drama of Living: Becoming Wise in the Spirit*, are the two main companion books for this commentary.

Christian Wisdom (2007) integrates my developing understanding of John with other biblical books, especially Job, Psalms, Song of Songs, Isaiah, Wisdom of Solomon, Sirach, Luke, Acts, 1 Corinthians, Ephesians, and Revelation, and gives an account of the approach to Scripture used in this commentary. It gives much fuller discussions of particular theological topics than is possible in a commentary, the most important being on evil and suffering; God, Jesus, and the Spirit; tradition; and worship. Of themes running through the book the most relevant here are wisdom, knowledge, learning, meaning, and discernment; reading and rereading; cries and desire; faith and love; Judaism; the kingdom

6. See Ford and Pecknold, *The Promise of Scriptural Reasoning*, and also the more recent Ford and Clemson, *Interreligious Reading after Vatican II*. See, too, the foreword to what I consider the most significant book on Scriptural Reasoning to have been written so far, Ochs, *Religion without Violence*; and, in addition, many occasional writings, addresses, and web-based material, as on www.scripturalreasoning.org and the Rose Castle Foundation website, www.rosecastle.com.

of God and abundance; community and church; and being human. Likewise not appropriate in a commentary are the three detailed case studies, each of them partly shaped by my reading of John: interfaith wisdom in Scriptural Reasoning; interdisciplinary wisdom in universities; and interpersonal wisdom in relation to learning disability.

The Drama of Living (2014) is aimed at a wider readership, takes John as its primary text, and focuses mainly on what this commentary calls the ongoing drama of living and loving. It is John applied to ordinary daily life; to work, love, and sex; to Christianity and other faiths; to community and disability; to aging and dying. Besides John, the poetry of Micheal O'Siadhail is the main conversation partner. *The Drama of Living* is my interim account, partly autobiographical, of how John can shape life now.

Those two books are very different genres. The first is constructive theology, an account of themes and topics accompanied by case studies; the second is spirituality, a practical guide to the formative and transformative potential of John and other sources of meaning. I am fascinated by the fruitfulness of diverse genres (the Bible has many), but I believe that the interpretation of Scripture is primary for Christian thinking, praying, living, and writing. Unless that pervades all the other genres, Christian understanding, worship, and action are not nourished from their deepest and most widely shared source. That is by no means an original conclusion—it is common ground among most Christians down through the centuries and around the world today. But such interpretation can take many forms. I have had two main aims.

First, I have read John in conversation with a good many other commentaries and interpretations. I have tried to learn from them and to be as sure-footed as possible in scholarly terms, but without being too occupied with the scholarly guild's detailed discussions. I have tried not to weigh the text down with footnotes, but to indicate in the bibliography which have been the writings on John that have been most important for me. Sometimes their influences have been very hard to separate out from one another or even recollect, and I apologize for the resulting unattributed insights.

Second, I have attempted to convey the sense of God's presence, in the past and now, in Jesus and the Spirit, and to connect that with the ongoing drama of following Jesus, within the horizon of God and all reality. There is no such thing as neutrality here—everyone stands somewhere in relation to these issues, and John continually invites readers to decide where they stand and which path to follow. I am a fallible follower of Jesus who has found John to be an incomparably helpful, surprising, and challenging text, and one result has been the writing of this book.

The sixth book, *Wording a Radiance: Parting Conversations on God and the Church*,[7] has been perhaps the most unusual, and most Johannine, of any publication in which I have participated. My father-in-law and long-term friend, conversation partner, and coauthor, Daniel Hardy, was diagnosed with cancer in early 2007 and given six months to live, which proved accurate. He was living next door to my wife, Deborah, and myself, and those months were an unprecedented period of intense interaction and conversation. He also had a contract for a book on the church with Cambridge University Press, and it was clear that he would not be able to write it. But Peter Ochs, a professor of Jewish philosophy at the University of Virginia, cofounder of Scriptural Reasoning, and a close friend of all three of us, was determined to elicit the book. Peter rang Dan nearly every day during the six months, till he finally announced, just before Dan died in November, "I've got it!"

Peter, Deborah, and I could not face the task for a couple of years, but when we eventually spent some days comparing notes and memories, we realized that we had what amounted to Dan's "farewell discourses." Each of us had a deep but also very different relationship with Dan, and our three testimonies both converged and diverged. But at the heart of them was the remarkable testimony of Dan to his experiences in the Holy Land, to his theological vision, and to what can happen through, in Dan's words, "allowing the divine to flood in without inhibition."[8] There was an intensely, and self-consciously Johannine, integration of theology and life, through which the golden thread was "the reality and superabundance of meaning in God."[9]

Jesus

The experience of writing this book has been most significant in the way it has enabled ongoing and repeatedly renewed relationship with Jesus in trust and love. If he is who John says he is—the "I am" who is present as God is present—then reading and rereading this Gospel is done in the presence of Jesus, an occasion for meeting him through faith and for being drawn deeper and deeper into a relationship of mutual knowledge, trust, and love. It has been an astonishing, humbling, and transformative gift to be able to experience this year after year, in conversation, community, and friendship with many others.

Since I am a theologian, the intellectual dimension of that experience has, of course, been important, with constant evaluation of the ways in which other

7. Hardy, with Hardy Ford, Ochs, and Ford, *Wording a Radiance.*
8. Hardy, with Hardy Ford, Ochs, and Ford, *Wording a Radiance*, back cover.
9. Hardy, with Hardy Ford, Ochs, and Ford, *Wording a Radiance*, 114.

theologians have thought about Jesus. The significance of works can increase or decrease, as they are reread, tested, and found to be more or less illuminating.

For me, one book has stood out beyond others. It is *The Identity of Jesus Christ* by Hans Frei. I had the privilege of knowing Hans Frei and consider him the twentieth-century North American theologian who has most to teach us in the twenty-first century. He proposed what I consider the best way of categorizing the variety of modern Christian theologians and theologies,[10] and he also made what I judge to be the single most important twentieth-century contribution to the interpretation of the New Testament Gospels in *The Eclipse of Biblical Narrative*. *The Identity of Jesus Christ* is mainly focused on the Synoptic Gospels, and I have in this book developed many of its findings and proposals[11] in relation to the Gospel of John. These include my approaches to the relationship of the identity of Jesus Christ (the "who" question) to his presence, the relationship of history to theology in John, how to understand the "plain sense" of John, and, above all, how to do both historical and theological justice to the resurrection of Jesus.[12]

Ongoing Drama

My little ongoing drama of writing this commentary has had a large cast of characters over the years.

Besides the people and authors already mentioned, I think with gratitude of numerous classes on John at Cambridge University, at the Community of St. Anselm, at Emory University's Candler School of Theology in Atlanta, and elsewhere, and of many gatherings of laity and clergy from the Church of England and other churches. Teaching is one of the best ways to learn. The problem is that many ideas come through the back and forth with students, or in reading good essays, and it is almost impossible to remember later where they came from—so my apologies are due to all those students and others who recognize their unacknowledged contributions.

There have been innumerable occasional conversations and other exchanges about John, including with authors of some of my favorite books on John—Susan Hylen, Dorothy Lee, and Margaret Daly-Denton. After nearly a decade on the project, in 2009 there was a sustained conversation around John that

10. Frei, *Types of Christian Theology*. It is used to map Christian theology since 1918 in the introduction to each of the three editions of Ford and Muers, *The Modern Theologians*.

11. Perceptively summarized by Mike Higton in his foreword to the 2013 edition.

12. The 2013 edition helpfully adds to the book an appendix containing Frei's essay, "Theological Reflections on the Accounts of Jesus' Death and Resurrection."

has acted as an inspiration and a benchmark. Richard Bauckham had just retired from St. Andrews University to Cambridge, and Richard Hays was in Cambridge for a six-month sabbatical. We put twenty-one three-hour sessions in our diaries, and the three of us read the whole Gospel together. That time has continued to be fruitful.

In 2014 the McDonald Agape Foundation generously sponsored a symposium on John to which I was able to invite a small group of those with whom I most wanted to engage over several days.[13] One was Jean Vanier, the founder of the L'Arche communities in which those with and without learning disabilities share life together. I had found his commentary on John illuminating; I was also part of a small group with him, Frances Young, my wife Deborah, and the international coordinators of L'Arche, that over several years had met to discuss matters related to L'Arche, especially its ethos and constitution as an international federation. He had also encouraged Deborah to found (together with others) Lyn's House, a L'Arche-inspired community in Cambridge (see below). He died in 2019; and then in 2020 an independent inquiry set up by L'Arche found that he had sexually abused several women who were in spiritual direction with him. Stefan Posner, the leader of L'Arche International, spoke for us all: "We have been deeply and painfully shaken."[14] Posner's full response expresses well the need to face the "heartbreaking truth," to have concern for the victims, to reassess the legacy of Vanier, and yet to continue to value the good in what he did and the wisdom in what he said and wrote. The question for this commentary (most of which was already written by then) has been whether to include references to Vanier. After taking counsel, I decided that the insights in the commentary that I owed to Vanier should be kept and attributed to him—they are not invalidated by what has been revealed about his behavior in spiritual accompaniment. But the wrestling with the complex legacy of Vanier continues, within and beyond L'Arche, and for me personally. It has led to further rereading of John, and to renewed recognition that the darkness continues (in ourselves, in others, in the church, and in the rest of the world), just as for John this was evident in Jesus's first disciples as well as in his opponents.

In 2015 I delivered eight Bampton Lectures at Oxford University on "Daring Spirit: John's Gospel Now." The preparation, accompanying discussions in

13. The participants were Jonathan Aitken, Richard Bauckham, Frances Clemson, Maria Dakake, Deborah Ford, Richard Hays, Peter McDonald, Peter Ochs, Micheal O'Siadhail, Jean Vanier, Justin Welby, and Frances Young.

14. Céline Hoyeau, "Stephan Posner, Standing Up When the Ground Slips from under You," L'Arche International, accessed March 10, 2021, https://www.larche.org/news/-/asset_publisher/mQsRZspJMdBy/content/when-the-ground-slips-from-under-you?, translation of "Stephan Posner, tenir debout quand le sol se dérobe," *La Croix*, August 3, 2020, https://www.la-croix.com/Religion/Stephan-Posner-tenir-debout-quand-sol-derobe-2020-08-03-1201107557.

Oxford, and feedback from the lectures, in addition to close collaboration with Giles Waller, who combined help with research, editorial expertise, and illuminating conversation, made these few years a concentrated time of coming to a range of judgments, especially regarding the academic work of others on John. Giles was the fourth in a series of remarkable research associates I had in the Faculty of Divinity at Cambridge University during the two decades of work on this commentary, and to each of the others—Paul Nimmo, Simeon Zahl, and Frances Clemson—I also owe considerable debts of gratitude. There are few things more valuable than intensive conversation and collaboration with colleagues in the rising generation in one's field.

Since my retirement in late 2015, I have been doing far more things beyond the academy that are concerned with John. There have been many more church-related study days, residential conferences, courses, and lectures. There has been more involvement with Scriptural Reasoning, especially in the United Kingdom, China, and India. There has been more time for the Cambridge-based Lyn's House community, in which people with and without learning disabilities come together in friendship.[15] There has also been an array of further conversations around John and related texts and topics, and Michael Volland, principal of Ridley Hall in Cambridge, has helpfully read with me whatever part of John I have happened to be working on. Especially illuminating have been regular meetings of a small group[16] on the interrelationship of psychotherapy and theology, which works mainly by reading and reflecting on Dante's *Divine Comedy*.

Two commitments in particular have opened up new and challenging implications of the Gospel of John. The Church of England has around a million pupils in its state-funded church schools. Taking part in the working group that produced the Church of England Vision for Education in 2016 was an unusually satisfying experience, and it has been even more satisfactory to see the way it has been welcomed, followed through, and embedded in thousands of schools. Its leading concept is from John 10:10, "life in all its fullness."[17]

The Rose Castle Foundation, based at an 800-year-old castle in Cumbria, northwest England, is dedicated to the formation of those committed to reconciliation across deep divisions and to interfaith engagement (it is the United Kingdom hub for Scriptural Reasoning), religious literacy, and the environment. I took part in a group, convened by its founding director, Sarah Snyder, that worked on a "Wisdom of Reconciliation" aimed at helping in the work being

15. See Ford, Hardy Ford, and Randall, *A Kind of Upside-Downness*.
16. Deborah Hardy Ford, Loraine Gelsthorpe, and Vittorio Montemaggi.
17. https://www.churchofengland.org/media/2532839/ce-education-vision-web-final.pdf.

done both through Rose Castle and through the Archbishop of Canterbury's Reconciling Leaders Network and its associated initiative, Women on the Frontline. That also led to fresh Johannine insights—above all into the encompassing significance of John 17:20–26.

The result of this latest phase has been much rereading of what had already been written in this commentary, and extensive rewriting.

God and All Reality

The horizon within which all this has taken place has increasingly been shaped by the interplay between the Gospel of John, its interpretation down through the centuries and around the world today, and those involvements in church, academy, and world just mentioned. But there has been one other experience that has contributed distinctively to the formation of that horizon and to my own perception of our twenty-first-century world and the appropriate reception of John within it.

In 2018 Micheal O'Siadhail published *The Five Quintets*. It is five long poems on each of five themes, moving from early modernity up to the present: "Making," on the arts; "Dealing," on economics; "Steering," on politics; "Finding," on the sciences; and "Meaning," on philosophy and theology. For nearly fifty years I have been the first reader of O'Siadhail's poetry, and he of my theology. *The Five Quintets* took over a decade to write, so my reading and responding to it, as it was being produced, was interwoven with the work on this commentary, just as his writing of *The Five Quintets* was accompanied by him reading and responding to this commentary chapter by chapter. I will not attempt to sum up the mutual influence of the two texts, but simply note that O'Siadhail's vision of God and all reality can illuminate and supplement that of the Gospel of John as I have understood it.[18] I hope in the future to write a sequel to *The Drama of Living* that will try to bring together the Bible and *The Five Quintets* in relation to twenty-first-century thinking, praying, and living.

Since the publication of *The Five Quintets* there have been major global developments in politics and economics, in the environmental crisis, in machine learning and our "information civilization," and in other areas, and it has been fascinating to discern time and again how relevant the Gospel of John is to shaping responses to them. Most recently, there has been the COVID-19, or coronavirus, pandemic. As I write, we are still in the midst of that, and the last section of the introduction has commented on it. The final revision of the

18. For my response to *The Five Quintets*, see Ford, "Seeking a Wiser Worldview in the Twenty-First Century."

chapters of this book has been done bearing in mind this new situation, but explicit treatment of it must await future publications.

The final note is from *The Five Quintets*, as the last canto heads for its climax in a vision of God:

> I can't yet understand but know by heart
> that nothing but desire can underwrite
> my passage through this vaulted light-led zone,
> that in this arch's eye all things unite.[19]

19. O'Siadhail, *The Five Quintets*, 355 (used with permission).

Bibliography

Not all the works read or consulted in the writing of this commentary can be listed. Typically, in studying a particular verse, chapter, or topic, I have consulted multiple sources and then come to a conclusion that cannot be attributed to any single author, so many sources are missing from the footnotes—it would overload the notes to name them all. This has the odd result that some authors who have been influential may get few explicit mentions, or even none at all. In the bibliography that follows, that is especially true (just to choose thirty that have been particularly important from around two hundred listed there) of the works by Adams, Aquinas, Ashton, Augustine, Barth, Bauckham, Bonhoeffer, Brodie, Bultmann, Coloe, Ecclestone, Ruth Edwards, Frei, Frey, Greggs, Hays, Hylen, Inge, Lee, Levertov, Ochs, O'Day, Quash, Reinhartz, Ricoeur, Ringe, Schneiders, Sonderegger, Westcott, and Young. Of the modern post-1918 commentaries, if compelled to name just a dozen that have, in very different ways, been most helpful to think with, chapter after chapter (which does not imply complete agreement with them), I probably would choose Barrett, Brant, Brown, Bruner, Daly-Denton, Gardner, Hoskyns and Davey, Lincoln, Newbigin, Schnackenburg, Vanier, and the short gem by O'Day and Hylen. And if John McHugh had lived to complete his commentary—of which we only have the posthumously published fragment on John 1–4, exquisite in both scholarship and historical theology—his certainly would be there.

The decision has been made mainly to list the works cited, but others are included that have been important. There are many more relevant works that could be listed, some of them cited in the other writings I have published during this period, as mentioned in the epilogue.

Abbott, Edwin A. *Johannine Vocabulary: A Comparison of the Words of the Fourth Gospel with Those of the Other Three*. London: Adam & Charles Black, 1905. Reprint, Eugene, OR: Wipf & Stock, 2005.

Adams, Nicholas. *Eclipse of Grace: Divine and Human Interaction in Hegel*. Oxford: Wiley-Blackwell, 2013.

Anderson, Paul N. *The Christology of the Fourth Gospel: Its Unity and Disunity in the Light of John 6*. Valley Forge, PA: Trinity Press International, 1996.

Anselm. *Proslogion*. In *St. Anselm: Basic Writings*, edited and translated by S. N. Deane. Chicago: Open Court, 1962.

Aquinas, Thomas. *Catena Aurea: Commentary on the Four Gospels Collected out of the Works of the Fathers*. Edited by John Henry Newman. 4 vols. Southampton: Saint Austin, 1997.

———. *Commentary on the Gospel of John*. Translated by Fabian Larcher and James A. Weisheipf. 3 vols. Washington, DC: Catholic University of America Press, 2010.

Ashton, John. *The Gospel of John and Christian Origins*. Minneapolis: Fortress, 2014.

———. *The Interpretation of John*. 2nd ed. Edinburgh: T&T Clark, 1997.

———. *Understanding the Fourth Gospel*. 2nd ed. Oxford: Oxford University Press, 2007.

Attridge, Harold W. "The Samaritan Woman: A Woman Transformed." In *Character Studies in the Fourth Gospel: Narrative Approaches to Seventy Figures in John*, edited by Steven Hunt, D. Francois Tolmie, and Ruben Zimmermann, 268–81. Wissenschaftliche Untersuchungen zum Neuen Testament 314. Tübingen: Mohr Siebeck, 2013.

Augustine. *Homilies on the Gospel of John 1–40*. Translated by Edmund Hill. Edited by Allan D. Fitzgerald. New York: New City Press, 2009.

Aulén, Gustav. *Christus Victor: An Historical Study of the Three Main Types of the Idea of Atonement*. Translated by A. G. Hebert. London: Macmillan, 1969.

Barker, Margaret. *King of the Jews: Temple Theology in John's Gospel*. London: SPCK, 2014.

Barrett, C. K. *The Gospel according to St. John: An Introduction with Commentary and Notes on the Greek Text*. 2nd ed. London: SPCK, 1978.

Barth, Karl. *Church Dogmatics*. Translated by G. T. Thomson. 4 vols. Edinburgh: T&T Clark, 1936–69.

———. *Witness to the Word: A Commentary on John 1*. Translated by Geoffrey W. Bromiley. Edited by Walther Fürst. Grand Rapids: Eerdmans, 1986.

Barton, Stephen C. "Johannine Dualism and Contemporary Pluralism." In Bauckham and Mosser, *Gospel of John*, 3–18.

Bauckham, Richard. *Gospel of Glory: Major Themes in Johannine Theology*. Grand Rapids: Baker Academic, 2015.

———. *The Testimony of the Beloved Disciple: Narrative, History, and Theology in the Gospel of John*. Grand Rapids: Baker Academic, 2007.

Bauckham, Richard, and Carl Mosser, eds. *The Gospel of John and Christian Theology*. Grand Rapids: Eerdmans, 2008.

Bayfield, Tony, ed. *Deep Calls to Deep: Transforming Conversations between Jews and Christians*. London: SCM, 2018.

Begbie, Jeremy S. *Resounding Truth: Christian Wisdom in the World of Music*. London: SPCK, 2008.

———. *Theology, Music and Time*. Cambridge: Cambridge University Press, 2000.

Begbie, Jeremy S., and Steven R. Guthrie, eds. *Resonant Witness: Conversations between Music and Theology*. Grand Rapids: Eerdmans, 2011.

Behr, John. *John the Theologian and His Paschal Gospel*. Oxford: Oxford University Press, 2019.

Bieringer, Reimund. "'I Am Ascending to My Father and Your Father, to My God and Your God' (John 20:17): Resurrection and Ascension in the Gospel of John." In *The Resurrection of Jesus in the Gospel of John*, edited by Craig R. Koester and Reimund Bieringer, 209–35. Wissenschaftliche Untersuchungen zum Neuen Testament 222. Tübingen: Mohr Siebeck, 2008.

Bieringer, Reimund, Didier Pollefeyt, and Frederique Vandecasteele-Vanneuville, eds. *Anti-Judaism and the Fourth Gospel: Papers of the Leuven Colloquium, 2000*. Jewish and Christian Heritage 1. Assen: Royal Van Gorcum, 2001.

Bonhoeffer, Dietrich. *Christ the Center*. Translated by Edwin Robinson. New York: Harper & Row, 1978.

Bouyer, Louis. *The Fourth Gospel*. Translated by Patrick Byrne. Westminster, MD: Newman, 1964.

Brant, Jo-Ann A. *John*. Paideia. Grand Rapids: Baker Academic, 2011.

Brodie, Thomas L. *The Gospel according to John: A Literary and Theological Commentary*. Oxford: Oxford University Press, 1993.

———. *The Quest for the Origin of John's Gospel: A Source-Oriented Approach*. Oxford: Oxford University Press, 1993.

Brown, Raymond E. *The Community of the Beloved Disciple: The Life, Loves, and Hates of an Individual Church in New Testament Times*. New York: Paulist Press, 1979.

———. *The Gospel according to John: Introduction, Translation, and Notes*. 2 vols. Anchor Bible 29, 29A. New York: Doubleday, 1966, 1970.

Brown, Tricia Gates. *Spirit in the Writings of John: Johannine Pneumatology in Social-Scientific Perspective*. Journal for the Study of the New Testament Supplement Series 253. London: T&T Clark, 2003.

Bruner, Frederick Dale. *The Gospel of John: A Commentary*. Grand Rapids: Eerdmans, 2012.

Bultmann, Rudolf. *The Gospel of John*. Translated by G. R. Beasley-Murray. Edited by R. W. N Hoare and J. K. Riches. Oxford: Basil Blackwell, 1971.

———. *Theology of the New Testament*. Translated by Kendrick Grobel. 2 vols. New York: Scribner, 1951, 1955.

Byrne, Brendan. *Life Abounding: A Reading of John's Gospel*. Collegeville, MN: Liturgical Press, 2014.

Calvin, John. *The Gospel according to John 1–10*. Translated by T. H. L. Parker. Edited by David W. Torrance and Thomas F. Torrance. Calvin's New Testament Commentaries 4. Grand Rapids: Eerdmans; Carlisle: Paternoster, 1994.

———. *The Gospel according to John 11–21 and the First Epistle of John*. Translated by T. H. L. Parker. Edited by David W. Torrance and Thomas F. Torrance. Calvin's New Testament Commentaries 5. Grand Rapids: Eerdmans; Carlisle: Paternoster, 1995.

Caragounis, Chrys. "'Abide in Me': The New Mode of Relationship between Jesus and His Followers as a Basis for Christian Ethics (John 15)." In *Rethinking the Ethics of John: "Implicit Ethics" in the Johannine Writings*, edited by Jan G. van der Watt and Ruben Zimmermann, 250–63. Kontexte und Normen neutestamentlicher Ethik 3; Wissenschaftliche Untersuchungen zum Neuen Testament 291. Tübingen: Mohr Siebeck, 2012.

Carnley, Peter. *Resurrection in Retrospect: A Critical Examination of the Theology of N. T. Wright*. Eugene, OR: Cascade, 2019.

Carter, Warren. *John and Empire: Initial Explorations*. New York: T&T Clark, 2008.

———. *John: Storyteller, Interpreter, Evangelist*. Peabody, MA: Hendrickson, 2006.

Cefalu, Paul. *The Johannine Renaissance in Early Modern English Literature and Theology*. Oxford: Oxford University Press, 2017.

Chafe, Eric. *J. S. Bach's Johannine Theology: The St. John Passion and the Cantatas for Spring 1725*. Oxford: Oxford University Press, 2014.

Coloe, Mary L. *Dwelling in the Household of God: Johannine Ecclesiology and Spirituality*. Collegeville, MN: Liturgical Press, 2007.

———. "The Nazarene King: Pilate's Title as the Key to John's Crucifixion." In *The Death of Jesus in the Fourth Gospel*, edited by Gilbert Van Belle, 839–48. Bibliotheca Ephemeridum Theologicarum Lovaniensium 200. Leuven: Leuven University Press, 2007.

Culpepper, R. Alan. *Anatomy of the Fourth Gospel: A Study in Literary Design*. Philadelphia: Fortress, 1983.

———. *The Gospel and Letters of John*. Interpreting Biblical Texts. Nashville: Abingdon, 1998.

Culpepper, R. Alan, and C. Clifton Black, eds. *Exploring the Gospel of John: In Honor of D. Moody Smith*. Louisville: Westminster John Knox, 1996.

Daly-Denton, Margaret. *David in the Fourth Gospel: The Johannine Reception of the Psalms*. Arbeiten zur Geschichte des antiken Judentums und des Urchristentums 47. Leiden: Brill, 2000.

———. *John: Supposing Him to Be the Gardener*. Earth Bible Commentary. London: Bloomsbury T&T Clark, 2017.

Dante Alighieri. *The Divine Comedy: Purgatorio*. Translated and edited by Allen Mandelbaum. Berkeley: University of California Press, 1982.

———. *The Divine Comedy 1: Inferno*. Translated and edited by Robin Kirkpatrick. London: Penguin, 2006.

———. *The Divine Comedy 3: Paradiso*. Translated and edited by Robin Kirkpatrick. London: Penguin, 2007.

Dauphinais, Michael, and Matthew Levering, eds. *Reading John with St. Thomas Aquinas: Theological Exegesis and Speculative Theology*. Washington, DC: Catholic University of America Press, 2005.

Devillers, Luc. *La saga de Siloé: Jésus et la fête des Tentes (Jean 7,1–10,21)*. Lire la bible 143. Paris: Cerf, 2005.

Dodd, C. H. *Historical Tradition in the Fourth Gospel*. Cambridge: Cambridge University Press, 1965.

———. *The Interpretation of the Fourth Gospel*. Cambridge: Cambridge University Press, 1968.

Dokka, Trond Skard. "Irony and Sectarianism in the Gospel of John." In *New Readings in John: Literary and Theological Perspectives*, edited by Johannes Nissen and Sigfred Pedersen, 83–107. London: T&T Clark, 2004.

Donahue, John R., ed. *Life in Abundance: Studies of John's Gospel in Tribute to Raymond E. Brown*. Collegeville, MN: Liturgical Press, 2005.

Ecclestone, Alan. *The Scaffolding of Spirit: Reflections on the Gospel of St John*. London: Darton, Longman & Todd, 1987.

Edwards, Mark. *John*. Blackwell Bible Commentaries. Oxford: Blackwell, 2004.

Edwards, Ruth B. *Discovering John: Content, Interpretation, Reception*. 2nd ed. Discovering Biblical Texts. London: SPCK, 2014.

Elowsky, Joel C., ed. *John 1–10*. Ancient Christian Commentary on Scripture: New Testament IVa. Downers Grove, IL: InterVarsity, 2006.

Engberg-Pedersen, Troels. *John and Philosophy: A New Reading of the Fourth Gospel*. Oxford: Oxford University Press, 2017.

Esler, Philip F., and Ronald Piper. *Lazarus, Mary, and Martha: Social-Scientific Approaches to the Gospel of John*. Minneapolis: Fortress, 2006.

Farelly, Nicolas. *The Disciples in the Fourth Gospel: A Narrative Analysis of Their Faith and Understanding*. Wissenschaftliche Untersuchungen zum Neuen Testament 2/290. Tübingen: Mohr Siebeck, 2010.

Farmer, Craig S., ed. *John 1–12*. Reformation Commentary on Scripture: New Testament 4. Downers Grove, IL: IVP Academic, 2014.

Ford, David F. *Christian Wisdom: Desiring God and Learning in Love*. Cambridge Studies in Christian Doctrine. Cambridge: Cambridge University Press, 2007.

———. *The Drama of Living: Becoming Wise in the Spirit*. Norwich: Canterbury; Grand Rapids: Brazos, 2014.

———. "Mature Ecumenism's Daring Future: Learning from the Gospel of John for the Twenty-First Century." In *Receptive Ecumenism as Ecclesial Learning: Principles, Practices, and Perspectives*, edited by Paul D. Murray, Paul Lakeland, and Gregory A. Ryan. Oxford: Oxford University Press, forthcoming.

———. *Meeting God in John*. London: SPCK, forthcoming.

———. "Meeting Nicodemus: A Case Study in Daring Theological Interpretation." *Scottish Journal of Theology* 66, no. 1 (2013): 1–17.

———. "Reading Backwards, Reading Forwards, and Abiding: Reading John in the Spirit Now." *Journal of Theological Interpretation* 2, no. 1 (2017): 69–84.

———. "Seeking a Wiser Worldview in the Twenty-First Century: Micheal O'Siadhail's *The Five Quintets*." *Studies: An Irish Quarterly Review* 110, no. 437 (Spring 2021): 59–83; no. 438 (Summer 2021): 213–30.

———. *Self and Salvation: Being Transformed*. Cambridge Studies in Christian Doctrine. Cambridge: Cambridge University Press, 1999.

———. "'To See My Glory': Jesus and the Dynamics of Glory in John's Gospel." In *Exploring the Glory of God: New Horizons for a Theology of Glory*. Edited by Adesola Joan Akala. Lanham, MD: Lexington Books / Fortress Academic, 2021.

———. "Ultimate Desire: The Prayer of Jesus in John 17." In *T&T Clark Handbook to Christian Prayer*. Edited by Ashley Cocksworth. London: T&T Clark, 2021.

———. "Who Is Jesus Now?—Maxims and Surprises." *Anglican Theological Review* 101, no. 2 (2019): 213–35.

Ford, David F., and Frances Clemson, eds. *Interreligious Reading after Vatican II*. Oxford: Wiley-Blackwell, 2013.

Ford, David F., and Ashley Cocksworth. *Glorification*. Grand Rapids: Baker Academic, forthcoming.

Ford, David F., Deborah Hardy Ford, and Ian Randall. *A Kind of Upside-Downness: Learning Disabilities and Transformational Community*. London: Jessica Kingsley, 2020.

Ford, David F., and Rachel Muers, eds. *The Modern Theologians: An Introduction to Christian Theology Since 1918*. 3rd ed. Oxford: Blackwell, 2005.

Ford, David F., and C. C. Pecknold, eds. *The Promise of Scriptural Reasoning*. Oxford: Blackwell, 2006.

Francis. *Laudato Si': Encyclical Letter of the Holy Father Francis on Care for our Common Home*. Rome: Libreria Editrice Vaticana, 2015.

Frankl, Viktor. *The Doctor and the Soul: From Psychotherapy to Logotherapy*. Translated by Richard and Clara Winston. London: Penguin, 1973.

Frei, Hans W. *The Eclipse of Biblical Narrative: A Study in Eighteenth and Nineteenth Century Hermeneutics*. New Haven: Yale University Press, 1974.

———. *The Identity of Jesus Christ: The Hermeneutical Bases of Dogmatic Theology*. Updated and expanded ed. Eugene, OR: Cascade, 2013.

———. *Types of Christian Theology*. Edited by George Hunsinger and William C. Placher. New Haven: Yale University Press, 1992.

Frey, Jörg. "'Die Juden' im Johanesevangelium und die Frage nach der 'Trennung der Wege' zwischen der johanneischen Gemeinde und der Synagoge." In *Die Herrlichkeit des Gekreuzigten*, 339–80. Wissenschaftliche Untersuchungen zum Neuen Testament 307. Tübingen: Mohr Siebeck, 2013.

———. "Edler Tod – wirksamer Tod – stellvertretender Tod – heilschaffender Tod: Zur narrativen und theologischen Deutung des Todes Jesu im Johannesevangelium." In *The Death of Jesus in the Fourth Gospel*, edited by Gilbert Van Belle, 65–94. Bibliotheca Ephemeridum Theologicarum Lovaniensium 200. Leuven: Leuven University Press, 2007.

Frey, Jörg, Jan G. van der Watt, and Ruben Zimmermann, eds. *Imagery in the Gospel of John: Terms, Forms, Themes, and Theology of Johannine Figurative Language*. Wissenschaftliche Untersuchungen zum Neuen Testament 200. Tübingen: Mohr Siebeck, 2006.

Gardner, Thomas. *John in the Company of the Poets: The Gospel in Literary Imagination*. Waco: Baylor University Press, 2011.

Gaventa, Beverly Roberts. "The Archive of Excess: John 21 and the Problem of Narrative Closure." In *Exploring the Gospel of John: In Honor of D. Moody Smith*, edited by R. Alan Culpepper and C. Clifton Black, 240–54. Louisville: Westminster John Knox, 1996.

Grayston, Kenneth. *Dying We Live: A New Enquiry into the Death of Christ in the New Testament*. London: Darton, Longman & Todd, 1990.

———. *The Gospel of John*. Narrative Commentaries. Philadelphia: Trinity Press International, 1990.

Greggs, Tom. *Dogmatic Ecclesiology*. Vol. 1, *The Priestly Catholicity of the Church*. Grand Rapids: Baker Academic, 2019.

Gregory Nazianzus. *On the Holy Passover*. Quoted in Dorothy Lee, "Ecology and the Johannine Literature," *St. Mark's Review* 212 (May 2010): 39–50, https://anglican.org.au/wp-content/uploads/2019/05/Ecology-and-the-Johannine-Literature-Dorothy-Lee.pdf.

Haenchen, Ernst. *John: A Commentary on the Gospel of John*. Translated and edited by Robert W. Funk. 2 vols. Hermeneia. Philadelphia: Fortress, 1984.

Hardy, Daniel W., with Deborah Hardy Ford, Peter Ochs, and David F. Ford. *Wording a Radiance: Parting Conversations on God and the Church*. London: SCM, 2010.

Harrington, Wilfred J. *John, Spiritual Theologian: The Jesus of John*. Dublin: Columba, 1999.

Harris, Elizabeth. *Prologue and Gospel: The Theology of the Fourth Evangelist*. Journal for the Study of the New Testament Supplement Series 107. Sheffield: Sheffield Academic, 1994.

Hawkins, Peter S. "All Smiles: Poetry and Theology in Dante's *Commedia*." In *Dante's* Commedia: *Theology as Poetry*, edited by Vittorio Montemaggi and Matthew Treherne, 36–59. Notre Dame, IN: University of Notre Dame Press, 2010.

———. *Dante's Testaments: Essays in Scriptural Imagination*. Figurae. Stanford, CA: Stanford University Press, 1999.

Hays, Richard B. *Echoes of Scripture in the Gospels*. Waco: Baylor University Press, 2016.

Hengel, Martin. "The Prologue of John as the Gateway to Christological Truth." In *The Gospel of John and Christian Theology*, edited by Richard Bauckham and Carl Mosser, 265–94. Grand Rapids: Eerdmans, 2008.

Higton, Mike. *The Life of Christian Doctrine*. London: T&T Clark, 2020.

Hill, Charles. *The Johannine Corpus in the Early Church*. Oxford: Oxford University Press, 2004.

Hofius, Otfried, and Hans-Christian Kammler. *Johannesstudien: Untersuchungen zur Theologie des vierten Evangeliums*. Wissenschaftliche Untersuchungen zum Neuen Testament 88. Tübingen: Mohr Siebeck, 1996.

Hoskyns, E. C., and F. N. Davey. *The Fourth Gospel*. London: Faber & Faber, 1947.

Howard, Wilbert Francis. *The Fourth Gospel in Recent Criticism and Interpretation*. Revised by C. K. Barrett. 4th ed. Eugene, OR: Wipf & Stock, 2009.

Howard-Brook, Wes. *Becoming Children of God: John's Gospel and Radical Discipleship*. Eugene, OR: Wipf & Stock, 1994.

Hunt, Steven A. "The Men of the Samaritan Woman: Six of Sychar." In *Character Studies in the Fourth Gospel: Narrative Approaches to Seventy Figures in John*, edited by Steven Hunt, D. Francois Tolmie, and Ruben Zimmermann, 282–91. Wissenschaftliche Untersuchungen zum Neuen Testament 314. Tübingen: Mohr Siebeck, 2013.

———. *Rewriting the Feeding of the Five Thousand: John 6:1–15 as a Test Case for Johannine Dependence on the Synoptic Gospels*. Studies in Biblical Literature 125. New York: Peter Lang, 2011.

Hunt, Steven, D. Francois Tolmie, and Ruben Zimmermann, eds. *Character Studies in the Fourth Gospel: Narrative Approaches to Seventy Figures in John*. Wissenschaftliche Untersuchungen zum Neuen Testament 314. Tübingen: Mohr Siebeck, 2013.

Hylen, Susan. *Allusion and Meaning in John 6*. Beihefte zur Zeitschrift für die neutestamentliche Wissenschaft und die Kunde der älteren Kirche 137. Berlin: de Gruyter, 2005.

———. *Imperfect Believers: Ambiguous Characters in the Gospel of John*. Louisville: Westminster John Knox, 2009.

Inge, Denise, ed. *Happiness and Holiness: Thomas Traherne and His Writings*. Norwich: Canterbury, 2008.

———. *Wanting Like a God: Desire and Freedom in the Work of Thomas Traherne*. London: SCM, 2008.

Jensen, Alexander S. *John's Gospel as Witness: The Development of the Early Christian Language of Faith*. Burlington, VT: Ashgate, 2004.

Karris, Robert J. *Jesus and the Marginalized in John's Gospel*. Collegeville, MN: Liturgical Press, 1990.

Käsemann, Ernst. *New Testament Questions of Today*. New Testament Library. London: SCM, 1969.

———. *The Testament of Jesus: A Study of the Gospel of John in the Light of Chapter 17*. Translated by Gerhard Krodel. Philadelphia: Fortress, 1968.

Keener, Craig S. *The Gospel of John: A Commentary*. 2 vols. Peabody, MA: Hendrickson, 2003.

Kierkegaard, Søren. *Philosophical Fragments*. In *Philosophical Fragments; Johannes Climacus*. Edited and translated by Howard V. Hong and Edna H. Hong. Kierkegaard's Writings 7. Princeton: Princeton University Press, 1985.

———. *Practice in Christianity*. Edited and translated by Howard V. Hong and Edna H. Hong. Kierkegaard's Writings 20. Princeton: Princeton University Press, 1991.

———. *Works of Love*. Edited and translated by Howard V. Hong and Edna H. Hong. Kierkegaard's Writings 16. Princeton: Princeton University Press, 1995.

Koester, Craig R. *Symbolism in the Fourth Gospel: Meaning, Mystery, Community*. 2nd ed. Minneapolis: Fortress, 2003.

Koester, Craig R., and Reimund Bieringer, eds. *The Resurrection of Jesus in the Gospel of John*. Wissenschaftliche Untersuchungen zum Neuen Testament 222. Tübingen: Mohr Siebeck, 2008.

Köstenberger, Andreas J. *John*. Baker Exegetical Commentary on the New Testament. Grand Rapids: Baker Academic, 2004.

Krznaric, Roman. *The Good Ancestor: How to Think Long Term in a Short-Term World*. London: W. H. Allen, 2020.

Kysar, Robert. *John: The Maverick Gospel*. 3rd ed. Louisville: Westminster John Knox, 2007.

———. *John's Story of Jesus*. Eugene, OR: Wipf & Stock, 2003.

———. *Voyages with John: Charting the Fourth Gospel*. Waco: Baylor University Press, 2005.

Labahn, Michael. "Simon Peter: An Ambiguous Character and His Narrative Career." In *Character Studies in the Fourth Gospel: Narrative Approaches to Seventy*

Figures in John, edited by Steven Hunt, D. Francois Tolmie, and Ruben Zimmermann, 151–67. Wissenschaftliche Untersuchungen zum Neuen Testament 314. Tübingen: Mohr Siebeck, 2013.

LaCocque, André, and Paul Ricoeur. *Thinking Biblically: Exegetical and Hermeneutical Studies*. Translated by David Pellauer. Chicago: University of Chicago Press, 1998.

Lamb, David A. *Text, Context and the Johannine Community: A Sociolinguistic Analysis of the Johannine Writings*. Library of New Testament Studies 477. London: Bloomsbury T&T Clark, 2014.

Lee, Dorothy. *Flesh and Glory: Symbolism, Gender and Theology in the Gospel of John*. New York: Crossroad, 2002.

Levertov, Denise. *Breathing the Water*. New York: New Directions, 1987.

———. *Candles in Babylon*. New York: New Directions, 1982.

———. *The Collected Poems of Denise Levertov*. Edited by Paul A. Lacey and Anne Dewey. New York: New Directions, 2013.

———. "A Poet's View." In *New & Selected Essays*, 239–46. New York: New Directions, 1992.

Lierman, John, ed. *Challenging Perspectives on the Gospel of John*. Wissenschaftliche Untersuchungen zum Neuen Testament 2/219. Tübingen: Mohr Siebeck, 2006.

Lieu, Judith. *I, II, & III John: A Commentary*. New Testament Library. Louisville: Westminster John Knox, 2008.

Lieu, Judith M., and Martinus de Boer, eds. *The Oxford Handbook of Johannine Studies*. Oxford: Oxford University Press, 2018.

Lincoln, Andrew T. *The Gospel according to Saint John*. Black's New Testament Commentaries. Peabody, MA: Hendrickson, 2005.

———. "The Lazarus Story: A Literary Perspective." In *The Gospel of John and Christian Theology*, edited by Richard Bauckham and Carl Mosser, 211–32. Grand Rapids: Eerdmans, 2008.

———. *Truth on Trial: The Lawsuit Motif in the Fourth Gospel*. Peabody, MA: Hendrickson, 2000.

Lindars, Barnabas. *The Gospel of John*. New Century Bible Commentary. London: Oliphants, 1972.

Luther, Martin. *Sermons on the Gospel of St. John: Chapters 1–4*. Edited by Jaroslav Pelikan. St. Louis: Concordia, 1957.

MacKinnon, Donald. *Borderlands of Theology*. London: Lutterworth, 1968.

Malina, Bruce J., and Richard L. Rohrbaugh. *Social-Science Commentary on the Gospel of John*. Minneapolis: Fortress, 1998.

Marissen, Michael. *Lutheranism, Anti-Judaism, and Bach's St. John Passion*. Oxford: Oxford University Press, 1998.

Maritz, Petrus, and Gilbert Van Belle. "The Imagery of Eating and Drinking in John 6:35." In *Imagery in the Gospel of John: Terms, Forms, Themes, and Theology of Johannine Figurative Language*, edited by Jörg Frey, Jan G. van der Watt, and Ruben Zimmermann, 333–52. Wissenschaftliche Untersuchungen zum Neuen Testament 200. Tübingen: Mohr Siebeck, 2006.

Marsh, John. *Saint John*. Westminster Pelican Commentaries. Philadelphia: Westminster, 1978.

Martini, Carlo M. *The Ignatian Exercises in the Light of St. John*. 2nd ed. Anand: Gujarat Sihitya Prakash, 1997.

Martyn, J. Louis. *The Gospel of John in Christian History: Essays for Interpreters*. Eugene, OR: Wipf & Stock, 2004.

———. *History and Theology in the Fourth Gospel*. 3rd ed. Louisville: Westminster John Knox, 2003.

McCracken, David. *The Scandal of the Gospels: Jesus, Story, and Offense*. Oxford: Oxford University Press, 1994.

McGrath, James F. *John's Apologetic Christology: Legitimation and Development in Johannine Christology*. Cambridge: Cambridge University Press, 2001.

McHugh, John F. *A Critical and Exegetical Commentary on John 1–4*. International Critical Commentary. London: T&T Clark, 2009.

Menken, Maarten J. J. *Old Testament Quotations in the Fourth Gospel: Studies in Textual Form*. Contributions to Biblical Exegesis and Theology 15. Kampen: Kok Pharos, 1996.

Minear, Paul S. *John: The Martyr's Gospel*. 2nd ed. Eugene, OR: Wipf & Stock, 2003.

Miranda, José Porfirio. *Being and the Messiah: The Message of St. John*. Translated by John Eagleson. Eugene, OR: Wipf & Stock, 2006.

Moberly, R. W. L. *The Bible, Theology, and Faith: A Study of Abraham and Jesus*. Cambridge: Cambridge University Press, 2000.

Moloney, Francis J. *The Gospel of John*. Sacra Pagina. Collegeville, MN: Liturgical Press, 1998.

———. *"A Hard Saying": The Gospel and Culture*. Collegeville, MN: Liturgical Press, 2001.

Moltmann, Jürgen. *The Crucified God: The Cross of Christ as the Foundation and Criticism of Christian Theology*. Translated by R. A. Wilson and John Bowden. London: SCM, 1973.

Montemaggi, Vittorio. *Reading Dante's* Commedia *as Theology: Divinity Realized in Human Encounter*. Oxford: Oxford University Press, 2016.

Newbigin, Lesslie. *The Light Has Come: An Exposition of the Fourth Gospel*. Edinburgh: Handsel, 1982.

Newheart, Michael Willett. *Word and Soul: A Psychological, Literary, and Cultural Reading of the Fourth Gospel*. Collegeville, MN: Liturgical Press, 2001.

Newton, Bert. *Subversive Wisdom: Sociopolitical Dimensions of John's Gospel*. Eugene, OR: Wipf & Stock, 2012.

Neyrey, Jerome H. *The Gospel of John*. New Cambridge Bible Commentary. Cambridge: Cambridge University Press, 2007.

Nissen, Johannes, and Sigfred Pedersen, eds. *New Readings in John: Literary and Theological Perspectives*. London: T&T Clark, 2004.

Ochs, Peter. *Religion without Violence: The Practice and Philosophy of Scriptural Reasoning*. Eugene, OR: Cascade, 2019.

O'Day, Gail. "Martha: Seeing the Glory of God." In *Character Studies in the Fourth Gospel: Narrative Approaches to Seventy Figures in John*, edited by Steven Hunt, D. Francois Tolmie, and Ruben Zimmermann, 487–503. Wissenschaftliche Untersuchungen zum Neuen Testament 314. Tübingen: Mohr Siebeck, 2013.

———. *The Word Disclosed: John's Story and Narrative Preaching*. St. Louis: CBP Press, 1987.

O'Day, Gail R., and Susan E. Hylen. *John*. Westminster Bible Companion. Louisville: Westminster John Knox, 2006.

Olsson, Birger. "*Deus semper maior?* On God in the Johannine Writings." In *New Readings in John: Literary and Theological Perspectives*, edited by Johannes Nissen and Sigfred Pedersen, 143–71. London: T&T Clark, 2004.

Origen. *Commentary on the Gospel according to John*. Translated Ronald E. Heine. 2 vols. Fathers of the Church 80, 89. Washington, DC: Catholic University of America Press, 1989, 1993.

O'Siadhail, Micheal. *The Five Quintets*. Waco: Baylor University Press, 2018.

Parsenios, George L. *Departure and Consolation: The Johannine Farewell Discourses in Light of Greco-Roman Literature*. Supplements to Novum Testamentum 117. Leiden: Brill, 2005.

———. *Rhetoric and Drama in the Johannine Lawsuit Motif*. Wissenschaftliche Untersuchungen zum Neuen Testament 258. Tübingen: Mohr Siebeck, 2010.

Patte, Daniel, ed. *Global Bible Commentary*. Nashville: Abingdon, 2004.

Placher, William. *Mark*. Louisville: Westminster John Knox, 2010.

Plantinga, Richard J. "The Integration of Music and Theology in the Vocal Compositions of J. S. Bach." In *Resonant Witness: Conversations between Music and Theology*, edited by Jeremy S. Begbie and Steven R. Guthrie, 215–39. Grand Rapids: Eerdmans, 2011.

Quash, Ben. *Abiding*. London: Bloomsbury, 2012.

———. *Found Theology: History, Imagination and the Holy Spirit*. London: Bloomsbury, 2013.

Rainbow, Paul A. *Johannine Theology: The Gospel, the Epistles and the Apocalypse*. Downers Grove: IVP Academic, 2014.

Reinhartz, Adele. *Befriending the Beloved Disciple: A Jewish Reading of the Gospel of John*. New York: Continuum, 2001.

———. "The Jews of the Fourth Gospel." In *The Oxford Handbook of Johannine Studies*, edited by Judith M. Lieu and Martinus C. de Boer, 121–37. Oxford: Oxford University Press, 2018.

Ridderbos, Herman. *The Gospel according to John: A Theological Commentary*. Translated by John Vriend. Grand Rapids: Eerdmans, 1997.

Ringe, Sharon H. *Wisdom's Friends: Community and Christology in the Fourth Gospel*. Louisville: Westminster John Knox, 1999.

Royce, Josiah. *The Problem of Christianity*. 2 vols. New York: Macmillan, 1913.

Ruprecht, Louis A., Jr. *This Tragic Gospel: How John Corrupted the Heart of Christianity*. San Francisco: Jossey-Bass, 2008.

Sanders, J. N., and B. A. Mastin. *A Commentary on the Gospel according to St. John*. Harper's New Testament Commentaries. New York: Harper & Row, 1968.

Sanford, John A. *Mystical Christianity: A Psychological Commentary on the Gospel of John*. New York: Crossroad, 1993.

Schnackenburg, Rudolf. *The Gospel according to St. John*. Translated by Kevin Smyth. 3 vols. Herder's Theological Commentary on the New Testament. London: Burns & Oates, 1980–82.

Schneiders, Sandra M. *Jesus Risen in Our Midst: Essays on the Resurrection of Jesus in the Fourth Gospel*. Collegeville, MN: Liturgical Press, 2013.

Schuchard, Bruce G. "Temple, Festivals, and Scripture in the Gospel of John." In *The Oxford Handbook of Johannine Studies*, edited by Judith M. Lieu and Martinus de Boer, 381–95. Oxford: Oxford University Press, 2018.

Segovia, Fernando F., ed. *What Is John?* 2 vols. SBL Symposium Series 3, 7. Atlanta: Scholars Press, 1996, 1998.

Skinner, Christopher W., ed. *Character and Characterization in the Gospel of John*. Library of New Testament Studies 461. London: Bloomsbury T&T Clark, 2013.

Smalley, Stephen S. *John: Evangelist and Interpreter*. Eugene, OR: Wipf & Stock, 2012.

Smith, D. Moody. *John*. Abingdon New Testament Commentaries. Nashville: Abingdon, 1999.

———. *The Theology of the Gospel of John*. New Testament Theology. Cambridge: Cambridge University Press, 1995.

Sonderegger, Katherine. *The Doctrine of God*. Vol. 1 of *Systematic Theology*. Minneapolis: Fortress, 2015.

———. *The Doctrine of the Holy Trinity: Processions and Persons*. Vol. 2 of *Systematic Theology*. Minneapolis: Fortress, 2020.

Soskice, Janet. *The Kindness of God: Metaphor, Gender, and Religious Language*. Oxford: Oxford University Press, 2007.

Soulen, R. Kendall. *Distinguishing the Voices*. Vol. 1 of *The Divine Name(s) and the Holy Trinity*. Louisville: Westminster John Knox, 2011.

Stevick, Daniel B. *Jesus and His Own: A Commentary on John 13–17*. Grand Rapids: Eerdmans, 2011.

Stibbe, Mark W. G. *John*. Readings. Sheffield: JSOT Press, 1993.

Tanner, Kathryn. *God and Creation in Christian Theology: Tyranny or Empowerment?* Oxford: Basil Blackwell, 1988.

Taylor, T. Kevin, and Giles Waller, eds. *Christian Theology and Tragedy: Theologians, Tragic Literature, and Tragic Theory*. Burlington, VT: Ashgate, 2011.

Temple, William. *Readings in John's Gospel*. London: Macmillan, 1955.

Thomas, R. S. *Collected Poems: 1945–1990*. London: Phoenix, 2000.

Thompson, Marianne Meye. *The God of the Gospel of John*. Grand Rapids: Eerdmans, 2001.

———. "The Raising of Lazarus in John 11: A Theological Reading." In *The Gospel of John and Christian Theology*, edited by Richard Bauckham and Carl Mosser, 233–44. Grand Rapids: Eerdmans, 2008.

Ticciati, Susannah. *Job and the Disruption of Identity: Reading beyond Barth*. New York: T&T Clark, 2005.

Torrance, Alan J. "The Lazarus Narrative, Theological History, and Historical Probability." In *The Gospel of John and Christian Theology*, edited by Richard Bauckham and Carl Mosser, 245–62. Grand Rapids: Eerdmans, 2008.

Toulmin, Stephen. *Cosmopolis: The Hidden Agenda of Modernity*. Chicago: University of Chicago Press, 1992.

Tsing, Anna Lowenhaupt. *The Mushroom at the End of the World: On the Possibility of Life in Capitalist Ruins*. Princeton: Princeton University Press, 2015.

Van Belle, Gilbert. "The Death of Jesus and the Literary Unity of the Fourth Gospel." In *The Death of Jesus in the Fourth Gospel*, edited by Gilbert van Belle, 3–64. Bibliotheca Ephemeridum Theologicarum Lovaniensium 200. Leuven: Leuven University Press, 2007.

———, ed. *The Death of Jesus in the Fourth Gospel*. Bibliotheca Ephemeridum Theologicarum Lovaniensium 200. Leuven: Leuven University Press, 2007.

Vande Kappelle, Robert P. *Truth Revealed: The Message of the Gospel of John—Then and Now*. Eugene, OR: Wipf & Stock, 2014.

Van der Watt, Jan G., and Ruben Zimmermann, eds. *Rethinking the Ethics of John: "Implicit Ethics" in the Johannine Writings*. Kontexte und Normen neutestamentlicher Ethik 3; Wissenschaftliche Untersuchungen zum Neuen Testament 291. Tübingen: Mohr Siebeck, 2012.

Vanier, Jean. *Drawn into the Mystery of Jesus through the Gospel of John*. London: Darton, Longman & Todd, 2004.

Volf, Miroslav. "Johannine Dualism and Contemporary Pluralism." In Bauckham and Mosser, *Gospel of John*, 19–50.

Webster, John. *Holy Scripture: A Dogmatic Sketch*. Cambridge: Cambridge University Press, 2003.

Westcott, B. F. *The Gospel according to St. John*. London: John Murray, 1898.

Wilbur, Richard. *The Mind-Reader: New Poems*. New York: Harcourt Brace, 1976.

Williams, Catrin H. "Faith, Eternal Life, and the Spirit in the Gospel of John." In *The Oxford Handbook of Johannine Studies*, edited by Judith M. Lieu and Martinus de Boer, 347–62. Oxford: Oxford University Press, 2018.

Young, Frances M. *Biblical Exegesis and the Formation of Christian Culture*. Cambridge: Cambridge University Press, 1997.

———. "Doctrine as Making Sense of Scripture: Clearing a Path through Early Christian Argument." Unpublished manuscript, 2020.

———. *Exegesis and Theology in Early Christianity*. Burlington, VT: Ashgate, 2012.

———. *From Nicaea to Chalcedon: A Guide to Literature and Its Background*. London: SCM, 1983.

———. "Prelude: Jesus Christ, Foundation of Christianity." In *Origins to Constantine*, edited by Margaret M. Mitchell and Frances M. Young, 1–34. Vol. 1 of *The Cambridge History of Christianity*. Cambridge: Cambridge University Press, 2006.

———. *Ways of Reading Scripture: Collected Papers*. Wissenschaftliche Untersuchungen zum Neuen Testament 369. Tübingen: Mohr Siebeck, 2018.

Young, Frances M., and David F. Ford. *Meaning and Truth in 2 Corinthians*. London: SPCK, 1987; Grand Rapids: Eerdmans, 1988. Reprint, Eugene, OR: Wipf & Stock, 2008.

Zahl, Simeon. *The Holy Spirit and Christian Experience*. Oxford: Oxford University Press, 2020.

Zimmerman, Ruben. "Eschatology and Time in the Gospel of John." In *The Oxford Handbook of Johannine Studies*, edited by Judith M. Lieu and Martinus de Boer, 292–310. Oxford: Oxford University Press, 2018.

Zuboff, Shoshana. *The Age of Surveillance Capitalism: The Fight for a Human Future at the New Frontier of Power*. London: Profile Books, 2019.

Scripture Index

Nehemiah

Job

Psalms

Proverbs

Song of Songs

Isaiah

Jeremiah

Acts

Romans

1 Corinthians

2 Corinthians

Galatians

Ephesians

1 Thessalonians

2 Timothy

1 John

Revelation

Author Index

Subject Index